I0894288

FAMOUS AMERICAN AIRCRAFT

Vought F7U-3

TOMMY H THOMASON
AND
ALFRED C CASBY

Vought F7U-3 Cutlass

Tommy H. Thomason and Alfred C. Casby

First published in 2024 by
Hikoki Publications Ltd
An imprint of Crécy Publishing Ltd
1a Ringway Trading Est
Shadowmoss Rd
Manchester
M22 5LH
England

www.crecy.co.uk

© Al Casby 2024
© Tommy H. Thomason 2024

ISBN 9 781800 352940

All rights reserved. No part of this book may be reproduced or transmitted in any form or by any means electronic or mechanical, including photocopying, recording or by any information storage without permission from the Publisher in writing. All enquiries should be directed to the Publisher.

Printed in Türkiye by Ozlem Print

MIX
Paper | Supporting responsible forestry
FSC® C176481

FRONT COVER A factory formation of three brand new F7U-3s, BuNos 129564, 129563 and 129562 fly over the verdant cotton fields near their Dallas, Texas birthplace. Pilots were Donald 'Mad Dog' Shultz, Leroy J 'Jack' Walton and Martin Collis, all Vought test pilots. *Chance Vought photographs H.P.F 115C by Arthur L. Schoeni*

BACK COVER Resplendent in their polished aluminium and freshly painted magnesium panels, the "Silver Streaks" utilized BAR Dallas-assigned aircraft like BuNo 129663 and 129648 pictured here. Vought's factory support personnel travelled to the airshows by automobile to attend to any minor maintenance work necessary. The team never missed a performance. *Casby Collection*

BACK BOTTOM LEFT In order to expedite availability for first flight to meet a schedule milestone, the airplane is often unpainted for the event; in this case the Navy had also decreed that the F7U-3 would be one of the subjects of its "Natural Metal Finish" test program. *VAHF*

BACK BOTTOM CENTRE The Navy's first two jet fighters with afterburning engines, the F6U-1 Pirate and F7U-1 Cutlass, in formation just south of the Vought plant located on NAS Dallas, Texas. *VAHF*

BACK BOTTOM RIGHT BuNo 129655 shared space with several aircraft and trains as part of the Travel Town Transportation display in Griffith Park, California. *Casby Collection via Aric Aldrich*

PAGE 3 The fourth F7U-3, BuNo 128454, was assigned to carrier-suitability testing, particularly the need to mitigate concerns with the initial forward fuselage design with respect to over-the-nose visibility for carrier landings. Seen here with the production canopy and radome configuration, it is resplendent in its patriotic-themed livery during a test flight over Dallas, Texas. *VAHF*

Contents

The

Edward Joseph Casby

Memorial Gallery
of
Chance Vought F7U Cutlass Art and Illustration

Dedicated to those who made the ultimate sacrifice operating and supporting the F7U Cutlass series aircraft for the advancement of Naval Aviation and the defense of the United States of America

IN MEMORIAM

Mr.	William Henry Bonynge Millar	CVA Flight Test	XF7U-1	122473	14 March 1949
Mr.	Warren Port Smith	CVA Flight Test	F7U-1	124416	06 July 1950
Mr.	William Patrick Harrigan	CVA Flight Test	F7U-1	124417	28 September 1950
LCDR	Bert Lynn Hendrickson, USN	NATC	F7U-3	128455	10 June 1952
Mr.	William Walker Sunday	CVA Flight Test	F7U-3	128460	09 December 1952
LT	Robert Clifford Woolverton, USN	BAR Dallas	F7U-3	129647	11 June 1954
Mrs.	Elaine House Branch, NCE	NATTC Memphis	F7U-3	129647	11 June 1954
AMC	Roland Francis Brousseau, USN	NATTC Memphis	F7U-3	129647	11 June 1954
AMC	George Francis Hurlburt, USN	NATTC Memphis	F7U-3	129647	11 June 1954
AMC	George Wright Woodruff, USN	NATTC Memphis	F7U-3	129647	11 June 1954
CAPT	Vincent Joseph Marzelo, USMC	VX-3	F7U-3	129644	28 September 1954
ENS	James Ray Sears, USNR	VF-124	F7U-3	129690	18 November 1954
LTJG	John Wylie Hood, USNR	VF-81	F7U-3	129659	11 December 1954
Mr.	James Robert Whitten	CVA Factory	F7U-3M	129743	13 May 1955
LCDR	Jay Alkire, USNR (XO)	VF-124	F7U-3	129595	14 July 1955
LT	Robert Walter Slezak, USNR	VX-4	F7U-3P	129756	29 July 1955
CDR	William John Manby, Jr., USN (CO)	VA-66	F7U-3	129673	01 August 1955
LTJG	George Barrett Milliard, USNR	VF-124	F7U-3	129586	01 November 1955
LT	Frank Asburn Downs, USN	NASWF	F7U-3	129546	21 November 1955
LT	Brooke Montgomery, USN	VX-4	F7U-3M	129712	01 February 1956
ENS	Patrick Edward Harwood, USNR	VA-151	F7U-3	129619	19 February 1956
LTJG	Roger Harley Butts, USNR	VA-83	F7U-3M	129738	09 May 1956
LTJG	Jerold Quigley Weaver, USN	VA-116	F7U-3M	139901	27 June 1956
LTJG	David Harry Chantler, USN	VA-151	F7U-3	129693	08 July 1956
CDR	Chester Wright Gates, Jr., USN (CO)	VA-86	F7U-3M	139883	10 July 1956
LTJG	William Milnes Austin, Jr., USN	VA-86	F7U-3M	129715	10 July 1956
LT	Samuel Wadsworth Morey, USN	VA-126	F7U-3	129583	13 July 1956
LCDR	Robert Lee Anderson, USN	VR-32	F7U-3	128475	01 August 1956
LTJG	Arthur Gerald Callahan, Jr., USNR	VA-212	F7U-3	129660	22 August 1956
LTJG	Frank James Carrig, USNR	VA-151	F7U-3	129633	12 October 1956
LTJG	John Anthony Shields, USN	VA-116	F7U-3M	139894	02 February 1957

Always Revered - Never Forgotten

Acknowledgements

A book on a single subject of the breadth and depth of this one is only possible with the help of other subject matter experts, aviation enthusiasts and the people directly involved with the aircraft. Paul Christiansen has written very detailed histories of the Westinghouse's development of aviation gas turbine engines from the first to the J46; he reviewed our text and provided knowledgeable comments and corrections. Patrizia Nava is the curator of the Aviation Archives at the University of Texas at Dallas; her unwavering support and willingness to 'look up just one more thing' was instrumental in navigating Vought's archives. Bill Spidle is a lifelong aviation enthusiast and former Vought employee who has dedicated many volunteer hours as a supporter of the Vought Aircraft Heritage Foundation (VAHF); his willingness to share his collection is greatly appreciated. CAPT Robert 'Barney' Ruble USN provided expert commentary on much of the draft text. Other individuals who provided information and material that we incorporated in some way are:

Aric Aldrich, Mark Aldrich, LT John 'Jack' Anderson USNR, Joseph Angelone, CAPT Carl 'Tex' Birdwell Jr. USN, Gerry Balzar, CAPT Jess Barker USN, Roger Besecker, CAPT WaLTer Blaseck USN, Paul Bless, Odilo Brand, Tony Buttler, Thomas Cathcart, CAPT Richard Cavicke USN, Paul Christiansen, LT John Curtis USNR, CDR Jack Dalby USN, West Doss, Ron Downey, Patrick Earley, VADM Donald D. Engen USN, RADM Edward L. Feightner USN, Mat Garretson, CAPT Dudley A Gillaspy USN, Steve Ginter, RADM John 'Mac' Gleim USN, Senator John H. Glenn Jr., John Griffith, Don Hinton, CDR Felton M. Humphreys USN, William T. Larkin, Don Linn, Kimble McCutcheon, CAPT Howard C. Mitchell USN, CDR John Moore USN, Mark Nankivil, Douglas Olson, Kathryn Partusch, CAPT Billy Phillips USN, CAPT Edward M. Porter USN, Ronald G. Puckett, CDR John W. Rademacher USN, RADM James D. Ramage USN, Angelo Romano, CAPT Walter M. Schirra Jr. USN, Arthur Schoeni, John Seal, RADM Alan B. Shepard Jr. USN, RADM Burton H. Shepherd USN, Paul Thayer, Barrett Tillman, LCDR Edwin Van Biesbroeck USN, Gary Verver, Allyson Vought, Leroy 'Jack' Walton, Jan van Waarde, Jerry Wells, Enid Wescott, Mike Wilson.

The research assistance provided by the volunteer staff at the National Naval Aviation Museum at Pensacola and the Naval History Center in Washington DC was also invaluable.

Taking full advantage of the spacious deck of the newly christened *Forrestal* (CVA-59), VA-86 conducted flight operations with their F7U-3Ms during the carrier's shakedown cruise to the Caribbean in early 1956 without incident or accident, demonstrating that the type was fully capable of safe operations on an angled deck guided by a mirror landing system. ***US Navy***

Author biographies

Al Casby

Assembling a proverbial 'glue-bomb' model aircraft at the age of 2 – despite not ever having seen an aircraft nor having the ability to read the instructions – author Al Casby was clearly predisposed for a career as a pilot. At the age of 8 he spotted an illustration of a Chance Vought F7U-1 Cutlass in his artist father's files and his life's goal became instantly clear. He set out to acquire an actual F7U and began a letter-writing campaign whose recipients included admirals, senators, astronauts, and more than two hundred former Cutlass pilots. From purchasing his first F7U-3 cockpit as a teenager to starting up Westinghouse jet engines on his father's driveway, the dream of owning (and flying) a Cutlass was always first and foremost. In October 2014, he finally acquired the only complete one that could be made flyable again and began the arduous ongoing task of restoring the aircraft to airworthiness. Employed as a senior commercial airline captain, to date he has amassed over 31,000 flight hours in DC-6s, Convair 640s, L-188 Electras, Boeing 737s and 757s, and Airbus A319/320/321 airliners in his forty-one-year career. With retirement around the corner, he looks forward to continuing to restore his F7U-3 with the hopes of achieving the goal he set his sights on fifty-six years ago.

Tommy H. Thomason

Now retired, author Tommy H. Thomason doesn't remember when he didn't want to be a pilot. He received his private pilot licence a few days before his 21st birthday. He subsequently graduated from Rensselaer Polytechnic Institute with a Bachelor of Aeronautical Engineering and earned graduate degrees from the University of Southern California and the Harvard Graduate School of Business Administration. His forty-year career in the aerospace industry included assignments as a flight test engineer, manager, and executive. He has an Airline Transport Pilot certificate; been a flight instructor for aircraft, gliders, aerobatics, and instruments; and flown more than 3,000 hours in eighty different airplanes, helicopters, and sailplanes with one guest pilot flight in the Goodyear blimp and another in the XV-15 tilt-rotor research aircraft. At one point, he had an FAA altitude waiver for aerobatic exhibition of the Fournier RF 4D motor glider. Another highlight was a week at the Reno Air Races as pit crew on a Vought F4U Corsair. Although thwarted by poor distance vision in becoming a Navy fighter pilot, he has maintained a very active interest in carrier aviation, authoring numerous articles and blog posts, five books, and seven monographs on US Navy aircraft (*see https://tommythomason.com*).

Foreword

The authors recommend that you turn the page with an open mind because anything derogatory that you've heard or read about the F7U Cutlass is probably incorrect, taken out of context, or misrepresented. The difference in that regard between what has been previously published and which you will find here is *that* significant. However, you can be assured that together we have researched, critically examined, vetted, and fact checked every word we have written and illustration we have created.

Doing research for his books, monographs, and blog posts on US Navy aircraft, Tommy Thomason has spent thousands of hours in research at the Vought Archives in Grand Prairie, Texas; the National Archives at College Park, Maryland; the Naval History and Heritage Command at the Navy Yard in Washington, D.C: the Buehler Library at the National Naval Aviation Museum in Pensacola, Florida; and the Grumman Archives at Bethpage, New York. The material he and others have found at those repositories has been added to a lifelong accumulation of magazine articles, technical reports, monographs, books, photos, etc. about aviation in general and naval aviation in particular. The resulting body of work has provided naval aviation enthusiasts with a wealth of accurate and often less well-known information because his choice of subjects tends toward forgotten or unfairly maligned naval aircraft.

In one way or another, Al Casby has dedicated most of his free waking moments to researching the history of the Vought F7U Cutlass ever since he was 8 years old. His extensive collection includes official reports, manuals, artwork, memorabilia, models, toys, and over 6,000 photos and slides. He has personally acquired the only totally complete F7U-3 in existence, the partial remains of four others, as well as eight J46 engines in his ongoing effort to restore his aircraft to flight status. In addition, he has interviewed over 200 Cutlass pilots and maintainers over the years as well as other individuals associated with the programme. He has acted as a consultant at the request of the National Naval Aviation Museum as well as the USS Midway Museum, assisting these organisations with the refurbishment of their F7U-3s. His knowledge of the aircraft is second to none. He was planning to write a book on the Cutlass eventually but his priority was on flying one.

Thomason wrote to Casby in December 2010 requesting his help in writing a monograph on the F7U-1 Cutlass to be published in Steve Ginter's Naval Fighters series. The result, with his generous assistance, was well-regarded. Skipping forward to January 2020, Steve Ginter was planning to update his F7U-3 monograph, which was to be co-authored by Thomason and Casby, merging their respective knowledge and resources. As work on the project progressed, it became apparent that the material available to us and essential for inclusion in a definitive history of the Cutlass exceeded the monograph format. At that point Crécy Publishing accepted our proposal to write this book.

We are confident that you can rely on what we have written and illustrated to be grounded in the most scrupulous use of contemporaneous official material and other primary source documents, i.e. journalism standards, as opposed to much of what has been presented in published works and online heretofore. Interpretations and analysis are based on our joint knowledge and experience as pilots and engineers. The text and illustrations have also been reviewed by subject matter experts, including naval aviators and historians, as appropriate.

In its time, the F7U represented the cutting edge of aviation, and has long deserved to have its history told *accurately*. We sincerely hope you find our work beneficial to increasing your understanding of the Cutlass.

Al Casby and Tommy H. Thomason, 14 January 2024

Although huge in appearance, primarily due to its girth and stance, even on axial-deck carriers the F7U-3s could be spotted four across on the deck (VF-124 on the way home aboard *Hancock* (CVA-19) at the end of the Cutlasses' first deployment). *US Navy*

Introduction

The Chance Vought F7U Cutlass was ahead of its time. In 1948, when it first flew, it could hardly have been more exotic, challenging the state of the art: a tail-less fighter to be powered by two afterburning jet engines. As a day fighter, it was not only to be carrier-based but also climb quicker and accelerate faster than the Air Force's new swept-wing North American F-86 Sabre. Development problems and a subsequent increase in mission capability resulted in it taking too long to reach operational squadrons, which partly accounts for its relatively short career. The F7U-1's empty weight growth during detail design and development necessitated its redesign as the F7U-2 to beef up the structure. Modification of the forward fuselage was also required to provide an adequate view of the carrier deck when landing. However, the -2 was stillborn due to military budget reductions. When funding was again available, the Navy elected to repurpose the Cutlass to be a larger, more capable, general-purpose fighter, the F7U-3. That required more thrust, which was to be provided by Westinghouse's new afterburning J46 engine, a scaled-up derivative of its J34 – a well-thought-of engine – with the benefit of F6U-1 and F7U-1 afterburner experience.

Ahead of its time also meant that the Cutlass was designed too soon to benefit from the discovery of the area rule, which doomed it to transonic performance in level flight. Similarly, its lack of a horizontal tail was intended in part to address the transonic pitch control difficulties being encountered at the time. They proved to be avoidable by having the horizontal stabiliser and the elevator function as a unit (i.e. stabilator) for pitch control and properly locating it with respect to the wing. Unfortunately, no horizontal tail resulted in it not only being radical in appearance but also requiring an appreciation of its particular handling qualities at approach speed.

When questions arose within the Navy's Bureau of Aeronautics about the feasibility of launching the F7U-3 with existing hydraulic catapults at its projected weight, it was made lighter by deleting mission functionality. That meant it was once again a day fighter but larger, more complicated, and costlier than swept-wing day fighters then in development with comparable performance. The introduction of the more powerful steam catapult allowed the Navy to add back mission functionality and order production of heavier, more capable

The Navy's first two jet fighters with afterburning engines, the F6U-1 Pirate and F7U-1 Cutlass, in formation just south of the Vought plant located on NAS Dallas, Texas. ***VAHF***

A thorn between two roses, the F4U and the F8U? Definitely not when the F7U's reputation is examined more closely. *Casby Collection*

variants, the A2U for medium tactical strike and the F7U-3M armed with guided missiles to defend the carrier against attacks by Soviet jet bombers. However, unfavourable opinions about the Cutlass had already begun to form and the weight increase required to arm the -3M with missiles was not accompanied by an increase in engine thrust, unfairly condemning it to be retrospectively considered underpowered.

The F7U-3's service introduction was also accomplished before the Navy perfected a rigorous process for transitioning pilots to new aircraft, even more important in the case of the Cutlass with its systems complexity, afterburning engines, and high angle of attack handling qualities. It was also first deployed before the introduction of the angled-deck carrier concept that greatly reduced the degree of difficulty in landing high-performance jet fighters back aboard. And perhaps worst of all, Westinghouse initially failed to meet the thrust and fuel economy that it had proposed and was never able to better them as was customary and expected of engine manufacturers.

In contrast, Vought's next fighter for the Navy, the F8U Crusader, benefited significantly from its timely gestation: supersonic aerodynamics, pilot check-out rigour, angled-deck carriers, and advanced engine technology. As a result, even though its low-speed handling qualities were more challenging than the F7U's and its accident rate worse initially, it is widely regarded as the best of the Navy's day fighters while the F7U Cutlass is usually included on shortlists of the world's worst jet fighters and inevitably in discussions among less-informed aviation enthusiasts, to be forever known as the 'Gutless Cutlass' and the 'Ensign Eliminator'.

Although its bright future was too soon behind it, the Cutlass did eventually deploy with the fleet, albeit to mixed reviews. Now a 'stepping-stone' aircraft, as were many in its day due to aerodynamic and engine technology advances, the F7U had its advocates and detractors. Some aviators who flew the -3 thought very well of it. Others who flew it and/or the -3M did not and were not reticent about saying so. As a result, some were intimidated by the stories they heard and not only avoided flying it, but perpetuated and exaggerated second-hand tales of its shortcomings, which proved popular as mean-spirited gossip will.

Nevertheless, the Cutlass also deserves to be remembered for its impressive innovation. In addition to being Vought's first production aircraft with a fully pressurised and air-conditioned cockpit, the -1 and -3 together accounted for these firsts:

1. Production tail-less fighter
2. Originally designed to incorporate afterburner thrust augmentation
3. US Navy swept-wing fighter
4. US Navy fighter to achieve supersonic flight in a dive
5. Designed with a high-pressure (3,000 psi) hydraulic system
6. Utilise full-power irreversible controls with an artificial feel system
7. Incorporate an automatic flight-stabilisation system
8. US Navy fighter to incorporate a powered steerable nose wheel
9. Release bombs in supersonic flight
10. Deploy at sea with guided missiles as its primary armament

CHAPTER ONE

It seemed like a good idea at the time

The uncommon tail-less configuration (so called at the time because it did not have a horizontal tail) that Vought chose to propose in the Navy's 1946 day-fighter competition was intended to avoid a problem already being encountered at transonic speeds, the loss of pitch control effectiveness due to shockwaves on the wing and horizontal stabiliser. It should be noted that Vought also proposed conventional swept-wing configurations with a horizontal tail – one a twin-engine version of its F6U – in case the Bureau of Aeronautics (BuAer) was risk averse. In fact, BuAer ranked Vought's tail-less design highest even though it was more expensive than the F6U derivative as well as swept-wing proposals from some of the other five companies that bid.

BuAer agreed with Vought that not having a horizontal tail was a straightforward solution to the reduction in pitch control at transonic speeds, with the additional benefit of reducing weight. It did result in a narrower acceptable range for the centre of gravity (CG), a limitation on the location of heavy disposable loads like fuel, ammunition, and bombs. For example, a multi-cell fuel system and careful sequencing of the usage of their contents would be required to keep the CG within that range.

Pitch and roll control was provided by control surfaces on the outboard trailing edge of the wings. Vought elected to call these 'ailavators', derived from AILeron And eleVATOR (sometimes, but rarely in Vought documents, spelled ailevators; other companies chose to call these surfaces 'elevons' in their tail-less designs). In order for them to be reasonably effective for pitch control and not be too large relative to roll control, the wing had to be swept so as to move them as far aft of the centre of gravity as possible. For high-speed

The Vought V-346A proposal model provided to BuAer in April 1946 with control surface annotations added. ***Thomason***

Before and during the Second World War, aircraft manufacturers were pursuing flying-wing designs to reduce weight and drag. The first operational one, albeit not a pure flying wing since it had a vertical tail, was a German rocket-powered interceptor, the Me 163 Komet. *National Museum of the USAF*

flight, sweeping the wing was also desirable in order to increase the critical Mach number, defined as the point when drag began to increase more rapidly with increasing speed.

The tail-less configuration did preclude the use of trailing-edge flaps to provide more lift at take-off and approach speeds. When extended, they produced a nose-down pitching moment for which there was no horizontal tail to counteract. Fortunately, leading-edge flaps or slats provided a lift increase without a corresponding pitching moment change. Leading-edge slats had also been proven to provide acceptable

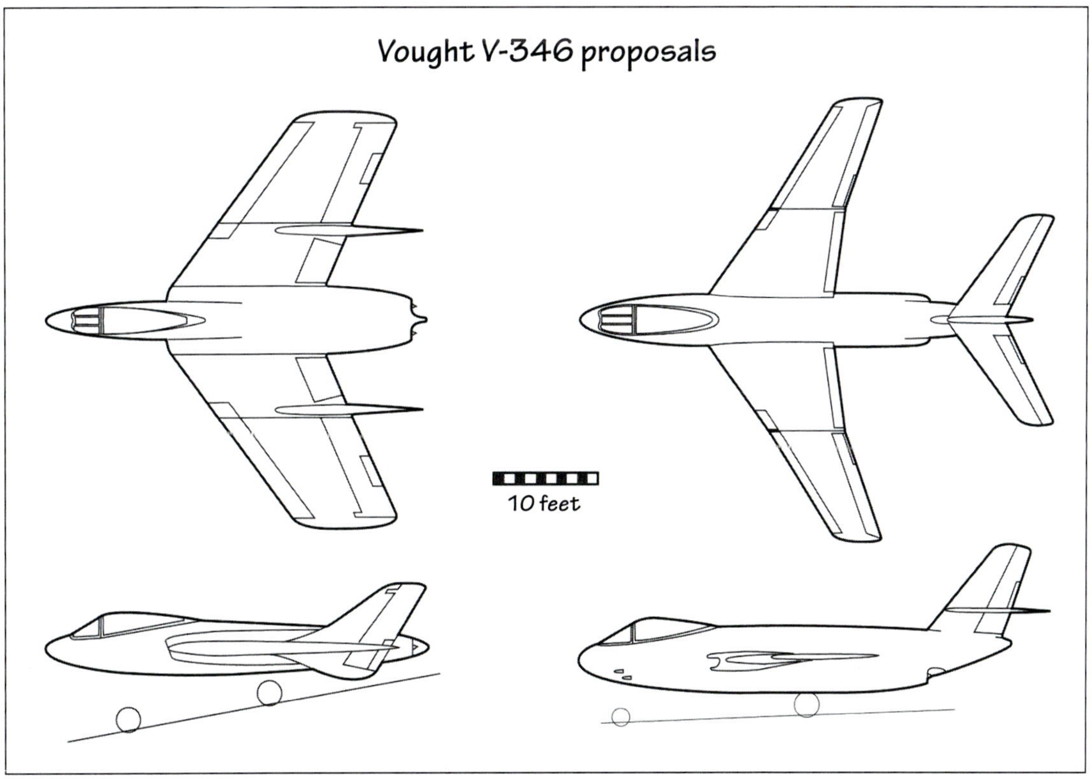

BuAer ranked Vought's tail-less V-346A proposal slightly higher than the V-346B. The latter was a swept-wing, twin-engine derivative of Vought's first jet fighter, the F6U, which had not yet flown. The V-346A met all the OS-105 requirements and exceeded most. It was lighter and slightly superior in performance than the V-346B as well as somewhat smaller, meaning more could be accommodated on an aircraft carrier. *Thomason*

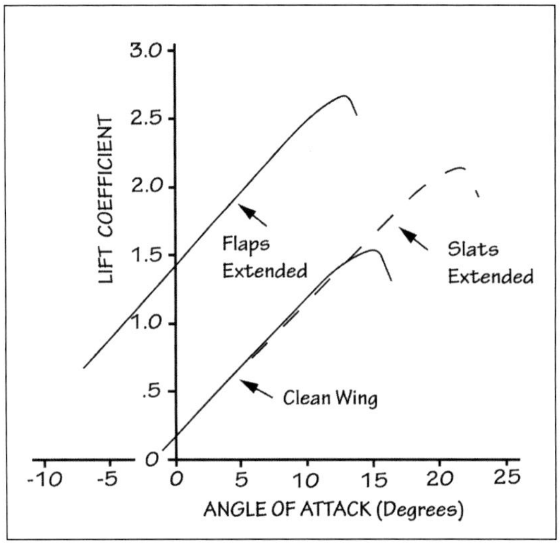

Extension of flaps on an aircraft wing to increase lift results in a large nose-down pitching moment, which has to be counteracted by increasing the download of a horizontal tail. Fortunately, extending leading-edge slats also increased lift but did not result in a significant pitching moment. ***Thomason***

swept-wing, low-speed handling qualities on a Bell P-63 King Cobra modified with a swept wing.

One consequence of not having trailing-edge flaps meant that F7U had to take off and land at a notably higher nose-up attitude than aircraft with them and/or the wing had to be relatively large in area to provide enough lift at carrier approach speeds. Vought chose to emphasise the nose-up attitude. In contrast, the Douglas F4D Skyray, another tail-less configuration developed roughly in parallel with the F7U, was able to be flown slowly enough for carrier landings at a lower nose-up attitude because it had a bigger wing for its weight, i.e. a lower wing loading, than the F7U. Vought chose to minimise the wing area and accommodate the pitch attitude required on take-off and landing with an unusually long nose landing gear.

Beginning with the F7U-1, one concern with a long nose landing gear strut that Vought engineers took into account was the kickback load caused by the initial sliding friction when a tyre touches down on landing, particularly on the non-skid surface of an aircraft carrier deck. This was minimised by rotating the nose wheel for landing, significantly reducing the kickback load to something approaching the lower rolling-friction drag. Similarly, the F7U-3's dual nose wheels were spun by bleed air from the engine's eleventh compressor stage impinging on buckets in a disc, similar to a waterwheel, mounted on the inner side of each nose wheel hub. The resulting rotation at 2,160 rpm was equivalent to a ground/deck speed of 77 knots (an airspeed of 107 knots at a typical wind-over-deck of 30 knots). The bleed air was automatically introduced when the landing gear was extended and shut off when the aircraft touched down, the throttles were advanced to military thrust, or the landing gear was raised.

One unanticipated, and belatedly realised, consequence of the F7U's nose-high stance was the inadequacy of the Navy's existing specification for the minimum over-the-nose visibility angle for a carrier-based aircraft. It had been established by experience with conventional aircraft configurations that did not

In 1946, BuAer contracted with Bell Aircraft to modify two P-63 King Cobras with swept wings as low-speed handling quality research aircraft. Without slats, the wing stall characteristics were unacceptable: abrupt, without warning, and resulting in a significant roll-off; with slats they were acceptable. ***US Navy via Hal Andrews Collection***

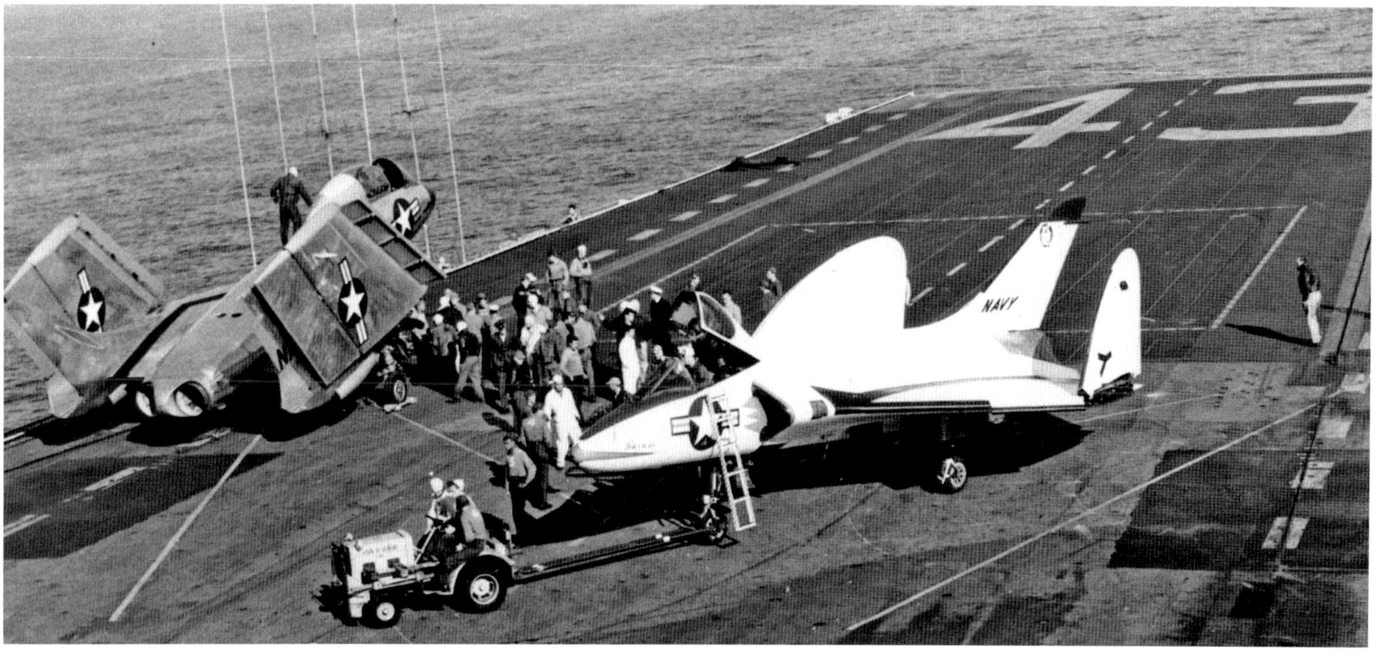

In October 1953 both F7U-3 BuNo 128475 (No. 25) and XF4D-1 BuNo 124586 were aboard *Coral Sea* (CVA-43) for carrier trials. Note the significant difference in nose-up attitude on the deck. *US Navy*

make an approach to land while pitched up to such a degree.

Another fallout of the tail-less configuration was the short fuselage, which necessitated the use of the wing for fuel tanks to a greater degree than usual. That resulted in a fairly thick wing relative to its chord. Both the low fineness ratio of the fuselage and thickness of the wing increased drag at transonic speeds that limited the aircraft's high-speed potential. Vought accepted the shortcoming in light of the configuration's other benefits and a jet engine innovation, afterburning, that was barely more than a concept.

Afterburning promised a significant increase in thrust for acceleration and rate of climb and, to a lesser

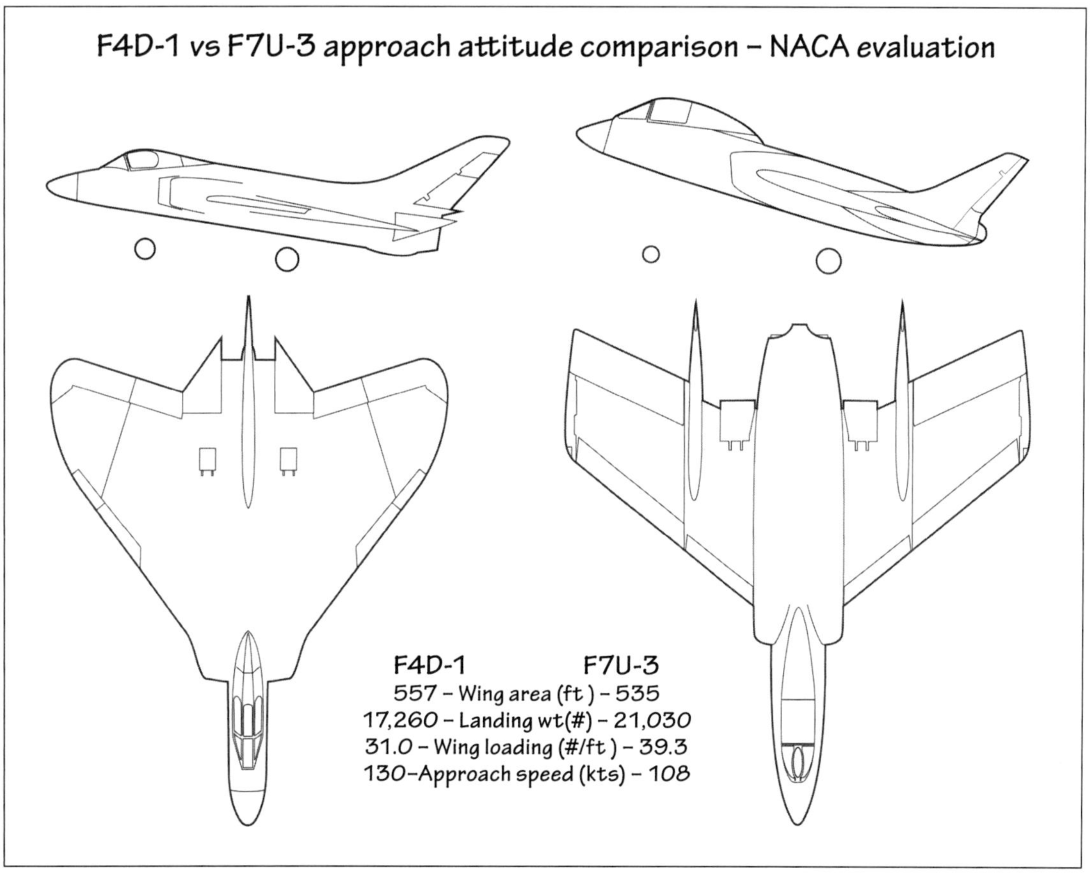

The pilot of a tail-less F4D could approach at a lower angle of attack because of its lower wing loading, albeit at a higher speed. Note that the F7U-3 pilot is sitting about 5ft higher than the F4D pilot, a significant difference given that the desired height of the wheels above the carrier deck during the flat approach was in the order of 20ft. *Thomason*

ABOVE A carrier-based fighter with no horizontal tail had to have a bigger wing than a land-based fighter of similar size since a slow approach speed was necessary and flaps could not be used to increase lift. Also note the nose-high stance of the tail-less V-346A compared to the F-86's. *Thomason*

RIGHT To provide roughly the same mission range and endurance, the Navy's first carrier-based jet, the FH-1 Phantom, had twice the internal fuel capacity of its last reciprocating-engine fighter, the F8F-1 Bearcat, but the jet had to be cruised much higher for the range and its engine could not be throttled back enough to reduce its fuel consumption for increased loiter time like the Bearcat's. *Thomason*

extent due to transonic drag, top speed. It also addressed a shortcoming of the basic turbojet engine at low speed relative to a propeller-pulled one: in automotive terms, a jet-propelled aircraft without an afterburner had no first or second gear, only a third gear. Acceleration on take-off or a wave off was therefore slow, although once a jet got up to speed, it had a fourth gear that the propeller plane did not. Afterburner added a second gear, albeit one that had a deleterious effect on range and endurance when employed. Not only could jet engines not sip fuel like a piston engine in any flight regime, the fuel burned each minute in afterburner (aka combat thrust), would be enough for three to four minutes of military (non-afterburning) thrust. On the other hand, acceleration from cruise speed to maximum speed in level flight would take less than a minute in afterburner but five minutes at military thrust. Likewise, rate of climb was significantly improved.

There was also a range benefit of afterburning for fighter missions: a jet engine's specific fuel consumption (lb of fuel per hour per lb of thrust) increased as thrust was decreased below its maximum. For the same take-off, top speed, acceleration, and rate of climb performance provided by an afterburning engine, a non-afterburning engine had to be bigger than optimal for cruise. This resulted in significantly higher fuel consumption at lower, i.e. cruising, thrust levels than that of a smaller engine with an afterburner added for the maximum performance required only occasionally and briefly. Lower fuel consumption during cruise, the greater part of a given mission, was a compelling argument for jet fighters powered by small afterburning engines instead of big, non-afterburning ones for the same combat performance.

Before jets were added to the carrier air group (CVG), endurance had not been a particularly challenging metric for a carrier-based aircraft. If necessary due to a landing deck availability problem, the fuel consumption of the reciprocating engine could be reduced significantly.

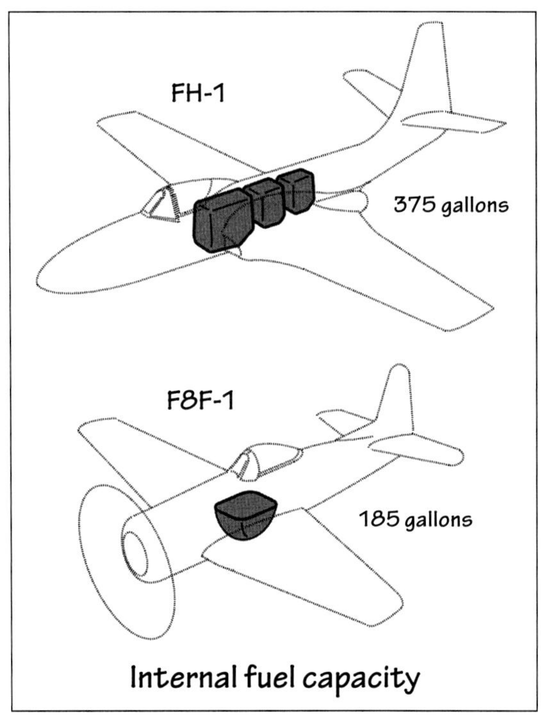

During the F4D mock-up review in March 1949 it was determined that its specification requirement of 18 degrees over-the-nose visibility was inadequate due to the high angle of attack on approach; the requirement was revised to 21 degrees and the forward fuselage modified accordingly. For some reason, this did not come up in the F7U-1 mock-up review two and a half years earlier and did not become a BuAer cause célèbre until its at-sea carrier trials in July 1951. *US Navy*

That was not possible with a jet engine, which had a very high basic metabolism: an Allison J35 burned twice as much fuel even when just idling as a Pratt & Whitney (P&W) R-2800 piston engine did at the minimum power required for maximum loiter time. A jet pilot therefore could not extend his time aloft very much by simply throttling way back. This was a critical difference from an operational standpoint because the number of aircraft in an embarked air group would fill half the flight deck of an axial-deck carrier and most of its hangar deck. It could therefore only either launch aircraft or land them. After the last landing of the day, all the aircraft on the flight deck would be parked aft in preparation for the first two launch events the next morning. The remaining aircraft on the deck would then be pulled forward to clear the landing area for the recovery of the aircraft in the first launch event. All the aircraft would then be pulled aft to allow the launch of the aircraft in the third event, after which they would be pulled forward for the recovery of the aircraft in the second event, and so on through the day. The interval between the launch and recovery of a group of aircraft was known as a cycle.

The introduction of jets resulted in the imposition of shorter and less flexible cycle times to minimise the risk of fuel exhaustion. Shorter cycle times meant more frequent re-spotting of the deck. The result was a scheduled cycle time of eighty to ninety minutes. That allowed some margin of jet aircraft endurance in the event the deck was fouled and recovery delayed. The combat radius for the basic jet fighter profile of take-off, climb, cruise, twenty minutes of combat, and return within ninety minutes was therefore about 300 nautical miles with a fuel reserve of twenty minutes at maximum endurance plus 5% of initial fuel.

The afterburner had shortcomings besides prodigious fuel consumption: somewhat finicky operability affecting use during an approach to landing and lack of reliable operation at high altitude. From the Navy's standpoint, the damage caused by the impingement of jet engine exhaust

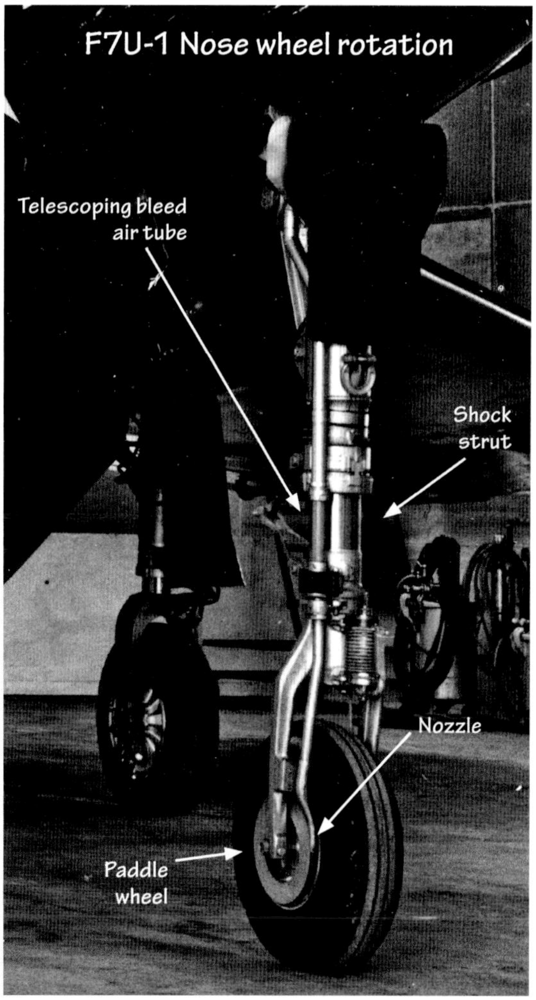

High-pressure bleed air to spin the F7U-1 nose wheel up to speed was carried down the right side of the F7U-1 nose landing gear strut in a telescoping tube. *Thomason*

on a wooden carrier deck during launch was already a problem; afterburning exacerbated it. The benefits were still perceived to be worthwhile for fighters. Development of one began at the United Kingdom's National Gas Turbine Establishment in 1943; limited flight tests were accomplished in 1944 as a result. Afterburning was initially adopted as an expedient way to increase the thrust of

Axial-carrier deck spots

Launch Recovery

When a full air group was aboard an axial-deck carrier, aircraft were normally launched or recovered at intervals, not at the same time. To switch from one capability to the other, almost all the aircraft on the flight deck had to flown off or the remainder moved forward or aft. *Thomason*

existing jet engines. The first US aircraft to fly with an afterburning engine, a Vought XF6U Pirate modified to add a Solar afterburner to its Westinghouse J34, flew on 28 July 1948. Similarly, the USAF added afterburning to the Allison J33 and J35 after the first flights of the Lockheed F-94 and the Northrop F-89 respectively. The Vought F7U-1 Cutlass, however, would be the first fighter to be designed with an afterburning engine, a leap of faith in 1946 by both Vought and the Navy.

Unrelated to the unconventional configuration choice but critical to the success of the programme was the Navy's reliance on the manufacturer of its first jet engine, Westinghouse, to design and qualify ones with greater thrust. Because 1) it took longer to develop and flight qualify engines than it did to design and build aircraft and 2) engines could be used to power aircraft from more than one manufacturer, it was customary for the military services to separately contract for the design, development, qualification, and production of aircraft engines in different power/thrust classes. They were then provided to the aircraft manufacturers as Government-Furnished Product (GFP), aka GFE substituting 'Equipment' for Product. Westinghouse had developed the J30 engines for the Navy's first carrier-based jet fighter, the McDonnell FH Phantom, and the J34 engines for its follow-on, the F2H Banshee, as well as Vought's F6U Pirate. In late 1947, Westinghouse won a Navy competition to develop the J40, a 7,500lb thrust (without afterburning) engine to power a twin-engine carrier-based bomber. With afterburning, it was be used in the Navy's forthcoming single-engine jet fighters. It was to have more than twice the thrust and mass flow of the J34. Westinghouse, however, had successfully more than doubled the thrust of the J30 with the J34 so the scale-up was not a cause for concern. In addition, the newly created US Air Force could be expected to contract with

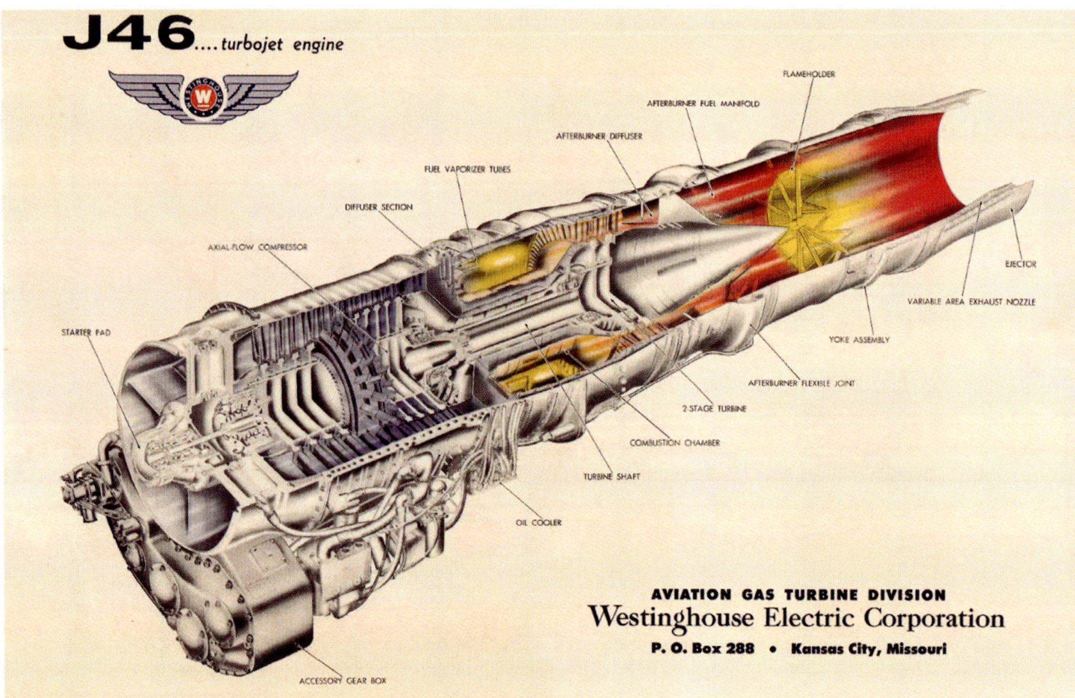

one or more of the engine manufacturers who had proposed an engine of similar performance, which would provide alternatives in the event that the J40 disappointed.

With the J40 programme in hand, Westinghouse submitted a proposal to the Navy for a scaled up derivative of the J34 in late December 1947. As a result, in April 1948 Westinghouse received a contract from BuAer for development of two different J34 derivatives:

- J34-WE-32: Aerodynamically and structurally similar to the -30 then in development, it would have a Westinghouse-furnished afterburner (the F7U-1 was originally to be powered by two J34-WE-22s and a government-furnished afterburner developed by Solar). Thrust ratings would increase to 3,500lb Military and 4,900lb Combat, about 17% and 15% better than the WE-22/Solar AB combination respectively.
- J46-WE-2: It was to be slightly larger than the J34 – limited to a 1.1in increase in diameter so it could potentially be retrofitted to J34-powered aircraft – and about 25% heavier with a twelve-stage rather than eleven-stage compressor providing a mass-flow increase to 73lb/second versus 58. The result was a predicted military-thrust rating of 4,200lb (20% more than the J34-WE-32), increased with afterburning to a combat rating of 6,100lb (24% more than the J34-WE-32). Westinghouse projected that the thrust of the J46 in afterburner would in time exceed 7,000lb.

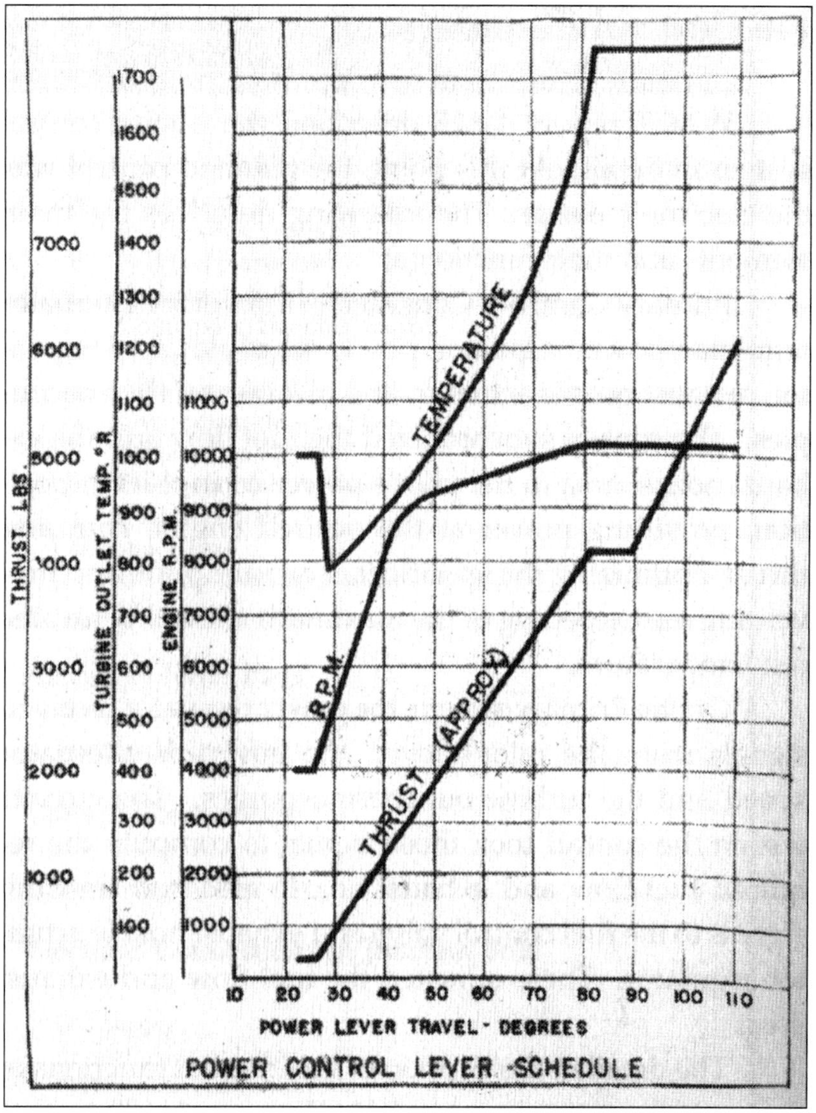

XJ46-WE-2 thrust schedule from WAGT report A-813: Note A/B thrust was to be fully modulated,; this proved to be unattainable: production engine afterburning was either on or off. However, the production-qualified fuel control maintained 100% rpm above about 50% of military thrust, resulting in minimal lag in response to throttle changes, particularly compared to centrifugal-flow engines.
Paul J. Christiansen

Both (as well as the J40) were to incorporate a Westinghouse electronic control system that kept the engine RPM at or above 90% of maximum above 40% of military thrust. Variation in thrust was to be accomplished primarily by increased or decreased fuel and nozzle area, resulting in rapid response to throttle movement (for a jet engine) as well as providing the pilot with linear throttle response from idle to maximum thrust even on afterburner-equipped engines, i.e. the afterburner thrust would be fully modulated rather than just on or off.

Several aircraft that were to be powered by two J34s would benefit from its replacement by the J46. The Navy's F3D Skyknight and F7U-1 were initially to be powered by J34s; derivatives of both aircraft would benefit from the J46's increased thrust, as would the Douglas D-558-II research aircraft, which relied on a single jet engine for take-off and climb and a rocket motor for high-speed flight. The J46 was also considered a prospective powerplant for the twin-engine Douglas predesign that resulted in the single-engine F4D Skyray. Convair proposed that the J46 power its jet-propelled seaplane fighter proposal that became the F2Y Sea Dart. The Air Force's McDonnell P-85, Curtiss-Wright P-87, McDonnell P-88, and Lockheed F-90 were all powered by J34s and therefore candidates to be powered by the J46. Finally, the Douglas X-3 Stiletto, a USAF supersonic research aircraft, was being designed to use two J46s.

The future for Westinghouse was bright if it could overcome production and systemic development weaknesses apparent during their earlier engine programmes. It was potentially brilliant at the end of 1948 when BuAer added a fourth major development programme to the company's plate, a 26% higher-thrust derivative of the J40-WE-2 that Westinghouse had only just begun to test. At this point, almost all of Navy's tactical jet aircraft to be developed in the next few years – seven fighters and a bomber – were to be powered by one or another of Westinghouse's four engines in development at the same time. The only exception was a swept-wing derivative of the Grumman F9F Panther that retained its P&W engine with a centrifugal-flow compressor.

CHAPTER TWO

1949 – Vought's Cutlass programme goes on life support

At the risk of oversimplifying the respective roles and responsibilities at the time, the Chief of Naval Operations (CNO) is the military head of the US Navy; reporting to him is a Deputy for Air Warfare (DCNO (Air)). BuAer, which is responsible for the development and production of aircraft that meet the needs of the Navy, and the Naval Air Test Center (NATC) at NAS Patuxent River, which is responsible for evaluating those aircraft, report to the DCNO (Air).

Two months before the XF7U-1's first flight on 27 September 1948, BuAer had ordered nineteen production F7U-1s via a letter of intent. Retrofit of changes to some or all of them resulting from XF7U flight testing was expected. This was indicative of the urgency of deploying a high-performance day fighter to match the Air Force's F-86 Sabre, which had flown for the first time a year earlier on 1 October 1947. The year 1949 began well, with the ferry flight of the first two XF7U-1s from

The F6U Pirate was Vought's first jet. Only three prototypes and thirty production aircraft were delivered. It was never carrier qualified; its major contributions were experience with adding an afterburner to a jet engine and its availability for a limited shore-based jet fighter operational evaluation. US Navy

Connecticut to a government-owned plant in Grand Prairie (a suburb of Dallas), Texas, where the Chance Vought Aircraft Division of United Aircraft was relocating its operations. The stillborn F5U programme was behind it; the F6U programme would disappoint but also provide significant jet design lessons learned. By contrast, the F7U programme was off to a good start.

However, in February the third XF7U-1 literally disappeared along with its pilot on a test flight from Patuxent River. The first Navy evaluation in June 1949 confirmed handling quality issues and other shortcomings that had already been identified by Vought. The modifications to correct them exacerbated a pre-existing empty weight challenge caused by Vought's optimistic weight estimates. The resulting increase meant that F7U-1 would no longer meet the minimum requirement for manoeuvring load factor strength at its combat weight.

Vought therefore proposed that some structural components and the landing gear of F7U number 20 and subsequent be redesigned. This would entail 'some sacrifice of speed and endurance' but restored the customary strength required for manoeuvring and high sink rate landings. The nineteen F7U-1s on order would be completed and used for qualification and operational evaluation. In September 1949, Vought received a letter of intent for production of eighty-eight F7U-2 day fighters, BuNos 125322–125409, as well as two somewhat larger and heavier F7U-3s, BuNos 125410–125411. The F7U-3, powered by J46 engines and with an APS-25 visual-assist radar, would provide the Navy with a back-up to the Grumman's XF10F, the Navy's first general-purpose fighter, in the event of problems in its development.

The CNO's requirement for a general-purpose fighter was based on carrier-warfare experience late in the Second World War. A carrier's air group had to have sufficient numbers of aircraft to both defend the carrier against attack and strike the enemy, taking into account the limited total quantity that could be aboard. The Japanese introduction of massed Kamikaze attacks from shore bases required a significant increase in the numbers of fighters in an air group at the expense of the number of bombers. A complement of night fighters also had to be added to the air group to provide around-the-clock protection, which again displaced some bombers. Fighters like the Vought F4U Corsair were therefore increasingly called upon to carry bombs and rockets to augment a strike force when air superiority had been attained.

The new general-purpose jet fighter requirement was developed over time during discussions with Grumman, which had a contract for its first jet fighter, the F9F-2, that included the development of a swept-wing day fighter prototype. The swept-wing version was

The XF5U configuration was even more unusual than the F7U's. Unfortunately, a combination of inferior performance compared to jet fighters and delay in the development of its interconnected propeller drive system and the propellers themselves resulted in the sole example being cancelled in March 1947 just as it was finally ready for its first flight. ***VAHF***

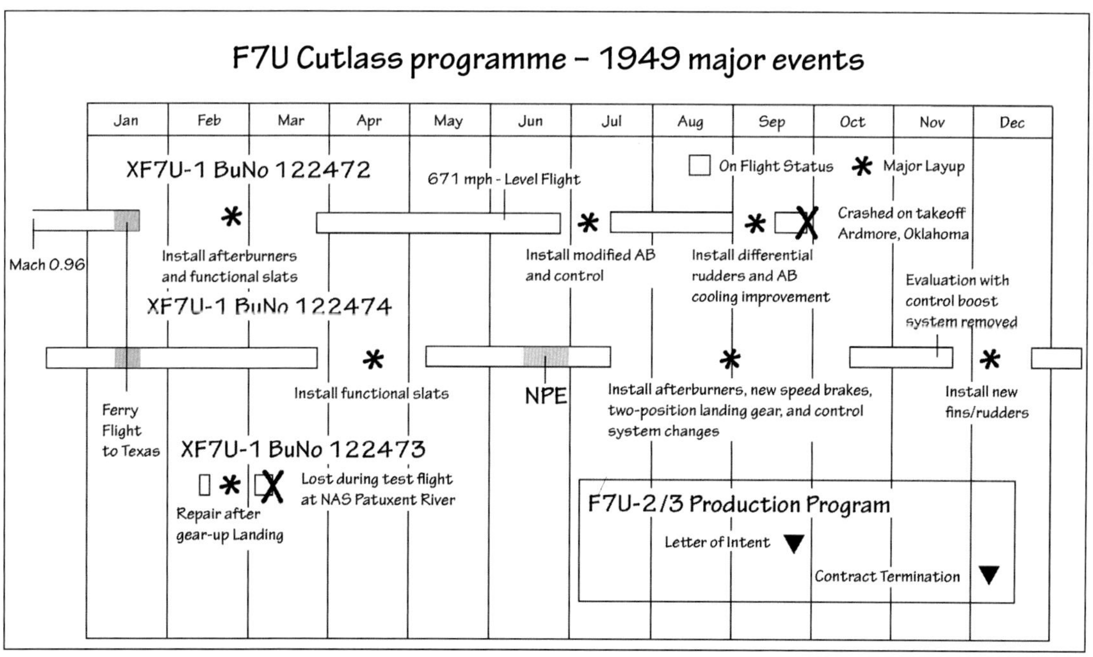

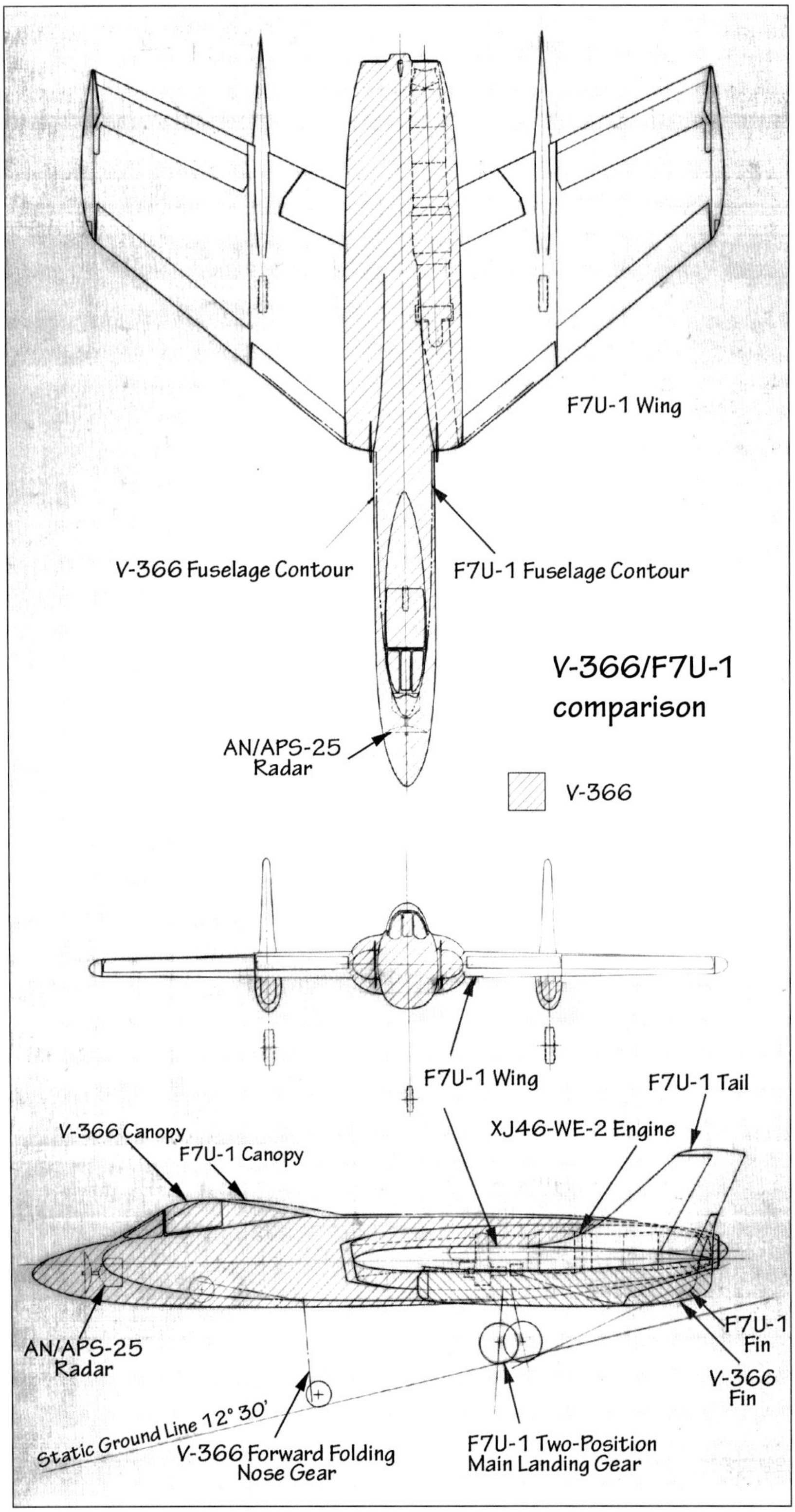

By March 1949, Vought had already begun to consider the addition of more thrust and a visual-assist radar to the F7U-1 to increase its performance and mission capability. Among other changes, the lower side of the main landing gear fairing was extended forward to house 2.75in folding-fin rockets as alternative armament to the 20mm cannon. To allow for a higher nose attitude on launch and landing, clamshell doors opened on the aft end of the fairing for ground clearance. This J46-powered variant was given the design number V-366. ***VAHF***

subsequently designated F10F and repurposed to be a general-purpose fighter; agreement on its configuration and mission capability was not completed until October 1949, more than a year after Grumman had received a letter of intent for it. Moreover, the aircraft's weight increase eventually necessitated the incorporation of a variable-sweep wing, an unproven feature: the USAF's experimental variable-sweep wing aircraft, the X-5, would not fly until June 1951.

The general-purpose fighter also addressed the problem of jet fighters being larger than piston-engine ones, reducing the number that could be included in the carrier air group. It was to fulfil the roles of an all-weather fighter (incorporating the visual-assist radar of a night fighter) and a strike escort (requiring it to accommodate lots of fuel for the necessary range) as well as directly augment a carrier's strike force by carrying bombs and rockets when air superiority had been achieved. This dictated a big and complex aircraft but it was believed to be the most effective use of the aircraft carrier's limited deck and hangar space that had to be shared with a squadron of day fighters (small, inexpensive but high-performance and manoeuvrable 'dog fighters') as well as some interceptors (very high rate of climb but limited endurance, launched in response to bombers getting through the combat air patrol); two-man night fighters equipped with more capable radar and fire control electronics; and airborne early warning aircraft as well as the carrier's raison d'être: the main battery consisting of dedicated attack aircraft including big bombers with a long-range, nuclear strike capability.

Contracting with Vought for F7U-3s was in accordance with the Navy's long-standing practice of developing aircraft from two different manufacturers for the same requirement, e.g. the Brewster F2A Buffalo and the Grumman F4F Wildcat, as a hedge against a failure of either one to meet specification or otherwise disappoint, not to mention the benefit to the Navy of competition between manufacturers, both in development and production. The Vought F4U Corsair and the Grumman F6F Hellcat are another example. In that case, wartime necessity resulted in both being produced in large numbers. In 1949, the Douglas F4D and McDonnell F3H were both candidates for the Navy's new short-range jet interceptor requirement.

The F7U-2s were to be powered by Westinghouse J34-WE-32 engines and be delivered between June 1951 and July 1952. One of the Westinghouse J46-WE-2 engine-powered F7U-3s would be delivered in October 1951 and the other a month later. To meet the general-purpose fighter requirement, the F7U-3s were to be equipped with an APS-25 visual-assist radar, additional stores pylons, and greater fuel capacity. The -3's wing area was somewhat greater than the -2's because the fuselage was wider, reportedly to

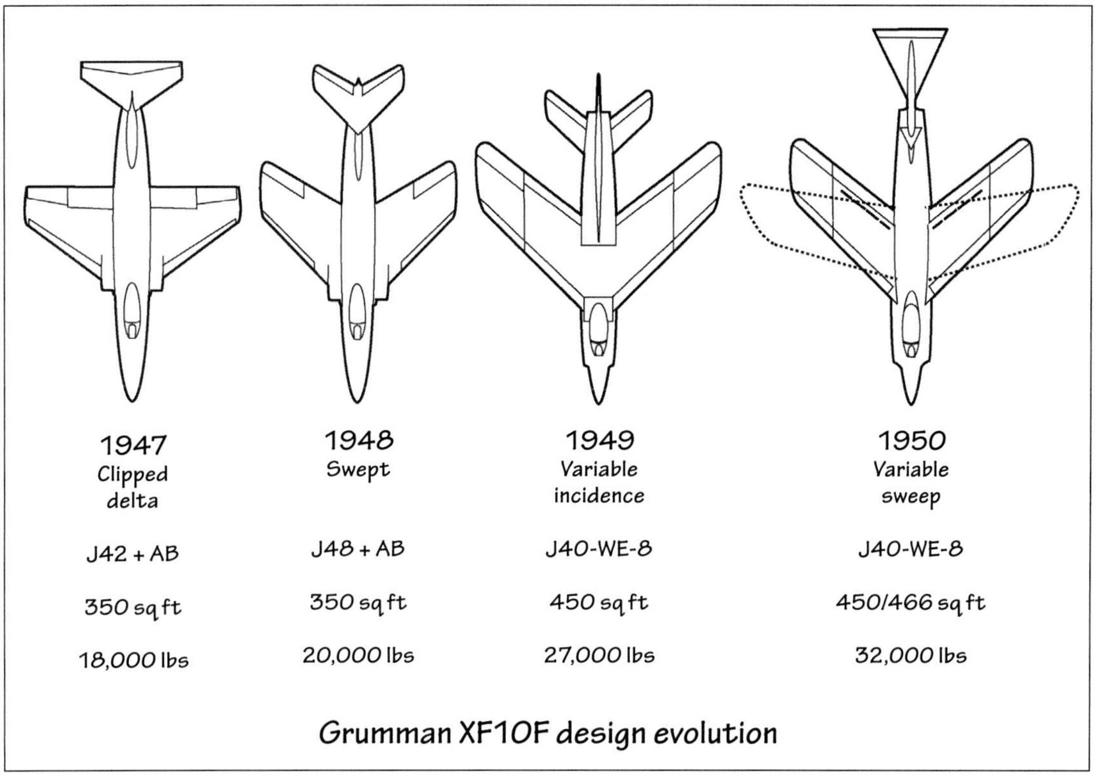

The Navy kept adding mission capability – avionics, armament, and range/endurance – to what was to originally have been a swept-wing day fighter until the Grumman F10F Jaguar's take-off gross weight exceeded 30,000lb. That resulted in the aircraft needing a variable-sweep wing to reduce its take-off and landing speed to accommodate existing catapult and arresting gear capability. ***Thomason***

accommodate the slightly bigger Westinghouse J46s even though its diameter increase had been restricted to allow it to be a relatively straightforward replacement for a J34 in an existing aircraft. The schedule was tight, particularly in the case of the engine, but the J46 mock-up review had been accomplished in mid-March 1949 and it was a derivative of the J34, providing confidence in Westinghouse's qualification and delivery commitments.

One prerequisite before a new engine would be approved for a first flight was completion of a Preliminary Flight Rating Test (PFRT) and subsequent teardown inspection. The PFRT consisted of a minimum of fifty hours' run time on a test stand – without replacement of any significant components – accomplishing a specific number of starts and shutdowns and hours at various high-power settings. The engine company would then disassemble the engine and inspect each part for any indication of damage as well as even a hint of incipient failure. After a customer review of the teardown report and on occasion, the parts, the engine would then be considered safe for flight with a limit of fifty hours of run time. However, since that was an unacceptable operational Time Between Overhaul (TBO), the engine company would then have to complete a similar 150-hour qualification test of an engine, again followed by a teardown inspection. (Splitting the qualification into two parts allowed for flight test to begin as soon as possible.) The condition of the parts subjected to the 150-hour test would establish an initial TBO for service use; inspection of overhauled engines and correction of any problems found would result in subsequent TBO increases.

Unfortunately, President Truman had become increasingly intent on not only eliminating ongoing budget deficits but also winding down the debt that the nation had incurred as a result of the Second World War. In June 1949, he reduced the DoD budget for the 1950 fiscal year beginning on 1 July 1949 by almost 10%. What was worse from the standpoint of the Navy's plans, his Secretary of Defense made additional draconian reductions in its account in November, almost halfway through the fiscal year, and made it known that there would be further reductions for FY1951.

Of all the Navy fighter development programmes on contract at that moment, the F7U-2 day fighter/ interim interceptor was the most vulnerable. The other new high-performance fighters – the F10F Jaguar, F4D Skyray, and F3H Demon – addressed important mission requirements that the F7U-2 fell short of. Vought management believed the inability of Westinghouse to meet its qualification and delivery schedule for the F7U-1's afterburning engines to be a major factor. However, the DCNO (Air) had told BuAer of back-channel reports that he had received of the F7U-1's unacceptable flight characteristics. He requested an evaluation of the likelihood that they were resolvable, probably lowering BuAer's inclination to continue funding the F7U-2 programme in light of the onerous budget reductions. On 8 December 1949, it was terminated along with the two F7U-3s.

The shortsightedness of the Navy's decision to postpone the availability of a carrier-based transonic day fighter in favour of only interceptors and general-

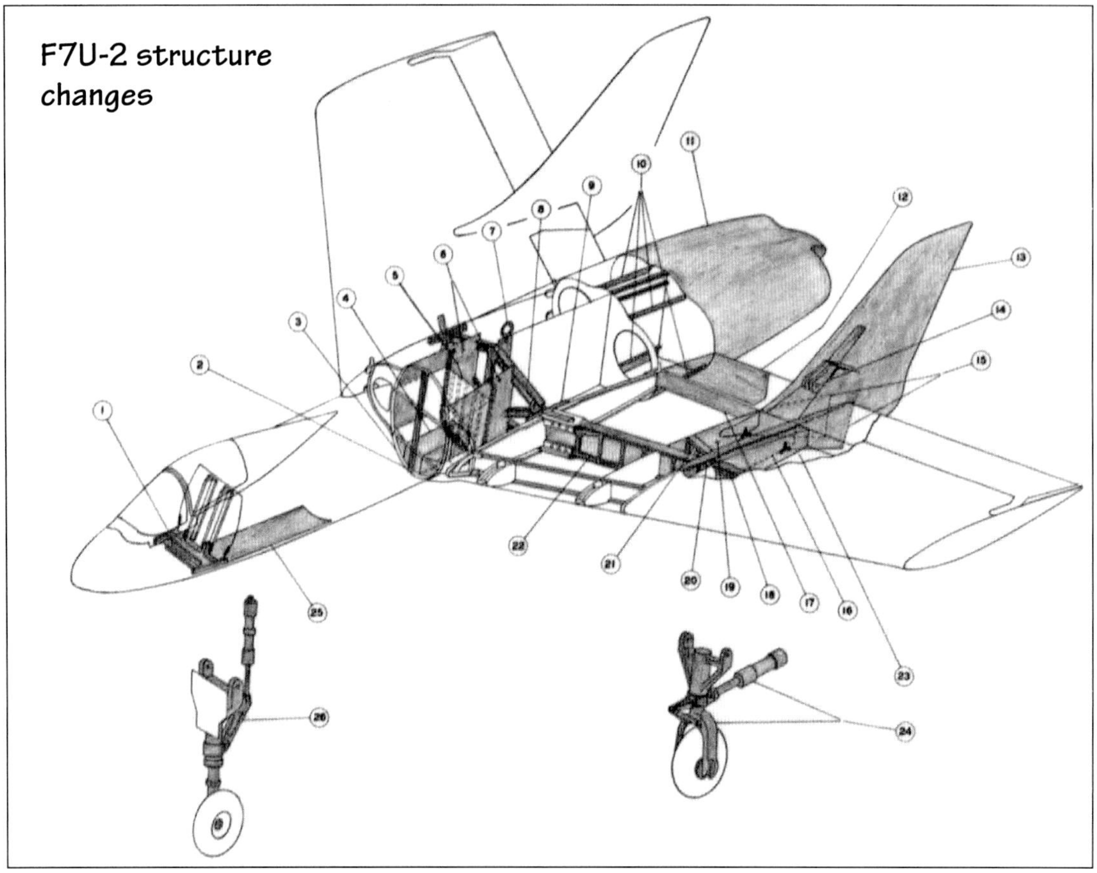

Beef up of portions of the F7U-1 structure and landing gear was required as a result of the gross weight increase that occurred during development. Not shown is a proposed modification to cant the forward fuselage downward for better visibility on approach. ***VAHF***

1 Bulkhead 70 – Change of the nose gear trunnion fitting the trunnion fitting tie to the seat tracks and the splice of the side members

2 Jacking Fitting and Support – Heavier fitting and attachment

3 Front Beam Bulkhead 184.5 – Increase gage of of lower web and centreline vertical member

4 Catapult Reel Assembly – Increase gage of keel webs and doublers – increase gage of vertical supports – change horizontal fitting, catapult hook, and holdback strut increase gage of holdback support channels increase strength of members attaching to bulkheads 184.5 and 215.2 – change location of catapult doors in lower panels – increase gage of ammo deck between keels

5 Bulkhead 215.2 – Increase gage of vertical web and vertical stiffeners at keel attachment

6 Internal Panels – 184.5 to 232.5 – Increase web gage and edge attachments

7 Hoist Sling Stud and support fitting strengthened

8 Increase area of struts on bulkhead 232.5

9 Change material of wing fuselage attaching fitting from 14ST to 75ST

10 Longerons from 306 to 344 to be redesigned

11 Fuselage aft of bulkhead 344 to be redesigned for production installation of "Flying V" type arresting hook consisting of skin and frame changes and longeron relocation

12 Redesigned short span airbrake and increased outboard fairing

13 General redesign of vertical tail – Skin gage change, beam relocation and and rudder changes

14 Drag Strut Support Fitting – Forging change and possible relocation of fitting

15 Lower Fin Tie to Wing – Heavier lower longerons

16 Rib 108 – Centre Section – Larger lower cap strip, heavier web and attachments

17 Rear Seam – Web and stiffener gage changes

18 Increase area of outer panel beam flange

19 Upper Wing Skin Panel – STA 92-106 Aft – Skin gage change and stiffener change

20 Increase bending strength of wing fold fittings

21 Main Landing Gear Support Fitting – Redesign involving new forging dies to strengthen fitting

22 Centre Section Main Beam – Increase web thickness and flange area

23 Main Landing Gear Doors – Strengthen

24 Main Landing Gear – General increase in strength

25 Nose Gear Doors – Strengthen

26 Nose Gear – Strengthened generally with possible increase in stroke

Vought test pilot Paul Thayer survived the crash of an XF7U-1 in September 1949 with minor injuries: he lost control on take-off with an experimental rudder control system and a significant asymmetric loading consisting of one large external fuel tank full of fuel. ***VAHF***

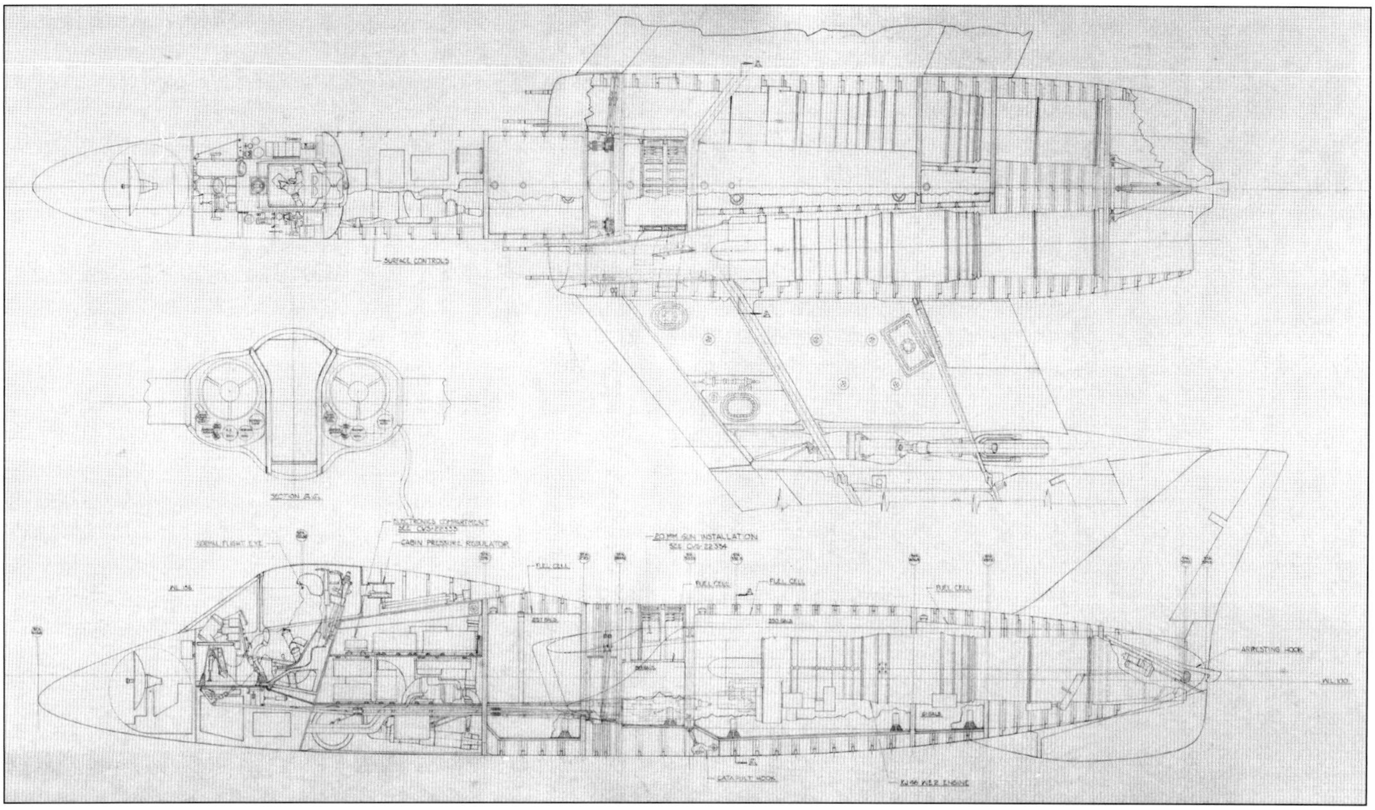

This V-366D inboard profile, created in October 1949, depicts a combination of features of the F7U-1, the future F7U-3, and some additional design innovations. For example, it still has the complex tail hook installation of the F7U-1 but J46 engines and a visual-assist radar. The 20mm cannon were relocated aft below the engine inlets with the barrels extending forward of them. It also has a forward-retracting nose landing gear with a shrink strut to minimise the size of the wheel well and 'solid' tires for weight reduction. The view directly over the nose is 19 degrees, somewhat greater off to the side. ***VAHF***

purpose fighters that had not yet flown would soon become apparent. Fortunately the contract for nineteen production F7U-1s had been funded by the FY1949 authorisation and so was not affected by the FY1950 budget reductions. Modifications were being developed or already satisfactorily being demonstrated for the issues that had been identified by XF7U-1 testing, even though there were never more than two on flight status at any one time and then only for a total of ten weeks during the year. A second XF7U-1 had crashed in September but at that point, the first production F7U-1 was in final assembly. The various Westinghouse engine-development programmes were also not affected.

The F7U-2/3 cancellation was very bad news but Vought hoped that BuAer was still desirous of a back-up to the XF10F for the general-purpose fighter requirement. Because the cancellation of F7U-2 production had significantly affected Vought's projected sales and revenue, management redoubled their efforts to reinstate the F7U-2 and/or F7U-3 programmes. With respect to the latter, the company provided an unsolicited proposal to the Navy on 4 November 1949 for its V-366D powered by two J46s and V-366E powered by one J40-WE-10. Although Westinghouse was projecting that J46 flight qualification would be accomplished in September 1950, Vought management thought that might be optimistic, particularly considering that the J46 programme was competing with the J40 for resources. It was a legitimate concern given the J40's importance to the Navy: it was to power the F10F, F4D, and F3H as well as the Douglas A3D Skywarrior bomber. After a detailed evaluation of several factors (Design, Aerodynamics, Power Plant, Structure, Weight and Balance, Armament and Electronic Equipment, and Cost and Fabrication), Vought concluded that the single-engine version was 'a better basic airplane design' (not to mention that there were now other engines in development for the Air Force in that size class in case Westinghouse was unable to successfully qualify the J40 for production). The Bureau did not agree, possibly because its dependence on the J40 for the success of its other transonic fighter programmes dictated an alternative one powered by a different engine. However, it also took no action on the twin-engine V-366D proposal.

CHAPTER THREE

1950 – The F7U-2 programme is dead; long live the F7U-3 programme

In late 1949, after the F7U-2 production programme was cancelled, Vought management was still hopeful, based on discussions with BuAer, that it would be reinstated at some point in 1950. It was not to be …

Vought therefore submitted an updated F7U-3 programme plan in early February 1950 that would result in a first flight on 1 November 1951 – absorbing at least one month of the hiatus caused by its cancellation in December – because of its similarity to the F7U-1 and work done to that point on the F7U-2. In contrast to its early 1949 recommendation that an F7U-3 prototype be flight tested that combined the new F7U-3 fuselage and nose landing gear with the F7U-1 wing and vertical fins, Vought now claimed that there was no need for a prototype phase since the F7U-3 was aerodynamically similar enough to the -1. Two XF7U-1s had been flying for more than a year and the first production F7U-1s were being readied for flight. BuAer did not disagree with this justification for not needing a prototype phase in the F7U-3 programme plan, which would expedite its availability for operational use.

Vought's proposal was for its V-366F, which was different in detail relative to the twin-J46 V-366D, probably in part as a result of feedback from BuAer. Gone were the solid tyres, the two-position main landing gear, the forward-retracting nose landing gear, and the complex, double-jointed arresting hook. The lower fin stub was smaller both in length (no longer housing rockets) and depth (no longer requiring doors for ground clearance). The cannon were now located above the engine inlets. The engines were to be installed and removed by removing the tail cone rather than from below. The launch attitude would be increased to 25 degrees by inflation of the main gear oleos to their fully extended position and pulling the tail down until small wheels in the lower fin stub fairings touched the deck. The cockpit was

Vought test pilot and future company president Paul Thayer in the cockpit of the first production F7U-1. Note the original, much shorter, vertical fins. ***VAHF***

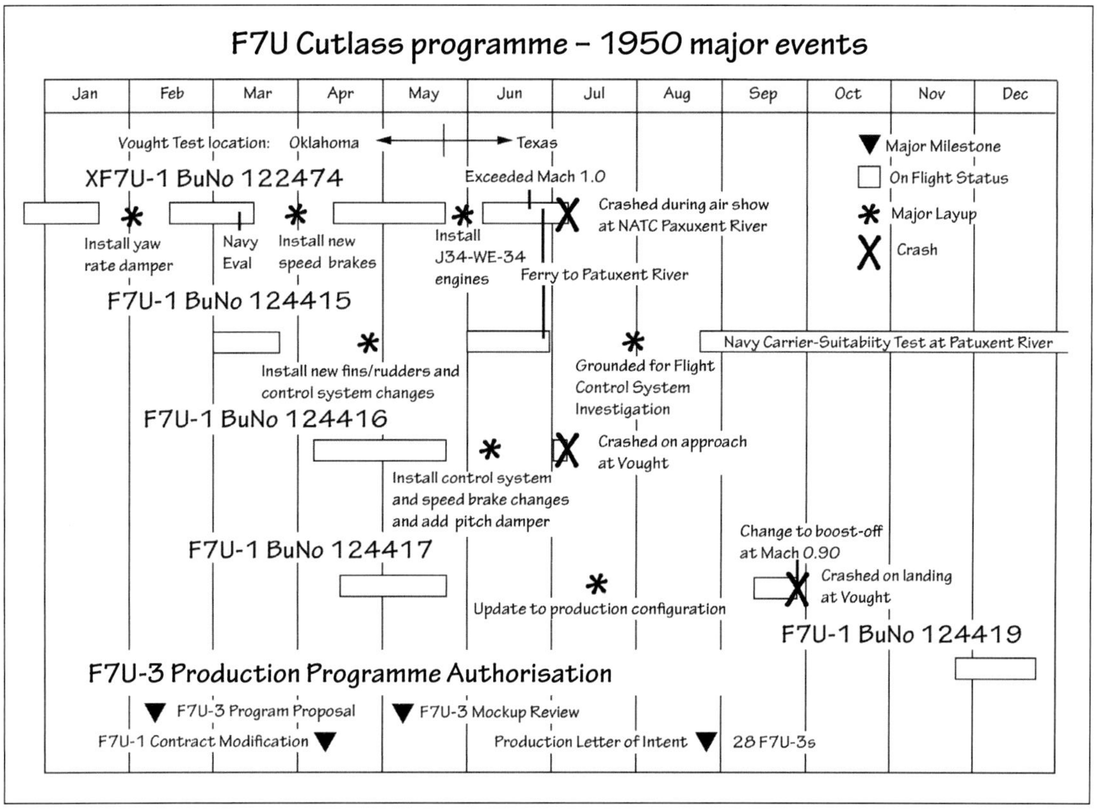

enlarged and tilted down about 6 degrees for the desired vision over the nose without requiring the pilot to lean forward. The take-off weight with full internal fuel and 800 rounds of 20mm ammunition was 27,000lb.

A production F7U-1 flew for the first time on 1 March 1950. Two NATC pilots, LtCol Marion Carl, USMC and LCDR Joseph Rees, and two BuAer pilots, CDR Noel Gayler and CDR Charles E. Gibson, flew it later that month, coming away with different opinions of its performance and handling qualities. According to Gayler, LtCol Carl specifically stated that the performance of the aircraft was not quite up to expectations, that the control stick force per *g* was unsatisfactory, that the aileron response was 'slow', and that 'certain things … certainly require additional investigation'. Fortunately the BuAer pilots – even though some of the planned modifications to rectify problems identified by Vought in XF7U-1 flight test had not yet been incorporated in the Cutlasses being evaluated – were impressed by its potential and therefore supported the continuation of the F7U-3 programme within BuAer.

It is easy for some to wonder in hindsight why BuAer kept funding the F7U programme. One likely reason for its 1950 reinstatement is that it was the only Navy carrier-based fighter being developed that was not powered by the unproven Westinghouse J40. Its J46 engine was not much of a stretch from the J34, certainly not as much as the J40's, and therefore lower risk. BuAer was also still desirous of a general-purpose fighter back-up to the XF10F, which had an unproven variable-sweep wing and was still at least a year away from first flight. Because of the ongoing F7U-1 flight test and evaluation, the likelihood of the F7U-3 being developed successfully– not to mention deployable earlier – than the F10F was clearly greater.

An article in the April 1950 Naval Aviation Confidential Bulletin written by CDR Gayler, then in charge of the Fighter Class Desk at BuAer, listed the desired and challenging characteristics of the general-purpose fighter:

Armament – Present aircraft cannon with higher cyclic rates and higher striking velocities. Salvos of 2.75-inch Mighty Mouse rockets capable of being fired on either a collision or a pursuit course with the target. Large, high-performance air-to-air rockets. Air-to-air guided missiles.

All-Weather Capability – Effective operation in all but the worst weather conditions, day or night, and therefore equipped with all-weather instrumentation, electronic navigation, automatic direction finding, high-performance radio altimeters, air-to-air homing devices, and radar capable of mapping and 'beaconry'.

Human Factors – A cabin pressure high enough at the highest flight altitudes to make the pilot entirely comfortable when wearing 'modern' oxygen equipment.

Performance – Transonic speed without serious buffet or control difficulties and supersonic in a

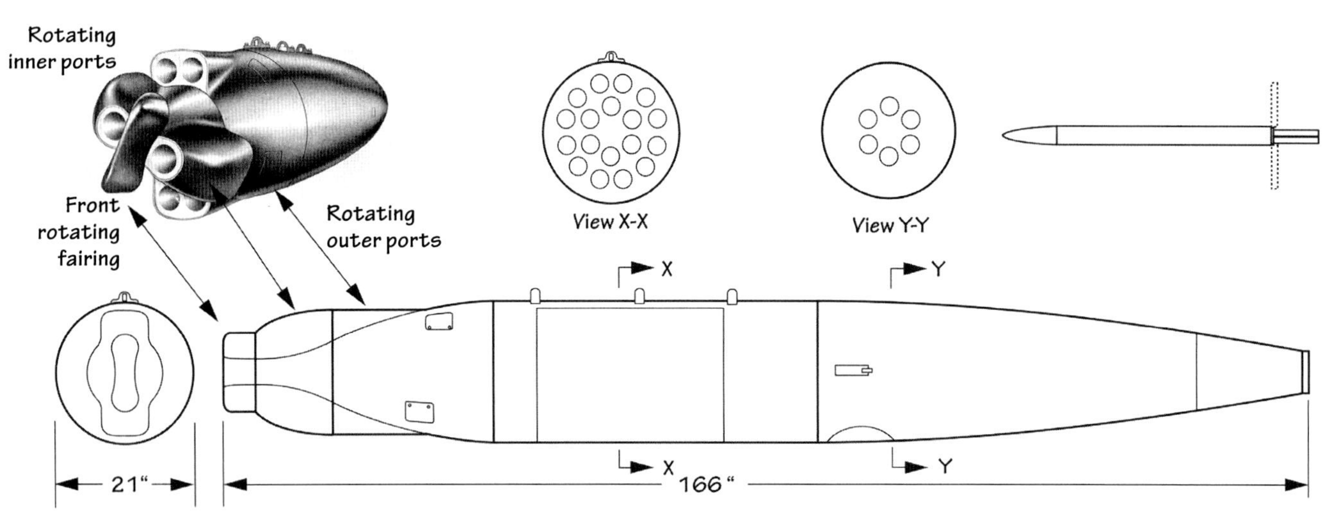

Mk 13 2.75" folding-fin rocket launcher

In the late 1940s, the Naval Ordnance Test Station (NOTS) at China Lake, California, began developing folding-fin aircraft rockets (FFAR) that could be loaded into pods rather than having to be individually carried on pylons. In the early 1950s, the Mk 13 Aircraft Rocket Launcher was in development to be carried by fighters as air-to-air armament. It was intended to be loaded with twenty-four 2.75-in FFARs, eighteen in the mid-section and six in the aft section. To minimise drag, the forward section was comprised of three rotating fairings, the aft two containing ports through which the rockets fired as they aligned with the rocket tubes. When loaded, the pod weighed nearly 800lb, of which almost half was the weight of the pod itself. The concept was abandoned in favour of a much simpler and lighter pod that had no moving parts and a frangible fairing on the nose. ***Thomason***

dive to intercept or to overhaul enemy bombers of the highest performance, a rate of climb less than that of interceptors but sufficiently high to meet the requirements of escort and combat air patrol, endurance comparable to our wartime propeller-driven fighters, a combat radius considerably greater than that of current jet fighters, and turning ability at high altitudes.
Carrier Suitability – Good slow-speed control, good stability, good stall characteristics, and good vision for carrier landing and take-off.

The author noted that these requirements would entail a significant increase in the fighter's size compared to the Grumman F9F Panther and the McDonnell F2H Banshee day fighters then being deployed. A take-off gross weight of up to 30,000lb was envisaged. Moreover, he recognised the degree of difficulty in combining the required high-speed performance of a fighter of this size with the low-speed capability necessary for carrier landings.

He went on to describe the two general-purpose fighters under consideration at that time. The Grumman F10F Jaguar was expected to 'be capable of very high speed performance, attaining considerably more than 600 knots in level flight, and it should be capable of operating in the transonic region without control difficulties. This aircraft will have high rates of climb even at full load and a combat radius in excess of 600 nautical miles.' The Vought F7U-3 Cutlass 'promises to have more than 600 knots true speed with a very high rate of climb, a combat radius of more than 500 nautical miles, and necessary radar and other equipment to make it a high performance, all-weather, general-purpose fighter'. Unstated was the intention that the general-purpose fighter would also be capable of delivering the tactical nuclear weapons then being developed.

Gayler's conclusion, part of which was emphasised in italics in the article, was: 'In some respects, the size of these aircraft will prejudice their employment, but this much can confidently be stated: *One or both models will provide the Navy with carrier-based general-purpose fighters of combat performance second to none*.'

Vought's parent, United Aircraft, shared its confidence that BuAer would reinstate the F7U-3 programme. As a result, the corporation funded resumption of engineering work in early 1950 in advance of a contract so Vought did not have to lay off engineers and could begin production as soon as possible. A fuselage-only mock-up review could therefore be held for the Navy in late April and progress made in long-lead tasks like tool design. United Aircraft subsequently approved funds for long-lead material as well.

In late March, prior to the mock-up review, Vought Chief Engineer Fred Dickerman and J.B. Schliemann visited BuAer to discuss and perfect the draft F7U-3 Detail Specification. For example, senior aviators suggested that the control stick have a lateral pivot point high on its column to avoid leg interference at full roll control throw. CDR Gayler expressed his desire for an angle-of-attack indicator for the pilot. A BuAer representative described a recent incident with an F2H

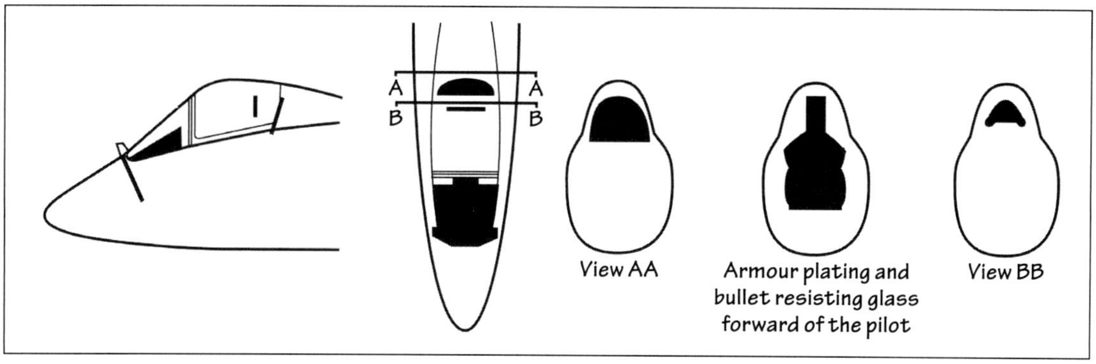

LEFT In the 1 April 1952 F7U-3 Standard Aircraft Characteristics chart (SAC), the total weight of the armour and bullet-resistant glass had been reduced to 190lb. *Thomason*

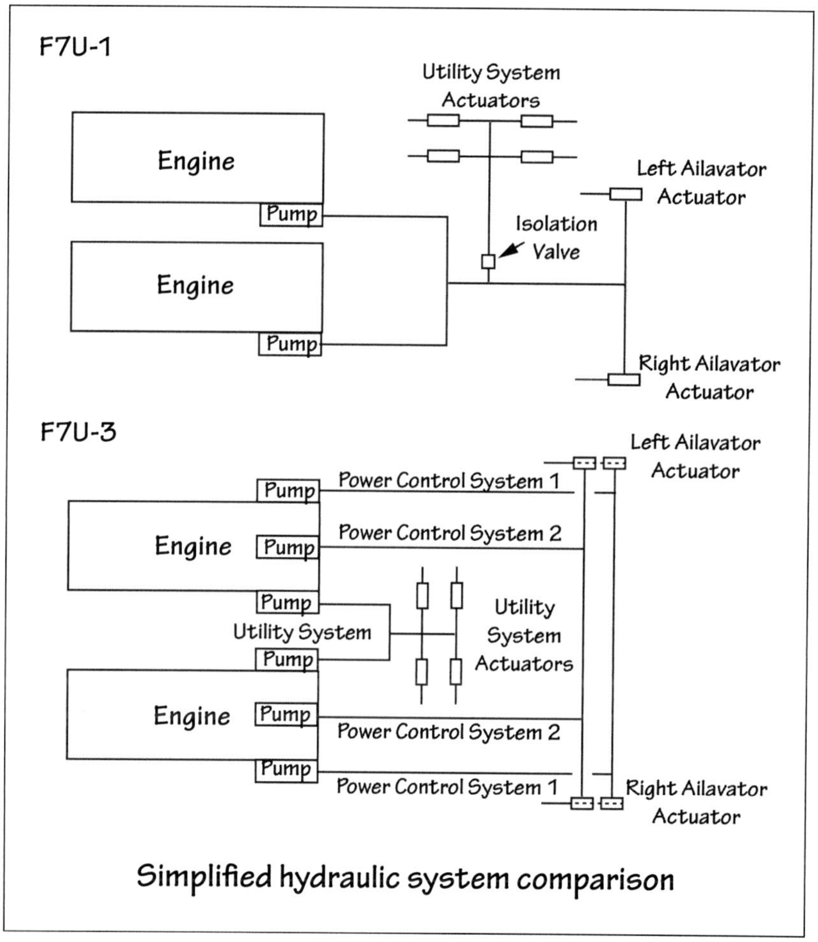

ABOVE This simplified comparison does not show many details such as return lines, filters, reservoirs, check valves, gages, auxiliary (emergency) pumps, etc, but does depict the significantly increased complexity of the F7U-3's hydraulic system compared to the F7U-1's, which was typical of jet fighters up until then with the exception of an increase in a flight control system pressure to 3,000 psi. *Thomason*

Banshee engagement with the new Davis barrier installed on carriers to stop aircraft with nose landing gears that failed to hook one of the arresting wires. Sharp edges on the main landing gear had sheared the barrier's cable, which then cut the brake line located on the forward side of the landing gear, leaving the pilot with no brakes. Schliemann took a note to have drawings available at the mock-up review showing generously rounded edges on all forward portions of the nose and main landing gear since the mock-up was only the fuselage itself.

In the first Armament Section meeting, the Vought engineers were told that as a general-purpose fighter, the F7U-3 was to be armed with four of the Navy's new Mk 12 20mm cannon and also have provisions to carry 'packages' of 2.75in and 5in rockets or Sparrow air-to-air missiles in addition to the necessary 'rocket computers'. A government-furnished search and acquisition radar, the AN/APQ-36, was to be assumed. However, any external stores and the rocket computer could be considered to be an overload for structural strength (g-capability) purposes to minimise empty weight. Although Vought had proposed ten pylons originally (most to carry one 5in rocket or small bomb each), the need for that many was obviated by the Navy's development of pylon-mounted pods with multiple tubes to house the small and more compact 2.75in folding-fin rockets. It was agreed that there would only be four pylons: one on each inboard wing section and one on the outboard (folding) panels. The inboard pylon would be stressed for a 2,000lb store; the outboard, a 1,000lb one. All four pylons were to be Sparrow capable. Guidance was also provided with respect to armament system management.

In a second Armament Section meeting, an updated BuAer policy on armour protection was discussed. Forward and aft protection from armour-piercing slugs was to be provided with a minimum ⅜in face-hardened steel although aft protection below the shoulders could be provided by hardware and components, e.g. the engines. The resulting protection totalled 214lb, almost twice that of the F7U-1 requirement.

The Airborne Equipment Section meeting covered Vought's proposed dual-boost control system. The F7U-1 had a single hydraulic system pressurised by one hydraulic pump on each engine. It provided hydraulic pressure to the ailavator control system as well as the utility system, e.g. actuators for the landing gear, leading-edge wing slats, etc. In the event of a hydraulic fluid loss in the lines to the utility system actuators, the system was designed to automatically only provide hydraulic pressure to the ailavator actuators. In the event of a total loss of hydraulic pressure, for example an

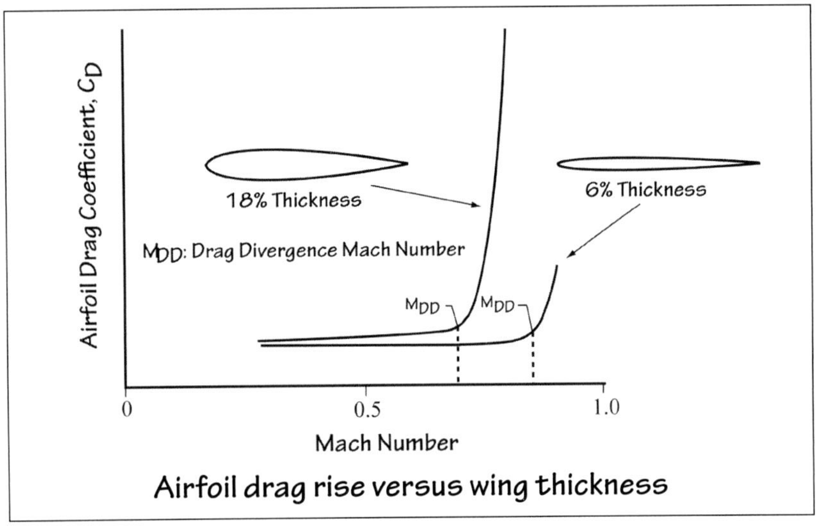

The thickness of an aerofoil relative to its chord had a significant impact on the so-called critical Mach number at which drag that had been increasing as a function of airspeed squared began to increase much more quickly with increasing speed. ***Thomason***

engine failure combined with the failure of the pump on the other engine, the control system was to automatically change over to a manual back-up using spring tabs on the control surfaces (while the changeover only took a few seconds, it seemed much longer to the pilot when it happened). This approach was typical of hydraulic systems in the early jets because the weight of hydraulic actuators, pumps, valves, accumulators, filters, pressure and return lines, the fluid itself, etc. dictated their minimisation. One innovation, introduced on the F7U-1, was to increase system pressure from 1,000 psi to 3,000 psi to minimise weight by reducing the diameter of the hydraulic lines and the amount of fluid required.

Pilot concerns about the F7U-1 automatic switchover concept and the Airborne Equipment Section's increasing reluctance to have the flight control system possibly compromised by the failure of non-flight essential components resulted in Vought going to the other extreme: three separate hydraulic systems, two for flight control with both supplying power separately to each ailavator actuator and one dedicated to the utility hydraulic system powering the landing gear, wing leading-edge slats, speed brakes, etc. Moreover, each of the three hydraulic systems was to be pressurised by two pumps, one on each engine, for a total of six hydraulic pumps, compared to the usual two (one per engine on a twin-engine jet, two on the engine of a fighter with only one). The result was an unprecedented degree of redundancy: if one flight control system pump failed, the other would provide adequate pressure to that system; if one flight control hydraulic system failed, the other would provide adequate power to the ailavator actuator; if one engine failed, the other would keep all three systems pressurised. However, the system was also heavy even at 3,000 psi and the total quantity of components and fittings ensured a higher incidence of leaks and potential failures than would be experienced with a simpler one.

After some discussion, it was agreed that a manual emergency system for flight control would not be needed, although there was concern whether there would be enough hydraulic power, in the event that both engines failed, provided by windmilling engines for flight control at landing or ditching speed. Another subject was the concept of a 'non-pressurised in-flight' utility hydraulic system: shutting off the hydraulic flow to some actuators after take-off until just before landing to reduce the risk that a component failure or battle damage would result in draining the utility system of fluid. Both features would subsequently be added to an already complex and heavy design.

In a typical BuAer example of conveying a manufacturer's best design practice or innovation (in BuAer's opinion) to competitors, the McDonnell XF3H instrument panel was described to Dickerman. Its desirable feature was the use of a curved Plexiglas panel to provide the lighting of the instruments and make them equidistant from the pilot's eye. The panel was basically a section of a cylinder 34in in diameter that was tilted forward 15 degrees. The desired standardisation by BuAer of instrument size and location was also discussed.

CDR Gayler raised concerns about the proposed wing thickness versus chord resulting in a low critical Mach number, doubtless as a result of technical reviews with other aircraft manufacturers. Dickerman explained that he hesitated 'to make any changes to the F7U-1 wing due to the lack of knowledge of what might occur aerodynamically were (Vought) to add tip area or even increase the chord over the centre section to match the increased ailavator chord on the outer panel'. He pointed out that, based on analysis by Vought's aerodynamicists, the thick wing did not penalise performance to any great extent. It was apparent to him that his explanation was not convincing (and in hindsight, should not have been). Nevertheless, BuAer did not request a reduction in wing thickness.

Discussions with the Power Plant Section primarily covered details like the refuelling shut-off switch design and a requirement for a fuel boost pump warning light in the cockpit. However, there was a recommendation that JP-3 fuel be considered as an alternative to the then-standard gasoline, which would result in an increase in gross weight as jet fuel, basically kerosene, was about 13% heavier than gasoline per gallon.

The exact configuration of Vought's February 27,000lb F7U-3 proposal is not known but the result of its review by and discussions with BuAer was a F7U-3 Detail Specification with a take-off gross weight of 28,244lb, an increase of almost 5%.

In April, BuAer, since the F7U-3 programme was likely to be reinstated, provided Vought with a modification to the F7U-1 production contract that, for the time being, substituted an F7U-3 for the fifteenth F7U-1 (the remaining four F7U-1s on that contract were subsequently cancelled). That allowed Vought to begin charging the Navy for F7U-3 engineering design and analysis as opposed to continuing to self-fund it, which likely would have lengthened the time to first flight. BuAer representatives reviewed and basically accepted the fuselage mock-up on 18–21 April.

On 19 May, Vought's General Manager, Fred Detweiler and United Aircraft Corporation Vice President Charles 'Mac' McCarthy, visited BuAer for a meeting with its Chief, Rear Admiral Alfred Pride. According to Detweiler's trip report, 'Admiral Pride made it clear that he could not, on that day, give us a positive commitment for F7U-3 production. He simply said that the Navy had in mind a final evaluation of the F7U-3 about August 1, 1950 based upon progress at that point with the XF7U-1 and the carrier suitability tests of the first F7U-1 aircraft at Patuxent. He indicated that, if progress then was satisfactory, we could expect a production order for 30 F7U-3 airplanes with 1951 funds. He made it clear that, if we failed at this check point with the F7U-1, the Navy would probably withhold its order for F7U-3 airplanes.'

Given that prerequisite, the F7U-1 programme could hardly have fared worse that summer. It began well, with XF7U-1 BuNo 122474 and the first production F7U-1 BuNo 124415 being ferried to Patuxent River in late June, a month earlier than Detweiler's commitment to RADM Pride at the May meeting. On 6 July, though, the second production F7U-1 crashed at Grand Prairie while making a precautionary single-engine approach due to an unforeseen combination of the circumstances and the control system design. The Vought test pilot, Warren Smith, was killed. The next day, the XF7U-1 caught fire during a flyby at an air show at NATC; Vought test pilot Paul Thayer was forced to eject. Instead of beginning carrier suitability testing, the first production Cutlass was grounded at Patuxent River pending the results of the investigation of Smith's crash. However, Vought expedited the crash investigation and resulting control system modifications so that 415 was modified and back on flight status in late August.

Even more troubling, BuAer's Military Requirements division expressed its concern in August that the F7U-3 was too heavy to be catapulted by existing hydraulic catapults at the desired maximum wind-over-deck (WOD) speed, whereas the heavier XF10F could be because of its variable-sweep wing. Although both the Essex and Midway-class carriers were capable of generating as much as 33 knots of WOD in zero-wind conditions, the maximum dictated by BuAer's Ships Installation Division for evaluating launch weight suitability was a more conservative 25 knots.

After discussions to clarify and correct BuAer assumptions, the comparison of a launch with full internal fuel and cannon/ammunition on 'a standard day' using afterburning thrust was:

	Catapult	F7U-3	F10F
Weight, lb		28,241	30,809
Speed for .9 C_{Lmax} plus 5%, knots		111.0	100.2
Required wind over deck, knots	H-4-1	31.5	23.5
	H-8	27	19

Essex-class carriers at the time were equipped with a pair of either the H-4-1 or H-8 catapult. The H-4-1 was capable of accelerating 28,000lb to 78 knots; if an aircraft of that weight had to be accelerated to an end speed of 110 knots, the ship had to provide 32 knots of wind-over-deck. The H-8 was the H-4-1's replacement, able to accelerate 15,500lb (a typical day fighter) to 105 knots or 100,000lb (the original take-off weight maximum for a long-range nuclear bomber) to 78 knots. BuAer, however, was unable to consider more powerful catapults in its analysis until BuShip committed to equip carriers with them. That wasn't happening: BuShip was not being provided with the funds to do so because of austere military budgets imposed following the end of the Second World War.

What was worse, this discouraging assessment did not include the weight of external loads such as fuel, bombs, or rockets, which would provide significantly increased mission capability. With respect to the accuracy of the projection or the possibility that it was overly conservative, Vought was informed that the Grumman F9F Panthers taking off from carriers in Korean waters were needing 35 knots of WOD instead of the 25 knots that the Ships Installations Division had estimated would be required. Vought engineering management committed to study ways to increase the maximum lift coefficient and expressed confidence in their empty weight estimate, which alleviated BuAer's concerns for the time being.

Nevertheless, the empty weight was to grow. According to a Vought sales representative's internal memo documenting a visit to BuAer: 'I agreed (with the admiral) that the airplane's weight had grown to the extent to where the capabilities of present catapults was extremely marginal, but that this could certainly not be blamed entirely on Vought. I mentioned the fact that there was not one Section or Division in BuAer that did not wish a Navy contractor to adhere 100% to the rules, regulations, requirements, and specifications as set up by such Section or Division and that it was extremely difficult for a Navy contractor to obtain satisfactory deviations or relief from such set patterns.' He went on to note that GFE vendors supplying armament, electronics, engines, etc. – a significant portion of an aircraft's empty weight – were also subjected to the unrestricted wants and desires of the Sections and Divisions. In effect, most of the BuAer engineering matrix treated empty weight as an independent variable that its contractors had to guarantee while meeting all of their other requirements.

Vought's sales and engineering efforts resulted in the F7U-3 programme being reinstated later that year as hoped. The company received notification on 27 August 1950 that it would receive Contract NOa(s) 51-156 (dated 21 August) for the manufacture and delivery of twenty-eight F7U-3s (North Korea's invasion of South Korea on 25 June may have also caused ADM Pride to consider F7U-1 development progress as satisfactory in spite of two XF7U-1 crashes in July). The Detail Specification was submitted in late July and returned to Vought on 18 September 1950. An external stores and cockpit lighting mock-up was held on 19 and 20 September. Only minor changes were required. As had been suggested by Vought, BuAer considered the F7U-1s to suffice for an F7U-3 prototype phase since they were similar aerodynamically.

There were many changes, however. The F7U-3 carried forward the proposed F7U-2 forward fuselage change that increased over-the-nose visibility, the long-chord ailavators, and its simpler, belly-mounted, V-frame tail hook that had been substituted for the -1's upper aft fuselage-mounted stinger hook. The most notable external differences were the location of the four 20mm cannon (moved from the forward fuselage to above the engine inlets) and the widening and deepening of the mid and aft fuselage to house the bigger J46s. The -1's two-position main landing gear feature (struts angled forward for take-off and aft for landing) was deleted because more pitch control power was to be provided by the bigger ailavators. Two wheels replaced the single wheel on the nose gear but the pre-rotation feature to reduce nose gear kickback loads was retained. Adding the second hydraulic system to power the ailavator actuators eliminated the need for reversion to a manual control system and therefore the second set of speed brakes under the mid-fuselage – required to quickly slow the F7U-1 so that stick forces in manual mode were not excessive – was deleted.

In response to criticism of F7U-1 maintainability, more access panels were added. For example, small doors were located on the outside of the forward fuselage to permit direct access to the components and wiring in the side consoles in the cockpit. Large doors, which also served as work platforms, were also added on both sides of the forward fuselage to provide access to avionics, batteries, pressurisation system, and air-conditioning components. The engines were to be installed and removed by first removing the tail cone and then sliding them in or out using an overhead track rather than having to raise and lower them through large access doors in the bottom of the aft fuselage. Smaller access doors on the belly were substituted for the servicing, adjustment, or minor repair of the engine and its accessories.

The resulting F7U-3 was significantly heavier than the F7U-1; thrust and wing area did not increase commensurately:

	F7U-1* (J34-WE-32)	F7U-3** (J46-WE-2)	% Increase
Combat weight, lb	17,707	25,698	45
Total thrust (both engines)			
Afterburner, lb	9,800	12,200	24
Military, lb	6,740	8,160	21
Fuel capacity, gallons	971	1,320	
Wing area, ft^2	496.0	535.5	8
Afterburner thrust to combat weight	0.55	0.47	
Time to climb to 30K ft, minutes	2.8	2.3	

* 1 June 1949 SAC

** 27 April 1951 performance estimate

The good news, the F7U-3 programme reinstatement, was offset by another fatal F7U-1 crash. On 28 September, Vought test pilot William Harrigan declared an emergency while test flying BuNo 124417. He reported having a left-hand engine compartment fire warning light and shutting down the engine. However, his approach was high and fast, with his judgment possibly impaired by anoxia due to an oxygen system problem. He ran off the end of the runway into the lake and was unable to get the canopy open before he drowned. However, as was often the case with aircraft development, the Navy did not let the tragedy deter it from continuing with the field carrier landing and shore-based catapult testing at Patuxent River with F7U-1 No. 1 in preparation for at-sea carrier suitability trials.

To hopefully shorten the F7U-3 flight test programme by identifying any problems requiring redesign as early as possible, an amendment to the production F7U-1 contract allowed Vought to modify two of them for specific F7U-3 engineering design support projects: BuNo 124421, No. 7 production aircraft, to evaluate catapult concepts; and No. 9, BuNo 124423, to be an 'Aero Prototype' of the flight control system changes. Vought eventually utilised at least three other F7U-1s for evaluation of F7U-3 design changes and issues, including two to evaluate Westinghouse J46 engine control development using J34 engines.

The major concern in late 1950 was the growing realisation that the J46 might not be available for installation in the first F7U-3s. In early 1950, Westinghouse had been working toward completion of its fifty-hour PFRT by 1 May 1950. However, the first XJ46 test runs in March were halted after only two hours when a first-stage compressor screw came loose and damaged 75% of the compressor blades. Testing finally resumed in early May 1950 but compressor stalling was experienced between

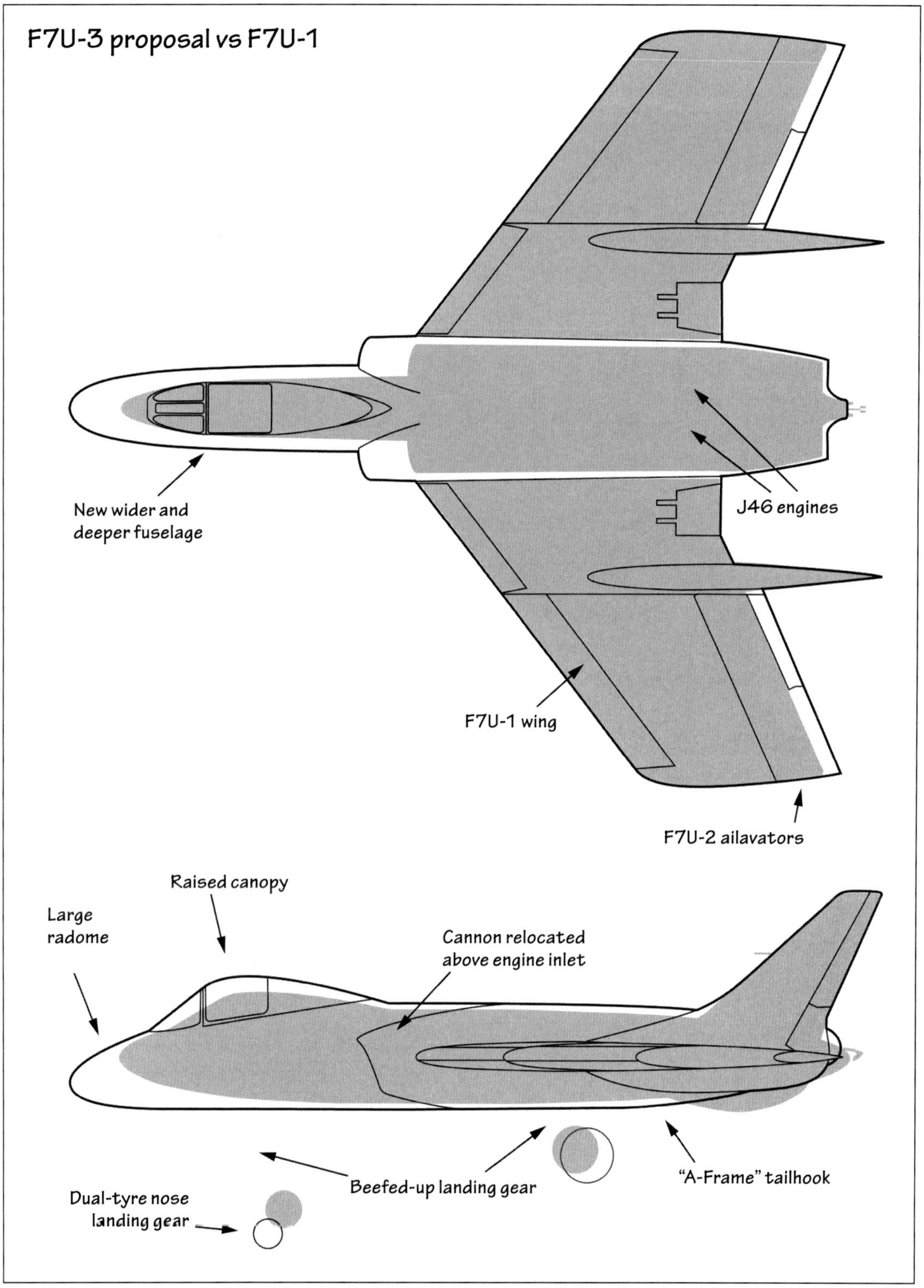

The F7U-3 incorporated the F7U-2 wing and structural changes along with a larger forward fuselage to accommodate a visual-assist radar system. *Thomason*

8,500 and 9,500 rpm, well short of the planned operating rpm of 10,100. Nevertheless, in August 1950 Westinghouse was projecting that the all-important PFRT would be complete by 31 March 1951 and initial production qualification, by 30 June 1951. Vought had therefore committed to BuAer that the first F7U-3 would be delivered at the end of 1951 and all twenty-eight would be delivered by the end of November 1952. The expected follow-on production order of 212 would be delivered by the end of 1953, with a maximum monthly production rate of twenty-two from July 1953 to December.

In early October 1950, even though Westinghouse was still projecting PFRT in March 1951 and production qualification in July, the Vought Sales Department was

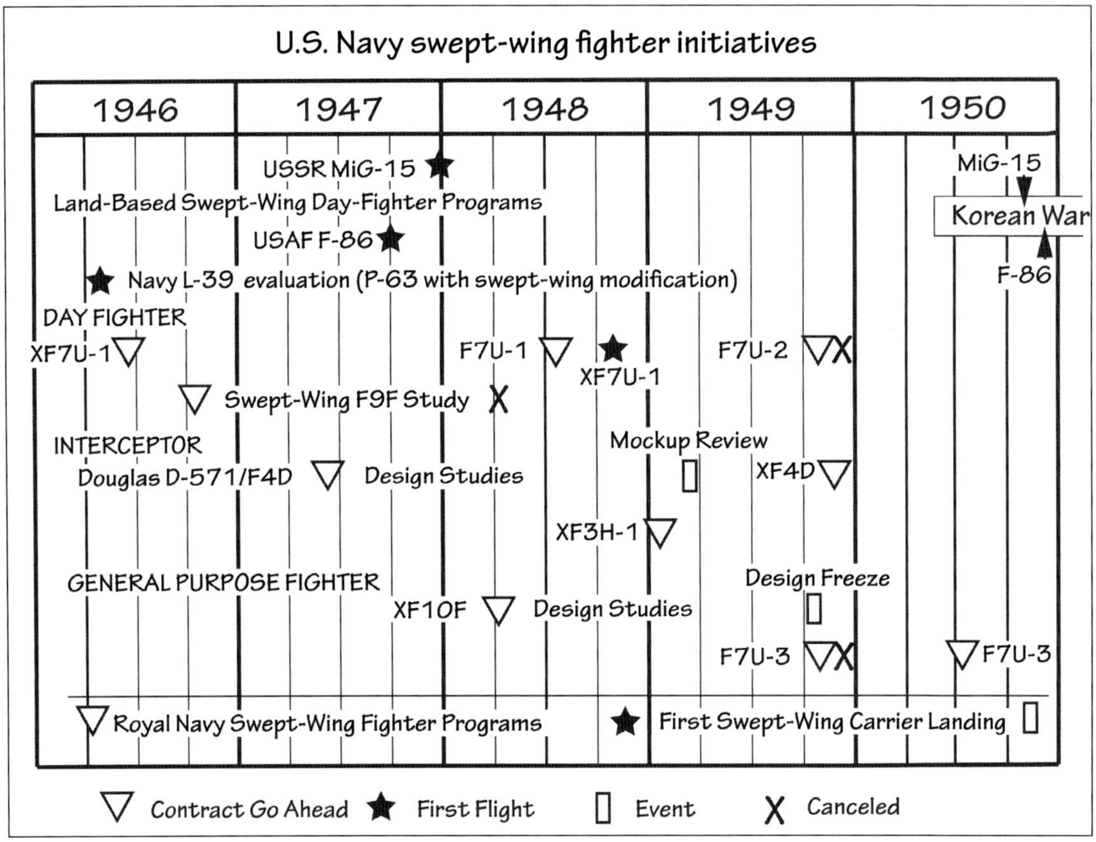

BuAer had initiated its first transonic fighter development programme, the F7U-1, in mid-1946 following the successful Bell L-39 demonstration of the swept wing's adequate low-speed handling qualities. By January 1949, it had contracted for three more. Nevertheless, when the USSR's swept-wing MiG-15 appeared in the skies over North Korea in late 1950, only the F7U-1 prototypes had begun flight test. ***Thomason***

concerned about 'the effect the completely indeterminate status of the Westinghouse J46-WE-2 engine has on the future of the F7U-3 airplane. There is today no realistic estimate of the availability of a satisfactory J46-WE-2 engine plus afterburner.' They also noted that Grumman was having similar concerns about the J40 for its F10F and was considering substituting the J57 that P&W had begun testing in January.

As a result, Vought engineering accomplished an evaluation of alternative engines that was provided to management and sales in a 6 October memo:

Two J48-P-5s (no afterburners)
One J57-P-1 with afterburner
Two J47-GE-23s (no afterburners)
Two '7,500-lb thrust engines' (no afterburners)

Substantial redesign of the aft fuselage and inlet ducts was required in all cases. The empty weight was higher and performance of each of the alternatives was never better than equal to two J46s, in part because at this point there was no reason to doubt that the J46 would provide 6,100lb of thrust in afterburner, with Westinghouse still projecting an increase to more than 7,000lb of thrust by the time the F7U entered service.

In addition, Fred Dickerman had written a memo to Detweiler expressing his concern about Vought's prospective initiation of a sales campaign to replace the J46, particularly with the J57. He noted that P&W was only then designing an afterburner for it so it was about six months to a year behind Westinghouse's delivery schedule commitment. Moreover, since the Air Force had contracted for its development, Air Force aircraft programmes would have priority for its production. However, given the J57's potential – 'I regard the J57 as the ultimate engine for the airplane' – he committed to continue to keep abreast of its development progress and update F7U-3 preliminary designs that incorporated it.

The appearance of swept-wing MiGs during the Korean War intensified the Navy's need to replace its two straight-wing carrier-based jet day fighters with higher-performance ones. The sense of urgency resulted in Vought receiving Contract NOa(s) 51-643 Letter-of-intent dated 10 February 1951 for 212 F7U-3s, twelve of which were to be the photoreconnaissance F7U-3P.

The year 1950 therefore ended well for Vought despite the cancellation of its nascent carrier-based ASW aircraft programme that BuAer had initiated to provide competition for Grumman's S2F. BuAer also took the crash of Vought's Regulus surface-to-surface missile on its first flight in its stride and gave the company a second chance on that programme. Benefitting from the design work previously accomplished on the F7U-2 and United Aircraft's pre-contract funding of the programme in early 1950, engineering had released the last of the F7U-3 structural drawings. And a December Westinghouse study was now projecting that an increase in J46 mass flow could result in an increase in its combat rating of up to 7,850lb!

CHAPTER FOUR

1951 – F7U-3 production cancellation and resurrection

In January 1951, several months before the XF3H-1's first flight, BuAer directed McDonnell to repurpose the F3H Demon, initiated as an interceptor back-up to the Douglas F4D Skyray, to be a general-purpose fighter as well. This entailed a significant redesign to add fuel capacity and external stores capability. The resulting increase in gross weight would be somewhat offset by Westinghouse qualifying a J40 with increased thrust; launching with less than a full internal fuel load would still result in interceptor climb performance. BuAer's redirection of the programme was probably done out of concern for the F10F's development risk and the F7U-3's weight and/or its J46 engine qualification status. It was not welcome news to either Grumman or Vought since it was not likely that the Navy would fund three different aircraft for the same mission requirement for long.

In February, Vought engineering decided that the planned ailavator hinge-moment capability of 8,660 foot-pounds was inadequate for the F7U-3's longer-chord control surfaces; the new

In order to expedite availability for the first flight to meet a schedule milestone, the aircraft is often unpainted for the event; in this case the Navy had also decreed that the F7U-3 would be one of the subjects of its 'natural metal finish' test programme. ***VAHF***

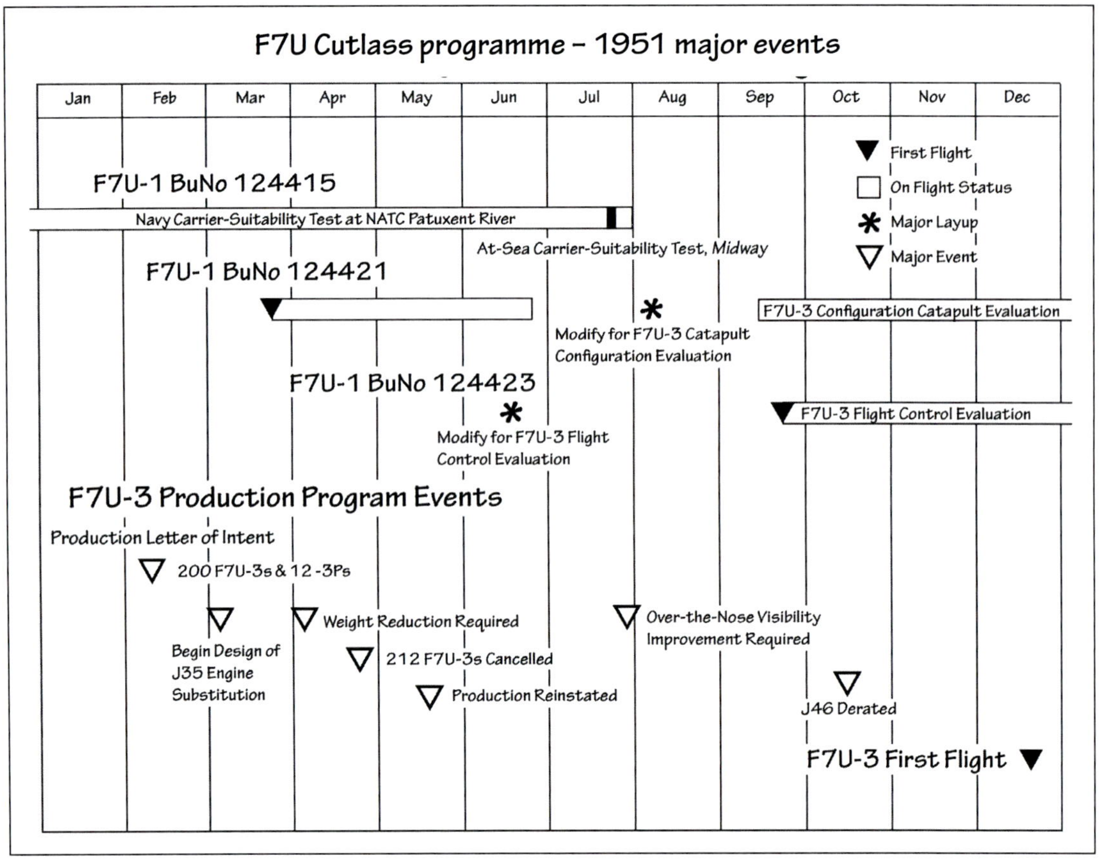

requirement was 30,000 foot-pounds. This resulted in a change from the dual actuators operating in tandem to acting in parallel and a redesign of the outer wing panel structure.

As a result of the performance inferiority of its existing straight-wing day fighters compared to the swept-wing MiG-15, the Navy also realised that it needed a carrier-based transonic day fighter as soon as possible. BuAer therefore provided sole source contracts in March 1951 to Grumman to modify the F9F-5 Panther to have swept wings and to North American for the modifications required to the US Air Force's F-86 Sabre so it was capable of taking off from and landing on a carrier.

BuAer finally agreed in early 1951 that Westinghouse's qualification of the J46 would not support Vought's ambitious but not unreasonable schedule for the F7U-3's first flight. An alternative was therefore required for at least the first sixteen F7U-3s. In January, Vought had provided BuAer with evaluations of the General Electric J47-GE-23 and Allison J35-A-29 as J46 substitutes for initial F7U-3 flight test. The Air Force refused to consider diverting any J47 engines to the Navy for this purpose but J35s were available. It provided significantly more thrust than the J46's Military rating, but not having an afterburner, a bit less than the J46's maximum (Combat) thrust. The pair of J35s also weighed about 1,078lb more than the projected weight of the J46-WE-2s but for initial flight test requirements like envelope expansion and handling qualities evaluation this was not consequential.

Thrust comparison	J35-A-29	J46-WE-2
Military (lb)	5,600	4,080
Combat (lb)	N/A	6,100

Vought began to create engineering drawings for mid and aft fuselage modifications in March to accommodate the interim engine. One exterior difference was that due to the greater J35 mass-flow requirement compared to the J46's, the fuselage boundary layer removal feature was deleted to enlarge the size of the engine inlets without changing the outer inlet lip profile.

The ongoing Westinghouse problems with J46 development prompted Vought to again re-examine other afterburning engines expected to be qualified in time to replace the J35s for production. The candidates were all single-engine alternatives: J57-P-1, J40-WE-10, J35-A-23 (which would evolve into the J71), J67-W, and J47-GE-21. The study, dated 27 April 1951, concluded that the J46 was still the best choice, *if* it met specification. The Navy concurred. (The fact that a carrier-based aircraft with two engines rather than one provided a safety benefit was not considered worthy of mention.) The only notable improvement with a J46 substitute was the mission radius projected for the J57

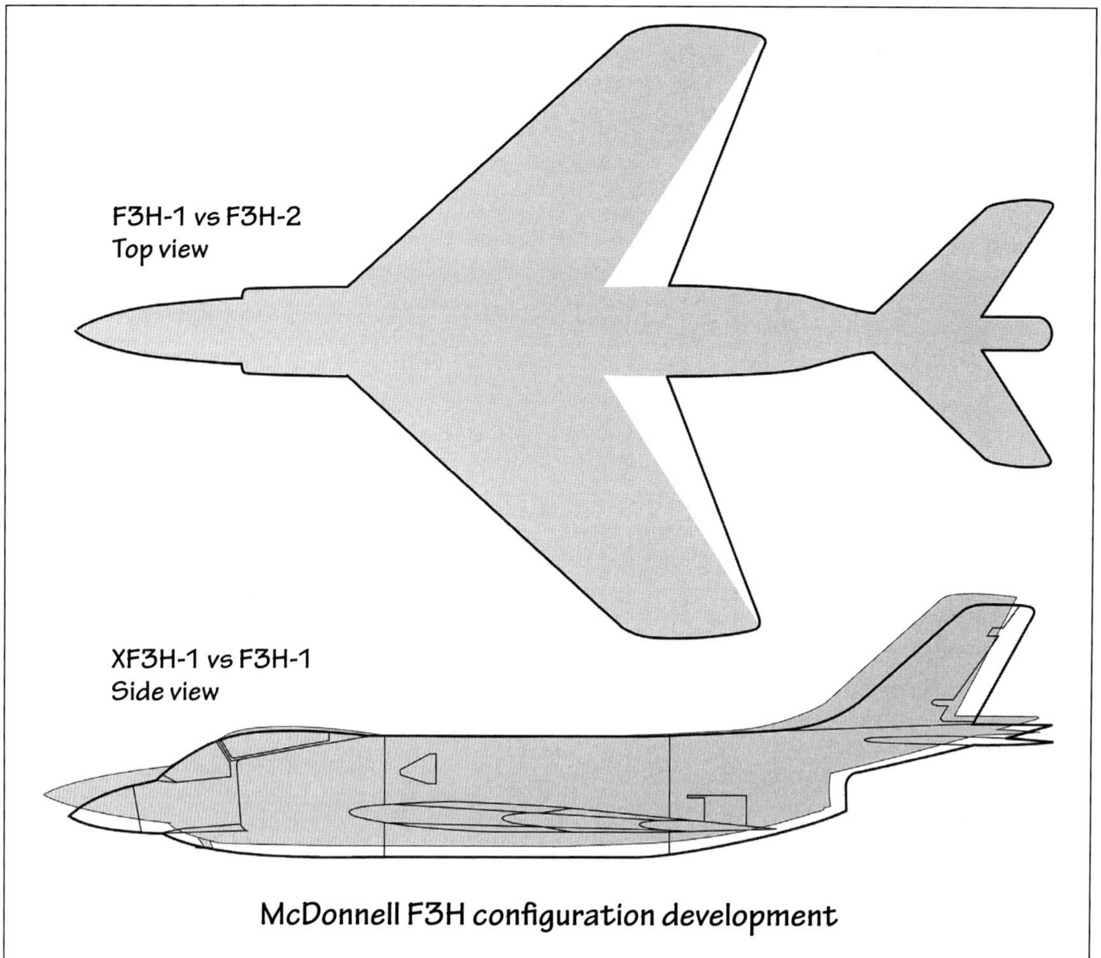

The XF3H-1 interceptor was repurposed to be a general-purpose fighter by removing the internal air-to-air rocket tray and deepening the fuselage to add more internal fuel; external store pylons were also added to the wings and fuselage. The increased weight was to be offset by a derivative of the J40 engine with more thrust. The resulting F3H-1 was subsequently modified to have more wing area as the F3H-2 in addition to replacing the J40 with the Allison J71. ***Thomason***

and the J67, although caution was expressed with respect to the latter as it was based on a preliminary performance estimate. Compared to the single-engine alternatives, the twin-J46 Cutlass was projected to be as fast or faster at all altitudes and as well as quicker climbing to 35,000ft. With the exception of the mission radius, all of the other performance numbers, including wind-over-deck for launch, were essentially the same. Another reason not to change engines was that it would delay development and deployment of the Cutlass, which still had a schedule advantage over the F10F and F3H.

No sooner had a workaround plan been established so J46 qualification schedule slippage would not delay F7U-3 flight test than another crisis arose. BuAer called Vought to a conference in Washington on 4 April. It was in effect an intervention, with Vought's concerned friends being representatives from BuAer, the CNO (CAPT Paul Ramsey, responsible for Military Requirements), and NATC Patuxent River. In particular, they noted that the F7U-3's continued empty weight growth had resulted in performance deterioration and unacceptably high wind-over-deck required for take-off.

However, it was also clear at the beginning of the meeting that BuAer 1) took some responsibility for the specification and requirements that led to the overweight condition and 2) wanted to try to save the programme, even to the extent of retaining magnesium structure (it had become apparent that it was too susceptible to corrosion) to minimise weight and redefining the amount of fuel protection required. One revelation to Vought was that BuAer had allowed Grumman and McDonnell to reduce compliance with some of the latest strength requirements on the F10F and F3H respectively that Vought was intending to meet in full. Since structure was almost 50% of the empty weight, the F7U-3 was at a disadvantage to its competitors in that regard.

Ramsey also admitted that BuShip's catapult development was lagging BuAer's need for the capability to launch heavier aircraft. CDR Gayler then divided the group into five subcommittees for detailed discussions of the areas of concern:

- Weight Allocation, Performance, Carrier Suitability, Design Philosophy
- Powerplant, Fuel Arrangement, Fuel Protection
- Stability and Control
- Maintenance
- Electronics and Electrical

The subcommittees would reconvene later in the day to discuss their findings with the entire group.

The major problem was renewed concern about the projected inability of the H-8 catapult to launch the F7U-3 at the maximum desired wind-over-deck speed of 25 knots. Vought proposed using JATO during the launch, which BuAer rejected out of hand.

The Powerplant meeting primarily addressed the plan to use J35-A-29s in at least the first sixteen F7U-3s. Although the candidates for a single-engine installation were discussed, their flight qualification dates were all considered to be about a year behind in comparison with the J46's and there was no significant performance gain. In fact, CDR Mercer of the Powerplant Division told CAPT Ramsey that the J46 had the potential to grow in thrust from 6,100lb to as much as 7,800lb based on a Westinghouse brochure created for an Air Force interceptor competition – if the Navy or Air Force funded the development.

BuAer's most significant Stability and Control concern was assurance that the F7U-3 would meet the specification requirement that the pilot retain enough control after a double-engine failure to successfully crash land or ditch the aircraft rather than having to eject (for one thing, the ejection seats at that time were bailout assists; an ejection below 1,000ft was unlikely to be survivable). The windmilling engines were now predicted to provide inadequate hydraulic pressure to the flight control actuators below 200 knots.

Maintenance, in Vought attendees' opinion, proved to not be a major issue. The F7U-1s being evaluated at Patuxent River was plagued with hydraulic leaks but Vought expressed confidence that the F7U-3 would be appreciably better from that standpoint, even though there were many more components and connections. Also, the number of maintenance access doors was being increased.

Electronics and Electrical represented the greatest opportunity and most straightforward approach to reducing weight. As much as 850lb could be removed by the simple expedient of removing all-weather mission equipment, although that relegated the F7U-3 to a day fighter role.

Vought attendees acknowledged the Navy's concerns and committed to returning to BuAer on 2 May with an action plan to allay them, particularly the launch weight. It was also agreed that while changes were required, BuAer did not expect them to all be incorporated on the first twenty-eight, even though they might not be carrier-suitable as a result. Ramsey volunteered that some of them could be assigned to a land-based squadron, 'maybe for the Marines'. (When the Navy procured aircraft that proved disappointing or surplus to its requirements for whatever reason, the Marines were frequently the beneficiary: the first Douglas SBDs; the big, slow, two-place Douglas F3D night fighter; the Vought AU-1, a Corsair optimised for ground attack in lieu of Douglas AD Skyraiders; and the underpowered North American FJ-2s are examples. As it happened, the Marine Corps never became interested in receiving Cutlasses.)

Vought was therefore shocked to be notified on 24 April that RADM Alfred M. Pride, the outgoing BuAer Chief, had ordered the cancellation of the production order for 200 F7U-3s and twelve F7U-3Ps that had been issued on 10 February. Fred Detweiler happened to be at United Aircraft's headquarters in Connecticut that day and rushed down to Washington to meet with Pride the next. The admiral explained that there would be a change of command on 1 May, with RADM Thomas Combs (who was also in the meeting) replacing him as chief, and he wanted to clear the deck for him, so to speak. In a personal letter to CAPT Ramsey dated 27 April, Detweiler quoted Pride, 'The decision was ... precipitated by a substantial cut ordered by the Department of Defense in Navy requests for appropriations for (fiscal years 1951 and 1952). Pride said that, in meeting the required cutback, it was necessary to cull out any soft spots in the programme. He felt that the F7U-3 was less likely to meet the Navy's general-purpose fighter requirements than the Grumman F10F or the McDonnell F3H, specifically the inability to launch the F7U-3 in no-wind conditions with existing catapults. He went on to say he thought the F7U was basically a good 'envelope' and for that reason he had not killed the programme entirely but had left the first twenty-eight on order.

Detweiler argued that steam-powered catapults – far superior to existing hydraulic catapults – being developed for the Royal Navy would be adequate to the task of launching the Cutlass when it reached the fleet (one had not yet, however, actually been used to launch an aircraft: HMS *Perseus* (R51), a Royal Navy Colossus-class aircraft carrier completed for an aircraft maintenance role without catapults or arresting gear, was in the process of been modified for an evaluation.) He also noted that the F7U-3 would be available sooner than either of the Navy's general-purpose fighter alternatives, which were also likely to be too heavy to be launched from existing catapults. In his letter to Ramsey, he went on to say: 'In this weight discussion, I pointed out to Admiral Pride that for two years he'd been telling me to give the Navy what it wanted. I remember that in January 1950 he told me a story about like this: When Chance Vought was alive, some airplane or other was delivered with black leather trim. Somebody in the Navy preferred red leather. So when Chance got the word, he saw to it that the next airplane delivered went down with red leather trim (red, I suppose, so the blood wouldn't show). This was his way of emphasising that Vought had recently been trying to argue the customer out of its desires and that it was important for Vought to change its point of view and give the customer everything it wanted. Paul, for the past year and one half we have been trying to do exactly that and I honestly believe this to be the largest underlying reason for the weight growth of the airplane.'

The Vought conference on 2 May at BuAer with the Piloted Aircraft Division could not have gone better. Vought presented a list of weight reduction suggestions that virtually eliminated the F7U-3's general-purpose fighter mission capability and range/endurance but provided the option for it to be reinstated in the future when carriers were fitted with more powerful catapults. In summary, carrier suitability was to be achieved by reducing the take-off gross weight to 27,500lb – about a ton – by deleting mission equipment and capability in addition to the redesign of systems and structure where feasible. As previously planned, Vought was also to test catapult hook/holdback alternatives on F7U-1 BuNo 124421 in the next few months to determine the most effective launch configuration, hopefully one that provided additional margin with respect to the 25 knots of wind-over-deck limitation.

The major changes were the deletion of the visual assist radar, autopilot, and other all-weather electronic components; the two outboard stores pylons; and the fuel cells in the outboard wing panels (the latter reduced both empty weight and gross weight but at the expense of range and endurance). The F7U-3 was also to be added to an experimental Navy programme being initiated to eliminate exterior paint, which somewhat reduced empty weight.

One addition, an emergency electrically driven hydraulic pump, addressed the concern about insufficient hydraulic power for flight control actuation from the pumps on windmilling engines at an airspeed of less than 200 knots. A dedicated battery would power the pump for at least five minutes. That was considered enough time for the pilot to crash-land or ditch 'dead stick' after descending to 2,000ft above the ground and slowing to 200 knots.

CDR Gayler committed to review BuAer Division suggestions or requests that resulted in additional weight increase and not allow any that were not 'positively necessary' or 'required because of military features'.

On 7 May, BuAer notified Vought that based on Westinghouse's ongoing development issues, initial J46 flight qualification would be for derated engines, with a military thrust of 3,960lb and combat thrust of 5,800lb, a modest decrease of about 3% and 5% respectively. These were subsequently designated J46-WE-8 (a higher dash number does not necessarily mean an improvement) to provide a revision to the Westinghouse contract specification for delivery acceptance.

After reviewing Vought's proposal with OpNav, BuAer reinstated the contract for 200 F7U-3s and twelve -3Ps in early May. Vought's Engineering Change Proposals (ECPs) for weight reduction were approved by BuAer and implemented at Vought by two Master Change Records (MCRs), -4 (changes to F7U-3s No. 1-16, i.e. J35-powered) and -5 (changes to F7U-3 No. 17 and subsequent). Vought engineering established a design weight goal of 26,900lb to provide a 600lb margin between drawing release and first flight

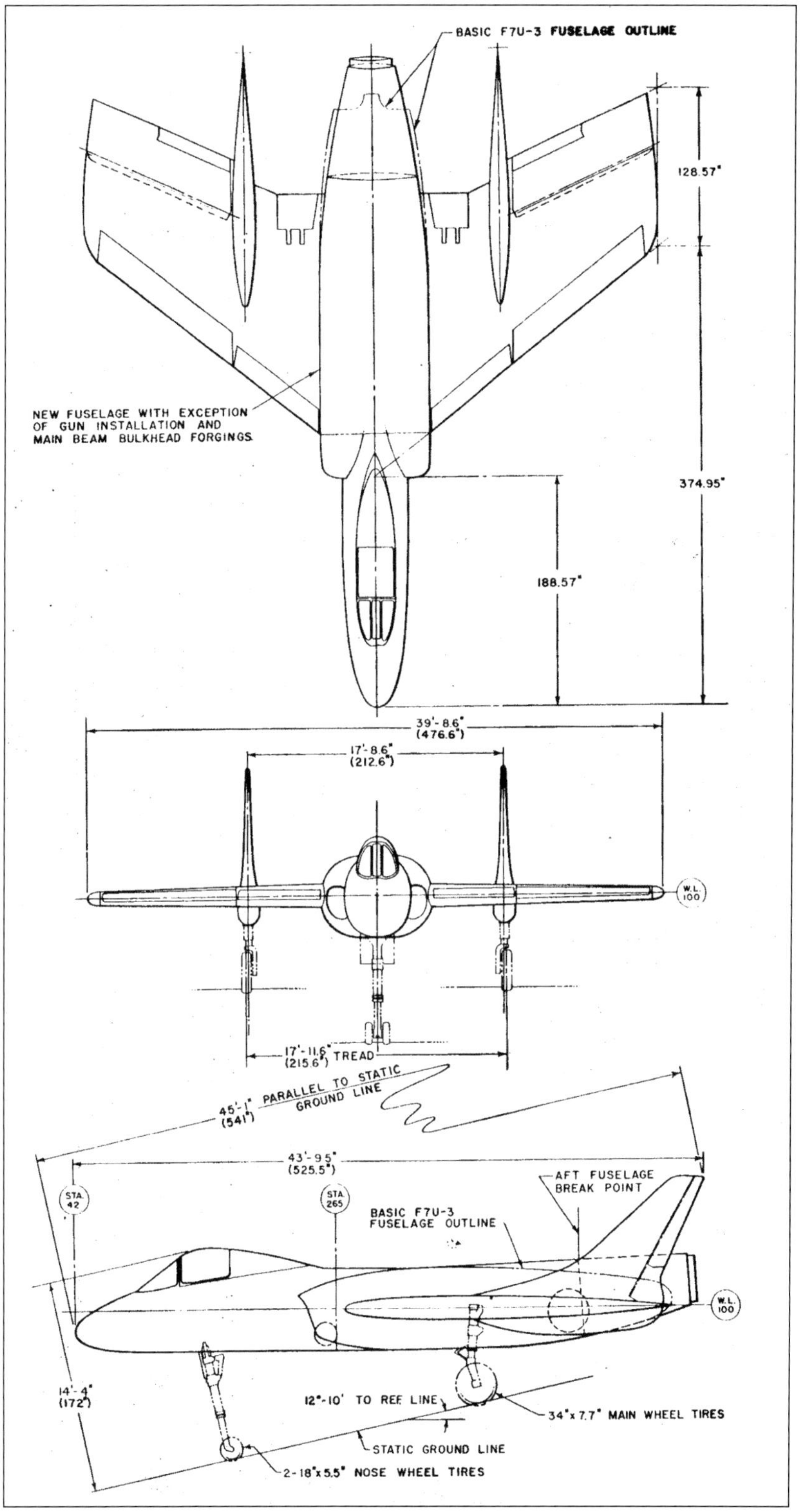

Single Engine F7U-3 three view. ***VAHF***

F7U-3 single-engine studies 27 April 1951

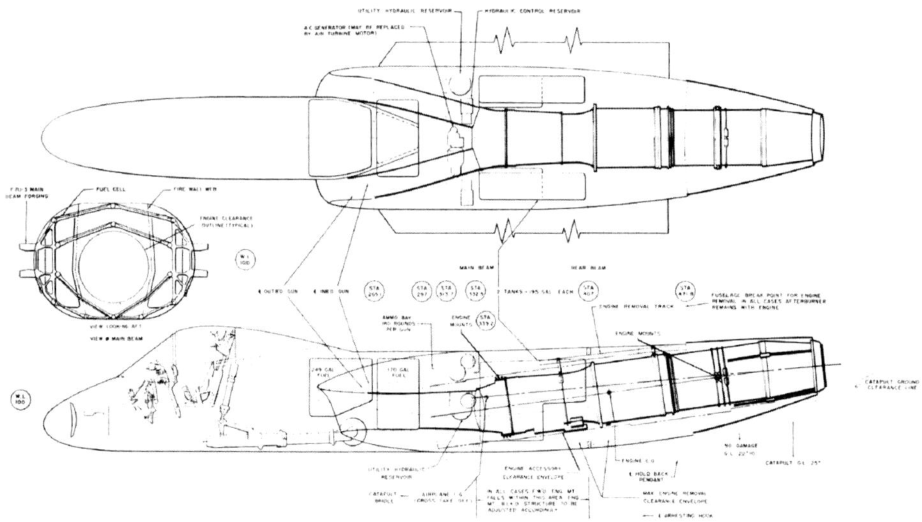

Westinghouse J40-WE-10
Navy specification
7 June 1950

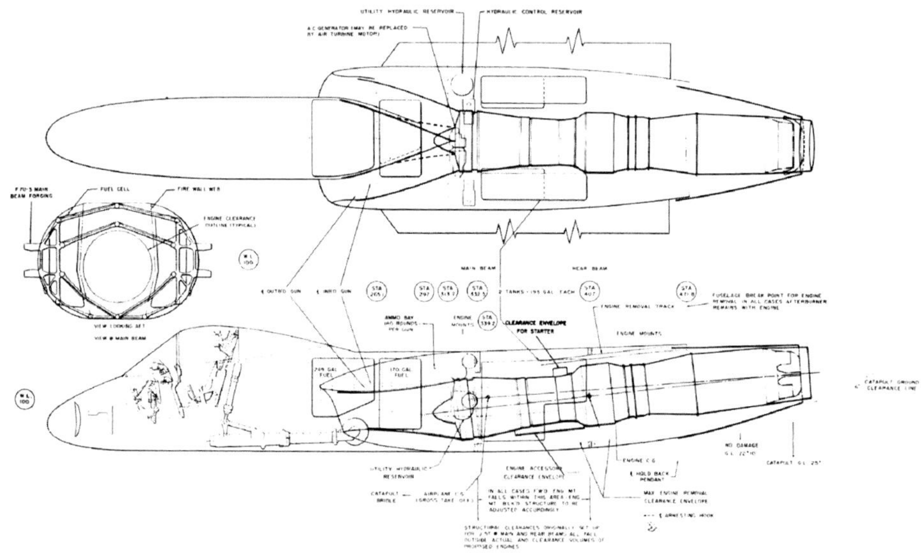

Wright J67-W
Preliminary estimate

	J46-WE-2	J57-P-1	J40-WE-10	J35-A-23	J67-W	J47-GE-21
Sea Level CRT (lbs)	12,200 (2)	15,000	13,750	13,000	14,000	13,050
Takeoff Weight (lbs)	29,286	30,275	29,593	29,965	29,082	29,425
Mission Radius (nm)	460	515	490	470	550	490
Time to 35K (min)	3.3	3. 7	3.6	4.3	3.8	4.1
Vmax, 35k ft (kts/MN)	543/.945	543/.945	540/.939	535/.93	540/.939	538/.935
Ceiling, 500 fpm (ft)	48,300	49,700	49,000	47,800	49,200	48,700

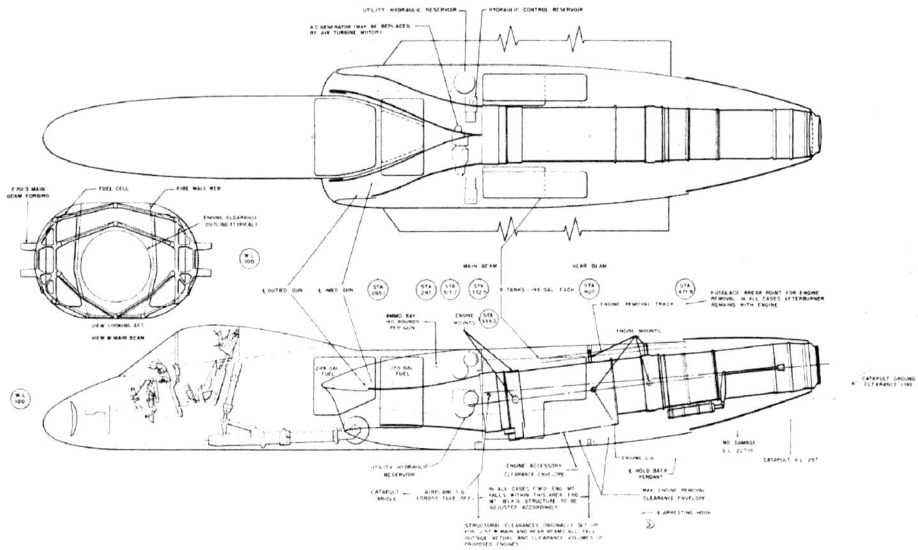

Allison J35-A-23
USAF specification
4Dec 1950

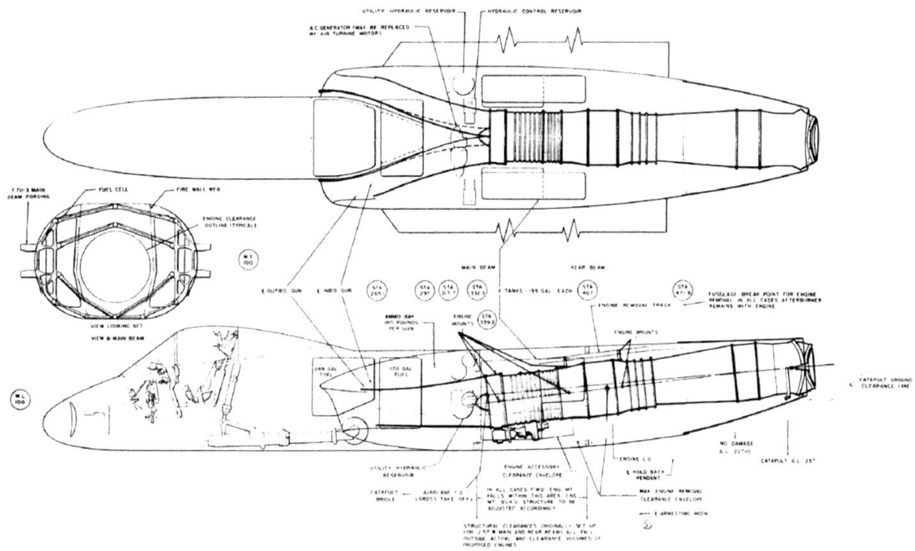

GEJ47-GE-21
GE bulletin
2 Nov1950

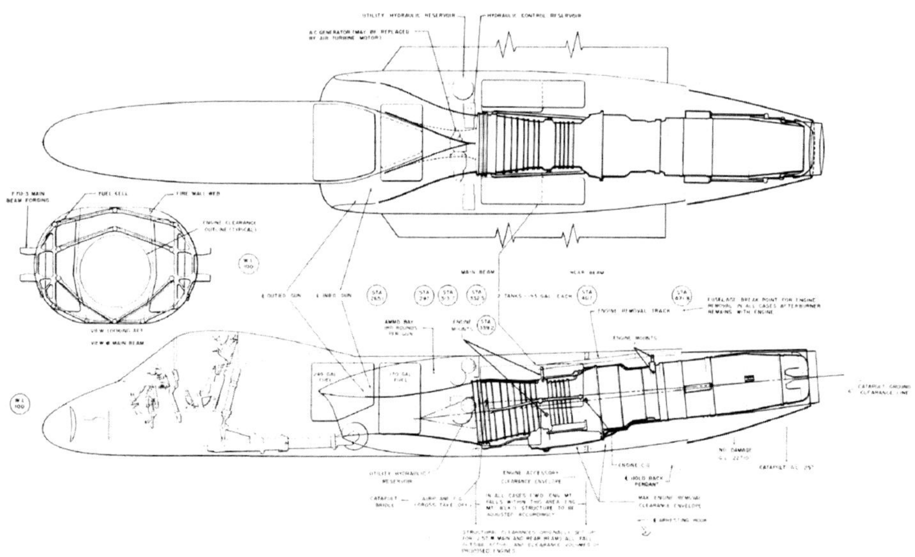

P&W J57-P-1
Installation memo
23 Mar 1951

On 29 June 1951, a conference was held with Vought, BuAer, and Westinghouse attendees, primarily to discuss the unsatisfactory status of development of the J34-WE-32 engine and its effect on the F7U-1 programme as well as the prospective delay of the J46 on F7U-3 development. One of Vought's concerns, seconded by BuAer's Power Plants Division, was that Westinghouse's electronic control system for the engine and afterburner was 'entirely unsatisfactory and would require too long to make reliable'. Vought strongly recommended that Westinghouse develop a simplified mechanical one. Vought also complained that Westinghouse did not have the ability to evaluate an engine in flight; instead, aircraft manufacturers like Vought were having to deal with engine problems in flight test that were not discernible during Westinghouse's development and qualification conducted solely in ground-bound test cells. The conference concluded with no change – according to Vought – in Westinghouse's 'obstinate attitude' and no direction otherwise from BuAer, which was responsible for the engines as Government-Furnished Equipment. However, Westinghouse subsequently proposed a 'Simple Hydraulic Control' (SHC) System option. On 6 August, BuAer directed Westinghouse to begin its immediate development and that both the derated J46 and the J40-WE-8 should be qualified with it 'at the earliest practicable date'.

Only a few months after resolving the issue of an unacceptable wind-over-deck requirement for a catapult launch by committing to a significant weight reduction, Vought was faced with a serious deficiency at the other end of the ship. NATC test pilot LCDR 'Whitey' Feightner came to Vought in late July 1951 immediately following his at-sea evaluation of the first F7U-1 to personally debrief Vought management and engineering on the need to redesign the F7U-3's forward fuselage to provide satisfactory visibility for a carrier landing. For some reason, NATC pilots had not found the -1 to be unacceptable in that regard during almost 200 field carrier landings at Patuxent River over the course of several months before taking it to *Midway* (although it had been noted in an April 1951 report that the LSO was barely viewable through the lower edge of the side panel and this view was distorted by the curvature of the Plexiglas). The lack of concern may have been because the pilots were accustomed to limited forward visibility for landing in fighters with reciprocating engines turning propellers, particularly the Vought F4U Corsair. It may also have been that the pilots were unconsciously using their peripheral view of the surrounding features shortly before and then after the throttle cut point to keep them oriented with respect to height and position, whereas the ocean on either side of a 200ft-wide deck offered no such assistance.

Vought's subsequent analysis of the F7U-3 pilot's view of the LSO and the deck on approach suggested that it was not absolutely necessary to improve it because of changes already made relative to the F7U-1. Nevertheless, management's decision was to once again not argue with the customer's wishes or concerns. Engineering began a redesign on 27 August that

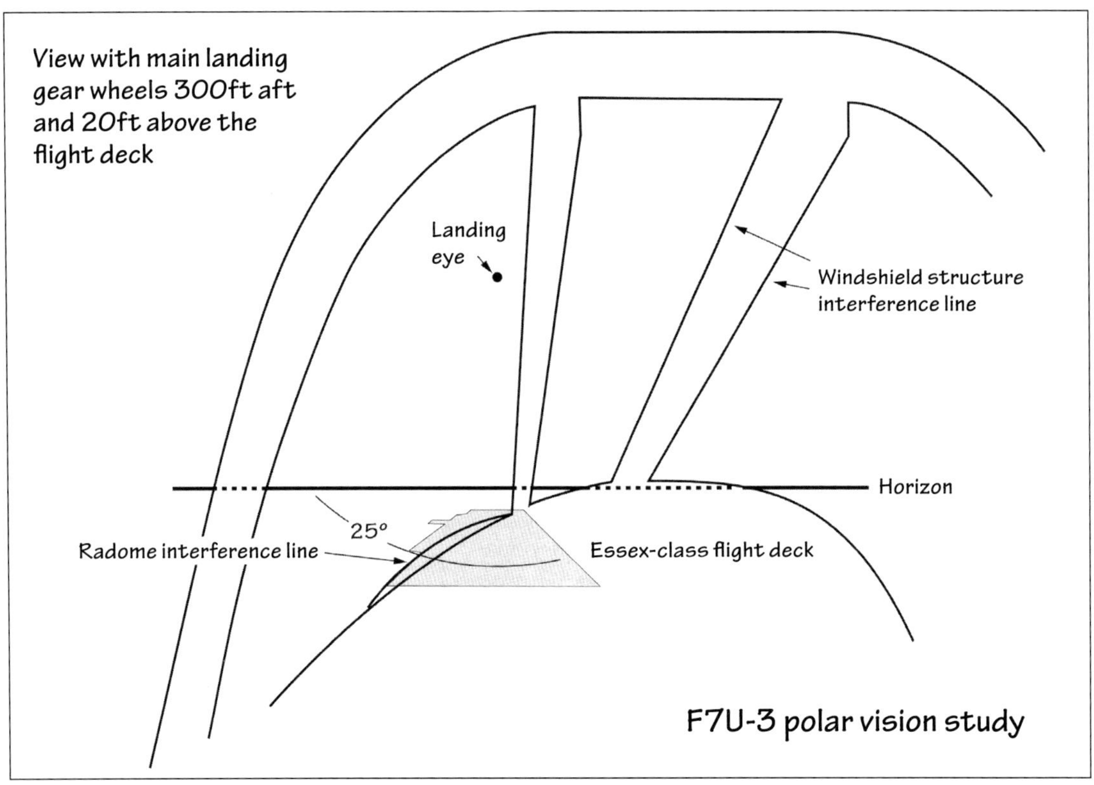

As part of the kerfuffle following the F7U-1 at-sea evaluation over the lack of visibility of the LSO and the deck, Vought analysed the visibility to the side of the original 'bulb' nose to determine how marginal it still was. *Thomason*

resulted in a new nose and canopy. Identified as MCR-8, the necessary changes included a fuselage modification from the aft cockpit bulkhead forward that included a tapered nose, a new windshield and canopy, and forward tilting of the cockpit seat. Vought created a mock-up of the redesigned forward fuselage that was installed on a specially constructed tower to simulate the view of the deck on approach for evaluation and approval by both BuAer and NATC. F7U-3 No. 4, BuNo 128454, which was scheduled for carrier suitability trials in July 1952, was selected for modification to this configuration. It was to be introduced in production with No. 17.

Another fallout of the disappointing F7U-1 carrier trials was the cancellation of tentative plans to assign three or four F7U-1s to VX-3 for an early operational and tactical evaluation both ashore and at sea. Given the bad reputation that the -1 would earn in early 1952 for reliability and frequency of in-flight emergencies as a result of its brief association with the Blue Angels flight demonstration team, that was probably a blessing. The last four F7U-1s were cancelled instead.

In August, Vought was dismayed to be informed by BuAer that F7U-3 No. 5 would no longer be utilised for the trial installation of the APQ-42 radar being considered for general-purpose fighters. It was behind schedule and therefore would be flight tested in the Grumman F10F instead. Worse case, this put the F7U-3 at a further disadvantage with respect to the Navy's eventual selection of the fighter to fulfil this mission requirement but as it happened, both the radar and the F10F development programmes would be cancelled.

In September 1951, long-lead items that could not be delivered in time to meet the final assembly schedule included the landing gear forgings produced by Wyman Gordon. This forced Vought to repurpose F7U-1 landing gear for use on the first few F7U-3s and modify them and the landing gear doors accordingly.

Vought was also making a full court press with the F7U-1s to be modified to provide early test and evaluation of F7U-3 design features:

F7U-1 BuNo 124421 (No. 7) that was assigned to be the F7U-3 catapult prototype had first flown in March 1951 and was briefly utilised for miscellaneous flight test assignments. It was then laid up in June to be modified for catapult optimisation tests, including an F7U-3 representative landing gear. It arrived at Patuxent River on 26 October to begin testing on the land-based catapult system there.

F7U-1 BuNo 124423 (No. 9) that was to be the so-called F7U-3 aerodynamic prototype flew on 21 September. From then through early June 1952 it was used for evaluation of the F7U-3 flight control system, including the long-chord ailavators; dual-power actuators; a feel system with a trimmable centring spring, viscous damper, and bob-weight; the wing-only speed brake configuration; an emergency feel system, etc. Redesign of the

Because of forging lead times, Vought was forced to complete the first few F7U-3s with modified F7U-1 landing gear and add holes in the landing gear doors to accommodate the larger wheels in order to maintain the F7U-3 programme schedule. *Thomason*

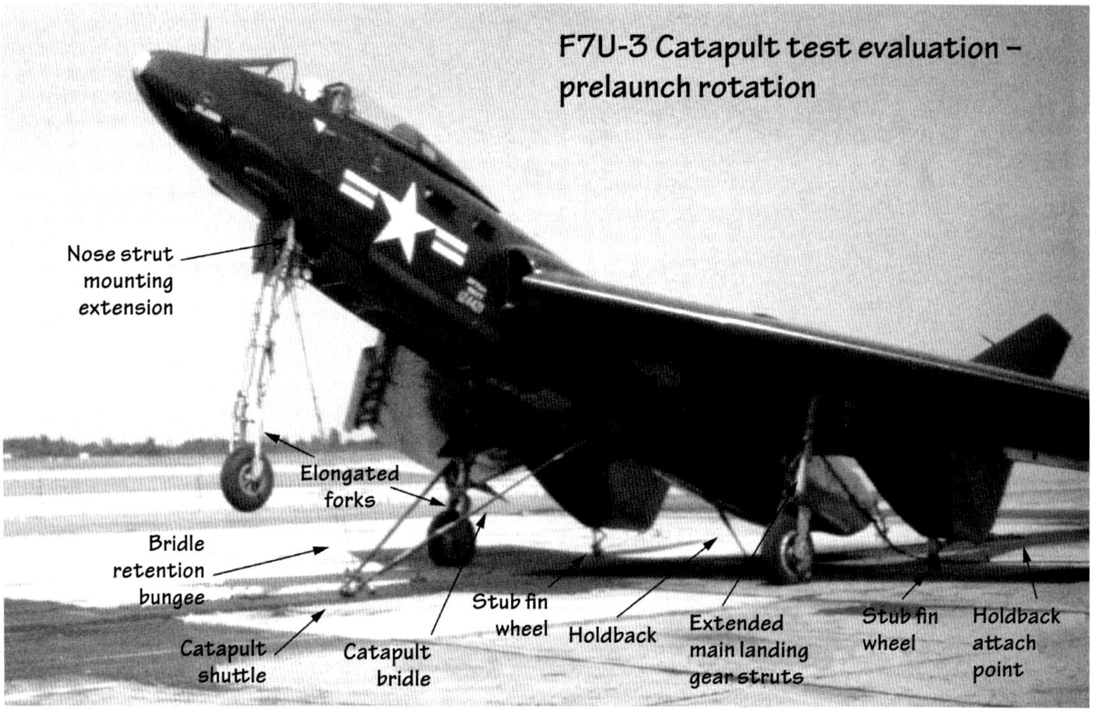

For F7U-3 catapult concept testing, BuNo 124421's landing gear was modified to represent the F7U-3's. Here, BuNo 124421 has been tensioned by the holdback cable to achieve the maximum nose-up attitude permitted by main landing gear oleo extension and the small wheels mounted on the bottom of the stub fins. The bridle-retention bungee line between the catapult bridle and the nose landing gear was a test-only expedient that shortened the time required to hook the Cutlass up for the next launch. *Thomason*

emergency feel system proved necessary and the speed brake configuration was modified to reduce buffeting. The desired changes would be implemented beginning with F7U-3 No. 5, BuNo 128455.

The optimum result of the catapult stroke was to have the aircraft nearing the angle of attack for maximum lift, at the speed required for level flight at that angle of attack, and in trim for that airspeed. It was also desirable that this be achieved with little or no pilot input, since the acceleration (and the response of some aircraft to it) was at least somewhat disconcerting. The two extremes to accomplish this were 1) accelerate the aircraft in a level, low-drag attitude and rotate to the desired angle of attack at the end of the catapult stroke and 2) position the aircraft on the catapult at the desired angle of attack at the end of the stroke, i.e. nose high. The level acceleration results in a higher end speed because aerodynamic drag is less and engine thrust is oriented directly aft during the catapult stoke; however, increasing the angle of attack at the end of the stroke requires a nose-up pitch input by the pilot and/or a compression of the nose landing gear shock strut during it that results in an upward rebound at the end of it. In either case, timely and exacting pilot input is required so the pitch up is neither too little (sink off the bow into the sea) nor too much (stall and crash into the sea). The nose-high acceleration, on the other hand, requires less

F7U-1 BuNo 124418 was also retained at Vought for miscellaneous development and evaluation efforts in support of the F7U-3 programme. The F7U-1 beyond it was painted and marked for its brief assignment to the Blue Angels. *VAHF*

pilot input at the end of the stroke but reduces the maximum end speed (and therefore the maximum weight that can be launched) possible due to higher aerodynamic drag and loss of some amount of the forward thrust component during the catapult stroke.

In view of the F7U-3's higher launch weight for a relatively small increase in wing area, F7U-1 No. 7 was modified to determine the optimum method to achieve

Vought continued to produce F4Us while developing the F7U-1, in this case a French F4U-7 (note the respective positions of the cockpits relative to the wing). The canopy of BuNo 124423, which was configured for F7U-3 flight control system design, appears to have been modified with a radio antenna. ***VAHF***

BELOW The J34 engines in F7U-1 BuNo 124425 (shown here in the foreground on the Vought flight line with J35-powered F7U-3s) as well as 124424 were used by Vought to evaluate Westinghouse J46 engine control development. ***VAHF***

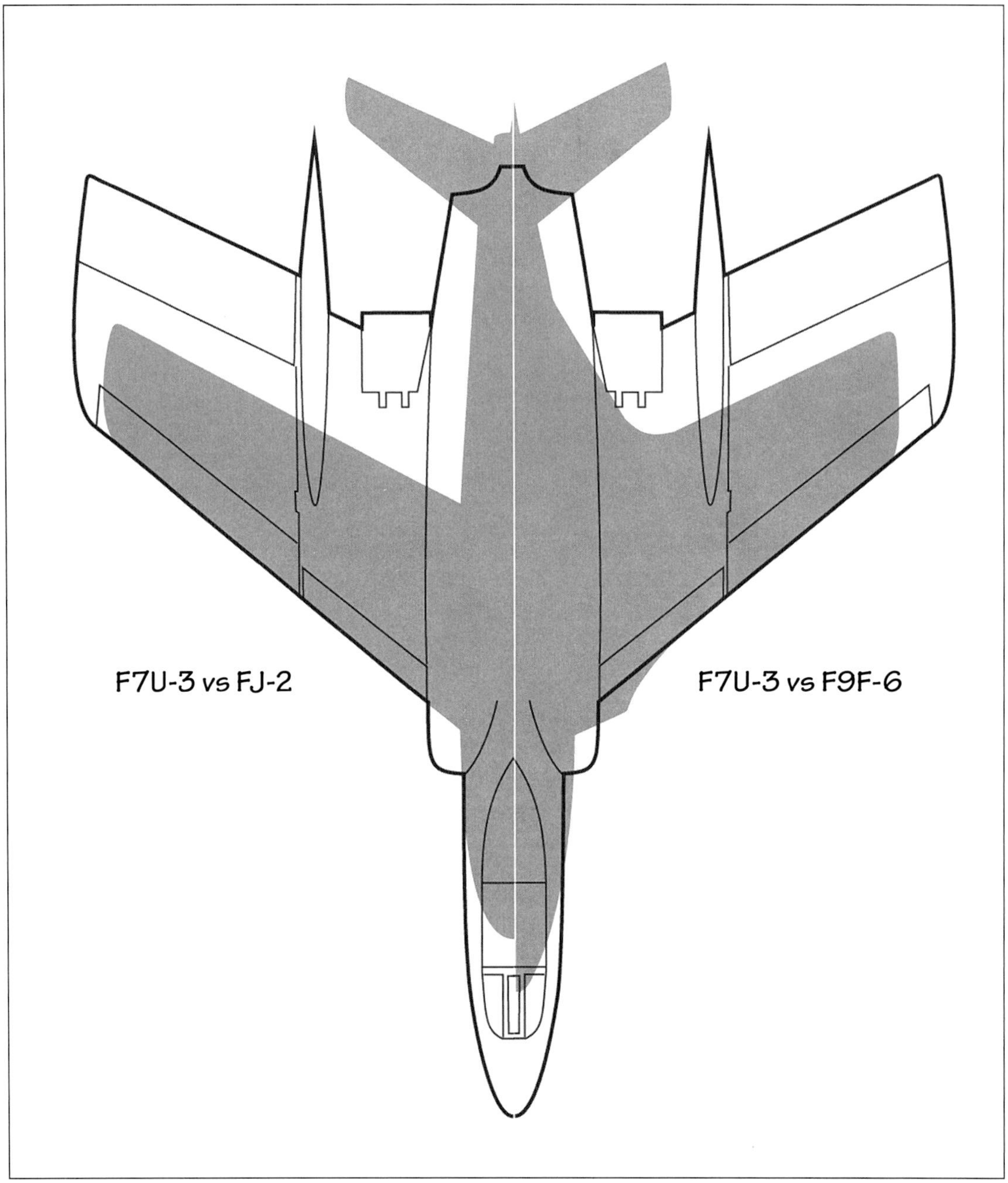

The F7U-3 was criticised for being big but it was not that much bigger in length or wingspan than the swept-wing day fighters being developed at the same time. It was significantly heavier, had a much larger wing area, and towered over them. The wing planform also meant not as many could be parked in the same amount of deck as the FJ-2 Fury or the F9F-6 Cougar. *Thomason*

the lift required at the end of the catapult stroke at the least wind over deck. Since the aircraft already had a nose-up attitude necessary for landing, the question primarily was whether increasing it further for take-off was beneficial. Pressurising the main landing gear oleos to extend them and increase the nose-up attitude attainable before the stub fins were resting on the deck, adding small wheels to the bottom of the stub fins to protect them, and then putting so much tension on the holdback cable that wheels were resting on the deck accomplished the extreme nose-up initial catapult attitude. As a result of shore-based F7U-1 catapult testing, the original single catapult hook on the belly of the F7U-1 had already been changed to two hooks, one under each wing adjacent to the fuselage, for its carrier trials. For the F7U-3 evaluation, this was changed to two spool-like knobs, one on each side of the fuselage under the wing for attachment of a bridle that was looped over the catapult shuttle.

The conclusion from F7U-1 No. 7 catapult-launch testing was that there was some benefit from the extremely nose-high position at the start of the catapult stroke, but the process of preparing it for launch took too long. Some shore-based catapult testing of an F7U-3 in this trussed-up configuration was accomplished but it was decided to simply increase the pressure in the nose landing gear strut for carrier operations and rely on the pilot to set pitch trim, hold aft stick for the launch, and pitch to the correct attitude at the end of the catapult stroke.

As 1951 ended, Vought was potentially facing no longer being an aircraft supplier to the US Navy. The Vought VE-7 was the first aircraft to take off from an American aircraft carrier (an Aeromarine 39-B was the first to land on). The Navy's first two fighter squadrons, VF-1 and VF-2, flew the Vought VE-7FS. The F4U Corsair was one of the all-time best propeller-pulled fighters and production of it was only just then ending after a decade. However, its next two attempts at fighters, the F5U and F6U, had come to naught.

While Vought was still one of the Navy's go-to contractors for carrier-based aircraft, Douglas and Grumman had also been for almost as long. Moreover, in the late 1940s two newcomers, McDonnell and North American, had successfully proved themselves to BuAer with their first carrier-based jet fighters. Budget limitations meant that funds would be available for fewer programmes and therefore fewer companies.

As a result of the mission-equipment and capability deletions, the F7U-3 was now relegated to competing for the swept-wing day fighter role that the F7U-2 was to have fulfilled. The Grumman F9F-6 flew for the first time in September 1951 and the North American XFJ-2, since an F-86 needed somewhat more modification to be carrier capable, was being readied for a first flight in early 1952. The F7U-3 was bigger, heavier, and more complicated than them and therefore more expensive. Its major competitive advantage was the superior acceleration and climb performance provided by afterburning engines but their qualification date continued to slip: in January 1951 Westinghouse had committed to delivering fourteen J46s to Vought by the end of 1951; none were.

Most humiliating of all, Vought was informally asked by BuAer in December if they would be willing to produce McDonnell F3H Demons as a second source to newcomer McDonnell instead of F7Us (OpNav was reportedly still second guessing the decision to continue with the Cutlass programme but supportive of Vought as a Navy contractor). Vought's General Manager was less than enthusiastic but couldn't just say no: 'If the Navy will not permit us to make F7Us and needed us to produce additional F3Hs, we would have little choice but to do the best we could for the Navy.' Fortunately for Vought, XF3H flight test delays caused by Westinghouse J40 engine problems caused BuAer to cut back F3H production plans and not pull the plug on the Cutlass powered by the J46. The swept-wing Douglas F3D-3 was terminated in early 1952 instead.

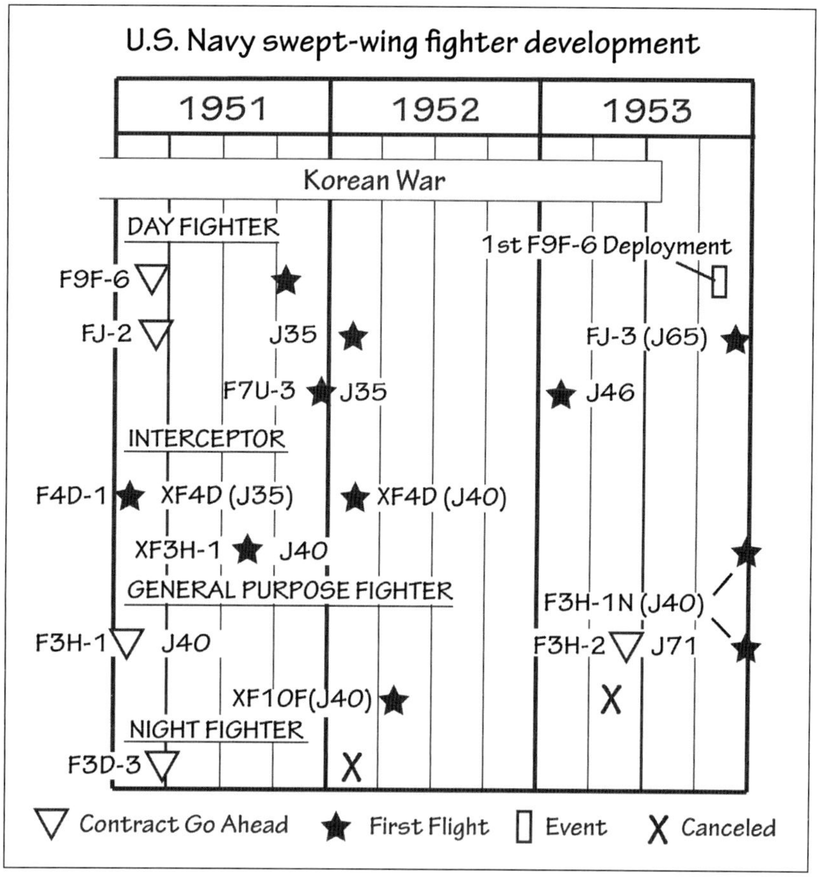

Prior to the Korean War, the Navy's plan for the introduction of carrier-based high-performance fighters consisted of big general-purpose fighters, and lightweight, fast-climbing interceptors. In early 1951, BuAer added two new day fighter programmes in addition to repurposing the F7U-3 as a day fighter. *Thomason*

However, 1951 ended on a high note with the first flight of F7U-3 BuNo 128451 on 18 December (20 December was the date of the 'formal' first flight), piloted by Vought chief test pilot John W. 'Mac' McGuyrt. First flight is always an uplifting milestone for the company and the programme team, but it was particularly gratifying for Vought. It was only a month later than Vought's ambitious early commitment to delivering the production F7U-3 in December and only sixteen months after the BuAer provided the company with a letter of intent for the programme. On the other hand, it was powered by J35s instead of J46s and rolling on F7U-1 landing gear; a new forward fuselage and outer wing panels were in work; and some systems like flight control feel were in the process of being re-evaluated. While it was therefore not entirely the production configuration, it should be noted that Vought had been handicapped by shortages and vendor lead time increases that resulted from the Korean War, which had begun in mid-1950.

A first flight only needs to result in a drama-free landing to be declared a success. By that standard, the F7U-3's was an outstanding success. *Casby Collection*

CHAPTER FIVE

1952 – The F7U-3 goes to sea for the first time

At the start of the 1952, Vought was expecting the delivery of the first flight-qualified J46 in July. One was finally delivered at the very end of the year …

CDR Pete Aurand, in charge of the Fighter Class Desk at BuAer in 1952, thought the best use of the F7U-3 was as an interceptor rather than a day fighter because of F4D and F3H programme slippage (the Skyray had flown in early 1951 but with an interim engine as the J40 was not yet flight qualified; the F3H was being redesigned so it could also serve as a general-purpose fighter). For one thing, he was a proponent of a day fighter being small and simple, which ruled out an afterburner. He was particularly enthusiastic about a carrier-capable USAF F-86 Sabre and by comparison, not supportive of a big, complicated F7U deploying as a day fighter. With afterburning engines, however, the Cutlass had the necessary rate of climb in addition to the internal volume required for missile/rocket fire control radar and avionics. In January 1952, on a visit to Grand Prairie, Aurand informally told Vought that he wanted to reinstate the all-weather missile-armed capability in the seventeenth and subsequent F7U-3s. As an interceptor placeholder, however, he would then limit total F7U-3 production to about 200 aircraft, ending in mid-1954 when the F4D was expected to be deployable. Vought was relieved that BuAer did not immediately implement Aurand's vision and continued with the procurement of the F7U-3 as a day fighter.

Also in January, because of concerns about additional slippage in the J46 delivery schedule, the F7U-3 Project Engineer, J.B. Schliemann, summarised three alternatives for continuing to utilise the J35 after the first sixteen F7U-3s:

A) Continuing with the non-afterburning J35-A-29
B) Same as A plus reinstating fuel in, and a pylon on, the outer wing panel as well as the radar and autopilot
C) Same as B plus adding an afterburner that Allison was in the process of qualifying for the J35.

Although any of these three alternatives would exceed the agreed take-off weight limit of 27,500lb, updated BuAer H-8 catapult capability studies had concluded that higher weights could be accommodated.

The second F7U-3, BuNo 128452, flew in January 1952. Note the F7U-1 landing gear wheels protruding slightly out of small openings in the landing gear doors. ***VAHF***

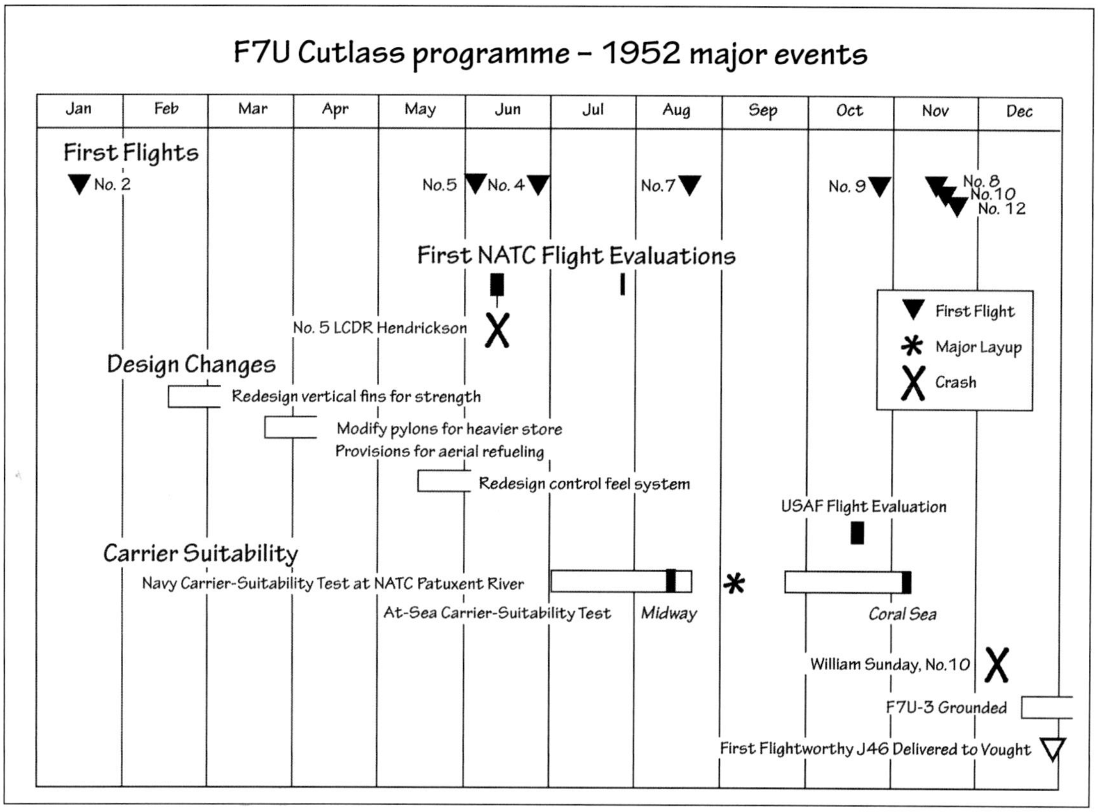

His recommendation, assuming Westinghouse was able to meet its most recent J46 schedule commitment, was to introduce alternative B into production in phases, first continuing to build F7U-3s with J35s and then implementing the other changes at a later date, retrofitting them to No. 17 and subsequent. If the Navy terminated the Westinghouse programme, then alternative C was the fallback.

A pair of afterburning J35s was the engine installation included in an unsolicited V-377 proposal to the Air Force for a fighter-bomber derivative of the F7U-3.

Initial flight tests of No. 1 and No. 2 revealed deficiencies in performance and handling qualities:

- Low buffet boundary
- High approach speed
- Low Vmax
- Poor clean condition stalling characteristics
- Low control forces above 200 knots IAS resulting in over-control

The low buffet boundary was a particular concern. As the angle of attack is increased at transonic speeds, the shock wave/turbulent boundary layer interaction and flow separation on an aircraft wing induce aerodynamic flow instabilities that the pilot senses as buffet due to the wing structure resonating in response to localised load changes. The effect was similar to driving down an unpaved washboarded road. Lines of *g* capability versus Mach number defined the buffet boundary. The degree of buffet experienced was subjective. The first detection of buffet by the pilot was referred to as Onset. The upper edge of the boundary was termed Limit or maximum tolerable, which basically was the warning of an accelerated stall or potential structural problems. Most important was the Tracking or maximum usable level of buffet, somewhere between the two, above which the pilot's ability to hold an aim point was unsatisfactory, a significant deficiency for a fighter.

As it turned out, the F7U-3's buffet boundaries were basically the same as the -1's and therefore lower than desired for a fighter. Flights with the airframe festooned with many tufts of yarn revealed disturbed flow on the upper surface of the outer wing panels, the trailing edge of the original canopy, and the aft outboard side of the fin stubs. An indication of the degree of difficulty in ascertaining the source of the buffet was that one F7U-1, BuNo 124420, had a higher buffet boundary between Mach 0.87 and 0.92 than the other -1s; its outer wing panels were installed on F7U-1 BuNo 124418 to see if they were the source of the difference; they did delay the buffet onset with *g* but it did not equal 124420's.

Vought engineers attempted to remediate the deficiencies with every aerodynamic trick in their toolboxes: fairings, vortex generators, wing fences, etc. Some tests were made of impractical fixes to see what the buffet improvement might be if they could somehow be implemented, such as sealing the wing fold joint. None

were successful in notably improving the buffet boundary. Fortunately it was only one of the manoeuvrability attributes desired in a jet fighter; judicious use of the extra thrust available using the afterburners somewhat made up for that particular shortfall.

The handling qualities above 200 knots were significantly improved by incorporating a redesigned feel system. The use of irreversible hydraulic controls required that feel of the air loads on the ailavators be artificially added to the control stick since there was no feedback of loads to the pilot from the control surfaces themselves. The first F7U-3s flew with the same feel system as the F7U-1: hydraulic loads on the stick shaped by ram-air

LEFT The Royal Navy's HMS *Perseus* (R51) was originally to be an aircraft carrier but was completed as aircraft maintenance ship without catapults or arresting gear. In late 1950, it was modified with an experimental steam-driven catapult mounted on top of its upper deck for an at-sea evaluation of the concept. Aircraft were craned aboard for launches; they landed back ashore. Testing of virtually every Royal Navy carrier-capable aircraft in service at the time, including the de Havilland Sea Vampire jet and the big twin-engine Short Sturgeon, were completed in late 1951. *UK Crown Copyright expired*

BELOW After Royal Navy tests were completed, HMS *Perseus* (R51) sailed to the US east coast in early 1952 for a US Navy evaluation of its steam-driven catapult using F9F Panthers, F2H Banshees, and the big F3D Skyknight. To evaluate the capability of the catapult at higher steam pressures than provided by *Perseus'* power plant, dock-side launches were accomplished with steam provided by a US Navy destroyer moored alongside: an F3D Skyknight weighing more than 20,000lb was reportedly launched with a 10-knot tailwind. *US Navy*

In April 1952, BuNo 128452 was positioned 25 degrees nose high (note the fork lift under the nose gear wheel) to determine the amount of unavailable fuel at this extreme but achievable attitude. *VAHF*

programming. This proved to be unsatisfactory and was replaced by a purely mechanical system consisting of spring struts (provides increase in force required proportional to control surface deflection), a bob weight (increases force proportional to *g*), and a viscous damper (increases force proportional to rate of stick movement). The spring struts were located in the wing; the bob weight and viscous damper were linked to the pilot's stick. A ram-air scoop under the nose reduced maximum roll control deflection with increasing air speed to keep structural loads within limits.

Other design changes continued to be required but were generally deferred in production to aircraft 17 and subsequent or even to No. 29. Some resolved deficiencies: the vertical fins were found to be under strength in proof-load testing. An external strap was added to existing Cutlasses; for new production, the fin structure was strengthened to no longer require the strap. Others added mission capability: ECP 16 resulted in the redesign of the pylons to carry the heaviest of the new lightweight 'special' weapons, i.e. nuclear bombs, and provision for in-flight refuelling via a nose-mounted probe. Utilising big North American AJ Savages as tankers, the Navy had committed to in-flight refuelling of jets armed with the recently developed smaller nuclear bombs. This resulted in a significant increase in a jet's combat range, allowing the carriers to stand-off farther from enemy airfields.

From 9 until 12 June 1952, three NATC pilots (LtCol Marion Carl, CDR Robert 'Bob' Elder, and LCDR Bert L. Hendrickson) conducted a preliminary, qualitative, fifteen-flight evaluation of three different F7U-3s (BuNos 128451, 128452, and 128455) at the Chance Vought plant. At this point in F7U development, the engines were non-afterburning J35s, the landing gear was still the modified F7U-1s, there were two different artificial feel systems (hydraulic versus mechanical) among the aircraft, and the forward visibility improvement was not yet available for evaluation.

In preparation for it, Vought engineering created a chart listing fifty-one reported XF7U-1/F7U-1 deficiencies (some of which were duplicates), the F7U-1 corrective action, and the applicability of the deficiency to the F7U-3. Of the fifty-one, only three were considered by them to continue to be of concern:

- Inadequate stall warning (the artificial system was deleted with BuAer approval as part of the weight reduction programme)
- Accelerated stall characteristics
- Rudder effectiveness in a crosswind take-off

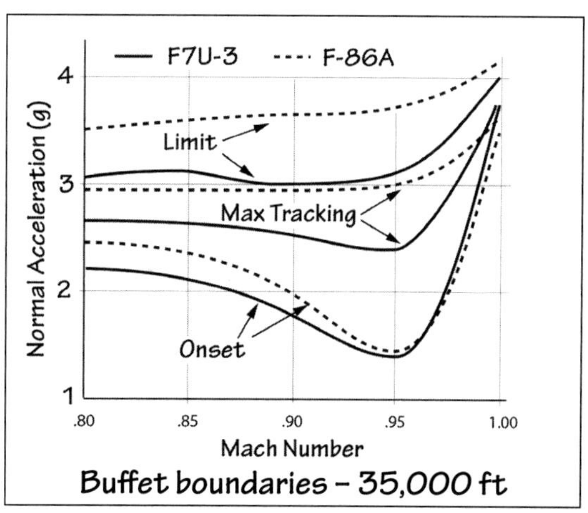

Vought was already concerned based on F7U-1 flight test that the F7U-3's buffet boundary might be inadequate, certainly compared to the swept-wing F-86. That proved to be the case. *Thomason*

RIGHT Tufting (the attachment of small strings by the end facing the airflow) is used to see whether the airflow over the aircraft's surface is behaving as hoped. This is the second F7U-3, readily identifiable by two red horizontal stripes on the vertical fin. For this flight, a flexible seal had been added over the gap between the wing and the ailavator to see if that resulted in an improvement in the buffet boundary and/or reduced approach speed. *VAHF*

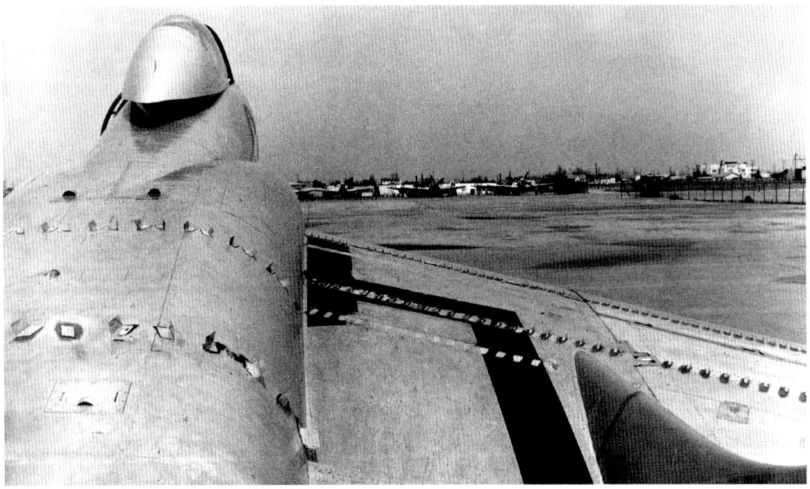

LEFT In the event that undesired unsteady or separated airflow is detected by the movement of the tufts, a likely cure is the addition of vortex generators, as shown here on the first F7U-3. These are angled slightly to the airflow to add energy to the boundary layer next to the airframe surface, which tends to delay separation. Although usually beneficial in that regard, they do increase drag. *VAHF*

BELOW Wing fences, frequently seen on swept-wing fighters to prevent undesirable span-wise airflow, were evaluated in the attempt to reduce the approach speed and also to improve the stall characteristics. They were not beneficial in this instance. *VAHF*

Approach speed reduction

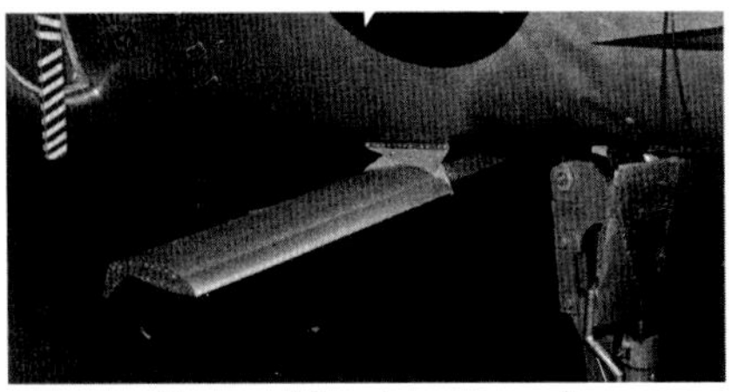

Forward fuselage canard

Engine inlet slat

Centre section trimmer

Extended chord ailavator

ABOVE Several significant modifications were evaluated to reduce the approach speed like these shown here, none of which were successful. *VAHF*

BuNo 128452 wing fences

Inboard

Outboard

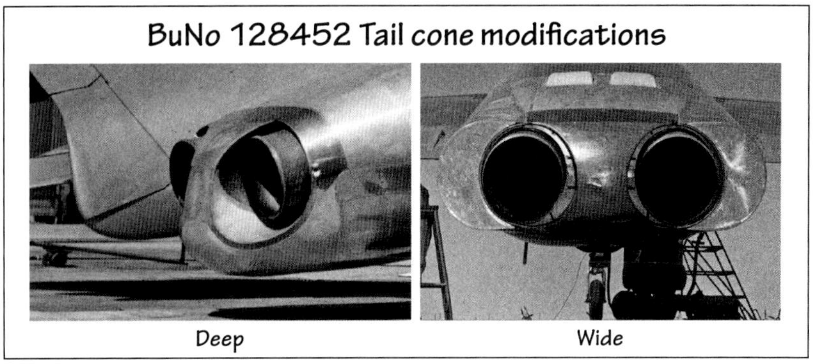

TOP LEFT The blunt trailing-edge modification to the ailavator had the effect of aerodynamically increasing its chord for greater control effectiveness as well as improving the clean-condition stall characteristics, enough to offset the increase in drag. It was therefore incorporated on the production ailavators. *VAHF*

ABOVE Several different slat configurations were evaluated in the attempt to reduce the approach speed, including this one with the slat nose rotated downward. Others included adding tiny vortex generators in the slot between the slat and the leading edge of the wing and sealing the gaps between the inboard and outboard slats and the inboard slat and the fuselage. *VAHF*

TOP RIGHT The second F7U-3 was evaluated with a modified inlet intended to increase the effective thrust of the J35 engines. The first F7U-3 was also temporarily modified to increase Vmax with the J35 engines with nose and canopy fairings, inlet vortex generators, and fairings over the openings in the landing gear doors for the F7U-1 landing gear. *VAHF*

ABOVE RIGHT Two major changes to the tail cone shape were evaluated in the attempt to increase the buffet boundary; neither was effective. *VAHF*

Nevertheless (and customary in these evaluations), the NATC pilots reported several more deficiencies and shortcomings, most related to handling qualities as before. Ironically, there was a nose-down trim change encountered between 0.89 IMN and 0.95, which the tail-less configuration was intended to avoid. Most significantly. the report noted that: 'The radius of action of the aircraft with a maximum fuel load of 1,140 gallons is extremely short.'

At least one dive was made to an indicated Mach number of 1.02, made specifically by Carl to 'sound bomb' the Vought facility.

One observation that would subsequently prove to be prescient was a large yawing tendency accompanied by a sudden reduction in rudder control force when approaching a stall with the slats retracted. Any attempt to counteract the yaw with rudder usually resulted in an extreme yaw reversal unless it was preceded by a reduction in angle of attack and increase in airspeed.

Overall, performance was regarded as similar or slightly superior to the F9F-6 except for the buffet boundary, which was not only 'disappointingly low' but 'considered to be a major deficiency'. The need for an improvement on the order of 1 *g* was stated. It was also noted that the NATC F-86A-5 being used for chase and pace during this evaluation 'demonstrated a significant margin in manoeuvring performance'. However, Vought engineers considered the F-86 to be exceptional in that regard.

The evaluation was tragically marred by the death of LCDR Hendrickson. On 10 June, on his third

ABOVE **The XF10F first flight was accomplished on 1 May 1952 at Edwards AFB, California, where it remained for its year-long flight test, often operating from the lakebed as shown in this take-off.** ***Grumman Archives***

BELOW **A May 1952 Vought F7U-3 study evaluated the weight impact of a tilting forward fuselage to maximise visibility over the nose on approach. The nose landing gear actuator would simultaneously lower the nose landing gear and tilt the forward fuselage down. The estimated increase in weight was 163lb.** ***Thomason***

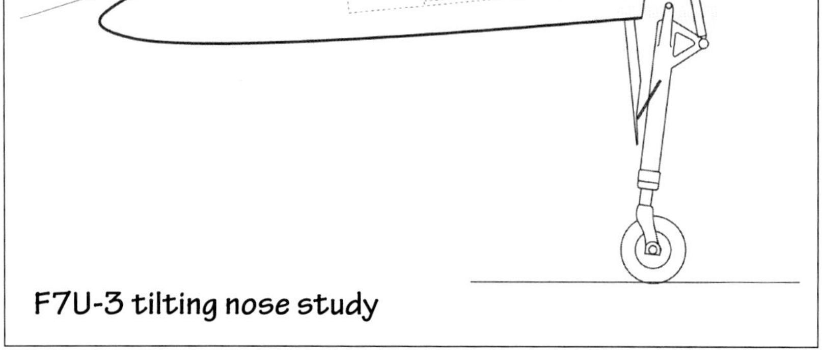

evaluation flight, he failed to extend the wing slats before take-off in BuNo 128455 (No. 5). After lifting off briefly a few times and then stalling back onto the runway, his last stall ended in the lake at the end of the runway and he was killed. However, since it was clearly pilot error, the accident did not appear to affect the Navy evaluation – it was not mentioned in the letter report from NATC to BuAer, not even in the paragraph recommending changes to slat control to avoid pilot error, which resulted in a landing gear-slat interconnect to ensure that when the landing gear was extended, the slats were too.

On 26 July 1952, LtCol Carl and CDR Elder returned to Vought to make one flight each in BuNo. 128451, now modified with blunt trailing-edge ailavators, F7U-3 landing gear with improved wheel brakes, improvements to the feel system and yaw damper, and the tailpipes tilted up 2 degrees to align the thrust line with the centre of gravity. Their report to BuAer noted some improvement in the handling qualities but 'little significant improvement in the buffet boundary'. Carl and Elder subsequently told Paul Thayer that Vought had 'made some very marked improvements in eliminating some of the deficiencies of the aircraft' but improvement in the buffet boundary was extremely desirable.

In mid-1952, Vought engineering accomplished yet another J46 replacement design study, this time a

CDR Elder on the left and LtCol Carl on the right in front of BuNo 128451 were well on their way to being legends in the test pilot community in 1952 when they made the first NATC F7U-3 flights. ***VAHF***

performance comparison and detailed assessment of the fuselage structure and fuel system modifications required if the two J46s were replaced by a single P&W J57-P-7. (At the time, both Chance Vought and P&W were divisions of the United Aircraft Corporation.) The heavier J57 had to be relocated farther forward, which fortuitously allowed an increase in internal fuel capacity of 136 gallons. The estimated empty weight increase was 1,150lb but the total thrust at combat rating compared to the J46-WE-2 increased by 2,600lb. However, on balance, except for range on the same amount of internal fuel, the performance improvement with the J57 was not significant or even less than would be provided by the J46s. In any event, the impact on the production schedule of such a significant redesign was also unacceptable.

Elder and Carl's flights were an early progress check by the Navy to determine whether an aircraft still had the potential to fulfil the mission that it was being developed for. The final exam was yet to come. It was conducted by the Navy's Board of Inspection and Survey (BIS), which dated back to wooden ships and represented the Secretary of the Navy. With respect to aircraft, the Board's task was to determine compliance with procurement contract specifications and guarantees; report all defects in material, performance, and design including those not necessarily covered by the contract; recommend design changes; and recommend final acceptance or rejection of the aircraft for service use. The responsibility for the evaluation itself was delegated, at the time to BuAer, which issued BIS project orders, assigned test aircraft, and provided engineering support. The actual testing was conducted by units like the Naval Air Test Center at Patuxent River, Maryland, and the Naval Air Special Weapons Facility at Albuquerque, New Mexico.

Aircraft were delivered for BIS flight test as soon as the BuAer and the manufacturer agreed that their configuration and flight envelope were suitable for an in-depth evaluation of a production-representative aircraft. Several were required, with at least one being assigned to each of NATC's test divisions: Armament, Electronics, Flight, Service, and Tactical (see pages 239-247). Typically, since the evaluation took several months, production of the aircraft was continued at a low rate so that operational squadrons could begin to be equipped with them as soon as the Board approval for service use was received. While modifications were likely as a result of this final exam, it was hoped that they could be readily accomplished by retrofit.

Because of the overriding significance of satisfactory carrier suitability, the Navy's at-sea evaluation of a new aircraft was accomplished as soon as possible. In the case of the Cutlass, the NATC Flight Test division received the fourth J35-powered F7U-3, BuNo 128454,

Added strap Cut back

Vertical fin modifications

First flight

Beef-up

Increased deck clearance

Initial canopy/nose change

BuNo 128452

BuNo 128454 (early)

BuNo 128451

BuNo 128454 (early)

on 2 July 1952 for initial carrier suitability tests, only six months after the F7U-3's first flight. It had the new radome with the upper surface slanted sharply downward to improve the all-important view of the LSO on approach. It also had modifications to the lower side of the vertical fin for greater ground clearance in nose-high landings.

Paul Thayer, now Vought's Vice President of Sales and Service, went to Patuxent River in late July to observe the shore-based carrier suitability evaluation of No. 4. It could hardly have been progressing better. For one thing, the Navy had flown it about seventy-five times in five weeks, remarkable reliability for a low-time prototype much less one being subjected to the loads of multiple high-sink rate landings. According to Thayer's trip report, CDR Feightner, who had been the pilot on the F7U-1 at-sea trials a year earlier, told him 'all of the deficiencies that existed in the F7U-1 for carrier suitability have been corrected in the F7U-3'. Moreover, Feightner stated 'if an inexperienced pilot asked him for a check out in the aircraft, with the intention of taking it aboard a carrier, I would have no hesitation whatsoever in doing so with only a normal amount of familiarisation'.

Initial carrier suitability tests commenced aboard *Midway* (then CVB-41), one of the three biggest US Navy carriers, on 11 August 1952. The NATC pilots were LCDR E.L. 'Whitey' Feightner and LCDR Andrew B. Connor Jr. Chance Vought F7U-3 test pilot William 'Billy' Sunday participated as the LSO.

Also aboard for NATC evaluation were the XFJ-2 Fury, F9F-5 Panther, F9F-6 Cougar, and F2H-3 Banshee. The other day fighters were notably lighter than the F7U-3: the F9F-5 with full internal fuel only weighed 15,000lb; the swept-wing F9F-6, with full internal fuel, 18,200lb; and the swept-wing XFJ-2 with full internal and external fuel, 18,900. The all-weather F2H-3 with full internal fuel was a bit heavier at 20,760 lb. The F7U-3 weighed 28,300lb with full internal fuel, at least 50% more than the other two swept-wing day fighters nearing introduction into service.

The existing carrier landing approach had been developed with biplanes in the 1920s. It was based on a short-field landing technique that resulted in a touchdown at stall speed as close as safely possible to the beginning of the runway but not before it! The pilot would slow to just above power-on stall speed in level flight (being flown on the 'backside of the power curve') with his wheels only about 15 to 20ft above the height of the flight deck, coached by the Landing Signal Officer (LSO) as to line-up, speed, and height. Just before reaching the deck, if the aircraft was lined up, on speed, and not too low or high, the LSO would make the cut signal, dropping his left arm to his side and slashing the paddle in his right hand across his throat. The pilot would respond by chopping the throttle to idle, which caused the aircraft to immediately begin a descent to the deck, ideally just beyond the first arresting wire or two. Operating on the backside of the power curve in level flight meant that the pilot had to add power if lower than desired. Simply pulling back on the stick would result in the aircraft losing altitude, not climbing.

Jet aircraft were very different in their approach and landing characteristics compared to aircraft with propellers. For one thing, they did not slow as rapidly when the throttle was cut since there wasn't the significant increase in drag of a now windmilling propeller. They also did not accelerate as quickly to climb speed when more throttle was added. The slowness of deceleration and acceleration meant that there was less margin of error in being fast or slow. Moreover, the jet's higher approach speed provided less time for the LSO to signal corrections. This also meant that the cut had to be given farther out; if the deck were moving due to the sea state, it might not be where the LSO had expected it to be when the jet was over the ramp. A wave off also had to be given farther out to allow for the jet to accelerate to climbing speed before getting too close to the ramp. Nevertheless, jet aircraft approaches and landings continued to be accomplished as they had been for aircraft with propellers. It helped the low-speed thrust-versus-drag curve of most jets – but not the Cutlass! – and resulted in them still being on the front side of the power curve at an approach speed providing adequate roll control power, so pulling back on the stick would result in a small rate of climb until adding throttle had an effect.

NATC reported that the F7U-3's approach, landing, and wave off characteristics were satisfactory. The other good news was that the predicted minimum wind-over-deck value for launch was not only demonstrated, the results indicated that it could be reduced by 5 knots using more aggressive pilot technique. Almost immediately following the evaluation, 454 was returned to Vought for the next set of modifications to make it more representative of the seventeenth and subsequent production F7U-3s.

TOP F7U-3 BuNo 128454 (No. 4) aboard *Midway* for a five-day evaluation in August 1952 along with F9F-6 BuNo 128257, among others. A swept-wing day fighter rival, the Cougar was about to be delivered to an operational squadron. ***US Navy***

ABOVE An F7U-3 pilot being 'cut' by the LSO during Field Carrier Landing Practice. ***US Navy***

ABOVE Four of the Navy's newest day fighters were on static display in late August 1952 at the International Aviation Exposition in Detroit, Michigan. F7U-3 BuNo 128457 leads a formation (from nearest to farthest) of the North American XFJ-2 Fury, Grumman F9F-6 Cougar, and Grumman F9F-5 Panther. *US Navy*

BELOW The most obvious external change to the F7U-3 before the *Coral Sea* trials was the significantly lengthened (almost 4ft) and therefore more tapered sliding canopy, an attempt to reduce canopy buffet and cockpit noise at high speed. *Thomason*

F7U-3 128454 sliding canopy, early iterations

The Navy put F7U-3 BuNo 128457 on display at Detroit's 5th Annual international Aviation Exposition from 30 August–1 September 1952 along with its other new jet fighters. This Cutlass' first flight had only been made a week earlier! LT Alan B. Shepard made three flybys during the show and LCDR Edward 'Whitey' Feightner led a formation flight of them in the F7U-3.

In September 1952, Vought management gave serious consideration to suggesting to the Navy that the last four of the sixteen J35-powered F7U-3s be sent to Korea in March 1953 for a land-based combat evaluation. After further discussion of the degree of difficulty and the risks involved versus the potential benefit, they decided not to pursue the effort. One concern, harking back to an earlier publicity stunt, was: 'The way the Blue Angels' F7U-1s were thrown out of Corpus Christi is an illustration of the rapid way things can happen, entirely out of our control.'

There were still doubters in the Atlantic fleet as to the operational suitability of the F7U-3 – notwithstanding the favourable report of the trials aboard *Midway* – based on the number of fatal crashes and NATC's unfavourable report following its flight evaluation in June. In October 1952, RADM Selden B. Spangler, on the staff of ComAirLant (Commander Air Force, Atlantic Fleet), stated in a memo to the ComAirLant Plans Department that his Material Section had no desire for the Cutlass 'due primarily to its inferior air performance, high catapult requirements, high excess weight in the form of undue complication, unduly high requirements for piloting skill, and excessive maintenance requirements'. In part as a result, ComAirLant, ADM John J. Ballentine, recommended to the CNO that his desired air group composition in the near future would be comprised of five squadrons, one each of McDonnell F2H-3s for the all-weather fighter (to be replaced by McDonnell F3H-1s when available), Grumman F9F-5s as a day fighter

ABOVE BuNo 128457 on the McDonnell Aircraft ramp at St Louis next to the eleventh production F2H-3, possibly flown by a Navy pilot on the way to or from the 1952 Detroit Aviation Exposition (inset). ***Casby Collection***

RIGHT At the Air Force's request, NACA evaluated the recovery of a jet fighter into a RB-36's bomb bay by either a towed drogue or the fixed coupling in this illustration. ***NACA RM SL52D07***

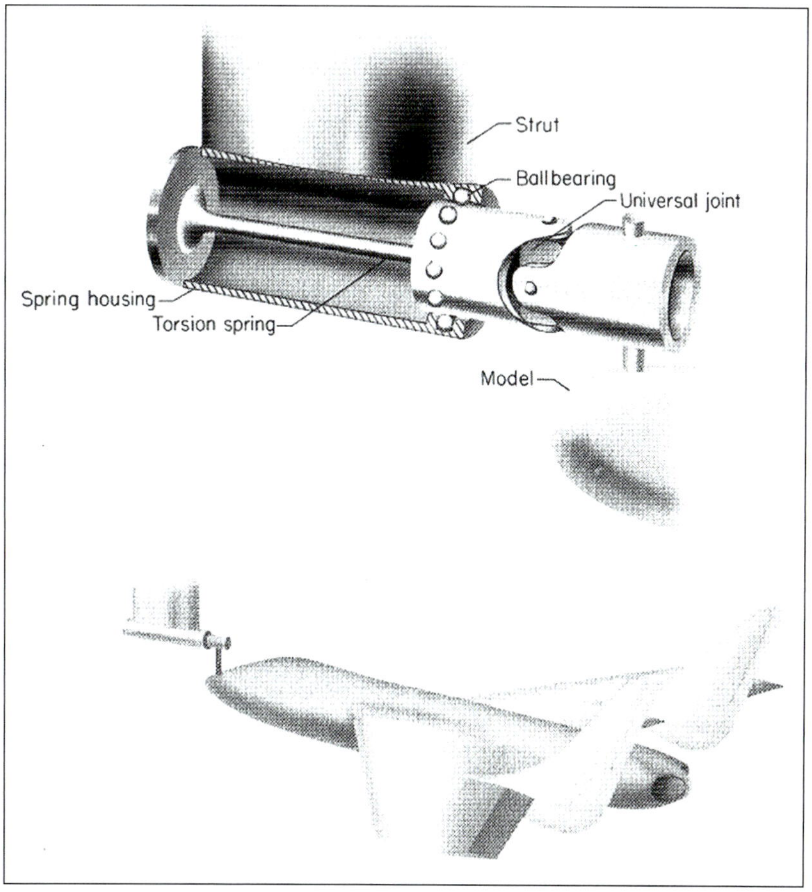

until replaced by swept-wing F9F-6s, Douglas AD-4s for interdiction attack to be replaced by the turboprop-powered A2D then in development, and Douglas AD-4s for close air support. The F7U-3 already had a serious image problem at NAS Norfolk.

In late October, in conjunction with Vought's proposal to sell an F7U-3 derivative, the V-377 powered by J35s with afterburning, to the Air Force, Col Fred Ascani, LtCol Frank Everest, and Capt Thomas Curtis flew two different J35-powered F7U-3s at Vought over three days. They were most impressed by the visibility from the cockpit, mentioning it more than once in their evaluation report, even though it was considered by the NATC to be marginal at best for carrier landings. Their handling qualities evaluation was not overly critical but affected to an unknown extent by Vought's discovery a week after their flights that both aircraft had binding in the feel control system. They noted that

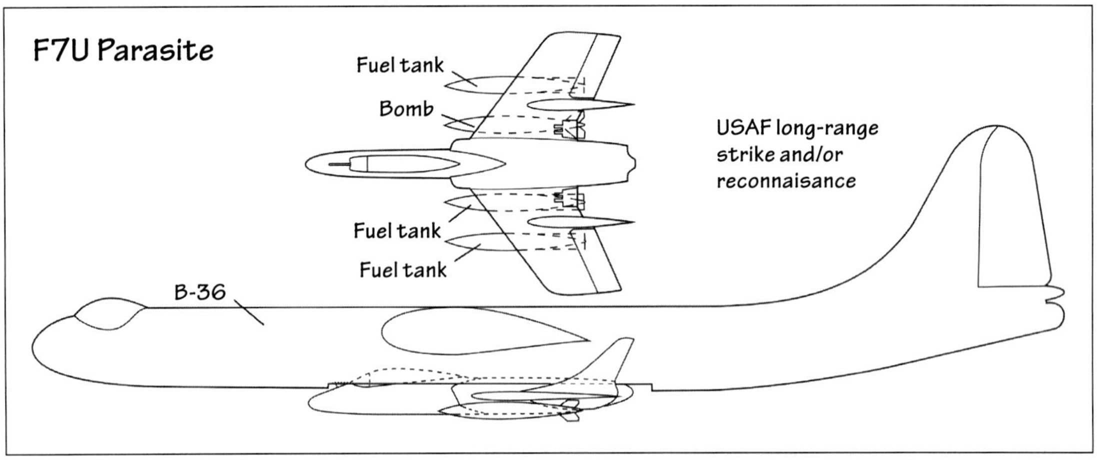

RIGHT The F7U was a good match for the B-36 as a parasite fighter-bomber. When housed in the bomb bay, its twin fins were located outside the fuselage and aft of the wing. *Thomason*

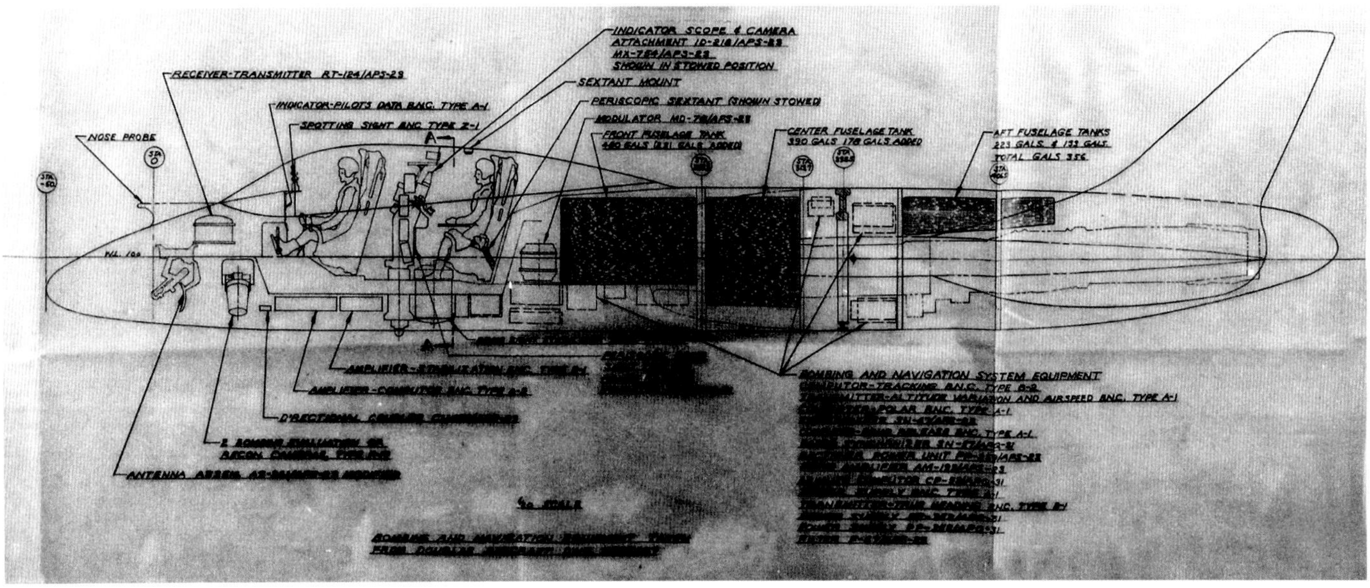

ABOVE The Vought proposal of an F7U-3 parasite fighter bomber to the Air Force added a second crew position for a mission specialist to operate all the navigation, bombing and reconnaissance avionics involved. One internal fuel option included the removal of the landing gear for the installation of two fuel cells in each vertical fin. Total internal fuel capacity would then be 2,193 gallons (70% more than the F7U3-M/P); adding three 500-gallon external tanks would raise the total to 3,693 gallons. *Thomason*

it was very difficult to achieve a stall with the slats extended and stall warning, except when the gear and slats were retracted, was clearly apparent due to airframe buffeting. Single-engine handling qualities were considered to be excellent, but 'the aircraft will not maintain level flight at any altitude on one engine with gear and slats extended'. At the other end of the flight envelope, at least one flight included a 75-degree dive from 40,000ft to an indicated Mach number of 1.0. The 3g pullout began at 20,000ft. As had already been noted, there was an extremely high noise level in the cockpit at Mach 0.84 and above.

While their F7U-3 evaluation was generally favourable, the Air Force passed on acquiring any, already having similar capability among its numerous fighters in service and in development. However, in conjunction with determining the feasibility of using a fighter as a 'parasite' in combination with a Consolidated Vultee RB-36 for long-range reconnaissance missions (Project FICON), the Air Research and Development Command Force – possibly in response to a Vought proposal – asked NACA to determine the stability and control characteristics of retrieving one in flight via a fixed probe engaging a fixed coupling or towed drogue rather that hooking on to a trapeze as was then being flight tested. It is not known whether they or NACA chose a F7U-3 model for the resulting wind tunnel test. The model proved to be unstable laterally when towed on either length of tow line tested; stability was acceptable with the fixed coupling with a spring restraint in roll. The Air Force continued its full-scale evaluations with the trapeze concept and one of its swept-wing fighters.

On 4 November, 454 went aboard *Coral Sea* (CVA-43) for a second set of trials, this time at higher gross weights, both take-off and landing, accomplished by NATC test pilots LCDR A.B. Connor Jr. and USMC Capt J. Lynn Helms. Changes from the *Midway* (CVA-41) trials in addition to the elongated sliding canopy were installation of the blunt trailing elevators, tilting the engine tailpipes up for an increase in nose-up thrust moment, ballasting the aircraft to move the centre of gravity aft to represent the seventeenth and subsequent F7U-3s, and increasing the nose gear servicing pressure to 50 psi from 40 for a higher nose-up attitude at launch.

F7U-3 BuNo 128454 (No. 4) being launched from *Coral Sea* in November 1952; the top of the vertical fins now sport red and white stripes preceded by a dark blue leading edge. *US Navy*

The North American XFJ-2 Fury was also aboard *Coral Sea* in November 1952 with the F7U-3, the second at-sea trials for both. *US Navy*

NATC test pilot J. Lynn Helms, Capt USMC, inadvertently exceeded the F7U-3 landing gear sink-rate limit aboard *Coral Sea* in November 1952. The failure was attributed to the loss of proper damping in the oleo due to the failure of the metering mechanism at higher than design loads on a previous landing. *US Navy*

One of the nine launches was made at 33,400lb, with almost full internal fuel and 4,950lb of external stores, albeit with a Wind Over Deck of 44 knots. Some of the landing sink rates were in excess of the design requirement of 17ft per second. Three arrested landings were accomplished at a gross weight of 24,250lb; one at 23,900lb was at a sink rate of 20.5ft per second, resulting in a main landing gear tyre blowout. The evaluation was concluded after three days when the ninth landing at 24,000lb and a sink rate of 20ft per second with a Wind Over Deck of 32 knots resulted in the left main landing gear strut failing at the axle due to an undetected shock strut oleo failure on a previous landing.

With the proviso that BuNo 128454 was not wholly production representative, the NATC report concluded, 'the test aircraft is satisfactory for catapult launchings and arrested landing up to the limits tested'. Based on the results, NATC 'estimated that an F7U-3 equivalent to aircraft 29 and subsequent can launch from an H8 4,000 psi catapult carrying 3,500 pounds of external stores with 25 knots of (WOD)', a significantly better result than the 1951 prediction that caused the F7U-3 to become a day fighter. The axle failure was not worthy of mention.

On 9 December, Vought test pilot William Sunday was killed on a production test flight of the tenth production F7U-3, BuNo 128460, when an aileron control linkage became disconnected on short final. The aircraft began an uncommanded roll, caught a wing tip short of the runway, and cartwheeled to destruction. The F7U-3s were grounded briefly while the cause of the accident and corrective action were established.

In August, Westinghouse had projected the delivery of six flight-qualified but derated J46s, three for F7U-3 No. 3 that was to be the first to fly with the J46 and three for No. 17. Westinghouse finally delivered a single flight-worthy YJ46-WE-8A engine to Vought on 29 December. The second one would be delivered five weeks later. The suffix letter identified it as being derated relative to the -8 specification in order to begin delivery of a handful J46s to Vought. At that time, Westinghouse projected that deliveries of engines that fully met the J46-WE-8 specification would not begin until November 1953. BuAer was still assuming that the -2 engine would be available for the completion and delivery of the 121st F7U-3.

The future was still bright, however. At the end of 1952 BuAer was reportedly planning to order F7U-3Ms to be armed with Sparrow I missiles – adding back much of the mission equipment and capability that had been deleted in mid-1951 – as well as A2U-1s, an F7U-3 modified for attack missions. Even better news was that Grumman flight test of the rival F10F was not going well (the programme would be terminated in April 1953) and neither was the Westinghouse J40 engine programme, which adversely affected Vought's other rival for the general-purpose fighter requirement, the McDonnell F3H-1.

CHAPTER SIX

1953 – Flight test with the J46 finally begins

The year 1953 began with the ungrounding of the F7U-3 after the determination of the cause of Billy Sunday's fatal crash and corrective action. Initial envelope expansion and a significant amount of development was essentially complete on No. 1 and No. 2: in March, Part I Power Plant demonstration had been completed on BuNo 128452; Part I Aerodynamic and Structural demonstration was in progress. When that was complete, it would be assigned to the spin demonstration. In general, the year represented a high watermark in the programme; its future remained bright throughout the year, a welcome change from previous ones.

Vought received the second fifty-hour qualified YJ46-WE-8A in January. In February, as Vought was beginning to 'provisionally deliver' F7U-3s complete except for the installation of the government-furnished J46 engines, Westinghouse provided the Navy and Vought with an updated J46 development plan. The 150-hour test of the -8A engine was to be completed in March, allowing deliveries to begin with the electric fuel control; it would be quickly followed by deliveries of the -8B engine with a new turbine design that increased the combat thrust from 5,500lb to 5,800lb. It also stated that Vought would receive the first ten -8 engines with the hydro-mechanical nozzle control in October, a month earlier than had been previously projected. Deliveries of the 6,100lb (combat thrust) -2, which required a redesign of the compressor and yet another turbine redesign, would finally begin in December 1953. Vought Power Plant engineering had no confidence

Depending on gross weight and the wind-over-deck speed, the catapult launch of the F7U-3 was made with up to full aft stick. ***US Navy***

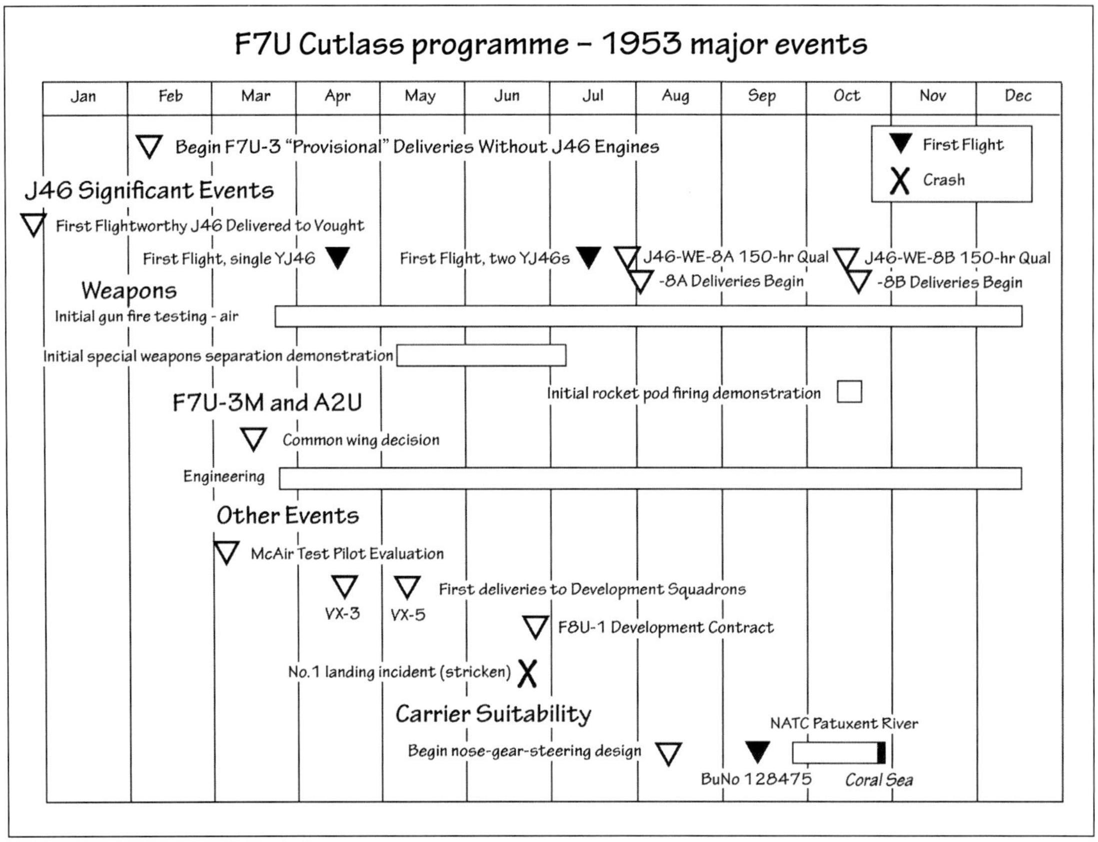

BELOW McDonnell test pilot Robert Little and the XF3H-1; the Demon may have had the best over-the-nose visibility of any Navy carrier-based aircraft. *Mark Nankivil*

in the schedule – justifiably so as it turned out: Westinghouse missed them all by months except for -2 deliveries that turned out to be never – but did not express concern about Westinghouse's ability to make good on the engine's performance thrust guarantee.

After directing Vought to repurpose the F7U-3 to be a day fighter in 1951, some in BuAer were still not convinced that the F7U-3 had a future as one. A 13 February evaluation prepared for CAPT Dietrich, head of the Plans Co-ordination Division, of near-term (within two years) day fighter options to replace the Grumman F9F-6 and North American FJ-2 in the air group didn't even mention the F7U-3, but did the F3H/J71 (so the Cutlass' size was not the reason for its lack of consideration) and F4D/J57. The latter was preferred over the former: that airframe/engine combination was predicted to result in satisfactory range (at least 300nm radius) with eternal tanks, performance matching that of the MiG-15/F-86/FJ-2, and the 'potential of being (the) best manoeuvring aircraft of those considered'. These were to be replaced in turn in the air groups by either the North American FJ-4 or the Grumman F11F (then known as the F9F-9), both being considered for development contracts. They would be replaced by the winner of the 1953 day fighter competition for which proposals were about to be received (it resulted in the Vought F8U programme). As it turned out, slippages in the F3H/F4D and FJ-4/F11F programmes required replacement of the F9F-6/FJ-2 with the F9F-8/FJ-3, which were

LEFT The 'V' windscreen somewhat reduced buffet but was incompatible with the gunsight. *VAHF*

CENTRE LEFT AND RIGHT Another variation of a fence on the outboard wing panel was no more successful than the previous one. *VAHF*

BOTTOM Another variation of the extended centre section concept also failed to provide significant benefit. *VAHF*

ABOVE Delta-tip ailavators evaluated on aircraft No. 4 resulted in no buffet improvement and apparently did not provide significant benefit expected from the increased aspect ratio. ***VAHF***

BELOW In the mid-1950s, the wings of some Navy carrier-based jets were modified to have a cambered leading edge to provide more lift for lower speed on approach and more manoeuvrability at altitude. Vought evaluated the concept on the F7U-3 but decided not to incorporate it. ***VAHF***

subsequently replaced by the F8U and to a limited degree, the F11F.

Nevertheless, the F7U's future was seemingly assured with respect to production. Vought had a 200-plus F7U-3 contract in hand. The development of the Navy's first air-to-air missile, the Sparrow I, was nearing completion; BuAer and OpNav needed to pair it with a big high-performance fighter for defence of the carrier battle group during attack by Soviet jet bombers. The other candidates, the Grumman F10F Jaguar and the McDonnell F3H Demon, were even farther behind schedule than the Cutlass. BuAer therefore contracted with Vought in March 1953 for the F7U-3M. Another requirement was for a big carrier-based jet to replace the AD Skyraider being flown by both the Navy from carriers and the USMC from shore bases. That resulted in a letter of intent for fifty A2Us, an F7U-3 optimised for close-air support missions.

In March 1953, McDonnell's Chief Test Pilot, Robert C. Little, visited Vought to make two flights in the No. 7 F7U-3. (BuAer encouraged the practice, in part to ensure that each company was fully aware of the performance of its rival's fighters and felt pressure to meet or exceed it.) He then provided Vought management and engineering with a qualitative comparison of its handling qualities and performance with those of the XF3H-1 prototype (the heavier production F3H-1 would not fly until the end of the year). He reported that the Cutlass was somewhat easier to fly on approach except for higher lateral control loads. The rate of roll at high speed was about the same but the F7U-3's lateral control loads were again higher, as was the adverse yaw with aileron. Since No. 7's engines were the non-afterburning J35s, Vmax was less but otherwise the performance was equivalent. Little evaluated the F7U-3's speed brake's effectiveness as good and considerably better than the XF3H's. The major handling quality difference in the XF3H's favour was the F7U-3's large and abrupt trim

In early June 1953, BuNo 128453, the J46 engine test bed, was in lay-up for maintenance. Note the 'J-Forty Six' logo on the nose. The canopy has been removed, revealing a fully extended sliding-canopy actuator. *VAHF*

change around Mach 0.9. He noted that the XF3H exhibited little if any trim change between Mach 0.9 and 1.05. Little's only comment on the buffet boundary was: 'It's pretty low, isn't it?'

At that point, Vought had resumed development and evaluation of prospective solutions to the low buffet boundary: seismic dampers (a dashpot in the wing tip that functions like a shock absorber), a 'V' windscreen, a revisit of the outer-panel wing fence and centre section trailing edge extension, a drooped and extended variant of the leading-edge slats, and delta-tip ailavators that had been proposed in 1952 for the A2U programme. No. 1 was dedicated to this effort supported by No. 4.

Vought finally flew F7U-3 BuNo 128453 (No. 3) with a YJ46-8A in April 1953, albeit only one, as a left engine, accompanied by a J35 on the right side. According to a Vought internal memo, the J46 had never been operated in flight on a test bed aircraft, nor run in an altitude chamber prior to any being provided to Vought for F7U-3 flight test. What was worse, in three weeks of test stand runs at Vought prior to installation in an aircraft, eleven major discrepancies were discovered, some of which were considered to affect safety of flight. Due to slippage in the J46 delivery schedule, BuAer reduced the peak F7U-3 monthly production rate from twenty-one to eighteen to reduce the number of aircraft that would be waiting on engines for completion.

Flight test with the J46 was not without problems, including compressor stalls and afterburner failures to light off or stay lit. The -8A engine didn't pass its 150-hour qualification test until 25 July 1953, two years behind Westinghouse's late 1950 schedule plan. Delivery of this interim engine began immediately and they were installed in some of the airframes that had been completed beginning in February. By the end of August, there were eleven F7U-3s assigned to the BIS activity at NATC, but only four were powered by J46s. As of 21 October, there were still twenty-eight F7U-3s parked on Vought's ramp, complete except for engines. What was worse, BuAer considered the engines in production to be unacceptable for service use because of high SFC and propensity to compressor stall. If the redesigned turbine and compressor being readied for flight test did not rectify the shortcomings, then the F7U-3 programme would again be in jeopardy of being cancelled.

A few of the first sixteen J35-powered F7U-3s were delivered to two Air Development squadrons in 1953: VX-3 at NAS Atlantic City, NJ, and VX-5 at NAS Moffett Field, CA. VX-3 received two, BuNos 128464 in mid-April 1953 and 128463 two weeks later, to familiarise itself with the type prior to a full operational evaluation. VX-5 received BuNos 128465 and 128466 in May as part of its assignment to develop and evaluate aircraft tactics and techniques for delivery of tactical nuclear weapons.

The highlight for Vought in 1953, winning the Navy's competition for a supersonic day fighter against all comers in May, had a little something to do with the F7U and vice versa. First, if configuration differences meant anything, the F8U owed a lot to the F7U lessons learned. It was long and sleek, not short and fat, including thinner wing aerofoils; it had a horizontal tail, all moving and placed low to avoid transonic effects; its single engine was the new P&W J57; and the nose landing gear was short, made possible by a variable-incidence wing. Vought probably benefited from the timing of the competition, because more F7U-3 disappointments were yet to come; those might have adversely affected BuAer's regard for Vought's ability to design and develop a supersonic jet fighter. The F8U returned the favour to an extent by incentivising the

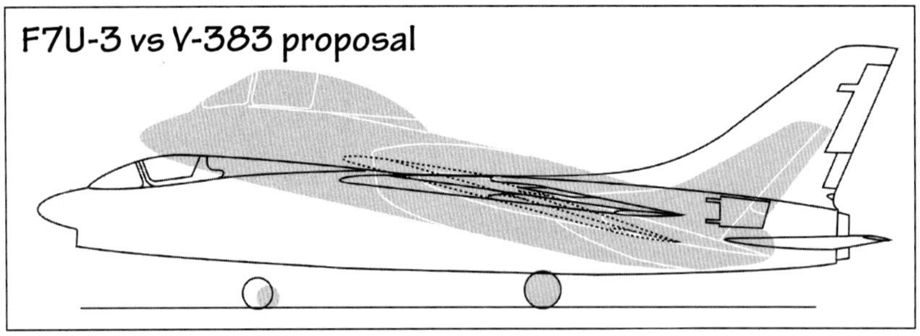

ABOVE Vought's J57-powered V-383 proposal for the Navy's 1953 carrier-based day fighter requirement could not have been more different from the F7U-3, beginning with its variable-incidence wing. *Thomason*

BELOW Several detail changes were made to Vought's proposed day fighter during detail design, particularly in the forward fuselage: the cannon were relocated aft on the fuselage in place of the speed brakes, which had been relocated from the aft fuselage and now became a single panel on the belly. The top of the fuselage aft of the canopy was widened to provide more volume for ammunition. *VAHF*

Navy to continue funding F7U problem-solving and production, thereby maintaining Vought as a viable design and manufacturing facility.

In September 1953, Vought had contracts for a total of 590 F7U-3s, F7U-3Ps, F7U-3Ms, and A2U-1s. The company was expecting a contract for an additional 297 A2U-1s at a minimum for a production total of 887 Cutlasses to be delivered up to the end of 1956. It was the high water mark from that standpoint. The actual total turned out to be only 290, with the last F7U-3M delivered at the end of 1955 and no A2U-1 production.

The first at-sea testing with a production representative Cutlass (BuNo 128475, No. 25) occurred aboard *Coral Sea* from 26 to 30 October 1953. The XF4D and XF3H were aboard at the same time but the F7U-3 was still well ahead of those programmes from a development standpoint since they were both prototypes powered by the troubled J40 engine. The most obvious F7U-3 external change was the final revision to the sliding canopy but one of the most significant differences from the prior at-sea evaluations was that the aircraft was now powered with afterburning J46 engines. It was also equipped with a pilot-operated steerable nose landing gear – a first for a carrier-based jet – determined to be necessary as a result of the carrier suitability evaluations with BuNo 128454. Detail changes were also made to the landing gears, arresting hook, and associated fuselage structure. While the fuselage and main landing gear weight was less than the first sixteen F7U-3s that had been powered by J35s as an interim engine, the arresting limits were reduced, with the maximum landing weight now being 24,200lb rather than 26,180lb.

As predicted, launches at high gross weights required more wind over deck than the desired 25 knots but even the H4-1, the least powerful hydraulic catapult, was capable of accelerating an F7U-3 with full fuel and a 3,250lb T-64 shape representing the Mk 8 nuclear weapon – a gross weight of 30,450lb – to a satisfactory end speed (albeit with a wind-over-deck of 40 knots) even with the derated J46-WE-8A engines.

At landing gross weights from 22,000 to 24,500lb and approach speeds from 107 to 120 knots depending on the weight, the aircraft response was adequate for answering the signals from the LSO and wave off characteristics were good with either military or combat power. The pilot's view of the LSO during the final portion of the approach was partially obscured by the frame between the forward and left windscreen panels even after the oval centre panel was incorporated but still acceptable.

The only notable shortcoming was that the single-engine carrier approach characteristics were unsatisfactory, although a successful landing was feasible. The problem was that when the Cutlass was configured for landing with the gear down and the slats extended, the thrust from one engine at Military thrust was insufficient to maintain level flight. However, employing the afterburner resulted in a minimum approach speed of 125 knots even with fully extended speed brakes since the thrust in afterburner could not be modulated. Intermittent use of afterburner on approach was to be avoided because of the risk of a failure of the afterburner to light off or worse, the possibility of a compressor stall when going into afterburner. As a result, the aircraft's attitude on approach would be lower than usual, which the LSO had to take into account and its speed higher than desired, which required more wind over deck if possible. One NATC suggestion for consideration was to have the pilot approach and land wheels up, which would reduce drag enough so military thrust would be adequate.

No discrepancies were noted in the deck-handling characteristics of the aircraft 'considering its size and weight'. Spotting the aircraft on the deck-edge lift 'was facilitated by the use of the nose gear steering'. 'The aircraft can be moved over normal obstacles on the

hangar deck by a plane-handling crew of approximately 15 men.' However, it was observed that sudden stops and starts that resulted in the nose gear strut extending needed to be avoided during movement on the hangar deck because of the minimal clearance with the overhead. Satisfactory wing folding and canopy closing were accomplished in winds of 40 to 58 knots from 45 degrees off the nose.

While there were F7U-3 programme successes in 1953, most notably the carrier trials of a production-representative aircraft, Westinghouse continued to be unable to meet either its schedule commitments for qualification and delivery of engines or the original contract specification for thrust, SFC, and weight.

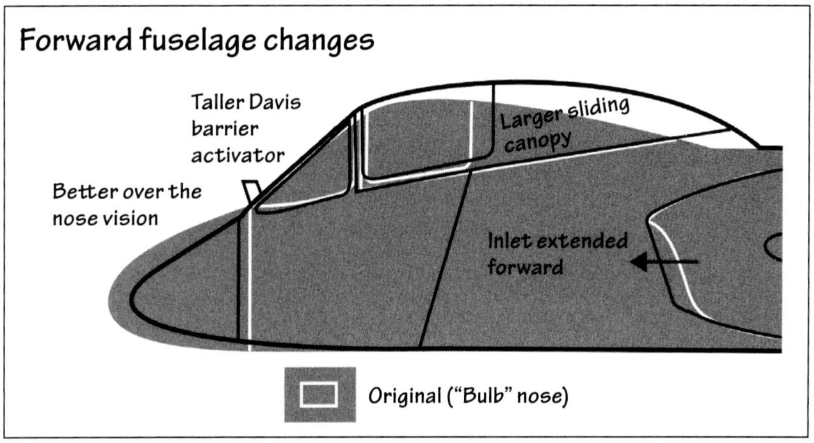

TOP LEFT AND RIGHT **The final shape of the canopy had an enlarged sliding section to reduce buffet and an oval centre pane in the windscreen that maximised visibility down and to the side of the nose. The Davis barrier activator was also increased in height.** ***Thomason***

LEFT **Apparently the engines were shut down so BuNo 128475 could not be taxied off the *Coral Sea* elevator into the hangar. Certainly the few deck hands that could push on nose strut would not be enough to turn an F7U.** ***US Navy***

Also aboard *Coral Sea* for carrier trials in October 1953 in addition to an XF4D-1 were the XF3H-1 Demon and a production F2H-3 Banshee. *US Navy*

At the beginning of 1953, having finally managed to get the first flightworthy J46 to Vought, Westinghouse planned to deliver a total of 348 J46 engines during the year. However, at mid-year Westinghouse was still testing engines with four different compressors and three different turbine combinations. Qualification of the production -8B engine was finally accomplished in mid-October to allow deliveries of that engine to Vought to begin. As a result, the actual number of engines delivered in 1953 was sixty-nine with eight in transit. BuAer had Vought slow its production rate but not by enough to match the Westinghouse shortfall. Vought had completed seventy-eight F7U-3s that were to be powered by J46s, meaning more than half of them lacked engines.

Not only were the J46s being delivered late and with lower thrust than the original specification, they were also heavier than specification, a contributor to the 600lb increase of the aircraft's weight during the year. What was worse, Westinghouse was still in the process of resolving significant engine issues at the end of the year:

- Compressor stalls during engine acceleration
- Compressor stalls during afterburner light-off
- Afterburner blow out at lower altitudes than anticipated

To be fair, Westinghouse's inability to meet its engine delivery schedule was not the only problem affecting the 1954 delivery of F7U-3s to fleet squadrons. The Navy decision to let Vought continue production during 1953, albeit at a reduced rate, while development and evaluation testing was still in progress meant that those F7U-3s were going to have to go through an update programme to incorporate modifications before delivery to fleet squadrons. While none of Cutlass issues approached the seriousness of Westinghouse's with the J46, the ever-increasing number of desired/required changes would soon become a cause for concern (to minimise the impact, Vought had begun making some known changes to the completed but engine-less F7U-3s beginning in April in order to shorten the time to prepare them for delivery after engines became available).

The fact that more Cutlasses were being built before the Navy had completed its formal acceptance trials was not unusual. In fact, it was not unknown for aircraft to be flying in fleet squadrons before the final BIS report was issued. However, the degree to which unresolved issues still existed and even more modifications were required to address shortcomings that would be identified by initial squadron-level operation in the coming year would sour some on the Cutlass ever being acceptable for service use.

CHAPTER SEVEN

1954 – Mixed programme and service test results

The year 1954 was a pivotal one for Vought and the F7U-3 programme. Because of the increasing reluctance of other engine and aircraft manufacturers to do business with United Aircraft's Chance Vought and Pratt & Whitney divisions respectively, due to concerns that their technology would find its way to a competitor, the corporation divested itself of the Chance Vought Aircraft Division. It was reformed as an independent company, Chance Vought Aircraft, Incorporated. Meanwhile, the Navy was completing the formal acceptance trials of the Cutlass and initiating the formation of squadrons that would deploy with it. At the same time, Vought was resolving issues with F7U-3 performance and function, building F7U-3s, and creating kits to accomplish changes required for service suitability in delivered ones. Westinghouse continued to disappoint in J46 engine development, qualification, and production.

An FJ-3 leads a VC-3 formation of two F9F-6s, two former *Project Cutlass* F7U-3s, and an F2H-3, the fighters that would be assigned to the mid-1950s air groups. *US Navy*

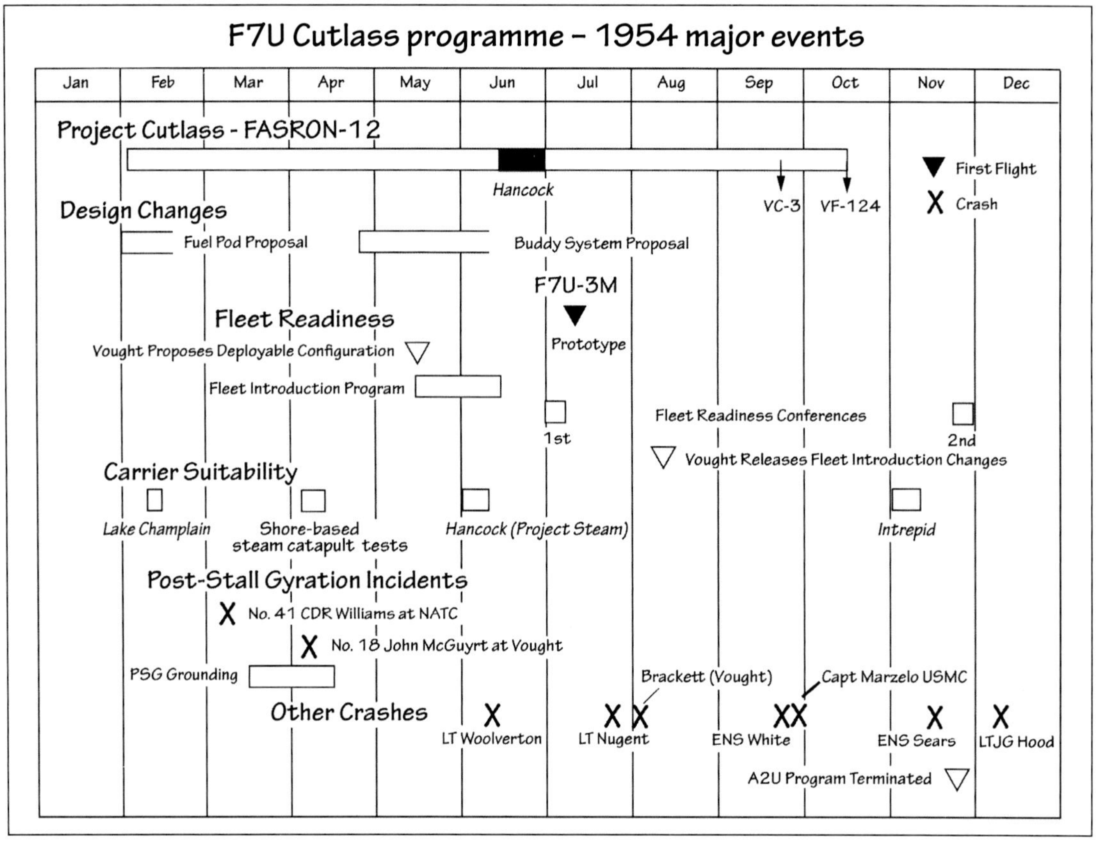

Carrier suitability

The penultimate set of F7U-3 day fighter carrier suitability trials was accomplished by NATC with No. 25, BuNo 128475, aboard *Lake Champlain* (CVA-39), an Essex-class carrier, on 8 to 13 February 1954. Up until then, these had been accomplished on the slightly bigger Midway-class carriers. *Champ* represented the smaller but more numerous flight decks that Cutlass squadrons would also have to operate from. It did, however, have the more powerful H-8 catapults. Somewhat belying the BuAer concern about hydraulic catapult capability, launches were accomplished safely, albeit at a gross weight of 27,200lb (full fuel but no ammunition) with a wind-over-deck of only 20 knots even with the -8 engines. The heaviest launches were made from the H-8 with full fuel, two 2,000lb bombs, and a rocket pack for a gross weight of 32,450lb, although the required wind-over-deck was 39 knots. 'The catapult launching characteristics are satisfactory.' Even if a launch was made with full back stick at end speeds significantly higher than the minimum, the resulting over-rotation did not result in a stall and the nose subsequently dropped to the attitude required for level or climbing flight.

With respect to landings, 'an approach speed of 115 kts IAS was considered … to be optimum for weights under 23,000lb under normal sea conditions with 30–35 knots of wind over deck', providing satisfactory approach and wave off characteristics. It was noted that the aircraft could be flown at slower speeds but much higher engine power was required to maintain altitude on the approach and therefore less margin for error existed. At higher gross weights (up to 24,350lb), an approach speed of 120 knots was recommended.

Following the last series of F7U-3 at-sea evaluations, NATC reported that the 'aircraft as finally tested was satisfactory for arrested landings and catapult launches' and was recommended for service use, although it should be 'restricted from carrier operations until structural modifications to the arresting hook installation are incorporated'. It also noted that the single-engine carrier approach characteristics were unsatisfactory and the exterior lighting was inadequate for providing sufficient aircraft attitude information to the LSO during night landings. However, correction of these and a few other deficiencies was only necessary 'to improve the operational suitability of the aircraft'.

In response to a March 1954 request from BuAer to provide a qualitative discussion of the catapult launching and arrested landing evolution of the model F7U-3 aircraft 'for dissemination to operating activities', i.e. fleet squadrons, the Naval Air Test Center provided F7U-3 carrier suitability information in a memo dated 4 May 1954. Its counsel reflected no undue concern about the aircraft's performance or handling qualities during either take-off from or landing on a carrier. It mentioned that the aircraft would over-rotate on launch if the trim were not correct for the end speed but 'the aircraft will not stall and the nose of the aircraft will drop to the attitude required

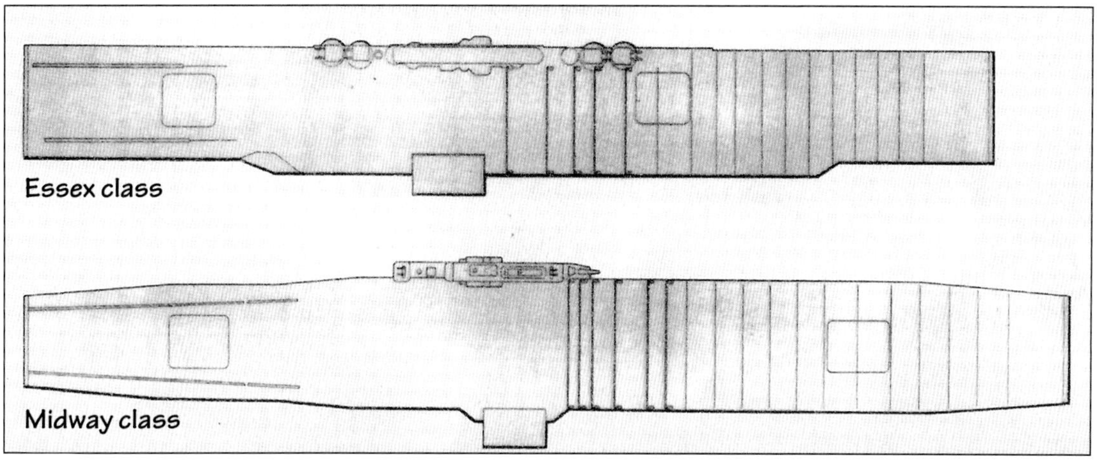

The three Midway-class carriers were longer but the deck was not notably wider than that of the more numerous Essex-class carriers or higher above the water. *Thomason*

Although the Midway-class carriers like *Coral Sea* were bigger than the Essex-class carriers in some respects, the view on landing wasn't all that different when they had axial decks: *Coral Sea* (CVA-43) on the left; *Essex* (CVA-9) on the right. *Thomason*

for level or climbing flight'. It cautioned that the leading slats should only be retracted after the minimum speed for the clean (i.e. wheels up) configuration was safely exceeded to avoid the risk of a stall.

The degree of difficulty in landing a Cutlass on an axial deck using the then-standard low, flat approach to an LSO-directed cut was clearly not considered to be particularly high relative to other jet fighters. It noted that the high angle of attack of the aircraft at the recommended approach speed versus weight required use of considerably more engine power than that required on the downwind leg when decelerating to approach speed and the margin for error was low; therefore, instead of reducing power, the extension of speed brakes was recommended for that purpose. The most idiosyncratic Cutlass characteristic was: 'The height of the cockpit above the landing gear, together with the high angle of attack of the aircraft during the approach, gives the pilot the impression of being too high as the aircraft nears the "cut" point. Therefore the pilot should avoid the tendency to drop the nose in the groove and to dive for the deck after the cut.'

The technique to be used after the cut was not dictated, as 'fleet pilots' should be capable of flying 'the aircraft to a landing rather than relying on a mechanical method', but 'as a guide', after the cut the pilot was advised 'to release back pressure on the control stick and if needed, exert a slight forward pressure to start the nose down to set up a sink rate. Before touchdown, increase back pressure on the control stick to develop a slight flare, and land on the main gear. Immediately after touchdown, apply forward pressure on the control stick to keep the aircraft on the deck in the event of a hook skip.' The memo continued: 'Wave-offs may be successfully executed with either military or afterburner power. However, if the wave-off is given under extremely critical conditions the afterburners should be used to improve performance.'

The LSO comments also provided Cutlass-specific recommendations (note that the height above the deck is with respect to the main landing gear wheels):

> The F7U-3 airplane makes an *excellent* [emphasis added] carrier approach and landing. There will be, however, a marked tendency for the pilot, during his initial field carrier landing passes and carrier qualification landings, to be slightly low. This is caused by the sense of being 'too high' due to the height of the cockpit above the landing gear. Similarly, the LSO should use the landing gear for altitude control and ignore the height of the cockpit. It will seem strange at first for the LSO to see the cockpit so far above the wheels as compared with other airplane. Last minute 'high dips' and 'lows' should be avoided. A constant altitude of 15 feet above the deck is considered ideal. The altitude of the airplane in the approach at a speed of 115 kts IAS at approximately 15 feet

The shore-based XC-11 steam catapult was used for initial compatibility tests in May 1954 of the carrier-suitability F7U-3, BuNo 128475, with the high-temperature air exhausting from the catapult track. Note the full 30in extension of the nose landing gear. ***US Navy***

> above the deck and at weights below 23,000lb as seen by the LSO is with the nose gear wheels approximately one-wheel diameter above the bottom of the tail cone.
>
> Cut depth cannot be a hard and fast rule in terms of feet. It will depend on the speed and altitude. A cut height of 15 feet is considered optimum with wind, sea, and weight conditions described earlier in this letter. Cut depth will be determined by the LSO during field carrier landing practice and 'touch and go' landings aboard ship. It will be approximately the same as F9F and F2H type airplane now operating in the fleet.

The final F7U-3 carrier suitability evaluation was accomplished with BuNo 128475, the instrumented carrier qualification F7U-3, aboard *Hancock* (CVA-19) from 14 to 30 June 1954 off San Diego. It was accompanied by BuNos 129522 and 129638, which were not instrumented and so provided only qualitative information. The F7U-3s were aboard along with several other aircraft types for the beginning of *Project Steam*, the evaluation of compatibility with the steam catapult (the potential deleterious effect of engine ingestion of steam on the launch was one concern). The carrier had only just been recommissioned in February 1954 following overhaul and upgrade. Although *Lake Champlain* (CVA-39) and *Hancock* were both Essex class, there was a significant difference between them at this time with respect to launch and recovery capability: the former had hydraulic H-8 catapults and the Mk 5 arresting gear. Since *Hancock* was already laid up in dry dock for overhaul and upgrade when the decision was made to add steam catapults and more capable arresting gear, it was the first US Navy aircraft carrier to be equipped with them in accordance with SCB-27C. Its C-11 catapult could accelerate a 39,000lb aircraft to an end speed of 136 knots, which eliminated concerns about the F7U-3's wind-over-deck requirement at its maximum take-off weight. *Hancock* also received the Mk 7 Mod 1 arresting gear, which was capable of stopping a 60,000lb aircraft touching down at 140 knots, far more than needed for the Cutlass. The only innovation that increased the ability of carriers to accommodate high-performance jets that was missing from *Hancock* was the angled deck.

Following the *Hancock* evaluation, high-speed barricade engagements were evaluated with BuNo 129567 in late August at NATC, the last hurdle to be cleared for full release. Several of the surviving J35-powered F7U-3s had already been transferred to the Naval Air Material Center in Philadelphia to be expended in barrier and barricade crash testing.

Formation of squadrons

At the time, part of the transition of a new aircraft into service use was accomplished with the Fleet Introduction Programme (FIP). This was a new concept intended to obtain spares usage data, evaluate the flight and maintenance manuals and ground support equipment,

NATC's carrier-suitability F7U-3, BuNo 128475, was ferried out to the west coast to participate in the at-sea trials of the new steam catapult installed on *Hancock* along with an example of almost every other carrier-based aircraft in the Navy inventory. *US Navy*

and establish cadres of pilots and maintainers for the first fleet squadrons. Six production aircraft were dedicated to an intensive four to six-week evaluation (approximately 800 hours' total flying time) in an operational squadron environment and flying tempo. The pilots and ground crews would come from the first fleet squadron or squadrons that were to operate the new type.

In early 1954, the Pacific Fleet command elected to establish *Project Cutlass*, a parallel effort to the Fleet Introduction Programme that was to be accomplished at Patuxent River, to gain 'operational familiarisation, maintenance knowledge, and logistic data prior to the Cutlass's assignment to the first operational squadron'. It was to be accomplished by Fleet Aircraft Service Squadron 12 (FASRon-12) at NAS Miramar, California, which received its first of several F7U-3s in February 1954. *Project Cutlass* is described in detail in the FASRon-12 section of Chapter 14.

BuNos 129558, 129559, 129560, 129562, 129563, and 129641 were assigned to the F7U-3 FIP at NATC to be flown primarily by five pilots from VF-81 and six from VF-83, both east coast squadrons scheduled to receive F7U-3s. Between mid-May and mid-June 1954 they logged 570 flights totalling 701.3 hours. The average number of Cutlasses ready to fly at 0800 was 3.1, or a little over 50%. However, the maintenance man hours per flight hour was calculated to be 8.6, far better than the 26.7 reported by the Service Test Division accomplishing the BIS Service Suitability evaluation of BuNo 129554. The difference was ascribed in the BIS report to be in large part due to the expected learning curve associated with first-time maintenance actions on one aircraft versus the improvement in performance over time in repetitive actions on six aircraft.

About 39% of the maintenance was considered non-routine, split one third/two thirds between the engine and the airframe (about half the airframe non-routine maintenance was hydraulic, a harbinger of fleet experience). Also notable was the need to replace fifteen engines (on average, every aircraft had both its engines replaced sometime within 117 flight hours, significantly less than the established 150-hour TBO), two afterburners, and eight afterburner fuel manifold rings.

VF-81 at NAS Oceana had received its first F7U-3s in April 1954 to begin its transition from F9F-5 Panthers. VF-83, also at NAS Oceana, traded in its F9F-5s for F7U-3s in August.

In late 1954, the Cutlasses, pilots, and maintainers from *Project Cutlass* were split between the first Pacific Fleet F7U-3 squadron, VF-124 at NAS Miramar, and VC-3 at NAS Moffett Field near San Francisco. VC-3 had been given the ongoing task of training officers who had spent the last few years in non-flying assignments but were now slated to command squadrons, and pilots and key enlisted men who were to be the cadre for those squadrons that were receiving high-performance jet aircraft like the F9F-6 Cougar. The first F7U-3 class from VC-3's *Project Check-Out* graduated in January 1955, the pilots having received 150 hours of ground school and fifty flight hours in the Cutlass.

Barrier and barricade

On axial-deck carriers, a series of barriers was used to protect the people and planes forward if a landing aircraft failed to be stopped by the arresting gear. They each initially consisted of two steel cables stretched across the deck about 3ft up between stanchions that were raised and lowered as required. Although they were attached to arresting 'engines' like the cross-deck pendants, the run-out was relatively short. The result could be very hard on the aircraft with 'conventional' landing gear, i.e. with a tail wheel, but rarely resulted in serious injury to the pilot since the cables would hang up on the propeller and/or the main landing gear ahead of him.

Jets (and for that matter, twin-propeller-engine aircraft with a nose landing gear) were not compatible with the traditional barrier. The nose landing gear was almost certain to collapse or be torn off upon encountering it and the succeeding barrier might take the pilot's head off before the first one had stopped the aircraft's forward progress by hanging up on the main landing gear.

The solution was a Rube Goldberg modification of the existing barrier system utilising its stanchions, cables, and arresting engine. The cables were now lying flat on the deck with a canvas actuator strap raised in their place by the stanchions. When the nose landing gear hit the strap, its forward motion yanked the cables up off the deck, after the nose landing gear passed over them, by means of vertical lifter straps attached between the actuator strap and the cables. As the aircraft continued forward, break-away fittings (in this

RIGHT This F8F Bearcat was being kept from proceeding farther up the deck in no uncertain terms by a barrier. *US Navy*

BELOW Testing at the Naval Air Material Center near Philadelphia, PA, of the Grumman F7F Tigercat confirmed the unsuitability of the conventional barrier set-up for aircraft with nose landing gears. *US Navy*

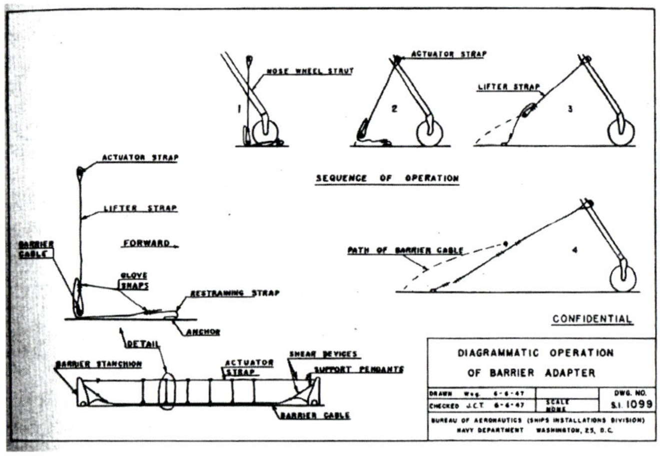

CENTRE RIGHT *US Navy*

RIGHT The Davis barrier ability to stop an F7F without significant damage (note the forward-facing nose landing gear door crimped by the actuator strap) was demonstrated successfully. *US Navy*

case, glove snaps) on the riser straps released the cables, which ideally were still in the air when the main landing gear struts reached them, thereby dragging the aircraft to a halt. The creation became known as the Davis barrier after its creator, an engineer at the Naval Air Material Center (NAMC).

The Davis barrier concept resulted in corresponding features on jets. The most obvious one was the requirement for a 'barrier guard' in front of the windscreen. This was a misnomer because its real purpose was to activate the Davis barrier via the actuator strap in the event of a nose landing gear collapse. This took different forms. On the F7U-3 Cutlass, it was a small fixed mast at the base of the windscreen. Another, a device to keep the actuator strap at a certain height and thereby assure proper lifting of the cable, might not be necessary; the need for it and the specific implementation was determined during actual barrier testing. In the case of the F7U-3, it was a hook hanging down from the front of the nose landing gear strut just above the oleo. F7U-3 barrier testing also resulted in the need for strap cutters between and above the twin nose wheels. And finally, it was important that the barrier cable become positioned properly on the main landing gear struts. On the F7U-3, this resulted in a pick-up extending forward on each landing gear strut. Its purpose was to direct the cable up high on the landing gear strut to reduce the loads on the drag link that kept it from collapsing.

There were two notable Davis barrier shortcomings. First, in the event of a hard landing and resultant main landing gear collapse, there would not be any struts for the barrier cables to snag. Second – and more likely – a jet travelling either too slowly or too fast would not properly activate the Davis barrier. Too slow, and the cable would drop back down to the

The tail hook has failed to pick up a cross-deck pendant due to hook skip. The Cutlass is about to engage the first Davis barrier. Note the position of the barrier activator strap detent on the nose landing gear and the position of the main landing gear barrier guard in front of the shock strut. *Tailhook Association*

deck before the main landing gear got to it; too fast, and the cable would not be pulled high enough in time to snag the landing gear struts. (Worst case, the cable only got high enough to hit the landing gear strut just above the tyres; this could result in the violent wrenching off of the wheels and little retardation.) The solution was the barricade. It was suspended from stanchions similar to those that raised the barriers but much taller. There was a horizontal strap on the deck and another stretched between the tops of the stanchions. Multiple vertical straps were attached between the lower and upper horizontal straps. If a careening jet got that far, it was unlikely to get much farther forward. The vertical straps would restrain the aircraft's wings as the barricade's arresting engine dragged the lower horizontal strap to a stop.

The barricade was introduced in the early 1950s on axial deck carriers operating jets, beginning with *Midway* in 1951. While it addressed the shortcomings of the Davis barrier, it was only idiot resistant, at least initially: A Panther pilot, too high and too fast on approach, managed to break through *Midway*'s and crash into parked planes forward in late 1951. With the advent of swept-wing jets, another barricade weakness was evident: more straps might slip off the end of one wing than the other; the unequal loading might cause the jet to slew into the island or off the deck into the ocean. As a result, there was a new requirement for barricade strap detents on the leading edges of swept-wing jets.

The advent of angled-deck carriers did away with the need for barriers. The barricade capability was retained but it was only erected in the event that an aircraft was unlikely to be able to make a successful arrested landing due to a landing gear or tail hook problem.

This F9F Panther pilot possibly attempted to take a very late wave off and flew into the barricade. Note that the upper horizontal strap has released as intended. The vertical straps will engulf the jet and it will be dragged to a stop by the lower horizontal strap, which is a steel cable attached to an arresting engine like the barriers and cross-deck pendants. *US Navy*

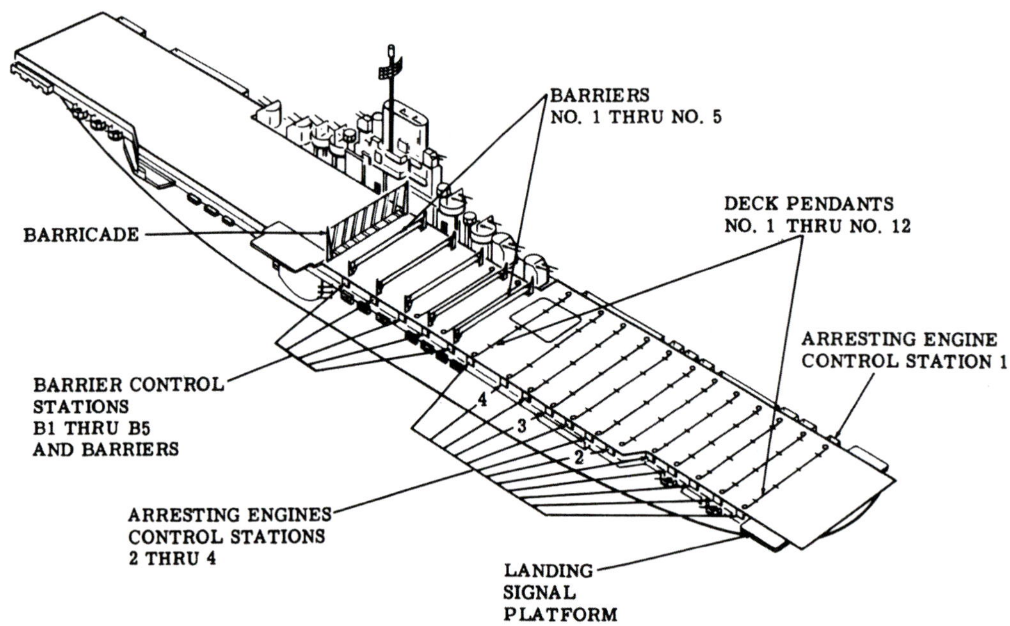

Typical Axial Deck Topside Arresting Gear Arrangement

In the mid-1950s there were twelve arresting cables (also known as cross-deck pendants) on the typical Essex-class axial-deck carrier. Forward of them were five barriers. Any barrier could be configured quickly before landings began to stop either propeller planes (steel cables stretched across the deck about 3ft up) or jet planes (the Davis modification); only the barriers that corresponded to the type of aircraft on approach were raised into position. Since the Davis-rigged barrier was not as effective as the original prop-plane barrier, the barricade, a giant net of vertical straps, was added in the early 1950s and raised for jet landings. *US Navy*

LEFT If this F9F-6 Cougar had not picked up an arresting cable, it would have continued up the deck to encounter two successive Davis barriers and finally, if still necessary, the barricade, the height of which was subsequently increased to accommodate the AJ Savage and the F7U-3. *US Navy*

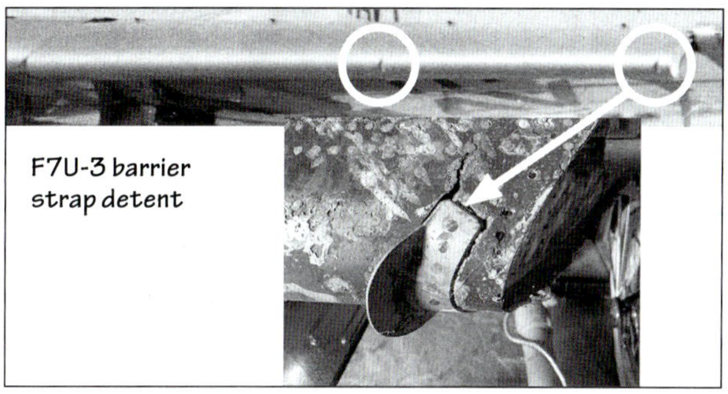

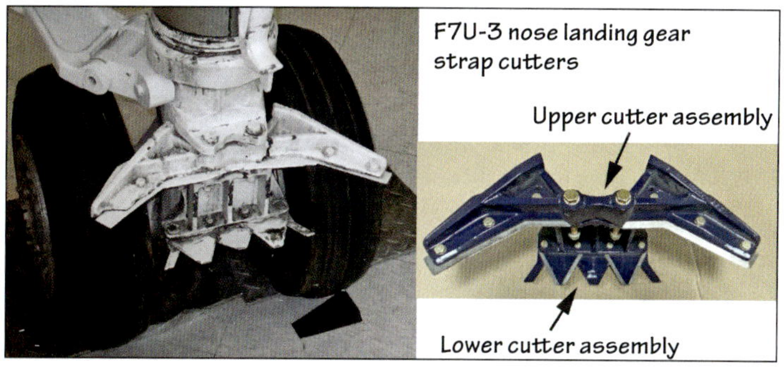

CENTRE LEFT On the F7U-3, two small metal fittings were added to the outboard leading edge slat to keep the barricade straps from sliding off the end of the wings. *Casby*

CENTRE RIGHT Razor-sharp blades between the nose wheels were another unique feature on the F7U-3 because otherwise vertical barrier/barricade straps might be jammed between them, resulting in an overload of the nose gear strut actuator. *Casby*

LEFT Unfortunately, not all F7U-3 barricade engagements were as innocuous as this one. Note that the tail hook had picked up a cross deck pendant so the Cutlass was being brought to a stop when it reached the barricade. *US Navy*

ABOVE Nose wheel steering allowed the F7U-3 pilot to manoeuvre without assistance. Note that the catapult bridle is rigged to remain attached after launch on these trials aboard *Hancock* to permit quicker set-up for the next launch. *National Archives RG-80-G-640354*

RIGHT An F7U-3 being launched from *Hancock*'s steam catapult, probably deliberately angled left to evaluate the response to slightly imperfect alignment. *US Navy*

F7U-3 production and deliveries

For Vought, 1954 was an F7U-3 production control and configuration management challenge. Engineering was designing fixes for problems revealed in BIS evaluations and initial squadron operations and capability improvements like a belly-mounted, 220-gallon fuel pod to address the endurance and mission radius shortfall. Manufacturing was building aircraft for which there were no engines. Due to the ongoing inability of Westinghouse to meet its J46 delivery schedule, in January the Navy had been forced to again slip the F7U-3 delivery schedule, reducing peak production to twelve Cutlasses per month (to meet fiscal year aircraft procurement budgets, it also reduced Vought's production contracts by fifty-two F7U-3Ms and two F7U-3Ps.)

Worse was to come. In May, the Navy temporarily halted production deliveries pending establishment of a configuration suitable for deployment of F7U-3s given all the changes in work as a result of BIS progress reports. BuAer convened a conference in June to review the readiness of the F7U-3 for delivery to additional operating squadrons and the recommended configuration in light of all the changes, product improvements, and ongoing development. It had been expected that the overlap of development/evaluation and production would result in modifications to the first aircraft that had been delivered but the Cutlass programme was proving to be exceptional in that regard – and not in a good way.

BuAer was not being draconian, however. Although Vought was still having problems (as were other manufacturers) with the Navy's new 20mm cannon, in July it allowed continuation of F7U-3 deliveries to Atlantic fleet squadrons VF-81 and VF-83 'for training purposes only', stipulating 'do not fire guns'. Definition and evaluation of fixes continued through the end of the year.

As a result, Vought delivered ten F7U-3s, BuNos 129666–129675, in July. Acceptances now totalled approximately 159 of 290 F7U-3/3P/3Ms on order, although some of these were 'provisional' because there were no engines, a government responsibility, to

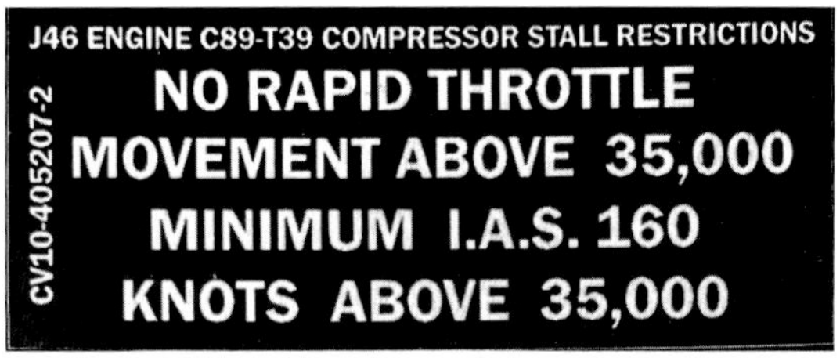

With respect to the ongoing J46 engine issues, the 15 July 1954 F7U-3 Maintenance Instructions stated that J46s had been delivered with combinations of two different compressors and two different turbines so that one of four different compressor stall placards was to be placed on the °instrument panel depending on the engines installed (the one here represented the subsequent production standard, the least restrictive, to which about 100 previously delivered engines were retrofitted). *Casby Collection*

be installed in them when they came off the final assembly line.

In August production was further reduced to nine per month. Delays in the qualification of the -18 engine to be installed in the A2U resulted in its planned production being reduced by fifty aircraft, which was offset by a production increase of fifty F7U-3Ms.

Also in August, Vought proposed a recommended F7U-3 configuration for Cutlass deliveries to fleet squadrons. It included J46 engine updates to resolve engine issues; several fuel system modifications; a hoped-for final cannon installation configuration; required rocket pack modifications; and a total of fifteen miscellaneous improvements.

The Industry Observer column in the 25 October 1954 issue of *Aviation Week* reported: 'Navy is ordering more Grumman F9F-8 swept-wing fighters to compensate for slow deliveries of the Chance Vought F7U-3 Cutlass and McDonnell F3H Demon.'

Matters came to a head on 22 November 1954 when BuAer again – in the terse vernacular of Navy messages – ordered the Dallas BAR to not accept F7U deliveries because: 'Numerous F7U-3 deficiencies recently uncovered through service usage indicate F7U-3, F7U-3P, F7U-3M (are) not ready for fleet operation.' While field installation of kits to correct the shortcomings were being accomplished, 'squadrons unable (to) cope with situation and maintain satisfactory routine availability and training'. BuAer therefore authorised a Vought field team to travel to NAS Oceana to assist VF-81 in the incorporation of the twenty-three changes required to their Cutlasses prior to being cleared for its imminent shakedown cruise. Previously delivered Cutlasses were also being returned to Vought for updating.

Many F7U-3s had to be provisionally accepted and temporarily preserved and stored until Westinghouse could deliver enough engines to complete their assembly. The storage requirement lasted a total of thirty-one months; at one point, sixty-four F7U-3s were awaiting engines. *VAHF*

Retrofit and kit examples

A comparison of the forward fuselages of BuNos 129626 and 129687 illustrates that post-production retrofits had to be tailored to each F7U-3 to ready it for service use (the refuelling probe was a kit). ***Thomason***

There were nine F7U-3 crashes in 1954, four of them fatal. Three were stalls while manoeuvring with the slats not extended that resulted in what became known as a post-stall gyration; it was not predicted by F7U-1 flight test and NACA model spin test of the F7U-3 but proved to be both avoidable and in the event of occurrence, easy to recover from if encountered at altitude. Two were a known issue: stall in low-speed flight with the slats in; one was pilot error and the other possibly a malfunction of the slat/landing gear interlock designed to ensure slat deployment for take-off and landing. Two were caused by maintenance errors, one fatal. One was the result of a design deficiency in the wing-fold mechanism and fatal. The cause of ENS Sears' fatal accident could not be determined.

The list of required changes continued to grow. In December, BuAer requested incorporation of additional changes involving Navy-responsible items becoming necessary for fleet deployment. They included replacement of the Aero 5B Fire Control System with the Aero 10D Fire Control System and the addition of both fuel meters and thrust meters. Moreover, a solution for the unsatisfactory engine operation when the 20mm cannon were fired at altitudes greater than 35,000ft was still required.

On 15 December 1954, then CDR James D. 'Jig Dog' Ramage, who commanded VC-3, wrote to CDR Bob Elder, then on the staff of the Commander, Naval Air Pacific as Training Officer, a personal letter with a scathing review of the F7U-3. It began with 'Cutlass has been giving us quite a bit of trouble' and went downhill from there:

> I haven't had a lot of time in the plane but have had at least enough experience to question fully its use aboard ship. My point is that even if the plane is working perfectly, that is, when many of the mechanical difficulties now confronting us are solved, what do you have? Is the task force commander ready to go to an hourly launch schedule? This will certainly be a requirement if the afterburner is used (without which the plane will do nothing that even an F2H-3 will do except by pointing the F7U-3 straight down). I feel that there has been too much apologising rather than facing the facts in this case. If we accept the speed and range limitations, the plane's inability to perform as a fighter (because of low speed) or a bomber (because of range) what have we?
>
> … As you may well gather, in spite of the nice control system on the plane, I feel that it could be best used as a replacement for the Civil War cannon on the various courthouse greens.

Fortunately, the future of the F7U-3 did not wholly depend solely on his opinion, which was, as he noted, based on limited time in the aircraft.

F7U Cutlass crashes – 1954

Date	Location	Pilot	BuNo	Cause
17Mar	Pax River	CDR Williams	129557	Post-stall gyration (ejected)
7 April	Dallas	J. McGuyrt CVA	128468	Post-stall gyration demo (ejected)
11 June	Memphis	LT Woolverton	129647	Slats retracted too soon on takeoff (fatal)
26July	San Diego	LT Nugent	129552	Landing gear damaged on launch (ejected)
4Aug	Dallas	H. T. Brackett CVA	129651	Inadvertent slat retraction on approach* (ejected)
24Sept	Oceana	ENS White	129560	Post-stall gyration (ejected)
28Sept	Atlantic City	Capt Marzelo	129644	Control jam on takeoff** (fatal)
18Nov	Miramar	ENS Sears	129690	Spiral dive due to loss of control (fatal ejection)
11 Dec	Newport News	LTJG Hood	129659	Control jam – high speed pass*** (fatal ejection)

Subsequent redesign
* Slat/landing gear interlock changed from mechanical linkage to hydraulic interlock
** Nose gear steering activation changed from depressurized inflight to landing gear down
*** Wing-fold centering mechanism modified

CHAPTER EIGHT

F7U-3P

BuAer usually contracted for a photoreconnaissance version of its day fighters to minimise spares and support requirements aboard ship. The F7U-3P was one result, even though at first glance the degree of difficulty in loading and servicing big cameras in a nose that was 13ft off the deck would seem to have ruled it out. Vought created a mock-up to demonstrate the capability to do so.

The F7U-3P nose contained two camera bays. The forward bay was for cameras that took pictures forward, downward, or to the side at a downward angle. In the aft bay, cameras could be installed to take pictures downward and/or directly off to the side. All the camera viewports were flat windows mounted in facets on the nose of the fuselage.

Seven different camera installations were possible. The F7U-3P could therefore be configured for four types of photographic missions: general reconnaissance; mapping and charting; beach, amphibious and offshore reconnaissance; and night reconnaissance. For the latter, upward-firing photoflash cartridge ejectors that could be loaded with a total of forty photoflash cartridges were installed in place of the 20mm cannon.

The F7U-3P's nose was 25in longer than the -3's. The view over the nose for carrier approaches and landings, however, was the same. ***VAHF***

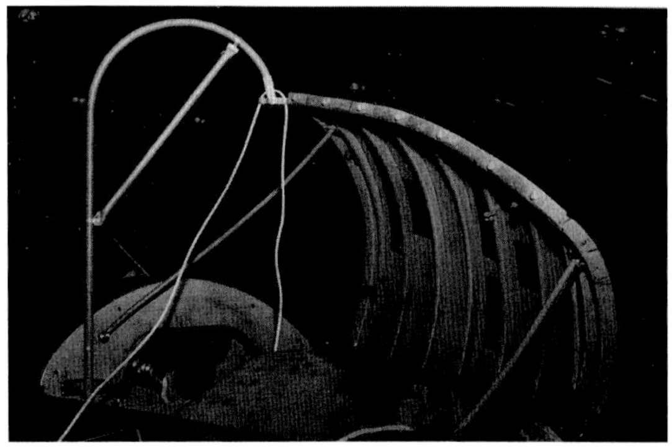

ABOVE The camera bays were to be accessed from above. *VAHF*

TOP RIGHT Raising and lowering the cameras was to be accomplished using a piece of ground support equipment like this conceptual mock-up of a swivelling boom and pulley. *VAHF*

RIGHT It is not clear why the access ladder is located on the left side of the nose in this photo because the hatch over the camera bays opened to the left. *VAHF*

BELOW All the camera viewports were located in facets on the lower half of the nose and its tip. *Thomason*

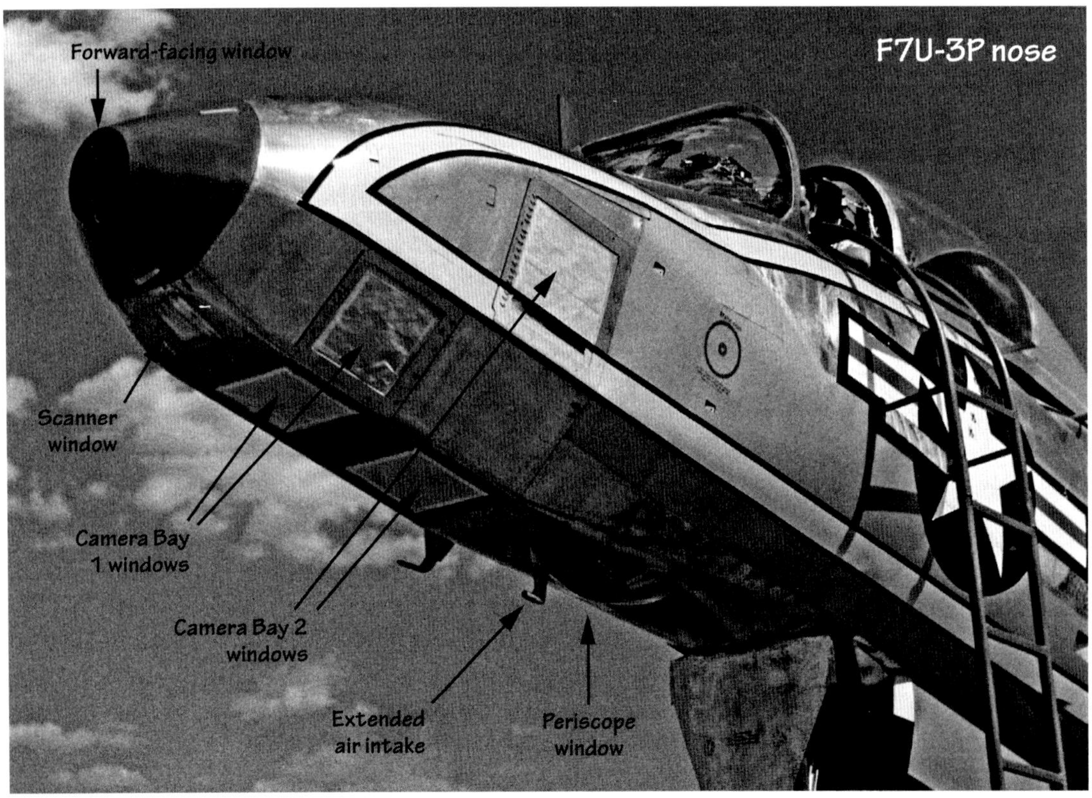

RIGHT A viewfinder for the periscope enabled the pilot to see what was directly under the nose. The light-sensitive scanner in the nose automatically detected the ratio of ground speed to altitude required to set the interval between still-camera exposures or film camera speed during daylight conditions below 5,000ft agl. Photoflash cartridges were loaded in a multi-barrel flare ejector for night photography. *Thomason*

F7U-3P camera options

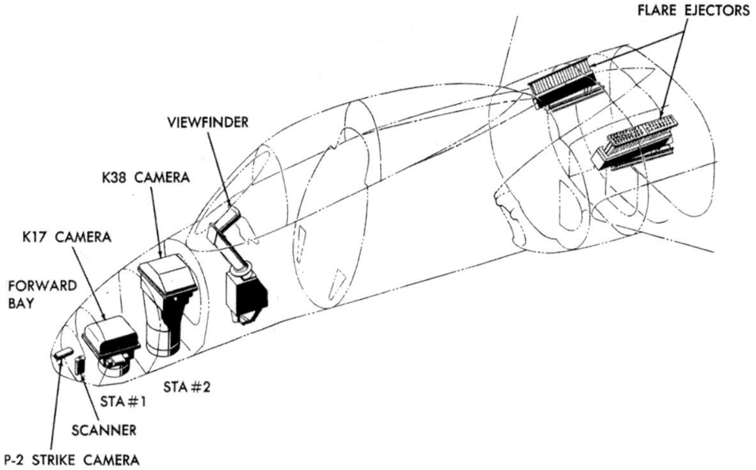

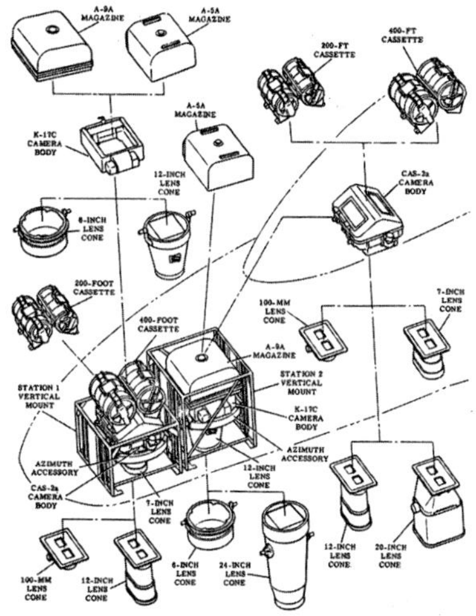

Azimuth

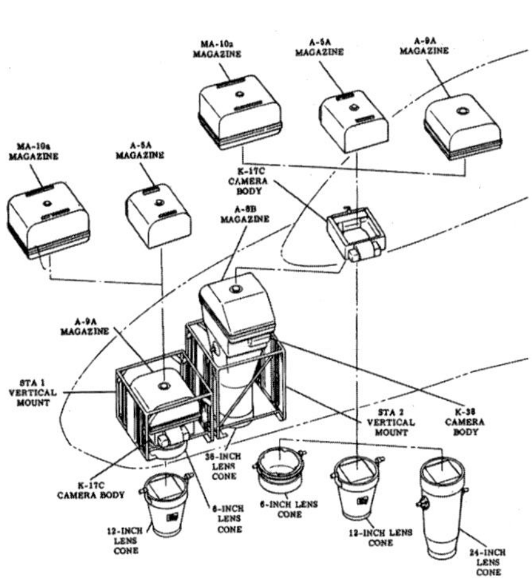

Fixed vertical

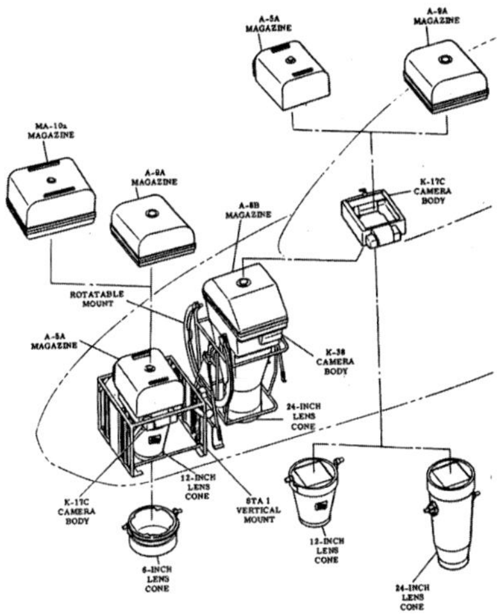

Rotatable

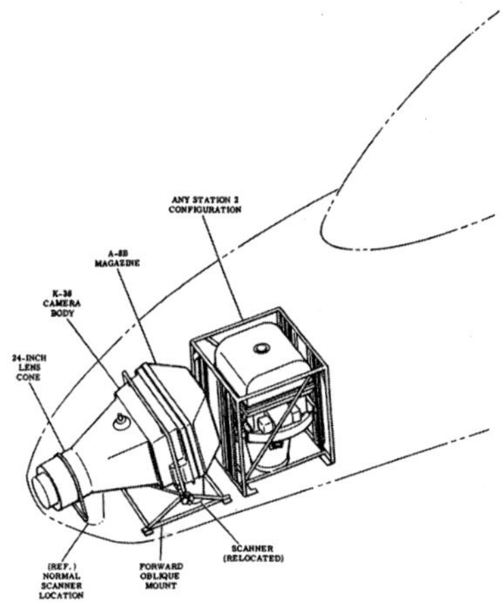

Vertical

General reconnaissance

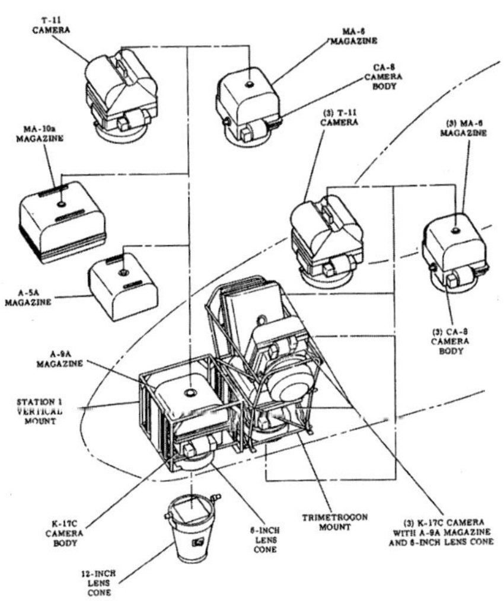

Mapping and charting

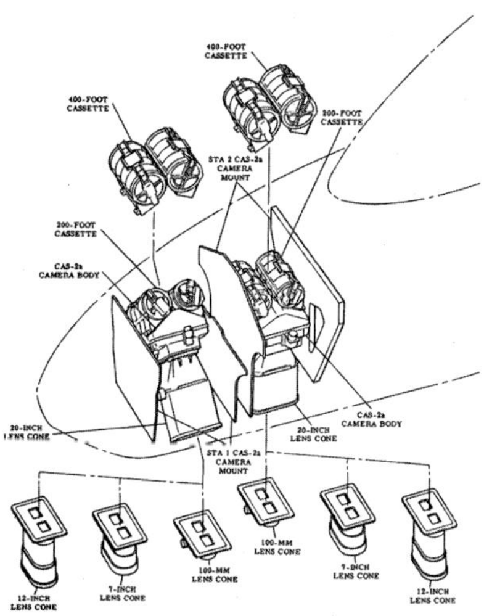

Beach/Offshore reconnaissance

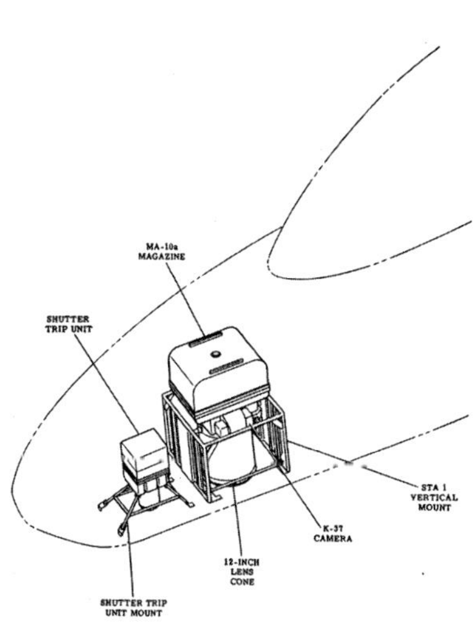

Night reconnaissance

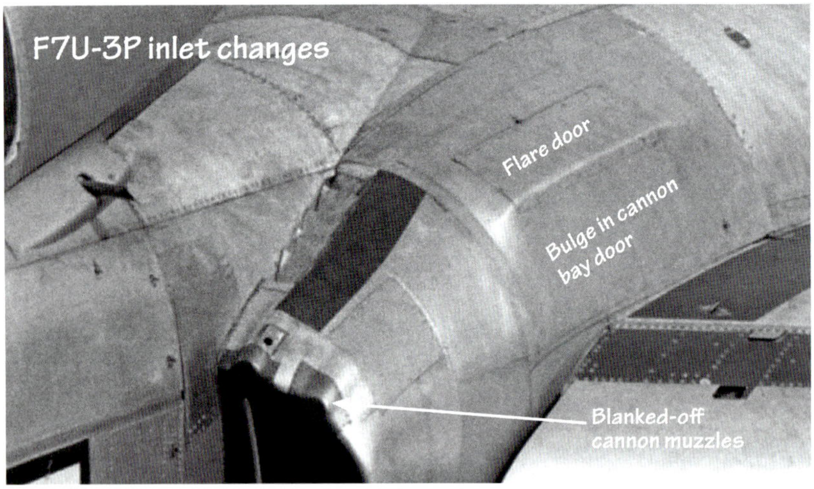

TOP The F7U-3P utilised the -3 engine inlet with the cannon muzzles blanked off and a bulge in the -3's gun bay door where a door was added for flare ejection. The dark panel on top of the inlet is a non-skid walkway. *Thomason*

ABOVE As in all of the Navy's photo-reconnaissance jets, the instrument panel was dominated by a viewfinder that displayed an image of what was somewhat ahead of and beneath the nose. *VAHF*

ABOVE RIGHT A sight was provided on each side of the canopy to position the aircraft for oblique photographs. *VAHF*

Cockpit controls allowed the pilot to position the general reconnaissance cameras as desired, set the interval controller, and adjust the film speed of the beach reconnaissance camera. Normal camera operation was automatic but the pilot could also make individual exposures by pressing the extra picture switch. Azimuth control was provided to enable the pilot to line up the film with the line of flight.

There was no provision for in-flight refuelling. Instead, in addition to the standard two 150-gallon drop tanks and the 220-gallon belly-mounted fuel pod, the -3P was configured with the outboard wing panels that contained fuel tanks. With full internal and external fuel, its gross weight was slightly more than 34,000lb. Using afterburning only for one minute on take-off and not descending below 15,000ft for photography, it had an estimated combat radius of 330nm, assuming twenty minutes at military-rated power at mid mission. On internal fuel only, mission radius was reduced to 200nm and would have been significantly less if pictures had to be taken at treetop level (an F9F-8P's combat radius at high altitude was cut in half if the flight involved mid-mission photography at sea level instead of 35,000ft).

F7U-3P BuNo 129745 was used to accomplish the type's first flight on 1 July 1954. The last of twelve was delivered in May 1955. Service acceptance trials began at NAS Patuxent River on 4 March 1955 with two F7U-3Ps. In November 1955, however, the CNO advised the Board and BuAer that the F7U-3P would be utilised only for research and development projects. The trials were therefore to be discontinued when sufficient information was available to establish compliance with contract guarantees and specifications.

The BIS report dated 13 July 1956 reflected the capability and shortcomings with the F7U-3 being experienced in its initial service: 'The F7U-3P airplane, when using afterburner, was found to be superior to other current Navy photographic airplanes in rate of climb and top speed. However, these good characteristics are more than offset by the limited range and endurance, low buffet boundary, and excessive maintenance requirements of the airplane. Like the F7U-3, its physical size, difficult deck-handling characteristics, and probable low availability would hamper the flexibility of an air group in which it is incorporated. The F7U-3P airplane does not appear to be suitable for full employment as a photographic airplane.' Most of the excessive maintenance activity was blamed on the Westinghouse J46 engines and accessories, although the report mentioned 'repeated hydraulic leaks'.

It also fell notably short of the three contract performance guarantees:

Guaranteed item	Guaranteed value	Test results
Weight empty	18,510.5lb	18,546lb
Maximum speed in level flight with MRT	553 kts	514 kts
Stalling speed, without power	113.5 kts	113 kts
Rate of climb, take-off, CRT	1,660ft/min	1,000ft/min
Service ceiling, normal thrust, combat weight	38,300ft	34,000ft

Although on balance the Cutlass itself was not considered satisfactory as a carrier-based reconnaissance aircraft relative to the smaller day fighter conversions, the BIS report conclusions stated, with somewhat faint praise,

Vought's John Konrad was the pilot for the F7U-3P's first flight on 1 July 1954. *VAHF*

The F9F-8P, a camera-equipped derivative of the Grumman Cougar day fighter, became the standard photo-reconnaissance aircraft assigned to air groups until it was replaced by the Vought F8U-1P. *US Navy*

NATC retained the F7U-3Ps it had used for BIS testing after the evaluation was complete for miscellaneous test projects. One F7U-3P was assigned to NADC for several months for reconnaissance tactics development before it was transferred to the NATC fleet. VX-3 received its four F7U-3Ps on 3 May 1955; one was used for the type's first at-sea carrier trials before being transferred to NAMTC at Point Mugu on 5 August for support of the Sparrow I missile programme. The other three were used for various projects, including the evaluation of the new mirror landing system, the first Cutlass night carrier landing on 25 August 1955, and photo chase of the Regulus I missile. VX-4 was also assigned three F7U-3Ps for a few months in mid-1955 to support F7U-3M missile tests. *Thomason*

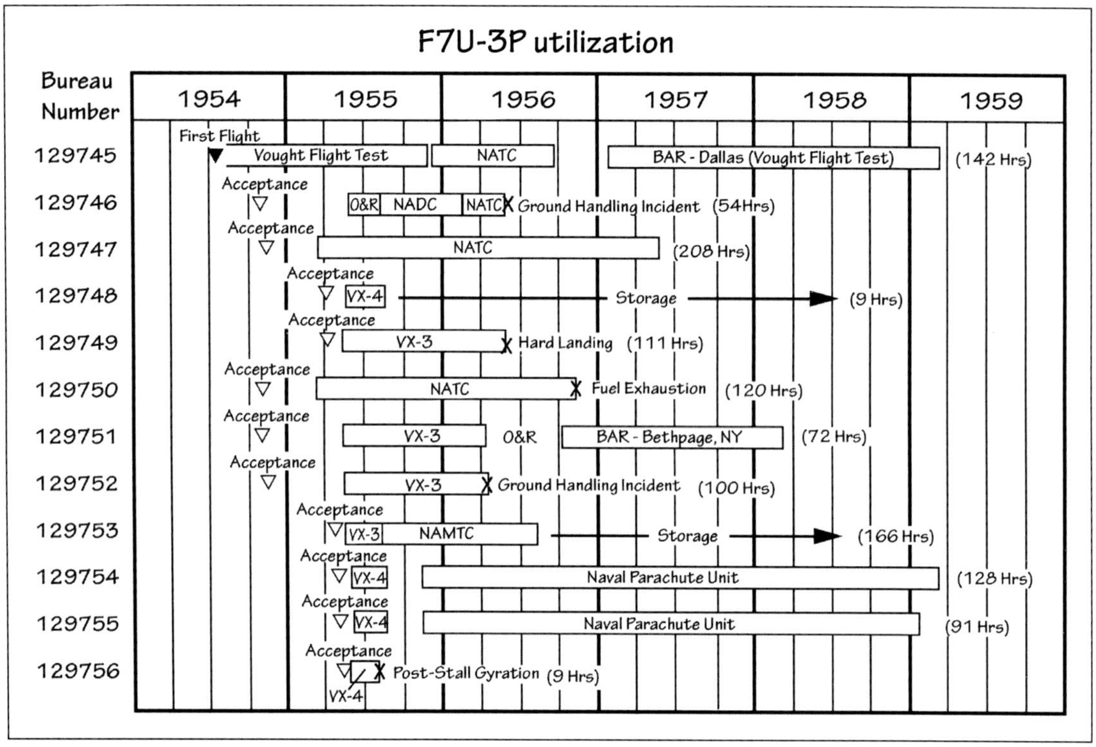

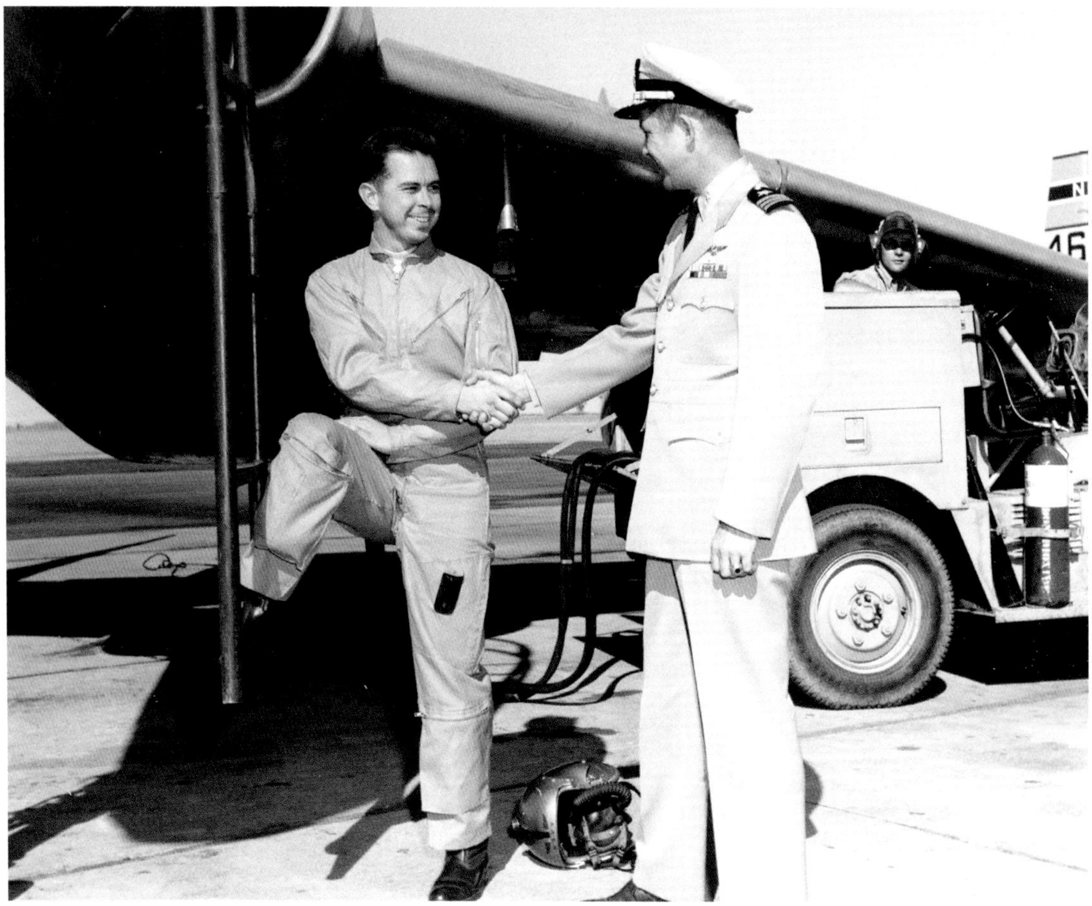

In this NPU publicity photo, LT Howard C. Mitchell, one of the first FASRon-12 *Project Cutlass* pilots, is preparing to board F7U-3P BuNo 129754 for the last flight of an F7U in naval service. *Casby Collection*

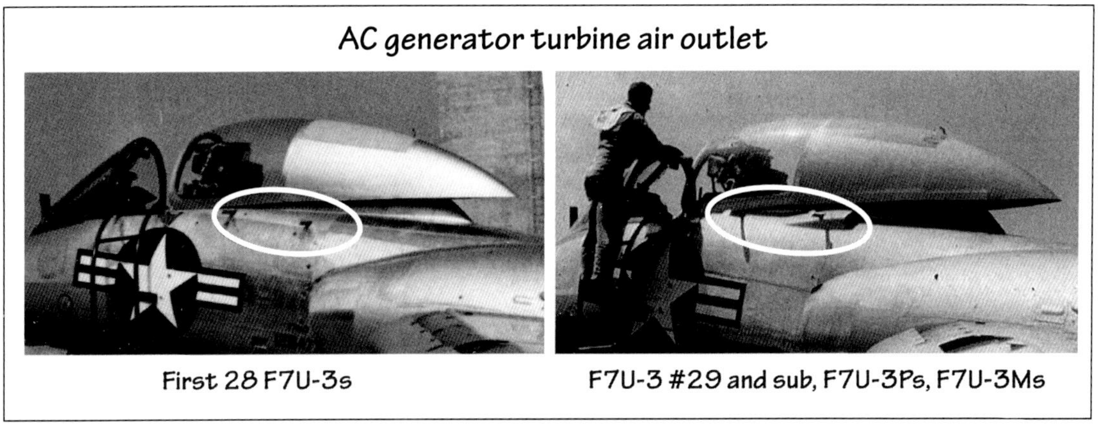

While this air vent on the left side of the fuselage is present on F7U-3s No. 29 and subsequent and all -3Ps and -3Ms, it is only functional on the -3Ps and -3Ms. Note that the foot pegs retracted and extended when the nose landing gear did. ***Casby Collection***

'No major deficiencies existed in the photographic installation and associated equipment.' In fact, its camera system, developed by Chicago Aerial Industries, was very advanced – especially considering that it was not computer controlled – and featured:

- Automated scanning that sensed the aircraft's speed-to-altitude ratio
- Automatic cycling rate of sequential cameras that adjusted for correct overlap using a newly developed intervalometer
- Exposure control for existing ambient light conditions
- 100-million candlepower ejectable photo-flash flares for low-altitude night photography with interval control to alleviate overexposure due to flash
- Four-billion candlepower droppable photo-flash bombs to allow photographs to be taken at night between 6,000 to 20,000ft
- Compensation for vertical to oblique camera shifting to ensure continuity of images during turns
- Automatic azimuth corrections
- Gyro-stabilisation to reduce distortion due to turbulence or pilot-induced oscillation

As a result, the Armament Division Test report on the photographic trials was very positive: 'Ability of the F7U-3P to take satisfactory pictures throughout the altitude and speed ranges (at up to 47,000 feet and 0.9 IMN) was excellent.' No mention was made of any degree of difficulty in accessing or replacing the camera equipment.

In any event, the fate of the F7U-3P had been predetermined. It was never assigned to a composite squadron to be deployed with an air group in a photo-plane detachment. The Grumman F9F-8P Cougar, which had flown for the first time in February 1955, was considered adequate for the requirement, not to mention being smaller and cheaper and that almost every air group was assigned a squadron of F9F-8s and/or -8Bs that were essentially identical except for the camera-laden nose. A few of the F7U-3Ps proved useful elsewhere. One made the last flight of an F7U-3 to date.

An unusual legacy of the F7U-3P was the addition of a fairing just under the sliding canopy on its left side (the aft extendable boarding step protrudes through it). Its electrical system included an air turbine-powered AC generator. The fairing was needed to vent engine compressor bleed air overboard after it had turned the turbine. This fairing is present and functional on all -3Ps and -3Ms. However, only the -3P and -3M were equipped with this generator. Nevertheless, the fairing is present on the F7U-3 No. 29 and subsequent for airframe commonality but it is not functional: its aft end is closed off by a blanking plate.

CHAPTER NINE

The stillborn A2U Attack-Cutlass programme

In June 1952, using funds that had been earmarked for the troubled A2D programme, BuAer awarded Douglas a contract for the development of a bespoke jet-propelled, nuclear strike aircraft, the A4D. While the big turboprop-powered A2D was to have replaced the AD Skyraider in carrier air groups, the little A4D's sole *raison d'être* was delivery of a nuclear weapon at a jet's cruising speed. The Skyraider had excellent range and payload capability but its low cruise speed meant that a nuclear war could conceivably be over before it reached its designated target. The opportunity to replace the AD for all its missions, not just the nuclear strike, inspired Vought to discuss an

This artist's concept depicts an attack on a fleet oiler (used for replenishment of combat ships) armed with anti-aircraft guns. The A2U is carrying seven four-shot Zuni pods. *NHHC Photo Archives*

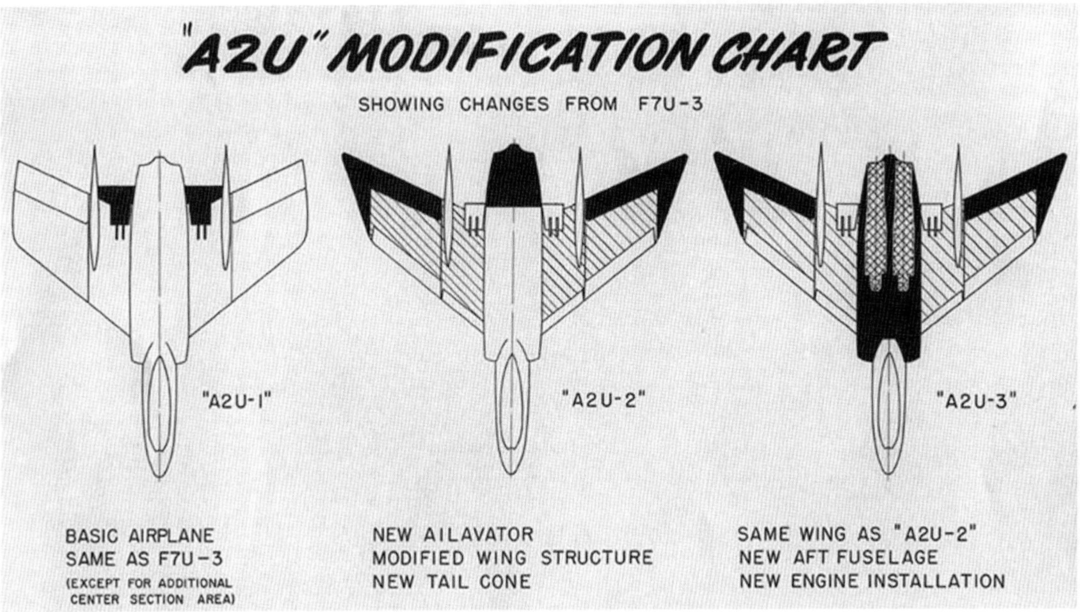

Vought proposed a minimal modification of the F7U-3 for the earliest availability of an attack derivative of the F7U-3 to be followed in production by one with more significant changes for increased mission capability. ***VAHF***

F7U-3 derivative with BuAer that month. It was a logical role for the Cutlass. It was big and so could carry a lot of bombs and rockets. It also had two engines, which reduced its vulnerability to anti-aircraft defences.

In late August 1952, following the successful F7U-3 at-sea carrier trials aboard *Midway*, Vought presented three options of an attack version of the F7U-3 to BuAer to meet the perceived need in the fleet for, as Vought described it, a 'high-performance, unrestricted, jet attack aircraft with good load-carrying ability' (unrestricted was a somewhat snide commentary on the A4D's limited usefulness). Vought unofficially identified these as the 'A2U' (a close-air-support derivative of the F4U produced for the Marine Corps had been designated AU). The least modified of the three options from an airframe standpoint, the A2U-1, was to be powered by the J46-WE-8 with provisions for the J46-WE-2 when it was qualified. Fuel capacity would be increased by fuel tanks in the outboard wing panels. The chord of the inner wing panels was extended aft along with the speed brakes for centre of gravity considerations.

Because the 'A2U-1' changes were relatively minimal, Vought claimed that deliveries could begin one year after go ahead. It would be followed in production by either of two options with more extensive changes, both with the previously demonstrated extended-tip ailavators to permit a higher gross weight. The centre section chord increase would be deleted in favour of relocating the engines farther aft. The 'A2U-2' was to be powered by the original J46-WE-2. The 'A2U-3' would have the J46 engines replaced by two non-afterburning engines, either the Wright J65 or the General Electric J47.

Consistent with its philosophy of maximising the likelihood that state-of-the-art carrier-based aircraft would be available in a few years for each of the air group's fighter and attack missions by issuing contracts for the development of two alternatives for each one, BuAer awarded Vought a letter of intent for Contract Noa(s)-53-603 on 31 December 1952 for fifty A2U-1s, BuNos 138368–138417. For some reason, it was not publicly announced until 29 April 1953. The Detail Specification was signed in July. The initial order was followed by one for ninety-six, BuNos 139822–139917. There were reportedly plans to potentially buy a total of 593, with the next lot of 150 already assigned BuNos 140161–140310.

The A2U-1 that the Navy ordered was basically the same as Vought's 'A2U-1' but with the J46-WE-2 engine, which was still in development at Westinghouse. During 1953, BuAer worked with Westinghouse to redefine the -2 as having the -8 hydro-mechanical control system; a modified -8 compressor (thirteen stages instead of twelve); a new, slightly larger, combustion chamber design; and the latest -2 turbine and

The different powerplant installations addressed engine availability uncertainty: The J46-WE-2, if it met specification, provided the best performance; the J65, as yet unproven, was an alternative if no J46 became qualified; the J47-GE-2 represented a sure thing from an engine availability standpoint. ***VAHF***

"A2U" characteristics summary

		"A2U-1"	"A2U-2"	"A2U-3"
ENGINES		TWO J46-WE-8	TWO J46-WE-2	TWO J65-W (TJ3B)
GROSS WEIGHT PLUS EXTERNAL LOAD	LB LB	27,880 3,570	28,350 3,570	30,525 3,570
MAX SPEED - SEA LEVEL	KNOTS	607 (614)	614	607 (595)
RADIUS OF ACTION	N MI	450 (500)	520	450 (410)
RATE OF CLIMB - SEA LEVEL (COMBAT WEIGHT)	FT/MIN	13,600 (18,600)	18,400	14,100 (9,530)
CATAPULT		H-8	H-8	H-8
WIND-OVER-DECK	KNOTS	25	18	24
		( ) J46-WE-2		( ) J47-GE-2

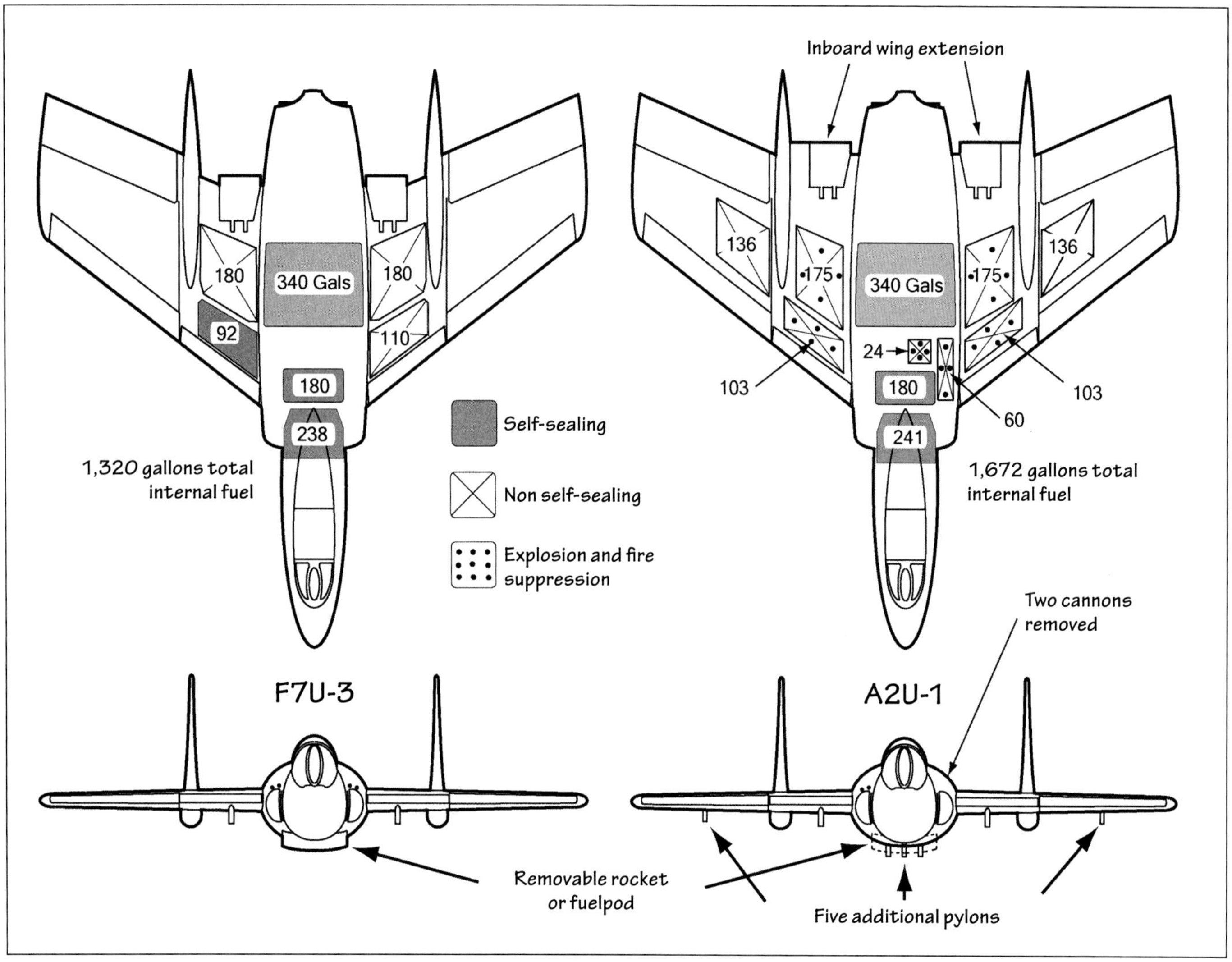

Like the Vought AU derivative of the F4U Corsair, the A2U was optimised for the low-altitude air-to-ground mission with increased fuel system protection and more stores stations. ***Thomason***

afterburner with a larger nozzle. This configuration was expected to provide the J46-WE-2's specified thrust and SFC, both slightly better than the -8's. A test engine ran for the first time in January 1954. BuAer subsequently designated it J46-WE-18 and ordered termination of the work on the -2.

In addition to the restoration of fuel cells in the outboard wing panel already planned for the F7U-3P, the A2U was to have a modified fuel system to provide increased ballistic protection, larger main landing gear wheels/tyres to accommodate the increased gross weight, additional armour protection for the pilot, and a Mk 3 Mod 4 bombing system. To reduce the weight increase, two guns and their ammunition were to be deleted along with the radar-ranging fire control system; four hydraulic pumps were to be utilised instead of six for the flight controls and utility hydraulic systems; and Vought was to replace the GE pitch and yaw damper system with a lighter in-house design. The number and capability of the stores stations changed over time but the final configuration provided for three (one on the centreline and under each inboard wing panel) with up to 2,000lb capacity each and four (one under each outboard wing panel and two on the belly of the fuselage) with up to 500lb capacity each. The three pylons on the belly could be replaced with the rocket pack or fuel pod.

The A2U is probably the '30,000lb' jet attack aircraft that Douglas Chief Engineer Ed Heinemann disparaged in comparison to his diminutive A4D Skyhawk that weighed less than half as much since it was optimised for the nuclear-strike mission. To be fair, the A2U was big and heavy because Vought had incorporated every design requirement and specification that BuAer's multiple engineering divisions insisted upon (or in some cases, just desired/preferred) whereas Heinemann, with the acquiescence of the responsible BuAer Class Desk Officer, ignored many that he considered unimportant relative to achieving the lowest possible weight and therefore cost. The result was an empty weight of only 8,400lb (the A2U's was more than twice that, about 18,500lb).

A2U-1 tactical versatility

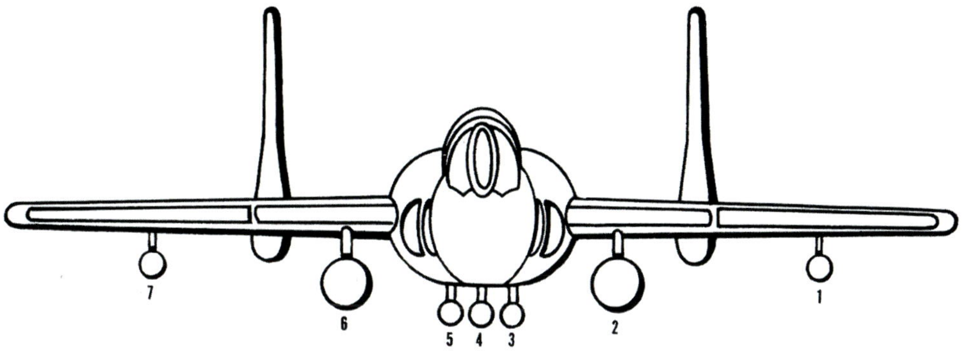

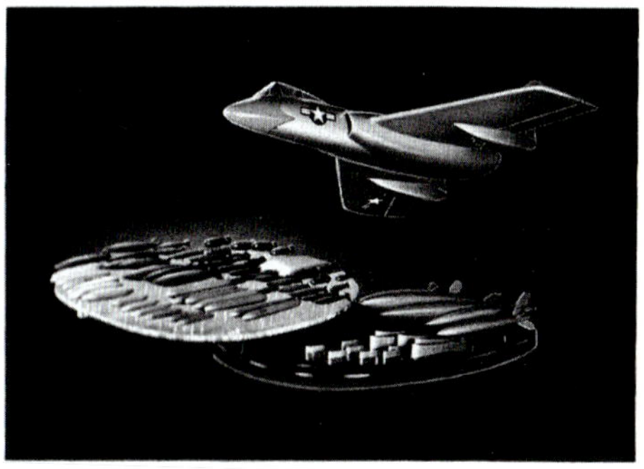

MODEL A2U-1 EXTERNAL STORE LOADINGS

ITEM	OP STA 1	CS STA 2	FUSELAGE STATION 3	FUSELAGE STATION 4	FUSELAGE STATION 5	CS STA 6	OP STA 7	TOTAL NO STORES	STORE WEIGHT	GROSS WEIGHT
ROCKET PACK 32 2.75″	0	0	0	X	0	0	0	1	579	31,037
ROCKET PACK 19 2.75″	X	X	X	X	X	X	X	7	2,695	33,190
ROCKET PACK X-6A 7 2.75″	X	X	X	X	X	X	X	7	994	31,489
ROCKET PACK ZUNI 4-5″	X	X	X	X	X	X	X	7	3,360	33,855
BOMB 250 LB GP OR DAC	X	X	X	X	X	X	X	7	1,750	32,245
BOMB 500 LB GP OR DAC	X	X	X	X	X	X	X	7	3,500	33,995
BOMB 1000 LB	0	X	0	X	0	X	0	3	3,000	33,501
BOMB 2000 LB	0	X	0	0	0	X	0	2	4,000	34,404
BOMB 2000 LB	0	X	0	X	0	X	0	3	6,000	36,501
BOMBS 500 LB AND 2000 LB	500	2,000	0	2,000	0	2,000	500	5	7,000	37,541
BOMBS 500 LB AND 2000 LB	500	2,000	500	500	500	2,000	500	7	6,500	36,995
DROP TANK 150 GAL	0	X	0	0	0	X	0	2	2,204	32,608

	A4D	A2U
Engines	One	Two
Afterburning	No	Yes
Wing folding	No	Yes
Flight control hydraulics	One pump, manual back-up	Four pumps
Electrical system	One AC	One AC, Two DC
VHF navigation	External store	Yes
Battery	No	Yes
Turnover angle specification	Ignored	Met
Leading-edge slats extension	Aerodynamic	Hydraulic power
Load factor (combat weight)	5.9	7.2
Stores pylons	Three	Seven
20mm cannon	Two	Two
Maximum external load (lb)	5,000	7,000
Ammo (rounds)	200	360
Armour protection (lb)	50	200
Engine start	Pneumatic GSE	Electrical
Self-boarding	No	Yes
Nose gear steering	No	Yes
Emergency gear extension	Gravity	Pneumatic

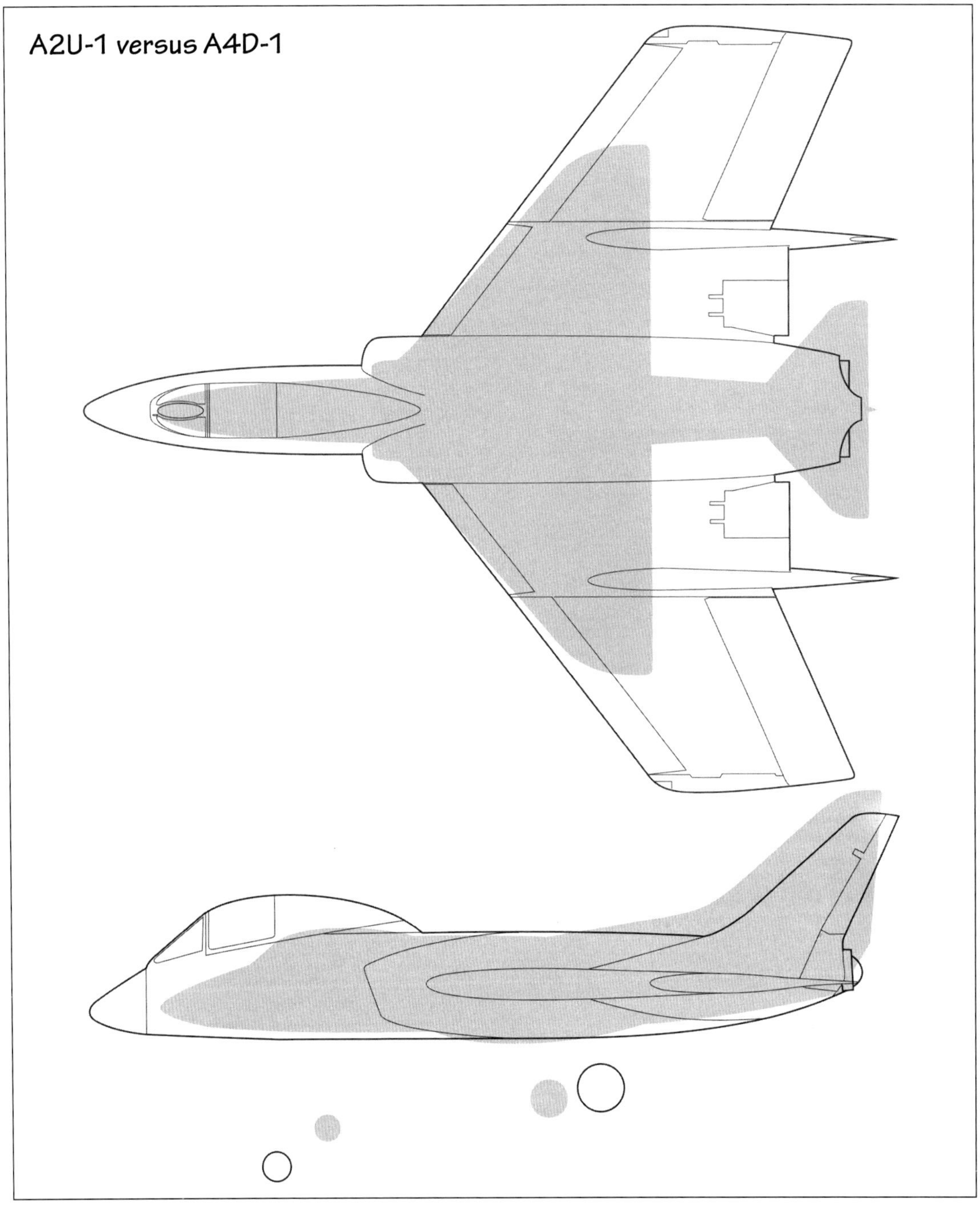

Although the A4D was significantly smaller than the A2U, since its wings did not fold only twenty-seven Skyhawks versus twenty-five Cutlasses could be parked in a 96ft wide, 200ft long area on the flight deck, one of the standard measures of relative size. ***Thomason***

In addition to leaving stuff out, Heinemann insisted on minimising the weight of what had to be kept in. One example was the ejection seat. All the existing designs were fully compliant with detailed BuAer requirements; he insisted on one that met the essential requirement of bailout assist but was designed with his rigorous attention to minimising weight. His rule of thumb was that for a given mission, every pound of equipment being taken along resulted in a 10lb increase in gross weight because of the necessary wing area, power plant, fuel and structure to do so. As a result, the A4D's ejection seat was assembled from only eighty parts and weighed 40lb when installed compared to its Douglas-designed predecessor comprised of 240 parts that weighed 92lb.

Nevertheless, the A4D was a one-trick pony – 'one man, one bomb, one way' – while the A2U had many of the features and capability of a general-purpose fighter. However, since the A4D was small, simple, and powered by only one engine, its procurement and operating costs were far less than the A2U's. Its take-off gross weight was about half that of the A2U, enabling it to be launched from an H-8 catapult with 25 knots wind-over-deck carrying its maximum external load of 5,000lb; the A2U would be limited to 2,000lb of payload in that event and also not have as much range as the

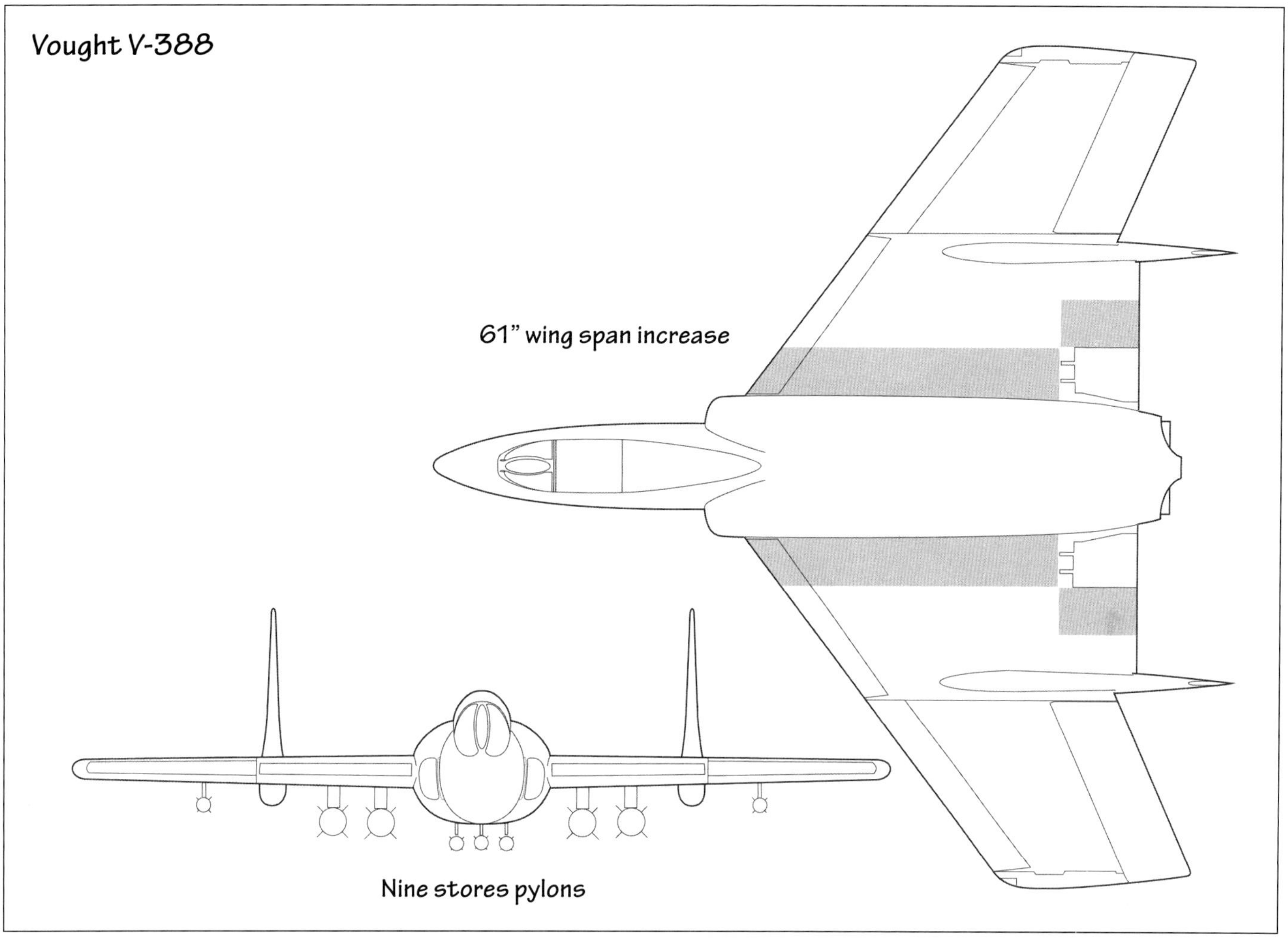

A4D. Of course, the A2U could carry much more when taking off from a land base or when launched by a C-11 steam catapult, including a predicted unrefuelled combat radius twice that of the A4D with two 150-gallon drop tanks.

Vought was confident that because the A4D was an entirely new design, its development – even if relatively trouble-free – would delay its production deliveries by a year or more relative to the A2U since the Attack Cutlass was a relatively low-risk derivative of the F7U-3. Vought was, on the other hand, very concerned about meeting the A2U mission performance it had predicted. A 1 October 1953 internal memo from Vought to United Aircraft's president highlighted significant shortcomings, 'principally lack of radius in the attack mission and inadequate cycle time for carrier operation'. For example, the desired cycle time (take-off to landing) was 1.7 hours; the A2U's was 'nearly half an hour short of this'. 'The A2U has deteriorated in these respects because of gradual total weight increases and significantly increased SFC now indicated for the J46-WE-8 engines.' Vought was therefore discussing an A2U-1 weight reduction programme with the Navy and also proposing its Model V-388, which would replace the A2U-1 in production in March 1955 after fifty had been delivered.

The major V-388 change was the addition of a wing section, 30.5in wide, between the side of the A2U-1's fuselage and its wing root. The existing wing, vertical tail, and landing gear would be repositioned 14.1in aft, maintaining the centre of gravity. The new inboard wing sections would contain two fuel cells each that would increase the total fuel capacity by 320 gallons. An additional increase of 62 gallons would be provided by removal of the honeycomb pads above the wing fuel tanks that provided ballistic tolerance since it was assumed that they would be empty when the shooting started. A second pair of stores stations would be added to the wings.

In addition, Westinghouse had developed a programme of successive J46 improvements, Blocks II (the J46-WE-18), III, and IV (III and IV benefited from its 1953 licensing agreement with Rolls-Royce for engine components and technology). In early February 1954, Vought responded that the Block III engine was 'a step in the right direction' to 'something approaching the predicted values with the original J46-WE-2 engine'. Unfortunately, that step was more than offset by an

ABOVE Probably the best fix for the range and endurance shortfall of the twin-J46 powered F7U-3 was the V-389, which substituted a single P&W J57. ***VAHF***

BELOW The most significant performance improvement was the increase in range and endurance made possible by the J57 engine's superior SFC relative to the J46's. ***VAHF***

AIRPLANE	V-389		A2U—1*	
ENGINE	J57-P-4		TWO J46-WE-18	
Loading	Two 2,000-Lb Bombs	3,500-Lb Store 520-Gal External Fuel†	Two 2,000-Lb Bombs	3,500-Lb Store 520-Gal External Fuel†
Gross Weight, Pounds	34,830§	38,170	33,950	37,330
Wind Required C-11, Knots	—1§	15	—3	15
Combat Radius, Naut Mi‡	605	815	325	500
Cycle Time, Hours‡	2.8	3.9	1.6	2.4
Max Speed (SL, Clean) Knots	598	598	593	593
Max Rate of Climb (SL, Clean) FPM	18,500	18,500	14,800	14,800
Takeoff Distance over 50-Ft Obstacle, Ft	3,500	4,050	3,850	4,750

* A2U-1 Including ECP-1 (Weight Saving Program)

† 300-Gallon Drop Tank plus 220-Gallon Fuel Pack

‡ "Low Altitude Attack and Ground Support Bomber" Mission

§ By Removing 278 Gallons of Internal Fuel from LH Center Section Tanks at the Option of the Ground Crew, the Gross Weight is 33,020 lb, the Wind Required by the 4,000 PSI H-8 Catapult is 24 Knots, the Radius of Action is 460 Nautical Miles, and the Cycle Time is 2.2 Hours

increase in A2U airframe drag predicted by subsequent wind tunnel and flight test analysis. A 19 March 1954 internal Vought memo reported that the drag resulting from the new extended wing centre section reduced the radius of action by almost 100 nautical miles compared to the original A2U-1 estimate, more than the increase predicted with the Block III's better SFC. The maximum speed was also affected.

To solve the range problem, Vought had also proposed its V-389, a J57-powered A2U, to BuAer in February 1954. A new fuselage section from the inlets aft would be required for a single-engine configuration but it would incorporate major components of the A2U-1 including wings, vertical tails, landing gear and forward fuselage. The inlets were relocated a few inches forward and enlarged to accommodate the J57's greater mass flow. Armament was to include two cannon over the right inlet duct with provisions for two on the left; These were relocated farther aft of the inlet lip and the inboard cannon were to be staggered aft of the outboards rather than slightly forward as on the F7U/A2U, possibly an attempt to avoid the engine problems that were occurring when the cannon were being fired, affecting engine inlet conditions. The wings along with

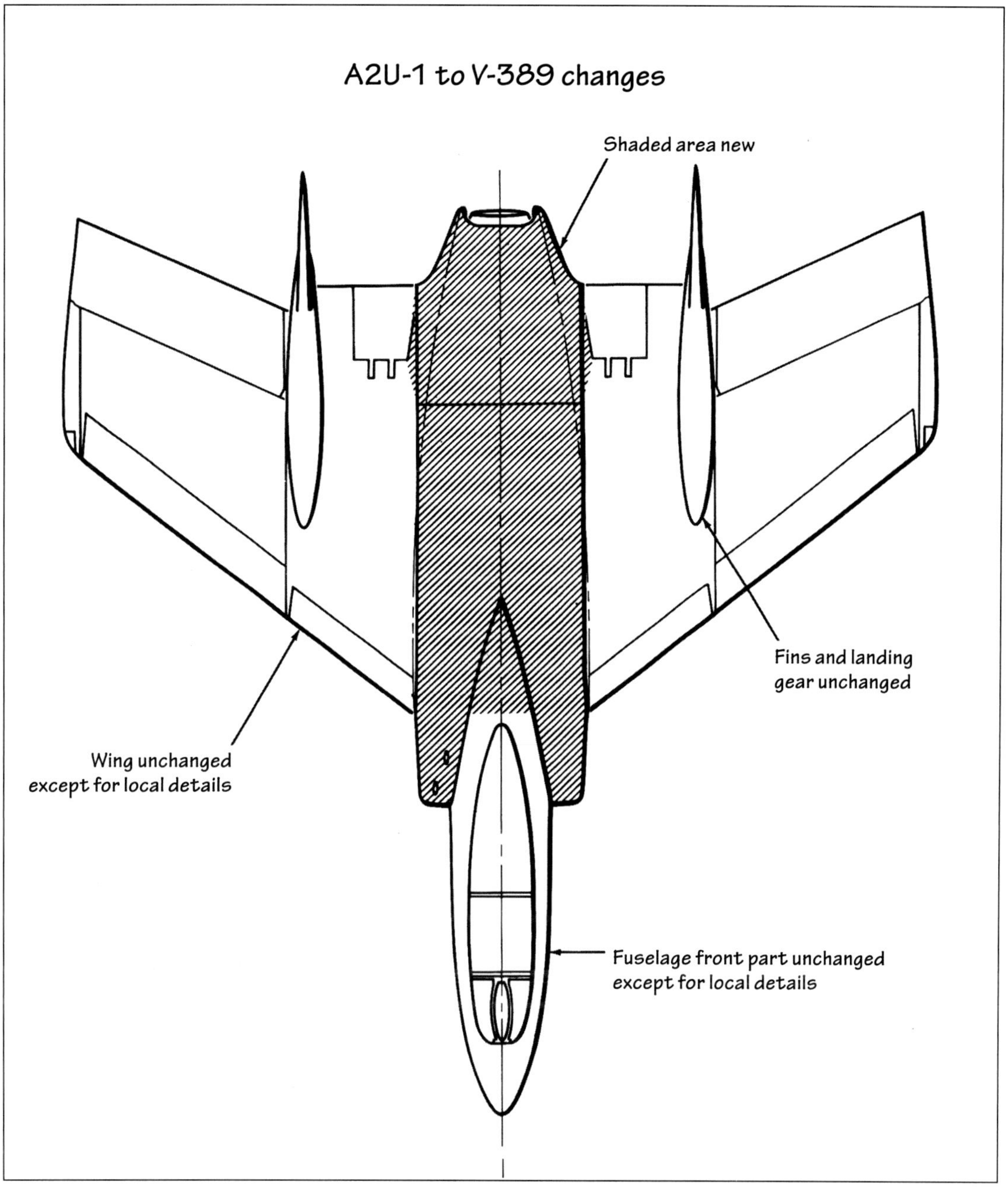

The single-engine V-389 featured a new centre fuselage that would have required a relatively straightforward design and tooling effort. ***VAHF***

the vertical fins were to be relocated slightly aft. Several electrical and hydraulic changes were proposed as well to reduce weight. The J57-P-4's thrust in afterburner was 16,000lb compared to two J46-WE-18s at 12,000lb; the increase in thrust did not do much for speed because of the F7U transonic drag but rate of climb, acceleration, and useful load all benefited. Even more importantly, the J57's cruising SFC was only 0.815. That translated to a dramatic increase in range and endurance compared to the J46-powered A2U-1: a combat radius of 605nm and cycle time of 2.8 hours – an increase of 86 and 75% respectively – while using only internal fuel and carrying two 2,000lb bombs. Adding external fuel resulted in a radius of 815nm. BuAer reviewed the proposal but by 3 March had decided to take no action on it.

In April 1954, BuAer asked for Vought's comments on the feasibility of a 'Buddy' mission refuelling system for the Cutlass. Vought reported back on the results of its initial flight test and design studies in June 1954. As expected, the conclusion was that there would be a significant increase in the receiver's mission radius. The pilots recommended that the drogue, in order that the receiver avoid the wake of the tanker, be placed approximately 7ft below and 6ft behind the refuelling store. This was done by rotating an articulated pipe, at the end of which was another pipe and then the drogue (all linked by ball joints), out of the store. (A simpler concept pursued by Douglas was to simply stream the drogue at the end of a long hose deployed from a reel in the pod.) Chance Vought subsequently contracted

An artist modified an in-flight photo of an actual F7U-3 to depict the buddy system concept of increasing the strike radius of the A2U. The Cutlass tanker is carrying an in-flight refuelling store, the belly fuel pod, and an external fuel tank under the left wing; the receiver has a Mk 7 under the right wing and an external fuel tank under the left. *VAHF*

with the Schulz Tool and Manufacturing Co. of San Gabriel, California, to design and manufacture the store (see pages 154-155).

Vought's expectation that the Douglas A4D schedule was optimistic proved to be incorrect. It flew ahead of schedule on 22 June 1954. The initial impression was quite good, which significantly reduced the Navy's need for a back-up to it and eventually made for an easy decision to terminate the A2U programme, particularly after the first production A4D-1 flew in September 1954, about two months ahead of schedule. Meanwhile, the A2U first flight had slipped to January/February 1955.

If BuAer had any confidence that Westinghouse would meet the -18's qualification schedule, it had to have been

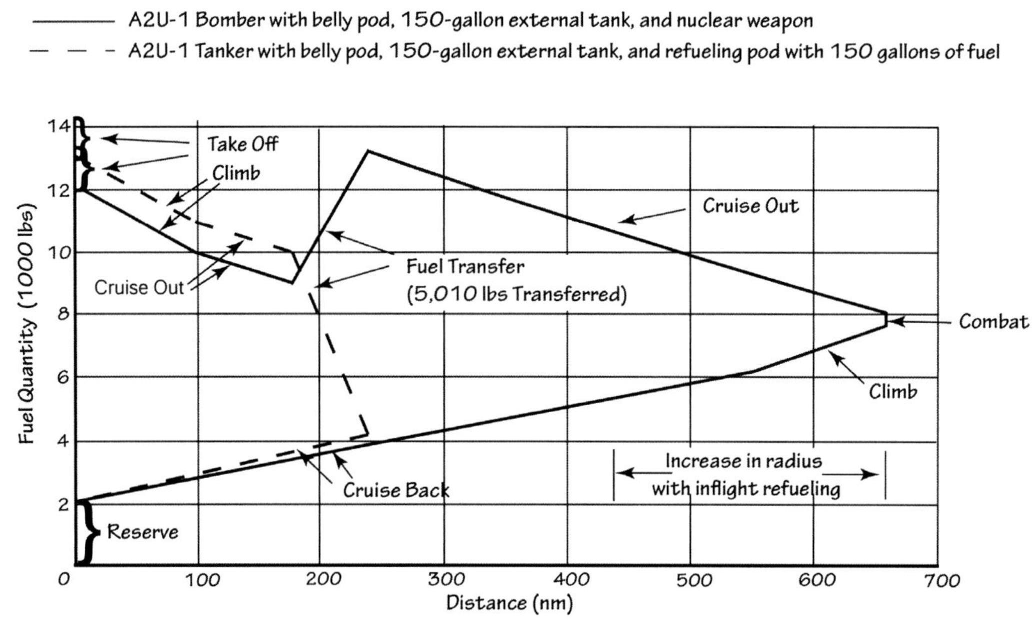

A2U buddy-tanked radius of action

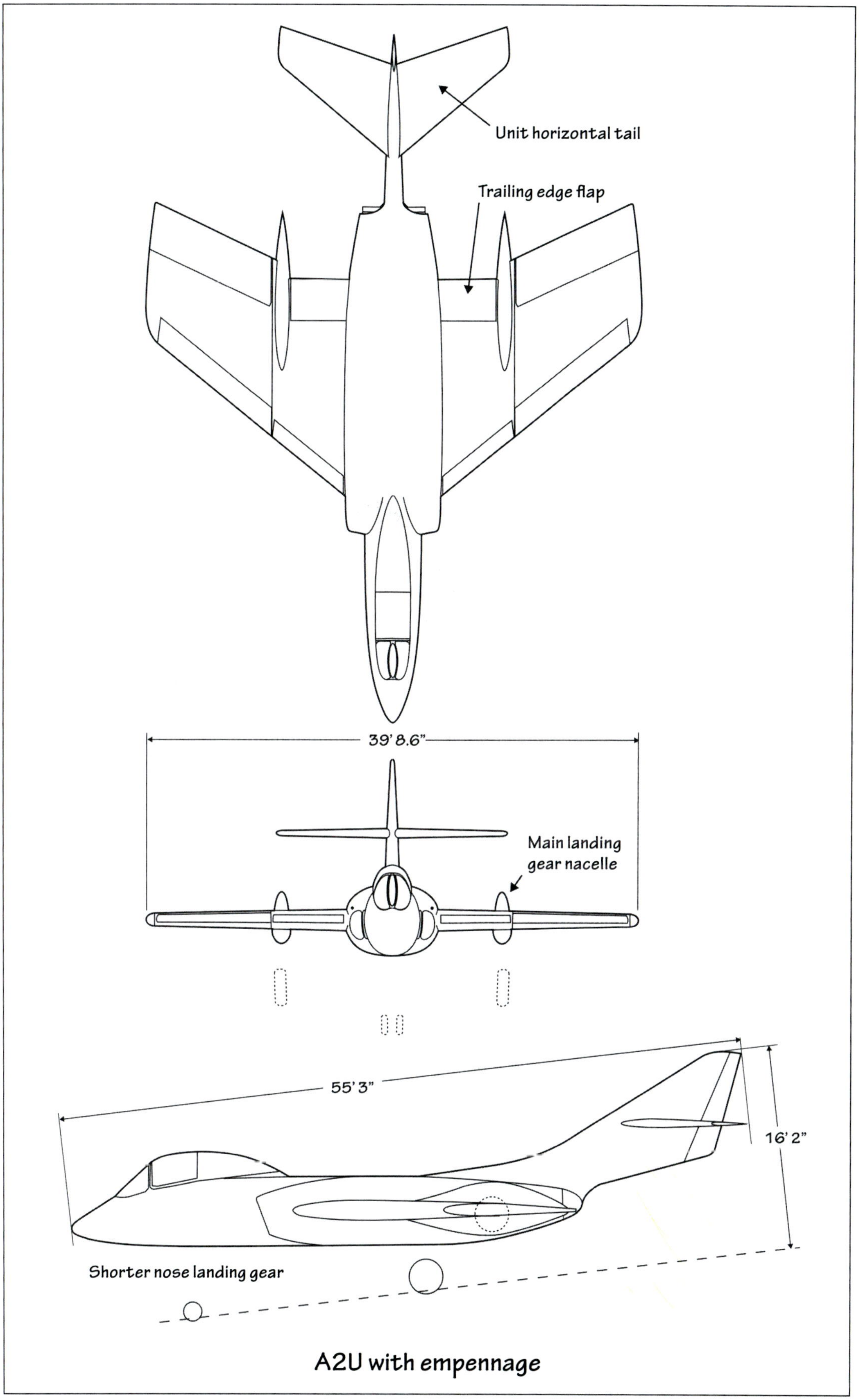

At some point, Vought Predesign speculated on what an A2U would look like with a conventional empennage, wing flaps, and stance. *Thomason*

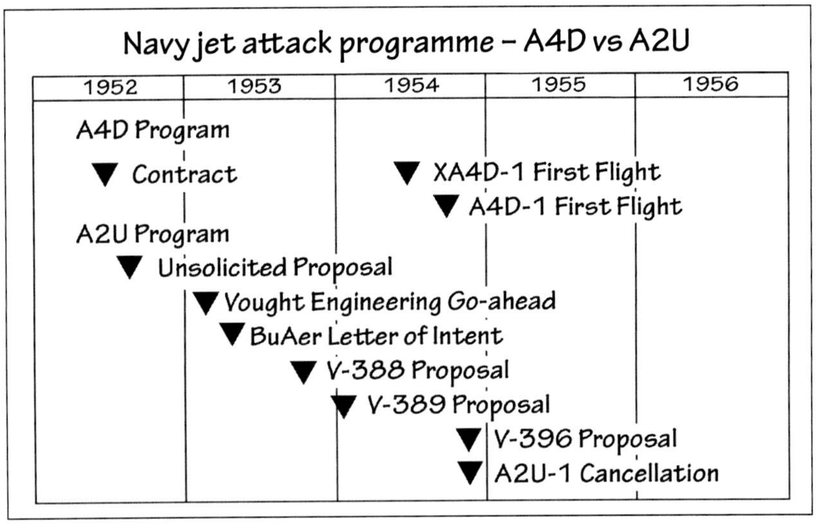

dimmed when one suffered a catastrophic compressor disc failure during a ground run at Vought in F7U-3 BuNo 128453 (No. 3) on 21 July 1954. The subsequent fire damage resulted in the F7U-3 being stricken. It was replaced with BuNo 128452 (No. 2) for flight test of a -18 prototype engine again on the left side and a -8B on the right. (As a Vought test bed, it was one of the last F7U-3s on flight status, being ferried to Litchfield Park in May 1957.)

The first A2U-1 was nearing completion – if not already complete – about two or three months behind schedule when the programme, including further test and development of the engine, was terminated in November 1954. According to the Navy's press release: 'The cancellation is caused by a delay in the development programme of the A2U-1 airplane and the J46 (-WE-18 engine).' Westinghouse had not able to successfully complete any of the 150-hour qualification tests of the -18 that it conducted between May and October 1954. However, one last attempt in December was successful and demonstrated engine performance above guarantees by a margin of 5 to 8%. Nevertheless, the Navy chose not to procure -18s for F7U-3 retrofit. It would have required some redesign of the engine installation and a lack of enthusiasm for further investment in both the F7U-3 and the J46 (its only remaining application being the F7U) was becoming evident.

It is unlikely that Vought was surprised when BuAer ended the A2U programme. In any event, concurrent with its cancellation, they made one last attempt to stretch out Cutlass production for a few more years by proposing the V-396 Cutlass Missile Carrier. Although it combined components and mission capability of the F7U-3M and A2U-1, it was actually more A2U than F7U-3M. Armed with Sparrow missiles, however, it would have a significant increase in combat radius of action and small increases in ceiling and maximum speed compared to the F7U-3M, while allowing the air group

Although the first A2U-1, BuNo 138368, does not have engines installed in this photo, Westinghouse had assembled eight YJ46-WE-18s and acceptance tested at least some of them for delivery to Vought for flight test of the first few A2U-1s. *VAHF*

commander to utilise it for attack missions like an A2U if desired. The F7U-3M provided the forward fuselage, wing pylons, Sparrow launch rails, and aft inboard wing. The remainder was A2U-1 structure and centre fuselage pylons as well as the latest A2U-1 design improvements:

- An increase in maximum landing weight from 21,000lb to 25,000lb
- Simpler power control, pneumatic, and flight stabilisation systems
- A lighter weight, redesigned fuel gauging system
- A simpler fuel system: two fuel pumps and four vent valves were deleted, which increased the amount of gravity-feed fuel by 234 gallons

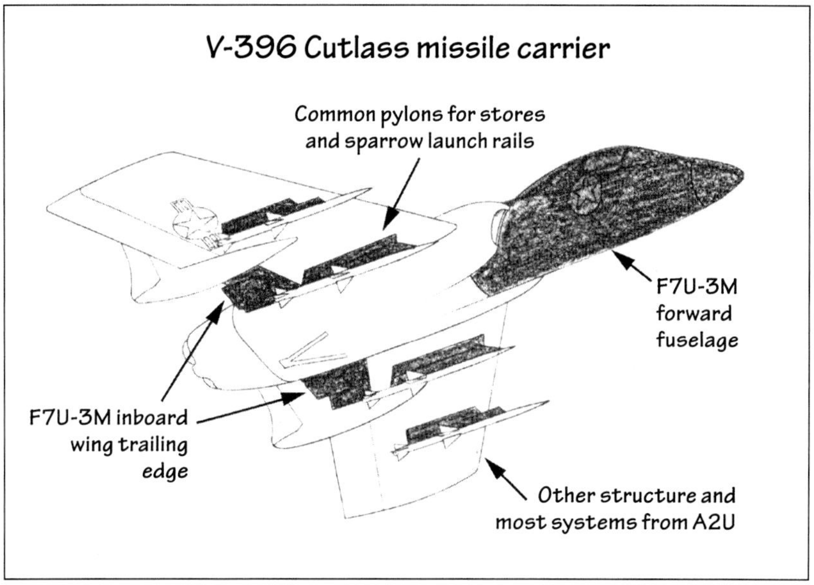

The utility hydraulic and emergency pneumatic systems were from the A2U. However, the F7U-3M's electrically driven emergency power control system was to be utilised rather than the A2U's wind-driven pump, and the F7U-3M's air turbine generator was to provide AC power rather than the A2U's inverter. The cannon were deleted to allow an increase in fuel capacity of 84 gallons. In the event that the aircraft was assigned a nuclear strike mission, some APQ-51 radar components and control panels would have to be removed to provide space for the requisite Low Altitude Bombing System (LABS) instrument and controls.

In recognition of BuAer's loss of interest in continuing with the J46-WE-18, Vought provided performance projections on the -8 as well, noting that the airframe would accommodate either.

The Navy decided not to purchase any V-396s, but fifty airframes from the second lot of A2Us, BuNos 139868–139917, were to be completed as F7U-3Ms. Even though the Navy might have been leaning toward the F7U having a short service life at the end of 1954, the F3H Demon was only just beginning flight test with the Allison J71 engine replacement for the Westinghouse J40. Buying more -3Ms was consistent with their belt-and-braces approach to ensuring the fleet would have an up-to-date mission capability in the event that the F3H development programme failed like the F10F Jaguar's had.

Before formally cancelling the A2U, BuAer had decided that a back-up to the A4D programme was still required, if for no other reason than to ensure that Douglas' chief engineer, Ed Heinemann, paid more attention to its concerns about Skyhawk handling qualities and other issues. The result was a modification of the North American FJ-4 Fury (a subsonic day fighter eclipsed by the F8U Crusader) for nuclear strike as the FJ-4B. A total of 222 were produced but it was eventually phased out in favour of upgrades to, and additional production of, the A4D.

The last F7U-3M, BuNo 139917, during its factory rollout. The dark skins are unpainted magnesium. Accepted on 8 December 1955, the aircraft served with VA-116 aboard Hancock (CVA-19) before retiring to NASF Litchfield Park, Arizona with 164 hours accumulated flight time. ***Chance Vought photograph by Arthur L. Schoeni via Casby Collection***

CHAPTER TEN

Surprise! The F7U-3 gyrates rather than spins

A spin can result when an aircraft is at or near its angle of attack for a stall (a loss of lift and increase in drag) and a yawing or rolling motion is present so that one wing stalls before the other (note that the stall occurs at a specific angle of attack, not a specific speed). A spin is a fully developed autorotation in the direction of the wing that stalls first because of its lower lift and higher drag. The classic recovery for an erect spin is to eliminate the differential in lift and drag between the wings by applying roll control into the spin (counterintuitive, but it results in increasing the angle of attack on the wing on the outside of the spin and therefore causes lower lift and higher drag) as well as rudder against the spin (reducing the angle of attack on the wing on the inside of the spin). When the rate of autorotation decreases enough, i.e. the spin is 'broken', forward stick completes the recovery. However, the recommended flight control movements for spin recovery in a particular aircraft type can vary significantly.

BuNo 128452, the F7U-3 assigned to spin test, utilised the traditional location at the rear of the fuselage for the deployable spin-recovery parachute. However, while the parachute was housed in a container under the aft end of the fuselage, when deployed it was tethered to a hard point on the top of the aft fuselage. ***VAHF***

NACA Langley had pioneered initial evaluation of an aircraft's susceptibility to spinning and determination of an appropriate recovery technique beginning in 1935, utilising small free-flying balsa wood models in a vertically oriented wind tunnel. This became a standard early step in the design phase of an aircraft development programme. Since this testing does not always predict an aircraft's spin and recovery characteristics accurately, an evaluation of them early on in the contractor's flight test programme is usually a high priority. The aircraft used for spin testing is almost always modified with a spin-recovery device to break the spin if the recommended control applications are not effective and subsequent ad hoc ones aren't either. All this leads to a formal demonstration of spin susceptibility and recovery technique that is one of the requirements of an aircraft's readiness for service evaluation. NACA did spin tests on a 0.057-scale model representing the XF7U-1 configuration in 1948: 'The spin and recovery characteristics of the airplane will be satisfactory for all loading conditions.'

Vought utilised an unusual anti-spin parachute configuration for the F7U-1 spin programme consisting of a deployable parachute in a wing tip-mounted container. It was not needed when a Vought test pilot accomplished a total of sixteen spins in an initial evaluation. A spin recovery demonstration was then provided to the Navy at NATC on 22 August 1952, including a roll out from low-speed inverted flight with full lateral stick as well as erect power-on and power-off entries. 'With the exception of the power-off spin with ailerons against the spin, all recoveries were accomplished by neutralising the controls. Control forces required for recovery were negligible.' Since the F7U-3 configuration was very similar to the -1's, Vought and the Navy had expected its flight characteristics would be very similar to those of the F7U-1's. With respect to loss of control propensity and characteristics, they would be very surprised and disappointed.

A NACA Langley evaluation accomplished in 1951 of a 1/20th F7U-3 spin-test model determined that for an erect spin, which was readily obtained, the recommended recovery was to move the stick laterally with the spin (stick full right in a spin to the right) simultaneously with full rudder against the spin, followed by forward stick approximately one half turn later. In the case of inverted spins, the recommendation was rudder full against the spin and the stick neutralised longitudinally and laterally.

Given the benign spin characteristics of the F7U-1, Vought's F7U-3 spin evaluation programme did not begin until 6 November 1953 with BuNo 128452 (No. 2) equipped with an aft fuselage-mounted anti-spin parachute. The tests were conducted with slats retracted, as the F7U-3 was determined to not stall with them extended, only gently mush ahead. It consisted of nineteen practice and formal demonstration flights and eighty spin attempts. It concluded in early January 1954 with Vought test pilots being unable to force it into a fully developed spin following a stall, unlike the results obtained with the NACA spin model: the aircraft would not stay in a steady, sustained spin even with full pro-spin controls applied.

Nevertheless, on 17 March 1954 CDR Clyde A. Williams was flying BuNo 129557 (No. 41), the first of six F7U-3s to be assigned to the Accelerated Service Test Division at NATC. He had previously flown the J35-powered Cutlass five or six times, amassing 9.8 hours in

BuNo 124420, the F7U-1 spin test aircraft, was provided with a deployable drag parachute on each wing tip to 'break' a spin if it could not be accomplished using the flight controls. ***VAHF***

Two T-handles on the upper left side of the F7U-3 instrument panel were connected by cables to the spin-recovery parachute installation. Pulling on the left one deployed the chute; pulling on the right one jettisoned it. ***VAHF***

In hindsight, relying on the benign nature of the F7U-1's stall characteristics and reluctance to spin without compensating for the significant increase in the profile of the F7U-3 fuselage ahead of the centre of gravity by increasing the size of the vertical fins and/or moving them aft was a mistake. Note that the -3 fin below the wing, which would not lose directional stability effectiveness at high angles of attack, was also smaller in area. ***Thomason***

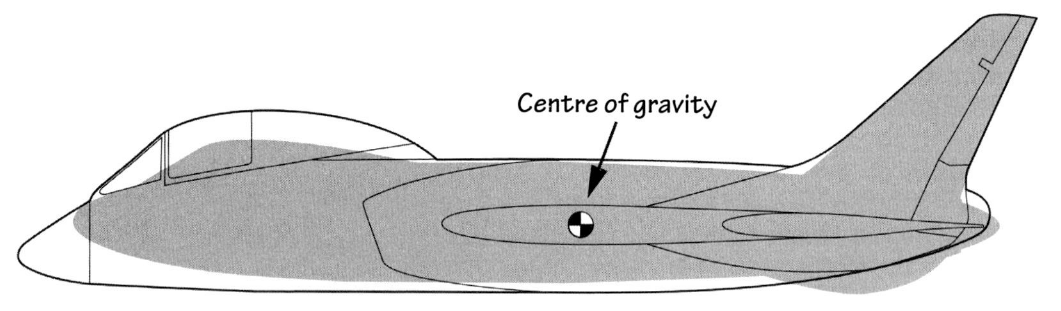

the type; this was his first flight in one powered by J46s. It was configured with a rocket pack on the belly and external stores pylons. His first two clean (landing gear and slats retracted) 1*g* stalls were as expected: the aircraft yawed left as it approached the stall and recovered when the stick pressure was released. The third was not: when Williams relaxed the back pressure, the nose pitched up and the aircraft rolled to the right, entering what he believed to be an erect (positive *g*), flat spin to the right: 'The spin was characterised by an extremely nose-down attitude and a rapid rate for 300-degree turn followed by a nose-high attitude and hesitation for the next 60 degrees.' When his attempts to recover were unsuccessful, he ejected at 7,000ft after at least seven turns by his count. The Navy promptly grounded its F7U-3s.

There were notable configuration differences between No. 2 that Vought had spin tested – e.g. original forward fuselage, flight-test nose boom, no rocket pack or stores pylons – and No. 41 that Williams was flying. Although Vought test pilots had accomplished clean stalls of No. 4, which had the tapered nose and larger canopy, without a loss of control while loaded with a rocket pack and a 2,000lb bomb on each stores pylon, there was a concern that the differences had altered the F7U-3 aerodynamics enough to make it susceptible to spinning and, worse, not recoverable from one.

In a little over a week, Vought removed the anti-spin parachute and associated cockpit controls from No. 2 and installed them on BuNo 128468 (No. 18), which had the production nose and canopy, along with a rocket pack and stores pylons, making it essentially identical to No. 41's configuration on Williams' flight. Vought Chief Test Pilot McGuyrt began spin-entry evaluation flights in it on 28 March. On 31 March, Vought's Sales and Service Manager, Paul Thayer, wrote a memo to the Dallas Bureau of Aeronautics Representative (BAR) requesting that it be forwarded to BuAer's Aircraft Division. It summarised the results of spin testing accomplished on No. 18 to that point (fifteen attempts in three flights) in terse Speed-Letter prose:

> Unable to produce continuous spin. Aircraft always recovers itself. Contractor satisfied no significant difference in spin characteristics No. 2 spin demonstration aircraft (BuNo 128452) and No. 17 and sub configuration. Contractor confident no risk in ungrounding aircraft with clean condition stall restriction. Contractor also confident in event steady state spin can be attained, NACA recommended recovery technique will recover aircraft. Contractor recommends all pilots be so advised. BuAer-contractor meeting scheduled 1 April to discuss contractor's flight test investigations to date and to establish satisfactory further spin demonstration programme. Contractor continuing investigation on highest priority.

The head of the Spin-Tunnel Section at NACA Langley, Anshal I. Neihouse, attended the 1 April meeting of Navy and Chance Vought representatives. McGuyrt was present along with CDR Williams. The main purpose of the meeting was to discuss how it was that NACA wind tunnel and Vought flight tests had not only come to very different conclusions about the F7U-3's propensity to spin, but neither predicted an unrecoverable spin. Neihouse suggested that the reason that McGuyrt had only been able to achieve incipient spins was that he had not explored the worst-case control applications, including yaw damper off (which meant the auxiliary rudders would not be counteracting a pro-spin yaw); full pro-spin rudders; and full pro-spin lateral control (stick left for a right spin). Williams noted 'it had not been sufficiently stressed to him how important it was to put the ailerons with the spin for recovery'. To further muddy the water, the original NACA spin-model had the bulb nose and smaller canopy of the original Vought spin test aircraft, not the production configuration that Williams was flying.

BuAer concluded the meeting with the request that Vought demonstrate spins to the left and right from both 1*g* and 3*g* stalls for five turns before recovery. This was to be accomplished with the yaw damper selected off as well as on (with the yaw damper off, the auxiliary

Vought test pilot John McGuyrt successfully provokes the bear

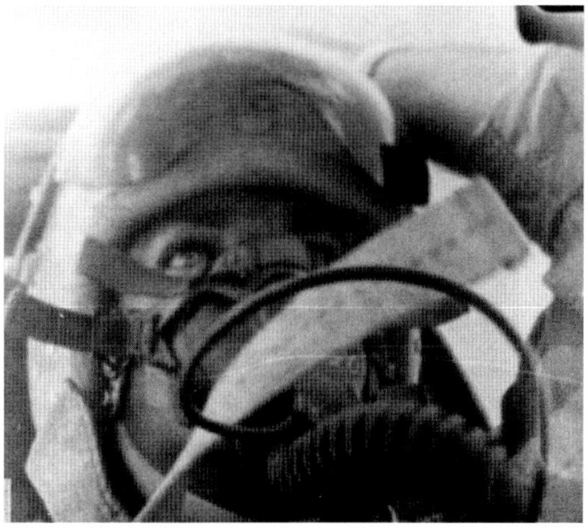

Inverted during a post-stall gyration, checking the location of the ejection seat's face-curtain handle

Spin chute deployment fails, visor down for ejection (Note strap and horizon indicating negative g and inverted)

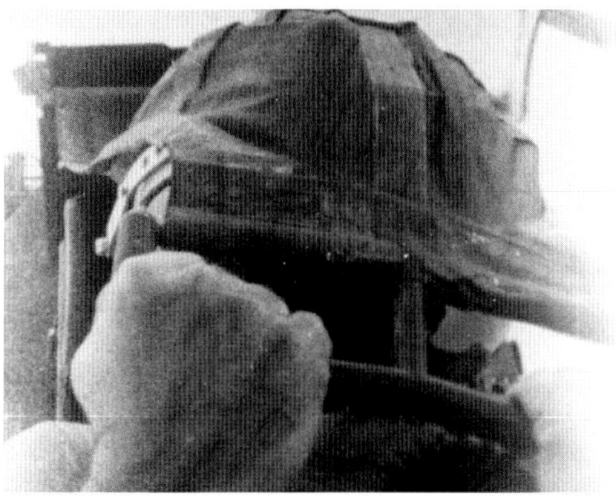

Pulling the face curtain, less than 5,000 feet above the ground at a high rate of descent

The ejection was successful

One of the motion picture cameras that Vought installed in the spin test F7U-3 BuNo 128468 provided what are now known as selfies. It survived the crash. *Casby Collection*

rudders were fixed in trail and therefore not acting against pro-spin yaw). If spins did not result, then Vought was to then mechanise the auxiliary rudders so they deflected with the upper rudders, since NACA spin testing indicated that they were very effective in promoting and recovering from spins. An inverted spin recovery was not addressed, although the model spin testing programme indicated that one 'could sometimes be obtained immediately after termination of the erect spin'. However, also according to those tests, the inverted spin was fairly steady and recovery deemed to be readily achieved.

After the 1 April meeting, McGuyrt made four more flights and another fourteen spin entries without being able to achieve more than some characteristics of a spin – which disappeared immediately after relaxation of pro-spin controls – much less a duplication of the Williams incident. Subsequent events suggest that one reason clean stalls in the F7U-3 were often non-events and even attempts to force the Cutlass into a spin had initially been unsuccessful was that the conditions had to be just right for a loss of control to occur. It was like poking a bear: sometimes the bear is hibernating and can't be aroused; sometimes the poke is too light to elicit a reaction from the bear. But sometimes the bear feels the poke and takes offence. It was to become apparent that if the F7U-3 was not prevented from stalling in the clean configuration, it usually yawed to one side or the other and then sometimes – but not always – began a violent series of twists, turns, and tumbles. Initially referred to as a 'flip-flop', the result soon became known as a 'Post-Stall Gyration' (PSG).

On 7 April, worst-case (pro-spin) auxiliary rudder proved not to be required to duplicate Williams' loss of control. With the yaw damper simply off, and reportedly by being as aggressive as possible with the controls, McGuyrt well and truly poked the bear. He began by applying full rudder in same direction as the uncommanded yaw that was characteristic of the clean-condition stall, followed by full forward stick. He

ABOVE The attachment of the anti-spin parachute to the fuselage of BuNo 128452 was proof-loaded but when its deployment was needed on BuNo 128468, the strength of the riser that connected the parachute to the fitting on the fuselage proved to be inadequate. *VAHF*

BELOW The third spin test F7U-3, BuNo 129566, was painted all white with a wide black stripe under each wing for easier determination of the aircraft's attitude during analysis of motion picture film of an event. *VAHF*

held the controls there for several turns of what he believed to be an inverted spin. After approximately fifteen more turns of not being able to recover with any control application he tried, he actuated the spin-recovery parachute. Unfortunately, the riser that connected it to the fuselage snapped, probably due to a higher than anticipated 'snatch' load when the parachute opened. McGuyrt attempted to break the spin for a few more turns but then had to eject at the last moment, 4,600ft above the ground.

Immediately after McGuyrt's crash, a meeting was convened at Vought and then at BuAer to review what had happened and determine what to do next. Based on chase plane and ground-based motion picture film of the manoeuvre, as well as cockpit-mounted camera footage of McGuyrt with a shoulder harness strap dangling upside down in his face, the F7U-3 had in fact been in an inverted spin but instead of recovering when the recommended control positions were employed, wound up spinning in the reverse direction and tumbling. In order for the Navy to justify ungrounding its Cutlasses, Vought defined flight restrictions that would avoid a loss of control, which in essence advocated not stalling the aircraft in the clean configuration. A Vought team, including McGuyrt, was

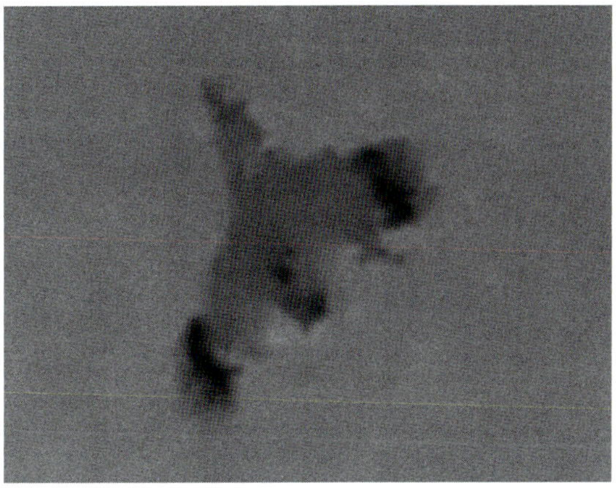

LEFT **The black stripe on the underside of the wing was clearly evident even in low-resolution images from a ground-based movie camera.** *VAHF*

BELOW **On the third spin test F7U-3, the spin recovery parachute was attached to the airframe much closer to its housing, possibly to reduce the snatch loads when the parachute opened.** *Casby Collection*

to visit units operating the Cutlass to brief them on the restrictions. NACA was asked to repeat the F7U-3 spin tunnel test programme with a model representative of the production configuration. It was also agreed that Vought would immediately start modifying another F7U-3, BuNo 129566, for the resumption of spin testing. The Navy accepted Vought's plan and stated that the F7U-3 would be ungrounded on 16 April.

Vought test pilot Don 'Mad Dog' Schultz was assigned to accomplish the F7U-3 spin test programme. He began with spinning a T-33 (bailed to Vought by the USAF) many times over four months:

> I had to acclimatise myself to motion ... we knew that in spin work, if you get really acquainted with it ... you do it at really short intervals, very frequent times per week, eventually you'll get used to the motion, and you get to the point of what they call 'transfer of motion'. Well, after you depart from controlled flight, it seems like the airplane is static and everything else is going around, and then you reach the point where you get so good you can read instruments.

In addition to adding a redesigned spin-recovery parachute system to the spin test Cutlass, its ejection seat was modified with a head restraint to be attached to Schultz' flight helmet. Otherwise, in the violent motions associated with the post-stall gyration, he would resemble a bobble-head doll on the dashboard of a car on a rutted road, unable to perceive accurately what the aircraft was doing in pitch, roll, and yaw. He was also provided with a quick disconnect stick grip that extended aft of the standard one. This ensured that he would be able to position the stick to its full-forward limit if required to either enter or exit a post-stall gyration. The quick disconnect feature was necessary in the event that he would have to eject with the stick fully aft, which would position the add-on grip over his crotch.

On 11 June 1954, another F7U-3 crashed and its pilot, LT Robert C. Woolverton of BuAer Dallas, was killed immediately following take-off from NAS Memphis during an airshow practice session. The cause was established to be his premature retraction of the slats during climb out, an error with potentially catastrophic consequences. The result was a clean-condition stall and loss of control (the Cutlass was seen to yaw from side to side and pitch up and down rapidly before yawing violently and crashing into a schoolhouse on the base).

On 24 September 1954, Chance Vought engineers and chief experimental test pilot John W. Konrad visited NACA Langley to discuss the results of the F7U-3 spin model tests. Before resumption of F7U-3 spin tests, Vought's Don Schultz was conditioning himself in spin entry and recovery in a T-33. The urgency of finding a solution was underscored when on that same day, ENS Marshal W. White ejected successfully following a loss of control at 10,000ft while flying a VF-81 Cutlass for the first time from nearby NAS Oceana, Virginia.

Here, Vought test pilot Don Schultz is discussing with German Second World War fighter pilot Karl Bauer the stick grip aft extension he helped design to be used when full forward stick was required during spin testing. The test grip is in Bauer's right hand and the mounting point to the aircraft's stick is in his left. *Casby Collection*

More evidence of the F7U-3's unusual behaviour after a clean stall was to come as a result of VC-3's role in *Project Check-Out*. It did not help that only limited information on the subject was provided to the students: 'You have read about it and you have heard about it ... but please prove it at a safe altitude. We're talking about the F7U-3 clean-condition stall characteristics. Remember, don't retract your slats too soon on take-off (150 knots minimum recommended), and be sure to extend them at an airspeed high enough to prevent loss of control near the ground. Be sure to study thoroughly the flight handbook section on stalls and spins.'

Surprisingly, the first VC-3 F7U-3 familiarisation flight was the only one in the fifty-four-and-a-half-hour syllabus that included any stall manoeuvres and it was limited to the take-off and landing configuration: 'practice stalls in "dirty" condition only, with various power settings and note rate of descent prior to stalls'.

It did not take long for a VC-3 student to get into trouble. On 11 January 1955 LTJG John D. Lindsay lost control during an air-to-air combat-related manoeuvre (a hard nose-down turn at 230 knots); he ejected successfully, reportedly with 'no definite recovery attempt.' The Cutlass 'recovered by itself and crashed wings level'.

LCDR Horatio G. 'Bud' Sickel Jr. was one of VC-3's senior officers and an experienced test pilot. He had received the Outstanding Student award at graduation from the Navy's Test Pilot School in 1951. He was subsequently involved in the evaluation of the North American XFJ-2 Fury, including spin testing. He was concerned as to whether the F7U-3 training syllabus was safe or should be altered to 1) stop pulling the stick at the onset buffet and 2) eliminate most of the air-to-air tactical work. He felt qualified to personally investigate the circumstances behind Lindsay's snap-spin manoeuvre, reportedly despite admonition not to.

His first flight on 18 January 1955 with that objective was to establish the onset and limit buffet boundaries in both symmetrical (no yaw) and asymmetrical (yawed) flight as well as the yaw resulting from the use of only one afterburner with the yaw damper on or off. He noted that the F7U-3's high adverse yaw with roll (rolling to the right required right rudder to keep the nose from yawing to the left) and weakening of directional stability with increased angle of attack was likely to result in an asymmetrical flight condition during a hard turning manoeuvre. The result was a roll in the same direction as the yaw. It was, however, relatively slow and the recovery immediate upon relaxation of back stick pressure and a return to symmetric flight.

He made a second flight on 20 January to evaluate the effect of symmetric and asymmetric flight while making a hard downward turn and pulling into limit buffet, essentially repeating the conditions that preceded Lindsay's PSG. The first manoeuvre in symmetric flight was uneventful. He climbed back to the same starting conditions and repeated the manoeuvre to the left with some left rudder so the ball in the turn and bank indicator was about ¼ to ½ out of centre:

> At the moment of left snap the controls were held momentarily fixed and then neutralised. The wing drop stopped immediately at about 135° (i.e. about 90 degrees of roll from my estimated 45-degree left bank). I had little or no sensation of yaw or any other feeling other than the mild manoeuvre was finished and I had only to gain a little airspeed to roll gently out and climb for the next point, which was to be a full-ball yawed repeat. *BUT* as I relaxed pressure the airplane went very suddenly into a tremendous right yaw with extreme yawing velocity. The onset of this manoeuvre felt as if I had been in a left yaw, which was returning to neutral but overshot and gained momentum. The airplane continued this slice to the right in an arc above the horizon to a right bank. The slice continued to the most extreme yaw angle that I have ever experienced. Roll due to yaw developed slowly. I had immediately cut throttle to about half, applied full rudder against the yaw automatically and pushed the stick very slightly forward of neutral, being very careful not to put in too much forward stick as advised against.
>
> The next slice to the left had a tremendous potential start from this yawed angle and gained extreme yawing velocity. The roll was again mild and secondary. This slice continued until the airplane was pointed straight down. I reversed rudder against the yaw and completely neutralised the stick. These reversing yaws continued about four or five times with the same or slightly increasing ferocity. Roll was mild in rate. The longitudinal axis of the airplane pointed alternately 30° about the horizon to straight down. At one time while pointed down I tried speed brakes for a while but they produced no noticeable effect and I felt that perhaps more speed rather than less would be better so I closed them again.

According to the rest of his lengthy Pilot's Statement, with Test Pilot School quality/detail in some respects but unsupported by the customary research instrumentation recording, Sickle tried various combinations of roll, yaw, and pitch input. He finally set the pitch trim to 7 degrees nose up and let go of the controls; however, before that could take effect he observed that he was descending nearly straight down at 350 to 400 knots and passing through 10,000ft, which meant that he was less than twenty seconds from hitting the ground. He ejected successfully.

It seems odd that at the very last – rather than first – he tried the recovery technique that Schultz was then demonstrating successfully at Vought. Perhaps he thought he could establish a different, more aviator-worthy solution than just releasing the controls. In any event, the Navy quickly decided that for the time being, existing F7U-3 flight restrictions, if followed, were sufficient to prevent entry into the 'pre-stall yaw condition' that preceded the loss of control. As a result, the Cutlass was not re-grounded.

On 1 February 1955, BuAer held a meeting in Washington with representatives from Vought, NACA Langley, squadrons operating the F7U-3, NATC, and the Naval Aviation Safety Activity, to discuss the F7U-3's control loss problem as a result of the VC-3 crashes. Fortunately, by then Vought's Schultz was near the end of determining how to avoid the loss of control and failing that, recover from it. According to a NACA memorandum of the meeting, the loss of control resulted from a directional divergence (described by Sickel as a 'slice' for its quickness) as the Cutlass approached a stall in a clean configuration. 'After yawing the airplane may go into a rolling motion, which may be difficult to control,' clearly an understatement.

Schultz had explored stalling the spin test Cutlass from all corners of the V-n envelope in a comprehensive test programme, including jerking the stick full aft and to the left or right corner in a dive at Mach 1.1. The result was a pitch up into an accelerated stall and then 'tremendous adverse yaw and cartwheel into this post-stall gyration so rapidly … at rates over 270 degrees per second, which no human could perceive'. As a result, Vought could now confidently report that PSG avoidance was accomplished by recognising the beginning of the 'slice' and immediately relaxing back pressure on the stick.

If the aircraft did go out of control, recovery was to be accomplished by neutralising the lateral and directional controls (i.e. stick and pedals centred) and positioning the stick longitudinally slightly aft of centre. The recommended aft-stick position equated to about 7 to 10 degrees nose up, the setting for a normal take-off, and depending on the phase of flight, just aft of the normal level flight trim. In other words, if the F7U-3 was in trim in all axes, just letting go of the controls would result in a PSG recovery.

The NACA attendee this time was Walter Klinar, who was an Aeronautical Research Scientist assigned to the Langley spin tunnel. His conclusion was that:

> Apparently no changes are planned for modifying the airplane to prevent the divergence, just more education of Navy pilots on how to deal with it. The spin-test programme will be a continuation of the past programmes with stronger effort being placed on getting an erect spin. Past tests have

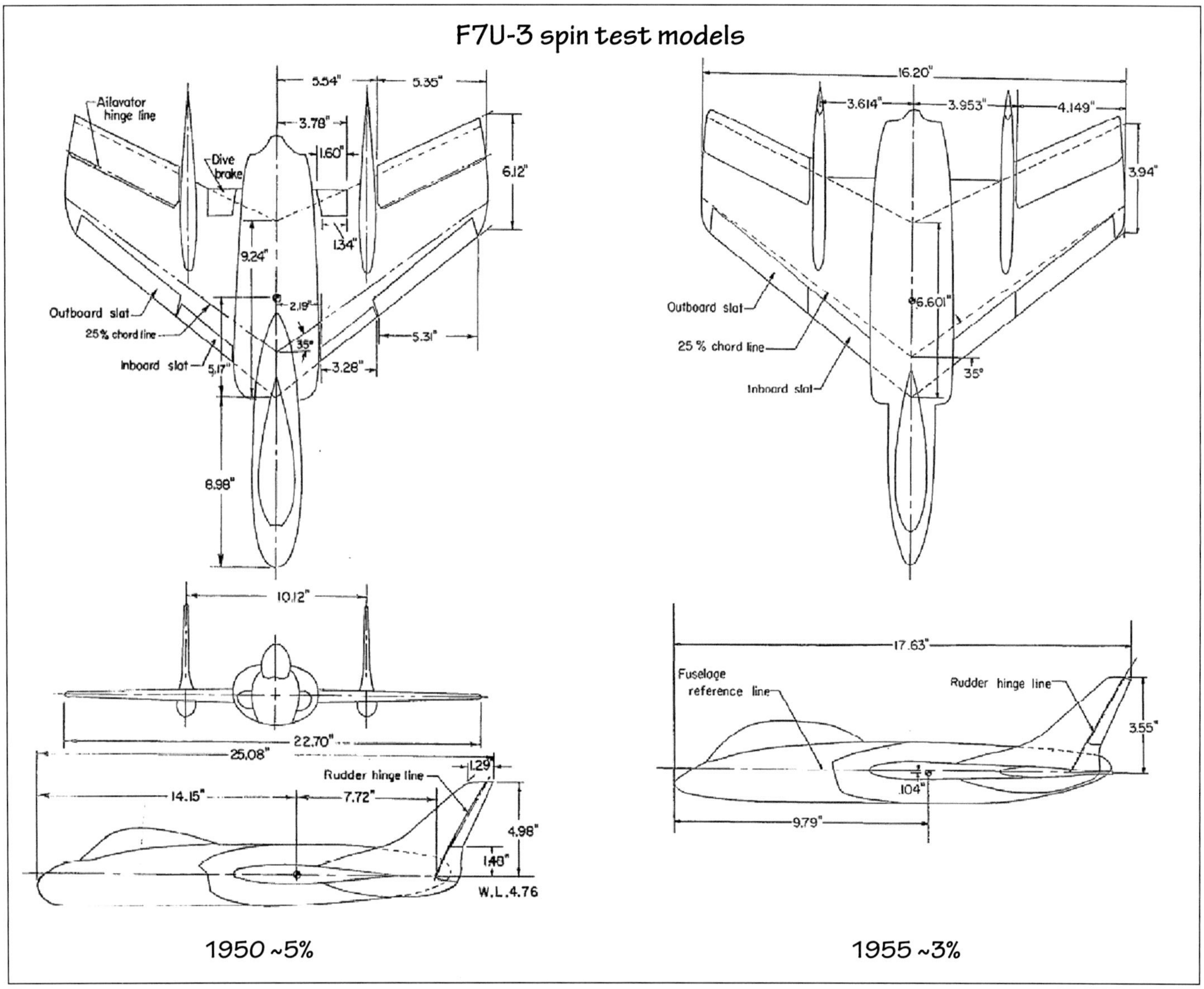

The first and second NACA F7U-3 spin models are depicted here as being the same size, although in fact the earlier model was bigger. The second one reflected the slightly shorter forward fuselage, larger canopy, longer tail cone, and decreased deflection of the ailavators of the production F7U-3 compared to the initial configuration; nevertheless, the new model could still not be coaxed into something resembling the post-stall gyration of which the full-scale aircraft was capable. ***Thomason***

shown that a true erect spinning condition was impossible to attain possibly due to a yaw damper … Inverted spins are also included in the programme and these have been obtained previously by pushing the stick forward once the rolling motion after the stall was encountered. Satisfactory recoveries from fully developed inverted spins on the airplane have not been demonstrated and two airplanes have been lost possibly as a result of inverted spins. Model results have indicated the proper control movements for recovery from erect and inverted spins and Chance Vought Aircraft personnel and the Bureau of Aeronautics are fully cognisant of these results.

NACA acknowledged in its spin test reports that its spin susceptibility and recovery predictions based on model testing were sometimes wrong, by their assessment about 10% of the time. The F7U-3 predictions appear to have been one of those instances. NACA's F7U-3 spin test models – including a retest in 1955 with one that more closely reflected the production F7U-3 configuration – entered classic spins while Vought test pilots were never able to force an F7U-3 into a fully developed conventional spin.

On 2 March 1955, Vought conducted flight demonstrations for representatives of BuAer, NATC, and various fleet commands at the Vought plant. A Flight Handbook revision was quickly prepared advocating clean stall avoidance and failing that, the PSG recovery technique of fixing the controls at recommended positions or just letting go of the controls. In addition, a briefing team of Vought personnel (including test pilots) was again sent out to visit all commands operating the aircraft.

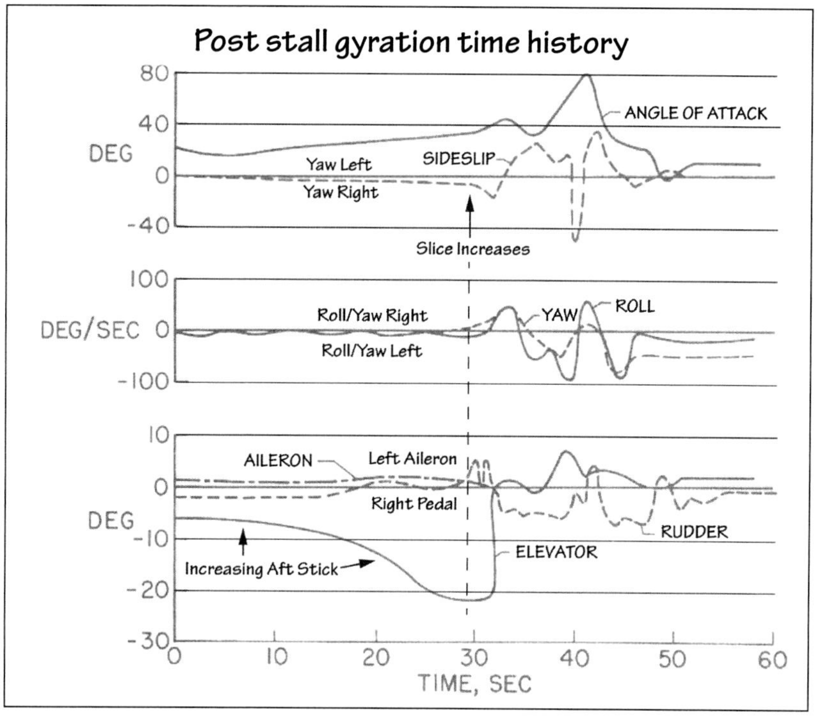

A time history of a post-stall gyration illustrates the potential result of approaching a stall in the clean configuration and allowing a yaw (or slice) to occur. The angle of attack reached 80 degrees and the sideslip, more than 40 degrees. Rates of yaw and roll approach 100 degrees per second with rapid reversals of direction in spite of (and perhaps exacerbated by) flight control movement. Recovery was accomplished after a loss in altitude of about 7,000ft by basically neutralising the controls. *Thomason*

The F7U-3/-3M/-3P Supplemental Flight Manual identified three uncontrolled manoeuvres along with the admonition that 'intentional gyrations or spins are prohibited':

- **Post-Stall Gyration:** 'These gyrations involve heavy buffet, snap rolls, partial turn spins, extreme angles of attack and yaw and, rapid erratic reversals in rolling, yawing, and normal accelerations.' 'The pilot can distinguish between this post-stall gyration and the steady-state inverted spin … by virtue of the erratic behaviour in a gyration in contrast to the smooth steady behaviour in the inverted spin.'

- **Inverted Spins:** 'Steady-state inverted spins may be attained from an inverted stall or as a result of improper recovery techniques from post-stall gyrations … the steady-state inverted spin is characterised by lack of airframe buffet and smooth non-oscillatory motion about a vertical axis.'

- **Normal Spins (Upright):** 'In 100 attempts the Contractor's pilots have been unable to enter a steady-state upright spin … it appears doubtful that any technique will be discovered for entry into normal upright spins.' It goes on to state 'the general characteristics of all aft-stick attempts were an extreme oscillatory post-stall gyration …'

One problem with trying to recover from the out-of-control gyrations with classic spin recovery control movements was that the aircraft was also trying to recover, resulting in an overreaction to the pilot's intent similar to a pilot-induced oscillation. According to a PSG description, 'In all cases, the rapidity of the reversal motions about all three axes and the associated buffet, (will) jostle and confuse the pilot beyond his ability to oppose any particular motion with control deflections in proper sequence to affect recovery.' The flight manual reinforced that warning with the admonition 'fighting the controls or manipulations other than the recommended technique (i.e. essentially letting go of the controls) will prolong or prevent recovery'.

In contrast, classic inverted spin recovery could be easily effected by full reverse of the rudders and both lateral and longitudinal neutralisation of the stick. The manual continues, 'The contractor is presently investigating prolonged inverted spins, the recovery from which will be supplied when flight tests are complete.'

At the risk of further confusing and/or scaring the pilot about to fly an F7U-3 for the first time, later revisions to the manual also discussed a 'gyrodynamic manoeuvre' that was an, 'Uncontrolled manoeuvre that may occur on rare occasions with pro-inverted spin control positions … it can be differentiated from post-stall gyrations by its smooth, buffet-free, non-oscillatory spiral flight path at positive *g*s. The airplane rotates smoothly in an upright yawed flight attitude, with nose low, about a comparatively steep flight path.' It would sometimes occur following a recovery from a classic inverted spin, manifesting itself as a tight, smooth 'grave-yard spiral' with increasing airspeed. However, 'immediate recovery from the gyrodynamic manoeuvre is accomplished by neutral ailerons and rudders with full forward stick'.

PSG and clean stall accidents were rare thereafter. On 29 July 1955, VX-4's LT Robert W. Slezak was killed shortly after take-off from NAS Point Mugu in an F7U-3P for a ferry flight to NAF Litchfield for its storage; his wingman reported that he entered a post-stall gyration at 3,500ft, probably due to retracting the slats too soon and too low to recover. He failed to eject. In December 1955, VA-34's ENS John G. Curtis attempted a loop that resulted in a PSG entry: he ejected successfully. In August 1956, VA-212's LT Arthur Gerald Callahan Jr. failed to extend his landing gear (which automatically extended the slats) while slowing in the pattern to land on *Bon Homme Richard* (CVA-31); a pre-PSG slice resulted followed by an out-of-control crash into the sea. Finally, ENS Henry H. Strong was able to recover successfully from a post-stall gyration while flying a VA-83 F7U-3M from NAS Oceana, Virginia, in November 1956 but over-temped both his engines in the process (airflow into the engine inlet was badly distorted as the Cutlass tumbled at a high angle of attack and rate of yaw and he had failed to retard the throttles). He ejected successfully rather than attempt a crash landing or ditching.

The hard-won knowledge of the PSG avoidance and recovery provided to F7U-3 pilots doubtless minimised the incidence of crashes after March 1955. However, one unexplained omission from the Cutlass instrument panel that would have been especially useful in that regard and others was an angle-of-attack (AoA) indicator. It had become a standard feature on Navy jets following an evaluation by VMF-122 during their deployment with F9F-5s in 1953 on *Coral Sea* (CVA-43) and was in fact incorporated on the first F7U-3s. It provided a direct, real-time indication of stall margin. An aircraft in a specific configuration, e.g. flap and slat position, will always stall at the same angle of attack but at different indicated airspeeds depending on the aircraft's gross weight and whether it was pulling up or turning hard, in effect significantly increasing 'weight' by adding *g* loading. The landing weight of a prop plane did not vary significantly with the amount of fuel remaining when returning from a mission because fuel was a much smaller fraction of take-off weight compared to a jet's and fuel consumption in the landing pattern was also much lower. For a prop pilot making a carrier approach, a single airspeed number plus a few knots for greater than usual retention of the disposable load would suffice. In contrast, a slow but safe approach airspeed for a jet differed significantly because fuel was a significantly higher fraction of gross weight; ideally, it required the jet pilot to calculate his approach speed based on the weight of external and internal stores retained and fuel on board in order to determine an airspeed that was slow but not too slow. Being too slow reduced control responsiveness and increased the risk of a stall with little chance for recovery on the low final approach to a carrier; too fast and the LSO had less time to signal corrections and the pilot to make them as well as increasing the risk of overshooting the landing area, which meant a trip into the barriers/barricade.

Having an angle of attack indication would have been particularly beneficial to an F7U-3 pilot on his approach to a landing because its Achilles' heel was the steep backside of the power curve. It would warn him that he was slowing to the point where he would not be able to maintain altitude, much less climb, even in afterburner. Another benefit was the potential for avoiding PSG during combat manoeuvring. While attacking or evading his opponent, instead of having to also be alert for the nose slice that preceded it, a pilot could glance at his angle of attack indicator or see a red warning light in his field of view that signalled him to reduce back pressure. Moreover, it would allow him to safely maximise his turning performance instead of being conservative in pulling *g* due to the undesirability of inducing a post-stall gyration. Another is the use of angle of attack for optimum endurance (particularly useful to maximise loiter time while waiting for a flight deck to land on) or range performance. Nevertheless, the pilot's angle-of-attack indicator was removed in the production F7U-3s and the aircraft's angle of attack only provided to the fire control system. Several Cutlass pilots have remarked that they could not understand why there were AoA indicators in every jet they flew for pitch control guidance while approaching to land except the one that needed it the most.

It should be noted that the F7U-3 was not the only 1950s jet to fall foul of unknown or unappreciated configuration-induced aerodynamic consequences. For example:

- The first North American F-100 Super Sabre configuration featured a long, dense fuselage that resulted in high pitch inertia, relatively low roll inertia, and a vertical fin that proved to be too small. It was therefore susceptible to a catastrophic coupling of aerodynamic and inertial forces when the aircraft was yawed or rolled at high speed, generating uncommanded pitch and yaw excursions that exceeded the ultimate strength of the airframe. North American Aviation's chief test pilot, George S. Welch, was fatally injured on 12 October 1954 when the F-100 he was flying for a structural demonstration disintegrated as he pulled out of a Mach 1.55 dive targeting 7.3 *g*. The short-coupled Cutlass traded that configuration shortcoming at high speed for one at high angles of attack.

- Somewhat late in its development, the F4D Skyray was discovered to have an unacceptable nose-up pitch change when abruptly slowed from its maximum level-flight speed (which, contrary to almost every article written about it, was not supersonic at any altitude) at sea level. An inadvertent and worst-case encounter with it during a Douglas test flight resulted in a 9.1*g* pitch up, causing sufficient structural damage to the airframe that it had to be scrapped. Automatic transonic trim compensation was incorporated in the flight control system as a result.

- The F3H Demon did not suffer from inertial coupling or experience significant transonic pitch trim changes but roll rate shortfalls at high speeds were encountered by fleet pilots due to the inadequate torsional stiffness of the wing relative to the force generated by the deflected ailerons. The lower weight and cost solution compared to beefing up the wing was to add an inboard spoiler system. The lateral control system automatically switched to the spoilers from the ailerons at the speed above which the roll rate generated by the ailerons began to diminish.

In April 1957, the Navy bailed the third spin test F7U-3,

After F-100 deliveries had commenced, the vertical fin had to be enlarged by 27.5% when investigation of a fatal flight test accident revealed that it was inadequate during high-speed rolling or yawing. *NACA*

BuNo 129566, to the Cornell Aeronautical Laboratory (CAL, subsequently Calspan) for evaluation of a proposed means of post-stall controllability by automatic and very powerful control of sideslip. It was modified with two very large, vertically mounted control fins on the nose ahead of the cockpit, one above and one below, positioned by an automatic yaw-prevention control system. When the sideslip that tended to occur during a clean stall was detected, the system quickly pivoted the fins to eliminate it and therefore preclude a spin. CAL's flight tests were accomplished in mid-1959. On flight twenty-four on 4 June, with the nose fins removed but the aircraft's pitch and yaw damper system engaged, CAL Chief Pilot, John C. Seal, deliberately induced a post-stall gyration:

> The second stall configuration was to enter a left turn at 38,000 feet and 240 KIAS. The pilot was then to accelerate the stall by rapid application of full up elevator, at the same time applying full top rudder and full aileron opposite to the rudder. The aircraft snapped over the top of the turn and then performed a series of violent pitching, rolling and yawing motions that the pilot could not follow due to the high rate and severe buffet. The chase pilot stated that the aircraft seemed to be in a violent spin, with the nose pitching up and down and with yaw and roll reversals. He also stated that the test plane lost 5,000 feet of altitude so quickly that he was barely able to stay with it in a steep dive. The recovery technique instituted by the pilot of the test plane resulted in almost immediate damping of the manoeuvre and final recovery was made from a steep dive. Although this is a violent manoeuvre the pilot feels it is not dangerous if the recovery is not postponed for too long a time. Also at this point, the pilot feels that the best recovery technique for this manoeuvre is to just relax all forces on the control stick and let it return to the neutral trim point. This he finds easy to do and it has worked very well thus far.

Flights with the CAL yaw control fins on and functional eliminated the post-stall gyration. Seal noted 'for some reason the stall manoeuvres entered from low speed (140 KIAS) are more violent and non-linear than those entered at high speed (240 KIAS). It is entirely possible that the entry of the post-stall gyration by service pilots have been inadvertently made from manoeuvres like the top of a loop where the aircraft speed is very low, controls are ineffective, and large yawing motions are built up before a gain in speed allows some control effectiveness. In the opinion of this pilot, post-stall gyrations are not possible on every entry and apparently are impossible with the CAL nose surface engaged and functioning.'

Even more confusing was the result of an attempt made on flight thirty-two on 19 June 1959 with the yaw control fins off to again induce the post-stall

BuAer awarded a contract to the Cornell Aeronautical Laboratory for evaluation of active control of sideslip minimisation at high angles of attack utilising Vought's spin test F7U-3, BuNo 129566. The canopy is an unpainted replacement. *Casby Collection*

gyration obtained on flight twenty-four on 4 June. The pilot tried to poke the bear five times, at least one considered to be identical to the one that had resulted in a post-stall gyration. The bear was not provoked on any of them. The worst result was a 'tight spiral with yawing and pitching accelerations which reversed direction quite rapidly. Recovery was effective immediately'. The project engineer noted, 'The records showed that the airplane's motions in this flight were similar to those of a normal upright spin rather than post-stall gyrations. No reason has been found to explain why the post-stall motions (without the control system) in this last flight were so much less violent than in the early flight.'

Walter O. Breuhaus, the Vought engineer who headed up the Aerodynamic Department's Stability and Control Section during the F7U-1 development and later went on to serve twenty-five years at Cornell Aeronautical Laboratories including work on the F7U-3's post-stall gyration problem recalled 'certainly one of the things we missed (at Vought) was the very rapid decrease in vertical tail effectiveness at angles of attack at and beyond the stall. This was a big contributor to the post-stall gyration problems that we encountered later.'

Having the distinction of being the last F7U Cutlass to fly, at least to date, BuNo 129566 was returned to Navy administrative control on 24 August 1959. It was subsequently stricken and scrapped at Buffalo.

CHAPTER ELEVEN

F7U-3 armament

The primary armament for Navy jet fighters at the time was four 20mm cannon, each provided with 180–200 rounds of ammunition. Moving the cannon from the nose of the F7U-1 to above the engine inlets on the F7U-3 was a good idea from the standpoint of minimising CG travel after the ammunition was expended, dumping the cases and links overboard behind the engine inlet, and not subjecting the radar to shock and vibration. As it turned out, the relocation had a deleterious effect on engine operation when the cannon were fired; that and other installation problems combined with teething problems with the Navy's new Mk 12 cannon required significant test and modification to resolve.

Fighters were also to be armed with unguided rockets. The employment of 5in diameter rockets for close-air support, one rocket per pylon, was being superseded by reusable pods containing several smaller (2.75in diameter) 'Mighty Mouse' folding-fin rockets loaded in tubes in the pods (the fins were spring loaded so they deployed as they left the tube after being fired). This increased significantly the number of rockets that could be carried and allowed their use as an air-to-air weapon to shoot down enemy bombers at near-sonic speeds while remaining out of range of the bomber's defensive guns. However, the deletion of all but two of the underwing pylons in an early empty weight reduction exercise initially placed the F7U-3 at a disadvantage with respect to stores capability.

In order to augment an air group's strike force when air superiority considerations permitted, its fighters were capable of being armed with bombs in addition to rockets. If some cases, Navy jets were also

The F7U-1's cannon were located in the forward fuselage like those of most Navy jet fighters. The loose cases and links generated as they were fired were jettisoned overboard into long, external, open-ended troughs on each side of the lower fuselage that funnelled them aft past the engine inlets. The F7U-3's cannon were relocated to be above and behind the engine inlets. ***VAHF***

The standard radar system for day fighters in the mid-1950s was the APG-30 that provided range data to the fire control system creating a gunsight presentation for aiming the 20mm cannon and the 2.75in rockets; range data was also used to generate an 800-cps tone in the pilot's headset when he was within effective range. *Casby*

being tasked with the collateral duty of delivering nuclear weapons, beginning with the F2H-2 Banshee. Like the other general-purpose fighters begin developed at the time, the Cutlass was to have that mission capability. As it happened, the size and stance of the F7U-3 made it well suited to carry big and heavy stores.

The F7U-3 was never retrofitted – as every other deployable Navy jet fighter at the time was except for the obsolescent F9F Panther – with the heat-seeking Sidewinder air-to-air missile that required very little modification to the aircraft to employ. Moreover, the outer wing panels of the derivative -3P, -3M, and A2U could easily have been retrofitted to the -3, adding two more pylons. In 1954 Vought had recommended that the F7U-3 be equipped with the Sidewinder, advocating that the 'fire-and-forget' missile system would represent a simpler, lighter alternative to the F7U-3M due to its self-contained homing capability. This would have provided a missile-armed Cutlass that retained the existing in-flight refuelling capability. Nevertheless, no evidence exists that the Navy ever considered, much less flight tested, a Cutlass with the Sidewinder. It seems likely that this was an early indication of the Navy's decision to minimise further investment in the Cutlass in favour of its other fighters in development.

Fire Control System

The armament control system on the first 159 F7U-3s was the AERO 5A, which consisted of the APG-30 Ranging Radar, the Mk 6 Mod 0 Fire Control, and the then standard Mk 8 Sight. Number 160 and subsequent were delivered with the Aero 10D Armament control System that consisted of the APG-30 radar, the Mk 16 Mod 4 Fire Control System, and the Mk 11 sight, which used the inside of the windscreen as the reflector of the reticle image. All but the first sixteen F7U-3s were to be retrofitted to this standard. The F7U-3M armed with Sparrows required the AERO 10E system, which substituted the APQ-51 radar for the simple APG-30.

The Mk 8 Mod 0 gunsight was a carryover from the F7U-1. *US Navy*

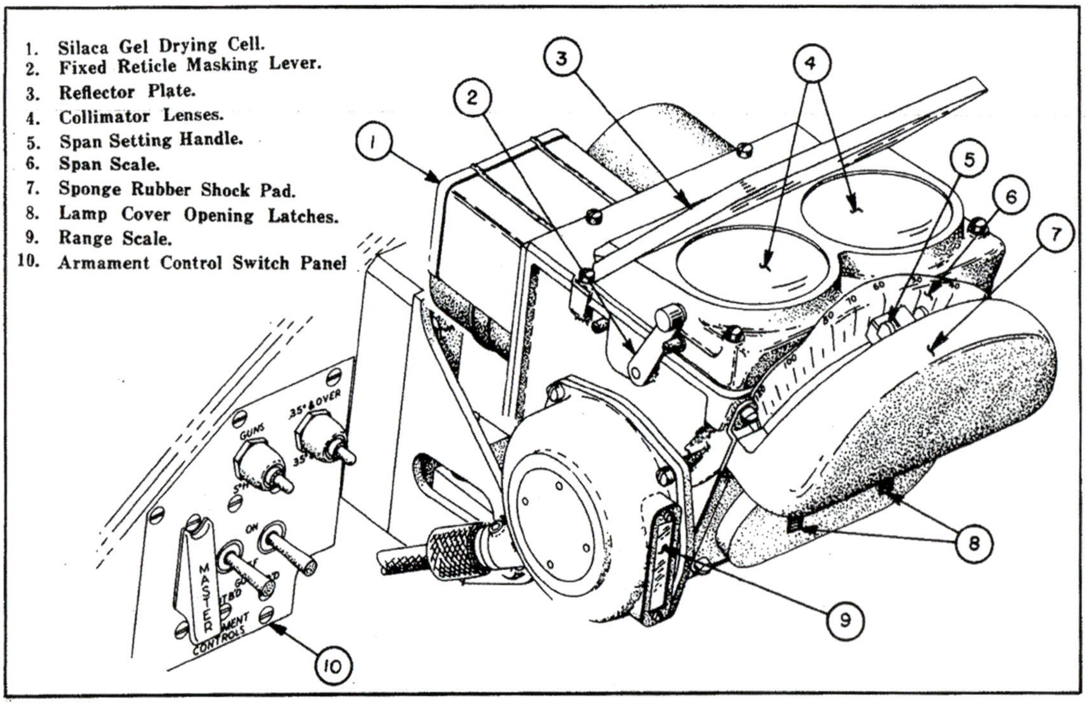

Figure 54—MK 8 Mod 0 Sight Unit

The Mk 11 gunsight projected the aiming reticle onto the inside of the windscreen. *Thomason*

F7U-3 BuNo 129545 and subsequent had provisions for the Low Altitude Bombing System (LABS) required for accurate delivery of a nuclear weapon. None of the F7U-3Ms did.

Automatic Yaw and Pitch Damping

One system critical to the handling qualities of the Cutlass in combat was the G-4 yaw and pitch damping system, one of the most misunderstood in the aircraft. Its purpose was to damp oscillations to make the aircraft more stable for gunnery, photography, and missile deployment. It was utilised to check uncommanded movements of the aircraft caused by wind gusts, turbulence, gunfire recoil, and missile launch. While it was sometimes referred to as an 'autopilot', it was not one per se but instead simply a stability augmentation system. The pitch corrections would never oppose the inputs of the pilot; the yaw function, however, might

Angle of attack was provided to the fire control system by a weather vane-type sensor mounted on the right side of the forward fuselage. *VAHF*

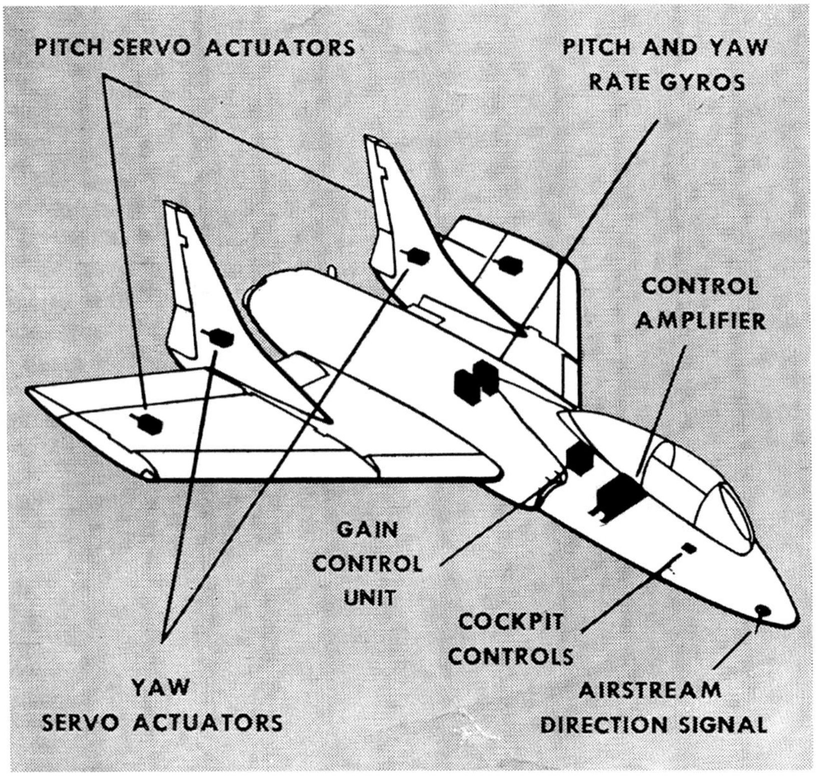

The F7U-3 flight stabilisation system was originally furnished by General Electric; it was replaced on the last fifty F7U-3Ms by a lighter Vought-designed system with the same functionality. ***Thomason Collection***

also oppose the pilot's inputs to a limited degree to correct for slips and skids. It was intended to reduce the pilot's workload and provide stabilisation for weapon deployment; the pilot could turn it off if it was not functioning properly. It was not, as is sometimes stated, necessary for adequate handling qualities on approach. In fact, pitch augmentation was automatically turned off when the slats were extended.

The system used gyroscopes mounted amidships for pitch and yaw input as well as a yaw vane (a rotating probe originally) under the nose to more accurately detect skids and slips at approach speeds. The yaw system controlled the position of auxiliary rudders to eliminate any skid or slip. The command was modulated when the leading-edge slats were retracted and larger when they were extended. Initially the input to the system's analogue computer switched from the yaw gyro to the yaw probe when the slats were extended but when the yaw probe was replaced by a vane, the yaw gyro and the yaw vane both provided input at all times. It was a very reliable system – most Cutlass pilots rarely moved the rudder pedals, allowing the auxiliary rudders to co-ordinate their turns, except for take-offs and landings when a slip for crosswind correction might be needed.

The G-4 system was replaced in F7U-3M No. 49 and subsequent by a Vought-furnished FC4-U1 stabilisation system originally intended for the A2U-1. It functioned the same way using the same protocols but was almost 100lb lighter as a result of the redesign of the pitch and yaw amplifier and actuators.

Cannon

The government-furnished Mk 12 cannon was a development of the Second World War M3 that had armed the early Navy jets. It was designed to fire a cartridge containing a lighter projectile and a larger powder charge at a higher rate of fire and an increased muzzle velocity. The North American XFJ-2B Fury was the test bed for the Mk 12.

Initial gunfire testing by Vought in 1953 with BuNo 128456 (No. 6) was disappointing, as it had been with the Mk 12 cannon installation in the FJ-2 Fury. The muzzle location immediately above the engine inlet induced engine over-temperature and compressor stalls

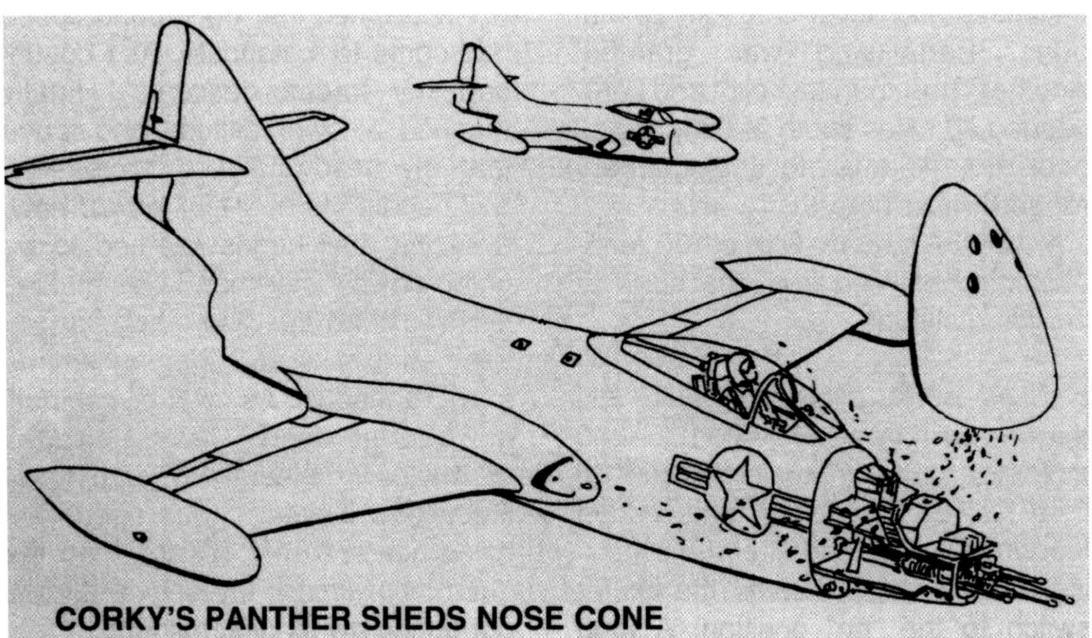

There doesn't appear to have been much attention paid initially to the build-up of potentially explosive gases in the gun bay. BuAer, however, was concerned about the consequences after a few F9F Panther nose cones had been blown off early in the Korean War. Grumman test pilot Corky Meyer demonstrated that ignition of gun gases was the cause. ***Ginter***

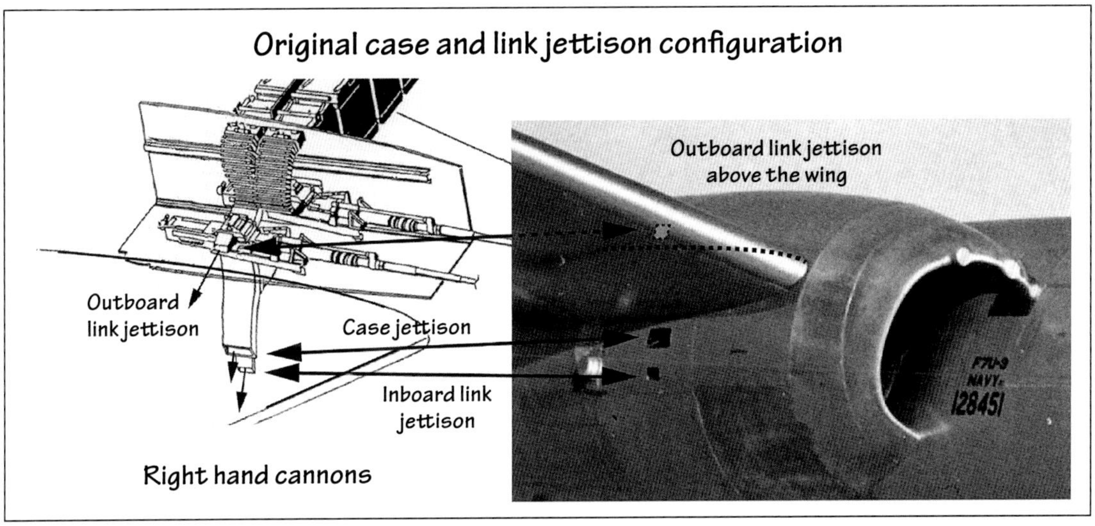

The original 20mm cannon case and link jettison was via simple rectangular openings in the fuselage skin. As with just about every aspect of the cannon installation, it would change. *Thomason*

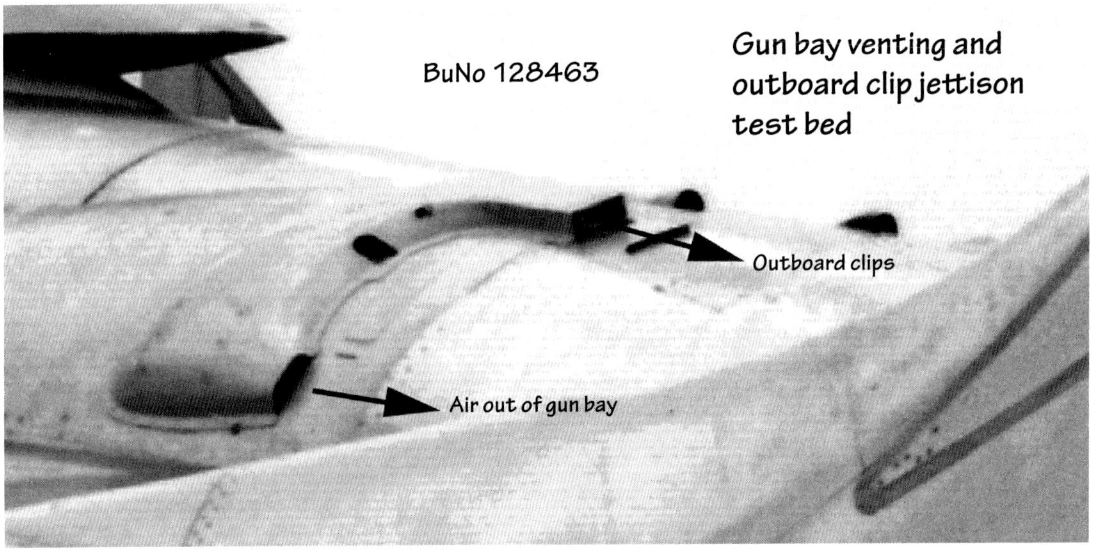

Two J35-powered F7U-3s were modified with a scabbed-on fairing on the top of the mid fuselage to evaluate the effectiveness of venting explosive gases from the gun bay and relocation of the jettison port for the outboard clips. *Thomason*

in the J35 engines. Other problems included an unacceptably low fire out percentage, inadequate gun bay venting of gun gases and unburnt powder; jamming of links and cartridge cases; and links and/or cases striking the fuselage after ejection. BuNo 128467 (No. 17), the first Cutlass powered by J46 engines, was added to the cannon installation test programme in September.

Vought quickly designed scab-on changes to evaluate prospective solutions to the case/link strike and gun gas build-up problems. These were 1) a large fairing on the upper fuselage that rerouted the upper link port to the top of the fuselage and provided ducting for a venturi effect that would suck the gunfire products out of the gun bay, 2) a fairing over the case jettison port, and 3) an extension downward of the inboard cannon link chute. Two J35-powered F7U-3s, BuNo 128456 (No. 6) and 128463 (No. 13), were modified for cannon installation development.

Two structural problems caused by the cannon firing, damage to the canopy attach/actuation structure and the fuselage adjacent to the gun muzzles,

In an early attempt to minimise contact of the cases and outboard links with the airframe surfaces, a fairing was added in front of the case ejection port and another added below it to move the inboard link port downward. *Thomason*

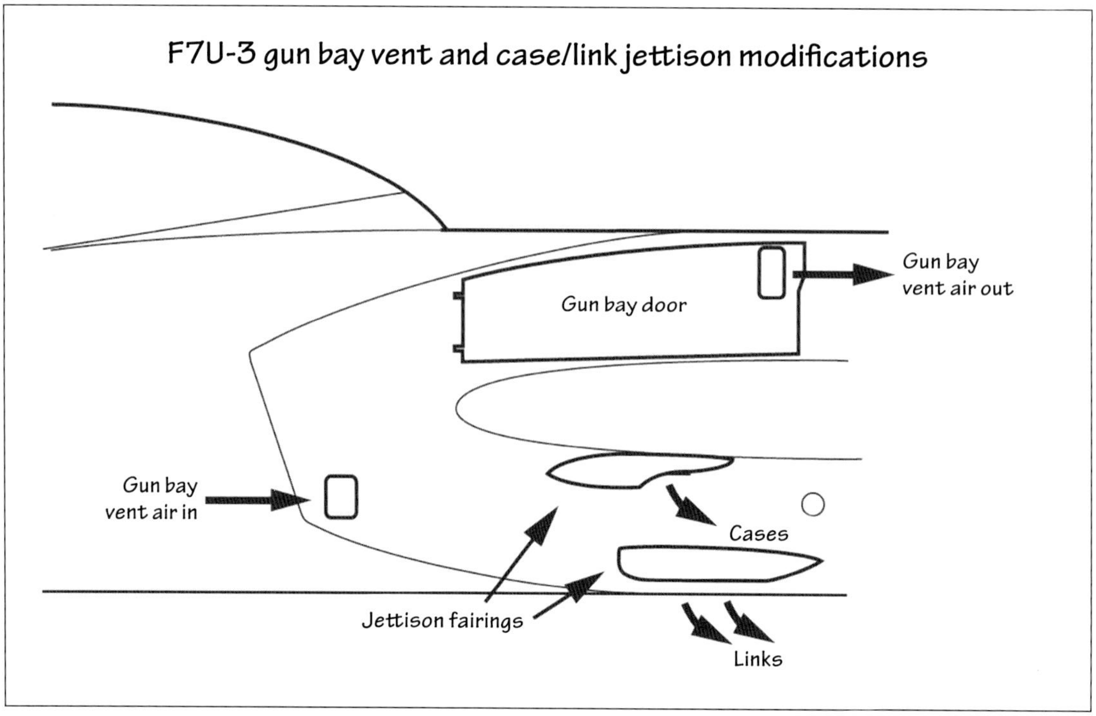

Except for the fairing initially added over the case jettison port, the production (and retrofit) embodiment of the test bed modification was very different: both link chutes were rerouted to a fairing on the lower corner of the fuselage. Instead of relying on the venturi effect, gas and unburnt powder were forced out of the gun bay by adding a hydraulically operated ram air duct on the outside of each engine nacelle near the engine intake lip. The air exited though a hydraulically operated door on the top of each engine bay access door. ***Thomason***

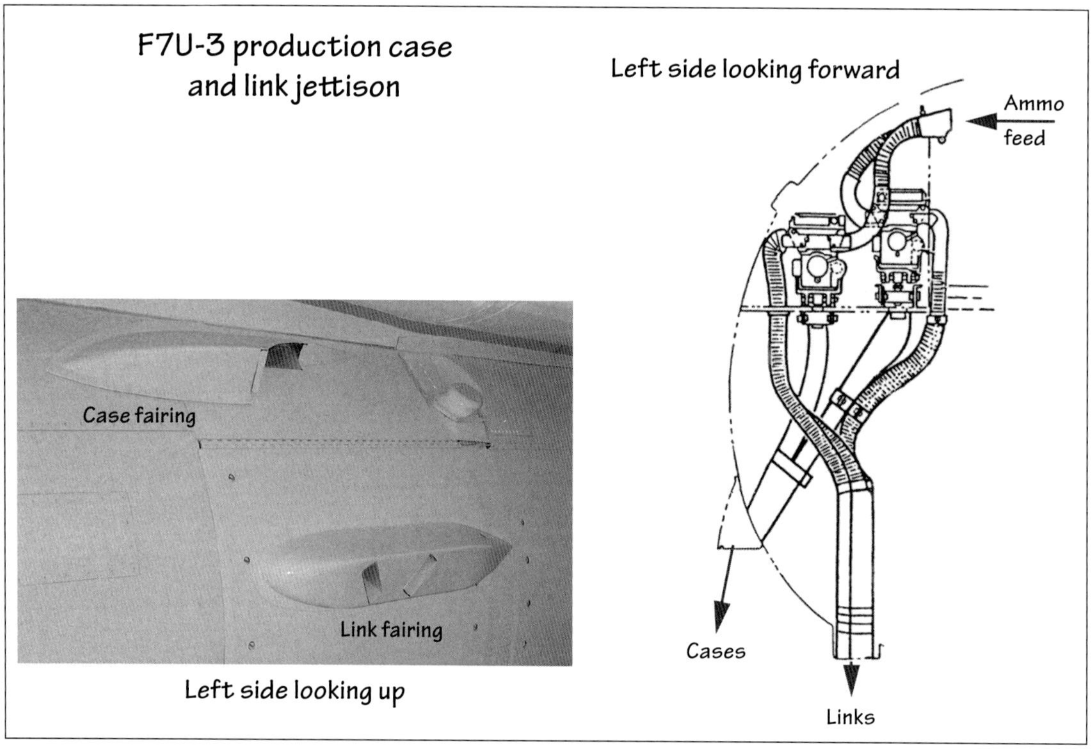

were dealt with by beefing up the canopy actuating cylinder support brackets and a stainless-steel plate respectively. The tendency of the gun feed mechanism to jam was an ongoing problem for which modifications were developed; significant improvement did not result.

Minimising the adverse effect of firing the cannon on engine operation was also not as readily solved. Early modification included the elimination of the muzzle fairing bulges on the inlet lip. The tubes were also laterally scarfed. A 'chimney' vent of the blast tube was added just aft of the inlet. These were inadequate so the top of the forward end of the blast tubes was cut back and two 'steam turbine'-type vanes were added to direct the gunfire blast upwards away from the inlet.

This set of modifications was evaluated by NATC using BuNo 129553 (No. 47) in BIS armament trials in mid-1954. BuNo 129640, which incorporated additional

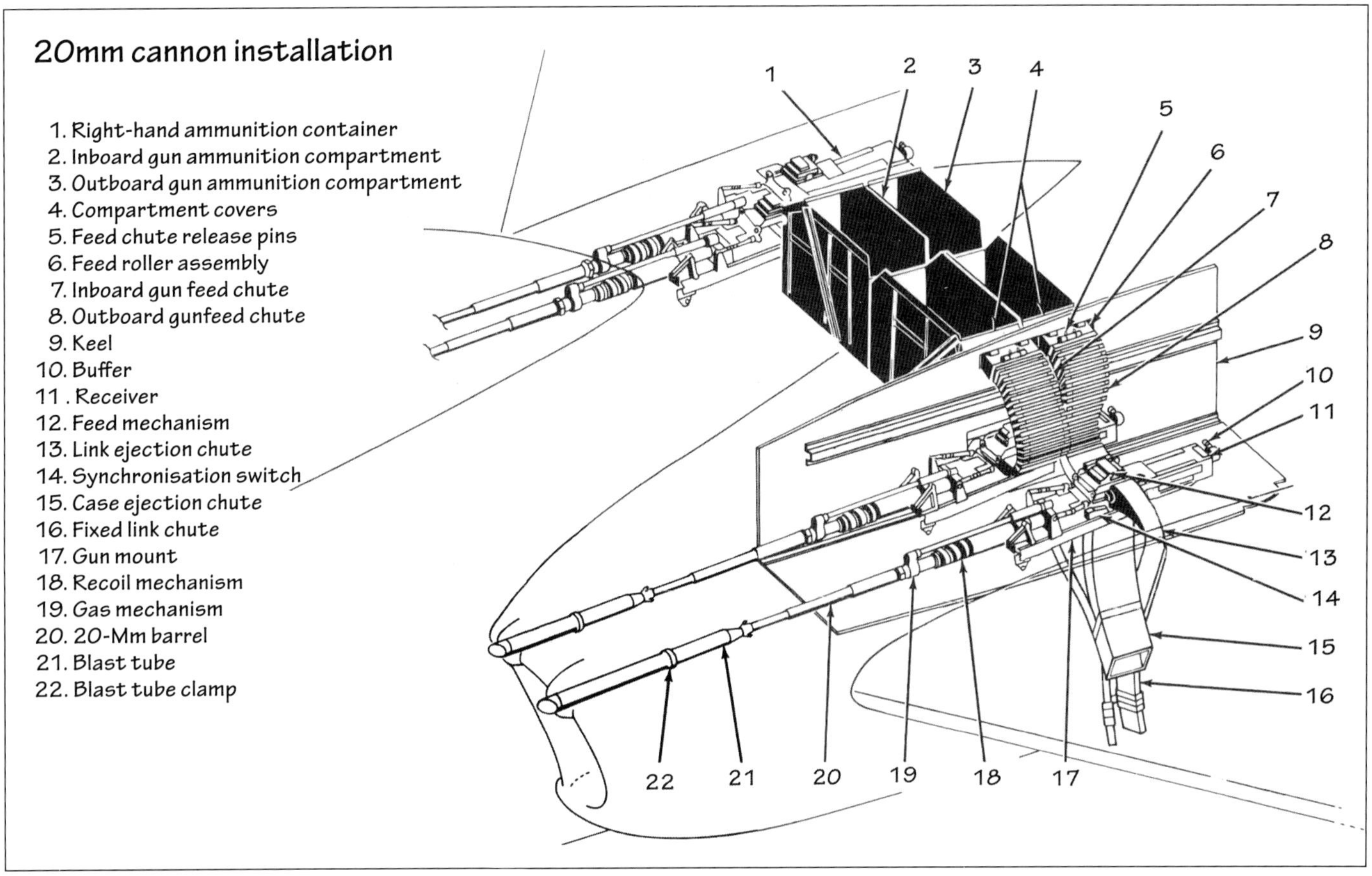

ABOVE After development of the 20mm cannon installation was complete, only the location of the cannon and the ammunition compartments remained unchanged. *Thomason*

LEFT F7U-3 BuNo 129553 was photographed on 28 May 1954 while assigned to the Armament Test Division at NATC. It incorporates all but the final engine inlet modifications and is carrying the belly-mounted rocket pack unique to the Cutlass. *US Navy*

installation modifications, was delivered to NATC on 30 May 1954.

The muzzle modifications did not completely resolve the gunfire-induced engine compressor stall and over-temperature, so Vought resorted to reducing the compressor sensitivity to gun gas ingestion: when the pilot pulled the trigger to fire the guns, the RPM of the engines was immediately reduced by 5% for six seconds after the trigger was released. At the same time, the engine trim system would also keep the exhaust nozzle open to prevent a compressor stall. While it was effective, it also reduced engine thrust by 15 to 20%, causing an unacceptable deceleration, and was not effective in eliminating engine over-temperature at altitudes below 10,000ft. Fortunately a fix for the latter shortcoming, developed by future

F7U-3 20mm cannon muzzle development

Original muzzle fairings in extended inlet upper lip (J:35 engines and therefore no boundary layer splitter)

Laterally scarfed blast tube openings in extended inlet upper lip but lip cut back below muzzle fairings (J:35 engines; gun bay-vent test bed)

Nozzle fairing cut back with laterally scarfed blast tubes and addition of "chimney" vent behind each muzzle (J46 engines with final gun bay venting and case/link jettison provisions)

Inboard

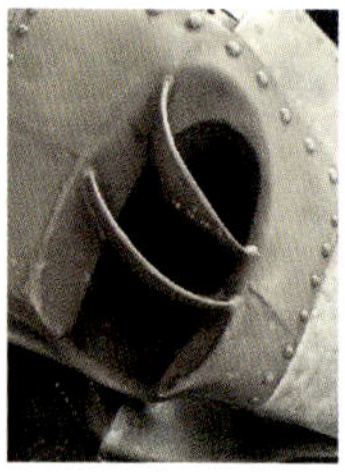

Outboard

Left hand muzzles

Replaced laterally scarfed blast tubes and chimney vents with longitudinally scarfed blast tubes cut back to inlet lip; added "steam-nozzle" turning vanes

Final muzzle configuration: Added troughs over blast tubes and gun barrels to minimize inlet ingestion of gun gases at all altitudes (the troughs are different lengths because the cannons are staggered by the width ofthe ammo boxes)

A Vought mechanic poses with the F7U-3 rocket pack that could be mounted on the belly of the Cutlass and loaded with thirty-two 2.75in folding-fin rockets. The exit door is open, exposing the tubes the rockets were loaded into. The mechanic's right hand is at the side of the row of openings for the exhaust of the forward rockets' blast. ***VAHF***

astronaut John Glenn at VX-3, was successful. It reduced the shockwave effect on an inlet when both guns on that side fired simultaneously by providing an electrical pulse to each gun on alternate sides at a frequency of approximately 16 pulses per second to desynchronise the firing of a pair of guns. It also reduced canopy buffet during firing. In late 1954, evaluation of the system proved that it alone solved the engine compressor stall and over-temperature, allowing the undesirable thrust-reduction kludge to be deleted. However, engine over-temperature and compressor stalls were still likely above 35,000ft, which was acceptable for training but not for combat.

The final blast tube modification increased the altitude for firing the cannon to 45,000ft, just in time for modification of VF-124 Cutlasses that would make the first F7U-3 deployment. It included the addition of a trough just above and outboard of each cannon barrel that created a negative pressure and funnelled off the gun gases. After an evaluation was accomplished on BuNo 129654, BuAer approved the contractors ECP 400, 'Gun Blast Port – Redesign of (Trough Type)' in March 1955.

The BIS report noted that air-to-air gunnery tracking was satisfactory to Mach 0.88 but affected by directional trim change with speed; acceptable to Mach 0.94 but with nose-down trim changes and decreasing pitch control effectiveness with increasing speed; unusable from Mach 0.95 to 0.97 for tracking purposes (but still usable for maintaining position advantage or disengagement) due to directional instability; and then acceptable again to the limit Mach number of 1.08. Some modification of the standard pursuit curve attack was required above 20,000ft for effective tracking in order to not exceed the F7U-3's relatively low buffet limits and the need for large 'elevator' deflections to increase *g*s that caused deceleration.

Air-to-ground strafing was judged to be accurate with no adverse pendulum effect noted due to the depressed sight line (the guns were mounted at a 3½-degree downward angle), which was beneficial in avoiding a tendency to steepen the dive angle.

Rockets

Vought addressed the lack of pylons to carry more than two of the standard multi-shot 2.75in folding-fin rocket pods (and thereby preclude the use of external fuel tanks) by designing a bespoke rocket pack that could be attached to the F7U-3's broad flat belly. It was loaded with thirty-two of the rockets in sixteen tubes, two rockets in line per tube. An exit door opened at the front of the pod when rockets were fired. Openings were provided just aft of both the forward and aft rockets to relieve the heat and pressure within the pack

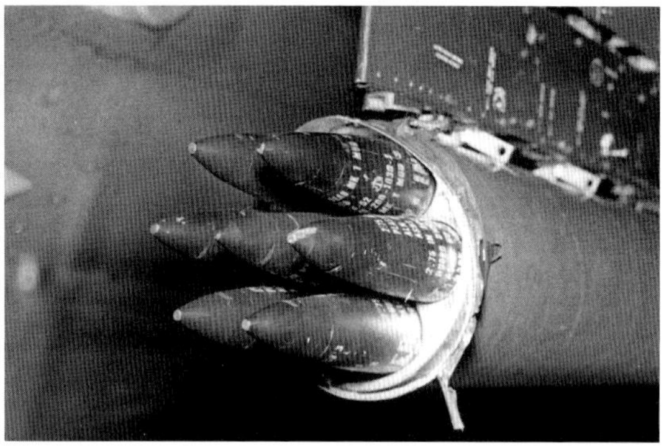

Vought also conducted flight test evaluation of the standard rocket pods like this AERO 6A loaded with seven 2.75in folding-fin rockets. *VAHF*

when they were fired. The pilot could fire groups of eight or sixteen rockets or salvo all thirty-two.

In contrast to the unsatisfactory results initially with firing the cannon and lengthy redesign and test effort to resolve problems, the qualification of the rocket pack required relatively little redesign and modification. In October 1953, Vought test pilot Joseph Angelone ferried BuNo 128463 (No. 13) to the Naval Ordnance Test Station, Inyokern, California, for an initial evaluation and demonstration. It was instrumented with eight 16mm movie cameras; four air-to-ground and eight air-to-air flights were accomplished. Only minor changes to the pack were required. After the usual corrections were made to the yaw and angle of attack data provided to the Mk 16 fire control system, accuracy, both air-to-ground and air-to-air, was satisfactory. The kill probability of a thirty-two-rocket salvo fired at a non-manoeuvring B-47-size target at 500 yards was estimated (no B-47s were harmed) to be 97%, primarily because only one or two hits might be enough. Accuracy was reported to be within 5 mils (30ft at 2,000 yards). Highlights included firing all thirty-two rockets in the pack in only 0.6 seconds compared to the contract specification of no more than 0.75 seconds.

However, additional testing with an F7U-3 powered by J46s was required due to the potential flow differences with the production nose/canopy/inlets and possible susceptibility of the J46 to rocket or gun gas ingestion. In August 1954, Angelone returned to Inyokern with the No. 17 F7U-3, BuNo 128467, the first production Cutlass with the J46 engines installed. He demonstrated air-to-ground rocket attacks from 4,500 to 6,000ft range at speeds of up to 575 knots. During his second series of tests, Angelone hit the K-17 camera installed in the centre of a 150ft ground target dead centre – considered to be an almost impossible feat at the time. He commented that during his wartime service flying P-47s, he 'only achieved one hit with 5-inch rockets using a ring sight. However, in the F7U-3 I had achieved an overall success rate of 87 percent.' He fired more than 1,000 rockets during this demonstration phase, recording over 60,000ft of high-speed movie film for review and analysis. He also got 25% hits firing the cannon at a towed banner, although he hadn't done any air-to-air gunnery since the Second World War.

Minor changes to the rocket pack were subsequently required as a result of the BIS evaluation and initial squadron utilisation. These included modification of the aft blast doors and removal of the forward blast doors to improve the exhaust of burned gases, installation of stainless steel sheeting over the rear rocket tubes to reduce the possibility of a rear rocket penetrating the engine bay or cockpit area if fired into a jammed front rocket, and reinforcement of internal webs of the rocket pack fore and aft spars to prevent excessive internal damage and burning of adjacent tubes.

As a result, the BIS armament test report stated that 'rocket pack performance during these trials has been outstanding and a considerable improvement over contemporary packs now in service. Extremes of speed, altitude, acceleration, and firing selection do not appear to appreciably affect pack performance and the effect of the rocket pack on aircraft performance is negligible.'

Further, NATC reported, 'The airplane is considered an excellent rocket platform with no adverse effects apparent with release of any of the rockets. In dives of 30 degrees or more and slant ranges of less than 3,000 feet, firing is essentially pipper to target with no lead allowance necessary. It is considered entirely feasible to fire both guns and rockets simultaneously during an air-to-ground attack.'

Nuclear weapons

By January 1952, two types of relatively small and light nuclear bombs had been qualified and were being stockpiled. The Mk 7 was a spherical implosion-type device, which meant it was relatively large in diameter. The Mk 8 was a gun-type device, smaller but much heavier, of interest to the Navy because it could withstand the shock of hitting the ground or water at a high incidence angle and speed, making it effective against submarine pens and ships/submarines. The subsequent improvements were the Mk 11, replacing the Mk 8, and the Mk 12, which was notably lighter and smaller than the Mk 7.

The availability of these bombs that could be carried by single-seat tactical jets resulted in a new technique to deliver them, a high-speed (500 knots), low-altitude (100ft) run-in followed by a 4*g* pull-up. The subsequent release of the bomb caused it to go high and/or far, allowing time for the pilot to reverse course and speed away before it detonated. To provide more accuracy for this loft-type delivery, he was provided with the Low Altitude Bombing System (LABS). It consisted of 1) a simple instrument with vertical and horizontal needles, the former to keep him straight in the pull-up and the latter to maintain 4*g* in the process, and 2) a timer to be activated over an obvious reference point relative to the target to let him know when to start the pull-up (it also released the bomb at the right moment after the start of the pull-up for it to hit the target).

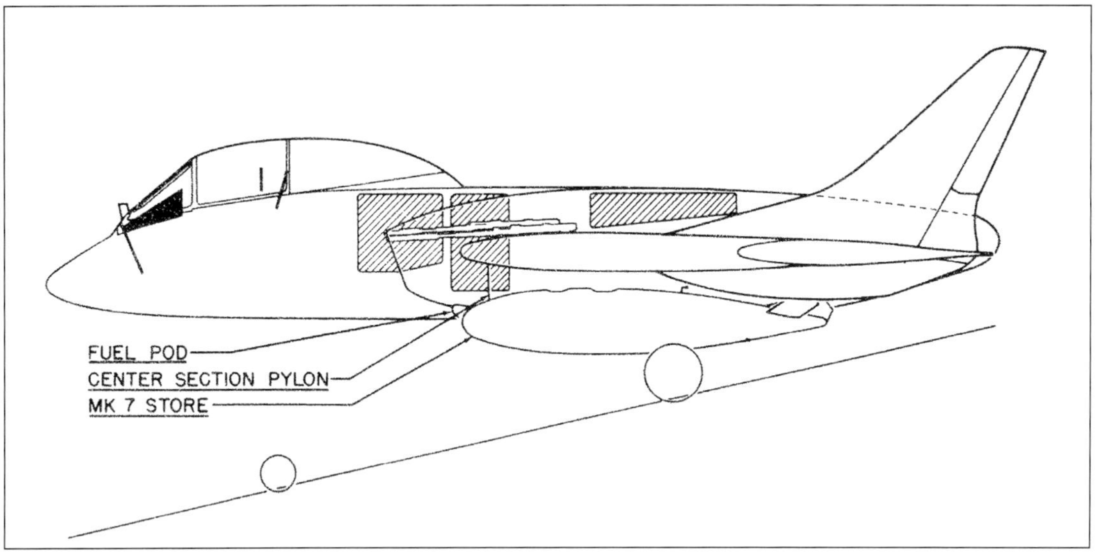

LEFT As it happened, one benefit of the F7U-3 size and configuration was that the big Mk 7 could be loaded on its existing stores pylon with no need for gimmicks like the F2H Banshee landing gear extension. *US Navy*

Service Acceptance Trials of special (i.e. nuclear) weapons were accomplished at the Naval Air Special Weapons Facility (NASWF) at Kirtland Air Force Base, Albuquerque, New Mexico. Between 6 May and 7 July 1953, Vought test pilots satisfactorily demonstrated separation of special stores shapes with BuNo 128462 (No. 12). Several airframe-mounted cameras were used to record them. There were four test conditions: dive with speed brakes open, dive with speed brakes closed, toss with speed brakes closed, and a lob (a high-speed, low-altitude run-in followed by a 4*g* pull up and store release). Four different shapes were evaluated: Marks 7 (all conditions), 8 (dive and lob conditions), 11 (dive only), and 12 (lob, toss, and high Mach number). One

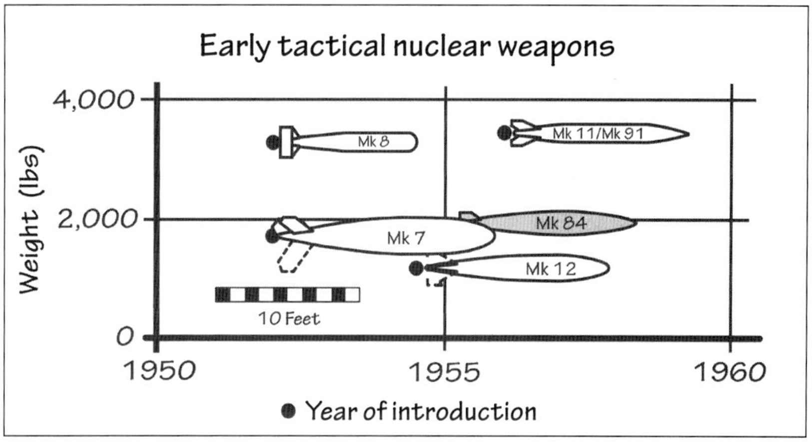

ABOVE The Mk 84, a conventional 2,000lb non-nuclear bomb, is provided to illustrate the difference in size of the 'special' weapons. *Thomason*

A TX-11 (Mk 91 shape) had just been released from an F7U-3 during this China Lake evaluation flight on 7 April 1955. *US Navy via China Lake Alumni*

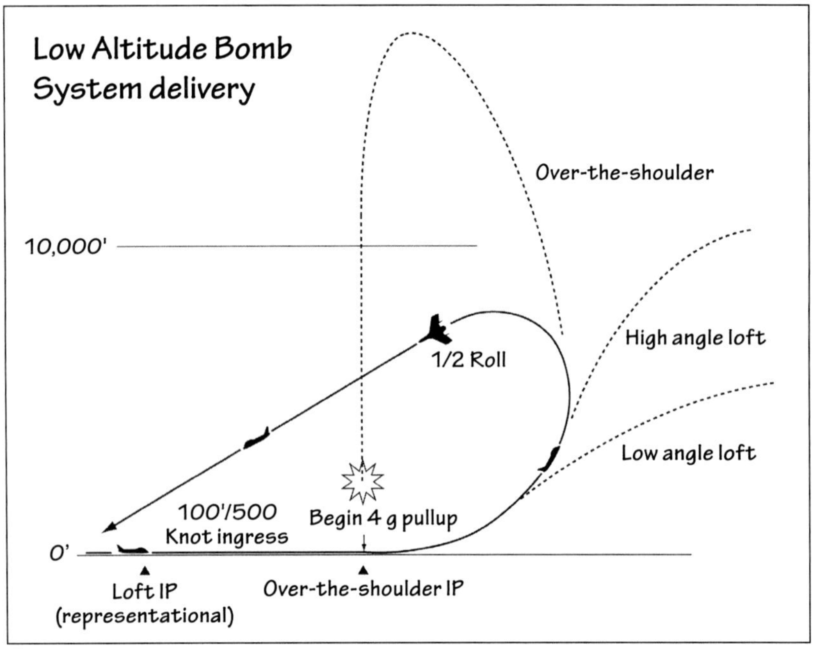

ABOVE **One of three different bomb delivery profiles could be preselected for LABS employment.** ***Thomason***

BELOW **LABS provision was added to F7U-3 BuNo 129545 and subsequent aircraft after incorporation of ASC 7 (ECP 223). It provided pull-up guidance to the pilot for the selected delivery type and automatically released the store.** ***US Navy***

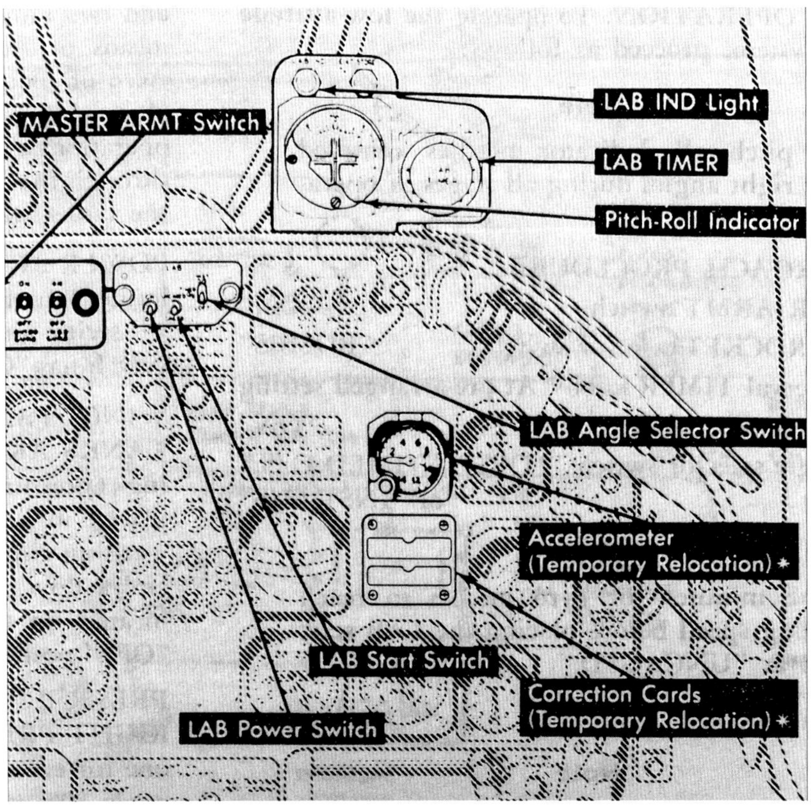

highlight was the separation of a Mk 12 shape at 24,460ft in a 47-degree dive at Mach 1.01, believed by Vought to be the first supersonic release of any type of bomb from any aircraft. The pylon used was representative of the one added to the twenty-nineth and subsequent F7U-3s. No weight was required on the pylon on the opposite wing. The accuracy of the drops was not part of the demonstration: a separation was considered satisfactory if the release conditions were attained, the operation of all equipment was normal, there was no damage to the delivery aircraft, and there were no abnormalities in the trajectory of the store after release.

BuNo 129546 arrived at NASWF on 23 April 1954 and was used for the remainder of the evaluation, which was primarily loading and fit tests of the special weapons and then flight test to evaluate the handling qualities during weapon delivery, verify proper function of the in-flight bomb control and monitoring equipment, and check the performance data provided in the Pilots Handbook. The final report stated: 'It is concluded that the Special Weapons Installation is satisfactory and that the F7U-3 can successfully carry and deliver the Mk 7, Mk 8, Mk 91, and Mk 12 atomic weapons.'

The F7U-3 was better suited for special weapons delivery than the Navy's other fighters at the time that were modified to carry nuclear bombs. Its high ground clearance required no added complexity for landing gear extension or bomb-fin retraction. Its afterburner thrust minimised the loss of speed in the pull-up for the release of the store and increased its distance from the target after its release. Maintaining the exact speed for accuracy during the time-critical run-in was accomplished by having one engine in afterburner and the other modulated below military thrust.

Conventional Bombing

NATC evaluated all modes of bomb delivery including dive, dive toss, lob (horizontal loft) and over the shoulder with all classes of conventional bombs to 2,000lb. The G-4 yaw and pitch damper unit was required on all dives because of the change in directional trim with speed and the possibility of initiating a longitudinal oscillation during pull out. Visibility of the target during a bombing run was considered excellent and it was easily tracked. Lateral control was considered excellent throughout all the bombing runs, including high-speed run-ins to the push-over point. All stores were carried to an indicated airspeed of 550 knots at 1,000ft pressure altitude and in accelerations between 0 and +6 *g*s. Anti-fogging, a concern during dives beginning at 28,000ft, was good, with fogging of the canopy and windshield being quickly and easily cleared by the use of the defog switch. In summary, the report stated: 'The F7U-3 is considered an excellent platform for both medium altitude (12,000ft and below) and high altitude (20,000ft and above) entry bombing runs.'

F7U-3 BuNo 129545 was photographed at NAS Patuxent River on 13 October 1954 (but still assigned to BAR R&D Dallas) while loaded with two 1,000lb GP bombs with T-143 fins, the predecessor of the low-drag Douglas shapes. Note that the nose gear scissors link is disconnected for towing. *US Navy*

BuNo 128454 was loaded with two 1,000lb GP bombs for flight 116 in September 1952. *VAHF*

CHAPTER TWELVE

F7U-3M

The US Navy began initial research into air-to-air guided missiles in 1946 after fleet defence studies indicated it was the most effective way to shoot down jet bombers. The so-called beam-riding Sparrow I was the first successful one. Its rearward-facing antennas detected a radar transmission, the beam, aimed by the pilot of an interceptor at an enemy aircraft; its flight control system adjusted its control fins so as to track within the beam to the target.

Testing of what was to become the Sparrow I commenced as 'Project Hot-Shot' in 1947 at the Naval Air Missile Test Center (NAMTC), Pt Mugu, CA, in co-ordination with Naval Ordnance Test Station (NOTS) Inyokern, CA. The Sperry Gyroscope Company of Great Neck, NY, was given the responsibility for the overall system development and was also chosen as the prime contractor for both the missile (the airframe was subcontracted to Douglas Aircraft, the die-formed stabilisation fins to Kaiser Aluminum) and the guidance system. The company's team arrived at NAMTC in late 1947, achieving the air launch of over 100 prototypes between 1948 and 1951. Grumman F6F Hellcats and F7F Tigercats were initially used as launch platforms. A pre-production example of the 12½ft long, 300lb missile was tested successfully on 2 April 1951.

The 1,500mph AAM-N-2 – as it was officially designated – was unveiled to the press on 12 May 1954 at Sperry's newly built missile manufacturing facility in Bristol, Tennessee. The first pre-production demonstration 'kill' occurred on 18 June 1954. However, Bureau of Ordnance (BuOrd) fleet evaluations held in conjunction with Bureau of Aeronautics demonstrations were delayed until 6 April 1955 due to Pacific test area clearance delays. After that, NAMTC test bed aircraft, including Douglas F3D Skyknights, successfully downed both USN Regulus I and USAF Matador target missiles, as well as various remotely controlled aircraft throughout the autumn of 1955. In November 1955, for a demonstration to the Chief of Naval Operations, Admiral Arleigh Burke, NAMTC fired a Sparrow I from F7U-3M BuNo 129700. RADM John E. Clark, the Navy's Director of Guided Missiles, declared subsequently: 'In ten short years, our scientists and engineers

An F7U-3M in flight armed with two test Sparrow Is. The belly-mounted fuel pod has been modified with camera ports for photo documentation of the missile launch. ***US Navy***

produced guided missiles of amazing performance and reliability.'

A fighter armed with air-to-air guided missiles needed to be big. Four Sparrow Is and their launch pylons weighed almost 1,700lb in total; the electronics (radar and missile control system), another 800lb or so, significantly more weight than a day fighter's range-only radar and gunsight, not to mention the volume needed for it within the airframe. The F3D Skyknight was selected to be the Navy's initial missile-armed fighter. It was a two-place, carrier-based, all-weather fighter for which development had begun in the late 1940s. While a handful of Sparrow-armed F3D-2Ms became operational, flown by two shore-based Marine Corps squadrons, the Skyknight with its big straight wing and lack of afterburners did not have the desired climb and speed performance that the Navy believed was required for the fleet air defence requirement. It was also not big enough to lug around an additional 1,000lb of 20mm cannon and ammunition that the Navy wanted as a back-up to the air-to-air missiles.

The Navy had planned to procure a variant of the McDonnell F3H-1 Demon for this mission. However, the F3H programme fell behind schedule and was in danger of cancellation because of ongoing qualification problems with its Westinghouse J40 engine. The decision to switch over to the Allison J71 for production aircraft further delayed the Demon's availability. That opened a window of opportunity for Chance Vought's F7U-3, since only a fighter of that size could carry aloft the weight of the radar, missile control system, and four Sparrows and their launch pylons as well as the standard 20mm cannon armament (the only other possibility, the Grumman F10F Jaguar, was even more behind schedule than the F3H and would soon be cancelled).

The F7U-3M would be provided with the newly developed AERO 10E armament control system that utilised the Sperry APQ-51 radar and be armed with four Sparrow Is, two on launchers on the existing inboard wing hard points and two on pylons added back on each outer wing panel. In partial compensation for the drag of the Sparrows, fuel cells with a 124-gallon capacity were added within each outer wing panel. Take-off gross weight increased to almost 35,000lb when the aircraft was launched with four Sparrows and the 220-gallon belly-mounted fuel pod. Even then, mission endurance was still only one hour and twenty-three minutes, assuming a few minutes of afterburner usage, less than preferred for the carrier operating cycle.

Vought received a change request from BuAer on 24 March 1953 for modification of one F7U-3 to be an F7U-3M prototype, as well as the construction of an initial production lot of thirty-five F7U-3Ms. The number of prototypes created from F7U-3s was subsequently increased to two; the seventy-third and seventy-fourth aircraft in the F7U-3 production

ABOVE The F3D Skyknight was featured in a 1954 Sperry advertisement launching a Sparrow I at an enemy bomber. *Thomason Collection*

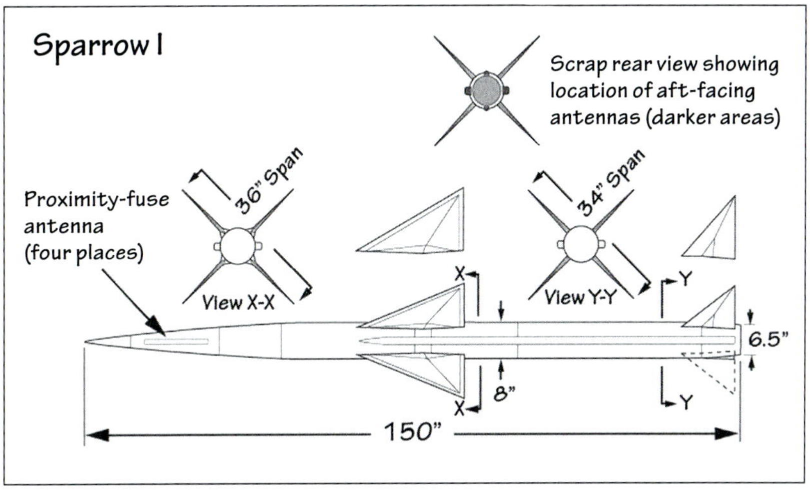

The Skyknight was the first Sparrow-armed fighter assigned to operational units, albeit shore-based Marine Corps squadrons like this VMF(aw)-542 F3D-2M. The 20mm cannon were deleted to reduce weight. *Paul Bless Collection*

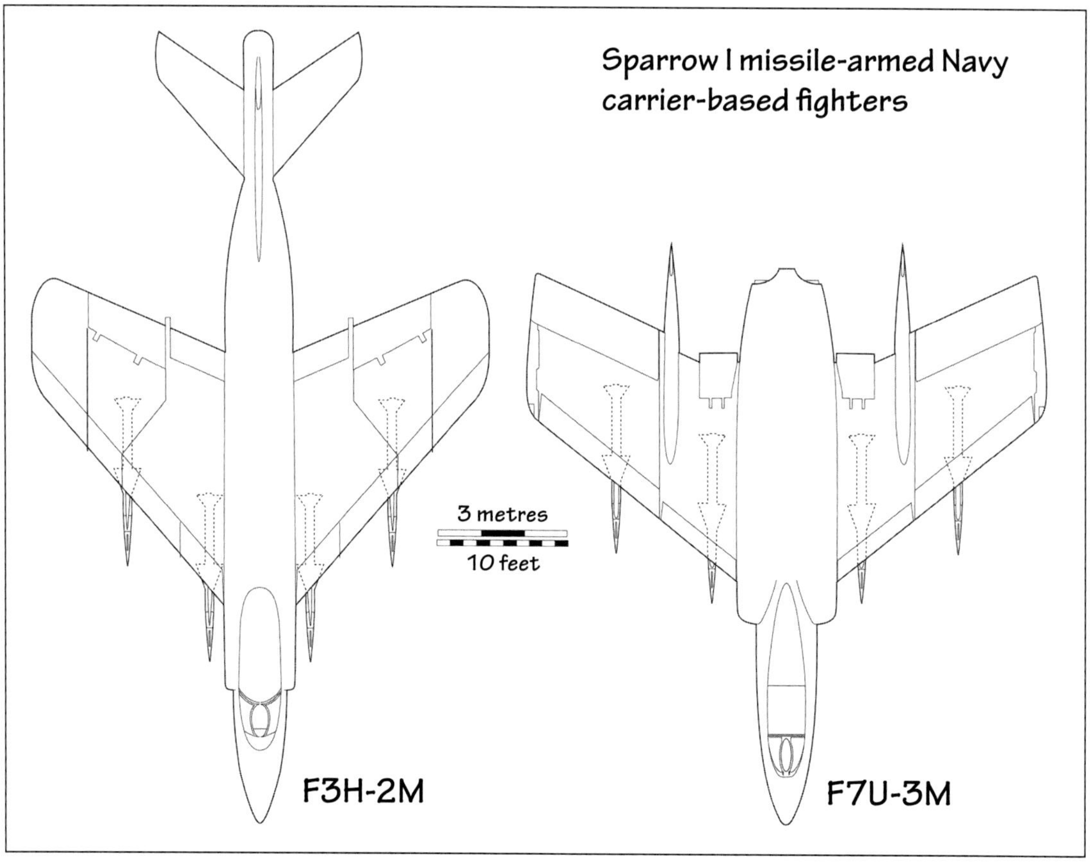

It took a big aircraft to carry four Sparrow air-to-air missiles and the fire control system to aim them. *Thomason*

sequence, BuNo's 129589 and 129590. A total of ninety-eight production F7U-3Ms were eventually delivered.

Although it was equipped with a missile-control radar, the F7U-3M was not, strictly speaking, an all-weather fighter because BuAer decided not to provide the pilot with a radarscope that enabled him to locate a bogey on his own in poor visibility conditions and, moreover, make it more likely that he would 'see' it in any event. He therefore had to rely on a fighter director (either on board a ship or in an airborne early warning aircraft) to provide vectors to bring him within sight of the bogey.

The design work was completed in late 1953 with CVA test pilot Jack Walton accomplishing the initial flight of the first F7U-3M prototype, BuNo 129589, on 12 July 1954. However, while production of -3Ms was proceeding apace, the J46 engine shortage meant that the first production F7U-3M, BuNo 129677, could only be provisionally accepted on 20 August 1954. It was subsequently completed and delivered to the Naval Air Missile Test Center on 16 December. The next production F7U-3M, BuNo 129700, was flight accepted at Vought on 30 December 1954, after which completion of several more F7U-3M 'gliders' was accomplished rapidly. The Navy's Pt Mugu-based VX-4 received its first F7U-3M, BuNo 129701, for test and evaluation with the Sparrow I missile on 26 January 1955.

ABOVE Adding the AERO 10E's radar to the nose of the F7U-3M precluded the incorporation of the F7U-3 in-flight refuelling probe kit. ***National Archives 80-G-669157***

BELOW F7U-3 BuNo 129589 (pictured here) and 129590 were converted to the F7U-3M configuration for initial flight test and evaluation. ***VAHF***

ABOVE **VX-4 pilot LT Walter M. Earley Jr. delivered F7U-3M 129701 to VX-4 at NAS Point Mugu in January 1955, fresh from training and a check out at Vought.** ***US Navy***

BELOW **F7U-3M BuNo 129700 loaded with two Sparrow Is taxiing out from Pt Mugu for a test flight. A belly-mounted fuel tank has been modified with two forward-facing movie camera ports to record the fly-out trajectory of the missiles.** ***US Navy***

The F7U-3M's Sparrow I was a short-range missile in practice, not because of the 8-mile range of the missile itself, but because the guidance beam 1) widened with distance and the missile tended to snake within the beam rather than maintaining a straight course down the centre of it, the deviations increasing with distance from the Cutlass and 2) was not necessarily pointed directly at the target.The system determined the range to the target through the echo pulses of the high-frequency energy emitted by the narrow beam emanating from the antenna and also provided range for the gunsight system like the APG-30 in the F7U-3 (indeed, when the pilot fired his cannon, it was capable of tracking and ranging the 20mm slugs outbound until they dropped below the radar's energy beam). A green Lock-On Indicator light would illuminate when the target was acquired and ranged successfully.

Because the Cutlass pilot was not provided with a radar scope, instead of selecting a blip himself for the fire control system to track, he had to first visually acquire a target, aim his aircraft directly at it using his gunsight, and then identify it as one he should shoot at, for example by comparing the readout on his Range Search Indicator to the fighter director's estimate of his distance to the bogey.

Once the pilot was visually tracking the target and had reduced the distance to it to a maximum of about 6nm, the radar could lock on to it and be switched to a conical scan that enabled it to automatically track the target through a relatively narrow +/- 7 degree limit, providing guidance to the Sparrow.

When in track mode, the panel-mounted Antenna Position Indicator displayed the radar antenna's aim point with respect to the gunsight's 'line of sight'. It was critical that the pilot not only manoeuvre as required to keep the antenna within its ability to track the target but

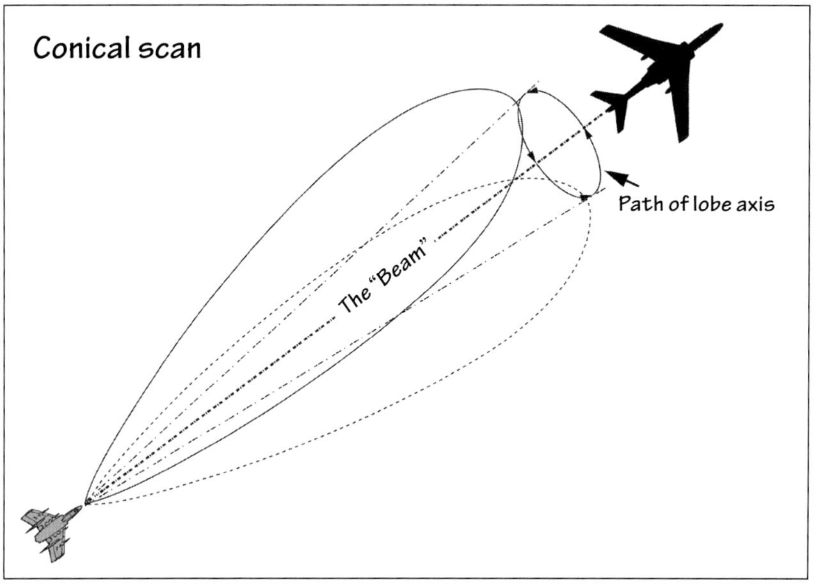

also keep the missile within the limits of the conical scan because if it 'lost' the beam there was no way for it to regain it. Maintaining that tracking angularity within the prescribed limits, even when attacking from the rear, also meant that neither the pilot nor the target should manoeuvre much, preferably not at all. An abeam attack was the least likely to be successful as it required the beam to be moved constantly to bear on the target. A head-on attack was problematical because maximum lock-on distance was about 6 miles; with closing speeds in the order of 1,000 knots, there was only a few seconds available to lock on and fire the missile in time for it to arm before it reached the target.

If the pilot was satisfied that the system could track the target within its limitations during the flight of the missile, he fired while continuing to keep the Cutlass pointed at the target. The missile's rocket motor would only burn for two seconds after leaving its launcher rail (about 3ft long rather than zero length to ensure that the missile went the way it was aimed initially in order to capture the beam) but the Sparrow would still attain a terminal velocity between Mach 2 and 3 depending on altitude. During this initial stage of the launch, the missile was unguided, but kept flying straight by its own stabilisation system. The Sparrow launch rails were angled slightly inboard to ensure that the missile, after motor burnout, would be within the beam emitted by the radar and thus be guided while it 'glided' unpowered to the target. If the missile did not pick up the beam or lost its guidance pulses thereafter, it was designed to destroy itself within two seconds.

TOP LEFT The pilot of the F7U-3M did not have a visual-assist radar presentation. He made do with these two instruments, one which provided the range (in yards) to the target and the other that depicted the position of that target with respect to his gun sight bore sight. ***US Navy***

TOP RIGHT The conical scan for automatic target tracking and the creation of a beam that the Sparrow I could follow involved the rotation of the radar antenna in a small circle. The radar used the relative position of the target within the scan to recentre the beam on it; the missile determined its location by reference to the lobe as it rotated to determine which way to turn to stay within the beam. ***Thomason***

ABOVE A bench test of the F7U-3M's missile control system avionics and gunsight at NAS Pt Mugu in July 1955. ***NA 80-G- 669163***

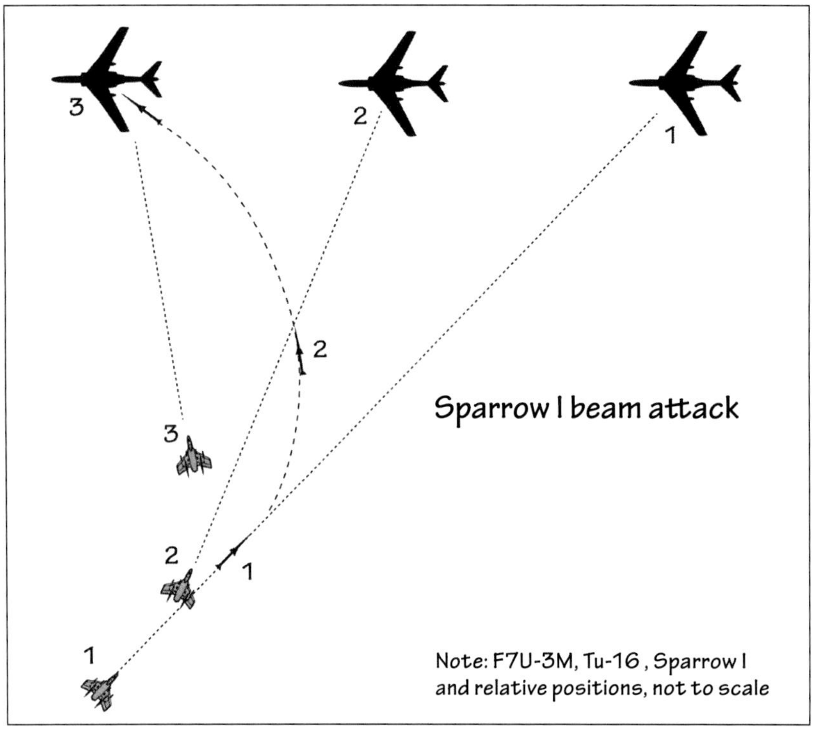

If all went well, following the rocket motor burnout the Sparrow would be within the beam (and as importantly, not passing through it at much of an angle) so the missile's control system could switch to beam guidance. Even with a Mach 2+ initial speed, however, the Sparrow took several seconds to get to the target, which under the visual conditions that had to prevail for an F7U-3M pilot to employ it meant that the target's crew, e.g. the tail gunner, or wing men had to ignore the initial plume of smoke headed their way and not call for evasive action. As a result, the missile could be guiding perfectly but miss if the target was able to make an abrupt and significant enough change in heading or altitude that exceeded the attacking aircraft's tracking and/or the missile's manoeuvre capability. The missile might also miss if in the process of snaking back and forth in order to stay within the beam, it happened to be on the far side of it relative to the target and therefore not close enough to trigger its proximity fuse. (On the other hand, at long ranges when the beam was much larger and not necessarily centred on the target, by happenstance the missile might still be passing by it close enough to detonate.

ABOVE **A beam attack would likely exceed the Sparrow's ability to turn at the rate necessary to stay within the radar beam.** ***Thomason***

The Sparrow I rocket motor only fired for two seconds but it produced an enormous plume of smoke while accelerating the missile to Mach 2+. Note that the launch rail was angled slightly inboard so the missile flew into the 'beam' that it used for guidance. The picture was taken by the pilot of an F7U-3P flying in trail. ***US Navy***

This actually happened during one Sparrow I test; the missile was tracking the beam erratically but zagged at just the right time to pass near enough to the target drone for a kill.) Nevertheless, the Sparrow I was demonstrated to be effective when employed against a target drone maintaining a constant heading and altitude during early testing and system qualification that was managed by BuOrd.

Vought and BuAer may have thought that the similarity of the F7U-3M to the F7U-3 would result in a relatively quick carrier suitability demonstration. If so, they would be disappointed. The *Coral Sea* trials in late 1952 proved that the 1951 removal of all-weather mission equipment had been overly conservative from a launch weight standpoint. The increase in landing weight attributable to the missile control system, the added pylons and launch rails, the additional internal fuel capacity, and four Sparrows was apparently considered to be acceptable based on the same carrier trials. With respect to the mission, fleet air defence with long-range air-to-air guided missiles, maximum speed and rate of climb performance may not have been considered critical. As a result, there was no need to increase the thrust available. In any event, the admirals wanted to deploy the Sparrow I as soon as it was qualified; replacing the J46 would delay the F7U-3M introduction by two or three years, which was when the F3H-2M might finally be deployable.

Better is often the enemy of good enough. However, in this case, the military-rated thrust of the J46 was not always adequate for an F7U-3M pilot making a traditional low, level approach to a cut for a carrier landing. While the weight might have been acceptable, the extra drag of missile pylons and certainly the missiles themselves was apparently not taken into consideration. Fortunately, two more British innovations in carrier operations, the angled flight deck and the mirror landing system, became available on US carriers. They resulted in acceptable landing approaches at higher weights. Westinghouse and Vought were also able to tweak the engine and inlet respectively to provide more thrust at approach speed.

The start of at-sea qualification on the west coast aboard *Shangri-La* (CVA-38), newly equipped with an angled deck, was originally scheduled for late May 1955. NATC test pilot LT John Long, who had been assigned to accomplish it, crashed F7U-3M BuNo 129699 on landing at NAS Dallas on 13 May while ferrying it from Patuxent River to San Diego. He was low on a turning approach to a short final and touched down just before the beginning of the runway, which tore off part of the left main landing gear. The aircraft continued down the runway and sheared off all three of its landing gears when it departed the paved surface travelling almost completely backwards, leaving LT Long with a serious back injury.

The angled-deck concept allowed an aircraft to take off again if it wasn't stopped by the arresting gear rather than being ruthlessly (and hopefully) brought to a stop by the barriers and barricade before reaching the crewmen and aircraft farther forward on the deck. ***US Navy***

Another NATC pilot, LT John Moore, replaced him, arriving at Vought a few days later to make his acquaintance there with F7U-3M BuNo 129736. Moore was familiar with the F7U-3, having been involved in *Project Steam*, as well as maximum sink rate testing of the Cutlass at Patuxent River. His initial evaluation of the F7U-3M during his acceptance of it at the Vought plant adjacent to NAS Dallas was unpromising, as he wrote in his biography, *The Wrong Stuff*:

> While making my (flat carrier-type) approach from the 180 about 100 feet above the rooftops, and at an acceptable approach speed, i.e. 135 knots, I found that I was at full Military Rated Thrust (MRT) trying to maintain airspeed. It was not enough. At the 90 in a lovely approach, my airspeed was rapidly decreasing to such an extent that I went into afterburner to accelerate out of the Dallas Econo Lodge. Once up to 150 knots, I resumed the simulated carrier approach, finding myself at MRT again just to stay airborne. The landing was uneventful, it turned out. I made four more approaches and landings, according to my logbook, and each time I was forced to use afterburner to make it around the pattern. It was troubling.

What was worse, afterburner thrust couldn't be modulated as originally planned: it was either on or off. This resulted in the likelihood of over-correction in addition to the possibility that the afterburner would not light off when needed, not only not adding thrust but if the nozzle had opened as required for maximum afterburner thrust, reducing it.

Nevertheless, Moore ferried 736 out to San Diego for their rendezvous with *Shangri-La*. The F7U-3M was hoisted aboard in late May 1955. Shipboard evaluations were accomplished between 27 and 30 May 1955. After additional FCLP work, he elected to increase the approach speed to 155 knots (since the approach was being made

Initial at-sea testing with F7U-3M BuNo 129736 was accomplished aboard *Shangri-La* in May and June 1955. *US Navy*

on the backside of the power curve, a higher approach speed reduced the thrust required for level flight). Additional at-sea trials were then accomplished between 8 and 11 June. The approaches were made with the equivalent weight of cannon and full ammunition as well as four Sparrow Is along with the fuel that resulted in a landing gross weight of 26,000–27,000lb.

The test report dated 19 July 1955 stated, 'At gross weights between 25,000lb and 26,000lb, the margin of thrust available over thrust required becomes critical. At gross weights above 26,000lb the thrust required in the approach turn may exceed that available at full military thrust in angles of bank greater than 30°.' Also, 'Should the airspeed drop as much as 5 kts below the desired approach speed, the pilot must be prepared to use (afterburner) on either one or both engines to recover the desired approach speed.'

Although the F7U-3 carrier suitability evaluation had found it acceptable for carrier landings at up to 24,500lb gross weight, the significant increase in drag from the two additional pylons and the Sparrows resulted in the F7U-3M in being unacceptable for fleet operations at gross weights greater than 23,000lb. The standard reserve on return to the carrier (twenty minutes at sea level at maximum endurance speed plus 5% of initial fuel) of about 2,000lb for the F7U meant that landing back with all four of the big and expensive Sparrows and a full load of 20mm ammunition resulted in a landing weight of at least 25,000lb, probably requiring afterburner on approach when returning back aboard on a 72°F day.

The restriction to 23,000lb turned out to be a revelation to senior NATC pilots, who subsequently agreed after essaying the existing low, level approach in the F7U-3M at higher gross weights themselves: 'Rough air, stack wash, or inadvertent over-rotation could cause dangerous approach situations' because getting low and/or slow was all too likely and recovery too reliant on the use of afterburning. It also caused consternation in BuAer. As Moore humorously put it in his book, 'The Bureau-crats were unified at being horrified: they had ordered ninety-eight of these mothers and were being told that they could not go aboard ship. Chance Vought was horrified that the Bureau was horrified. The world's largest conference outside of the United Nations was thereby convened at Flight Test, Pax River, with the ever-smooth "Duke" Windsor deftly moderating this menagerie.'

The prospective solution was to re-evaluate the F7U-3M using the mirror-landing system that the British had created along with the angled flight deck. Instead of utilising the 'flat' approach technique to ensure touchdown among the arresting wires, it provided guidance to the pilot for a constant speed and rate of descent approach

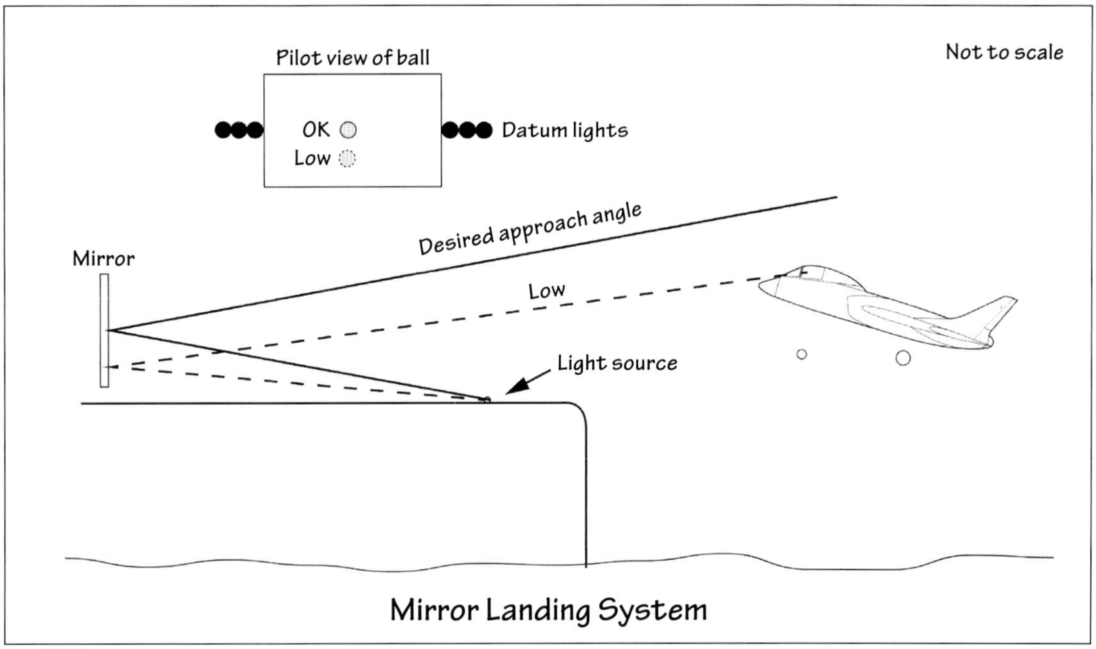

Because the angle of incidence and reflection in a mirror are equal, a pilot who is below the desired approach path will see the reflection of the fixed light, aka ball, below the centre of the mirror. *Thomason*

to a no-flare touchdown there. The mirror reflected a bright light located well aft of it. If the pilot approached at the desired speed and rate of descent, the light (termed the ball) would be centred vertically in the mirror at the same level as the datum lights on either side of it. If the pilot was too high, the light rose above the centre of the mirror, directing the pilot to increase his rate of descent. Too low, and the ball sank. The position of the ball was visible from farther out than the LSO signals, resulting in an earlier opportunity for the pilot to set up for the approach.

US Navy pilots attending the Empire Test Pilot School in England had made approaches guided by the mirror system in November 1953 at the Royal Aeronautical Establishment, Farnborough, England. Their enthusiastic recommendation for its adoption by the US Navy resulted. After evaluation aboard US carriers, begun with *Bennington* (CVA-20) in August 1955, OpNav directed in November that all angled-deck carriers were to have mirror landing systems.

The accuracy of the touchdown point relied on a carrier-based aircraft's heavy-duty landing gear; instead

The production mirror landing system installed on *Lexington* (CVA-16) for its deployment in 1956. *NA 80-G-1027729*

The view of an axial deck on approach versus that of an angled deck. At this time the *Bennington* (CVA-20) had both port and starboard mirrors for the initial evaluation; the port location of the mirror was subsequently selected as being preferable. The photo on the right was taken from a VX-3 F7U-3P that was slightly above the glide path. *Thomason*

of a potentially misjudged flare intended to provide a gentle touchdown, the pilot simply maintained a constant rate of descent all the way down to the deck as guided by the ball. The no-flare touchdown also eliminated the need for sudden and precise stick position changes following the flat approach's throttle 'cut' necessary to control the aircraft's pitch attitude while descending so the touchdown was on the main landing gear in the landing area among the wires. In fact, the LSO would admonish a pilot even suspected of anticipating the touchdown – 'spotting the deck' – and flaring to soften it.

The likelihood of a crash was further reduced by the angled deck in conjunction with the mirror system since there was still the possibility of missing all the wires due to the deck heaving or pitching away at the wrong moment, a hook skip, a late or inadequate correction by the pilot back to the glide slope, etc. In that case, instead of winding up in the barrier and/or barricade, the pilot simply took off again (a 'bolter') for another attempt.

The descending approach was particularly beneficial in the case of the F7U-3M because it required less

The first at-sea evaluation of the mirror landing system by VX-3 included BuNo 129752 F7U-3P (XC 02) flown by LTs James P. Buckner and John H. Cover. *USN 680156 via Casby*

A VX-4 F7U-3M armed with two Sparrow Is and carrying a refuelling pod modified with a camera makes a descending approach to CVA-16 in April 1956. *US Navy*

thrust than the flat approach and therefore provided more thrust margin. If the pilot got low, i.e. below the indicated glide slope, instead of having to transition to a climb, which was problematical (even more so if he was also slow and did not add throttle before aft stick), he only had to add enough thrust to reduce his rate of descent until he reached the glide slope. The descending approach also provided more over-the-nose visibility. Afterburner would not be required except possibly for a late wave off or a single-engine approach.

However, at that time the mirror-landing system was just then undergoing preliminary evaluation by the US Navy. CDR Robert G. Dose, flying a VX-3 FJ-3, made the first 'official' US Navy at-sea landing using the prototype system when he came aboard *Bennington* (CVA-20) on 22 August 1955. At least one VX-3 F7U-3P was also involved in the evaluation, taking pilot-eye pictures of the approach using its forward-facing camera.

In June 1955, while waiting for a carrier equipped with a mirror-landing system to become available for an evaluation of the descending approach with the F7U-3M, Moore and BuNo 129736 were assigned to trials of an improved arresting gear system that was being tested ashore at NAS Patuxent River. It malfunctioned, bringing the F7U-3M to a virtually instantaneous stop and causing the nose gear to collapse. The Cutlass had to be written off but Moore was not seriously hurt.

Furnishing the replacement, YF7U-3M BuNo 139868, only delayed resumption of carrier suitability testing for a few weeks but qualification eventually required at-sea trials on four different carriers between mid-September 1955 and mid-January 1956 in order to finally clear the F7U-3M for carrier operations. The first, aboard *Ticonderoga* (CVA-14), ended prematurely after four landings due to buckling of the nose gear actuator support structure when landing at a weight of 26,300lb. Ominously, while Moore was endeavouring to complete F7U-3M carrier qualification, also aboard for carrier suitability evaluation were early production examples of aircraft that would soon supplant it: an F4D Skyray (still painted overall blue), A4D-1 Skyhawk, and F3H-2N Demon.

The next at-sea evaluation, after an initial shore-based one in late September using a portable forklift-mounted mirror system set up at NAAS Mayport, Florida, was therefore scheduled aboard *Shangri-La* in late October 1955 back out on the west coast. (*Bennington* had already departed from Mayport, Florida, for a western Pacific deployment on 8 September.) Unfortunately the conditions were decidedly not pacific and the portable mirror was not gyro-stabilised. As Moore wrote, 'the mirror on the forklift was of little use on the pitching deck given to us by the Pacific Ocean. In two days, I made 29 approaches and 25 landings including 19 touch-and-goes and 6 traps using the mirror as a glide-slope starting point, since with the deck going up and down, the mirror might as well have been in the wardroom.'

These first trials with a descending approach guided by the mirror system were promising, with one landing

Vought determined that an extension of the lower side of the engine inlet – aka Ubangi Lip – would avoid an existing decrease in maximum thrust due to the higher angle of attack at speeds below 125 knots, where maximum thrust was critical to recovering from being slow on approach. ***US Navy***

accomplished at 25,000lb. In the meantime, Vought and Westinghouse were evaluating engine modifications to increase the military thrust of the -8 and -8B engines so that afterburning would be required less frequently on approach. One was to allow an increase in the turbine inlet temperature to 1,600°F for short periods of time. Another was to modify the afterburner flame holders to reduce their restriction on basic engine thrust. Modified engines were installed in F7U-3M BuNo 129705, which had been bailed to Vought in May 1955 for flight testing. NATC pilots subsequently determined that the modifications added about 350lb to the total military thrust. Vought also developed a modified engine intake on BuNo 129698. It had an extended lower inlet lip, which precluded a decrease in maximum thrust below 125 knots due to an increase in duct losses as the angle of attack increased and therefore provided a bit more margin if the aircraft became low and/or slow on approach (it was also determined in a Pax River evaluation to reduce the incidence of engine foreign object damage that had been experienced ashore at Atsugi and Port Lyautey, the Western Pacific and Mediterranean Naval Air Stations from which F7Us operated frequently).

Brief at-sea trials with BuNo 139868 were accomplished aboard *Intrepid* (CVA-11) in early January 1956 and *Forrestal* (CVA-59) in mid-January 1956, which concluded the testing. However, in its report on F7U-3M carrier suitability trials dated 19 March 1956, NATC recommended that the model F7U-3M aircraft be restricted from carrier operations until the following unacceptable items were corrected:

- High rate of fuel consumption in conjunction with limited landing fuel reserve imposed by landing gross weight limitations.
- Insufficient margin of thrust available over thrust required for a standard carrier approach.
- Static thrust variation of 680lb between different F7U-3M/3/3P aircraft at MRT.
- Design of the nose gear actuating-cylinder attaching structure.
- Deck-crew actuation of the hydraulic starting by-pass valve (a safety hazard).

Further, the F7U-3M was restricted to a landing weight of 24,000lb when flown from axial-deck carriers using a flat approach to a cut.

The formal NATC report was days from being issued when *Intrepid* (CVA-11), still an axial deck carrier, departed for the Mediterranean on 12 March 1956 with VA-83's Sparrow I-armed F7U-3Ms in its air group. It would be the first carrier deployment of guided-missile-equipped fleet-defence fighters. It did not go well. Even before the deployment began, there were six incidents, including three runway excursions, a total loss of hydraulics with the pilot ejecting, an engine failure culminating in the first ditching of an F7U-3, and a barrier crash during carrier qualifications. The deployment itself began badly with a nose gear collapse due to the failure of the drag link for which a beef-up was available but not yet incorporated in that Cutlass. Another was lost as a result of an electrical failure during launch: the pilot had to eject. Nevertheless, VA-83 continued to provide four-plane detachments aboard *Intrepid* during the deployment.

All subsequent F7U-3M deployments were from angled-deck carriers. NATC raised the maximum arrested landing gross weight of the F7U-3M to 25,300lb when 'using a mirror-type approach under landing signal officer control' and the incorporation of engine thrust improvements and nose landing gear beef-ups.

As it turned out, the Sparrow I-armed McDonnell F3H-2M programme only lagged that of the F7U-3M by a year or so. The prototype F3H-2M flew for the first time on 23 August 1955, a year later than the F7U-3M. The next major milestone, delivery to the Naval Air Missile Test Center at NAS Point Mugu, California, also lagged the F7U-3M by only a year. VF-61 was the first to take the F3H-2M to sea in September 1957 for a shakedown cruise aboard *Saratoga* (CVA-60), only eighteen months after VA-83 deployed aboard *Intrepid*. Unlike the F7U-3M, the F3H-2M had a radar scope, a really big one, in the cockpit. While this still required that its pilot close to within visual range to guide the Sparrow I, the scope allowed him to get into position to do so on his own rather than rely completely on a fighter director.

According to the respective Standard Aircraft Characteristics charts, the underpowered F7U-3M was also inferior to the F3H-2M from a performance standpoint in almost every way (and the F3H was considered to be underpowered by the changing expectations at the time, with the nickname 'lead sled'). However, the most significant and downright damning F7U-3M shortcoming was its range and endurance.

In late 1955, BuAer chose to go forward for missile-armed fleet air defence solely with the Sparrow III. It had become apparent that it was significantly better than the Sparrow I: it guided on the fighter's radar emissions

ABOVE F3H-2M BuNo 137037 fresh off the McDonnell assembly line with the build number still on the vertical fin. ***US Navy***

LEFT The F3H instrument panel was dominated by a large radar scope with a glare-reduction hood. ***Don Hinton***

	F7U-3M (1)		F3H-2M (2)
	Internal fuel	+ Fuel pod	
Take-off weight* (lb)	32,974	34,704	33,112
Combat weight** (lb)	27,522	28,710	27,859
Combat thrust to weight	42%	40%	52%
Combat speed/altitude (kts/ft) @CRT	543/23,750	541/22,300	558/31,500
Combat ceiling (ft) @CRT	44,400	42,800	47,800
Combat radius/mission time (nm/hr)	160/1.15	205/1.39	388/2.2
Sea Level to 30,000 ft @MRT (minutes)	32.4	N/A	13.3
ROC (fpm) @combat weight/altitude/thrust	5,680	5,370	5,500

* Four Sparrows
** Sparrows expended
(1) F7U-3M SAC dated 15 May 1955
(2) F3H-2M SAC dated 15 May 1955

reflected from the target (semi-active radar homing), which made it much more likely to hit it – the accuracy increased as the Sparrow III closed on the target rather than decreasing like the Sparrow I's. More importantly, the pilot didn't need to see the target to shoot it down and could therefore fire one at a much longer range and with more latitude as to relative target heading.

It was first to be employed on the McDonnell F3H-2, which first flew in 1956. As a result, McDonnell only built eighty Sparrow I-armed F3H-2Ms. Only a handful of operational squadrons were equipped with them and fewer deployed. When the F3H-2 was ready for deployment beginning in 1957, it replaced the F3H-2M and F4Ds. The F7U-3Ms were replaced by A4D-1s and FJ-4Bs consistent with their assignment to attack squadrons.

Nevertheless, starting with VA-83's F7U-3M missile-laden *Intrepid* deployment in 1956, and ending with VA-116's in September 1957 on *Hancock*, the F7U-3M paved the way for future advancements toward achieving the US Navy's goal of employing guided missiles as the primary armament system for fleet air defence.

CHAPTER THIRTEEN

1955 – Deployments begin

Although 1955 began badly with the loss of two F7U-3s at VC-3 in post-stall-gyration incidents, Vought had been able to promptly address that problem to the Navy's satisfaction. Much more significant was the urgent need to modify the aircraft in VC-3 and the first three deployable squadrons (VF-81, VF-83, and VF-124) to correct unacceptable or undesirable deficiencies identified during the service acceptance tests. Modifications continued to be added to the list that existed at the end of 1954. For example, in March 1955, BuAer approved the final corrective action for engine over-temperatures and compressor stall due to gun firing. Aircraft Service Change (ASC) No. 134 reinforced the arresting hook dashpot support assembly. ASC No. 79 added a fuel sump pump to the gravity feed line from the aft fuselage fuel cell to increase the amount of fuel when the aircraft was in a nose-high, e.g. landing, attitude.

The formal Board of Inspection and Survey evaluation of the F7U-3 had begun with the delivery of J35-powered BuNo 128454 (No. 4) to NATC in July 1952 for initial carrier suitability trials. Several more Cutlasses would follow and be assigned to the test divisions at NATC and other test agencies for evaluations that would be documented in the following trials reports:

Vought created a test stand that would place the F7U-3 at its extreme nose-up and down angles for fuel system calibration and CG determination. ***VAHF***

- Armament
- Carrier Suitability
- Aircraft and Engine Performance
- Stability and Control
- Electrical and Electronic
- Service Suitability

By the end of 1954, almost all of the required F7U-3 testing had been completed and reports issued. It should be noted that the Navy evaluators were responsible for determining whether an aircraft met contractual requirements and more importantly, was 'acceptable for service use' by pilots and maintainers. As a result, the reports focused heavily on problems, disappointments, and shortcomings. In accordance with the process, BuAer would receive early feedback and periodic status reports that would be provided to the aircraft and GFE manufacturers, who would develop modifications and improvements that corrected or at least alleviated the unsuitable characteristics and then propose them to BuAer for incorporation in production. Sometimes these changes could be incorporated in the aircraft assigned to BIS but often were not.

The Board report on the F7U-3 Service Acceptance Trials provided to the Secretary of the Navy in March 1955 was more critical than would have been expected from some of the interim reports:

> *The completion was delayed far beyond the time normally required for a day fighter. The most significant were:*
>
> - *Two years elapsed between the delivery of the first and last test aircraft.*
> - *Two basically different configurations, one J35 powered and the other J46, required duplication of much of the test flying. Only one J46-powered Cutlass had been delivered to NATC by the end of 1953. About 18 Cutlasses, far more than the usual number of airplanes assigned to BIS, were used in the trials including two flown at the Navy's Special Weapons Facility.*
> - *Periodic grounding and lack of spare parts: one J46-powered F7U-3 was grounded for cause or lack of parts for a total of 80 days during the seven months it was assigned to Service Suitability.*
> - *Low availability for test due to excessive and difficult maintenance requirements.*
>
> *An evaluation of the F7U-3 airplane shows little to recommend it for service use in comparison with other Navy fighter aircraft currently being delivered. Flight handling characteristics are generally acceptable although they deteriorate sharply beyond a limiting tactical Mach number of 0.92, which is low by present tactical standards.*

One example of a duplicative but still worthwhile evaluation was the accelerated service test of this J35-powered F7U-3, BuNo 128461 (No. 11) prior to the availability of J46-powered production Cutlasses. ***Gary Asher***

> *The radius of action of approximately 138 miles is unsatisfactorily low. Gains in performance by use of the engine afterburners are limited in time at low altitudes and result in markedly reduced range and endurance.*
>
> *The F7U-3 is satisfactory as a bombing, rocket, or strafing platform and as a gun platform up to Mach 0.92. The complicated systems and poor accessibility of the airplane result in excessive maintenance requirements and probably will result in below average combat availability for fleet units to be equipped with the F7U-3. The physical size of the airplane, its difficult deck handling characteristics, coupled with probable low availability will hamper the flexibility of an air group in which it is incorporated. The F7U-3 airplane does not appear to be an aircraft suitable for full employment as a day fighter nor, because of its limited range and endurance, a satisfactory fighter attack airplane.*

In contrast, the preliminary Service Suitability and Tactical Trials evaluation dated 10 July 1954 – accomplished with BuNo 129554 (No. 38) – had stated:

> The F7U-3 *without afterburner* [emphasis added] has a low combat ceiling, low rate of climb, low maximum level flight speed, short combat radius, and a low single-engine service ceiling. The F7U-3 airplane performance with the engines in afterburner is *very much improved* [emphasis added]. The combat ceiling with afterburner is increased from 35,000 feet to 45,000 feet and the time to climb to 35,000 feet is reduced from 27 to 7 minutes, while the fuel used is approximately the same. The time to climb and the fuel used to 45,000 feet in afterburner is 10 minutes and 3700 pounds. The Vmax at 35,000 feet is increased by afterburner operation from .83 IMN to .92 IMN.

With respect to manoeuvrability, the report stated that the F7U-3 had better high Mach characteristics than the FJ-2 and the F9F-6 type aircraft and could better these two types in air-to-air combat as well as better climb performance and acceleration when using its afterburners. In tracking trials at Mach 0.85 and higher with the lead aircraft making level flight and descending turns pulling maximum tolerable *g*, the buffet boundaries and turning radii were approximately the same but the F7U-3 had a higher rate of roll and more excess thrust when in afterburner, giving it the advantage.

The report concluded: 'The F7U-3 will be a satisfactory interim interceptor and will be a satisfactory medium-altitude, medium-speed attack plane when equipped for in-flight refueling or with external fuel.'

The final Performance report provided with the March 1955 letter to the Secretary of the Navy as an attachment also stated that none of the guarantees with the J46-WE-8 engines were met by the F7U-3 as tested:

	Guarantee	Test result
Weight empty (lb)	16,513	18,130
Maximum speed* (kts)	557	505
Stall speed, power off** (kts)	111.5	116
Take-off rate of climb*** (fpm)	1,650	1,110
Service ceiling**** (ft)	38,400	34,450

* Military thrust, combat load
** Sea level, landing gear and flaps extended
*** Maximum thrust, 95°F day, catapult end speed 115 kts, landing gear and flaps extended
**** Normal thrust, Combat load

Failure to meet guarantees, however, was not unusual. Not mentioned was the fact that problems identified in initial BIS testing – structure, systems, engine, etc. – were being corrected. BuAer, in its comments on the final BIS report, also noted that the deficient performance could 'be attributed directly to the many modification and additions required to make the F7U-3 aircraft satisfactory from the standpoint of mechanical reliability and handling characteristics'. Some examples cited were:

- Increased thickness of the trailing edge ailavator to eliminate marginal response at high Mach number pullouts.
- Cutting off the lower fin stubs to reduce the damage to the fin by the cross-deck pendant during arrested landings.
- Installation of an unfaired arresting hook, essential for reliability.
- Allowance for a larger magnitude of cooling airflow due to initial underestimate.
- Addition of miscellaneous vents and masts.

BuAer also pushed back on the BIS conclusions by documenting additional changes that were being made in the F7Us to be delivered to operational squadrons. For example, the rocket pack was repurposed to be an early example of a low-drag conformal external fuel tank, the engine problems with gun gas ingestion were virtually eliminated, development was in work at Westinghouse to increase thrust and reduce fuel consumption, etc.

In a letter to the Secretary of the Navy dated 20 September 1955, the Chief of Naval Operations, ADM W.L. Rees, split the difference, formally concurring with the final BIS report and recommending its approval. He, however, also accepted the F7U-3 for service use, noting that: 'Despite the F7U-3 aircraft's poor competitive position as a day fighter – largely attributable to its inordinately long development time and deficient performance – it has limited capability as a carrier-based jet special weapons delivery vehicle and it partially fills an urgent need now.' He stated that BuAer had completed appropriate action to ensure the correction of reported deficiencies 'where feasible and practical'. A reduction in contract price for the uncorrected deficiencies in contract guarantees that were clearly the contractor's responsibility was to be negotiated.

The phrase 'its inordinately long development time' seems a bit unfair except when using the first flight of the XF7U-1, a day fighter, as a starting point rather than the first flight of the F7U-3, similar in appearance but very different otherwise. If development time is considered to be the months between the F7U-3's first flight and delivery to the first operational squadron, the Cutlass was delivered quicker than improved versions of the Grumman F9F Cougar and the North American FJ Fury measured from the first flights of the F9F-6 and XFJ-2, which were minimal conversions of the proven F9F-5 Panther and F-86 Sabre respectively:

Type	F9F-6/8	FJ-2/3	F7U-3
Months	36	32	28

Even when evaluated against the other transonic fighters that the Navy had initiated in the late 1940s and based on the first flight of the XF7U-1, the F7U-3 does not fair badly from the standpoint of months from first flight to delivery to an operational squadron:

Type	F10F	F4D	F3H	F7U-3
Months	Never	62	55	67*

* *Including* Vought's lock, stock, and barrel move from Connecticut to Texas and a four-month F7U-3 programme timeout.

In a lengthy 21 October 1955 letter to BuAer, Vought's President, F.O. Detweiler responded to a BuAer letter dated 30 August 1955 requesting a price reduction for the first twenty-eight F7U-3s and the subsequent 150. He opened by stating that most of the deficiencies other than performance identified in BIS testing had been corrected and that he could therefore not agree that the F7U-3 was 'marginally acceptable for interim use only as a carrier-based day fighter'. His rebuttal quoted many favourable statements in the Final BIS Conference Report of F7U-3 Service Acceptance Trials:

- In general, the cockpit is roomy, comfortable, and well arranged.
- To eject, the pilot has only to pull the face curtain, which performs all pre-ejection procedures and fires the seat.
- Forward and side visibility is excellent.
- The instrument panel is concave, giving the pilot an excellent panoramic view of all instruments.
- No annoying windshield or canopy reflections were observed during night operations.
- The taxi characteristics are satisfactory.
- Vision during taxiing is excellent.
- The airplane is satisfactory for crosswind take-off and landings.
- There is no possibility of over-rotating on take-off in the fighter configuration … The stick can be held full back against the stop on take-off, and since the elevators do not pitch the aircraft up beyond the angle of attack of CL max, the airplane becomes airborne and climbs out.
- The high landing attitude is not bothersome on the initial landings if the airplane is flown at the proper speeds.
- Rudders and rudder trim are effective in handling the yaw associated with asymmetric flight.
- The airplane, because of high angle of attack, decelerates very satisfactorily on the landing roll-out.
- There is a slight nose-up trim when the landing gear is raised and a more pronounced nose-down trim change when it is lowered. Neither of these trim changes is objectionable.
- Speed brake effectiveness is excellent, better than any of the current Navy fighter airplanes. There is no trim change associated with either opening or closing. However, when they are opened at high speeds, a mild rudder buffet is felt.
- The high Mach characteristics are good when compared to the FJ-2 and F9F-6.
- Slow speed characteristics are good.
- A major advantage in the J46 type engine is that there is no lag in thrust response to throttle movements.
- The airplane makes excellent field carrier passes.
- The F7U-3 has good night flying characteristics.
- The F7U-3 possesses satisfactory all-weather flying characteristics.
- GCA approaches pose no particular problems and require average instrument flying ability
- Live rocket and bombing runs were made using dive angles from 15 to 60 degrees and at speeds up to 480 knots. Throughout the entire range tested the F7U-3 is considered a good rocket and bomb platform.
- The airplane is considered a satisfactory gun platform for strafing.

A major issue in the report was the excessive maintenance requirements and low reliability of a Service Test Cutlass, BuNo 128461. LT Don B. Shelton, who was assigned to Service Test at NATC, had given the F7U-3 his thumbs down from the standpoint of availability. His preliminary report, submitted after his reassignment and departure to *Project Cutlass* in January 1954, stated that the fleet would be unable to satisfactorily maintain the F7U-3. He reportedly received a lot of pressure from higher command to change the report but he refused and was backed up in that regard by CDR Heber Badger, NATC's Director of Flight Test at the time. In response, Detweiler noted that the Service Test report – based on the more representative six-aircraft Fleet Introduction Programme – had resulted in 8.6 maintenance man hours per flight hour, which closely approximated recent Fleet squadron experience with the F7U-3.

Another major F7U-3 operational problem mentioned was the low combat radius (the combat radius without external fuel in accordance with the MIL-C-5011A general-purpose fighter mission had been 355nm; it was now approximately half that). Detweiler placed the majority of the blame for the decrease on Westinghouse (higher SFC – 105nm) and BuAer (the 1951 reduction in fuel capacity – 40nm). He accepted that 38nm of the decrease was due to an increase in drag but that it was 'due to configuration changes made to improve the airplane or to correct deficiencies' acknowledged by BuAer.

His letter also quoted complimentary ComAir Pac statements as of May 1955:

> In a comparison of special stores capabilities between the F2H-3 and the F7U-3, the continued use and deployment of the F7U-3 is justified by its own merits. The speeds attained during approach and retirement and during delivery of stores are particularly attractive for the F7U-3. This data was obtained from actual flights using one 150-gallon drop tank and a store. These flights also covered a useful radius of 325 to 375 nautical miles, depending on type of delivery, which could be extended 60 to 80 miles by carrying the fuel pod.
>
> The F7U-3 has a good outlook with respect to rocket pack and fire control system. A kill on a bomber is considered to be highly probable when firing within stated ranges. Maintenance of the armament control system is not considered

difficult. The Mark 12 gun installation is giving good service and a high percentage of fire-out has been experienced by the squadron. The Contractor notes that squadron fire-out percentages within both ComAirPac and ComAirLant have been better than the BIS Armament Test results.

Good reliability is predicted for the Phase II J46 engine and afterburner light-offs are reported as consistent up to 40,000 feet.

Control system difficulties have been experienced but are said to be not even close percentage-wise to those of the F9F-6, for example.

ComAirPac has no basis for concurring in the BIS opinion that 'the structural integrity of the airframe is poor' and says the airframe has been subjected to 6*g* negative and 12*g* positive without structural damage.

Maintenance of modernised aircraft is less than 10 man-hours per flight hour and is considered acceptable in comparison to other jet aircraft. *The squadron considered, VF-124, has only 20% experienced personnel with the other 80% being initially unfamiliar with the Cutlass.* [Emphasis added]

The post-stall gyration is not considered serious and is familiar to all pilots. After entering it inadvertently, Fleet pilots have effected recovery by using proper techniques.

Detweiller's letter went on to summarise a VX-3 report on F7U-3 range potential dated 19 July 1955:

Range extension of the F7U-3 aircraft in a stores configuration by employing air-to-air refueling is practicable and desirable. It was recommended that this be adopted as standard operating procedure.

The F7U-3 can make a dive delivery with a store at a radius of 350 nm using one 150-gallon drop tank.

The F7U-3 can be refuelled without difficulty in this configuration at altitudes ranging from 300 feet to 25,000 feet; the radius of 350 nm in the high-altitude problem can be extended to 660 nm with one refueling or to 1,225 nm with two. The radius of action of the AJ-2 tanker presently reduces this 1,225 nm radius capability of the F7U-3 to 1,100 nm.

The low-altitude (500ft) cruise radius in the above stores configuration can be extended from 215 nm to 500 nm with one refueling, utilising loft delivery and high-altitude return to base.

The F7U-3 in the clean condition can be refuelled in flight at 30,000 feet without difficulty. This clean-condition refueling would occur during the return phase of the mission.

As was common at the time, the unfavourable final BIS report was being overcome by events: the F7U-3 had already been delivered to three fighter squadrons, two of which would deploy later that year. However, the report might also have been reflecting the opinion of some senior Navy leaders that the Cutlass' bright future was behind it. As subsequent events would prove, BuAer was in the process of reducing its investment in the programme with an eye toward an early withdrawal in favour of the other alternatives it had for the day fighter, fleet air defence, attack, close air support, and nuclear strike missions.

In sharp contrast to the difficulties to be experienced by two of the first three squadrons equipped with the F7U-3, there were few concerns in the BIS reports about its carrier suitability, none significant. On 2 June 1955, the Board of Inspection and Survey officially cleared the F7U-3 for unrestricted shipboard operations subject to the incorporation of ASC No. 177 (e.g. the addition of barrier/barricade strap cutter on the nose gear and wing leading edge detents to engage the barricade straps as well as strengthening of the vertical fin leading edges) and No. 53, a redesigned nose gear barricade detent (see page 77). Prior to that, the Cutlass had been restricted to clear-deck operations until the NAMC barrier/barricade evaluation had been accomplished.

A rocky introduction in fleet squadrons

Unfortunately, the introduction of the F7U-3 in deployable squadrons revealed how a lack of standardisation and adequate pilot check out in new types could affect safety. NATC pilots (the best of the best) had no cause for concern with respect to landing it on a carrier. There had been only minor carrier landing incidents during carrier suitability testing or *Project Cutlass*. Nevertheless, there was increasing evidence that fleet pilots were not receiving adequate preparation for making carrier landings in the F7U-3 given its somewhat different handling qualities and lift/drag characteristics at low speed. Avoiding the very real hazard of being low and slow and concerned whether there was enough additional thrust to accelerate without losing altitude, some pilots tended to be high and/or fast. (Even though the aircraft wasn't high, it certainly looked that way from the pilot's viewpoint until he became accustomed to the location of his perch relative to the wheels.) What was worse, it appeared that the pilots in each squadron that received F7U-3s had to establish the proper technique the hard way, by experimentation.

Although VF-83 in November 1954 was the first deployable squadron to carrier qualify in the F7U-3 and had little difficulty doing so, the second, VF-81 experienced three landing accidents in two weeks between 21 March 1955 and 5 April aboard *Ticonderoga*

(CVA-14). Two were hard landings and one the result of the hook engaging a non-flush flash plate on the deck. After BuAer and Vought recommended minor adjustments to both pilot and LSO technique, the squadron qualified successfully with only one accident on the subsequent deployment (as VA-66), a nose gear collapse due to a miss-rigged barrier.

VF-124 was next, with three accidents between 14 July and 31 August on *Hancock* (CVA-19). The first was a horrific and fatal ramp strike, LCDR Jay Alkire's, prior to its deployment, followed by two more within three weeks after the deployment began. There was a second VF-124 landing accident resulting in a fatality, LTJG Milliard's, on 1 November (see page 309).

The degree of difficulty with carrier landing being demonstrated by fleet pilots was an unwelcome surprise to NATC and BuAer given BIS and *Project Cutlass* experience. In December 1955, BuAer's Ships Installation Division obtained the following carrier-landing accident statistics for the day-fighter fleet from the Navy's Aviation Safety Center for the period 1 July 1954 to 30 September 1955:

	Carrier landings	Accidents	Accidents/1,000 landings
FJ-2/3	2,264	5	2.2
F2H	24,920	48	1.93
F9F-2/5	17,289	55	3.18
F9F-6/8	25,609	107	4.18
F7U-3	886	6	6.77

Of the six F7U-3 accidents, one was fatal and two resulted in minor injuries. Five were the result of bad landings, including two ramp strikes, one of which was disastrous. As a result, the F7U-3 was gaining a reputation for being hard for fleet pilots to land on a carrier.

It is difficult to argue that it was unfair to compare a new aircraft's accident rate to those with many more landings because of the FJ-2/3 data: fewer accidents in spite of almost three times as many carrier landings. Moreover, the Cutlass accidents were considered to be more severe than the average. However, the preponderance of the FJ-2/3 carrier landings during this period were probably made by a single Marine Corps squadron flying FJ-2s led by a commanding officer who placed an emphasis on training and proficiency, e.g. at least one flight per day per pilot during his transition to the Fury.

In part based on this data and another fatal carrier landing accident, Milliard's on 1 November, BuAer's Ships Installations Division documented its concern about the F7U-3's carrier suitability:

> Increased gross weight – Changes in the airplane have admittedly resulted in a significant weight increase in the airplane. The minor changes directly resulting from carrier suitability deficiencies are not significant, however. Changes involved are the revised arresting hook snubber back-up structure and increased catapult holdback strength.
>
> Decreased engine thrust – The result has had a detrimental effect on the airplane's carrier suitability.
>
> Allowable margin for error during the launching and recovery evolutions – This is of primary concern in the carrier approach and landing, since by employing proper pilot technique and using the prescribed catapult launching pressure, wind-over-deck, and trim setting, the airplane can be launched with no undue hazard. In the approach the increased weight and decreased thrust make slight errors in airspeed, altitude, and power setting very critical in comparison with other contemporary aircraft models. By flying too slowly and/or with slightly insufficient power, the airplane can easily commence to settle. This is true of other carrier aircraft, but the hazard in the F7U-3 is that recovery from a slow, settling approach requires immediate application of combat power coupled with extra skilful flying by the pilot. Answering a 'high' or 'high dip' signal from the LSO must be met with an increase in thrust to halt the rate of descent and yet not lose or gain airspeed. This manoeuvre is true of other swept-wing aircraft, but again is not as critical in execution. Pilot landing technique is not unduly difficult, however, slight variations from the optimum result in rapid deterioration of any margin for error.

However, there would only be one more ramp strike (more like a ramp slap) in August 1956. It resulted in a bolter and a successful recovery. Moreover, not including that accident, there were only eight more carrier-landing accidents (one fatal) before Cutlass deployments ended in 1957. Three were the result of pilot error, three were caused by tail hook failures and one was due to a nose gear drag link failure because ASC 231 had not yet been incorporated. The cause for one is unknown but it was concluded with a successful recovery using the emergency barricade. While the number of F7U-3 carrier landings between 1 October 1955 and the end of deployments is not known, a rough estimate is that the F7U-3 carrier-landing major accident rate after 1 October 1955 was in the order of one per 1,000 hours. While that may seem high, it was not out of line with the Navy's average carrier-landing major accident rate in Fiscal Year 1957 was 0.97 per 1,000 landings and been higher, 1.75, the prior fiscal year, possibly related to a significant increase in the transition to jets and swept-wing jets in particular.

LCDR Jay Alkire's fatal ramp strike

No F7U-3 incident is used to justify the Cutlass' undeserved reputation as being dangerous more than LCDR Jay Alkire's horrific ramp strike on 14 July 1955. As was customary, enlisted movie and still photographers documented it from the island and the port-side catwalk. Contrary to uninformed speculation, the Navy's accident report clearly stated that it was a case of pilot error; second-hand accounts suggest that Alkire was an accident waiting to happen, given his limited experience flying from carriers combined with an apparent lack of concern about it.

The VF-124 pilots were qualifying on *Hancock* (CVA-19) in preparation for the first F7U-3 deployment. LCDR Alkire was flying F7U-3 BuNo 129595. He had accumulated almost 1,000 hours total flight time, most in multi-engine land-based aircraft as a patrol squadron (VP) pilot. As the new Executive Officer of VF-124, he had flown the Cutlass for 146 hours and made sixteen carrier landings with it. On his last flight, he had already made one approach and arrested landing. His second approach ended tragically.

According to the accident report, Mother Nature and *Hancock* were providing a total of 39 knots wind over deck. The sea was calm and the deck was steady, perfect conditions for trouble-free qualification. On this second approach, Alkire's F7U-3 was slightly above the maximum weight for an arrested landing with full main tanks and 1,600lb in the transfer system: it had been even heavier, about 500lb, on his first uneventful one. Upon reaching the groove (basically short final), the Cutlass 'was observed to settle to a "low and slow" flight condition'. The LSO, LT Ted Reilly, gave Alkire a series of low and come-on (you're too slow) signals, followed by a wave off when the pilot did not respond appropriately to them.

Because it had no horizontal tail and needed to approach on the backside of the power curve (also referred to as the region of reversed command) for a low landing speed, the F7U was somewhat less forgiving of imprecise piloting technique than the Navy's other

RIGHT The outstanding photographic documentation of Alkire's ramp strike was the work of PH2 Jim Binkley, who took the still pictures of the accident from the 07 level, while the still photos and movie footage taken from the port catwalk were recorded by PH2 Jerry White and PH2 Jack Hanson respectively. *US Navy*

BELOW This is what a good position after the cut from a flat approach to an axial deck looks like: the Cutlass is settling toward the deck after the LSO 'cut', on centreline, no yaw, wings close to level, and pitched up enough so the nose wheels do not touch first – and most if not all of the arresting wires are in play. *US Navy*

ABOVE The LSO, Ted Reilly, made a non-standard departure from the LSO platform to the starboard side of the flight deck when it became clear that the Cutlass was coming directly at him and going to sink below deck level. ***US Navy***

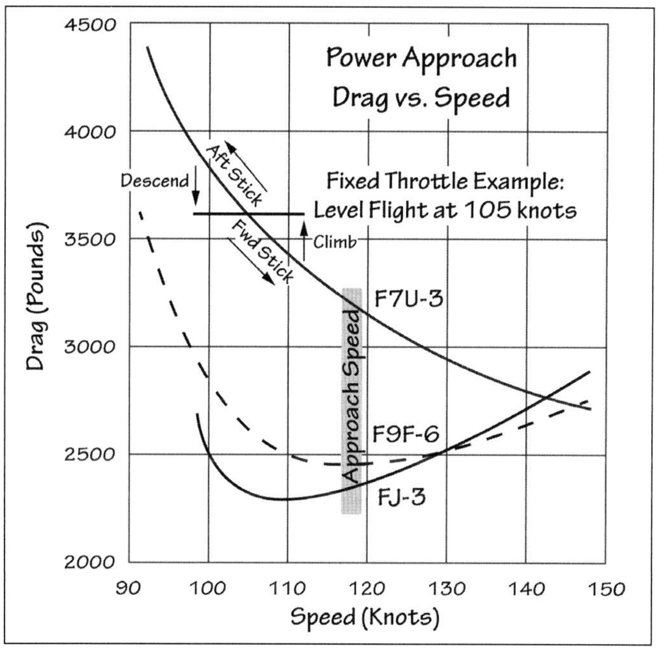

RIGHT While the F7U-3 had the same approach speed for a carrier landing using the low, flat technique as the Navy's other two swept-wing fighters, unlike them (but like aircraft with reciprocating engines and propellers) it was deep into the 'region of reversed command', also known as the backside of the drag or power curve. As a result, if the pilot attempted to climb by only pulling back on the stick, the result was a descent due to insufficient thrust/power for that airspeed; in order to climb, the pilot needed to add thrust/power and, counter-intuitively, avoid raising the nose. ***Thomason***

swept-wing jets that did not have to. In a Cougar or Fury, pulling back on the stick at approach speed, gear and flaps down, without adding thrust would result in at least a momentary decrease in the rate of sink if not a continuing – albeit slow – climb. In the Cutlass, on the other hand, pulling back on the stick on approach resulted in increased drag, slowing the F7U, which reduced lift, exacerbated by a slight initial loss of lift due to the increase in the negative camber of the wing before the increase in angle of attack increased it. If thrust was not added at the same time, preferably a bit before, the result was a descent. Another factor affecting the amount of thrust available to accelerate from a nose-high attitude was the relationship of the thrust vector, which was increasingly angled downward as the nose-up angle increased, reducing its effect on opposing the drag vector, which was horizontal or even angled slightly upward.

While a pilot might not notice a somewhat slow response to aft stick on a descending approach to a landing and if he did, not find it objectionable, the necessary precision required for a level approach only 100ft above the water (pilot's eye) and 20ft above the flight deck (wheel height) was affected. It was therefore imperative that during the then-standard low, flat approach for a carrier landing in an F7U the altitude and airspeed be controlled by a combination of throttle and stick, with the emphasis on throttle being used to avoid a loss of altitude or airspeed as soon as either was perceived. This had been well documented by NATC after its F7U-3 carrier suitability trials and not considered to be beyond the capability of a fleet pilot to accomplish. For one thing, flying in 'the region of reversed command' was routine for Navy pilots 'hanging on the prop' while making carrier landings in aircraft powered by reciprocating engines. The degree of difficulty for a pilot on the backside of the power curve in a jet was somewhat higher because the thrust response to a throttle change, even the J46's, was not nearly as immediate as it was when a big propeller was providing it (in fact, it was best to not be too abrupt with a large throttle increase then, lest the aircraft roll out of control due to torque and P-factor).

Just before reaching the aft end of the ship, Alkire appears to have pulled the nose up as far as possible, to an angle of about 30 degrees in a futile attempt to climb. Even though he had finally,

RIGHT At least a few jet pilots had survived ramp strikes on an axial flight deck when the cockpit stayed aboard (one even crashed into the fantail below the ramp and was not seriously injured); going over the side out of control was almost always fatal. LCDR Alkire was not an exception. ***US Navy***

BELOW The sailors in the carrier's catwalks next to the deck had access to openings that led under the deck, which allowed them to scramble to safety if necessary and avoid serious injury. ***US Navy***

belatedly, selected afterburning, the Cutlass was continuing to settle, with the landing gear and aft fuselage now below the deck.

Alkire *may* have been attempting to miss the ship to port but was unable to. The F7U-3 broke up and caught fire upon striking the ramp. Most of it, including the forward fuselage and Alkire, travelled up the deck but subsequently went over the port side and into the sea. The flaming wreckage still on the flight deck and catwalk was thrown or shoved overboard during fire-fighting operations. Neither the aircraft or LCDR were recovered. As a result, no material cause for the accident could be established. However, based on the eyewitness accounts and photographic coverage, none was suspected.

Contrary to most published accounts, Alkire was the only fatality according to the official accident report: 'A total of eleven men and officers were treated in sickbay … for minor burns and abrasions.'

LSO Reilly made a decidedly nonstandard but successful run across the deck to the starboard side; he was halfway there when the F7U obliterated the LSO platform. The other LSOs had jumped into the escape net to the side of the platform and rolled to safety into the ship under the deck. The enlisted hook/gear spotter missed the net and went into the water; he was subsequently rescued. All the deck hands and photographers in the port catwalk who were in harm's way were able to duck under the deck and into the ship.

The Navy's accident report attributed responsibility for the ramp strike to Alkire and exonerated the Cutlass' handling qualities and performance: 'Although variances do exist among individual F7U-3 aircraft in acceleration time from normal to military to afterburner power, this is considered a characteristic rather than a material failure. The pilot had what is considered adequate flight time in this aircraft to have become completely familiar with this characteristic and to make allowances for it in an approach for a carrier landing.'

Its summary was unequivocal:

1. It is concluded that this accident was caused by errors in pilot judgment and failure of the pilot to expeditiously answer signals from the Landing Signal Officer.

2. Although the afterburners were operating, it is possible in swept-wing aircraft to establish an angle of attack such that the power required is greater than the power available with a resulting uncontrollable rate of sink.

3. It is recognised that squadrons that are equipped with swept-wing aircraft employing afterburners stress pilot training for complete familiarisation with time lags in power acceleration and the curves for power required versus power available.

In fact, the J46 acceleration from normal to military power was somewhat better than other jet engines at the time, particularly the F9F-6 Cougar's P&W J48, which was handicapped by the inertia of its big centrifugal-flow compressor. The J46 operated at 100% rpm at throttle settings above about 75% of normal rated thrust; it was therefore always 'spooled up' on an approach requiring power. Instead of having to overcome the inertia of the compressor and turbine for changes in thrust, the J46 thrust changes at approach power were accomplished by varying the nozzle area, which took significantly less time. If the additional thrust from afterburning was needed, however, that was not a sure thing. For example, the nozzle might fully open again as it needed to for full afterburning thrust but the afterburner might not light off: the result was actually a reduction from military power thrust. Another was the nozzle not opening but the afterburner lighting off: that virtually guaranteed a compressor stall and loss of thrust. Even when the afterburner functioned as intended, the thrust increase was not achieved immediately. According to the F7U-3 flight manual, where 'MAXIMUM' meant afterburner:

> 'MAXIMUM' should be used in wave-offs executed from low, slow, and/or settling approaches. Because increases in angle of attack from flight conditions such as making a turn, stopping a rate of descent, and initiating a climb increases drag, caution should be exercised to assure that the airplane is accelerating prior to entering the afore-mentioned manoeuvres. The above recovery, however, must be initiated relatively early because selection of 'MAXIMUM' is accompanied by a thrust delay lasting up to 2 seconds. For the first 3 seconds following power increase, better airplane acceleration is attained in MILITARY POWER'; after 3 seconds a marked acceleration advantage is obtained in 'MAXIMUM'.

As part of his preparation to someday fly his F7U-3, Al Casby has spoken to many F7U pilots over the years. With respect to getting low and slow at the same time, the predominant theory for getting oneself out of that hole, specifically with respect to a carrier approach, was:

1. Don't dig the hole to start with!

2. Full afterburner and wave off at the first sign of dipping into the 'hole'.

3. If necessary, turn and pitch down to keep the aircraft flying and miss the fantail. If you strike the water you have a better chance of living than if you hit the ship.

Colourful F2H Banshee arrivals

Hard landing

Into the barricade

Ramp strike

Into the spud locker

Landing jets on axial-deck carriers was challenging. The pilots of even the relatively docile straight-wing F2H Banshee would sometimes find themselves overmatched. One even crashed into the fantail (aka spud locker) below the flight deck and survived without significant injury. *US Navy*

F7U-3 deployments begin

In mid-1955, VF-124 was deemed ready for the next *Hancock* deployment with its F7U-3s as a day fighter in company with VF-121's F9F-8 Cougars, also a day fighter that was new to the fleet. Deploying with two day fighter squadrons in addition to the customary all-weather fighter was unusual, perhaps a reflection on the uncertain suitability of the Cutlass at that point. The -8 Cougar was a second-generation swept-wing F9F, the -6 having first flown in late 1951, a few months earlier than the F7U-3's first flight and first deployed two years earlier. Another second-generation swept-wing day fighter, the FJ-3, had already deployed for the first time in June. In other words, the F7U-3 was late getting to the fleet.

According to the Standard Aircraft Characteristics charts for those three day fighters, they were similar in capability in most respects. The F7U-3 was decidedly inferior to the F9F-8 and the FJ-3 in range and endurance but certainly not 'gutless' in performance: its thrust-to-weight superiority resulted in a higher rate of climb and quicker acceleration to maximum speed from cruise/loiter – the similarity in maximum speed at 35,000ft is misleading from a thrust-to-weight standpoint, the result of the rapid increase in drag at transonic speeds (none of them was supersonic except in a dive).

In August 1955, the F7U-3 was not only the first US Navy fighter to deploy with an afterburning engine, for well over a year it remained the only one. VF-14 did not deploy with F3H-2N Demons until January 1957 and VF-141, with F4D-1 Skyrays, in July 1957. Afterburning during launch was not popular with the ship's captain and his engineering officer: it significantly increased the blast – both pressure and temperature – that had to be mitigated during launch. Carriers had wooden decks at the time; it was not unknown for this area to catch fire even when it was protected with steel plates. What was worse, the F7U-3's nose-up stance made its afterburner operation even harder on the deck than that of the Demon or Skyray would be. However, afterburning for launch was becoming necessary for a high-performance jet fighter so carriers were modified with improved jet-blast deflectors.

Pilots needed to learn to use the extra thrust judiciously and make mission trade-offs appropriately. For example, it took the same amount of fuel to climb to 35,000ft in both afterburner and military thrust, but took twenty minutes less in afterburner. However, that reduced endurance relative to the climb in military thrust. Unfortunately, the F7U was already at a disadvantage in that regard. Even without refuelling in flight, the F9F-8 and FJ-3 could easily stay away from the carrier for two hours while an F7U-3 pilot wanted to be landing back in ninety minutes.

The other major F7U-3 difference was size, a significant metric since an aircraft carrier was limited in deck and hangar space. One standard of size comparison at the time was how many could be parked, wings folded, on the flight deck and hangar deck of an Essex-class carrier, leaving the aft half of the deck clear for landing one more. An all-F9F-8 air group would total 103 Cougars; the FJ-3, 78; the F7U-3, only about 60. What was worse, in the early 1950s more mission-specific aircraft were being added to the air group. *Hancock* set sail for the western Pacific with not only F9F-8, F7U-3, and AD-6 squadrons, but also a Regulus cruise missile unit and detachments of F2H-3 night fighters, F9F-6Ps for photo reconnaissance and Regulus chase, AD-5Ns for night attack, AD-5Ws for airborne early warning, and HUPs for plane guard. At various times during the deployment, big AJ-2 tankers were aboard and, for some reason, a Marine Corps detachment of F2H-2Ps. All things being equal, the captain of the ship and the commander of the air group would prefer the smaller day fighter: In warfare, some believe that 'Quantity has a quality all its own'.

The F7U-3's multiple and leak-prone 3,000 psi hydraulic systems as well as complex pitch/yaw stabilisation and fuel management systems also meant that it would require more maintenance man hours per flight hour than a simpler day fighter, which also entailed more personnel, special test equipment, and spare parts as well as the space to accommodate them.

As it happened, VF-124 would be the only fighter squadron, per se, to deploy with the Cutlass. All subsequent deployments would be by attack squadrons, some equipped with F7U-3Ms, and two unusual deployments by four-plane detachments from VX-4, a development/evaluation squadron, flying F7U-3Ms. The urgent need cited by Rees in his letter to the Secretary of the Navy in September 1955 stemmed from the availability of nuclear weapons light enough to be carried by tactical fighters and bombers and the desire to replace the propeller-pulled AD Skyraiders and straight-wing F2H Banshees then assigned the mission with a swept-wing jet.

The Navy's first carrier-based tactical aircraft for the nuclear-strike mission were the Douglas AD-4B Skyraider and the McDonnell F2H-2B Banshee, with the B suffix standing for the armament changes necessary to carry, arm, and drop the Mk 7 and Mk 8. While modifications to the Skyraider were relatively minimal, the Banshee required a larger strengthened pylon, in-flight refuelling capability, and landing gear modifications to increase the ground clearance in order to taxi and take-off with the Mk 7 even with its retractable fin.

The propeller-pulled AD had excellent range (a combat radius of almost 900 nautical miles with external tanks) but a cruise speed of only 163 knots, which meant a maximum range mission required thirteen hours or more in the saddle. The F2H-2B had equivalent range with in-flight refuelling and a cruise speed more than twice that, 411 knots. The other Skyraider shortcoming was that it could only accelerate to a speed of 270 knots on the run-in to the target and for egress, which meant that the pilot being 'hoist with his own petard' was a real possibility. The Banshee, even with its straight wing, could accelerate to 500 knots in level flight: it could loft the nuke further and be miles more away when it detonated.While the Navy continued to assign the Skyraider to prospective nuclear strike missions, it was clear that jets were the preferred delivery platform. The F2H-2B was supplanted with F2H-3/4 Banshees. The exclusive assignment of the Cutlass to VA squadrons, including the redesignation of fighter squadrons that had been training with them, began in mid-1955. To fill the remaining need for swept-wing jets in attack squadrons before the A4D and FJ-4B became available, many swept-wing F9F-8 Cougars were modified for the nuclear strike mission as F9F-8Bs. These were only capable of carrying the Mk 12 since it provided adequate ground clearance with all four of its fins folded.

As the first fighter squadrons were being equipped with F7U-3s in 1954, BuShips was having Essex-class carriers modified with the two major changes, the steam catapult and the angled deck: the former eliminated any remaining concerns about the Cutlass launch weight; the latter, combined with a descending approach guided by the mirror landing system, allowed an increase in landing weight and a decrease in degree of difficulty as described in the F7U-3M chapter.

As a result, all Cutlass squadrons deployed on carriers with steam catapults beginning with *Hancock* (CVA-19) in August 1955. Angled decks, however, required a more extensive rebuild, so the F7U-3's first three deployments – VF-124, VF-81 (as VA-66), and VF-83 (as VA-83) – were on axial-deck carriers.

1955 Day-fighter comparison

	F9F-8	FJ-3	F7U-3
SAC	15 Apr 57	30Apr58	15 May55
Take-off gross weight (lbs)	20,098*	20,287**	28, 173***
Rate of climb SL (ft/min)	4,840	5,750	9,450
Combat radius (nm)	385	560	245
Mission time (hrs)	2.06	2.8	1.49
Combat at 35,000 ft, drop tanks off			
Weight (lbs)	17,328	17,189	24,741
Speed (kts/MN)	515/0.90	537/0.94	523/0.92
Rate of climb (ft/min)	2,200	3,600	4,000
Ceiling (ft)	42,500	47,200	46,500
Approach Stall Speed (kts)	94	103	96

*Internal fuel **two 200-gallon drop tanks ***two 150-gallon drop tanks

The assignment of the F7U-3M to three attack squadrons that did make a deployment (and one that did not) seems counterintuitive. Although the -3M did have two additional stores pylons and the Sparrow I capability was available if needed, it could not be refuelled in flight because the existing F7U-3 probe location was incompatible with the -3M's radar installation. That meant its usefulness as a strike aircraft was limited from a range and endurance standpoint,

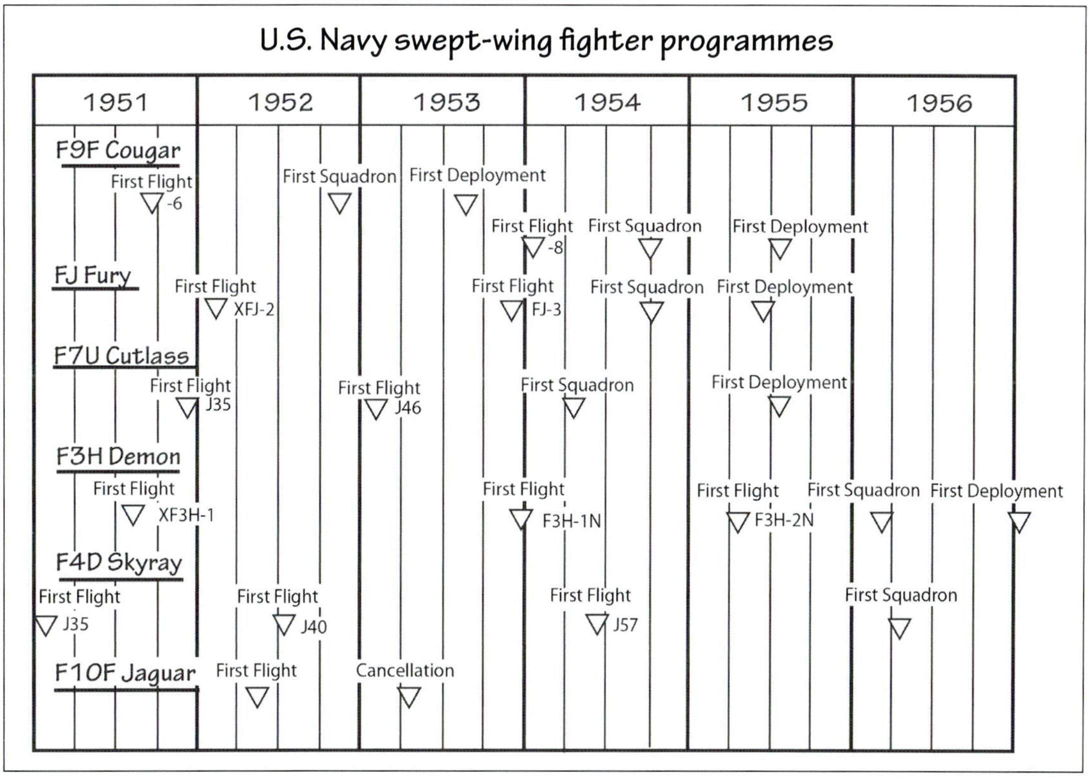

The Mk 12 with its folding fins was a replacement for the Mk 8 for the subsurface-penetration mission requirement. Its folding fins enabled it to be carried under the wing of the F9F Cougar. *US Navy*

not to mention that it did not have provisions for LABS for nuclear bomb delivery.

In September 1955, after a few incidents of jet pilots almost having to ditch due to too low a ceiling for landing on a carrier or a badly fouled deck, BuAer dictated that all carrier-based jets were to have the capability to be refuelled in flight. At the time, the only carrier-based tanker capability was provided by the big AJ Savage. However, efforts were already under way to develop and qualify an external refuelling store so smaller carrier-based aircraft could be configured as a tanker. In late 1955, Vought had installed a 'dry' flight test version of its rigid tube, buddy mission, in-flight refuelling rig that had been proposed for the A2U programme (see pages 97-98) on one of the prototype F7U-3Ms, BuNo 129589. Simulated refuelling flights were accomplished in December 1955. By the fourth flight, the receiver pilot was able to maintain an engagement for up to fourteen minutes. The biggest problem noted was 'the "mental" block of the receiver pilot due to his proximity to the tanker'. Another was that the upper portion of the left-hand fin of the receiver was in the jet wake of the tanker's right-hand engine, resulting in a cyclical yawing motion during refuelling. A third problem was the turbulence and downwash behind the tanker. However, none of them were considered to be 'major deterrents to the use of the Buddy System for service operations'. In-flight refuelling was estimated to increase the combat radius of an F7U-3 by 170nm.

The vendor for the operational store was to deliver the first one to Vought in mid-February 1956 with formal demonstration of the capability at NATC scheduled for 20 July. However, it appears that BuAer cancelled further evaluation of the complex Vought in-flight refuelling rig in favour of the simpler Douglas and North American designs that utilised a retractable hose that extended from the buddy store. Vought also proposed an F7U-3M in-flight refuelling receiver modification but BuAer elected not to fund it, another indication that the Cutlasses' bright future was behind it.

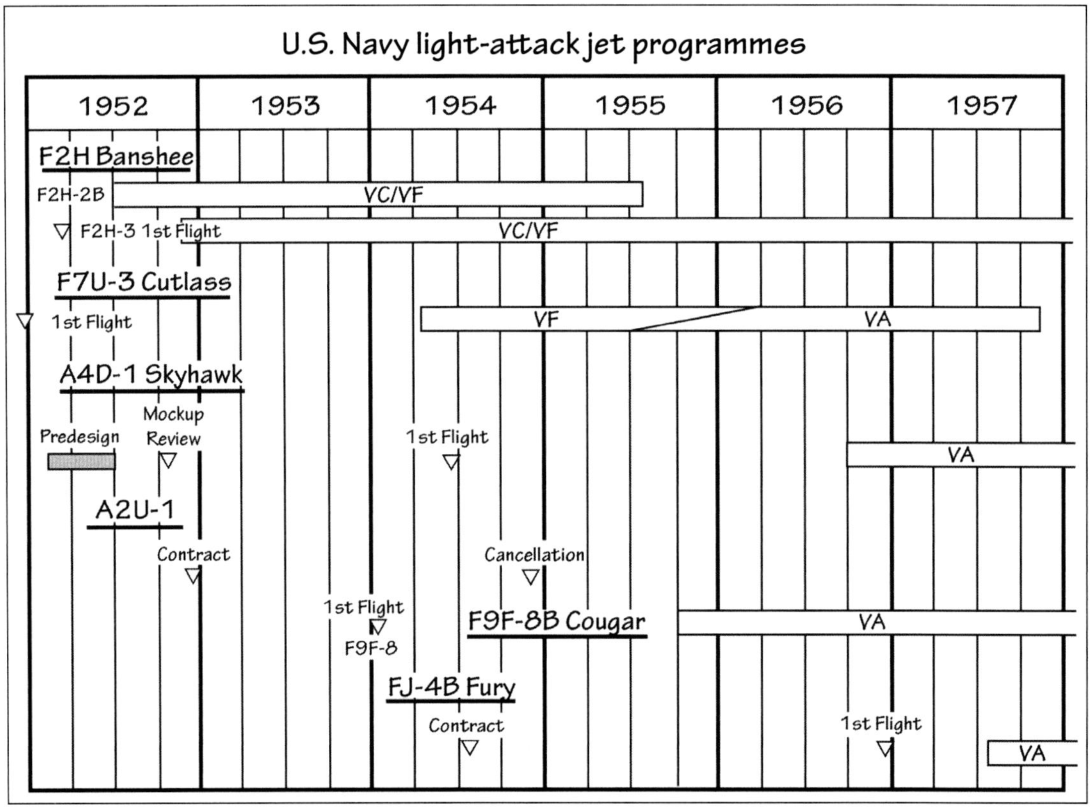

The Cutlass and F9F-8B became placeholders for the A4D Skyhawk and FJ-4B Fury that were in development for the light jet attack mission requirement. *Thomason*

Some F9F-8B conversions might have been accomplished in order to allow for an early removal of the F7Us from service; they were smaller and simpler to maintain. Cougars replaced the Cutlasses in four of the nine attack squadrons that had been assigned them. *US Navy*

This 1955 aerial photograph of piers and dry docks at the Puget Sound Naval Shipyard, Bremerton, Washington, illustrates the status of the transition between axial and angled-deck carriers. *Lexington*, *Shangri-La*, *Yorktown*, and *FDR* are in the process of receiving the angle-deck conversion. *Midway* and *Essex* still have axial decks. *R.D. Bean Collection*

Vought accomplished a successful initial evaluation of its in-flight refuelling concept but BuAer elected not to fund its full qualification. *VAHF*

Ditching the F7U-3

The first instance of the F7U making a water landing, aka 'ditching', albeit unpiloted occurred on 26 July 1954. The capability of an aircraft to be ditched was particularly important in Naval Aviation and somewhat of a concern with the introduction of jet aircraft because of their higher stall speeds. Ejection at low altitudes was not an option early on: the first ejection seats were simply bailout assists required because of the high speeds easily attained by jet aircraft. Before ejecting, the pilot had to actuate a pre-ejection lever that readied the seat for ejection, depressurised the cockpit, and jettisoned the canopy; position his feet in the stirrups; sit with his spine straight and head back on the headrest; and if necessary depending on the altitude, activate the bailout bottle. Navy pilots then pulled a face curtain down over their faces to fire the seat. After ejection, he then had to open his seat belt, push away from the seat, and once clear of it, open his parachute.

By the time the F7U-3 was introduced, the pre-ejection lever requirement, instituted as a prerequisite to ease pilot concerns about a seat misfiring on its own, had been deleted. All the pilot had to do was put his feet in the footrests, activate the emergency oxygen supply if necessary, and pull the face curtain. The first few inches of face curtain movement caused the seat to reposition to cruise-eye level, the safety harness to lock, and the canopy to jettison. Completing the downward pull of the face curtain then fired the seat. However, before the implementation of ASC 179–ECP 472, which automatically unfastened the safety belt immediately after ejection, the pilot still had to release it himself (in fact, it was recommended that if feasible when ejecting below 2,000ft, before pulling the face curtain, the pilot released his safety belt along with disconnecting the oxygen-radio tube and shucking off the shoulder harness straps). Once clear of the aircraft, however, he was still required to roll forward out of the seat and advised to delay pulling the rip cord to open his parachute for at least five seconds to reduce the opening shock and avoid entangling the seat in the parachute. As a result, an ejection initiated below 500ft in level flight was unlikely to be survivable; ejecting at 1,000ft was still only marginally likely to be successful. In other words, during take-off and landing from the carrier and even in the traffic pattern, the pilot would want to ditch the aircraft in the event of a loss of power due to engine failure or fuel exhaustion.

During F7U-3 specification development, BuAer therefore required Vought to add an emergency, battery-powered, electric hydraulic pump to an already complex flight control system because below 150 knots IAS, the windmilling engines would not provide adequate hydraulic pressure to the flight controls in the event that the pilot had to ditch or crash land due to the failure of both engines or fuel exhaustion. It provided hydraulic power for only three minutes, however.

At BuAer's request, NACA Langley conducted ditching tests of a large, 1/11th scale model of the F7U-3 with the landing gear retracted. Touchdown nose-up attitudes evaluated were 28 degrees (near stall), 23 degrees (near maximum tail down on deck), and 18 degrees with corresponding level flight, power-off speeds. In addition to testing a model with no damage, configurations that represented damage incurred after the initial contact with the water followed by a skip were:

Crumpled bottom
Crumpled bottom and no main landing gear doors
Crumpled bottom and no landing gear doors

NACA concluded that the F7U-3 should be ditched at the highest nose attitude consistent with adequate control in order to touch down at the lowest speed (higher speeds were likely to result in more violent motions). The report predicted that in calm water with the lower aft fuselage damage and no main landing gear doors, the aircraft would probably pitch down, skip slightly once, and then porpoise (pitch up and down but remain in contact with the water) for the remainder of a run of about 500ft. Maximum longitudinal decelerations would be in the order of 3.5*g*; maximum normal accelerations would be about 7*g*. Rough-water ditching was expected to be about the same if made parallel to the waves or swells.

As it turned out, NACA predictions for ditching behaviour based on model test were more accurate than those for spin recovery. The F7U-3 was ditched successfully at least a few times. The first one was actually unpiloted when LT Floyd Nugent was forced to eject after a maintenance-induced loss of the right main landing gear when he

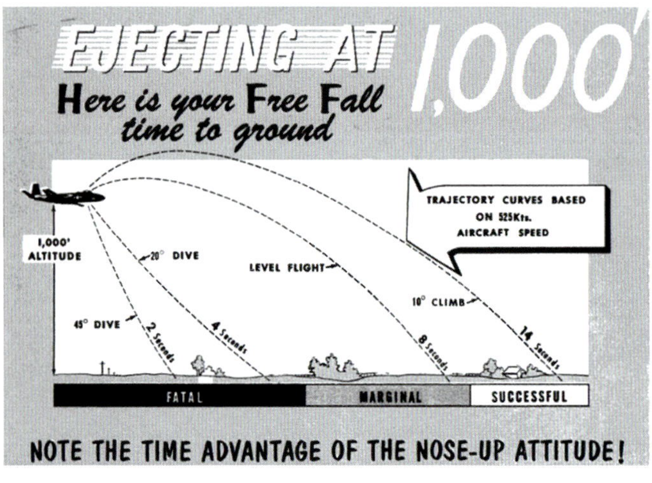

Worse-case ditching-model damage

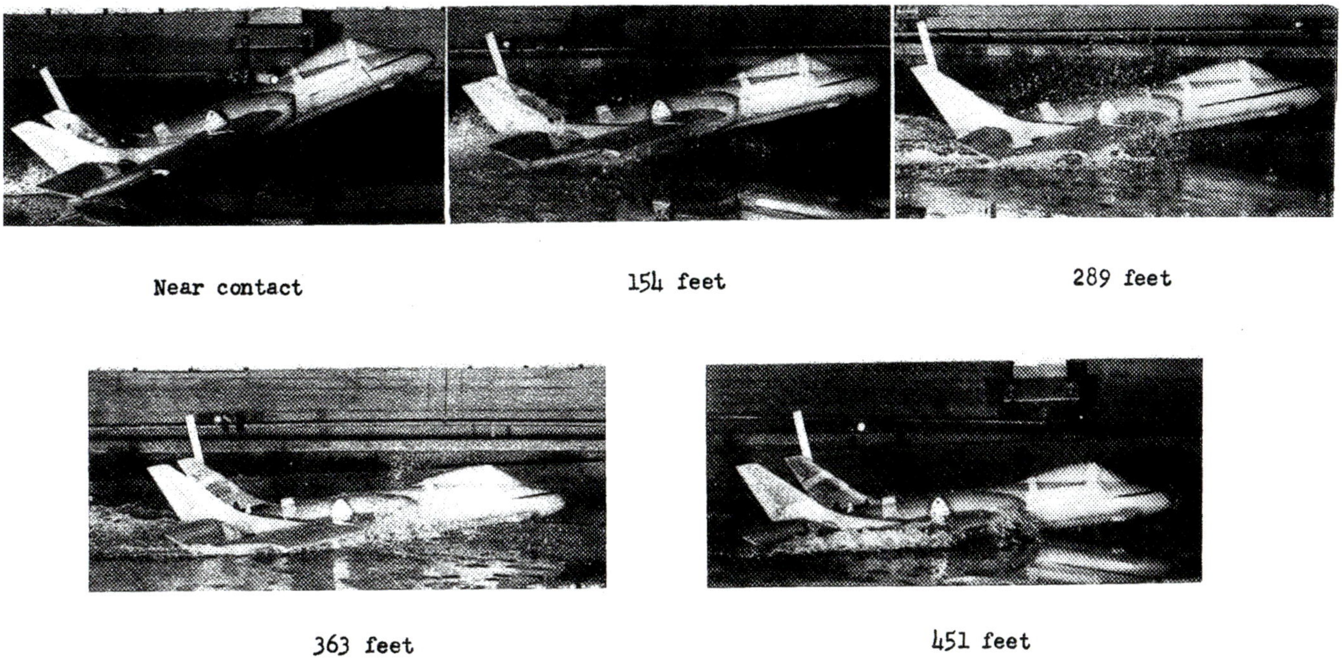

was launched from *Hancock* off San Diego on 26 July 1954. The lack of damage indicated that he would have survived ditching it even with the nose and main landing gear still down.

The flight manual recommended keeping the aircraft at the speed recommended for flameout approaches until making a flare to a nose-high attitude to minimise sink rate just before contact with the water tail first at an airspeed between 106 and 111 knots. With a relatively smooth sea, the Cutlass was expected to settle down smoothly and not nose under. The forces were predicted to be similar to an arrested landing. With 1,500lb of fuel or less remaining, the Cutlass was expected to float from one to three minutes, allowing adequate time for pilot egress.

ABOVE NACA took high-speed photographs of a ditching test to determine what the aircraft might do following initial contact with the water. ***NACA***

RIGHT Considering that LT Floyd Nugent's F7U-3 was unpiloted and its nose and right main landing gears were down when it crashed into the sea, the lack of damage is surprising. ***Casby Collection***

FAR LEFT A mid-1950s cautionary poster on ejection seat capability. ***US Navy***

LEFT Although the illustration quality is poor, this model appears to be a worst case representation of the initial damage expected upon contact with the water: a crumpled lower aft fuselage and no landing gear doors. ***NACA***

CHAPTER FOURTEEN

Squadron histories

Transitional Training Units

The Atlantic and Pacific Naval Air Forces were semi-autonomous. With respect to the introduction of the F7U-3 operationally, the Commander, Naval Air Force, Pacific Fleet assigned two existing squadrons an additional responsibility of facilitating it, first FASRon-12 and then VC-3.

Fleet Aircraft Service Squadron Twelve's *Project Cutlass*. The squadron with the most F7U-3s assigned to it over time was FASRon-12, with a total of forty-six F7U-3s in its custody between February 1954 and July 1956, because it had the unprecedented FASRon assignment of introducing a new aircraft type to the fleet: in addition to its usual responsibilities, it was to establish a unit that

A group of naval aviators watching future astronaut LT Walter M. 'Wally' Schirra making Field Carrier Landing Practice approaches and landings under the critical eye of the LSO in the checkered cap. ***US Navy***

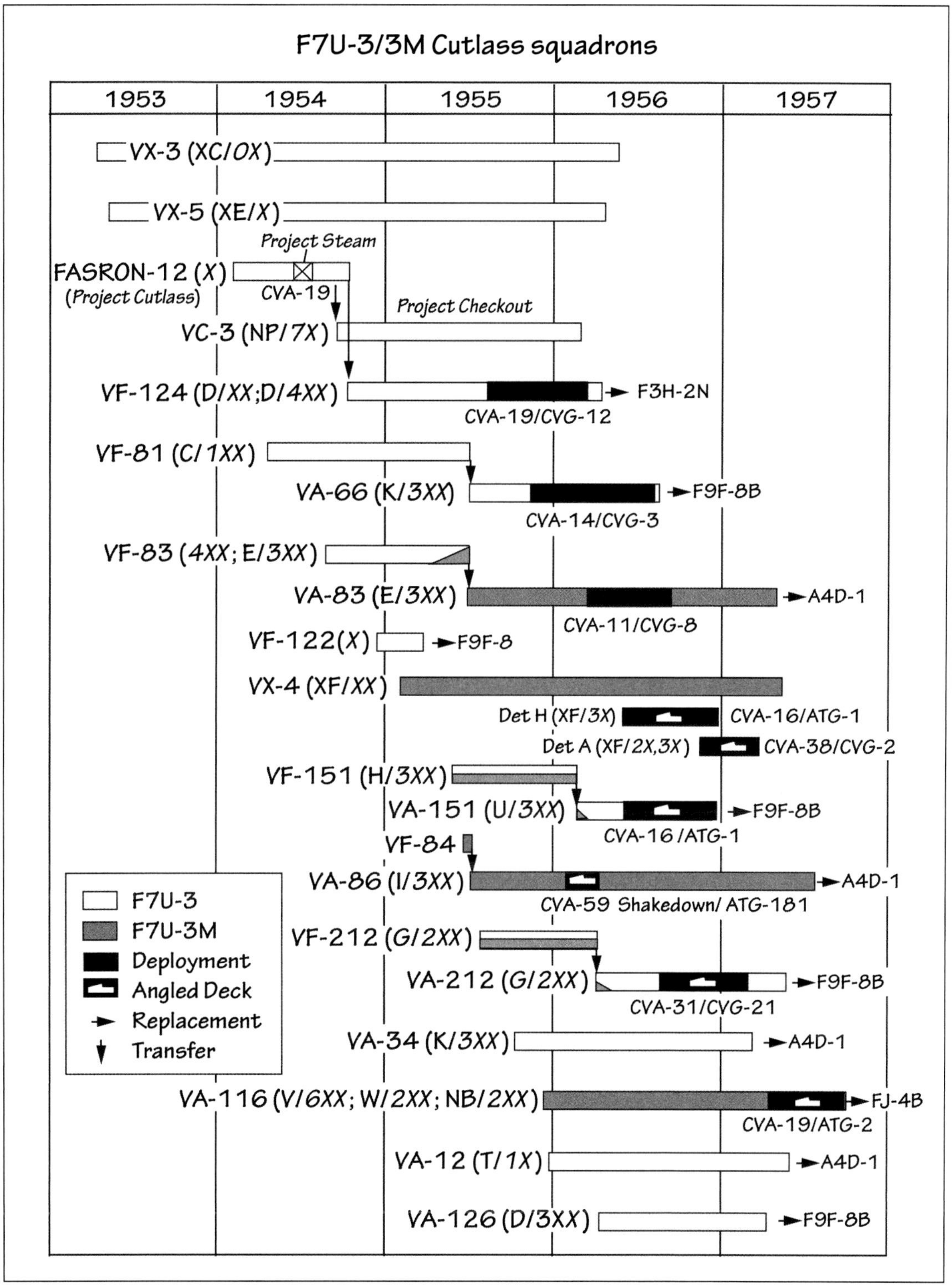

While the F7U-3's reputation had suffered from its initial accident rate in service, all the unique reasons for them were addressed successfully subsequently, either by modifications or training. It continued to have shortcomings in range and endurance, but the Navy still had almost 200 of them in early 1955 and production of new ones planned through the end of 1955. As a result, a total of eleven deployable fighter/ attack squadrons were assigned F7U-3s and -3Ms between mid-1955 and the end of 1957; six made full deployments. *Thomason*

operated like a deployable squadron and document any procedural changes required for maintenance and operation. In the process it was to train the pilots and maintainers who would became the nucleus of VF-124 and VC-3's *Project Check-Out* transitional training unit. The aptly named *Project Cutlass* was the west coast-initiated equivalent of the formal F7U-3 Fleet Introduction Programme (FIP) accomplished at Patuxent River in mid-1954.

Acquiring its first F7U-3 at 11.16 a.m. on 2 February 1954 when LCDR Ronald G. Puckett from BAR Dallas delivered the brand-new BuNo128477 from the Chance Vought factory to FASRon-12's home, NAS Miramar, California, the squadron went on to initially take delivery of nine more F7U-3s and need for the formation of *Project Cutlass*, commanded by LCDR James S. Brown. FASRon-12 provided not only the maintenance and administrative support personnel for the project, but

The reception committee for LCDR Ronald G. Puckett (center), who flew the first of *Project Cutlass*'s F7U-3 fighters to NAS Miramar from Chance Vought Aircraft's Dallas, Texas factory, included (from left) CAPT Donald L. Mills, NAS Miramar's Commanding Officer; Mr William P. Thayer, head of Chance Vought Aircraft Sales and Service; LCDR Puckett; LCDR James S. Brown, FASRon-12's *Project Cutlass* Officer-in-Charge; and CDR Archie R. Fields, FASRon-12's Commanding Officer. *USN Photo NARA 80-G-679274 via Casby*

A FASRon-12 F7U-3, BuNo 129662, is ready for launch from the *Hancock*'s new steam catapult with a fully extended nose landing gear during *Project Steam*. At this point, the unit's only distinguishing markings were the black top on the vertical fins. *US Navy*

also seven pilots, which included future astronaut LT Walter M. Schirra as gunnery officer, LT Donald Christianson – project flight officer, LT Robert D. Belt – maintenance officer, LT Doniphan B. Shelton – operations officer, LT Floyd C. Nugent – personnel officer, LT Edwin Van Biesbroeck – administrative officer, and LTJG Burton H. Shepherd – Assistant Administrative Officer. Additionally, five pilots from Air Transport Squadron Thirty-Two (VR-32) joined in the initial training, as they would be tasked with Cutlass deliveries to the fleet squadrons and other units. These twelve pilots were all recent graduates of factory indoctrination training on the F7U-3 aircraft performed at Vought's facility in Dallas. In addition, a semi-trailer containing a complete Cockpit Procedures Trainer (CPT) was provided to the *Project Cutlass* pilots to assist in maintaining familiarisation and procedure proficiency. The initial cadre of maintenance personnel were also trained at Vought, and later utilised hands-on systems simulators acquired from the Training Device Division of the Naval Air Technical Training Command (NATTC) in Memphis, Tennessee.

As *Project Cutlass* training progressed, the Jam Handy Company of Detroit, Michigan, was contracted to produce familiarisation training films that would assist future Cutlass pilots in transitioning to the aircraft. Known as *Operation Shutterbug*, the project involved both ground and air-to-air photography. LT Shelton was tasked with starring in this cinematic endeavour and his efforts allowed future F7U pilots to familiarise themselves with flying the Cutlass prior to their first solo take-offs.

Following Field Carrier Landing Practice (FCLP) operations conducted at Naval Outlying Field (NOLF) Crows Landing, two of the initial-batch aircraft – BuNos 129552 and 129637 – took part in the *Project Steam* C-11 catapult evaluation aboard *Hancock* (CVA-19) between 14 June to 30 July 1954. Three other aircraft, BuNos 129657, 129662, and 129678 joined them wearing FASRon-12's *Project Cutlass* black-tipped fin livery but were not technically in FASRon-12's custody until two months later. BuNo129678 had not even been accepted by the Navy until 31 August 1954, a full month after the carrier trials ended. The fast pace of the trials, coupled with the limited stock of F7U-specific launch bridles, caused the testing to be conducted with the bridles temporarily fastened to the aircraft with long bungee cords attaching the forward portion of the bridle to the extended nose gear. This necessitated that the aircraft be operated gear down for each launch-to-landing circuit, as the retained bridle would foul the nose gear upon retraction.

One aircraft was damaged beyond repair during these trials following maintenance conducted on the left main landing gear. Upon reassembly following a pneudraulic cylinder seal replacement, the retaining gland nut was threaded onto the upper gear assembly only one half-turn. On 26 July 1954, when LT Nugent's BuNo 129552 was catapulted off of *Hancock*, the weight of the extending oleo following launch tore through the minimal threads holding the retaining nut. The lower portion of the landing gear – complete with wheel and brake – dropped into the sea. With no ability to retract the landing gear due to the bridle configuration, a gear-up landing was ruled out – a gear-down landing aboard ship or at NAS North Island was deemed too risky as the possibility of the left gear leg digging in and causing a cartwheel was envisioned. Nugent was ordered to head the aircraft out to sea and eject. He was rescued by helicopter and deposited at North Island, wet and shaken, but unharmed.

However, following his successful ejection, the aircraft – minus canopy, seat, and pilot continued to fly and circled back toward San Diego's Coronado Island. Several aircraft were scrambled from NAS North Island to intercept the errant F7U-3, but the proximity to the city and the fact that the aircraft had entered a slow circling of the famed Hotel del Coronado precluded the option of shooting it down. Several attempts were made to aerodynamically steer the Cutlass away from populated areas, each failing. Eventually the aircraft ran out of fuel and made a picture-perfect 'landing' in the water offshore, staying afloat long enough for a Navy tugboat to tow the aircraft to the beach. Contrary to many repeated stories of this incident, the aircraft was damaged extensively in the ditching and was not repairable, much less flying again within days as many reports state erroneously. It did, however, provide a demonstration of the ability to ditch the Cutlass successfully in the worst possible configuration, i.e. gear down with flamed-out engines.

Following the formation of VF-124 and VC-3's *Project Check-Out*, nine of FASRon-12's initial group of ten aircraft – minus Nugent's BuNo 129552 – were transferred to these respective squadrons in late September and early October 1954, ending its very successful implementation of *Project Cutlass* with only one major incident and no injuries or fatalities during eight months. Unfortunately, the depth and breadth of the transition to the F7U provided to its pilots and mechanics was not yet standard practice within the Navy.

Composite Squadron Three (VC-3) Interceptors and Transitional Training Unit Pacific *Project Check-Out*/Cutlass Classroom. The storied VC-3 legacy began on 20 May 1949 when they were established to provide specialised night fighter detachments to augment Pacific Fleet deployed air groups. These consisted of four to five aircraft, five to six pilots, and a number of enlisted personnel. Serving with distinction during the Korean Conflict, VC-3 detachments provided night interdiction of enemy aircraft as well as supplementing night-time ground attack operations. On 16 July 1953, VC-3's LT Guy Bordelon became the only Navy ace during the conflict.

Carriers operating in the Pacific would offload crash-damaged aircraft in Japan and pick up replacements. Here, three VF-191 F9F-6 Cougars are on the barge of shame compared to only one each of the other types in *Oriskany*'s air group, indicative of initial problems with landing swept-wing jets on carriers, although obviously, straight-wing aircraft were not immune to accidents. The higher accident rate was the impetus for the creation of *Cougar College*. *US Navy*

VC-3 was known as the *Chukar Pups* and their squadron insignia consisted of an angry bulldog armed with a lance and bat-adorned shield against a towering white storm cloud – the bat indicating the specialised night mission of the squadron, and the cloud representing the perilous environment in which they performed their mission. Their aircraft carried the two-letter 'NP' tail code.

In December 1950, the squadron had been the first to receive the Navy's first jet night fighter, the Douglas F3D-1, but did not provide any detachments of them or the F3D-2s that they received subsequently to deploying air groups. Following the Korean War armistice in 1953, VC-3 continued to provide night fighter detachments to Pacific Fleet carrier deployments, having transitioned from Vought's F4U-5N Corsair to the McDonnell F2H-3 Banshee. A unique feature of VC-3 was that they remained home-based at NAS Moffett Field at all times.

In June 1954, VC-3 welcomed CDR James D. 'Jig Dog' Ramage as its new commanding officer following his service as the Commander of CVG-19 while deployed aboard *Oriskany* (CVA-34). Ramage would soon be tasked with transforming the squadron to include a specialised training unit for the newest jet aircraft joining the fleet. VADM Harold M. 'Beauty' Martin, the Commander Air Force, Pacific Fleet (ComAirPac), was concerned with the mounting number of fatal accidents experienced by squadrons equipped with the Grumman F9F-6 Cougar. Although the accident rate increased with the advent of jet propulsion, the Navy had been able to arrest it for the straight-winged Grumman F9F-2/-5 Panther and McDonnell F2H-2/-3/-4 Banshee with little training effort – mostly centred around teaching the lag experienced during a turbojet's power application. However, the swept-wing Cougar presented the Navy with a conundrum – its systems were basically that of its straight-winged predecessor, with few identifiable technical differences to adequately account for the losses that the fleet was experiencing. A new training approach was needed.

It had been determined that the prevailing wisdom of placing new naval aviators into even newer and more complex aircraft types – particularly swept-winged jets – without specialised training was at least a contributing factor to the unacceptable accident rate that the Navy was experiencing. The concept of a Transitional Training Unit (TransTU) that would provide type-specific training for pilots slated to fly these new aircraft types was developed. This training would be standardised and ensure a common knowledge base delivered by experienced instructors. However, there were not enough experienced instructors to provide this training to each and every pilot assigned to squadrons slated to receive these new aircraft. Therefore, the concept was only to train the squadron's senior pilots – prospective commanding officers and executive officers – who would then themselves become the instructors for their junior underlings. It was acknowledged that this was not optimal training, and that problems with mis-relayed information could potentially undermine the intended goal. Nonetheless, with limited experienced instructors and limited available aircraft (none of which included two-seat, swept-wing, training-specific versions), the TransTU was seen as the best available option for addressing the ever-growing accident rate plaguing the Navy's aviators.

In August 1954, VC-3 was chosen by ComNavAirPac to become the parent squadron of Transitional Training Unit-Pacific (TransTUPac). This mission was in addition to the squadron's regular duty to provide the Pacific Fleet with all-weather fighter and attack detachments, and was increased in difficulty due to the multiple aircraft types soon to be assigned to VC-3. Assisting CDR Ramage was Executive Officer CDR Robert W. 'Duke' Windsor, Jr., a seasoned naval aviator who had previously graduated from the Naval Test Pilot School (NTPS), as well as having commanded VF-24 – the navy's first swept-wing jet squadron. Windsor took responsibility for selecting the best potential instructor pilots and forwarding his suggestions to BuAer for review. The multiplicity of types was not new for Windsor, as NTPS exposed its students to multiple aircraft types in an effort to foster an understanding of various planforms and their performance. As a result, many of Windsor's selectees were fellow NTPS graduates. VC-3's maintenance personnel had to become proficient with using a multitude of specialised equipment needed for each particular type, as well as learning and understanding the complexities of systems and avionics that were being seen in the fleet for the first time. This resulted in CDR Ramage dedicating twenty-one maintenance personnel to the TransTUPac programme separate from the maintenance staff assigned to the

The F7U-3's J46 afterburner in action was particularly impressive at night. ***Casby Collection***

squadron's F2H and F3D night fighter detachment fleet. Moffett Field provided VC-3 with access to both the maintenance expertise at FASRon-10 as well as the seasoned maintainers at several of the squadrons that their pilot students would soon be joining, although the new assignment was daunting nonetheless. VC-3 was absorbed into CVG-21 as a 'supplemental' squadron and renamed themselves the *Interceptors* shortly after receiving their TransTUPac assignment, however they retained the *Chukar Pup* insignia and 'NP' tail code.

The training unit was tasked initially with schooling pilots and maintainers in the beleaguered Grumman F9F-6 Cougar, followed by the North American FJ-3 Fury and Vought F7U-3 and -3M Cutlasses. It operated under the programme name *Project Check-Out* and initially consisted of seven pilot-instructor pilots. With over 1,500 flight hours in jet aircraft, LCDR Horatio G. 'Bud' Sickel was chosen as Officer-in-Charge of the programme, assisted by Operations Officer LT James F. 'Tut' Tuttle.

VC-3's F9F-6 training effort was known as the *Cougar College of Supersonic Knowledge* and was commanded by its 'Dean', LCDR Sickel. LT Tuttle acted as his assistant. The FJ-3 programme was nicknamed *Fury Finishing School* and its programme leader was LT Robert B. 'Bob' Baldwin, assisted by LT Addison H. Brown. The F7U programme was known as the *Cutlass Classroom* and its Programme Officer was *Project Cutlass* alumnus LT Doniphan B. 'Don' Shelton, assisted by LTs Walter M. 'Wally' Schirra Jr. and Burton H. 'Burt' Shepherd, also *Project Cutlass* alums.

In addition, VC-3 operated the Lockheed TV-2 Shooting Star as an initial jet-exposure trainer for students who were to transition to the new jets from piston-powered aircraft. Although the programme's instructor pilots were assigned to the individual respective programmes, they each flew all the aircraft within *Project Check-Out*'s fleet. As the programme progressed, additional instructor pilots were added. The *Cutlass Classroom* absorbed LT J.D. Ward from his initial assignment as VC-3's Assistant Personnel Officer.

Between 23 September and 5 October 1954, LTs Shelton and Shepherd ferried six FASRon-12 F7U-3s from Miramar, California, to Moffett Field following their transfer to VC-3. LT Schirra was unable to participate because of illness but joined them at VC-3 on 14 October. The *Project Cutlass* aircraft were soon stripped of their black-tipped fins. Retaining the natural metal finish that they wore while in FASRon-12, VC-3's Cutlasses soon displayed two medium blue chevron stripes added to the upper fuselage mid-wing. Additionally, 7X series side numbers were added in front of the fuselage national insignia and the fins had medium-blue stripes painted below their fin tips – each adorned with three white stars – above the 'NP' tail code.

In November 1954, VF-122 was the first squadron to begin F7U-3 transition training at TransTUPac, with LCDR John W. Eash completing the programme with no difficulty. Changes were instituted following VF-122's completion of their senior pilot's training, which refined the syllabus and streamlined the ground school instruction. Representatives from Vought – including their test pilot cadre – made visits to Moffett Field to discuss items deemed relevant to the continued success of the programme. Discussions regarding the stability of the aircraft following clean stall manoeuvres were only lightly touched upon in spite of Vought's ongoing efforts to develop a solution to the problem identified several months earlier.

On 11 January 1955, LTJG John D. Lindsay was training in section tactics at 28,000ft when he entered a post-stall gyration following an accelerated stall in F7U-3 BuNo 128476. Stunned by the tumbling, spinning manoeuvre, he effected a successful ejection without attempting a recovery. Nine days later, LCDR Sickel purposely entered a PSG in an attempt to verify his contention that normal spin recovery techniques would be effective in abating the PSG phenomena. They were not. Ejecting from BuNo 129548 at 10,000ft, Sickel actuated his parachute prior to releasing himself from the ejection seat. The seat entangled his parachute and ripped one side while fouling the other. With a partially streaming chute, he landed in a recently ploughed field and sank up to his waist, narrowly escaping a fatal injury. Within three months, VC-3 was down to four aircraft to provide training for its students. On 15 February, F7U-3 BuNo 128473 was delivered from BAR Dallas to replace the one Lindsay ejected from. Although VF-122's senior pilots were the first to train with VC-3, their squadron was reassigned the F9F-8 Cougar and their F7U-3 aircraft were soon made available for reassignment (see page 209). One month later, VF-122's F7U-3 BuNo 129648's custody was transferred to VC-3 to replace 548.

LT Schirra was tasked with training LCDR Payton O. 'Po' Harwell, a FASRon-10 pilot based next door at Moffett Field's Hangar 1. Harwell had been pestering LT Schirra to check out in the F7U-3 in spite of his having no assignment-related need to train in the Cutlass. Following repeated pleadings to CDR Ramage, Harwell was allowed to attend the 'Cutlass Classroom' ground school and was scheduled for his first training flight for 28 March 1955. Inclement weather delayed his first flight taking place until 30 March. Unfortunately, as subsequent events would prove, he was assigned F7U-3 BuNo 128474 that had just had its port engine replaced. With Instructor Schirra on his wing in BuNo 128478 – he selected afterburner and commenced the take-off roll. Soon streaming flames, Harwell climbed to just under 10,000ft and was instructed to eject after Schirra witnessed Harwell's tail cone departing the aircraft following an explosion. The aircraft subsequently

VC-3's BuNo 129550 on static display next to a VC-3 FJ-3 Fury at San Francisco International Airport in July 1955 *Larkin*

crashed into the salt flats in San Fransisco Bay and was unrecoverable due to the muddy bottom. Harwell landed in the bay and was rescued, although he suffered a serious injury to his arm due to making contact with the ejection seat after a delayed separation. The explosion was initially attributed to a possible faulty fuel strainer cover, but subsequent analysis of later similar incidents revealed the great probability that the afterburner fuel line was left disconnected following the engine change. This theory was subsequently validated decades later after the engine was found and examined: there was no evidence of the fuel line connection having been made, with no fasteners being found at the fuel line flange's interface.

With guided missile-armed F7U-3Ms reaching squadron strength, VC-3 took custody of two, BuNos 129708 and 129744 from VA-151 on 7 Nov 1955 to conduct transitional training in the heavier -3M. The use of the -3Ms was short, as both aircraft were transferred to VA-116 a month later on 9 and 7 November respectively to round out their complement of fighters.

VC-3 continued to conduct transitional training in the Cutlass up until January 1956 without incident. BuNo 129565 became the last F7U-3 to be relinquished to BAR Dallas on 28 February. The squadron began taking custody of Douglas F4D-1 Skyrays on 16 April 1956, in anticipation of continuing transitional training in this new bat-winged fighter, as well as the Douglas A4D-1 Skyhawk. However, fiscal year re-appropriations soon resulted in a mission redesignation. VC-3 was redesignated VF(AW)-3 on 1 July 1956. Adopting a new insignia and name – *Blue Nemesis* – the squadron relinquished their Skyhawks in 1957 and continued to provide Skyray-based all-weather interceptor training until its dis-establishment on 2 May 1958, when Fleet All Weather Training Unit-Pacific (FAWTUPac) assumed its designation and name.

The concept of a transitional training course in the Navy's latest jet fighter and attack aircraft proved to be sound. However, it was quickly noted that the potential for miscommunication of important procedural information was evident when senior squadron mentors relayed their newly acquired skills to their junior pilots. The need for a fleet-wide system of training all naval aviators in the aircraft they were assigned to operate – by competent designated instructor pilots – led to the introduction of the Replacement Air Group (RAG) squadron concept. The successes gleaned from the institution of RAGs resulted in a marked decrease in accidents and incidents. VC-3's efforts in spearheading the training squadron concept (particularly with advanced jets like the Cutlass) provided the necessary data to substantiate the need for this advanced training across the spectrum of Naval Aviation.

Development Squadrons

Each of the Navy's Air Development Squadrons was assigned specific mission development responsibilities and received early production aircraft in order to evaluate and create type-specific recommendations to fulfil those missions prior to their deployment. F7U-3s were assigned to VX-3, VX-4, and VX-5.

Air Development Squadron Three (VX-3) *Developers.* Established on 20 November 1948 at NAS Atlantic City, New Jersey, VX-3 was assigned a three-fold mission: 'to evaluate new and already existing naval aircraft, airborne equipment, and operational methods'; 'to recommend methods for the most effective tactical deployment of aircraft and equipment'; and 'to recommend training procedures and countermeasures for these aircraft and methods'. The squadron absorbed elements of disestablished Attack Squadron One L (VA-1L), as well as Fighter Squadron One L (VF-1L) and some material assets of Light Carrier Air Group One (CVLG-1). Their attractive squadron insignia was approved in April 1949 and featured a winged sundial with a stylised jet aircraft flying vertically from its centre with the Roman numerals VXIII centred on the dial. Under the administrative control of the Commander Operations Test and Evaluation Force (COMOPTEVFOR), CDR Noel A. Gayler assumed command of the squadron, and soon experienced aviators with NATC and Test Pilot School experience began to be transferred into VX-3.

In anticipation of the acquisition of the F7U-3, CDR Gayler brought aboard LCDR Edward L. 'Whitey' Feightner – who flew the F7U-1 at NATC and with the Blue Angels Flight Demonstration Team – in September 1952 as the squadron's Chief Project and Development Officer. Feightner had the most flight time in the F7U series, and was a welcome addition to VX-3.

VX-3 was assigned two of the first sixteen F7U-3s built to familiarise itself with the type prior to a full operational evaluation. The first one, BuNo 128464, arrived on 17 April 1953 (it had an early gun compartment purge system). A second, BuNo 128463, was delivered on 1 May 1953. These early aircraft were used to evaluate gun gas ingestion and armament compartment venting issues noted with the interim J35 engine installation. All VX-3's aircraft carried two-digit squadron nose numbers beginning with '00' and the 'XC' tail code. These particular early-production -3s also had large red warning areas painted on their intakes.

BuNo 128463 did not last long, having experienced a land-short accident fifteen days later at the hands of VX-3's LTJG Jack H. Stephenson on 16 May 1953. He touched down 100ft short of the runway and the nose gear struck the edge of the concrete, which caused the actuator link to shear. Stephenson sustained minor injuries, and 128463 was damaged beyond repair. It was held by VX-3 until 15 November 1954, when its custody was transferred to O&R Norfolk prior to being trucked to NAMC Philadelphia for use in barricade testing. BuNo 128464's custody was also transferred to O&R Norfolk seven days later.

A gun gas ingestion issue plagued the early F7U-3s. LCDR Feightner as well as pilots from NATC Patuxent were keen to determine the cause of – and solution to – the problem of engine flameouts experienced when the cannon were fired at high altitudes. Marine Colonel George M. Chinn from Dahlgren, Virginia's Naval Ordnance Depot developed a slotted baffle for the F7U-3's four 20mm auto-cannon and felt that this would adequately solve the issue by allowing the expanding gasses to be redirected aft of the intake lip of the F7U-3. Tested extensively by NATC's Maj John H. Glenn, Jr, the new screw-on stainless steel blast deflectors worked as advertised, however the issue remained when firing the guns at very high altitude. Glenn enlisted the help of several engineers at Patuxent and developed a close liaison with VX-3's Feightner and LCDR Thomas J. 'Tom' Gallagher. After much in-flight testing by NATC and VX-3 pilot's, it was determined that Glenn's idea for an intervalometer installed in the cannon's electronic firing circuit would provide a milli-second lag between the firing of each gun per side. This interrupted the formation of a shock wave in front of the intake leading to the compressor stalls being experienced. VX-3 pilots continued to test this apparatus in the early model F7U-3s and recommended to BuAer that the intervalometer be adopted for use in future F7U-3 deliveries, which it was.

CDR Gayler relinquished command of VX-3 to CDR Hawley M. 'Monk' Russell on 1 January 1954. CDR Russell was assisted by Executive Officer William 'Bill' Leonard and soon welcomed LCDR Donald D. Engen following his return from Exchange Officer duty at England's Empire Test Pilot School. Engen had previously flown both the F7U-1 and F7U-3 during his time assigned to BAR Dallas. In March 1954, Engen began a project to re-ignite BuAer's interest in the in-flight refuelling concept – testing that they had earlier conducted at NATC in 1951–52, as well as sporadic testing conducted by VX-3 in March 1953. His persistence resulted in Flight Refuelling Limited from Dorset, England, to create a US-based branch named Flight Refueling Incorporated (FRI) located at Baltimore's Friendship Airport to more easily provide the Navy with the company's probe and drogue products.

On 30 April 1954 BuNo 128458 arrived from NATC and one month later four production-series F7U-3s were delivered in the form of BuNos 129643, 644, 646, and 649 – all newly produced and ferried by VX-3 pilots from BAR Dallas. These aircraft soon were fitted with prototype (FRI A-12A-1) in-flight refuelling kits modified by Vought for F7U-3 use from FRI's newly designed probe and drogue system. These production series aircraft had an orange day-glo vertical stripe painted aft

Vought modified BuNo 128463 to have a temporary gun compartment purge system before it was delivered to VX-3. Note the red inlet warning marking, rare before the implementation of the grey/white paint scheme. *Nick Veronico Collection*

of the radome and their refuelling probes were striped in orange and black. COMOPTEVFOR Project V-168 had VX-3 evaluate the Cutlasses' air-to-air refuelling compatibility with AJ Savage tankers. Working closely with Vought's Atlantic City-based Field Service Representative (FSR) Supervisor Malcolm 'Mal' Raffo, and his assistant FSR Edward 'Ed' Scott, the personnel of VX-3 spearheaded the implementation of the system. Vought test pilots John W. Konrad, Martin 'Marty' Collis, and L.J. 'Jack' Walton participated, flying both BAR Dallas aircraft as well as those belonging to NATC and VX-3.

Then-CAPT Russell remembered a particularly eventful flight during the testing of this new system. The following is translated from an interview with Stephane Nicolaov in April 1981:

> On 13 April 1954 I was flying F7U-3 BuNo 129649 in company with an AJ-2 tanker and a F2H-2P Banshee at an altitude of 25,000 feet east of Chincoteague. The very low position of the short refueling probe obliged me to remove my safety belt so that I could stand up and look over the nose of the Cutlass to be able to plug into the basket. After the transfer was complete, I sat back down and prepared to separate from the tanker. At this point I was still unfastened in my seat. I bled off a few knots to disconnect the probe from the basket only to see the hose unreeling under the Savage. When the whole hose was extended, I was still hooked up.
>
> My position was even more uncomfortable because the basket was hiding the airspeed indicator [author's note – most likely was affecting airflow to the pitot tube]]. Several attempts to disconnect were unsuccessful, having the only result to decrease rather dangerously the airspeed of both airplanes. Finally I popped the airbrakes to their full extension again; the probe left the basket but at the same time the hose broke and suddenly everything went just over the canopy. I feared that all this stuff was going to tangle on the fins but thank God it didn't.
>
> On the way back to base, I had reached an altitude of 10,000 feet when I selected landing gear down. Immediately the Cutlass turned crazy: rolling, tumbling, throwing me from one side of the canopy to the other, head down, feet up, hell I was grabbing, pulling, pushing every

ABOVE **VX-3 accomplished one of the first evaluations of in-flight refuelling of an F7U-3 from an AJ Savage tanker. The pilot's view of the tip of the refueling probe was marginal.** ***Thomason***

OPPOSITE TOP **VX-3's F7U-3 BuNo 129646 and two FJ-3s escorted the squadron's AD-5N carrying the Royal Navy's VADM Barnard to NAS Atlantic City, New Jersey, on 2 April 1955. Note the blue (not commonly seen on F7U-3s) 150-gallon external fuel tanks.** ***NASAC Photo NA113/10520(L)2-55 Casby Collection***

> kind of switch and handle I could reach and in the earphone the Banshee's pilot was screaming 'eject, eject, eject'. How could I do that? I was not even on my seat!
>
> Suddenly, after five turns the plane became perfectly still again. Without knowing it I had put the landing gear up. On the ground my critical position had been immediately felt in the operations room where a Cutlass specialist advised me that the automatic yaw dampener had been sprung by the hose or the basket departing the aircraft. He told me to turn off a switch on the left back under the seat… you know that little switch you never notice before an emergency.
>
> I was then able to get the gear down. My approach was very, very fast. I touched down at about 200 knots. All the tires blew off and the wheels produced huge sparks. When the Cutlass stopped, the fire truck was at my side. I jumped on it as it was dangerous to jump from the very high cockpit. That was my last flight in a Cutlass.

VX-3's evaluations were instrumental in providing recommendations to FRI for the necessary modifications to the system. These resulted in the FRI A-12-C unit – equipped with a MA-2 coupling – which accelerated the delivery of the probe and associated tubing, in kit form, to fleet squadrons preparing to take the Cutlass to sea.

On 2 August 1954, VX-3's Capt Vincent J. Marzelo, USMC, aborted his take-off in BuNo 128458 while conducting a check-flight that followed an extended maintenance lay-up of the aircraft. During the take-off roll, Marzelo noted no airspeed indication and applied full braking. Due to moderate rain, gusty surface winds, and poor braking conditions, Marzelo left the runway. He was unhurt but the aircraft sustained major damage to the left wing and landing gear, as well as the lower fuselage. Investigation into the accident revealed that the airspeed indicator's pitot line had been capped during maintenance and not reconnected. His aircraft's custody was administratively transferred to O&R Quonset Point on 13 December, but the airframe was actually trucked to the BuAer pool at Philadelphia to potentially be used for barrier and barricade testing.

Tragically, Capt Marzelo's luck would run out on 28 September when he was killed in F7U-3 BuNo 129644 following a return to NAS Atlantic City after an orientation flight with the intention of doing touch and goes. Retracting the gear after the first one, Marzelo then turned to the downwind leg for his next landing. His Cutlass snap-rolled during the turn and plunged into the woods adjacent to the runway. Only the aft fuselage and fins remained semi-intact when crash crews – assisted by NAS Atlantic City's Piasecki HUP-1 rescue helicopter used to fan away the flames – arrived on the scene. Investigators initially focused on a failure within the nose gear's steering system that allowed the nose gear to turn within the gear well and impinge on the ailavator's push-pull control tube.

Vought conducted extensive tests culminating in the release of an engineering report suggesting changes be made to the design to potentially prevent a repeat occurrence, however they were unable to replicate the failure. Following a similar impingement that occurred later during a VA-151 'gear swing' hangar test, it was determined that the cause of the accident was the failure of ground personnel to fully seat the quick-release ball-lock pin used to reconnect the nose gear scissors following towing. It was presumed that the scissors became unconnected and the lower scissor arm jammed Marzelo's ailavator control tube.

VX-3 was honoured to escort VADM Sir Geoffrey Barnard of the Royal Navy when he visited the squadron in anticipation of their involvement in testing and evaluating the British-developed mirror-assisted landing system. Barnard was flown to Atlantic City in VX-3's Douglas AD-5N Skyraider while two VX-3 FJ-3 Furies and F7U-3 BuNo 129646 provided the escort.

VX-3 received four F7U-3Ps on 3 May 1955, BuNos 129749 and 129751–753. The squadron was tasked with

Capt Marzelo's fatal accident cause

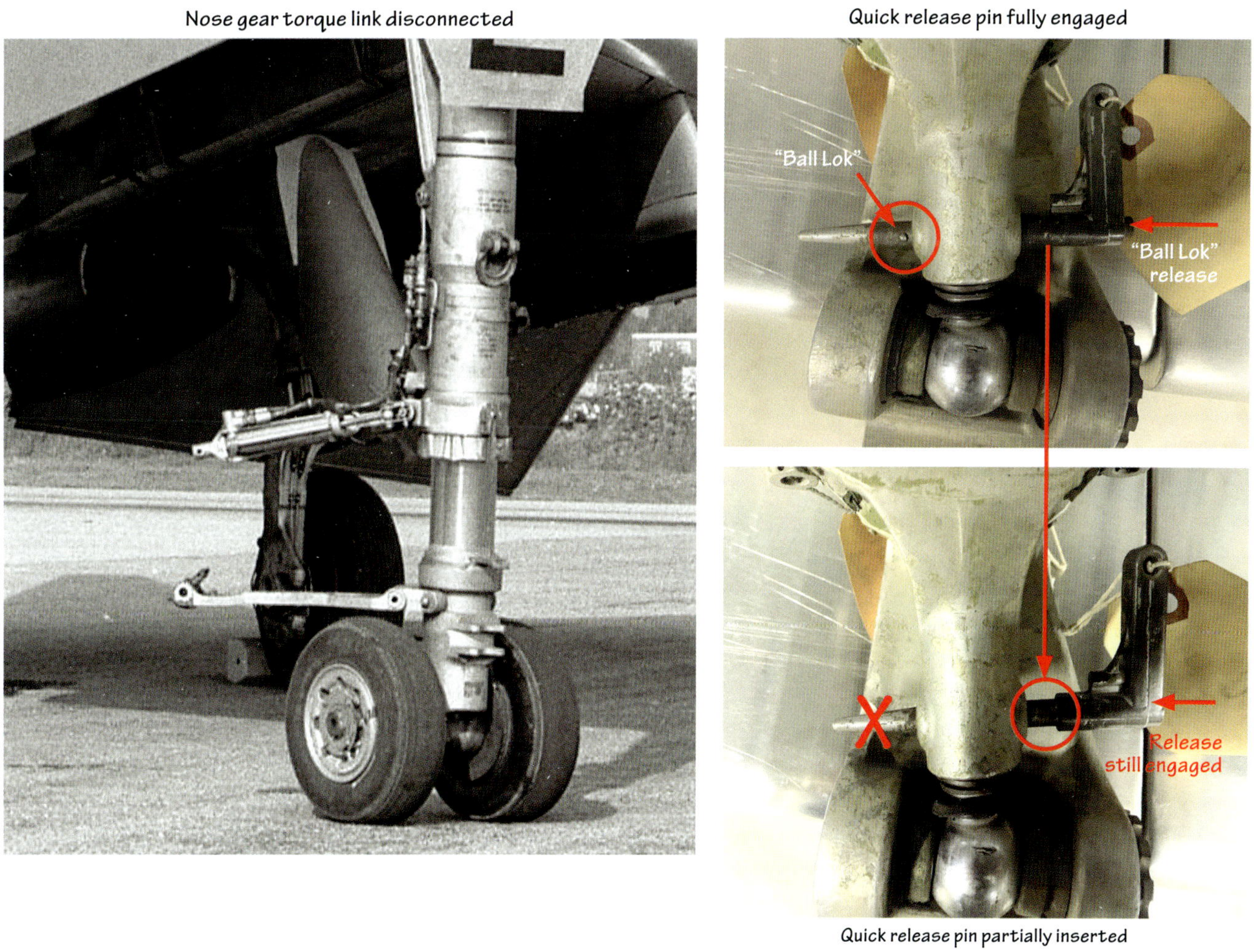

HN 9

XC
NAVY
04

determining the best practices for implementing the F7U-3P into the fleet, with an emphasis on carrier-based operations with the type. They kept their -3Ps in natural metal finish, but some had an orange day-glo vertical stripe just behind the aft edge of the photo-nose, mimicking the squadron's late-model -3s. Once again, squadron numbers were two digits, starting with '00' (as aircraft left VX-3, replacements would be painted with their squadron nose number. As a result, several aircraft (early bulb-nosed F7U-3s, production -3s, and F7U-3Ps) displayed the same nose numbers during their tenure with the squadron).

LT James P. Buckner accomplished the first F7U-3P carrier take-offs and landings in BuNo 129753, operating from *Lake Champlain* (CVA-38) on 1 to 4 June 1955. VX-3 transferred custody of 753 to NAMTC Point Mugu on 5 August for support of the Sparrow I missile programme.

CDR Robert G. Dose took command of VX-3 on 1 July 1955 and began to prepare the squadron for the Vought F8U-1 Crusader, which the squadron was expected to begin testing. In the meantime, VX-3 was busy with continued testing and evaluation of the mirror-assisted landing system and in-flight refuelling, utilising all the aircraft types in its custody.

The late summer of 1955 found VX-3 forced to fly their aircraft inland to escape the unparalleled wrath of Hurricane Diane, which pounded the Atlantic seaboard from 7 to 20 August. The squadron used this 'bug out' to its advantage, recording many photographs of their aircraft taken in flight from their F7U-3Ps. Once the threat of the storm had passed, VX-3 returned to NAS Atlantic City and began preparations for additional carrier qualifications involving its photo-Cutlasses.

Tests involving the British mirror-landing system were conducted aboard *Bennington* (CVA-20) on 22–26 August. These tests included the first utilisation of the mirror, which was accomplished by CDR Dose landing a North American FJ-3 Fury on 22 August. VX-3's LCDR Harding C. MacKnight followed up when he accomplished the first night mirror-assisted landing on 24 August in a Grumman F9F-8. LT Buckner again made history, the first night carrier landing of any Cutlass, when he brought F7U-3P BuNo 129752 aboard *Bennington* on 25 August 1955. He took part in further mirror-assisted landing evaluations on *Bennington* on 15–20 September 1955. (see pages 138-139)

The last two F7U-3s to join VX-3 were transferred from VA-66. F7U-3 BuNo 129556 joined VX-3 on 16 September 1955, but was involved in an unidentified incident on 17 November that resulted in its custody transfer to O&R Quonset Point on 21 December 1955. F7U-3 BuNo129571 arrived on 29 September 1955, but was transferred to VA-34 on 23 March 1956.

BuNo 129749's excellent photographic capabilities were also put to use by VX-3 when they were assigned to document Vought KDU-1 (the high-speed target drone version of the Regulus I missile) testing in April.

TOP PH3 N.F. Hansen loading a K-38 film magazine in VX-3's F7U-3P BuNo 129749 on 5 July 1955 prior to its first photo op at NAS Atlantic City, NJ. *NA113/67(L)7-55 NAS Atlantic City via Casby*

ABOVE Vought KDU-1 Regulus target missile as photographed in flight by VX-3's LT James R. Dillingham on 23 April 1956 while flying F7U-3P 129749. *NA113/2147(L)4-56 Casby Collection*

OPPOSITE TOP One of the most iconic photographs ever taken of the F7U-3 was accomplished by VX-3's LT John H. Cover while flying F7U-3P BuNo 129749. On 28 May 1955, Cover snapped the shot of his squadron mate, LT Randy Prothro while he was in-flight refuelling from a VAH-7 AJ-2 Savage tanker. The photo, which was taken from directly above, appeared in magazines and newspapers all over the world, and demonstrated the advances in both fighter design as well as long-range capabilities. From a viewpoint seldom seen, this photo became instantly iconic for not only its subject, but also its unique perspective. *US Navy*

OPPOSITE BOTTOM Although NATC did not do any at-sea testing of the F7U-3P during the type's abbreviated BIS trials, it was considered carrier qualified by similarity to the F7U-3. *CVA-39 1718 via Casby*

ABOVE VX-3 FJ-3 flown by LCDR Donald D. Engen takes the lead with LT Frank Austin flying wing in F7U-3 BuNo 129646 on 12 May 1955. Dr Austin was the first Naval Flight Surgeon to dual-qualify as a naval aviator and test pilot. *NA113/100(L)7-55 Casby Collection*

RIGHT LT James R Dillingham of VX-3 climbing aboard F7U-3P BuNo 129749 on 4 April 1956 for a Regulus I missile chase flight. Note the blanked-off muzzle openings on the inlet and the -3P unique flare compartment bulge and door. The anti-glare panel is green and the VX-3 fluorescent orange vertical stripe around the nose is discernible. *NA113/2053(L)4-56 via Casby*

VX-4 BuNo 129704 photo shoot with four test Sparrow Is in April 1955. *US Navy*

It was the last F7U to be relinquished by VX-3 when its custody was transferred to O&R Norfolk on 22 May 1956. This followed the transfer of BuNos 129751 and 752 on 10 April and 12 April 1956 respectively, also to O&R Norfolk.

Air Development Squadron Four (VX-4) *Vanguards*. Home-based at NAS Point Mugu, California, the VX-4 *Vanguards* worked hand-in-hand with the scientific, engineering, and flight test personnel at the co-located Naval Air Missile Test Center (NAMTC). Utilising multiple aircraft types, NAMTC conducted the theoretical evaluation and initial functional testing of air-launched missiles. BuAer – which had previously fought with the BuOrd for control over guided missile development – identified the need for close co-operation between NAMTC and a developmental squadron that would aid in the integration of these missiles to the fleet.

Established on 15 September 1952, VX-4's mission statement clearly outlined the scope of its responsibilities: 'To conduct projects that evaluate air-launched guided missiles and special weapons development as related to air launched missiles. To conduct tests and evaluations of aircraft weapons systems and support systems in an operational environment, and to develop all-weather intercept tactics utilising air-launched guided missiles.'

A co-located developmental squadron dedicated solely to this mission allowed BuAer to comprehensively evaluate both NAMTC's data and the squadron's test results. This facilitated the timely formulation of fleet integration plans that would have been difficult had the NAMTC and VX-4 been geographically separated.

CDR Harold Henry 'Swede' Larsen commanded VX-4 when custody of their first F7U-3M, BuNo 129701, was transferred to the squadron on 26 January 1955. He oversaw VX-4's early flight evaluations of the Sparrow I missile fired from the F7U-3M, as well as two Douglas F3D-2M Skyknights. Two shore-based Marine Corps squadrons were equipped with the F3D-2M – however, the F7U-3M was selected by BuAer as the chosen platform for the first operational deployment of a carrier-based, guided missile-equipped Navy fighter. VX-4 eventually held custody of twenty-nine individual Cutlasses between January 1955 and May 1957, including four F7U-3Ps to be used for photographic documentation of the missile's firing tests. Acting as the operational liaison between NAMTC and the individual companies involved in the Sparrow I's manufacture, VX-4 provided the NAMTC with timely operational feedback during the F7U's launch platform development, as well as simultaneously providing Sperry, Douglas (the Sparrow's airframe manufacturer), and Vought with direct progress reports through their individual Field Representatives.

Two months into VX-4's tenure with the F7U-3M, they experienced their first accident when Executive Officer CDR Raymond J. Devito landed BuNo 129725 short of the Point Mugu runway during his eighth familiarisation flight on 25 March 1955. Striking the edge of the runway, the nose landing gear failed and the aircraft caught fire due to broken hydraulic lines. Devito safely evacuated the aircraft but incurred a hand injury when the canopy rolled closed following his disengagement of the canopy actuating cylinder to manually open the canopy. Attributing the cause to pilot error, the investigators did note that a lack of a thrust indicator may have contributed to the accident.

VX-4 took part in F7U-3M carrier suitability trials aboard *Shangri-La* (CVA-38) in May 1955. Two months after Devito's accident, LT Walter M. Earley Jr. suffered a nose gear scissor failure during an otherwise normal carrier landing on 25 May. The resultant shimmy caused by the disconnected scissors caused extensive structural damage, wrinkling the lower fuselage skin from behind the cockpit to the aircraft's mid-section. The Cutlass was offloaded to O&R San Diego and subsequently sat on its ramp until finally being struck off charge over three years later. The first of VX-4's two fatal accidents occurred on 29 July 1955 when LT Robert Walter Slezak is presumed to have entered a post-stall gyration at 3,500ft following his take-off from Point Mugu. His aircraft impacted the sea in a wings-level dive, but there was no attempt to eject. Slezak was flying one of VX-4's F7U-3Ps, BuNo 129756, on a four-plane flight to NASF Litchfield Park when he lost control.

In September 1955, command of the squadron was transferred to Second World War ace CAPT Roger Richards 'Rog' Hedrick. He was assisted by Executive Officer CDR Howard J. Silberstein. In February 1956, Hedrick requested the transfer of F7U-3M-qualified CDR Edward S. Park from VF-151. Park was the commanding officer of VF-151 while it was equipped with F7U-3Ms. However, the squadron had been redesignated VA-151 and was being re-equipped with F7U-3s. Park assumed the role of VX-4's Developmental Operations Officer and oversaw the testing and evaluation of the procedures and tactics that the squadron's pilots developed. He was instrumental in counselling the squadron's pilots on adherence to safety protocols and standard procedures.

VX-4's aircraft initially appeared in a natural metal finish, with variations of the squadron's livery depending upon when they arrived. Wearing the fin code 'XF' and using two-digit unit numbers, the squadron's aircraft appeared with insignia blue fin tips, wing tips and aft canopy bordered by a tapered red stripe. The blue field of the fins and canopy were further adorned with white stars, which varied in number depending upon the individual aircraft (some VX-4 Cutlasses never received the stars on the canopy trim). In January 1956, VX-4 was selected to deploy a five-plane detachment aboard *Lexington* (CVA-16) the following May to operationally evaluate the F7U-3M's capabilities and service requirements aboard ship. In preparation for this deployment, the chosen aircraft (BuNos 139873, 874, 875, 881 and 898) received the newly adopted new light gull grey over gloss insignia white paint scheme. Pre-deployment carrier qualifications (carquals) took place aboard *Lexington* in mid-March 1956 while it was operating out of Bremerton, Washington, and on 13 April 1956 near San Diego concurrent with family cruises for the ship's company. Several of the VX-4 F7U-3M's still wore their shore-based 1X and 2X unit numbers during the carquals, but deployment aircraft would soon be painted with 3X numbers.

In preparation for the upcoming deployment, LT William Mohlenhoff and wingman LT Brooke Montgomery were involved in section tactics training at 40,000ft off the coast of Ventura, California, on 1 February 1956. They collided prior to initiating a practice run on a towed target. Mohlenhoff's BuNo 139878 was struck on its underside by his wingman's canopy after he initiated a right turn while still in formation. Montgomery was most likely fatally injured immediately upon contact, and his BuNo 129712 spiralled into the sea with no attempt at ejection. A Naval Academy graduate, Montgomery was the son of VADM Alfred E. Montgomery, the former Commander Air Forces Pacific (ComAirPac). Following this tragic loss, VX-4 suffered yet another incident during carquals aboard *Bon Homme Richard* (CVA-31) on 28 February 1956. LCDR Morris A. Esmiol Jr. was advised by his wingman of a hydraulic leak from his nose gear well. He landed aboard the ship, but his arresting hook point broke off after running the cross-deck pendant out 132ft. He applied both afterburners and successfully became airborne but was unable to close the canopy – an indication that his landing gear had not fully retracted – most probably due to loss of hydraulic fluid. Unable to reach land with his remaining fuel load, he elected to ditch his Cutlass. The ditching was perfect in all aspects – the only visible damage incurred was to the radome and the shearing of the tail cone attachment points. LCDR Esmiol was rescued uninjured. F7U-3M BuNo 129723 remained afloat for thirteen minutes following the ditching.

An unadorned VX-4 F7U-3M being prepared for engine start on *Shangri-La* (CVA-38). *US Navy*

VX-4 F7U-3M BuNo 129740 was acquired from VA-151 just prior to the deployment of both squadrons aboard *Lexington* (CVA-16). This aircraft occupied the ship's hangar deck as a spare during the CVA-16 deployment, and was subsequently left in the custody of NAF Atsugi's FASRon-11. Note the newly applied black parel-keytone anti-corrosion coating on the landing gear. *Casby Collection*

With the loss of or heavy damage to six of the squadron's aircraft, the spectre of potential deployment accidents weighed heavy on the pilots selected to participate. LCDR Leland D. Venable was to be the Officer-in-Charge of VX-4's Detachment H with LCDR Esmiol acting as his Executive Officer. Rounding out the pilot roster were LTs Lawrence P. Morgan and William Mohlenhoff. They deployed on 28 May 1956 with forty enlisted men and three chiefs in support of their deployment activities. Despite those early concerns, the Detachment H team conducted all operations during the deployment with few operational problems up until 17 August. LT Morgan launched from *Lexington* in F7U-3M BuNo 139875 and following retraction of the landing gear and slats, noticed a hydraulic leak, which was also witnessed by observers on the deck during his catapult launch. Morgan immediately used emergency air to deploy the slats followed by an attempt to use a similar method to extend the landing gear. The nose gear locked in the down position, but the main gear trailed in the slipstream and refused to fully extend and lock. Morgan climbed to 8,700ft and ejected without injury. He was rescued by *Lexington*'s plane guard helicopter and returned to the ship. Following this loss of one of their five aircraft (four were operational and one held as a spare), Detachment H completed the cruise without incident and returned with their four remaining F7U-3Ms on 20 December. Detachment H holds the honour of completing the first deployment of a Navy missile-equipped air group to the Far East.

While Detachment H was busy in the Pacific, CAPT Hedrick decided to check out in the F7U-3M following mentoring by CDR Silberstein. On 20 July 1956, Hedrick was completing his second flight in the Cutlass with three touch-and-go landings at Point Mugu. Following the third landing, he inadvertently selected only the left engine's afterburner during the attempt to take-off. Hedrick interpreted the resultant slight yaw as a loss of his right engine's thrust and aborted the take-off after already becoming airborne. Returning to the runway surface, he blew both main tyres and lost

On the hangar deck, four ordnance men lift a 300lb Sparrow I up to the launch rail of a VX-4 F7U-3M while a fifth secures it in place. *US Navy*

A VX-4 Cutlass, BuNo 139871, is armed with four dummy Sparrow Is for static display at an airshow. *US Navy*

directional control of 706, coming to a stop partially off the side of the runway. Although uninjured, Hedrick's aircraft sustained enough damage to transfer its custody to O&R San Diego, where it was subsequently stricken following the salvage of usable parts.

With multiple accidents still plaguing the squadron's record, VX-4 again prepared for their second deployment to the Far East aboard *Shangri-La*. Following his graduation from Line Officer's School at Monterey, California, famed BAR Dallas demonstration pilot LCDR John S. 'Jack' Christensen, joined VX-4 as their Maintenance Officer, bringing with him his extensive experience with the Cutlass. He was immediately selected to participate in CVG-2's upcoming deployment as a member of VX-4's Detachment A. Joined by Officer-in-Charge LCDR Benjamin W. 'Ben' Adams and Administrative Officer LCDR Andrew P. 'Andy' Stirnweiss, along with Operations Officer LT Charles E. 'Chuck' Hathaway, the Detachment A team prepared to exceed the operational readiness statistics as well as the actual numbers of missiles fired during the previously conducted evaluations by Detachment 'H' aboard *Lexington* (due in part to their limited Sparrow I availability during that cruise). Prior to their carquals aboard *Shangri-La*, LCDR Christensen was involved in a minor ramp incident in BuNo 129742 while at NAF El Centro, California, on 11 October 1956.

With four squadrons and six detachments on board, CVG-2 was comprised of eleven different aircraft types – a definite operational challenge for any air group. Following their shakedown cruise off San Diego, California, in October, Detachment A embarked on *Shangri-La* on 13 November 1956 with the four aviators and forty-four enlisted maintainers under Aviation Maintenance Chief J.P. Craig. Using VX-4's call sign *Vanderbilt*, the detachment conducted every scheduled mission and shot down six drones with the Sparrow I. They enjoyed full support from Vought, Westinghouse, Sperry, and Raytheon Field Service Representatives (FSRs) who accompanied the squadron during the deployment. Raytheon was involved as they had been chosen to take over the future development of the Sparrow platform.

According to RADM Christiansen in a 1989 rebuttal to CDR John Moore's salty review of the Cutlass that appeared in the Tailhook Association's *The Hook* magazine, he remembered '... in general had a most enjoyable cruise during which we accumulated many hundreds of carrier landings. I don't think there was any concern among any of us that the aircraft was difficult to bring aboard and that included Andy Stirnweiss, who was a (Test Pilot School) graduate.' Indeed, VX-4's Detachment A conducted all missile-firing evaluations that they had set out to accomplish, but not without one incident that marred their perfect record. On 2 February 1957, LT Hathaway lost control of BuNo 129704 after completing a successful arrested landing. He had taxied forward at what was deemed an excessive speed and skidded into

VX-5 was second only to VX-3 in being assigned a F7U-3 for an initial operational evaluation. ***US Navy***

several parked aircraft as a result. His aircraft sustained substantial damage and had to be craned off at Yokosuka, Japan. Its custody was transferred to FASRon-11 at Atsugi on 29 April. Having achieved their planned goals, on 2 May 1957 the Detachment transferred custody of its remaining aircraft to NAF Oppama, Japan, to provide spare F7U-3Ms for future deployed squadrons. BuNos 129590, 129700, and 129703 were towed to the NAF, but were eventually returned stateside. The members of Detachment A were flown home on Naval Transport Service aircraft.

While Detachment A had been busy in the Far East, VX-4 was wrapping up their testing with the F7U at Point Mugu. F7U-3M BuNo 139871 suffered a blown tyre during ENS John C. Tibbs' landing roll-out on 3 January 1957, causing it to run off the side of the runway. It incurred only slight damage and was repaired quickly in time for the retirement of the squadron's stateside Cutlasses scheduled to occur later that month. On 30 January 1957, BuNo 129742 was the last of VX-4's five remaining F7U-3Ms to be flown to NASF Litchfield Park, Arizona.

Air Development Squadron Five (VX-5) ***Vampires.*** VX-5 was established on 18 June 1951 at NAS Moffett Field, California, to accomplish the development and evaluation of aircraft tactics and techniques for delivery of airborne 'special weapons' in all-weather conditions, day or night. Although training flights for pilot check out and proficiency – as well as all heavy maintenance work on the aircraft – remained at Moffett, most of the developmental flying was accomplished on ranges located at Naval Ordnance Test Station (NOTS) Inyokern (later China Lake), California. Nicknamed the *Vampires*, VX-5 occupied permanent office and hangar space, as well as detachment quarters, at Inyokern's Armitage Field.

The squadron assumed custody of its first F7U-3 on 6 May 1953 with VX-5's Commanding Officer, CDR Thomas J. Walker, flying BuNo 128465 from BAR Dallas to Moffett Field the following day. Ten days later, F7U-3 BuNo 128466 would also be transferred to VX-5, providing the squadron with the opportunity to begin training its seven special project pilots on the two early J-35-powered Cutlasses. Both aircraft – carrying the side numbers 1 and 2 respectively – retained their

BuNo 129665 was one of the last of the F7U-3s to be assigned to VX-5 for the operational evaluation of special weapons, here with a TX-11 shape under its left wing. ***US Navy via Premselaar***

natural finish and wore the 'XE' tail code assigned to the squadron. F7U Project Officer LTJG Joseph Ellison led tactics evaluations with the two aircraft beginning on 15 June 1953.

VX-5's command would soon change on 18 June 1953 – the second anniversary of its establishment – when CDR Walker handed the reins to CDR Horace H. Epes, Jr., who would oversee the arrival of two additional F7U-3s in late April 1954 – joining the squadron's F3D, F2H, and F9F jets, along with piston-powered AD Skyraider aircraft used in their development projects. These two aircraft, BuNos 129549 (XE/1) and 129555 (XE/2) – both final production variants – would replace the early bulb-nosed models. Command of the squadron would once again change with the arrival of CDR William N. Leonard in June 1954. VX-5 would relinquish 128465 and 128466 to O&R San Diego by August 1954, while two additional aircraft, BuNos 129682 and 129695, would arrive on 14 October bringing the VX-5 complement to four aircraft. However, these last two aircraft were quickly transferred to VF-124 at NAS Miramar on 22 November. Replacement aircraft began arriving on 23 November with BuNo 129670 (XE/3) and 129674 (XE/4), soon followed by 129661 (XE/1) and 129665 (XE/2), which replaced 549 and 555. VX-5 applied the squadron's new and distinctive green and white banding to the nose and fins of these four Cutlasses.

Under Senior Projects Officer LCDR William W. Dyer, VX-5 returned to Armitage Field to conduct development and testing of the Low Altitude Bombing System (LABS). Working closely with Chance Vought Technical Representative William Watson, Project Officer LCDR Atlee F. Clapp was tasked with the evaluation of the F7U's loft-bombing capability and the development of a preliminary manual for use in training fleet pilots in the technique.

In addition to LABS development, VX-5's F7U-3s were assigned to evaluate the release characteristics of tactical nuclear bombs being developed at the NOTS, in concert with the efforts of the Naval Air Special Weapons Facility (NASWF) at Kirkland AFB, New Mexico, and the Special Weapons Unit – Pacific (SWUPAC) at Moffett Field. Using up to an 80-degree dive angle, Project Officers LT S. Joel Premselaar and LT Joseph M. McFadden evaluated release techniques for nuclear stores ranging from 12 to 60 kilotons. The largest weapon still required the folding of one of the store's fins to accommodate ground clearance, but all smaller stores could be carried with their fins fully spread due to the copious ground clearance afforded by the F7U-3 – an ability not available on any other aircraft involved in the testing. These aircraft featured red paint added to the upper and underside outboard wing surfaces to assist in photographic analysis.

Along with NOTS pilots, VX-5 took part in 104 simulated nuclear store releases from F7U-3s between March and October 1955. For example, a loop recovery was evaluated for the over-the-shoulder delivery rather than a half-Cuban 8 in order to minimise the Y-effect (the shock wave reflected by the ground augmenting the force of the initial wave). The F7U-3's afterburners provided the thrust necessary for this escape manoeuvre to be feasible.

CDR Filmore B. Gilkerson assumed command of VX-5 in June 1955 and presided over the custody transfer of the squadron's four F7U-3s back to BAR Dallas between 23 January and 19 April 1956.

Fleet Squadrons

F7U-3s were assigned to a total of eleven fleet squadrons. In some cases, the initial assignment was as a fighter squadron that was subsequently redesignated as an attack squadron with essentially the same personnel and at least initially the same aircraft. The redesignation was primarily to change the squadron's mission assignment within an air group and therefore its specific training emphasis.

Fleet squadrons were assigned to numbered Carrier Air Groups (CVGs) or to Air Task Groups (ATGs). The two were functionally identical but ATGs were relatively temporary units formed with 'surplus' squadrons from existing carrier air groups when the Navy's need for them exceeded the Congressional statutory limit on carrier air groups.

Attack Squadron Twelve (VA-12) *Flying Ubangis*. Originally established as Bombing Fighter Squadron FOUR (VBF-4) flying the F4U Corsair and designated VF-2A in May 1947, the squadron transitioned to the F8F Bearcat in May 1947 and was redesignated VF-12 on 2 August 1948. In September 1950, the squadron joined the jet age when they transitioned to the McDonnell F2H-2 Banshee. VF-12 became the first jet-equipped squadron to completely carrier qualify at night. After flying the Banshee for five years, on 1 August 1955 they were again redesignated as VA-12 with their new mission changing from 'jet intercept' to 'special weapons attack' under the command of CDR Paul H. Durand. He was expecting that his F2H-2 Banshees would be replaced by the new A4D-1 Skyhawk as soon as deliveries began. Instead, he was advised that he would be receiving F7U-3s. He recalled: 'Neither the Air Group Commander nor the Squadron Commander had been advised or consulted before this action was taken.' Not only that, he was under the impression that the Navy had decided 'sometime in 1955 … not to assign available F7U-3s to any more squadrons and to store them' because 'nose gear, hydraulic system, engine and other problems had curtailed its use aboard carriers and ashore'. He subsequently opined in an unpublished article that the decision had been reversed so the Navy did not have to admit to Congress that they were having difficulties fielding yet another aircraft as they were with the R3Y Tradewind, the F3H Demon, and the F4D Skyray. 'In an effort to relieve political pressure, the Navy made a decision to assign F7U-3s being held out of service to at least four squadrons. After all, of all the programmes in trouble only the Cutlasses were flyable and ready for assignment.'

While that interpretation may be at least somewhat correct (VA-34 in the adjacent hangar had also just received F7U-3s even though its air group already included VA-66 that was equipped with F7U-3s), the first delivery of the Skyhawk to a fleet squadron was not imminent; in fact, the first one did not occur until September 1956. In the meantime, the jet attack squadrons being tasked with nuclear weapon delivery needed to be flying aircraft that were capable of that.

VA-12 received their first F7U-3s on 21 December 1955 when four aircraft were delivered from VA-83 in preparation for that squadron's transition to the F7U-3M. Seven more F7U-3s arrived in January–February 1956, and in March 1956 the squadron received the last two Cutlasses to form its initial complement of thirteen aircraft. Home-based at NAS Cecil Field, Florida, VA-12 became the primary east coast special weapons squadron under the Commander of Fleet Air Jacksonville (COMFAIRJAX). Adorned with CVG-1's 'T' tail code, and having previously adopted the nickname *Flying Ubangis*, VA-12's aircraft featured their distinctive 'Kiss of Death' squadron insignia on the upper fins, as well as blue fin tips, rudders, lower fin surfaces, wing tips, and a unique blue lightning bolt on the aft canopy. In addition, the squadron's side number was painted in large numerals on the aircraft's dorsal spine, although not all squadron aircraft received this side number treatment.

VA-12 suffered seven accidents during their operations with the F7U-3, beginning in June 1956. On 8 June LCDR J.D. Kidd departed NAS Cecil Field in BuNo 129667 (T/12) and immediately suffered a flight stabilisation system trim amplifier failure. Experiencing heavy adverse stick forces – but failing to engage the emergency trim system – he elected to land on a 3,300ft auxiliary airstrip and applied emergency air brakes to effect a stop within the confines of the paved area. Blowing both tyres, his aircraft departed the right side of the runway and sheared off the port main gear. The aircraft was sent to O&R Jacksonville for evaluation and was struck off charge on 10 July. Two weeks later, LTJG William J. 'Bill' Doody was forced to eject from BuNo 129645 near Starke, Florida, on 22 June. Flying at 10,000ft, he was busy purging the belly fuel pod when both afterburner fire warning lights illuminated. Retarding the throttles to idle, Doody noted that both engine's RPM and tailpipe outlet temperatures (TOT) were reacting normally. Advancing back to military thrust, the port engine's fire warning light illuminated. He ejected at a very low altitude and landed in a field, where he was rescued by a civilian light aircraft pilot who saw him eject and landed his own aircraft to aid the shaken aviator.

On 29 August LT E.D. Howell in BuNo 129572 (T/10) was preparing to land at Cecil Field and upon deploying the landing gear, the starboard main gear remained up and locked with that gear's doors closed. Emergency air was selected in an attempt to blow the gear down, but this failed and a landing was attempted using the field's arresting gear. Engaging the arresting pendants, the aircraft swerved off the runway and struck an arresting chain, which sheared the nose gear and collapsed the port main gear. Howell was uninjured, and the accident

ABOVE CDR Paul H. Durand's BuNo 129669 seen at NAS New York's Floyd Bennett Field in 1956. Note the unique position of the squadron C.O.'s name on the canopy. *Casby Collection*

LEFT A very rare in-flight photograph of BuNo 129694 (T/12) showing the squadron's side numbers painted in extremely large font on the aircraft's dorsal spine. Note also the stylised 'T' on the starboard wing. *Casby Collection*

VA-12's forlorn crash victim, BuNo 129572 (T/10), 'photo bombing' rival VA-34's 'class photo'. *Casby Collection via RADM James M. 'Mac' Gleim USN*

VA-12 F7U-3 BuNo129559 on display at a NAS Pensacola airshow prior to its runway excursion at NAS Cecil Field, Florida, on 7 December 1956. *Joe Gryson photograph via Casby*

was attributed to a faulty sequence or shuttle valve in the landing gear hydraulic circuit. Humorously, VA-12 took some pleasure in the stricken aircraft appearing in the background of rival Cecil Field-based VA-34's official squadron roster photographs.

VA-12 participated in multiple exercises involving the dropping of special weapon-shaped stores, and conducted gunnery exercises at the Avon Park, Florida, bombing range with regularity. However, an inability to simultaneously field two four-plane divisions, much less an entire squadron, resulted in changes being made to the intended plan for VA-12's utilisation within the air group. They had initially been chosen to deploy to the Mediterranean in August 1956, but in assessing the recent mishaps and lengthy maintenance-related delays in maintaining an 'up' status for the majority of VA-12's F7U-3s, ComAirLant made the decision to cancel any additional F7U-equipped squadron's involvement. It had become clear that, unlike ComAirPac on the west coast, by then ComAirLant had decided that F7Us were more trouble than they were worth. As a result, no east coast air group deployed with an F7U-3 squadron thereafter. VA-12 did not even go aboard *Forrestal* with CVG-1 for a one-month shakedown cruise to the Azores that began on 7 November 1956; the jet attack squadron that participated was VA-76 from ATG-182 (tail code 'O') flying the F9F-8B; VA-12 was also left behind in favour of VA-76 when *Forrestal* made its first deployment with CVG-1, departing for the Mediterranean on 15 January 1957. VA-12's morale degraded as they witnessed west coast-based attack squadrons deploying successfully

with the Cutlass, while they struggled to maintain section strength.

Adding to the woes, on 5 October 1956 F7U-3 BuNo 129558 (T/8) was ground-looped during landing and subsequently struck off charge, followed by LTJG Bill Doody blowing a tyre during landing with BuNo 129559 (the 'new' T/8) on 7 December. His aircraft departed the left side of the runway and sheared off the starboard main gear. Fortunately, Doody suffered no injury. An investigation concluded that the newly resurfaced runway contained some 'slick spots', which may have caused unequal braking conditions.

CDR Marshall P. 'Pete' Deputy, Jr. assumed command of VA-12 in January 1957. He was involved in a ground-loop accident on 7 March 1957 with BuNo 129573, resulting in it being stricken on 21 March. The same day, BuNo 129576 was involved in a ground-equipment accident which resulted in it being struck off charge the same day due to heavy damage.

The squadron began the transition to the A4D-1 in April 1957. Ten of their remaining F7Us were flown to Naval Air Reserve Training Units (NARTUs) to become maintenance trainers and gate guardians in May, with four additional Cutlasses being flown to NAF Litchfield Park for long-term storage. Although they did not enjoy a deployment with the type, and the learning curve (especially for the mechanics) was steep, the opportunity to fly the F7U was generally met with enthusiasm. CDR Durand's reminiscences were not all negative: 'Since the early days of the Cutlass, much had been learned about (its flight characteristics) and this helped overcome pilots' concerns about flying this strange-looking aircraft with a bad reputation. The transition was made with minimum difficulties …' He also reported 'the Cutlass handled the transition through the sonic region very smoothly. The rate of roll was fantastic; the turning radius was excellent; the speed brakes were smooth and efficient. The Cutlass was a fun airplane to fly!'

Attack Squadron Thirty-Four (VA-34) *Fighting Tigers*. VF-34 was established on 15 February 1950 and began to replace their Grumman F8F Bearcats with jets, the Grumman F9F-2 Panther and subsequently the McDonnell F2H-2 Banshee. In April 1953, they were one of the first squadrons to evaluate the new angled deck aboard *Antietam* (CVA-36). In November 1953 they were assigned to the newly formed ATG-181 and subsequently made one shakedown cruise aboard *Hornet* (CVA-12) and one deployment aboard *Randolph* (CVA-15) from November 1954 to June 1955. Once back at NAS Cecil Field, Florida, they were reassigned to CVG-3 and redesignated VA-34 on 1 July 1955 to begin the process of gearing up for the arrival of the F7U-3 Cutlass with the assigned mission of 'special weapons attack'. They received their first F7U-3s, BuNo 129621 and 129625 on 6 October. Since they were only just beginning their transition to the Cutlass, VA-66 took their place on the CVG-3 deployment that began on 4 November and they fell under the administrative control of COMFAIRJAX along with VA-12. By the end of November they had added twelve more Cutlasses, achieving squadron strength, but were still in the process of training pilots and maintainers on the Cutlass. As the third squadron in CVG-3, VA-34 was assigned side numbers in the 300 range and the tail code 'K', with medium blue wing and fin tips. The radio call-sign 'Fighting Tiger' pluralised became the de-facto squadron nickname, and pilots wore orange-painted helmets with black tiger stripes fashioned out of electrical tape; their flight jackets adorned with the already popular cigarette-smoking skull insignia approved in 1949. Although it is widely assumed that VA-34 were known as the 'Blue Blasters' while operating Cutlasses, this moniker was not adopted until the squadron transitioned to the A4D-1 Skyhawk in March 1957.

VA-34 was initially helmed by acting commanding officer CDR Austin L. Detweiller, but by 28 October 1955 he had turned over the reins to CDR Charles W. Pittman Jr. Assisted by Executive Officer LCDR Ernest L. McClintock, Pittman made the squadron's first F7U-3 flight on 4 November 1955. Many of his pilots were first-tour aviators who were eager to fly the Navy's newest jet fighter. It has been surmised that the relative inexperience of the squadron's new pilots upon arrival at VA-34 actually served them well, in that they did not have to shed bad habits and were eager to learn to fly the Cutlass without any predispositions. Asked by his CO if he was scared to fly the Cutlass on his first day reporting for duty, ENS John T. (then nicknamed 'Andy') Anderson responded, 'I don't even know what a Cutlass is yet, so how could I be scared of it?' Checking out without issue, he amassed 115 F7U-3 hours before transitioning to the A4D Skyhawk and enjoyed flying the aircraft immensely while acknowledging its limitations in the nuclear delivery role compared to the A4D.

The squadron's mid-level officers were mostly retained aviators from VF-34's assignment to the F2H-2 Banshee. LTJG Duane L. 'Zeke' Varner, considered by many to be one of the finest natural pilots they had ever witnessed, had previously set a record flying non-stop from NAS Los Alamitos, California, to NAS Cecil Field in Jacksonville, Florida, in three hours fifty-eight minutes – a record for the F2H-2. Recalling his time in VA-34 flying the Cutlass, RADM James M. 'Mac' Gleim, then a LTJG who amassed 350 hours of F7U-3 flight time, opined: 'The Cutlass was a real "Cadillac" to fly, and a showstopper wherever it went.' VA-34 pilots generally enjoyed the Cutlass and with the exception of three accidents in seventeen months, they and their maintenance crews performed exceptionally well.

VA-34 operated successfully in their role as the air group's special weapon deliverymen, participating in

VA-34 roster photo taken soon after the arrival of the first two F7U-3s, BuNo 129621 and 129625. *Casby Collection via RADM J.M. Gleim, USN*

gunnery and bombing exercises throughout 1956 and early 1957. Flying a full attack syllabus that included low-level navigation, rocketry, strafing, and LABS exercises, the pilots became proficient in all methods of ground attack. VA-34 participated in *Operation Tenderfeet* in the third week of March 1956 at Camp Mackall in North Carolina – in competition with Army and Air Force aviation units, they scored at the top in ground attack and bombing exercises. Additionally, they completed in-flight refuelling qualifications on 26 June 1956. When the week-long Suez Crisis started on 29 October 1956, it was VA-34 pilots who were ordered to fully armed alert status, sitting in their cockpits around the clock in shifts with ground power units ready to start the aircraft.

In a stunning display of the all too typical bureaucratic thought process, COMFAIRJAX overlooked the obvious fact that none of the aircraft could make it to Bermuda – let alone the Middle East – if ordered to 'attack', as there were no tanker aircraft available to them.

The squadron's pilots routinely participated in many airshows around the eastern portion of the country, usually performing a forty-five-minute flight demonstration and then fielding questions from the crowds in front of their Cutlass. Single aircraft demonstrations were held in celebration of Armed Forces Day at Dobbins AFB, Craig AFB, Moody AFB, Shaw AFB, Hunter AFB, Lovell Field in Chattanooga, Tennessee, and NAS Jacksonville between 19 and 20 May 1956. A full squadron flight of all thirteen VA-34 F7U-3s to NAS Glynco in Brunswick, Georgia, resulted in ten aircraft completing the trip and appearing in an impressive flyover during the airshow there, while three returned to Cecil Field with maintenance issues.

VA-34 experienced three accidents and three incidents during their tenure with the F7U-3. On 16 December 1955, ENS John G. 'Curty' Curtis was attempting to perform a loop above 25,000ft when he stalled the aircraft and entered a post-stall gyration. Despite initiating the proper recovery technique, he prematurely ejected at 20,000ft, thinking he was at 10,000ft. His aircraft, BuNo 129628, recovered from the PSG on its own, and impacted the ground in a steep dive. On 23 July 1956 ENS John T. Anderson ran BuNo 129623 (K-109) off the left side of Cecil Field's runway after blowing a left main tyre following heavy braking during landing. The aircraft dug into the muddy ground, but the landing gear did not collapse and it was back in service within days.

LT George B. 'Scott' Ball Jr. was flying BuNo 129621 (K-310) during a section training mission on 21 September 1956. His canopy inexplicably opened in flight at 16,000ft, necessitating his immediate descent into Cecil Field. He landed without incident or injury. The

VA-34 was well represented at airshows around the country. Here, first Executive Officer LCDR Morris Lovern's BuNo 129620 (K-309) is admired by a bevy of onlookers. *Casby Collection*

Ten VA-34 F7U-3s headed to NAS Glynco in Brunswick, Georgia. VA-34 Photo. *Casby Collection via RADM J.M. Gleim, USN*

RIGHT ENS Anderson's runway excursion in BuNo 129623 following a blown tyre during the landing rollout. *NAS Cecil Field NA117-9393(L)7-56 photo, Casby Collection via John Anderson*

BELOW ENS Ira Lewey ran BuNo 129624, named to LTJG Varner, off the taxiway while taxiing for take-off on the evening of 2 October 1956. It is seen here with a VA-34 mechanic aboard following systems checks on 2 November 1956. *NAS Cecil NA117-9900 (L)-11/56, Casby Collection via RADM J.M. Gleim*

aircraft was transferred to FASRon-9, repaired and reassigned to VA-12. Five days later, ENS Ira D. (Dale) Lewey – on his second flight in a F7U-3 – blew a left main tyre on BuNo 129623 during his take-off roll at Cecil Field on 26 September 1956. The tyre separated from the wheel and he was forced to execute a field-arrested landing. He touched down to the right of centreline and proceeded to depart the runway – after crossing a portion of the arresting chains the aircraft was substantially damaged. Lewey was not injured and the aircraft was repaired and put back into service. ENS Lewey was again involved in an incident following a cross-country trip to NAS Pensacola, Florida, on 2 October 1956 when he accidentally ran off the taxiway while preparing to take-off that evening. His aircraft, BuNo 129624 (K-313) was not seriously damaged and was repaired prior to his departure the next morning. On 2 November 1957, LTJG Frederick W. Grupp, while landing BuNo 129630, touched down too fast and blew his left main gear tyre. He elected to go around and the field's arresting system was rigged for his landing. However, Grupp bounced over the arresting wire and departed the runway, shearing off both the left main gear and the nose gear upon contact with the soft earth. Grupp was not injured, but the aircraft was struck off charge due to the extensive damage.

VA-34 was rightfully proud of sustaining no injuries to its pilots during its F7U-3 operational period. Through constant training they met or exceeded all mission responsibilities assigned to them. In January 1957, Executive Officer (now-CDR) McClintock was selected to assume the Commanding Officer duties for VA-34 in preparation for the arrival of the squadron's new A4D-1 Skyhawks. With the exception of three aircraft transferred to their Cecil Field neighbour – VA-12 – the squadron's F7U-3s were flown to NASF Litchfield Park in late February 1957.

Fighter Squadron Eighty-One (VF-81)/Attack Squadron Sixty-Six (VA-66) *Waldomen*. Established at NAS Atlanta, Georgia, during the height of the Korean War, VF-671, a Naval Reserve fighter squadron, was called to active duty on 1 February 1951 equipped with the venerable Chance Vought F4U-4 Corsair. The squadron was assigned to CVG-8 on 9 April 1951 and its aircraft wore CVG-8's 'E' tail code. VF-671 transitioned to Grumman's F8F-2 Bearcat and later the Grumman F9F-5 Panther prior to being redesignated VF-81 on 4 February 1953. Now home-based at NAS Oceana, Virginia, VF-81 adopted an iconic insignia that was approved on 28 September 1953 featuring a 'fighting rooster' toting a smoking machine gun. The insignia's artist named the rooster 'Waldo' and VF-81 adopted the squadron nickname 'Waldomen'.

With previous experience operating jets from carriers gleaned from participating in the angled-deck evaluations aboard *Antietam* (CVA-36) in early 1953, VF-81 deployed aboard *Coral Sea* (CVA-43) to the Mediterranean between April and October of that year. Upon their return to Oceana the squadron continued to train with the F9F-5 in anticipation of transitioning to the Grumman F9F-6 Cougar in early 1954. Much to the squadron member's surprise, they were chosen to be the first of two Atlantic-based fleet squadrons to receive the highly anticipated F7U-3 Cutlass. CDR Herman J. 'Dixie' Harders, a recent participant in the Naval Air Test Center's F7U-3 Fleet Introduction Programme (FIP), was chosen to take command of VF-81. Assisting him in preparing the squadron for the new aircraft was Executive Officer LCDR Charles B. Smith, who also had extensive experience in the F7U-3 at Patuxent River. Along with VF-83, their Oceana-based sister squadron, the Waldomen began preparations for the daunting task of integrating this new aircraft into the fleet. On 22 April 1954, CDR Harders delivered F7U-3 BuNo 129560 to NAS Oceana from BAR Dallas. Six days later, four more new F7U-3s (BuNos 129558, 559, 562 and 563) were delivered. Custody of BuNo 128641 was transferred to the squadron on 14 May 1954 and rounded out VF-81's initial complement of six aircraft.

Intensive training began immediately as the members of VF-81 anticipated joining CVG-8's planned Mediterranean deployment aboard *Lake Champlain* (CVA-39) in September 1954. However, on 1 July 1954 CVG-6's VF-61 was transferred to CVG-8, and VF-81 was transferred to CVG-6 to allow them to gather more experience with the F7U-3 while ensuring that CVG-8 had an operationally ready day fighter squadron for the upcoming deployment. This was contrary to the generally accepted protocol of having each squadron's designator starting with the number of the air group. VF-81's aircraft would now feature the CVG-6 'C' tail code on their gleaming natural finishes with no other livery or painted trim. Their aircraft displayed 1XX squadron numbers consistent with their former position as the first squadron within CVG-8, but not within CVG-6.

As VF-81's senior pilots and maintainers became more comfortable with the F7U-3, they also welcomed new members. On 1 September 1954 the squadron experienced their first of many incidents with the Cutlass. Newly checked out in the Cutlass, LTJG William N. Phillips was climbing out of NAS Oceana when an explosion rocked BuNo 129562 as he passed 30,000ft. Facing an in-flight fire, Phillips (who only had 11.6 hours in the F7U-3) managed to land the Cutlass successfully. An investigation revealed a design issue with the Marmon clamp used to secure the fuel vent line in the tail cone compartment. Custody of the aircraft was transferred to O&R Norfolk, where it was stricken due to extensive damage. A replacement aircraft, F7U-3 BuNo

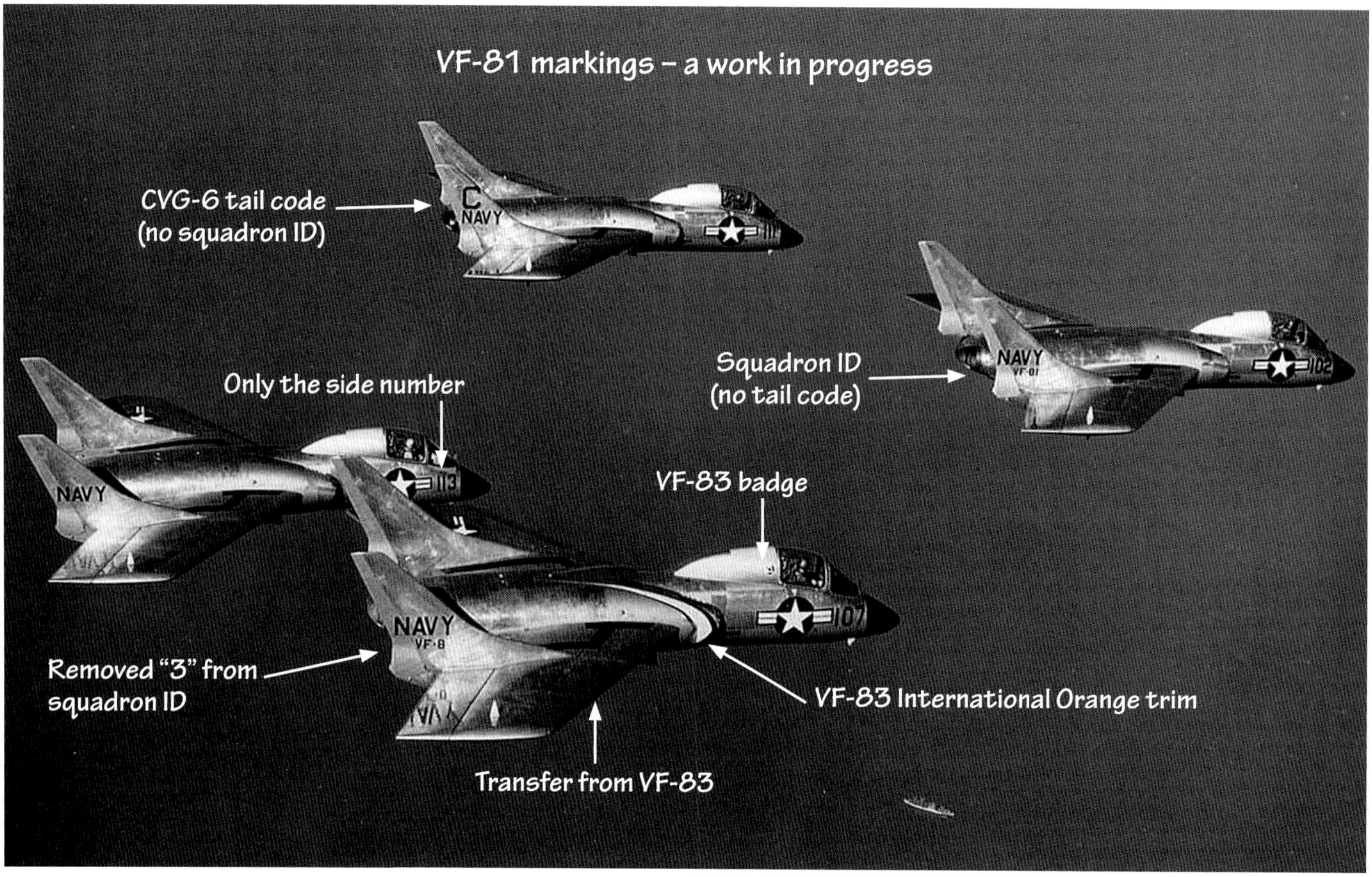

VF-81's early days, already demonstrating Blue Angel-like formation flying even before their aircraft were adorned with the squadron's markings except for the side numbers (107 in the foreground was a transfer from VF-83). *US Navy*

129642, was delivered from BAR Dallas on 18 September along with two additional aircraft, BuNos 129659 and 129664, arriving two days later.

Later that month, ENS Marshal W. White was forced to eject from BuNo 129560 on his initial flight in a Cutlass. On 24 September 1954 White was accelerating from 200 to 250 knots at an altitude of 10,000ft when he felt a 'jolt' following the selection of the second afterburner. He described entering an uncontrolled 'spin manoeuvre' from which he was unable to exit after retarding the throttles. Recovery of the wreckage found no evidence of engine failure, fire, or structural failure that would have caused the loss of control, so White's insistence that it was caused by the reduction in thrust was doubted. A post-stall gyration was suspected. With two of their original six aircraft destroyed, CDR Harders requested additional Vought Field Service Representatives to assist his pilots and maintenance personnel in adapting to the new aircraft and its idiosyncrasies.

Additions to the squadron's fleet arrived with the delivery of nine new Cutlasses from BAR Dallas as well as the transfer of three from VF-83. VF-81 returned three of their original six F7U-3s to BAR Dallas in late November along with two transfers to VF-83. By 1 December 1954, VF-81 was at full squadron strength with fifteen aircraft. The total would be reduced by one within a week and a half. On 11 December 1954, pilots from VF-81 and VF-83 were participating in the commissioning ceremonies for the new 'super carrier', *Forrestal* (CVA-59) at Newport News, Virginia. During a high-speed formation flyby of the reviewing stands, VF-81's LTJG John W. 'Foggy' Hood experienced a control-lock situation later determined to be caused by the ailavator centring device (used to prevent damage to the ailavators and fins during wing folding) becoming engaged in flight. With no ability to control his aircraft, Hood ejected 200ft above the bay at a speed of 450 knots. Although Hood achieved seat separation, he was too low to deploy his parachute and suffered fatal injuries upon impact with the water. His F7U-3, BuNo 129659 crashed between two civilian piers, with the wreckage narrowly missing the Pocahontas Steamship Company's *Pocahontas Fuel*, a 7,828-gross-ton collier (ex-Victory Ship SS *Lynchburg Victory* MC-853), which was being refuelled at Pier 13. Flaming debris from the crash careened past fuel hoses on the dock, but miraculously did not strike the fuelling lines. The condition of the river bottom precluded recovery of any significant wreckage. Comprehensive investigation and post-incident modelling of the accident by Vought engineers resulted in a modification to the wing-fold's centring device and BuAer ordered the modification implemented in all F7U-3 series aircraft.

In January 1955, VF-81's aircraft received medium blue fin tips consistent with their position as the third squadron within CVG-6, but inexplicably continued to display their 1XX squadron numbers. On 2 January

1955, F7U-3 BuNo 129572 joined VF-81, soon followed by BuNos 129669 and 129696 on 17 January. Custody of BuNo 129641 was transferred to FASRon-5 at the end of the month. Squadron strength stood at sixteen aircraft when CDR Harders confirmed that VF-81 had been selected to participate in *Ticonderoga*'s (CVA-14) shakedown cruise, scheduled to commence on 3 February 1955. With little time for preparation, VF-81's personnel worked tirelessly to acquire and box the needed spare parts for this two-month Caribbean excursion. Logistical support for the squadron was hastily arranged at NS Guantanamo Bay, Cuba's Leeward Point Field. By the end of January the squadron was ready.

Initial carrier operations with the F7U-3 went surprisingly well during the voyage to Cuba. However, during 22 February gunnery exercises 50 miles south-south-west of Guantanamo Bay, Ensign Robert B. Leslie's BuNo 129676 collided with the tow target's banner bar. The bar slashed into an outboard slat, but the damage did not impede its function. Leslie had already accumulated sixty-seven hours in the Cutlass, and had little difficulty handling the landing at Leeward Point. The aircraft was subsequently repaired and returned to service.

On 21 March, CDR Harder's BuNo 129684 received damage to its lower fuselage when its tail hook snagged a flash plate on the deck during an arrested landing. The incident identified the propensity for hook bounce and the need to redesign the tail hook damper. The aircraft was damaged beyond the squadron's ability to repair it, and it was relegated to the hangar deck until VF-81 returned to Norfolk. One day later, LT John H. Wise's BuNo 129686 suffered a nose gear scissor failure following a skewed off-centre landing. The lower nose gear wheel assembly then engaged an arresting wire while cocked 90 degrees to the trajectory of the aircraft. Stressed beyond any anticipated load, the nose gear actuator failed at the trunnion attachment point and the nose gear collapsed, resulting in Wise receiving a serious spinal injury. The aircraft was stored for transfer to O&R Norfolk, but was eventually stricken. Thirteen days later, ENS Eugene L. Schnebelt landed aboard *Ticonderoga* with an extreme nose-high pitch resulting in a bounce. BuNo 129668's arresting hook had already engaged the cable resulting in a subsequent pitch-down and nose wheel-first landing, which resulted in the nose gear collapsing. Although the aircraft's nose wheel pre-rotation system was inoperative, the sheer force with which the nose gear struck the deck was determined to be the cause of the failure. ENS Schnebelt received only minor injuries, but 129668 was stricken following its transfer to O&R Norfolk.

With the loss of three aircraft due to landing accidents, VF-81 was put ashore at Leeward Point for the duration of *Ticonderoga*'s Caribbean cruise. The squadron was unwittingly the first to experience nose gear-related issues in the fleet – but it should be noted that each nose gear failure was precipitated by pilots subjecting the aircraft to stresses outside those anticipated in normal carrier operations. VF-81's thirteen functional aircraft launched from *Ticonderoga* on 16 April 1955 prior to the ship making port. CDR Harders was now tasked with assessing the squadron's difficulties encountered (and suggesting fixes for future F7U carrier operations) before handing the reins of command over to incoming commanding officer CDR William J. 'Bill' Manby, a seasoned jet pilot himself. Manby took command in June 1955, and immediately began implementing Harder's suggestions, which included increased liaison with Vought's engineers and test pilots, as well as NATC's Service Test branch.

The beginning of the 1956 fiscal year ushered a major realignment of the composition of many of the Navy's air groups. Fighter squadrons were transitioned to the attack role, and vice versa to meet restrictions imposed by Congress. On 1 July 1955 a new attack squadron was established at NAS Oceana, Virginia, designated VA-66. Later that same day, this newly established VA-66 was redesignated VF-81. Simultaneously, CDR Manby's existing VF-81 was redesignated VA-66 and custody of all fifteen of their F7U-3s were effectively transferred to the new attack squadron on that date. These aircraft were scheduled to be replaced with new F7U-3s being readied at Dallas for delivery to the squadron in August. F7U-3 BuNo 129572 was the first ex-VF-81 Cutlass to be returned to BAR Dallas on 26 July 1955, with BuNo 129669 following a day later.

On the morning of 1 August, tragedy struck the Waldomen when their new skipper was killed while returning BuNo 129673 to BAR Dallas. CDR Manby and his wingman – LT Stephen O. Hesla flying BuNo 129685 – encountered a line of heavy thunderstorms over Tennessee. Manby (who had only accumulated a total of 19.3 flight hours in the Cutlass). Hesla became separated after they entered instrument flight conditions while attempting to divert to Dobbins AFB in Georgia. LT Hesla's attempts to contact Manby failed and he continued on to land at Dobbins, but Manby's aircraft did not arrive. Wreckage of 129673 with Manby's body were discovered that afternoon near Jasper, Tennessee. Although the cause of the crash was listed as 'undetermined', inspection of the aircraft's wreckage indicated a near-vertical impact consistent with a stall/spin trajectory, which led investigators to theorise plausibly that Manby may have entered a post-stall gyration while in the clouds. There was no indication that CDR Manby had attempted to eject. LT Hesla returned 129685 to NAS Oceana, and it was subsequently ferried to BAR Dallas on 8 August. Second

Word War veteran CDR Uncas L. Fretwell was chosen to replace CDR Manby, and assumed command of VA-66 on 2 August.

Between 9 August and 29 September, the remainder of VA-66's ex-VF-81 F7U-3s were relinquished, with two aircraft's custody transferred to VX-3 and the remainder returned to BAR Dallas. While the squadron's pilots were busy returning their old Cutlasses to Dallas, VR-31 and VR-32 pilots ferried new aircraft to them. From 27 July to 5 September 1955, VA-66 took custody of fourteen factory-fresh F7U-3s with sequential Bureau numbers from 129602–129614 and 129616. The aircraft were initially delivered to NAS Cecil Field in Jacksonville, Florida, as it had been intended to assign them to VA-34. However, it was still in transition to the F7U-3 and its pilots just beginning their training. It was not anticipated that they would be prepared adequately to be available for CVG-3's deployment planned for the late autumn of 1955.

As a result, these fourteen aircraft were assigned to VA-66 and CDR Fretwell ordered to move his squadron operations and administrative staff to Jacksonville, Florida. CVG-3 desired to deploy a Cutlass squadron aboard *Ticonderoga* (CVA-14) in early November, and hurried carrier qualifications (carquals) took place between 27 September and 12 October 1955 off Jacksonville's coast, with the carrier spending three of those days at Naval Station Mayport. Carquals were completed for all VA-66 pilots with no adverse incidents or accidents. VA-66 was subsequently transferred to CVG-3's administrative control on 1 November 1955, again contrary to desired air group/squadron numbering protocols.

Prior to their deployment, VA-66 aircraft received CVG-3's 'K' tail code and were painted in a simple livery consisting of medium blue wing and fin tips. It should be noted that VA-34's aircraft were painted identically, including the 3XX squadron number. They differed only in their respective squadron designator painted under the fin's 'NAVY' branch of service designation – this makes correct identification of the two squadron's aircraft difficult. However, the F7U-3s were initially delivered to VA-66 without in-flight refuelling kits installed, but gloss white-painted probes were soon installed on them, while VA-34 displayed red-and-white-striped probes, aiding in their differentiation. VA-66 painted their 3XX squadron numbers on the forward fuselage ahead of the national insignia, as well as the inside of the fins. The last one or two digits were replicated on the nose gear fairing and tail cone stinger. These squadron numbers mimicked the aircraft's BuNo with 129602 being aircraft 302, BuNo 129603 being aircraft 303, etc. In another diversion from standard practice, VA-66 did not paint the squadron number or the air group's 'K' identification letter on the starboard wing's upper surface.

One day prior to deployment, VA-66 transferred custody of two aircraft, BuNos 129607 and 129616 to VA-34 on 3 November. This resulted in a squadron complement of twelve aircraft numbered 302–314 but missing 307. On 4 November, *Ticonderoga* departed Mayport beginning a ten-day voyage bound for the Mediterranean with VA-66 providing CVG-3's jet attack and interceptor capability. Notably, VA-66 was the first F7U-3 squadron to deploy with the Sixth Fleet to the Mediterranean. Although their carrier qualifications were completed with little difficulty, VA-66's deployment would not follow suit. Troubles began on 24 December 1955 when the starboard wing of F7U-3 BuNo 129604 was badly damaged during a post-landing taxi collision with the carrier's on-deck recovery crane (affectionately known as 'Tilly'). The aircraft's damage was assessed and its administrative custody transferred to FASRon-6 in Jacksonville – the aircraft was used for spare parts and eventually stricken aboard ship. On 27 October BuNo 129602 was damaged by a landing F9F-8 from VF-32, which, after taking the barricade, struck and pushed the Cutlass into a VA-35 AD-6 and an AD-4Q from VC-33 Detachment 39. It was repaired and put back into service.

Three days later, LTJG Kevin R. Daley's BuNo 129611 suffered a complete electrical failure while conducting a formation flight. Daley's subsequent failure to follow established procedure and secure unnecessary electrical loads caused the starboard engine's temperature to increase dramatically – prompting Daley to shut the engine down and return for landing at Naples, Italy. Although he attempted to restart the windmilling engine, it would not relight due to insufficient remaining emergency electrical power. Slats and landing gear were extended using the emergency air bottles and an approach to the airfield was initiated, however Daley misjudged his position and began to overshoot his final approach path. Additional bank angle to line up with the runway caused an excessive rate of descent, resulting in Daley not being able to make the runway. He elected to land in a pepper farm's field, shearing off all three landing gear. Daley suffered only minor injuries from the crash.

With two aircraft already damaged beyond repair, the new year brought more heartache for VA-66 when LTJG Thomas A. McGuyre suffered a nose gear collapse in BuNo 129613 aboard *Ticonderoga* on 7 January 1956. The LSO cut McGuyre at a higher than normal approach speed, 136 knots. He floated over nine arresting cables, finally snagging the tenth. However, the cables had been mis-rigged by the ship's crew, resulting in an inadequate run-out. This caused the nose wheel tyres to bottom out and catch the number twelve arresting cable, resulting in an over-stress of the nose gear actuating cylinder's down locks and subsequent collapse of the gear. The violent drop to the deck dislodged the canopy, which hurtled forward and just missed McGuyre's helmet. McGuyre suffered a severe

Seen on 28 September 1955, BuNo 129604 was one of VA-66's brand new deliveries from BAR Dallas directly to their new base at NAS Cecil Field in Jacksonville, Florida. ***Cecil Field Photo NA117-7160 (L) 9-55 Casby Collection via Jack Anderson***

back injury, which initiated an investigation into the development of a frangible seat cushion and energy-absorbing strap to lessen similar injury in nose gear collapse incidents. The accident was attributed to a combination of excessive speed, mis-rigged arresting gear, and the bottoming of the nose gear tyres, the last of which precipitated the subsequent increase of nose gear tyre pressure to 325 psi for carrier operations. BuNo 129613 was stricken aboard ship following its custody being transferred to FASRon-3 and O&R Norfolk.

Following McGuyre's accident, and knowledgeable of the history of nose gear collapses that VF-81 had endured, CDR Robert N. Miller, the commander of CVG-3, decided to base VA-66 ashore at Naval Air Facility (NAF) Port Lyautey, Morocco. With the intent of mitigating repeat nose gear collapses aboard ship, the decision was not met with much consternation, and the squadron departed *Ticonderoga* in early February. However, being temporarily land-based did not provide VA-66 with the accident-free operations that they had hoped for.

On 16 February 1956, LTJG Donald E. Schuh departed the wet runway surface while attempting to land at Port Lyautey. During a formation landing in BuNo 129610, Schuh began to overrun his flight leader and applied heavy braking with no apparent result. He selected emergency air brakes, which caused an uncontrolled skid – Schuh's Cutlass departed the runway facing backwards and sheared the left main gear's lower casting. The aircraft's custody was transferred to FASRon-104 on 5 March 1956 and it was subsequently struck off charge at Port Lyautey due to an overstressed structure.

On 5 March, LTJG Eugene W. Jones, flying BuNo 129609, struck a target banner while recovering from a gunnery practice run but escaped injury. The banner's tow bar made contact with 609's starboard outboard slat – part of it remaining imbedded in the slat and part of it damaging the starboard gear's fairing and doors. An uneventful landing was accomplished at NAF Port Lyautey. The accident was attributed to pilot error, and was a virtual repeat of ENS Leslie's incident with VF-81.

Gear-up landing of VA-66's F7U-3 BuNo 129608 and subsequent fire followed LT Edward D. Jackson's failure to utilise a before-landing checklist on 10 April 1956 at NAF Port Lyautey, French Morocco. *Casby Collection*

VF-83 was initially assigned F7U-3s. Here BuNo 129676 is aboard *Intrepid* in November 1954 for carrier qualifications. The nose landing gear torque link has been disconnected to tow the aircraft. Note that the trim is orange with a black border, consistent with its assignment at the time as the fourth squadron in CVG-8. *NA 80-G-652939*

Despite the substantial damage, BuNo 129609 was repaired and operational within ten days.

One week after LTJG Jones' collision, LTJG Stephen O. Hesla was conducting a cross-country flight in BuNo 129603on 12 March 1956 when he experienced an in-flight explosion. Reducing the throttles to idle, Hesla noticed that the instrument power failure warning light and left engine generator warning light were illuminated. Carefully advancing the throttles back to full military power, Hesla then experienced another explosion and noted that the left engine and afterburner fire warning lights were glowing. LTJG Hesla ejected successfully and parachuted to a landing in the Moroccan desert. While awaiting rescue, he was approached by a band of Bedouin nomads. Hesla began to fear for his life when the bits and pieces of his equipment that he offered to dissuade them from doing him harm did not satisfy their desires. However, they seemingly were enthralled with his gold wristwatch, and having secured his watch they eventually moved away a short distance. However, the Bedouins appeared to again become agitated when they spotted a FASRon-104 P2V Neptune circling and an Air Force search-and-rescue helicopter that appeared. Hesla fortunately managed to board the helicopter without being attacked. The wreckage of BuNo 129603, which most likely crashed in the desolate desert, was never located.

Final woes came in the form of LT Edward D. Jackson Jr.'s gear-up landing on Port Lyautey's duty runway on the night of 10 April 1956 after twice reporting his landing gear down and locked in the landing pattern. Relying on memory instead of using a written checklist, Jackson compounded the error by ignoring the red warning light from the NAF wheel watch crewman. A normal flare for landing was accomplished so when the aircraft dropped to the runway surface, Jackson suffered a serious back injury. Once the aircraft stopped, it began to catch fire. Jackson extricated himself from the cockpit and hobbled across the field to the nearest hangar. When firefighters arrived at the scene, they could not find the pilot and feared that he had been thrown from the aircraft. Jackson was located at the hangar and diagnosed by a Corpsman to have multiple fractured vertebra. F7U-3 BuNo 129608 was struck off charge due to its extensive damage, but this action inexplicably did not occur until 1 November 1957.

The remainder of VA-66's time in the desert was without incident, however they were down to six functioning aircraft when they returned aboard *Ticonderoga* on 18 June 1956. Cutlass flight operations were limited during the remainder of the deployment, and on 1 August the squadron flew their aircraft to NAS Oceana a day before *Ticonderoga* docked. Between 10 and 16 August 1956, custody of all VA-66 F7U-3s were transferred to O&R Norfolk. VA-66 immediately began the transition to the Grumman F9F-8B Cougar, and CDR Fretwell handed off command to CDR Robert J. Selmer on 1 September 1956.

Fighter/Attack Squadron Eighty-Three (VF-83/VA-83) *Strike Eagles*. VF-961, a Naval Reserve fighter squadron, was established in April 1950. The *Roaring Bulls* were called to active duty on 1 February 1951 in anticipation of deploying for service in Korea. Equipped with Vought F4U-4 Corsairs, they were instead chosen to cover Sixth Fleet obligations in the Mediterranean while deployed with CVG-8 aboard *Tarawa* (CV-40). Upon return to NAS Oceana, Virginia, on 11 June 1952, the squadron transitioned briefly to the obsolescent propeller-driven Grumman F8F-1 Bearcat, but by September of that year received Grumman F9F-5 Panther jets. CDR William R. Sisley took command of VF-916 on 16 December 1952.

On 4 February 1953, VF-916 was redesignated VF-83. They made a Mediterranean deployment, again with CVG-8, aboard *Coral Sea* (CVA-43) from 26 April to 21 October 1953. Executive Officer LCDR David S. Stear modernised the squadron insignia to depict a diving winged form, reminiscent of the emblems and logotypes from then-popular television series such as *Space Patrol* and *Tom Corbett, Space Cadet*. CDR Sisley relinquished command of the squadron to CDR Raymond J. Swanson in December 1953. After receiving praise for the outstanding operational readiness with their F9F-5s, VF-83 was chosen to be one of two east coast-based fighter squadrons to receive the Vought F7U-3 Cutlass. As the second Atlantic Fleet squadron to receive the Cutlass, VF-83 took custody of five F7U-3s on 24 August 1954. Three more aircraft arrived on 18 September, followed by an additional seven arrivals between 27 September and 22 November. One, BuNo 129639, was transferred to NATC on 8 September, but was returned on 20 January 1955. With fifteen F7U-3s on hand, and twenty-six pilots, VF-83 was fully prepared to begin their integration of this new aircraft type into the fleet as 1955 approached.

VF-83's natural finish F7U-3s initially were painted with an attractive orange-yellow 'swoosh' trimmed in black that began on the intake sides and spread back along the fuselage above and below the wing. This design was taken from Greek mythology's symbolic 'Wing of a Goddess' shape. The trim format was continued on the leading edges of the fins, and although they were an integral member of CVG-8, initially no air group letter was displayed. The VF-83 designator was painted below the branch of service designator on the fins, and the 4XX squadron numbers were added forward of the national insignia on both sides of the fuselage, as well as on the upper starboard wing surface.

Departing Norfolk, Virginia, on 1 November 1954, VF-83 became the first Atlantic Fleet squadron to take the F7U-3 aboard a ship. Following intensive training during the first three months of operations with the Cutlass, four VF-83 pilots participated in what Fleet Air Atlantic

(AirLant) termed *Project Steam I* aboard *Intrepid* (CVA-11). This evaluation followed that of Fleet Air Pacific's (AirPac) *Project Steam* aboard *Hancock* (CVA-19), which took place on the west coast the previous June. Four VF-83 Cutlasses – BuNos 129645, 129653, 129676 and 129679 – as well as an NATC F7U-3 and other types attached to CVG-4, conducted operational testing of the steam catapults that were installed during *Intrepid*'s SCB-27C modernisation. The VF-83 pilots involved with *Project Steam I* were LT Frederick C. 'Fox' Turner, LT James P. Buckner, LTJG John J. Chambers, and LTJG Francis E. O'Conner. These same pilots created an aerial demonstration team nicknamed the 'Dandy Ganders'. This team performed during impromptu airshows conducted at NAS Oceana, as well as participating in the commissioning ceremonies of *Forrestal* (along with F7U-3s from VF-81), and the Army's change of command ceremonies at Fort Story, Virginia.

Rumours abounded that the squadron would be redesignated as an attack squadron in anticipation of receiving the Vought A2U-1 Cutlass, a ground attack version that was nearing its first flight. BuNo's 129676, 129679 and 129686 had been transferred to their Oceana neighbour, VF-81, on 23 November 1954, which fuelled those concerns. BuNo 129667, a replacement, was received from NATC on 21 January 1955, but it was not painted in the squadron's yellow/black livery. This would be the new protocol from this point forward, as the squadron expected to lose their F7U-3s.

On 1 February 1955 VF-83 participated in *Project Steam II* aboard *Ticonderoga* (CVA-14). They conducted steam catapult operations with their F7U-3s until 18 February, when the squadron retuned to NAS Oceana. *Ticonderoga* continued *Project Steam II* qualifications until 9 April 1955.

On 18 March 1955 LTJG Allan L. Bioff was practising a Ground-Controlled Approach (GCA) in actual instrument conditions when BuNo 129660 unexpectedly suffered a servo trim failure during the approach. Bioff landed long and fast on the rain-slicked runway and was not able to stop the aircraft before departing the paved surface, collapsing the nose gear when it encountered the soft rain-soaked earth. The aircraft was uncharacteristically repaired, requiring a new forward fuselage from Vought. Less than a month later, on 11 April, ENS Jacob E. 'Jake' Boelhouwer was taking off in BuNo 129652 when he began to overrun the lead aircraft. Boelhouwer applied the brakes aggressively, blowing both main gear tyres. Although he departed the runway surface to the left, Boelhouwer advanced the throttles into afterburner and became momentarily airborne. The aircraft settled back to the ground, hitting a deep ravine's berm, which caused the aircraft to catch fire. Boelhouwer escaped with burns to his hands. Four days later, LT William E. Brewer was returning to NAS Oceana following a flameout of BuNo 129561's port engine. When he extended the slats and landing gear, the aircraft began a high rate of descent, prompting Brewer to attempt to restart the port engine. Unsuccessful, Brewer placed the starboard engine into afterburner and retracted the landing gear. He continued to attempt to start the port engine and repeatedly re-selected afterburner on the starboard engine, believing it was not lighting off. Running out of altitude, Brewer successfully ditched in Norfolk, Virginia's Linkhorn Bay. He successfully inflated his pararaft and paddled to shore. Brewer maintained that the engines would not respond to his attempts to start them or select after-burning. The Cutlass was recovered by a Navy salvage barge and an extensive investigation into the accident concluded that the left engine's fuel control unit was indeed mis-adjusted, preventing it from windmill starting. However, the cause of the accident was determined to be that Brewer had failed to address the engine shutdown in a timely manner, and simply ran out of fuel during his attempt to avoid a single-engine landing.

The rumours of A2U-1s equipping VF-83 proved false, but the squadron received word that they would indeed be redesignated as an attack squadron. Beginning in April 1955, VF-83 took custody of thirteen F7U-3Ms. By 30 June, the squadron had given up custody of all but two of its F7U-3s. Official redesignation as VA-83 took place at the beginning of the 1956 fiscal year, 1 July 1955. On 8 July, now-LCDR Turner experienced a progressive loss of hydraulic fluid in both of F7U-3M BuNo 129738's Power Control (PC) systems while engaged in air-to-air rocket training. He returned to NAS Oceana with three PC warning lights illuminated. When Turner extended his slats and speed brakes to commence his descent, the fourth PC warning light illuminated and he began to experience a loss of flight control response. He ejected at 4,000ft and parachuted to earth safely, with only minor injuries. Post-crash investigation revealed that a pressure regulator was damaged internally, however it was determined that the aircraft had been over-serviced with hydraulic fluid as a result of a shift change among VA-83's personnel during routine maintenance. One additional full gallon had been added to the #2 PC system immediately before Turner's flight. A fleet-wide memorandum cautioned maintenance personnel to use a written checklist to verify that overfilling of fluids does not occur.

Following the squadron's redesignation, F7U-3 BuNo 129667 was returned to BAR Dallas on 13 July, and BuNo 129660 was transferred to BAR Dallas on 9 August. VA-83 was now completely equipped with F7U-3Ms. These aircraft carried no squadron markings outside of 'VA-83' painted under the 'NAVY' branch of service designator on the fins. As time progressed, each aircraft received a large 'E' on the tail to designate its CVG-8 affiliation.

VF-83 F7U-3M BuNo 129738 before the unit was formally redesignated as an attack squadron, VA-83. *Gene Sommerich*

On 3–5 September 1955, members of the squadron participated in the National Aircraft Show held at Philadelphia International Airport. It was touted as 'AirPower '56' and showcased almost every new fighter and bomber in the US inventory at the time. In a unique spectacle, *Ticonderoga* tied up at the Gulf Oil Company berth located a mile from the airport, but well within view of the airshow attendees. As thousands of onlookers watched, several VA-83 F7U-3Ms catapulted from the deck of the ship while it was berthed. At that time, few civilians had ever witnessed a catapult launch of Navy jets, much less in afterburner, and the sight of the Cutlasses launching was met with awe. However, four press reporters and a Civil Air Patrol representative received burns as they stood 100ft aft of BuNo 129735 as the pilot advanced its engines to full afterburner prior to its launch. United Press Photographer Phillip McMullen had to be rushed to the Philadelphia Navy Yard Hospital with severe burns to his hands after the men retreated to the deck's edge with no ability to gain shelter. The other men had suffered superficial burns to their hands and face, and were treated aboard the ship.

CDR Swanson turned over the reins of the squadron to Second World War ace CDR Harold E. Vita on 28 January 1956. Vita selected LCDR Turner as his Executive Officer. The new command team was informed they would need to prepare for deployment in March. VA-83 began carrier qualifying aboard *Ticonderoga* during a 1 February 1956 cruise to the Caribbean. Arriving at Guantanamo Bay's Leeward Point Field on 3 February, VA-83 began extensive gunnery exercises off the Cuban coast. LT William A. Lebert was a first-hand source for the notorious Cutlass story, 'Roger, you're number three in the emergency pattern'. By his account, it was on his first flight in air-to-air gunnery training. He was the wingman of the division leader who reported a hydraulic PC warning light and that he was returning to base. Lebert joined up on him to look him over but suddenly had problems of his own when both his engines flamed out. He quickly discovered that fuel was not transferring to the main fuel system from the transfer fuel system and managed to get that corrected and relight both engines while gliding back to land. Meanwhile, a third pilot in the flight of four Cutlasses had declared an emergency due to an electrical problem. All three aircraft landed safely. Subsequent investigation revealed these abnormalities were all caused by electrical issues – eventually traced to a single NC-5 self-propelled power plant used to start all three aircraft. The unit was creating a reverse current that caused the engine's starter generators to reverse their polarity and affect the aircraft's normally robust voltage regulators, as well as electrical components in the fuel and hydraulic system's control architecture. This subsequently affected almost every system in each aircraft, and lengthy inspections were required to clear these three aircraft to flight status. Unfortunately, these events would be revisited during the squadron's upcoming deployment.

Although the majority of VA-83's pilots had carrier qualified previously in the Cutlass aboard *Ticonderoga* earlier, several pilots still required qualification. With *Ticonderoga* now unavailable, *Intrepid* was tasked for this purpose. This required the ship to leave port in the midst of supply provisioning for the upcoming six-

VA-83 F7U-3M BuNos 129737 and 129709 are readied for start-up using Consolidated Diesel NC-4 self-propelled power units at NAS Oceana in early March 1956. Note VA-83's *Strike Eagles* patch on the maintenance Chief's G-1 jacket's shoulder, as well as the CVG-8 patch on his back. *Casby Collection*

month cruise, making the schedule even tighter. During his last qualification approach to *Intrepid* on 7 March 1956, LTJG Robert G. Pipkin held off following the LSO's cut and floated over the first seven arresting cables before making contact with the deck. The arresting hook bounced and did not pick up any of the remaining cables. BuNo 129729 triggered the Davis barrier followed by engaging the barricade – which sheared off both main landing gear. Pipkin injured his back in the accident, but was able to subsequently qualify in another aircraft. Transferred to Norfolk's FASRon-3 upon the carrier's return, 129729 was stricken on 23 March. Post-accident analysis of the aircraft revealed a leaking arresting gear dashpot, which failed to dampen the hook's bounce as designed.

With their date for deployment looming, VA-83 personnel had scrambled to paint their aircraft in an attractive adaptation of VF-83's old livery. As the third squadron within the air group, they changed their primary trim colour to medium blue and applied white-trimmed blue 'swooshes' to the fuselage intakes with the fin's leading edges and wing tips matching. They also adopted the name *Strike Eagles* as well as a new insignia showing a swooping eagle holding two fire-spouting Sparrow I missiles in its talons. As the first fleet squadron to equip with air-to-air missiles – as well as deploy overseas with them – the Navy desired to make a positive impression on those who would have the opportunity to witness their employment.

Departing Norfolk on 12 March 1956, CAPT Paul P. Blackburn Jr. and the crew of *Intrepid* steamed for Gibraltar with twelve VA-83 F7U-3Ms aboard. Flight operations for the squadron were routine during the Atlantic crossing. On 25 March 1956, CVG-8 dispatched a detachment of fourteen aircraft from VF-61 (four aircraft), VF-82 (four aircraft), and VA-83 (six aircraft) to NAF Port Lyautey near Kenitra, French Morocco. VA-83's LCDR Turner was the Officer-in-Charge (OinC) over the three-squadron detachment. Two additional F7Us subsequently joined the detachment, leaving four aboard the ship. The offloaded detachment enabled *Intrepid* to accommodate the large North American AJ-2 Savage tanker/bombers from VAH-9 that joined the air group. VAH-9 was to conduct in-flight refuelling practice for CVG-8's aircraft. VA-83's F7U-3Ms could not participate, as their AN/APQ-51 radar dish precluded the installation of an in-flight refuelling kit probe.

On 17 April, LT Lebert was landing BuNo 129713 aboard the carrier when his nose landing gear actuator's drag link cracked and allowed the gear to collapse (see page 310). Lebert suffered a serious back injury, while his aircraft received substantial damage and was stored in *Intrepid's* hangar deck until near the end of the deployment. Its custody was transferred to FASRon-5 on 9 August but it was subsequently stricken aboard ship on 30 August 1956. This was the only Cutlass nose gear collapse that could be attributed to a failure of the gear installation under conditions not found to be in excess of design specifications.

Nine May 1956 saw the VA-83 detachment in Morocco suffer their first accident when LTJG Roger H. Butts inexplicably began circling the city of Taza, Morocco, at 1,500ft above the ground during a cross-country training sortie. His flight leader observed the aircraft flying in the clean configuration and a nose-high attitude toward a mountain pass that was 3,900ft high. Radio communication could not be established with Butts, who was by all accounts an experienced pilot that had amassed 282 flight hours in the Cutlass. Failing to clear the pass, Butt's F7U-3M BuNo 129738 impacted a ridge and burned. Two paramedics from the Air Force's 56th Air Rescue Squadron at Sidi Slimane Air Base were dropped by helicopter and recovered Butt's body. The Navy's accident board concluded that the aircraft was functioning normally prior to the crash and that anoxia – possibly from a compromised oxygen mask – was a potential cause of Butt's bizarre flight path.

The Port Lyautey-based 'African Trotters', or 'Camel Herders' as they humorously nicknamed themselves, continued their operations until 25 June when VF-61's Grumman F9F-8 Cougars and VF-82's McDonnell F2H-4 Banshees returned to *Intrepid*. VA-83, however, remained in Morocco due to CAPT Blackburn's continued need for deck and hangar space to accommodate VAH-5 – which relieved VAH-9 on 16 May – for continued in-flight refuelling training and heavy bombing exercises.

LTJG John B. Barnes was seriously injured when he landed F7U-3M BuNo 129732 with the landing gear retracted on 28 June 1956 at Port Lyautey. While performing a night approach, Barnes failed to use his before-landing checklist in spite of being twice instructed by the GCA controller to do so. Additionally, the sailor acting as the control tower's wheel watch monitor failed to issue a wave off due to not being properly briefed and therefore unprepared for the assigned duty. Barnes retarded the throttles at 20ft above the runway and struck its surface in a nose-high attitude. The subsequent violent slamming down of the forward fuselage onto the runway caused Barnes

BuNo 129735, side number 301, has the white-striped blue wing tips that distinguished the VA-83 F7U-3M nominally assigned to its Commanding Officer, CDR Vita, from the rest of the squadron's Cutlasses. *US Navy*

A VA-83 F7U-3M BuNo 129733 being prepared for launch from *Intrepid*. LTJG H.C. Arnold is not necessarily flying and in fact another aviator's name might be on the other side of the fuselage. *US Navy*

to suffer a severe spinal injury. The aircraft's custody was transferred to FASRon-3 and stripped for parts, but not stricken until August.

The VA-83 detachment's accident record in Morocco was not limited to the flying of their Cutlasses. LTJG Dudley A. 'Dud' Gillaspy recalls, 'I broke my left foot after kicking a barstool that had been thrown at me during a party', while his OinC LCDR 'Fox' Turner broke his right ankle while playing a game of softball aboard the NAF. Both were off flight duty for a month. As Dud Gillaspy reminisces, 'Between us we had a good left foot and a good right foot.' Several detachment personnel photographs picture two crutches proudly displayed.

Back aboard ship, another incident occurred on 10 July 1956 when LCDR John P. 'JP' Murray experienced a loss of all electrical power immediately after his catapult launch from *Intrepid*. After circling for twenty-six minutes while troubleshooting the issue, he climbed to 3,500ft and headed for land. However, 20 miles from the ship, BuNo 129731's port engine failed. Unable to relight the engine after several attempts – and experiencing surges in his starboard engine – he elected to eject and suffered a spinal compression during the seat's catapult stroke. Safely parachuting into the sea, he was rescued by the *Intrepid*'s plane guard helicopter and returned to the ship. His aircraft sank after crashing, making post-crash investigation impossible. The loss of Murray's electrical system was not understood until five days later, when LTJG Thomas E. Quillin experienced a similar electrical anomaly during the starting of his engines aboard the ship. Fortunately Quillin's aircraft started to exhibit problems before he was launched. It was discovered that the starter power cables had been reversed during maintenance performed five days before on *Intrepid*'s deck edge power receptacle box. The resultant field reversal caused within both of the affected aircraft's starter generators damaged much of their fuses and equipment. The ship's cables had not been used during the four days between Murray's and Quillin's launches due to maintenance being performed on the nearby catapult itself. These two shipboard incidents – virtually identical to the ground equipment errors identified during VA-83's pre-deployment operations in Cuba – resulted in directives to all operators to ensure proper inspection and checklist usage in the maintenance of ground/ship-based power plants.

Notwithstanding those incidents, the squadron became proficient with downing F6F drones with the new Sparrow I missile: during its OpDev Four evaluation, the squadron fired about thirty missiles, each pilot firing at least two. According to LT Lebert – the squadron's missile officer – all four 20mm cannon had been removed from the aircraft during the deployment; the resulting reduction in weight made 'it safer to come aboard ship', particularly since *Intrepid* did not yet have an angled deck. Maintainers worked

hard to keep the aircraft in an up status. Every effort was made to ensure reliability – shipboard engine changes were performed after only forty hours – especially in light of the constant parade of foreign dignitaries and newspapermen invited to watch CVG-8's new missile-equipped fighters. As press reports of the United States' new capability were making their way to the Soviet Union, CVG-8's CAG, CDR Pierre N. Charbonnet was under a lot of pressure to put on a flawless show of strength.

On 18 July 1956 the pilots of CVG-8 had a new experience. The North Atlantic Treaty Organisation's (NATO) *Maltex '56* exercise involved cross-deck operations with the British aircraft carrier *HMS Eagle*. These exercises afforded the pilots of VA-83 their first taste of angled-deck operations as well as providing exposure to the British version of the mirror-landing system, known as the Optical Glide Path Indicator (OGPI). Following the conclusion of *Maltex '56*, VA-83's Executive Officer 'Fox' Turner received orders to assume a staff position with the Commander in Chief, Atlantic Fleet (CINCLANTFLT), and departed *Intrepid* to be flown to Norfolk early. Flight operations continued throughout August and *Intrepid* returned to Norfolk on 5 September 1956 – the eight remaining VA-83 F7U-3Ms were flown off a day prior. CDR Vita relinquished command of the squadron to CDR James L. 'Jim' Holloway, III on 12 September 1956. October 1956 brought the addition of three replacement F7U-3Ms – BuNos 139906, 907, and

ABOVE **ENS Nils A. Swenson photographed taxiing F7U-3M BuNo 129739 forward to *Intrepid*'s port catapult in preparation for launch. VF-61's F9F-8 Cougars are spotted along the deck's edge wearing both overall blue as well as the new grey over white liveries. Note Swenson's APH-5 helmet, which was just being issued at this time to replace the earlier Gentex H-4. *Casby Collection***

BELOW **VA-83 F7U-3M BuNo 129737 armed with a Sparrow on both inboard pylons and empty rails on the outboard pylons is being prepared for launch from *Intrepid* in June 1956. *US Navy***

E
NAVY
306

307
139908
E
304
E

908 – and the squadron began the arduous task of repainting all its aircraft in the mandated light gull grey over gloss insignia white livery. Gone were the blue and white fuselage chevrons and leading edge trim, replaced instead with simple medium blue fin tips.

Several new pilots joined the squadron and began their initial training in the Cutlass. ENS Henry H. Strong – on a 14 November 1956 familiarisation flight – was forced to eject from F7U-3M BuNo 139872. Strong attempted a 180-degree maximum g turn at 35,000ft and stalled the aircraft with the slats retracted. The aircraft entered a post-stall gyration and in spite of only having sixteen hours in the Cutlass, ENS Strong reacted appropriately and recovered. However, he failed to reduce engine power during the recovery and both engines suffered extreme compressor stalling with resultant turbine over-temperatures. The turbine outlet temperatures (TOTs) climbed to at least 1,000°C in spite of Strong finally reducing the throttles to idle, and subsequently to the cut-off position. Strong ejected without injury at 9,000ft. F7U-3M BuNo 139895 was obtained from FASRon-5 on 12 December to replace Strong's crashed 872.

VA-83 operated without incident through 1957, and the squadron's pilots continued to practise with the Sparrow I missiles over the Atlantic. The squadron was advised in January that they would be transitioning to the Douglas A4D-1 Skyhawk. F7U-3M BuNo 129737 was the first VA-83 Cutlass to be flown to storage at NASF Litchfield Park, Arizona. In total, nine F7U-3Ms were flown to the desert between 9 March and 14 April 1957. BuNo 139906 was flown to NAS-NART Dallas for display outside the base operations building, providing Vought's workers with a visible memory of their manufacturing efforts. Custody of BuNo 139907 was transferred to the Naval Air Reserve Training Unit (NARTU) Norfolk and flown its last five minutes to NAS Norfolk from NAS Oceana. (pages 274 and 282 for disposition of 906 and 907 respectively). Following the March 1957 arrival of the A4D-1s, the Strike Eagles renamed themselves the *Rampagers* and adopted a ram's head insignia, which was approved on 12 April 1957.

VA-83's LT Leonard H. Eisner summed up his F7U experience when he recounted, 'All in all I enjoyed my tour in the Cutlass. It was truly ahead of its time!'

Fighter Squadron Eighty-Four (VF-84)/Attack Squadron Eighty-Six (VA-86) *Sidewinders*. In preparation for the introduction of the F7U to fleet, four deployable squadrons (two east coast based, and two based on the west coast) were envisioned to be the initial recipients of the type. The intended east coast squadron selectees included VF-84, which prior to 4 February 1953 had been a Naval Reserve fighter squadron, VF-921. However, a late-1954 transition to the F7U-3 conflicted with the deployment schedule of CVG-8 to which they were assigned. VF-83 was therefore substituted as an initial F7U recipient. The *Sidewinders* of VF-84 completed their Mediterranean deployment aboard *Lake Champlain* (CVA-39) on 22 April 1955 while flying the Grumman F9F-5 and were told to anticipate transition to the Grumman F9F-6 Cougar in late 1955. Squadron Commanding Officer LCDR Herbert V. Ladley turned the reins over to CDR Chester W. 'Pearly' Gates Jr. in late May 1955, with LCDR R.J. Burns assuming the Executive Officer position. Just days later, on 1 June 1955 VF-84 received word that they would now be assigned the F7U-3M Cutlass, and on 29 June, F7U-3M BuNo 139870 arrived on the VF-84 ramp at NAS Oceana, having been ferried there from BAR Dallas.

One of the most convoluted squadron establishment/redesignation shuffles occurred three days later on 2 July 1955 when VA-86 was established at NAS Oceana. The same day, it was redesignated VF-84. Simultaneously, CDR Gates' VF-84 was redesignated VA-86. With less than a month to prepare for the new aircraft type, the former members of VF-84 found themselves preparing for the transition to the attack role as VA-86. Additionally, VA-86 would leave CVG-8 and become a component of ATG-181.

BuNo 139870's custody effectively changed to VA-86 on 2 July, and it was soon joined by BuNo 139869, which arrived from Dallas' BuAer storage pool on 15 July 1955. Between 8 August and 7 December, VA-86 took custody of eleven more F7U-3Ms, bringing the squadron complement to thirteen. While the majority of VA-86's aircraft were natural finish and adorned in squadron markings consisting of wide medium-blue stripes trimmed in white on the fins and fin tips, two of their aircraft came directly from the factory in the new light gull grey over gloss insignia white livery. BuNo 129714 was received from BAR Dallas on 24 October 1955 with a unique wave-shaped, hard-edged demarcation line between the grey and white finish. On 7 December, BuNo 129715 arrived – also in grey over white – but with a straight feathered-edge demarcation line. Both of these attractive aircraft were subsequently painted with VA-86's squadron markings, complete with the 'I' tail code assigned to ATG-181.

Representative of the newest advances in Naval Aviation, it was no wonder that Cutlass-equipped VA-86, as a component of ATG-181, was selected to participate in the shakedown cruise of *Forrestal* (CVA-59). Departing Norfolk, Virginia, on 24 January 1956, *Forrestal* hosted press reporters, photographers and newsreel motion picture cameramen to document the new 'super carrier' and its display of American sea-borne air power. VA-86 operated its thirteen Cutlasses without accident or incident while aboard CVA-59, exploiting the new carrier's angled deck and mirror landing system with no adverse issues. In spite of the squadron's stellar operational readiness and accident-free display of their

OPPOSITE TOP While evaluating HMS *Eagle*'s angled deck and mirror landing system in July 1956, VA-83 pilots made touch-and-go landings, affording the British crew who lined the flight deck and island their first sight of the radical Cutlass. *Thomason Collection*

OPPOSITE BOTTOM The new grey and white livery that VA-83 adopted post-deployment ushered in the loss of their splashy blue and white chevrons that were displayed proudly during their cruise aboard *Intrepid*. The new and rather austere markings simply consisted of blue fin tips. Note the difference in the application of the squadron numbers and air group codes on these two F7U-3Ms carrying Sparrow Is on 7 December 1956: '307' remained parallel to BuNo 139908's longitudinal axis, while '304' was applied to remain parallel to the ground when BuNo 139907 was parked. Their fin codes were applied with an opposite protocol. *Casby Collection*

ABOVE Contrary to misinformed opinion, the F7U-3M, like the one shown here above the aft end of *Forrestal*, was perfectly capable of taking a close-in wave off when flown properly. *US Navy*

OPPOSITE TOP All thirteen VA-86 Cutlasses parked on the bow of *Forrestal* as she heads to sea on 24 January 1956 (only the canopy of one is visible at the lower left side of the photo). Note that only 312 (left foreground) has a swept national insignia on the lower wing. *CVA59(L)-96/Casby Collection*

OPPOSITE BOTTOM Even an F7U-3 looks small on *Forrestal*. A VF-42 F2H-3 is on the starboard bow catapult while a VF-21 FJ-3 is waiting behind. *US Navy*

modern missile-capable fighters, *Forrestal*'s skipper, CAPT Roy L. Johnson ordered the squadron ashore at NAS Guantanamo Bay's Leeward Point Field. Johnson's decision could have been the result of reading reports that filtered in from *Ticonderoga* (CVA-14), which was concurrently deployed to the Mediterranean with Cutlass-equipped VA-66 aboard. VA-66 was experiencing multiple accidents aboard their ship, most notably nose gear collapses, hence a precautionary move to avoid similar accidents aboard *Forrestal* as the world's press corps – as well as visiting dignitaries such as the Royal Navy's Sea Lord of the Admiralty, Admiral Mountbatten – watched and recorded each round of air operations. Johnson's slight likely stung CDR Gates and his men but, as ordered, the entire squadron left the ship and made Guantanamo Bay, Cuba, their home for the remainder of the cruise, conducting combat air patrol (CAP) and intercept training. With *Forrestal* operating off the coast of Cuba, VA-86 made it a point to visit the ship at sea with high-speed passes and impressive formation fly-bys. During onshore operations at Leeward Point, VA-86 suffered only one incident – ENS Stanley J. Krieder departed the end of the runway following a blown tyre during a landing roll-out. The aircraft suffered no damage as a result of the incident, however, it received slight damage during its hurried extraction from the soft sand using improper recovery equipment.

Ignominiously (but unfairly so) craned back aboard the ship at Guantanamo on 20 March 1956, VA-86 conducted no air operations during the return trip to Norfolk. The squadron launched their aircraft when *Forrestal* was off the Virginia Capes for their return flight to NAS Oceana.

Ten of VA-86's F7U-3Ms seen on the transient ramp at NAS Guantanamo Bay's Leeward Point Field on 19 March 1956. Some F2H-3s and FJ-3s from ATG-181 are also on the ramp along with aircraft from ATG-182 (tail code 'O') and ATG-202 (tail code 'X') as well as resident Leeward Point F6F target drones. *NA56-2317-L-3-56/Casby Collection*

On 10 May 1956 F7U-3M BuNo 139900 arrived from FASRon-5. This was the third VA-86 aircraft in the new grey over white scheme and it was anticipated that the entire squadron would soon adopt the livery. However, with the exception of one additional arrival of a grey and white Cutlass early in 1957, the refinishing of the squadron's natural-finish aircraft did not materialise.

Marring what would have been a near-perfect operational record for a Cutlass-equipped squadron, VA-86 suffered a double tragedy on 10 July 1956 when CDR Gates and fellow Naval Academy graduate LTJG William M. Austin failed to return from a four-plane instrument condition training flight off the coast of Norfolk. Following an interval take-off from NAS Oceana, a report of icing conditions at the planned operating altitudes resulted in CDR Gates' order to descend into instrument conditions and home in on Oceana's Auxiliary Landing Field (ALF) Fentress. Gates' BuNo 129715 is presumed to have collided with wingman Austin's BuNo 139883. A single damaged Fabrilite canopy panel from 139883 was located 50 miles out to sea, but neither plane nor pilot was found despite an intensive two-week search using search and rescue assets from NAS Oceana, NAS Norfolk, NAS Jacksonville and several ships in the area. LCDR Grant 'Red' Boice was installed as VA-86's new Commanding Officer in September 1956 and oversaw the squadron's accident-free operations in the wake of Gates' and Austin's loss. VA-86 received its last F7U-3M on 6 February 1957 when BuNo 139897's custody was transferred from FASRon-5 to bring the squadron back to full strength.

Six brand-new F7U-3Ms were being held at O&R Norfolk for a planned transfer of custody to VA-86 as replacement aircraft. However, on 25 March the squadron received orders to prepare all their F7U-3Ms for transfer to NASF Litchfield Park, Arizona, for storage and disposition, and that the squadron would transition to the Douglas A4D-1 Skyhawk. They began to fly their Cutlasses to the NASF on 29 March 1957. On 30 June BuNo 139888 (the last VA-86 Cutlass bound for the boneyard) arrived at the NASF – however the squadron still retained the last two F7U-3Ms they received until 15 July, when their custody was turned over to the BuAer storage pool at Oceana and both aircraft stricken the same day.

In retrospect, VA-86 operated the F7U-3M for two full years – including operations aboard ship – with no operational losses attributable to the aircraft, no carrier accidents or incidents, and only one minor shore-based incident. The cause of the loss of CDR Gates and LTJG Austin will always remain a mystery, however interviewed squadron members of VA-86 spoke highly of their Cutlasses and did not implicate the aircraft in their disappearance.

ABOVE Former VA-86 F7U-3M BuNo 139897 sits forlornly on a corner pad at NAS Oceana, Virginia, on 30 August 1958. In the custody of Oceana's BuAer pool, the Cutlass was used as a static display piece during airshow events. Noteworthy are the day-glo-painted Sparrow I missiles on the inboard pylons. *Casby Collection*

LEFT Part of ATG-181 parked on the bow of *Forrestal* on 27 March 1956 during its return to Norfolk: The picture exemplifies why it is known as a 'pack' and demonstrates why folding wings and short fuselages were almost essential. Note that the big AJ Savages in the foreground had a manual wing and vertical tail fold process that was so onerous one was rarely folded unless it had become a 'dud' and needed to be taken down to the hangar deck. *NARA 80-G-689588/ Casby Collection*

Attack Squadron One Hundred and Sixteen (VA-116) *Road Runners.* The last of the Navy's squadrons to take the F7U aboard ship was VA-116, home-based at NAS Miramar, California. Established on 1 December 1955 under the command of CDR John L. 'Jack' Callis, the *Roadrunners* first assigned aircraft was the F7U-3M. Assisted by Executive Officer LCDR Daniel H. Stinemates, Callis had sixteen months to mould his pilots and non-flying officers into a capable attack squadron before a planned deployment. Callis and Stinemates had already attended VC-3's *Cutlass Classroom* in late October 1955 and both were students of VC-3's pre-eminent instructor pilot LT Walter M. Schirra, Jr., a veteran of *Project Cutlass*. They were followed by VA-116 LTs

Rudolph L. Kraus and David W. Pogue and were Schirra's last students before he transitioned to fly VC-3's F3H-2N Demons. Final division tactics training took place on 18–29 November in F7U-3M BuNo 129744, which would soon become VA-116's first aircraft.

VA-116 took custody of VC-3's 129744 just six days after establishment. By the end of the month the squadron had custody of five aircraft. These five aircraft enabled initial training of the junior officers to commence by 1 January 1956, with thirteen pilots, two ground officers, and 162 maintainers (known as 'Callis' Cutlass Coolies') cutting their teeth on the new aircraft. Although established as a unit of ATG-2, the aircraft initially carried the 'V' tail code assigned to CVG-11, with no additional markings or trim outside of the VA-116 designator on the tail fins and 6XX series nose numbers assigned to them as the sixth squadron in CVG-11. In late March 1956, VA-116 began to change their markings to reflect ATG-2's 'W' tail code and 2XX series nose numbers. As the second squadron in ATG-2, their trim colour was now orange-yellow and this was reflected in the wing tips and nose gear fairing, as well as the leading edges of the fins, which scalloped back along the fin–wing joint and had a thin black border.

VA-116 performed at many airshows throughout the country. Beginning with the Armed Forces Day Air Show at NAS Whidbey Island, Washington, they followed up with performances at the Los Angeles Air Fair, the San Diego Air Games, and the National Air Show at Oklahoma City, Oklahoma, where they put on an impressive full squadron fly-by. Interspersed between these was the Mrs US Navy Beauty Pageant, the USS Hancock Change of Command Ceremony, and a performance for the *Wide Wide World* television programme that was seen by thousands of viewers across the nation. While immersed in preparations for their deployment aboard *Hancock*, the squadron participated in two ADEX air-defence exercises in 1956, as well as *Operation Ski-Jump* in January 1957 – an eighteen-day exercise involving 20,000 Navy and 30,000 Marine Corps personnel in the largest naval training exercise performed up to that time. These operations culminated in a large-scale amphibious landing at Camp Pendleton, California, with VA-116 F7U-3Ms providing combat air patrol (CAP).

As exemplified by their *Ski-Jump* assignment, despite their designation as an attack squadron, VA-116 also trained in air-to-air defence and day interception duties. Their pilots qualified in high- and low-altitude gunnery, both air-to-air and air-to-ground rocketry, and Sparrow air-to-air missile operations. VA-116 broke all previous Cutlass-equipped squadron records for flight hours per day, total flight hours, and aircraft availability during their pre-deployment training.

Although VA-116's performance set a new benchmark for Cutlass equipped units, it was not without its problems or losses. In fact, VA-116 endured more accidents than any other F7U-equipped squadron. However, as usual, all were the result of pilot or maintainer error. On 23 March 1956 two aircraft were damaged when LTJG William A. Tarpley in F7U-3M BuNo 129708 clipped wings with LTJG Ronald L. Stoddart's BuNo 139893 during a section take-off from NAS Miramar. Both aircraft sustained repairable damage and were sent to FASRon-116 for repairs. On 24 April, LTJG Richard D. Mullen was conducting night touch-and-go landings at NAS Miramar in BuNo 129744 when he failed to extend the landing gear during his second approach. A normal flare resulted in the aircraft dropping to the runway with an extreme vertical velocity, which fractured Mullen's vertebra, effectively removing him from the squadron's roster.

The first loss of life for VA-116's pilots came with the crash of LTJG Jerold Q. Weaver in BuNo 139901 on 27 June 1956. Following take-off from NAS Miramar, Weaver reported fire warning lights illuminated for both the left engine and afterburner compartments. He attempted to return immediately for landing but developed an excessive sink rate and struck Miramar's Chief Petty Officers' Club roof before impacting short of the runway. Subsequent investigation of the wreckage revealed that an afterburner fuel line was left disconnected following an engine change – an inspection quality control issue that was responsible for several F7U-3 series accidents.

Ironically, thirteen days later on 10 July, LT David Meek walked away unscathed after crashing F7U-3M BuNo 129716 following a simulated flameout approach that he allowed to develop into an excessive sink rate. Unable to stem his rate of descent with the application of power, Meek impacted the ground 728ft short of the runway, collapsing all three landing gear, and skidding to a stop, where his aircraft then caught fire.

On 19 October 1956, LTJG James B. Brown suffered a loss of the utility system's hydraulic pressure during his roll-out following landing at NAS Miramar. He applied the emergency air brake, which resulted in the left wheel locking up and causing the left main gear's drag link to shear. The gear collapse caused substantial damage to BuNo 139876. The aircraft was transferred to O&R San Diego's custody but stricken on site.

On 26 November LT Walter M. Earley Jr. needed to eject from BuNo 139892 after being informed by NAS Miramar's tower that his right main landing gear was neither fully retracted, nor fully extended. Attempts to cycle the gear and exert high G-forces to effect its full extension were in vain. Due to inclement weather and low visibility, he was advised to climb to 10,000ft and eject. Earley did so and was unhurt. His Cutlass ditched itself and sank in the shallow waters off San Diego – the second time an unmanned F7U had effected a water ditching. It was raised from the sea floor two days later and found to be the victim of yet another mechanic's oversight. The right main gear's actuating cylinder

For some reason, VA-116 was marked as the second squadron (usually a fighter squadron) in ATG-2 although the trim colour in this photo looks more like the international orange assigned to the fourth squadron than the orange-yellow of the second squadron. In August 1956, when this picture was taken at Miramar, the ATG-2 was assigned tail code 'W'. *US Navy*

ATG-2 (tail code 'NB') deployed aboard *Hancock* in 1957 with VA-116's F7U-3Ms as well as squadrons/detachments of FJ-3Ms, F2H-4s, F2H-2Ps, AJs, and a variety of ADs. *US Navy*

piston rod bolt's securing nut had not been re-installed following maintenance in the gear well.

LTJG John T. Carroll made a hard landing in BuNo 139896 during his carrier qualification aboard *Hornet* (CVA-12) on 30 November 1956, which resulted in damage to the left main gear's axle. The aircraft was repaired.

LTJG John A. 'Jackie' Shields holds the unfortunate distinction of being the last pilot to lose his life in a Cutlass. On 2 February 1957, Shields lost control of BuNo 139894 following a section take-off from NAS Miramar. Shields ejected at only 1,000ft, and his parachute failed to blossom in time before he impacted the ground on the Marine Corps' Camp Matthews rifle range near La Jolla, California. Investigation of the wreckage revealed that excessive contamination in the #1 power control system's hydraulic fluid was the most probable cause of the accident. The aircraft had not flown previously for eight months and it was speculated that silting of the flight control system's slider valves had caused the contamination.

F7U-3M BuNo 139877 experienced an unknown problem during carquals aboard *Hancock* (CVA-19) that required it to be recovered by an emergency barricade engagement, which resulted in its being stricken with only 202 flight hours on 4 March 1957. LTJG Stoddart damaged BuNo 139912 eight days later but it was repairable, as evidenced by its ferry flight to NASF Litchfield Park for storage and disposition.

With carrier work-ups nearing an end, VA-116 began to reassign the unit's nose numbers in preparation for their deployment to the Far East aboard *Hancock*. (Example: BuNo 139896, which carried the unit number 212, now was renumbered 208. BuNo 139890, formerly 213, was now painted as 210). As a result of a fleet-wide revision of the unit tail code assignment, ATG-2's was changed from 'W' to 'NB' and all its squadrons were instructed to repaint their aircraft. VA-116 chose to stagger the new code letters, to better fit the narrowing width of the fins as they reached the tips, and not interfere with the black-trimmed yellow fin leading edges that they had adopted. The squadron's insignia, a black field with a red lightning bolt piercing an atomic electron ring symbol was replicated in small size under the windscreen harp, and pilot/plane captain names were painted inside a white banner on each side of the aircraft.

VA-116 boarded the *Hancock* on 18 March 1957. The ship left port on 6 April to begin its six-month cruise with thirteen F7U-3Ms aboard. VA-116's fourteen pilots conducted day fighter operations from the ship throughout the deployment, and also maintained a three-pilot detachment at NAF Atsugi, Japan. In the last three months of the deployment, 116 tallied 343 flights for a total of 458 flight hours. They broke all available carrier-borne Cutlass squadron records for total hours flown, total carrier landings, and total carrier sorties flown, but not without operational mishaps – they experienced ten more accidents during the deployment. All were minor in nature and repairable aboard ship or at NAF Atsugi, with the exception of LTJG George W. Baird's successful ejection from BuNo 139905 following unknown difficulties on 18 April 1957, just days into the deployment.

In spite of the plethora of accidents, in addition to the outstanding flight rates achieved the squadron chalked up at least two notable positive events: LTJG John T. Carroll joined the 'Centurion Club' after making his one hundredth landing aboard *Hancock* on 28 August 1957; LTJG Ron Stoddart became the only pilot to ever make a single-engine carrier landing with an F7U-3M when his starboard engine suddenly seized due to a total loss of oil in early June 1957. He burned his remaining fuel load down to the single-engine approach weight and conducted a mirror-assisted landing using his remaining engine's afterburner throughout the approach. He controlled his airspeed and descent rate with careful modulation of the speed brakes. Stoddart's landing made him one of only two pilots to land an F7U aboard a carrier while operating with a single engine – VA-151's LTJG Frank Carrig previously performed the feat twice in an F7U-3.

Prior to departing the western Pacific, VA-116 conducted on-station operations off the coast of Taiwan following the detection of a Communist Chinese build-up of forces opposite the island. No engagements occurred and the ship left the area on 6 September for its return voyage home. Following their fly-off from *Hancock* on 18 September 1957, VA-116 returned to Miramar and readied their aircraft for their transfer to NASF Litchfield Park, Arizona, for long-term storage and eventual reclamation. The fly-off marked the last time a F7U Cutlass would operate from a carrier. ATG-2 and VA-116 markings were painted over in preparation for the custody transfer, and four aircraft were delivered to the NASF on 24 September, followed by the remaining aircraft being flown out between 2 and 28 October.

Their deployment aboard *Hancock* would mark the last usage of the F7U-3 series aboard ship.

Fighter Squadron One Hundred and Twenty-Two (VF-122) *Black Angels*. VF-783, which had been established as a Naval Reserve fighter squadron at NAS Los Alamitos, California, the 'Minutemen' were redesignated as VF-122 on 4 February 1953 and renamed the *Black Angels*. Along with the change from reserve squadron to a fleet squadron status, they also moved to NAS Miramar, California. The squadron deployed aboard *Boxer* (CVA-21) with Grumman F9F-5 Panthers. Upon their return to Miramar on 11 October 1954 they received word that they were chosen to become one of the first four fleet squadrons to equip with the F7U-3 Cutlass – two on the east coast (VF-81 and VF-83) and CVG-12's VF-122 and VF-124, both based at Miramar.

VF-122's second F7U-3, BuNo129658, was quickly adorned with the squadron's livery consisting of insignia blue stars against a red-bordered white field on the aft canopy and fin tips. This photo depicts the first (and only) VF-122 class of pilots and maintainers to attend VC-3's *Project Check-Out.* They were the first of many to be trained in the F7U-3 by the Moffett-based Transitional Training Unit. *Casby Collection*

VF-122's commanding officer, CDR Robert M. Disque, chose four squadron pilots in addition to himself, along with twenty-one of the squadron's enlisted maintenance men, to train in the F7U-3 at VC-3's TransTUPac, and this was completed in January 1955. The squadron had received their first F7U-3 aircraft on 15 December 1954, with BuNo 129675 being towed from FASRon-12's Miramar ramp to VF-122's flight line. The next day, VF-122 received BuNo 129658, the second of five F7U-3s to be transferred from FASRon-12. BuNo's 129648 and 129671 arrived on 14 January 1955, and BuNo 129672 arrived on 2 February 1955. Both 129675 and 129658 received the squadron's intended paint livery, a very flashy red-bordered white field, resplendent with blue stars adorning the rear canopy and fin tips. They were to be the only two to receive these markings.

This initial complement of five former FASRon-12 aircraft was to be joined by seven more from the same source. However, plans soon changed. The squadron was notified by the Commander Air Forces Pacific (ComAirPac) on 14 February 1955 that they would now transition to the Grumman F9F-6 Cougar, in preparation for the F9F-8. This change in squadron type allocation occurred as ComAirPac came to the realisation that VC-3, VX-5, and VF-124 all needed F7U-3 aircraft to complete their squadron complements, while the fleet was in need of an additional west coast F9F-8 squadron.

As a result, VF-122 transferred three aircraft directly to Miramar-based VF-124 on 9 March 1955, and two aircraft, BuNos 129648 and 129675, went to VC-3 on 15 March and 24 March 1955 respectively. Although VF-122 returned from a successful deployment with the F9F-5 to begin transition into the F7U-3, they would no longer have any involvement with the Cutlass.

Fighter Squadron One Hundred and Twenty-Four (VF-124) *Stingarees.* VF-784, a Naval Reserve fighter squadron, was equipped with Vought F4U-4 Corsairs and based at NAS Oakland, California, when they were called to active duty on 20 July 1950 following the invasion of South Korea by North Korea. Prior to entering action in Korea, the squadron moved to NAS Miramar, just outside San Diego California. VF-874 deployed to Korea aboard *Bon Homme Richard* (CV-31) from 10 May to 17 December 1951 as a member of CVG-102. They deployed again aboard *Oriskany* (CVA-34) on 15 September 1952. On 4 February 1953, the squadron was redesignated VF-124 while still in Korean waters.

Following their return stateside on 18 May 1953, VF-124 began exchanging their tired Corsairs for Grumman F9F-2 Panther jets. Led by CDR Jack L. Morrissey, the squadron made their conversion to jet aircraft in a remarkably short time. They adopted the new nickname *Stingarees*, and designed a colourful insignia featuring a ray. Although a stingaree is a type of stingray found in inshore waters off eastern Australia, VF-124's use of this moniker was actually derived from an area of San Diego in the 1880s that was populated with gambling halls, saloons, and brothels. Those who frequented the area were known as 'stingarees', as it was postulated: 'you could be stung by the area's vice faster than by a stingray in the harbour'. The pilots of VF-124 apparently enjoyed the bawdy connotation.

From 3 March to 11 October 1954, they deployed aboard *Boxer* (CVA-21) with CVG-12. Upon their return, CDR Morrissey handed the reins of command to CDR James S. 'Bud' Brown – the former Officer-in-Charge of FASRon-12's *Project Cutlass*. VF-124 was now to be the first west coast squadron to transition to the F7U-3 and Brown was selected for its command as a result of his extensive experience with the aircraft. Many of VF-124's pilots were reassigned, but four of them stayed with the squadron and prepared for their transition to the Cutlass: LCDR Jay Alkire, LTJG Georges E. 'Frenchy' LeBlanc, ENS Howard C. Mitchell, and ENS Fulton M. 'Hump' Humphreys. CDR Brown also brought three experienced *Project Cutlass* pilots with him: LT Edwin Van Biesbroeck, LT Floyd C. Nugent, and LT Donald L. Christianson. The remaining twelve pilots and two support officers would be transferred from other squadrons or newly assigned. VF-124 could have benefitted from the inclusion of the remainder of the experienced *Project Cutlass* cadre, however they were assigned to NAS Moffett Field's VC-3 to train future Cutlass squadron senior officers. Worse, many *Project Cutlass* maintenance personnel who had become highly adept at maintaining and repairing the F7U-3 after intense training at Vought were dispersed to the fleet with the exception of a few. Nevertheless, before VF-124's one and only Cutlass deployment, the maintenance man hours per flight hour were considered to be acceptable.

Like VC-3, it received its first Cutlasses from FASRon-12's *Project Cutlass*, with custody of six transferred on 13 October 1954. Nine additional F7U-3s arrived between 2 and 12 November, from FASRon-12 (non-*Project Cutlass* aircraft), BAR Dallas, and VX-5. Two of the oldest FASRon-12 aircraft, BuNos 128470 and 128473, were returned to BAR Dallas on 1 December, bringing the squadron complement to thirteen. These Cutlasses retained FASRon-12's black paint on both sides of each fin tip. Squadron numbers, initially one to two digits, were painted on the nose of the aircraft in front of the national insignia.

F7U-3 training for the original VF-124 pilots, as well as the newly assigned ones, started immediately and proceeded rapidly. *Project Cutlass* alumni shared their expertise with the pilots who were new to the Cutlass, and in some instances, new to squadron life itself. ENS James R. Sears, in his first fleet squadron assignment since earning his wings, was eager to fly the Cutlass, albeit understandably somewhat nervous. On 18 November 1954, Sears began his initial flight in a Cutlass while manning F7U-3 BuNo 129690. Within five minutes, he would be dead. During a normal climb out from NAS Miramar, Sear's aircraft was observed by LT Christianson, his wingman-instructor pilot, to enter a slow spiral from 6,500ft to somewhere between 1,000 to 3,000ft as he crossed the coastline abeam the Torrey Pines golf course, north-west of Miramar. The Cutlass stopped its spiral, went inverted, and nosed over to a 60–75 degree dive angle. No radio contact was made between Sears and Christianson. Sears ejected at very low altitude and failed to clear the seat. The Cutlass crashed in the Pacific in relatively shallow water, so its wreckage was recovered. Although the Navy's Accident Board could not positively identify a cause for the accident, it was believed in many quarters to be caused by pilot disorientation while attempting to change radio frequencies – either by a deflection of the control stick or the inadvertent application of roll trim while switching gloved hands to enable adjustment of the radio controls located on the right-hand console. Vought engineers offered the possibility of a G-4 stabilisation system malfunction (which is addressable in flight), or a stuck slider valve in the ailavator power control installation. Needless to say, the crash focused the minds of those waiting to accomplish their first flights on being fully prepared for them, which in part resulted in the remainder of them qualifying in the Cutlass without incident.

Custody of three additional F7U-3s were transferred to VF-124 on 9 March from Miramar-based VF-122 just after that squadron painted them with their own markings. F7U-3 BuNo 129697 – the last of the 180 F7U-3s delivered to the Navy – joined the squadron a day later from O&R San Diego. A stylised yellow skull above crossed pirate-style scimitars (also known as cutlasses) was adopted as the squadron's trim marking and painted on the outer surfaces of the existing black fin tips.

Training continued, including section tactics, instrument flying, and air-to-air gunnery practice, throughout the first four months of 1955. A deployment to NAF El Centro, California, in April afforded the squadron's pilots the opportunity to practise air-to-ground gunnery, rocket firing, and bombing. On 6 April, LTJG Thomas P. Conroy was returning from a tactics training flight when he encountered gusty wind conditions as he began his approach to NAS Miramar. As he passed over the threshold of the runway he extended the speed brakes, causing BuNo 129637 to descend abruptly. The hard landing blew the left main tyre and resulted in an uncontrollable swerve. Excessive side loads imposed on the nose gear during the swerve caused it to fail at the trunnions and collapse. Conroy was not injured,

At least one VF-124 aircraft (BuNo 129637) was painted with a trial squadron marking consisting of three large yellow stars surrounded by field of six smaller yellow stars against the fin tip's black background on both sides of each fin. This livery was ultimately rejected. *Casby Collection*

and his aircraft was sent to O&R San Diego via FASRon-12. The aircraft was eventually repaired. The following week, ENS Lewis N. Mitchell Jr. had a 2.75in Mighty Mouse rocket from the rear bank slide forward and jam the rocket pack's door on BuNo 129682 while he conducted air-to-air rocketry training at El Centro. When the next rocket was fired from an adjacent tube, it could not exit: its flame burned through the tube and caused the jammed rocket's motor to ignite. With two rockets burning out within the pack, considerable damage was done to it, as well as the underside of the aircraft, but Mitchell was able to bring it back to base. The incident resulted in design changes to the pack.

ENS Richard J. 'Dick' Cavicke, humorously nicknamed 'Nose' by CDR Brown, recalled some of the training flights that enabled the squadron's pilots to proudly show off the capabilities of their Cutlasses, while simultaneously relaying their good-natured 'respect' for their counterparts in the Air Force:

> USAF B-47s would make frequent navigational flights over San Diego and they felt rather secure, cruising at 35K+ and above Mach 0.82; they were seldom overtaken. However, the Cutlass could go faster at that altitude and I participated in many a long drawn-out chase, in afterburner (with a fractional Mach overtake) for the opportunity to come out of afterburner and 'casually coast past' while exchanging appropriate hand signals!

Project Cutlass graduate LT Van Biesbroeck received his promotion to LCDR on 1 January 1955 (and it was CDR Brown's desire that he assume the Executive Officer (XO) role, given his experience in the Cutlass). However, LCDR Alkire had seniority over him, having been promoted six months earlier on 1 July 1954. Alkire was a former land-based, multi-engine pilot who had some difficulties transitioning to the Panther jets in VF-124. His troubles were said to have been related more to his attitude than to his aptitude. When VF-124 transitioned to Cutlasses, the experienced F7U-3 pilots from *Project Cutlass* were eager to assist each pilot who joined the squadron to transition smoothly. LCDR Alkire reportedly had difficulty adapting to the Cutlass, but remained aloof and unwilling to accept advice. Later, when discussing the upcoming carrier qualifications required in preparation for the squadron's deployment, LCDR Van Biesbroeck offered his assistance related to

The classic skull and crossed cutlasses in place of bones was a fitting Cutlass squadron marking. *Thomason Collection*

approaching the carrier in a low-energy state caused by a low, slow final to an LSO-mandated cut or wave off. He later stated in an interview with an author: 'I mentioned that if you get low and slow, don't keep pulling back. Take the wave-off and come back around … don't push it.' Alkire reportedly responded: 'I've never taken a wave-off in my life, and I never will.' Van Biesbroeck was surprised and stunned by Alkire's curt dismissal of his advice.

June–August 1955 brought a fleet of replacements to the VF-124 ramp. Beginning on 10 June with F7U-3 BuNo 129585, VF-124 took custody of twelve recently updated Cutlasses from FASRon-12 (non-*Project Cutlass* aircraft) to replace their tired jets. An additional two aircraft were accepted from BAR Dallas, as well as BuNo 129601 from O&R San Diego on 1 August 1955. All the squadron's original fleet of aircraft were transferred back to FASRon-12 for maintenance/modification and redistribution to other squadrons and units. In anticipation of their planned deployment aboard *Hancock*, the new aircraft were assigned 4XX-series squadron numbers from 401 to 415, omitting 413 for an unknown reason, possibly superstition. As the deployment grew near, CDR Brown realised that he had absorbed too many pilots. LTJG Conroy, LTJG Charles Wyatt, LTJG Paul N. Pflimlin and ENS Donald G. Crabtree were transferred to other squadrons.

In July 1955, the squadron began their carrier qualifications (carquals) aboard *Hancock* (CVA-19). Their work-ups were proceeding without incident when on 14 July 1955 tragedy befell the members of VF-124. After progressively getting lower and slower in his approach to the ship, LCDR Alkire repeatedly ignored Landing Signal Officer Ted Reilly's wave off signals. BuNo 129595 struck the deck's ramp, or 'round down', and exploded in a ball of fire. Seemingly stunned by the impact, Alkire rode the flaming cockpit section over the deck's port side and perished (see pages 148-150). He was replaced as XO by LCDR Van Biesbroeck, who had just months before sincerely suggested to Alkire alternative attitudes – one related to the aircraft's pitch, and one related to arrogance. Both were ignored. The squadron experienced another minor accident of unknown cause during its work-ups aboard *Hancock* when LTJG Robert O. Angle landed aboard ship on 28 August 1955. The aircraft was subsequently repaired and ready for its deployment thirteen days later.

Hancock departed San Diego on 10 August 1955 with fourteen VF-124 Cutlasses proudly displayed on her deck. Vought Field Service Representatives Lawrence E. Burney and Billy R. Browning accompanied the squadron to provide factory support for the first F7U-3 deployment. Once operating in Hawaiian waters, trouble started on 25 August when ENS Lew Mitchell Jr. had BuNo 129585's starboard main gear axle break upon landing aboard the carrier, resulting in the tyre and wheel assembly rolling forward down the deck. The aircraft was repaired aboard ship and returned to service. ENS Cavicke snagged the edge of the ramp with BuNo 129592's arresting hook point – as well as the port main gear tyre – during 31 August flight operations. Cavicke fortunately made it onto the deck but with the hook point gone, and a blown tyre, he was along for the ride. The aircraft triggered the Davis barrier, and proceeded to the barricade that was protecting the pack of aircraft and personnel forward. The left main gear failed at the gear's trunnions and collapsed. Offloaded at Pearl Harbor, the aircraft's custody was transferred to FASRon-117 at NAS Barbers Point, where it was subsequently stricken. The squadron conducted additional Fleet Carrier Landing Practice (FCLP) at NAS Barbers Point prior to an Operational Readiness Inspection (ORI). Operations between Hawaii and Japan were conducted without incident, outside of a few fin stubs making contact with the deck during landings. As they are 'sacrificial', constructed of laminated wood, the *Hancock*'s carpentry shop was kept busy. Once in Japanese waters, LT Floyd C. Nugent experienced a tail cone strike during one landing aboard *Hancock*, but this damage was repaired aboard the ship.

Upon their arrival in Japan, the squadron was offloaded to operate out of NAF Atsugi. Adversely affecting the Cutlass's reputation as being suitable for its purpose, much has been made of VF-124 being 'beached' at Atsugi. To at least some extent, it reflected the fact that the *Hancock* air group was unusually large and varied for an Essex-class carrier: two day fighter squadrons, VF-121 and VF-124, instead of the usual one; from time to time three of the huge AJ Savages for nuclear strike and air-to-air refuelling, particularly important in the western Pacific (as the cruise book noted, 'Our beloved Cutlasses left us, making room for the massive AJ's of VC-6'); a detachment of four Regulus I surface-to-surface nuclear-armed cruise missiles with their accompanying F9F-6Ps for en route guidance; and a USMC photo Banshee detachment at one point, all in addition to the customary AD attack squadrons and the now standard proliferation of special mission 'cats and dogs' for ECM, airborne early warning, etc. The four Regulus missiles, their launch carts, and support equipment were easily the equivalent of five carrier-based aircraft alone. As a result, to reduce overcrowding that would affect efficient operations, it was appropriate to leave one squadron behind at times.

The logical candidate for offloading was VF-124, the redundant day fighter squadron with not-quite-ready for primetime F7U-3s. However, if VF-121's F9F-8s had been grounded for some reason (although the -8 was very similar to the -6, there were detail differences and this was the -8's first deployment), VF-124 would almost certainly have remained aboard. Groundings,

Although VF-124 was a fighter squadron, the F7U-3 was qualified to deliver nuclear weapons. Here BuNo 129463 is carrying a 150-gallon fuel tank under the right wing and a Mk 12 'shape' under the left as it is being prepared for launch from Hancock. *US Navy*

primarily due to problems with a particular engine type, were not unknown: VF-91, equipped with Grumman F9F-8s, was a last-minute addition to CVG-5 deploying on *Kearsarge* (CVA-33) in October 1955. It replaced VF-51, which was flying North American FJ-3s plagued with J65 engine problems at the time. It should also be noted that during that seven-month deployment, VF-91 had eleven major accidents with one pilot killed. In any event, VF-121's deployment on *Hancock* was far from trouble free: The squadron had fourteen major accidents with its F9F-8s aboard the carrier between 20 June 1955 and 18 February 1956, including two in June before the deployment began. The F7U was not the only swept-wing jet that carrier-based aviators found to be challenging.

The F7U's maiden voyage abroad was not as trouble free as Vought and the Navy hoped it would be based on the *Project Cutlass* initiative and success. However, contrary to the reputation that the aircraft has acquired over the years, none of the shortcomings encountered were due to its performance, handling qualities, or a propensity for accidents. They were also not surprising

The AJ Savage was invaluable for in-flight refuelling of jets but because folding its wings and vertical fin was onerous and time-consuming, they generally weren't. The deck space to park one was significant, not to mention the need to tow it fore and aft between recoveries and launches on an axial-deck carrier. *US Navy*

given its unprecedented complexity compared to existing carrier-based jets, combined with the challenge of maintenance aboard an aircraft carrier at sea, where there is limited space for maintenance personnel billeting, below-deck parking, and spares storage. As a result, up to half of the squadron's aircraft were 'duds' (not flyable) at times. The only significant maintenance issue, however, was reportedly the unsuitability aboard ship of the engine removal/installation capability, for which Vought created a more user-friendly alternative. Another recommended change was that the plane captain, the only seaman dedicated to taking care of a particular aircraft as advanced as the Cutlass, be provided with an assistant.

Once acclimated to their new surroundings at NAF Atsugi, the pilots of VF-124 settled into a relatively routine shore-based deployment. With an unusually harsh Japanese winter predicted, the squadron conducted extensive daily flight operations in an attempt to capitalise on the relatively benign autumn weather. When *Hancock* was at sea, and the opportunity arose, VF-124 pilots made visits to the carrier to practise in-flight refuelling and additional carrier operations to keep their shipboard skills honed. Consideration was given to VF-124 being added to the air group aboard *Bennington* (CVA-20) that was also deployed in the western Pacific in late 1955/early 1956. This suggests that it was not in effect restricted to shore-based operations after November 1955. However, *Bennington* had not received steam catapults during its angled-deck modifications, which would have restricted the F7U-3's operational capability so the squadron remained at Atsugi.

The late autumn of 1955 saw VF-124 become one of the first deployed fleet squadrons to receive the new light gull grey over insignia white paint liveries as mandated by the fiscal year 1956 directives from BuAer (see Appendix A). Painting of the aircraft was conducted at FASRon-11's hangar as well as at the local Atsugi Nippon Services company. Additionally, the application of black parel-keytone to the landing gear and gear wells in the Fleet's ill-conceived attempt to mitigate corrosion proved to be a disaster for the VF-124 maintenance personnel, who could longer identify wire bundles and hydraulic lines after they had been coated in the tar-like substance. However, a case can be made that the paint and parel-keytone may have been beneficial once the winter of 1955 was upon them.

Although VF-124's operational record was good while based at Atsugi, two accidents occurred that tarnished the otherwise successful remaining portion of

VF-124 F7U-3's BuNo 129585 and 129580 share the ramp at NAF Atsugi in the winter of 1955. The harsh conditions experienced during Japan's winter kept VF-124's plane captains busy. ***Casby Collection***

the deployment. On 5 October 1955, following a normal landing, VF-124's Communications Officer, now-LT Angle departed the runway surface while taxiing due to inattention. The nose and port main gear dug into the soft earth. Stressed beyond design specifications, the nose gear failed at the trunnion attachments and collapsed. Angle escaped injury, but his aircraft, BuNo 129577, received overhaul-grade damage and its custody was transferred to Atsugi's FASRon-11. It was eventually stricken following inspection at NAF Advance Base Oppama by representatives from O&R San Diego. BuNo 129577 had accumulated only forty-five flight hours at the time of the accident.

The second was a tragedy that occurred on 1 November 1955 during carrier operations off the coast of Japan involving LTJG George B. 'Barry' Milliard. His accident resulted from a combination of poor pilot technique, a mis-rigged barrier, and an unforeseen consequence of a nose gear collapse triggering the ejection seat (see page 309). An example of the misinformation available online and in publications about the Cutlass is this statement: 'During this single 1955–1956 deployment aboard the *Hancock*, VF-124's *Stingarees* lost 5 of their 16 Cutlass pilots.' While it is true that five CAG-12 pilots were killed during the deployment, only one, LTJG Milliard, was flying a Cutlass.

On 23 November, BuNo 129599 was acquired from FASRon-11 to replace ENS Cavicke's BuNo 129592 that had been offloaded back in August at Barbers Point, Hawaii. This brought the squadron's complement to twelve operational aircraft.

The *Stingarees'* aircraft were craned back aboard *Hancock* for the return to San Diego. The squadron's section in *Hancock*'s cruise book concluded with this candid observation:

> VF-124's technical problems did not end with departure from San Diego aboard the HANCOCK. The ensuing months were paved with snafus and sorrow. The problems of fitting a plane as fast and heavy as the Cutlass into the fleet still caused persistent trouble. Yet, through it all, the officers and men of VF-124 have gained the satisfaction that, by using the data and experience gained during their cruise to West Pac, the fleet will overcome the difficulty in handling the complex monsters which have rolled off Chance Vought's assembly lines.

In his post-deployment Operational Report, the

Late in VF-124's deployment, BuNo 129584 is being respotted aboard *Hancock*. Note the 'black' landing gear and wheel wells. ***US Navy***

Commander of Air Group (CAG) Twelve, CDR Charlie N. 'Tex' Conatser, recommended changes to the process of introducing a new aircraft in an air group, particularly one as complex and different as the Cutlass. He wanted earlier and in-depth notice of a type's peculiarities, capabilities, and limitations, e.g. those associated with afterburning engines. He also recommended that instead of the air group's squadrons coming together from their home bases, which were in separate locations by mission type – only a week before deployment – that at least four weeks be dedicated to a shore-based, joint work-up at a single location under CAG control. Notably, this was not a specific criticism of the F7U-3, *per se*.

Following the *Hancock* deployment, the air group was expanded to have a second attack squadron, VA-126, which was established on 6 April 1956 at NAS Miramar, California, and assigned VF-124's twelve F7U-3s while VF-124 transitioned to the F3H-2M Demon.

Attack Squadron One Hundred and Twenty-Six (VA-126) *Tough Guys*. The last deployable squadron to be equipped with F7U-3s, VA-126, was established as an operational fleet attack squadron on 6 April 1956 at NAS Miramar, California. Skippered by CDR George L. Cassell and adopting the nickname *Tough Guys* and squadron motto 'Nulli Secundus' (Second to None), the squadron was formed around the F7U-3s that had returned on 15 March 1956 from VF-124's Far East deployment aboard *Hancock* (CVA-19). Miramar-based VF-124 was scheduled to transition to the McDonnell F3H-2N Demon, which facilitated the newest attack squadron in CVG-12 to instantly acquire a full squadron complement of F7U-3s. On 11 April 1956, all twelve remaining VF-124 Cutlasses were transferred to VA-126 custody. Along with the aircraft, three of VF-124's pilots brought their F7U-3 experience to the new squadron: LTJG Richard J. 'Dick' Cavicke, LTJG Willis Ivan Lewis Jr., and LTJG Samuel W. Morey.

On 26 April 1956, the squadron took custody of BuNo 129649 from O&R San Diego. This was followed by the acquisition of BuNo 129658 and 129678 in May, bringing the squadron complement to fifteen aircraft. With its new VA-126 paint still not fully cured, 129658 took part in the Armed Forces Day Open House held at Van Nuys Airport on 19 May, displaying the new squadron's flashy livery to the public for the first time. VA-126's F7U-3s retained the new light gull grey over gloss insignia white paint scheme that had been applied during VF-124's stay at NAF Atsugi, Japan, as well as CVG-12's 'D' tail code, but added an attractive medium blue trim with black stripes above and below the air group letter on the fin, all outlined in white. On some VA-126 aircraft the inner landing gear doors and the landing gear itself were finished in gloss white but others retained the silver lacquer. Like many squadrons during this transition to the new scheme, VA-126 was extended a certain amount of latitude in the application of the markings, as each individual squadron interpreted the directives differently. VA-126 was originally assigned a 3XX unit number within CVG-12, with the last one or two digits replicated on the nose gear fairing, but in late 1956 the squadron repainted the aircraft to display single and double-digit (1X) unit numbers, in anticipation of VA-126's unrealised transfer to a different administrative custodian.

The last F7U-3 to roll off Vought's production line, BuNo 129697, joined VA-126 on 20 June 1956 from O&R San Diego following an eleven-month overhaul at O&R Jacksonville. At sixteen F7U-3s, the squadron had reached its anticipated full complement, but that number would soon be reduced by one on 13 July 1956. Following a refuelling stop at Kirtland AFB in Albuquerque, New Mexico, during a flight from NAS Miramar to NAS Dallas, now-full LT 'Ivan' Lewis and his wingman LT 'Sam' Morey encountered adverse weather as they approached Amarillo, Texas. Morey had previously assumed the lead position due to a malfunctioning gyro horizon on Lewis' aircraft. Approaching a line of haze with imbedded thunderstorms, the two pilots attempted to climb above their 38,000ft cruise altitude by selecting afterburner. Both aircraft achieved light-off on the first selected afterburner, however Morey's second afterburner either did not ignite, or he encountered an afterburner blow out at the higher altitude on one or both engines. Morey was last seen descending into the overcast at 31,000ft.

LT Morey radioed Lewis that he was in trouble but did not indicate the nature of the problem. Lewis was unable to regain communication with Morey and continued on to a safe landing at Amarillo AFB with the hope that Morey had either already landed or would soon follow. However, LT Morey had ejected from BuNo 129583 and never achieved full separation from his seat. He deployed his parachute, which was found tangled around him and the seat after he impacted the ground on the Weymouth Ranch near Four-Way, Texas. State Highway Patrolmen reported finding the crash site of the aircraft 2 miles off Highway 136 near Fritch, Texas, but this initial report was in error, as the presumed crash site was an intentionally burned farm field. The aircraft was subsequently found 25 miles north of Amarillo two days later. The following week, VA-126's parachute rigger attempted to forensically untangle the parachute's

VA-126's F7U-3 BuNo 129658 on static display with its new squadron markings in May 1956. ***Casby Collection***

shroud lines (which had bundled up into a ball during Morey's tragic descent) in order to determine a cause for the ejection's deadly outcome. He found an unwrapped condom at the centre of the shroud line ball. No explanation for this strange find could be determined. BuAer and Vought engineers opined that the most likely cause of the unsuccessful ejection was the release of the parachute prior to full seat separation, allowing the seat to contact the billowing chute, possibly due to the rigours associated with a high-speed ejection within the thunderstorm. Custody of F7U-3 BuNo 129672 was assumed by the squadron on 14 August 1956 to replace Morey's aircraft.

Following this sombre loss, VA-126 concerned themselves with readying for the special weapons (nuclear) training they were about to begin in September 1956. Bypassed in the selection of squadrons to attend 1956's Fleet Air Gunnery Meet, the squadron set their sights on honing their bomb delivery skills during deployments to NOTS China Lake, California's Armitage Field, and NAAS Fallon, Nevada. Utilising the Low Altitude Bombing System (LABS) installed in their F7U-3s, the members of VA-126 excelled during the simulated nuclear bomb delivery training and subsequent Competitive Exercise (COMPEX) bombing competition held at Fallon.

During their two-and-a-half-week stay at Fallon, VA-126 flew more sorties, more hours, and dropped more ordnance than any previous F7U-equipped squadron. Logging 424 flight hours during 511 sorties, VA-126's pilots dropped more than 1,900 practice bombs, including the simulated nuclear shapes. Their average ground turnaround time was less than twenty minutes due to the exceptional performance of the VA-126 line crews. Following their training, eleven of the eighteen pilots participating qualified for the coveted individual Navy 'E' award for bombing, which authorised them to display the 'EB' adornment below their cockpits. This was the highest number of 'E's awarded to a single squadron's pilots in any type of aircraft.

October of 1956 saw VA-126 begin to trade their initial complement of aircraft for new replacements. Six aircraft were flown to NASF Litchfield Park, while six others' custody were transferred to O&R San Diego. One additional aircraft was ferried to Litchfield Park in December 1956. Meanwhile, deliveries of nine F7U-3s from O&R San Diego commenced in October and continued until January 1957, effectively bringing the squadron's new complement to thirteen aircraft. The Suez Crisis erupted on 29 October 1956 when Israel invaded the Gaza Strip and Egypt following Egypt's nationalisation of the Suez Canal. In anticipation of a possible deployment, VA-126 pilots conducted FCLPs at NOLF Crows Landing, California. It was anticipated that they would deploy aboard *Lexington* (CVA-16) if called upon. The crisis, however, ended on 7 November and the squadron resumed their normal stateside training activities. January 1957 brought the announcement of the Eisenhower Doctrine pledging military aid to the Middle East region, and with tensions increasing in Lebanon the squadron once again prepared for a possible deployment.

However, in February 1957 VA-126 received a directive from the Commander, Fleet Air Alameda, to trade their F7U-3s for F9F-8B Cougars in preparation for eventual transition to the FJ-4B Fury. F7U-3 flights to NASF Litchfield Park commenced on 7 February with BuNo 129658 and continued until the last six F7U-3s in VA-126 custody were flown to the NASF on 9 April 1957, their pilots putting on an impromptu airshow upon their arrival. After dropping off their Cutlasses, some VA-126 pilots were immediately transported to various Naval Air Stations to pick up their new F9F-8Bs for the delivery flights to Miramar.

Marred by only one unfortunate loss in the year they flew the Cutlass, the *Tough Guys* of VA-126 enjoyed a virtually perfect operational and safety record, exceeding that of most squadrons regardless of aircraft type. They were the go-to squadron if augmentation of nuclear strike capability was required at short notice by the President.

Fighter/Attack Squadron One Hundred and Fifty-One (VF-151/VA-151) *Black Knights*. VF-653, a Naval Reserve fighter squadron established in December 1949, was called to active duty on 1 February 1951. They were equipped with the Chance Vought F4U-4 and -4B Corsair and nicknamed the *Dragons*. Redesignated VF-151 on 4 February 1953, they traded their Corsairs for Grumman F9F-2/5 Panthers and assumed the name *Black Knights*. The squadron completed three Far East deployments after its establishment and returned from its last cruise aboard *Wasp* (CVA-18) to NAS Alameda on 11 April 1955. They immediately began preparations for transitioning to the F7U-3M Cutlass.

Originally intended to be Fleet Air Alameda's Cutlass-equipped interceptor squadron, VF-151 received their first -3M, BuNo 129742, on 26 May 1955. It was quickly joined by five more -3Ms by mid-July. CDR Edward S. Park accepted the aircraft following the completion of his F7U-3 flight training with VC-3 at Moffett Field and his assumption of command in June 1955. VF-151 began training with the -3Ms, but this did not involve Sparrow missiles as the squadron was advised on 6 June that they would become an attack squadron early in 1956 as a result of their air group's reorganisation. With the impending mission change, VF-151 began receiving F7U-3s on 25 June 1955 with the arrival of BuNo 129578 from BAR Dallas. Beginning in August, VF-151 would take custody of fifteen more F7U-3s with deliveries ending on 20 February 1956 with the custody transfer of F7U-3 BuNo 129618 from O&R San Diego. The F7U-3Ms began to be transferred to other squadrons on 7 November 1955, with the last two joining VX-4 in May 1956.

As a part of CVG-15, VF-151's F7Us wore the air group's

BuNo 129618 was still wearing the CVG-15 'H' tail code during carquals aboard CVA-16 on 23 April 1956. Note the added 'Ubangi' lip on the lower side of the engine inlet. ***Robert L. Lawson photo***

'H' tail code and the squadron's 300-series individual aircraft numbers on their natural finishes but little else in the way of squadron markings. The squadron was notified on 1 January 1956 that they would indeed be redesignated an attack squadron as planned and continue to be on loan to ATG-1 in preparation for its planned deployment to the Far East. As was customary for Air Task Groups, they retained their CVG-15 tail code 'H' for a time (ATG-1 was officially assigned its own tail code 'U' on 24 July 1956 but at least some of the F7U-3s had already been marked with it). The squadron also received orders to paint their aircraft in the new gull grey over insignia white livery being adopted for fleet aircraft, a time-consuming process. As a result, it operated with a mixture of aircraft liveries and tail codes during this transition period. They eventually adopted blue fin tips as their squadron's distinctive markings, which was consistent with a third squadron's trim colour in an air group.

On 7 February 1956 VF-151 was officially redesignated VA-151. CDR Park was reassigned to be the Operations Officer for VX-4 at Pt Mugu. Assuming command of VA-151 was LCDR Robert H. 'Salty' Moore Jr. assisted by LCDR Dixie J. Mays Jr. Squadron detachments conducted multiple training missions to the gunnery ranges at NAAS Fallon, Nevada, and NOTS China Lake, California, in preparation for the deployment aboard *Lexington* (CVA-16) scheduled for May. A full-squadron gunnery exercise was successfully conducted at China Lake's Armitage Field from 13 to 18 February. Starting the following day, two two-plane detachments per day were to conduct final gunnery qualification flights at Fallon. It was the initial detachment's departure on 19 February 1956 that would result in VA-151's first of seven accidents, three of which were fatal. Following a formation take-off from NAS Alameda, 21-year-old ENS Patrick E. Harwood inadvertently departed with his fully armed BuNo 129619's main fuel cell being fed by the external drop tanks instead of the internal transfer tanks in violation of checklist protocol. He remained in afterburner longer than necessary and the main cell – from which the engines drew fuel – was emptied in less than three minutes as the external tanks could not feed it fast enough. Both of Harwood's engines flamed out over the hills of Moraga, California. He attempted to eject.

Following the low-altitude procedure recommended for aircraft not yet modified with an automatic lap-belt release, Harwood unfastened his lap belt and shoulder harnesses, and pulled the face curtain to eject. Unfortunately, during maintenance on the seat, a mechanic erred by not fully screwing down the catapult's firing cap – this resulted in the firing pin not making contact with the explosive charge, so the seat did not eject. With the canopy already jettisoned, Harwood impacted a hillside and was thrown from the aircraft, his body coming to a stop against a fence, while the wreckage of his F7U showered a fifty-home area with exploding cannon ordnance.

Two months later, on 19 April 1956, LTJG David H. Chantler, who had been Harwood's wingman on his fatal flight, ground looped F7U-3 BuNo 129618 after returning from a post-maintenance test flight, although the aircraft only suffered minor damage and was able to participate in the April–May carrier-qualifications (carquals) aboard *Lexington*. During these carquals, LTJG Frank J. Carrig made history when he lost his starboard engine due to a malfunctioning fuel control unit while flying out to the *Lexington* off the California coast. With insufficient fuel to fly to a mainland airfield, Carrig requested permission to attempt a single-engine landing (with respect to a single-engine landing on a carrier, the Flight Handbook stated 'it is to be emphasised that the single-engine approach is difficult under ideal conditions and may be impracticable under adverse weather conditions. The circumstances will dictate whether such an approach is feasible or the airplane should be abandoned'). Reluctantly, CAPT Alexander S. Heyward Jr., the carrier's skipper, gave him the go-ahead. His first approach resulted in uncontrollable settling, requiring Carrig to execute a single-engine wave off. Using afterburner during the second approach and adjusting his speed and sink rate with use of the speed brakes, Carrig successfully brought his crippled F7U-3 aboard,

Unfolding the wings of F7U-3 BuNo 129653 while taxiing forward in accordance with the plane director's signals into position for launch from *Lexington* during carrier qualifications. ***US Navy***

earning him the nickname 'One Burner Carrig'.

With some VA-151 F7U-3s pre-marked with 'U' tail codes, while others still sported their 'H' code and VF-151 squadron identification (as well as some newly painted in grey and white and others still unpainted), the squadron's aircraft appeared somewhat of a hodgepodge during the qualifications. Notwithstanding, they qualified without incident and were ready to deploy.

CVA-16 left Alameda on its Far East cruise on 28 May 1956 with a now fully repainted VA-151 complement of eight F7U-3s aboard. During the first month of the deployment, VA-151 conducted air operations with few problems, but things would soon deteriorate. On 8 July 1956, during a launch from *Lexington*'s port catapult, a major fire erupted from the aft starboard side of LTJG Chantler's BuNo 129693, singeing several deck crew and enveloping an AJ Savage waiting its turn for launch. Chantler retracted the landing gear and climbed to 800ft. Although advised to eject, he elected to ditch the aircraft instead after turning into the wind. Just prior to touching down, the aircraft nosed over and disintegrated upon contact with the sea, claiming Chantler's life. Although no wreckage was recovered, analysis of the ship's launch films indicate that an afterburner fuel line either broke or was not properly reconnected following an engine change. Several witnesses aboard *Lexington* also reported that the landing gear was extended just prior to water contact, possibly causing the pitch over.

On 31 July 1956 LTJG Carrig made history once again when he repeated his carqual feat and landed successfully aboard *Lexington* after again losing the starboard engine, this time due to a fuel supply issue. Repeating what most thought impossible the first time, Carrig skilfully brought his F7U-3 aboard and stated, 'Same plane, same engine, same pilot ... last time!'

BuNo 129618 suffered a 3 August main gear collapse due to LT E.A. Corbett's extended float and hard landing at NAF Atsugi, which resulted in the aircraft's custody being transferred to FASRon-11 for subsequent scrapping. The squadron resumed carrier operations off the coast of Japan and on 12 September LTJG Carrig

This VA-151 pilot of BuNo 129664 is taking advantage of the angled deck of *Lexington* to 'bolter' after failing to 'trap', an option not available on axial-deck carriers with aircraft parked forward. *US Navy*

The customary air-to-air photo of a west Pacific deployment with Mt Fuji in the background. LTJG Hal Crandall, a future Mercury astronaut candidate, mans 129615 in the foreground. *US Navy*

Virtually all carrier take-offs and landings are documented by still and movie cameras, in this instance, the afterburner fuel-fed fire that occurred during BuNo 129693's launch on 8 July 1956. *Casby Collection*

accomplished *Lexington*'s first barricade engagement as an angled-deck carrier with BuNo 129664 following an arresting hook point failure during the prior landing attempt. This was successfully executed and the aircraft was subsequently offloaded and custody transferred to NAF Oppama for repairs upon the ship's return to port.

Tragically, one month later on 12 October 1956, LTJG Carrig – the hero of two single-engine carrier landings and a barricade engagement in the F7U-3 – encountered a rising deck resulting in an extremely hard landing that sheared off the starboard main landing gear. BuNo 129633 became airborne off the port side of the ship and settled into the ocean, breaking up on contact. The forward fuselage continued to float for several minutes, which allowed the carrier's plane-guard helicopter to drop a rescue crewman into the water. Tragically, Carrig had elected to land with his canopy closed due to inclement weather and was unable to open it after the impact. The rescue swimmer dived after the sinking cockpit section and remained in eye contact with Carrig until he sadly sank out of view.

LTJG Kenneth E. Behnke had a minor accident in BuNo 129666 on 26 October 1956 when he struck an NC-1 starter jeep while taxiing on the deck. The aircraft was repaired aboard ship.

Having left with eight Cutlasses, when CVA-16 returned stateside on 20 December 1956, VA-151 came home to NAS Alameda with only four. Awaiting on the Alameda ramp were the replacements for their Cutlasses, Grumman F9F-8B Cougars. All four F7Us were flown to NASF Litchfield Park within a week of their return, the last on 5 January 1957. CDR Bernard Sevilla assumed command of the squadron in January, taking custody of additional F9F-8Bs and F9F-8s, in preparation for the squadron's July 1957 transition to the FJ-4B Fury.

Fighter/Attack Squadron Two Hundred and Twelve (VF-212/VA-212) *Rampant Raiders*. VF-212 was established at NAS Moffett Field, California, on 20 June 1955 to provide Fleet Air Alameda with a second deployable air-to-air guided missile-equipped squadron following the assignment of F7U-3Ms to VF-151 in May 1955. The selection of a commanding officer to lead the squadron initially focused on LCDR Dixie J. Mays, however, he had assumed the Executive Officer position with NAS Alameda-based VF-151 a month earlier. With LCDR Mays already assigned, LCDR Douglas R. Hagood was selected to be the Commanding Officer of VF-212. Assisting Hagood as Executive Officer was LCDR Joachim F. 'Jack' Speciale.

On 1 July 1955, LCDR's Hagood and Speciale, accompanied by LT Bruce Cobb, attended Composite Squadron Three's (VC-3) *Project Check-Out* for their initial F7U-3 ground school training. On 15 July, LCDR's Hagood and Speciale began flight training with VC-3 instructors LT Doniphan B. 'Don' Shelton and LT Jacob D. 'Jake' Ward respectively, with LT Cobb assigned to VC-3's LT Walter M. Schirra Jr. By 10 August, VF-212's three senior officers had finished their division tactics training flights, making room for -212's LT Carl 'Tex' Birdwell Jr. to also benefit from *Project Check-Out*'s training programme.

VF-212 assumed custody of seven F7U-3Ms from FASRon-10, starting with BuNos 139871 and 139873 on 19 July 1955 and with BuNo 139879 joining them ten days later. August would see three more -3Ms arrive, with 129710 transferred on 8 August and BuNos 139876 and 139877 arriving on 25 August. BuNo 139880 was the last F7U-3M to join the squadron on 12 September 1955. VF-212's natural-finish aircraft were some of the most photogenic of F7U-3Ms, with bright orange-yellow tail tips and the unique location on the forward fuselage (under the sliding canopy) for the squadron's unit designator (side) numbers – unlike all other squadrons who placed them on the nose, forward of the national insignia. As part of CVG-21, VF-212 Cutlasses wore the 'G' tail code on their fins. 'VF-212' was painted below the 'NAVY' branch-of-service designator. With all their aircraft received within a two-month time frame from FASRon-10 (who received them directly from BAR Dallas following their factory completion) their aircraft's finish had not had any appreciable time to oxidise or dull. As a result, the squadron received many complimentary comments on the gleaming appearance of their aircraft, and LCDR Hagood insisted that the aircraft be waxed often to retain these honours. In addition to the F7U-3Ms, VF-212 also took custody of one F7U-3 from FASRon-12. F7U-3 BuNo 129692 was accepted by VF-212 on 19 August 1955 to be used as an additional training aircraft for the squadron's sixteen pilots.

Intensive in-house training of VF-212's junior aviators began in September 1955 with VF-212 making several shore deployments to NAAS Fallon for gunnery exercises once the squadron completed the initial check-outs. Unfortunately, Sparrow I missiles were not yet available to the squadron so they did not have the opportunity to conduct live fire exercises with the missile as intended. By mid-October 1955, LCDR Hagood had received word from the Commander of Fleet Air Alameda, RADM Frank T. Ward, Jr., that VF-212 would soon follow in the footsteps of VF-151 and be redesignated as an attack squadron equipped with F7U-3s. Two additional F7U-3s were transferred from FASRon-12 to VF-212: BuNo 129691 on 20 October and BuNo 129683 on 30 November. On 16 December 1955, F7U-3M BuNo 139873 was transferred to VX-4, followed by 139880 a month later. The remainder of the squadron's F7U-3Ms would be transferred to VA-116 between 29 December 1955 and 30 April 1956. By 9 January 1956, VF-212's early

F7U-3M BuNo 139880 assigned to VF-212 before the squadron was reequipped with F7U-3s and subsequently redesignated VA-212. Note the unusual location of the side number. ***US Navy***

complement of three F7U-3s would also be returned to BAR Dallas for modifications and eventual reassignment.

Beginning on 9 November 1955, VF-212 saw the arrival of its next complement of F7U-3s with the transfer of BuNo 129629 from FASRon-10. Eleven more -3s would arrive between 5 and 30 December, to bring the squadron's replacement F7U-3 aircraft-on-hand total to twelve.

Training in the F7U-3 resumed with an emphasis on section tactics, gunnery and bombing at NAAS Fallon and NOTS China Lake. The squadron experienced their first aircraft loss on 10 March 1956 when LT Birdwell was forced to eject from BuNo 129575 following a section take-off from NAAS Fallon. LT Birdwell noticed a starboard afterburner fire-warning light after relighting the afterburner following its intentional shutdown to allow his wingman, LTJG Conrad B. 'Connie' Olson, to maintain formation (following a blow out of one of his own afterburners during the take-off). Olson confirmed that Birdwell had a fire that was burning through the aft lower fuselage skin. Birdwell ejected successfully at 3,000ft and was uninjured. Subsequent crash investigation revealed that the right-hand afterburner fuel lines had loose nuts – most likely due to a maintenance oversight (and a seemingly common cause of F7U-3 afterburner fires). Custody of F7U-3 BuNo 129597 was transferred from O&R San Diego on 24 March 1956 to replace 575.

As anticipated, on 1 April 1956 VF-212 was redesignated VA-212 and all squadron aircraft were subsequently reassigned, however individual aircraft records did not initially reflect that at the time, probably due to it being a low priority given the other administrative duties involved in the transition. Although the squadron retained CVG-21's orange-yellow trim colour, the fin trim was now extended to cover the entire upper half of the fin with an insignia blue demarcation line on the lower edge. This trim treatment extended to both sides of each fin. The air group's 'G' tail code letter now appeared within the orange-yellow field and the squadron designator was changed to reflect the squadron's attack status.

CVG-21 was planning for a late-summer Far East deployment. LCDR Hagood therefore received word that his squadron would be scheduled for carrier qualifications (carquals) to commence in May 1956. A month prior, VA-212 began to paint their aircraft in the new light gull grey and glossy insignia white paint livery dictated by BuAer. The squadron embarked on the newly angle-decked *Bon Homme Richard* (CVA-31) in mid-May for carquals before all its aircraft were painted, with two aircraft still in natural finish. All pilots qualified, but not without incident. During a 14 May catapult launch, LTJG Carl J. 'Tate' Tatro's BuNo 129635 experienced a port bridle eye that failed to disengage from the aircraft following launch. The bridle's loose end continued to slap the underside of Tatro's aircraft, damaging the port fin, rudder, ailavator, wing trailing edge and engine bay door. Investigation revealed that the catapult hooks had not been greased, and that the fuel load signals given to the catapult officer were misconstrued, resulting in slower than normal end speed during the launch. LCDR Hagood also experienced bridle release issues when his BuNo 129555 failed to release its catapult bridle following launch on the same day. The bridle eventually released on the starboard side, causing the bridle eye to strike the right landing gear fairing causing minor damage. Two days later, LT Birdwell experienced a similar bridle separation failure in F7U-3 BuNo 129545 that caused the bridle to impact the fuselage's centre section, causing substantial damage. It should be noted that VA-212 had not been given instructions to grease the bridle eyes and catapult hooks prior to their carqual, as this issue had not been identified previously.

The summer of 1956 saw VA-212 continue to train in gunnery and bombing tactics at NAAS Fallon in preparation for their Far East deployment aboard *Bon Homme Richard*. On 16 August VA-212 embarked on CVA-31 with ten aircraft for a six-month cruise. Two days into the deployment, LCDR Speciale encountered a pitching deck during recovery operations. He initially struck the deck extremely hard with his starboard tyre, resulting in a blow out and loss of the wheel, brake, and axle. Selecting afterburner allowed Speciale to become airborne, and following assessment of the situation, he elected to ditch BuNo 129676 instead of attempting an ejection. Striking a large ocean swell, his aircraft nosed underwater. LCDR Speciale was able to release his harness and extricate himself from the sinking aircraft with only minor injuries. Four days later, tragedy struck when LTJG Arthur G. Callahan Jr. entered a low-altitude clean stall and pre-post stall gyration halfway through his turn to line up for landing following the break. His aircraft impacted the sea, causing fatal injuries and disintegration of BuNo 129660. LTJG Callahan's death was VA-212's only fatality, and the squadron solemnly welcomed LTJG David W. Doss from VA-151 as his replacement.

One day later on 23 August 1956, LTJG Richard 'Dick' Daleke struck the ramp with BuNo 129635's starboard landing gear and tail cone during a landing attempt following a mirror-assisted approach. His arresting hook did not engage a cross-deck pendant, and he became airborne again after selecting full afterburner. A subsequent approach and landing were successful, however his aircraft sustained overhaul-level damage and was offloaded to FASRon-117 at NAS Barbers Point upon the carrier's docking in Hawaii.

On 4 September 1956 the squadron's official insignia was approved and consisted of a round yellow-rimmed navy blue background with a yellow rampant lion. Later iterations included the VA-212 designator in a lower scroll while the squadron nickname *Rampant Raiders* was emblazoned in an upper scroll. The squadron's radio call sign was then switched from 'Bantam' to 'Raider'.

Pilots and support personnel of a VA-212 Special Weapons Training detachment at NAF China Lake, California, posing with F7U-3 BuNo 129549, *circa* April 1956. *US Navy*

VA-212's LTJG Ronald J. Carminati taxiing F7U-3 BuNo 129554 out for take-off at NAF Atsugi, Japan. This aircraft is currently being restored to airworthy condition by co-author Al Casby. *Casby Collection*

VA-212's LTJG Conrad B. 'Connie' Olson straps on Executive Officer LCDR Joachim F. 'Jack' Speciale's BuNo 129663 prior to a flight from NAF Atsugi. Note the jagged loss of paint along the panel line separating the upper Metalite panel from the lower magnesium panel. *Casby Collection*

Spotted amidships aboard *Bon Homme Richard* (CVA-31) while preparing for the return voyage home, VA-212's F7U-3's are lashed to the deck. Note the differences in intake warning markings and BuNo typeface and position on 129554. It was one of three replacement aircraft not equipped with the inflight refueling kit. ***Casby Collection***

Upon arrival in Japan, the squadron insignia was soon added to the aft canopy fairing on most aircraft.

As a result of the three aircraft losses VA-212 suffered during their less-than-stellar first leg of the cruise, a request was made for replacement aircraft once the squadron began shore operations out of NAF Atsugi, Japan. F7U-3 BuNos 129554 and 129564 were both transported in *Bon Homme Richard*'s hangar deck for delivery from Alameda's FASRon-8 to Atsugi's FASRon-11. Upon arrival in Japan, these aircraft were offloaded and quickly repainted in VA-212 markings, although the application of the livery was not identical to that of the rest of the squadron. Variations in air intake warning triangle shape and national insignia positioning was due to interpretation differences of the FASRon-11 applicator. In addition, the replacement aircraft did not have in-flight refuelling kits installed. Custody of both aircraft were transferred to VA-212 on 12 September 1956.

A sheared arresting hook point bolt caused LT Bruce Cobb to bolter following his attempt to land BuNo 129663 aboard *Bon Homme Richard* on 12 October 1956. Cobb requested that the barricade be rigged and he executed a picture-perfect landing into the barricade's straps, bringing him to a safe stop. BuNo 129663 sustained substantial damage from the engagement, but was eventually repaired in Japan and returned to service with the squadron. F7U-3 BuNo 129565 – which had also been transported aboard CVA-31 – joined VA-212 on 19 November 1956, bringing the squadron back to its ten-aircraft complement. Once again, its markings were applied in a unique fashion and did not match the squadron's existing aircraft exactly.

VA-212 operated without incident for the remainder of the deployment and shore operations conducted from NAF Atsugi. They participated in combat air patrols off the coast of Taiwan, Quemoy, and Matsu in a show of strength to dissuade Communist Chinese aggression in the region, and accumulated 493 flight hours during their six months deployed. Prior to *Bon Homme Richard*'s docking at Alameda on 28 February 1957, VA-212 launched their aircraft for their own homecoming to NAS Moffett Field. Selected as one of two squadrons (the other being VA-12) to provide aircraft for Naval Air Reserve Training use, VA-212 began preparations for the task of ferrying their aircraft to various NARTUs and NAS NART units throughout the western United States. These included the painting out of all squadron identifiers and air group markings, however, VA-212's pilot's names were allowed to remain painted on the aircraft.

On 5 March 1957, F7U-3 BuNo 129564 was administratively stricken to provide a parts source to facilitate the continued maintenance support of the squadron's aircraft, as all F7U-3 support parts had already been removed from VA-212's hangar in anticipation of the transition to the Grumman F9F-8B Cougar. Two aircraft, BuNos 129545 and 129634, were flown to NASF Litchfield Park for long-term storage and reclamation, while the remaining seven Cutlasses were flown to the various reserve units. Of those, three VA-212 aircraft still exist, as described in Chapter 16.

CHAPTER FIFTEEN

Summary facility/unit histories

Many more US Navy facilities and units were assigned F7U-3s besides weapons/tactic development (VX) squadrons and deployable (VC/VF/VA) squadrons than the type's relatively brief operational service would suggest. In addition to several test and evaluation facilities – NADC/NAMC/NAMTC/NAOTS/NASWF/NATC – involved in F7U development and evaluation, these included BARS (Bureau of Aeronautics Representatives), FASRons (Fleet Aircraft Service squadRon), and units in need of a large, fast, tactical jet for test purposes like NOTS, NPU, the Naval Liaison Office (NLO) at Edwards AFB, and the only USMC unit to be assigned Cutlasses. Fleet Air Transport Squadrons did not take custody of the F7Us that they flew but were nevertheless essential to Naval Aviation operations.

Test and evaluation facilities involved in F7U-3 development

Naval Air Development Center, Johnsville, Pennsylvania (NADC). Commissioned on 1 August 1949, the Naval Air Station at Johnsville, Pennsylvania, occupied land that was originally purchased by the Brewster Aircraft Corporation in 1939. Following Brewster's demise due to unsatisfactory aircraft completions during the Second World War, the Navy acquired their facilities and stationary equipment and moved the Naval Air Modification Unit (NAMU) – tasked with the development, modification, conversion, and prototyping of both fleet aircraft and their armament – there. The NAMU was a separate branch of Philadelphia's Naval Air Material Center (NAMC), itself involved in the testing and

While being ferried by a VR-32 pilot cross country from San Diego to NADC in August 1955, F7U-3P BuNo 129746 starred as a static display at the Rocky Mountain Airshow at NAS Buckley near Denver, Colorado. ***Casby Collection***

development of ship installations and airborne technology that would benefit Naval Aviation during the ever-changing early jet age.

August 1947 brought the redesignation of the facility from NAMU to the Naval Air Development Station (NADS), an autonomous entity under the administrative control of BuAer. The mission of NADS was adjusted to encompass airborne electronic development as well as gunnery, rocketry, and soon-to-appear guided missile prototyping and service integration. Small complementary units from other station's activities were absorbed into the NADS. On 1 August 1949 the station was redesignated as the US Naval Air Development Center (NADC) concurrent with the adjoining airfield becoming a full Naval Air Station.

The NADC was involved in multiple developmental projects, which directly affected the F7U programme, beginning with the F7U-1 and culminating in projects that determined the direction of F7U-3M and A2U pre-development. The vast majority of these projects did not require actual custodianship of F7U-series aircraft by the Center, but rather focused on theoretical and lab-based testing of F7U sub-assemblies, components, and equipment.

In 1953, BuAer determined that a study (along with improvement recommendations) be conducted to determine the vulnerability of naval aircraft to enemy fire, both airborne and ground-based. This study was deemed necessary by the review of after-action reports and damage assessments made in the field during the Korean War. Under the command of CAPT James A. Haley Jr., the NADC was instrumental in the determination of these vulnerabilities for all fleet aircraft, including the F7U-3 series. Dubbed 'Project Damage' by the Center's physicists, BAR Project TED-ADC-AR-8201.1 was the first investigation into then-current Naval aircraft's ability to withstand enemy fire.

The NADC report reviewed the analysis of F7U-3 vulnerability to both .50 calibre armour-piercing incendiary (API) rounds, 20mm high-explosive incendiary (HEI) rounds, as well as ordinary fragmenting anti-aircraft shells. Interestingly, the 2.75in Mighty-Mouse air-to-air rocket was not analysed, as it was assumed a single hit would result in the aircraft's immediate loss, categorised as a 'K' kill. The project concentrated on the vulnerability of the fuel system, engines, control systems, and pilot. Models produced in 1/35th scale were constructed in both complete form, as well as one model of the fuel tanks, engines, and pilot in their proper locations sans the remainder of the aircraft. All directions of fire and striking velocities were taken into account, with the .50 calibre and 20mm fire assumed to occur at 35,000ft while anti-aircraft rounds were analysed at 5,000–7,600ft.

The results were based upon an F7U-3 fuelled with aviation gasoline (AVGAS), which the Westinghouse J46 engine could operate on, but not optimally. This decision was due to a lack of available data regarding dedicated 'jet fuel'. This choice of fuel resulted in a higher than expected 'A' category kill rate (aircraft loss within five minutes) due to the volatility and extended burn time of gasoline compared with kerosene-based jet fuel. The loss rate attributed to in-flight fire was exacerbated by the lack of on-board fire suppression capability in accordance with BuAer's contract requirements.

The vulnerability of the J46 engines was found to be consistent with other aircraft installations of axial-flow engines, although the duplicative capability with a twin-engined fighter was deemed to decrease the 'K'-kill probability sharply. However, the report acknowledged that the aircraft would most likely not be able to complete its mission on a single engine. Recommendations included the shielding of the compressor sections (which BuAer objected to, as it would increase the weight of the aircraft by upwards to 500lb), but acknowledged that 'the J46 engine presents a very formidable number of pressurised fuel lines, most of which, when hit even by a very small fragment, will cause total engine failure'.

Pilot vulnerability in the F7U-3 was addressed by the NADC and they identified several potential improvements, all of which were eventually dismissed by BuAer. The proposed substitution of bullet-resistant glass in the entire windscreen and canopy, the addition of armour plate on the floor and cockpit sides, as well as additional armour plating behind the pilot were all shown to produce very small percentages of increased survivability, and were thusly rejected over concerns about total weight. However, the investigation into the addition of a 24lb 'flak suit' for the pilot was determined to decrease the pilot's mortality probability by 35–45%! Its implementation was also ultimately rejected by BuAer.

On 25 August 1955, the NADC took custody of its sole Cutlass, F7U-3P BuNo 129746. Following its construction, this aircraft had become one of the in-storage 'gliders' awaiting the delivery of J46 engines. Once completed, the aircraft was placed in the BuAer storage 'Pool' at San Diego until its initial assignment to the NADC. Its primary utilisation there was the development of reconnaissance tactics, specifically determining the best-practice use of the canopy-mounted aiming sights for taking oblique photographs. This research was conducted by the Aeronautical Photographic Experimental Laboratory (APEL), which became an NADC in-house lab in December 1953. This aircraft never carried any NADC markings during its tenure at the Center, nor did it fly often, as it had to be crewed by a pilot borrowed from nearby NATC. Instead it was primarily relegated to angular computations and visual vector analysis performed within NADC's hangar while perched on jack stands in various simulated angle-of-attack attitudes. Custody of 129746 was transferred to NATC on 13 February 1956 following the culmination of these experiments.

Other projects in support of the F7U programme included the development of a frangible pilot's seat cushion and a 'stretchable' stainless seat-catapult attachment (see page 310) in an effort to reduce spinal injuries incurred during nose gear collapse. In December 1956, under the command of CAPT Emerson E. Fawkes, the Center assisted in the analysis of the Sparrow I missile's combat capabilities following the successful deployment of VX-4's F7U-3Ms aboard *Lexington* (CVA-16). The results of this study were used to identify and correct deficiencies in the procedures and service implementation of the Sparrow in the fleet and contributed to improved operational readiness when VA-116 made the last F7U deployment with their F7U-3Ms in April 1957.

Naval Air Material Center, Philadelphia, Pennsylvania (NAMC). The Naval Air Material Center was the development, evaluation, and production partner of the Naval Aircraft Factory (NAF) located at Naval Auxiliary Air Station (NAAS) Mustin Field in Philadelphia, Pennsylvania. The Center was responsible for the design, prototype fabrication, testing, and evaluation of much Government-Furnished Equipment (GFE) as installed in Navy aircraft, as well as the development and integration of the Navy's aircraft and ship-installation systems as they pertained to Naval Aviation. The NAMC worked hand-in-hand with the Naval Air Development Center (NADC) at Johnsville, Pennsylvania, and was merged in 1954 with NADC to form the Naval Air Development and Material Center (NADMC) Johnsville, although both centres conducted their work at their original locations and remained independent entities under NADMC administrative oversight. NAMC's on-site laboratories, as well as the nearby NAF (now under the NAMC umbrella), enabled the Navy to identify adverse issues, design effective solutions, and build prototypes without the delay and cost involved in working through contractors.

Among a myriad of various projects, two of the main NAMC responsibilities in the mid-1950s were the development and refinement of catapult and barrier/barricade systems as they were envisioned for new carrier construction, as well as upgrades to existing ship installations. The Naval Air Testing Facility (NATF) was a separate but integral portion of NAMC, and was administratively responsible for the two onshore catapult installations, as well as the barrier and barricade runs used for refining the design of not only the ship installations themselves, but the carrier-based aircraft that would be operated using that equipment.

When the F7U-3 series attained its final production configuration, the sixteen J35-powered aircraft with the original 'bulb-nose' radomes quickly became obsolete for squadron utilisation in most, if not all, capacities. Starting with BuNo 128452 – the second F7U-3 constructed, a total of seven early-model F7U-3s were moved to Mustin Field between 2 September 1954 and 9 June 1955 to be used for F7U barrier and barricade testing. Of these seven aircraft, only four had their custody actually transferred to the NAMC, the reminder being airframes (BuNo 128452, 128456, and 128458) that were in the custody of the BuAer Maintenance & Storage Pool at NAAS Mustin. These three aircraft were used in the evaluation of the much taller barrier activator mast that appeared forward of the windscreen on F7U-3 No. 17 and subsequent, as well as the main gear's Davis barrier guards. Often fitted with wooden spoiler boards attached to their wings to preclude the aircraft from developing enough lift to achieve flight, these Cutlasses were propelled toward shore-installed Davis barriers and barricades to ascertain the effectiveness of the installations, as well as document the damage incurred to the aircraft structure during the engagements. This information was then relayed to Vought engineers to aid in the design or redesign necessary to achieve the performance desired.

Custody of BuNo 128459 was transferred to the NAMC from NATC on 2 September 1954 to take part in additional barricade testing. Repeated engagements with the barricade resulted in its being stricken due to excessive damage on 17 January 1955. Its intended back-up, BuNo 128461, had been delivered to the NAMC on 8 December 1954 and continued the barricade testing until 3 June 1955, when it too was stricken. BuNo 128463 officially joined the NAMC F7U complement on 16 March 1955 from O&R Norfolk, its custody previously changed five times following VX-3's LTJG Stephenson's landing short of the runway at NAS Atlantic City, New Jersey, two years earlier. NAMC's final acquisition was BuNo 128464 on 9 June 1955, however by this time testing related to the barrier and barricade effectiveness on the F7U-3 series was complete. The aircraft was struck off charge a day later and then languished for several years in Mustin Field's aircraft 'graveyard' until being scrapped on site.

In addition to the extensive barrier and barricade testing conducted at NAAS Mustin, the NAMC also hosted several NATC-assigned F7U-3s and -3Ms for testing and evaluation at NAMC's newly constructed steam catapult test facility. On 5 May 1954, F7U-3 BuNo 128475 conducted the first launch test of the XC-11 steam catapult, launching with a captive bridle for quick launch turnaround, which foreshadowed the first XC-11 shipboard launches a month later aboard *Hancock*.

Two years later, NATC's F7U-3M BuNo 139868 was shore-catapulted at both NATC and NAMC, this time at excessive weights in excess of 34,000lb – it became airborne in 200ft, a distance only five times its own length. These 6 August 1956 evaluations centred around determining the capability to launch at the high weights anticipated for F7U-3M carrier operations

A forlorn BuNo 128458 in the BuAer Maintenance & Storage Pool graveyard at NAAS Mustin following use as a barrier/barricade test subject at NAMC Philadelphia. Note the airflow spoiler board attached to the wing's top surface, as well as the ailavators being secured in the trailing position. *Casby Collection*

First launch test of the XC-11 steam catapult newly installed at NAMC's Mustin Field facility. F7U-3 BuNo 128475 from NATC's Service Test Division was equipped with a captive bridle for this 5 May 1954 evaluation. Note the deck angle and full up ailavators during this launch. *NAMC Photo NA46(1)-282830*

ABOVE Launching of F7U-3M BuNo 139868 during XC-11 steam catapult testing on 6 August 1956. Launch weights in excess of 34,000lb were eventually tested successfully. ***US Navy***

BELOW A comparison of Vought's mid-design F7U-3 ejection seat on the left and the light-weight F8U-1 seat without parachute, harnesses, and seat pack. The F7U/A2U seat with its foot rests, exterior frame, articulated head rest, etc. weighed 130lb. The F8U-1 seat weighed only 30lb. ***Chance Vought Photo CVA-26246 via H. H. Edwards – Casby Collection***

with a full complement of Sparrow missiles and a belly-mounted fuel pod. The results of these tests enabled NAMC's Catapult and Arresting Gear Field Service Unit (CAFSU), under the direct administration of the NAF, to provide technical advice and engineering assistance to the fleet that was specifically related to F7U-3M launch and recovery operations. CAFSU representatives worked closely with ship's personnel and VX-4 pilots when the F7U-3M was deployed aboard *Shangri-La* the following November, resulting in very successful operations of the heavy missile-laden Cutlasses.

The NAMC's Aeronautical Materials Laboratory, in close co-operation with NADC Johnsville, began an investigation into F7U-3 crash force loads in 1956, which culminated in the design and production of frangible seat cushions and stainless steel ejection seat mounting straps that would absorb vertical decelerations and mitigate spinal injuries suffered by pilots involved in nose gear collapse incidents. NAMC also designed the ejection seat catapult trigger guard following VF-124's LTJG Barry Milliard's tragic inadvertent ejection aboard *Hancock* in 1955. Although initially designed to be field-fabricated by squadrons and units, the guard retrofit kit was eventually produced by the NAF under NAMC oversight. Later, in an early attempt to achieve zero-zero ejection seat capability – the ability to eject at zero altitude and zero forward speed – the NAMC began addressing the need for ejection seat redesign to reduce weight. In co-operation with Chance Vought engineers, a new seat was designed and produced that was 100lb lighter than the F7U-3's seat. Although this new stamped aluminium seat did not make it into F7U-3 production or retrofit, it was incorporated into the F8U-1 Crusader. While not offering true zero-zero capability – it still utilised a ballistic cannon-propelled catapult – it did reduce the altitude for a successful ejection to 400 to 500ft.

In all, the NAMC played a pivotal role in the integration of the F7U-3 to the fleet and the mitigation of associated problems. Its involvement with the Cutlass provided the Navy with in-house derived solutions that were incorporated into almost every Navy fighter aircraft that followed.

Naval Air Missile Test Center, Point Mugu, California (NAMTC). The Naval Air Missile Test Center was commissioned at Naval Air Facility (NAF) Point Mugu, California, on 1 October 1946 to develop, test, and evaluate pilotless aircraft, air-launched guided missiles and other air-deployed guided munitions. Following its host's recommissioning as NAS Point Mugu on 1 August 1949, the NAMTC began to acquire multiple missile projects from BuAer and BuOrd. From a limited start with two projects in 1946, NAMTC was soon responsible for more than 220 separate missile and rocket projects for the Army, Navy, and Air Force, including both Regulus I and II, Nike, Thor, Honest John, Corporal and the air-to-air beam-riding Sparrow I (AAM-N-2) being developed by the Sperry Gyroscope Company. NAMTC testing of the Sparrow I primarily utilised Douglas F3D-1M Skyknights, as they had the capability to carry and launch four of the heavy missiles. Although approaching being obsolescent as a front-line fighter and determinedly subsonic, the straight-winged, two-place Skyknight allowed the NAMTC to advance the testing of the missile to the point where its launch system was developed adequately. However, for its intended use in the fleet as primary armament for fleet defence interceptors, the beam-riding Sparrow needed a new mother-ship.

NAMTC's Commanding Officer, CAPT Edward M. Condra, took NAMTC custody of two F7U-1 Cutlasses, BuNos 124422 and 124421, in October 1952 and August 1953 respectively. These aircraft were intended to be utilised in the development of the Sparrow I, although evidence suggests that no actual airborne missile testing occurred, as the weight-carrying capability of the F7U-1 was limited and underwing hard points had yet to be installed. They did, however, give the Center a taste of what was soon to come. The F7U-3 had transonic performance and the heavy-lifting capacity and physical stance to accommodate the four missiles as well as all associated systems. Contractor Sperry, along with Douglas Aircraft Company (the missile's airframe builder), and Chance Vought all assigned company representatives to the Center to assist in the development of the Navy's first operational air-to-air guided missile and its soon-to-arrive new launch platform – the F7U-3M.

CAPT J.E. Clark, NAMTC's new Commanding Officer, was tasked with four new missions: 1) aggressively test

F7U-3M BuNo 129700 with its new 'Point Mugu' fin markings and carrying test versions of the Sparrow I missile. Previously, this aircraft was assigned to the Flight test Division at NATC. ***Casby Collection via Terry Panopalis***

the new Sparrow I missile, 2) determine the best practices for integrating it to the fleet, 3) test the F7U-3M armed with the Sparrow I, and 4) perform a fleet integration analysis for the F7U-3M launch platform. On 27 September 1954, the NAMTC took custody of its first F7U-3M with the arrival of BuNo 129590, one of two F7U-3s modified into missile carriers and serving as the prototypes for the model. The following December, the first production F7U-3M, BuNo 129677, was also transferred to NAMTC custody. F7U-3M BuNo 129700 joined the NAMTC programme on 17 January 1955 and was equipped with a heavily modified belly-mounted pod containing two A-10 35mm motion picture cameras designed to record the firing of the Sparrow missiles. This camera pod was fitted to any F7U that was performing missile firings at the time. While in NAMTC custody, the F7U-3Ms had 'POINT MUGU' painted under the fin's 'NAVY' designator, but carried no other distinguishing markings of the unit on their natural finishes.

For such an important and complex assignment, Clark assigned CAPT Victor H. Soucek, the Center's Director of Tests, to develop a programme that would test and evaluate both projects at the same time – a forerunner to the modern concept of systems integration evaluation (SIE). Soucek named the endeavour *Operation Aesop*, and assigned Sparrow I Assistant Project Officer LTJG Alan R. Bedford as Project Test Conductor. Bedford's pilots, LTs Eugene F. Shine and Charles W. Griffing, fired more than 300 (of the roughly 2,000 missiles produced) during the evaluations. The NAMTC engineers and pilots co-ordinated with both Point Mugu-based Air Development Squadron Four (VX-4), as well as Guided Missile Unit Forty One (GMU-41), which supported VX-4's own evaluation work with the Sparrow and the F7U-3M. On 30 June 1955, BuNo 129590's custody was transferred to O&R San Diego in preparation for its assignment to VX-4, which would soon begin deploying detachments equipped with the F7U-3M and Sparrow for at-sea trials. Testing with BuNos 129677 and 129700 would continue at NAMTC through the end of 1955 – both aircraft were returned to BAR Dallas custody on 19 January 1956. Further Sparrow I evaluations, as well as Sparrow III developmental evaluations, were conducted with NAMTC-assigned McDonnell F3H-2M Demons.

In August 1955 NAMTC took custody of a sole F7U-3P, BuNo 129753. This assignment was originally intended to solely support the Sparrow I test programme, but was used instead to document photographically the testing of Vought's KDA-1 Regulus cruise missile undergoing trials at Point Mugu with Guided Missile Training Unit Five (GMTU-5). It was flown to NASF Litchfield Park on 3 August 1956 for storage and disposition.

Naval Air Ordnance Test Station, Chincoteague, Virginia (NAOTS). Similar in purpose to the Naval Ordnance Test Station (NOTS) at Inyokern, California (later NOTS China Lake), the Naval Aviation Ordnance Test Station at Chincoteague, Virginia, conducted development, testing and evaluation of air-launched munitions. Specialising in air-to-air rocketry and fixed gunnery, the NAOTS was the primary evaluation facility for these weapons on the United States' east coast. Where the NOTS concentrated on the development of missiles, rockets, bombs, and nuclear stores (through their close co-ordination with the Naval Air Special Weapons Facility (NASWF) at Kirtland AFB), the NAOTS concentrated on guns, auto-cannon, and rockets. While the NOTS and NASWF were under the administrative command of the BuOrd, NAOTS Chincoteague took their orders from BuAer.

The station took custody of four F7U-3 Cutlass aircraft between November 1954 and October 1956, initially evaluating the F7U-3's government-furnished 20mm Mark 12 Mod 0 auto-cannon installation in response to service reports from fleet squadrons. In spite of extensive Vought engineering efforts to perfect the cannon's installation, problems with ammunition feed, shell casing ejection, and accuracy persisted. Later, the NAOTS was instrumental in finding fixes for the F7U-3's rocket pack problems experienced by fleet squadrons (See page 124). F7U-3 BuNo 129638 was the first Cutlass to transfer to NAOTS custody on 22 November 1954 from NATC, where it had been assigned to the Armament Test Division. It arrived at Chincoteague a day later complete with its belly-mounted rocket pack.

This aircraft later received 'NAOTS' and 'Chincoteague' fin markings, as well as a large '638' repeat of its BuNo's last three digits on the forward fuselage. This Cutlass was primarily used for bore-sight procedural evaluations, and spent much of its tenure at the NAOTS raised upon levelling jacks adjacent to the gunnery range. This testing was in direct response to feedback acquired from VF-81 – the first fleet squadron to receive the F7U-3 – which noted problems with errant gunnery targeting results during exercises with the first batch of seven Cutlasses they received. With the direct involvement of VF-81's maintenance crew due to their close proximity at NAS Oceana, Virginia, the engineers at NAOTS determined that ambiguous bore-sighting instructions in the F7U-3's Handbook of Maintenance Instructions were the cause of the squadron's problems. Working in close co-ordination with Vought's Norfolk, Virginia Field Service Representative (FSR) Paul 'Eric' Ericson, and NAS Oceana's FSR Fred Zimmerman, the Handbook was revised.

Due to the requirement to re-rig the bore-sighting jigs every time 129638's position on the jacks was disturbed, it was deemed preferable to acquire a second Cutlass for the rocket pack testing. F7U-3 BuNo

A very clean F7U-3 BuNo 129638 photographed immediately following its arrival at NAOTS Chincoteague on 23 November 1954. Note early intake configuration. *NAOTS Chincoteague NP(5)18215*

Now wearing NAOTS Chincoteague markings on its fins, and a rather 'cramped' 638 nose number, BuNo 129638 is inspected by curious airshow attendees during the Armed Forces Day Open House in May 1955. *Roger Besecker*

Still wearing its squadron side-number from VA-66, F7U-3 BuNo 129681 prepares to leave NAS Dallas on 30 January 1956 for NAOTS Chincoteague, Virginia, after completion of gun trough modifications at the Vought factory. Note that this aircraft did not receive the air intake lower-lip extension modification. *VAHF*

129640 joined NAOTS from NATC on 3 February 1955 and was used in preliminary testing of the rocket pack concurrent with 129638's gunnery tests. With rocket packs in short supply, the pack that equipped 129638 was transferred to 129640 for these tests.

BuNo 129638 remained in the custody of the NAOTS until it was returned to BAR Dallas on 8 December 1955 for engine air intake and gun port modifications, and 129640's custody was transferred to BAR Dallas on 26 January 1956 to receive similar treatment at the Vought factory. Days later, on 29 January 1956, NAOTS took custody of F7U-3 BuNo 129681 from BAR Dallas following its gun trough modifications at Vought. This Cutlass had previously served with VF-81 and its later incarnation VA-66, and had 214 flight hours when it arrived in Chincoteague on 30 January. Unlike 129640, which primarily served as a static rocket-firing test bed at the NAOTS's bespoke rocket range, 129681 performed the aerial rocket firing duties.

The last F7U-3 to join NAOTS was BuNo 129591, which came directly from BAR Inglewood, California, on 3 October 1956 following its bailment to North American Aviation (NAA) in the ongoing development and testing of the Mighty Mouse Mk 4 folding-fin aerial rocket (FFAR). Equipped with fire control refinements developed by NAA, 129591 was then modified by Hughes Tool Company engineers for an evaluation of the 30mm Mk 4 cannon (a new armament option for British fighters) that was accomplished with three different types of ammunition feeders: a Hughes pneumatic feeder; an electric feeder designed by the Naval Gun Factory; and a mechanical feeder designed by Columbia Research similar to the Mk 9 feeder. After the subsequent NAOTS evaluation, the Navy decided not to switch from the 20mm standard. Originally intended to be flown to NASF Litchfield Park for storage, 129591 was instead cannibalised for parts to keep 129681 airworthy and stricken at NAOTS in November 1957 with only twenty-six hours' total flight time. In comparison, when eventually retired to Chincoteague's storage pool boneyard on 25 March 1958, the NAOTS's last remaining F7U-3, BuNo 129681, had amassed 418 hours on its airframe.

Naval Air Special Weapons Facility, Kirtland AFB, New Mexico (NASWF). The Navy's test and evaluation unit for special (i.e. nuclear) weapons was co-located with the Air Force Special Weapons Center at Kirtland AFB, Albuquerque, New Mexico. Situated on a sun-baked mesa overlooking the Rio Grande river and the City of Albuquerque, the base provided year-round environmental advantages for the development of atomic weapons and the integration of those weapons in both strategic as well as tactical aircraft types. Units at Kirtland provided support to the Atomic Energy Commission (AEC) Field Office, which oversaw all nuclear weapon development. The Naval Air Special Weapons Facility (NASWF), as a tenant at Kirtland AFB, provided the Navy with direct access to both the AEC as well as the Los Alamos Scientific Laboratories and the Sandia Corporation located at Sandia Base, New Mexico. In turn, as an integral component of the AEC's

F7U-3 BuNo 129546 prior to its final flight, which ended in disaster. Note the very early engine intake configuration. *Casby Collection via T. Panopalis*

Armed Forces Special Weapons Project, the NASWF provided the AEC with the ability to develop and evaluate the Navy's contribution to the overall nuclear deterrent capability. The NASWF was tasked with the engineering of special pylons, racks, release mechanisms (both manual and automated), as well as developing the procedures to be used for the handling, loading, and delivery of any nuclear stores carried by Navy aircraft. Aircraft types evaluated included the AD-4B, A3D, A4D-1, F3H-2, FJ-4, and the F7U-3.

Seven different F7U-3s were assigned for special weapon delivery testing and evaluation between March 1953 and October 1957 (See Chapter 11, Armament). These aircraft were utilised in support of AEC Project #67836, which was initiated to determine the optimal protocols for deployment of nuclear weapons from the F7U-3 series aircraft. AEC and Sandia project engineers reportedly loved the Cutlass. No matter what the size or the shape of their experimental store, it would fit beneath the aircraft. Working in close co-ordination with the Air Force's 4925th Test Group (Atomic), the NASWF conducted high- and low-altitude nuclear store (simulated) deployments at the Indian Springs AFB, Nevada Test Range, as well as test ranges at Naval Auxiliary Air Station (NAAS) Fallon, Nevada and the Salton Sea.

NASWF took custody of their first F7U-3, factory-fresh BuNo 128461, from BAR Dallas on 31 March 1953. This early Cutlass was intended to provide feedback to Vought for ongoing pylon development and to identify design changes required to accept extra-heavy and outsized stores; however, one week later on 7 April the aircraft was reassigned to NATC's Service Test Division. It was received at NATC the next day, 8 April. A second J35-powered F7U-3, BuNo 128462, was transferred to the NASWF on 29 July 1953 and resumed the delayed pylon evaluations until it was released on 7 September 1955 to FASRon-4's administrative custody. It was retired the next day and eventually transported by truck to the New Mexico Institute of Mining and Technology for rip-charge tests. On 23 April 1954 the facility accepted custody of BuNo 129546, which was used for stores separation testing except for a temporary transfer to the Naval Liaison Office at Edwards AFB for towed-target development on 31 July 1955 (see pages 264-265). Its pilot, LT Frank Asburn Downs accompanied the aircraft to Edwards for these tests. BuNo 129546 returned to NASWF custody one month later, and it was in this Cutlass that LT Downs lost his life on 21 November 1955 following a high-speed, low-level, simulated bombing run. Reporting an engine fire warning light, Downs secured the left engine but was

soon presented with a right engine fire warning. He declared an emergency and attempted to return to Kirtland AFB, however, the Cutlass exploded in flight while in an inverted attitude prior to impact on the Isleta Pueblo, an Indian village 12 miles south of Albuquerque. Downs had managed to eject from the aircraft, but he was too low. His body, still strapped in the seat, was found by Rev. Frederick Stadtmuller, a Catholic priest who heard the explosion and ran to the crash site from his rectory, arriving only in time to administer last rites to LT Downs postmortem.

F7U-3 BuNo 129551 joined the NASWF on 27 April 1955, after waiting months to receive engines in the BAR storage pool at Dallas. On 7 October 1955 custody of BuNo 129568 was transferred to the NASWF from NOTS China Lake, but its tenure with the unit was short-lived – it was returned to BAR Dallas on 9 January 1956 – the same day that BuNo 128467 (No. 17, the first production F7U-3 with J46 engines) arrived. Four months later, custody of BuNo 129569 was transferred to the NASWF on 24 April 1956; a rearward-facing camera was installed that replaced the small forward fuselage access panel – just aft of the radome on the left side – that normally allowed for disconnection of the in-flight refuelling tube (if installed). This camera was used to record separation characteristics of the nuclear-shaped stores. These last two arrivals remained at the facility until they, along with 129551, were flown to NASF Litchfield Park on 4 October 1957, ending the AEC's special weapons project with the F7U-3.

LTJG Georges E. 'Frenchy' LeBlanc Jr. was assigned to the NASWF in May 1956 following his tour with VF-124's F7U-3s. As an experienced F7U pilot, LeBlanc was assigned by NASWF Commanding Officer CDR Groom E. Marcus as the primary test pilot for all AEC development project tests using the F7U-3. He made 235 flights in the NASWF F7U-3s, mostly BuNos 128467, 129551 and 129569. LeBlanc, along with former VA-212 Executive Officer LCDR Joachim 'Jack' Speciale and LT J.T. Cockrill, flew these last three NASWF F7Us to Litchfield Park; his tenure with the F7U ended with having manned 602 flights and amassing 565 total F7U-3 flight hours.

All the facility's F7U-3s were marked with 'NASWF' and the full Bureau number above the outboard fin's NAVY service designator. They also carried the last three numerals of their Bureau numbers on the forward fuselage, much like a squadron's unit designator number. The NASWF Cutlasses remained in their natural finish, except that 129551 later received large red panels painted on its forward fuselage above the national insignia, the lower canopy, and outer wing panels to assist in motion picture assessment of the store release tests.

Naval Air Test Center, Patuxent River, Maryland (NATC). Commissioned on 1 April 1943, the Naval Air Test Center (NATC) at NAS Patuxent River, Maryland, was tasked by BuAer Materials Division to test, evaluate, and proffer recommendations to the Bureau concerning all phases of service acceptance and fleet integration of both new and modified Navy aircraft. With instrumented test ranges and large open-ocean operation areas, the Center's capability to conduct testing and evaluation of aircraft, aircraft systems, and turbine power plants was instrumental in the development and rapid integration of jet-powered aircraft into the fleet. Working in close co-operation with NADC Johnsville, NAMC Philadelphia, NAOTS Chincoteague, and other specialised units, NATC was also able to evaluate catapults, arresting gears, visual landing aids, ordnance, and airborne weapon systems that these new aircraft would utilise.

In the early to mid-1950s, NATC was comprised of five distinct divisions, each responsible for independent evaluation within their respective purview. Each division represented an expertise pool in their specific area, and was able to operate both independently or in concert with other divisions. Each division was further broken down into branches, dependent upon the aircraft and/or mission. Branches had their own project pilots, engineers, and technicians that would remain with that branch until the individual test project was completed and a Technical Report (TR) containing the branch's recommendations was published.

Heading up the division roster was the Flight Test (FT) Division, which acted as BuAer's in-house research and development department. The FT Division participated in Accelerated Service Trials (AST), Board of Inspection and Survey (BIS) evaluations, and Initial Operational Tests and Evaluations (IOT&E). Branches within the FT Division included the Carrier Suitability Branch (CS), which evaluated the aircraft's ability to be operated aboard ship, including not only launch and recovery operations, but hangar storage, deck manoeuvrability, and securement. The Flying Quality and Performance (FQP) Branch evaluated the aircraft's airborne characteristics in all flight regimes, and assessed the aircraft's overall performance characteristics as they related to other aircraft evaluated for potential fleet service.

The Service Test (ST) Division was responsible for evaluating the maintainability and reliability of tested aircraft in the fleet environment, as well as overall suitability for the missions assigned from a maintenance standpoint. Identification of serviceability deficiencies, material defects, and spare parts inventory requirements were primary responsibilities of the ST Division. In addition, engine reliability, ground-support equipment suitability, and pilot–aircraft interface issues fell within the responsibility of the Division. The ST Division included the Physiological Test Branch, which tested G-suits, oxygen systems, and parachutes used in Navy aircraft.

The Armament Test (AT) Division conducted armament trials of new aircraft, to include ordnance deployment under actual flight conditions. They developed solutions to armament-related problems encountered in the fleet's use of guns, bombs, rockets, and missiles. Branches within the Division were the Aerial Gunnery (AG) Branch, Un-guided Munition (UM) Branch and later the Guided Missile (GM) Branch.

The Electronics Test (ET) Division was responsible for the testing and evaluation of all airborne electronics and electrical equipment, determining their suitability and military usefulness. The Naval Aeronautical Laboratory (NAL) was brought under the ET Division umbrella and conducted testing of navigation avionics and landing aid systems. In late 1957, the AT and ET divisions began the process of merging to later become the Weapons System Test (WST) Division.

The Tactical Test (TT) Division was established to evaluate an aircraft's tactical use potential, and develop equipment and methods to allow pilots to physiologically withstand the implementation of these combat tactics. Evaluation of captured enemy aircraft also fell under the responsibility of the TT Division.

Due to the testing and evaluation requirements of an aircraft with the design advancements and complexity of the Cutlass, NATC F7Us became the most numerous of all shore-based F7Us assigned to custodians outside of NASF Litchfield Park. In addition to the five F7U-1s assigned from June 1950 to October 1953, NATC took custody of twenty-nine F7U-3 series aircraft, including eight -3Ms and four -3Ps. Although most Cutlasses joined NATC custody directly from BAR Dallas, four aircraft arrived at the Center after previous service with

OPPOSITE TOP F7U-3 BuNo 129551 shortly after arrival at the NASWF. Later the aircraft would have its full BuNo painted between the 'NASWF' and 'NAVY' on its fins, as well as red-painted panels. *Casby Collection*

OPPOSITE BOTTOM Left-to-right: LCDR Jack Speciale and LTJGs J.T. Cockrill and G.E. LeBlanc Jr. prepare to fly the NASWF's last three F7U-3s to retirement at NASF Litchfield Park. Note the red-painted panels above the national insignia and lower portion of the canopy on BuNo 129551, as well as the faint evidence of 'NASWF' removed from 128467's fin prior to its last flight. *Casby Collection via Jack Speciale*

NASWF Kirtland (128461), VF-83 (129639), NADC Johnsville (129746) and NAOTS Chincoteague, (which took interim custody of 129638 from NATC and returned the aircraft a year later).

Most F7U-3 aircraft in NATC custody typically retained their natural factory finish with the addition of 'NATC' markings applied to the fins above the NAVY service designator. Depending on division assignment, the letters FT, ST, AT, ET, or TT were applied to the forward fuselage sides above or in front of the national insignia's most forward bar on some, but not all, Cutlasses. Some F7Us received numerals following the division letters to designate which aircraft they were in the division's line-up. Some aircraft were shared among divisions, and may have taken part in division testing outside their actual assignments. Although most NATC aircraft did not carry any special livery, several Flight Test F7Us received insignia-blue arrows that ran from the air intakes to the radome, and in a couple of cases, black fin tips reminiscent of *Project Cutlass* aircraft.

NATC Flight Test Division: The division received their first F7U-3, BuNo 128454 (No. 4), when Vought test pilot William 'Billy' Sunday, arrived from BAR Dallas on 2 July 1952; however, its custody was not officially transferred to NATC until 1 August. BuNo 128454 was assigned to the Carrier Suitability Branch in anticipation of conducting initial BIS trials of the type aboard *Midway*, CVA-41. Seventy-two flights were conducted between its arrival and 31 July. Arriving from Vought already incorporating the sloped radome that would become standard on F7U-3 and -3Ms with aircraft No. 17 and subsequent, it featured a long insignia-blue arrow that bisected the branch of service designator and Bureau number located in front of the air intakes, and continued to the aft edge of the radome, which was painted silver with a stylised 'Cutlass' script rendered on each side in red with blue shadowing. Initial carrier suitability tests were conducted aboard *Midway* from 11 to 15 August 1952 (see page 57 for details).

Following the completion of this set of at-sea trials, 128454 was returned to Vought on 20 August for incorporation of additional canopy and windscreen modifications as outlined in the NATC evaluation. The new canopy utilised the existing early-design windscreen, but included a bulbous Perspex section and an elongated canopy fairing. A reposition and enlargement of the windscreen's barrier guard/trigger mast, a redesign of the nose gear's barrier strap detent, installation of blunt trailing edge ailavators, and the beefing up of the arresting gear hook point were also accomplished. In addition, the tailpipes were tilted up 3° 18', ballast added for a more forward CG with full fuel, increased nose gear servicing psi (to keep the nose from dipping during the catapult stroke), and additional stores capability was added (2,000lb capacity wing pylons and the rocket pack). BuNo 128454 returned to NATC a month later on 25 September 1952 sporting five alternating white and red stripes on each fin tip.

Preliminary armament evaluations were conducted with the addition of a rocket pack and 2,000lb bombs. Following them, an insignia blue leading edge was added to the existing fin tip stripes before testing resumed on 29 September 1952. Further BIS carrier trials were conducted aboard *Coral Sea* (CVA-43) between 4 and 6 November. Flight operations in support of the BIS evaluation were concluded on 8 November. BuNo 128454's custody was transferred back to BAR Dallas for further modifications to the canopy and windscreen on 15 February 1953, but 454 would not return to NATC custody.

BuNo 128458 was received by NATC on 28 March 1953 and assigned to the Flying Quality and Performance Branch of the Flight Test Division. It arrived with a factory-installed extended instrumentation boom mounted in its early bulb-nose radome that was uncharacteristically painted silver. BuNo 128458 was used for the preliminary phase of the stability and control testing of the F7U-3. The FQP Branch identified several improvements required for acceptance of the aircraft for fleet service, the identification of adverse pre-stall yaw and a low buffet-boundary being the primary deficiencies. The aircraft continued in flight testing for more than a year, with 128458 being transferred to VX-3 on 30 April 1954.

BuNo 128471's custody was transferred from BAR Dallas on 31 January 1954 and it joined the FQP Branch for Service Acceptance Trials to determine compliance with aircraft empty weight requirements as well as aircraft and engine performance guarantees. It remained with NATC until 5 April 1955, when its custody was transferred to BAR M&S Dallas before being returned to NATC the very next day. Custody was transferred permanently back to BAR Dallas on 31 August 1955.

BuNo 128475, marked as a YF7U-3, joined NATC on 26 September 1953 and took over the Carrier Suitability (CS) testing assignment. Featuring a similar blue arrow painted on its forward fuselage as well as an all-blue nose gear fairing, the CS branch took 128475 aboard *Coral Sea* between 26 and 30 October 1953 with LT Robert 'Rip' Rostine and LCDR James B. Verdin conducting multiple evaluation flights. Further carrier suitability evaluations were conducted aboard *Lake Champlain* (CVA-39) from 8 to 13 February 1954, and LT John M. Moore participated in *Project Steam* catapult testing in 128475 aboard Hancock (CVA-19) from 14 to 30 June 1954. This aircraft was returned to BAR Dallas Custody on 24 November 1954.

NATC's FQP Branch received F7U-3 BuNo 129569 on 8 June 1954, with custody transferred the following day. Comparative performance evaluations were accomplished with an asymmetric loading of one external fuel tank versus one along with a 1,000lb bomb on the other

ABOVE Although the first at-sea trials of a production representative F7U-3 went well, the F9F-6 Cougar behind it aboard *Coral Sea* was on its way to the fleet and a derivative, the F9F-8, would come to be preferred as a day fighter and a placeholder for A4D-1/FJ-4B for the tactical nuclear strike requirement. *NA 80-G-K-17595*

LEFT Along with LT Robert Rostine (who would go on to join the test pilot ranks at Vought), LCDR James B. Verdin conducted carrier suitability trials aboard *Coral Sea* (CVA-43) in F7U-3 BuNo 128475, seen here on 29 October 1955. *NA Photo 80-G-630058 Casby Collection*

ABOVE F7U-3 BuNo 129567 with barricade testing protective boards applied to the wings, belly pod and nose gear doors. The protuberances from the leading edge of the wing are temporary barricade strap detents to evaluate the area of the wing that the straps would land during a barricade engagement. NATC's F7U-3 129569 is in the background. Future astronaut Neil Armstrong was involved in similar tests with the FJ-3 Fury. *24 August 1954 NATC Photo via Neil Armstrong Casby Collection*

BELOW F7U-3 BuNo 129567 on 24 August 1954. Visible in the nose landing gear well are support boards creating a truss to ensure that the nose gear doors remain intact. Note protective covering on the outside of the doors and the elaborate protective sheathing of the belly pod and ammunition casing ports. *NATC Photo via Neil Armstrong Al Casby Collection*

pylon. The flight testing commenced on 29 September 1954 and concluded on 23 March 1955. Subsequent to these tests, an evaluation of the aircraft equipped with two Mk 51 pylon racks, one Aero-1A fuel tank, and the belly-mounted rocket pack was compared to only having the empty pylon racks installed. Following the conclusion of these tests a week later on 30 March, 129569 continued evaluations with various combinations of underwing and belly-mounted stores until it was transferred to BAR Dallas custody on 4 November 1955, prior to assignment to NASWF Kirtland AFB.

BuNo 129567 was received by the Flight Test Division on 17 July 1954 and used initially for high-speed barricade testing. The Cutlass had wooden protective coverings strapped over its wing leading edges, with large protruding wooden detents designed to catch and direct the barricade's vertical straps. A plywood protective shell was added to envelop the rocket pack and Vought-supplied screens were fitted over the engine's intakes to preclude foreign object damage during the test runs. Marked with the Division's 'FT' on its lower nose, it was involved in these tests in August 1954. Once completed, the aircraft was reassigned to the Service Test Division.

F7U-3 BuNo 129589 was the first to be converted for use as a test bed for the F7U-3M. It was subsequently redesignated as one. Its custody was transferred to NATC on 9 February 1955 and the aircraft arrived with a flashy scalloped red and white livery applied to its nose, wing tips and air intakes. Later marked with 'FT'

The first F7U-3M was a conversion of F7U-3 BuNo 129589 and unusually redesignated as such. *VAHF*

under its cockpit coaming, the new -3M remained with the Flight Test Division until it was returned to BAR Dallas custody on 21 September 1955. Additional F7U-3Ms assigned to Flight Test were BuNos 129699, 129700, 129736, and 139868. BuNo 129699 was involved in a landing accident on 11 May 1955 when NATC LT John Long landed short of the runway at Patuxent River and eventually sheared off all three landing gear after skidding off the runway into the soft dirt. BuNo 129700 only remained in NATC custody for one week before being reassigned to NAMTC Point Mugu on 17 January 1955 for support of the Sparrow I test programme conducted there, while BuNo 129736 took part in two evaluations of the -3M aboard Shangri-La (CVA-38) piloted by LT John M. Moore. Moore was involved in an impressive nose gear collapse episode (see pages 307-308) that destroyed this aircraft on 17 June 1955. The last of the NATC -3Ms, BuNo 139868, was involved in catapult testing at high weights at both NAS Patuxent River and NAMC Philadelphia's shore-based catapults before taking part in carrier suitability trials aboard three carriers including Forrestal (CVA-59) in January 1956 with LT Moore once again conducting the testing.

The first of its type, F7U-3P BuNo 129745, joined the NATC Flight Test stable on 7 December 1955 from BAR Dallas. Arriving with a factory test livery of black-bordered yellow striping, the photo-Cutlass remained in NATC custody until returned to BAR Dallas on 28 February 1957. It amassed seventy-three flight hours during its tenure with the FT Division.

NATC Service Test Division: The Service Test division of NATC was officially assigned six aircraft but also utilised shared aircraft from other divisions in their analysis of the type. NATC took custody of BuNo 128461 on 7 April 1953 from NASWF Kirtland AFB (who only held custody for one week). The aircraft was delivered the following day to the Service Test Division for immediate inclusion in the Bureau of Inspection and Survey's (BIS) Preliminary Evaluation Phase of the 'Accelerated Service Trials of Model F7U-3 Aircraft', Project No. BIS 21156. This J35-powered Cutlass began the trials on 17 April 1953 and they concluded on 13 July, with less than exemplary results. Delays caused by maintenance issues resulted in a failure to complete the testing within the prescribed sixty-day period allocated. Although the aircraft competed sixty flights, maintenance man hours required were considered excessive – the report concluded that 'the maintenance load imposed by this model aircraft, as indicated to date, can be justified only if the aircraft possesses outstanding performance and military usefulness'. It went on to recommend that the aircraft not be accepted for service use 'unless the twenty-ninth and subsequent configured aircraft can demonstrate satisfactory maintenance, servicing and operational reliability'. Many issues resulted from loose electrical leads, loose hydraulic fittings and other factory delivery discrepancies that led to the conclusion that the 'delivery status of the aircraft was unsatisfactory'. Vought clearly had work to do.

When Project 21156 tests resumed, a new J46-powered Cutlass was used to more adequately reflect the production model performance as well as address concerns identified in the first BIS report. F7U-3 BuNo 129554 was acquired by the division on 12 February 1954 direct from BAR Dallas and first flew in the second-round testing eight days later. Preliminary evaluations were completed on 2 June 1954, and it last flew on 16 September, however it was grounded for a total of eighty days due to various discrepancies found during the testing. The BIS final report titled 'Service Suitability Trials of Model F7U-3 Airplane' recommended that: 'If fleet squadrons continue operating the F7U-3, their complements be greatly increased,' in a nod to their findings that 'normally complemented Navy units do not have enough highly skilled maintenance personnel to quickly and effectively correct the number of discrepancies which arise'. It concluded that: 'The model F7U-3 not be accepted for service use.' This second negative evaluation would subsequently be countered by the results of the more representative six-aircraft Fleet Introduction Programme (see pages 74-75).

Project PTR AC-1305 concerned the 'Determination of Optimum Instrument Flying Procedures of Service Type Aircraft, F7U-3 and FJ-2/3 Phase'. Using F7U-3 BuNo 129567, which had recently been reassigned from Flight Test, LT Edward M. Porter evaluated the individual aircraft type's ability to perform instrument let downs, jet penetrations (rapid descents from altitude), thunderstorm penetrations, and standard range approaches including ground-controlled approaches (GCA). The final report concluded that the F7U-3s speed brakes were 'very effective' in controlling glide path on approaches (whereas those of the FJ series were found to be 'relatively ineffective'), as well as enabling very high descent rates when needed. The 18 October 1954 report identified optimal configurations, speeds, and altitudes for penetrations and landing pattern flying for incorporation to the aircraft's flight manuals.

Following the culmination of these tests, 129567 was predominantly used for evaluation of maintenance practices and the ability to integrate the type into fleet operations, with special consideration to turnaround times for various maintenance tasks. During the course of the aircraft's year and a half tenure with the NATC, 129567 experienced 218 engine changes in an effort to reduce the time taken to accomplish removal and subsequent re-installation. The aircraft was returned to BAR Dallas on 3 December 1955.

Project PTR AC-1301.13 was to be conducted on 10 November 1954 by the Navy's All-Weather Testing Programme Detachment at north Florida's Eglin Air Force Base to evaluate the effects of cold weather conditions on upgraded back-up rings used in the F7U-3's hydraulic and pneumatic systems. Leather back-up rings (AN6291) were originally used throughout the F7U-3 series for support of O-rings in practically every hydraulic, pnuedraulic, and pneumatic system in the aircraft, but were found to be susceptible to failure when aircraft transited various temperature regimes. An upgrade to Teflon back-up rings was advised to mitigate these issues. The Service Test Division was tasked to determine the extremes to which these upgraded components could operate effectively. Due to the unavailability of a suitable test aircraft, the intended 1955 evaluations were subsequently cancelled. The project was reactivated as PTR AC 1301.13.1 on 28 March 1956, and NATC provided a Service Test Division F7U-3, BuNo 129638, which it had received back from NAOTS Chincoteague custody on 14 April 1956. Following reconfiguration and instrument installation, the tests began on 19 April 1956 at Eglin's Climactic Laboratory. Although now back in NATC custody, 129638 wore its NAOTS Chincoteague fin, wing, and nose markings throughout the climactic testing. Exposed to varying temperature extremes of +70° F to -65° F, the Teflon back-up rings were found to be far superior to the leather rings, and recommended as replacements for all in-service aircraft. The testing further found that 'MS' (Military Standard) flare-less fittings were superior to their 'AN' (Army–Navy) counterparts. The F7U-3 was constructed with a combination of MS and AN fittings, however. To change to an all-'MS' configuration was deemed fiscally and practically unattainable, given the planned service life of the aircraft.

F7U-3M BuNo 129705 joined the Service Test Division on 9 March 1955 and was used in initial production variant evaluations of the -3M until NATC relinquished the aircraft to BAR Kansas City for bailment to the Westinghouse's Aviation Gas Turbine test facility at NAS Olathe, Kansas, for J46-WE-8 testing.

Service Test acquired custody of F7U-3P BuNo 129747 on 4 March 1955 for evaluation of camera accessibility and maintenance. Determining that the F7U-3P was unsuitable for carrier operations due to its high nose stance limiting the access to the cameras, NATC transferred custody of the aircraft to NARTU Glenview on 14 May 1957, where it was subsequently stricken.

NATC Armament Test Division: The division was assigned five F7U-3 series aircraft during its evaluations of the type. BuNo 129553 was acquired by NATC on 2 February 1954, and as part of Project No. BIS 21156, it was involved in both gunnery as well as rocket-firing evaluations. Carrying the Division number 'AT12', 129553 represented the first production series of the F7U-3. It was soon joined by BuNo 129640, which was configured with the latest armament installation modifications. These two aircraft conducted the initial service acceptability trials of the F7U-3's armament systems. LCDR Edward A. Gillespie flew forty-one project flights in Phase 1 of the testing. Evaluation of the test's data resulted in a recommendation that the F7U-3 not be accepted for service until several modifications were made to correct the gun's fire-out percentage, engine over-temperatures during gun firing, and a strengthening of the gun's blast tubes. The initial 21 October 1954 report did, however, praise the rocket firing and bombing performance of the aircraft.

Both aircraft were subsequently modified by Vought to address the NATC's Phase I issues. Phase 2 of the testing utilised the same aircraft. Its 20 December 1954 report determined that the majority of the modifications resulted in satisfactory performance of the gunnery

ABOVE NATC sometimes added the prefix 'Y' to designate a 'prototype' or test aircraft. Here F7U-3 BuNo 129567 shows one of several ways NATC aircraft were marked, with the Center's initialism located high on the fin and its Service Test Division 'ST' identifier located low on the forward fuselage. *NATC 3578-(A) 3104 Casby Collection*

LEFT LCDR Edward A. Gillespie retracts his landing gear after taking off from NAS Pensacola, Florida, following a refuelling stop while delivering F7U-3 BuNo 129640 to NATC's Armament Test Division at Patuxent River, Maryland, on 30 May 1954. *NATC NA9-8424(L)-5-54 Casby Collection*

LT John A. Chalbeck looks over his shoulder at his wingman after completing one of forty-one 'special weapons' evaluations in F7U-3 BuNo 129636, which wore the Armament Test Division's nose number 'AT13'. Note streamlined camera fairing located on the nose's in-flight refuelling kit access panel. ***NATC NA8-6545(L)-6-55 Casby Collection***

system, however the gun's fire-out percentage was still deemed unsatisfactory. Desynchronisation of the gunnery system's interlocks through the use of an intervalometer was determined to be satisfactory in mitigating engine compressor stalls during gun firing. It was recommended that this be accepted on an interim basis until the other remaining issues were resolved. However, it was found that these modifications became ineffective above 35,000ft.

Phase 3 of the tests required forty-five flights. The NATC final report dated 10 March 1955 concluded that the F7U-3's armament system was 'satisfactory for service use except for the fixed gun installation'. Although rocketry and bombing evaluations were deemed satisfactory (and in some cases, excellent), a failure of the guns to fire under negative *g* accelerations, low gun fire-out percentages, and compressor stalls above 35,000ft when the guns were fired were still unsatisfactory. However, additional 20mm cannon installation modifications developed by Vought resolved the last of these issues in time for the deployment of VF-124 (see page 123).

F7U-3 BuNo 129636 was acquired by the AT Division on 28 May 1954 and was assigned 'AT13' in the division's aircraft roster. Its use by NATC was primarily special weapons (i.e. nuclear) delivery evaluations and the determination of modifications required to mitigate issues that were being experienced by the engineers at NOTS Inyokern and the NASWF Kirtland AFB. LT John A. Chalbeck conducted forty-one flights with representative aerodynamic shapes, documenting the effect on aircraft performance and endurance with the simulated stores. Working separately, but in close contact with the west coast test stations, the NATC provided aircraft performance evaluations to the Board of Inspection and Survey as related to the carriage of these special stores.

F7U-3M BuNo 129698 joined NATC on 3 March 1956 and was used in the division's evaluation of the fire control system supporting the Sparrow I missile. It remained with NATC until 11 March 1957, when its custody was transferred to NASF Litchfield Park for storage. NATC's Maj Hal Vincent, USMC, conducted repeated trials of the fire control system, providing independent evaluation from the ongoing testing at NAMTC Point Mugu.

F7U-3P BuNo 129750 was transferred to NATC's Armament Test Division's custody on 4 March 1955 for use in the evaluation of 900lb delivery container drop tests. Unlike the belly pod dummy drop testing conducted at the Naval Parachute Unit at El Centro, California, these tests involved high-speed releases of large containers mounted on the underwing pylons. The use of the F7U-3P allowed camera documentation of these releases. Marked 'AT14' under the cockpit coaming, BuNo 129750 made use of NATC Patuxent River's test ranges, as well as on and off-shore ranges near NAS Quonset Point, Rhode Island. Following his 7 November 1956 take-off from Charlestown, Rhode Island, NATC's

LCDR Rutledge in the cockpit of F7U-3P BuNo 129750 (note the camera nose transition crease running through the '5' of the side number) prior to his ill-fated flight on 7 November 1956. ***Casby Collection***

LCDR Edward Rutledge experienced a total flameout during a 550-knot delivery run at 1,200ft above the ground. Because a steep turn would have been required to land on the airport's runway, he instead elected to land in an open field, where he touched down in a slight bank into soft dirt. He sustained serious injuries and was dragged from the aircraft by local firefighters who arrived on the scene. Although Rutledge believed the Cutlass had been refuelled prior to take-off due to seeing the airport fueller attending to his aircraft, the flameout was the result of fuel starvation as no additional fuel had been added.

NATC Electronics Test Division: F7U-3 BuNo 128459 was the first NATC aircraft assigned to the Electronics Test Division when its custody was accepted on 4 August 1953. Used for evaluation of avionics and weapon control electronics, the early -3 was transferred to NAMC Philadelphia on 2 September 1954. Six days later, F7U-3 BuNo 129639 was received from VF-83 and placed in the ET Divisions aircraft roster for testing of the General Electric flight stabilisation system. It was used for these evaluations until being returned to VF-83 on 20 January 1955. F7U-3M BuNo 129722 was the only -3M to be assigned to Electronics Test when NATC took custody on 13 March 1955. Receiving an 'ET' designation on either side of its nose, the aircraft was utilised by NATC engineers to determine modifications necessary to increase the effectiveness of the -3M's emitted radar beam for Sparrow I missile tracking. It was still wearing its NATC and 'ET' markings when transferred to FASRon-5 and eventually placed as a playground attraction in the Wheaton Regional Park in Montgomery County, Maryland.

NATC Tactical Test Division: The Tactical Test Division was only assigned one F7U-3P, BuNo 129746, used for initial evaluation of the photographic capabilities of the model, but several other F7U-3 aircraft were used by the division in spite of not being officially assigned. BuNos 129654, 129656, and 129667 arrived at NATC between 3 August 1954 and 1 February 1955, but were not assigned to any division. Tactical test (as well as other divisions) used these aircraft for small projects and temporary assignments.

Bureau of Aeronautics representatives

The United States Navy's Bureau of Aeronautics (BuAer) was established in 1921 to accomplish the development of naval aircraft and provide guidance and support for the design, testing, approval, procurement, and integration into the fleet of new, as well as existing, naval aircraft and systems. To facilitate communication between the Bureau and its contractors, Bureau of Aeronautics Representative (BAR) offices commanded by a naval officer were stationed in regions where BuAer contractors were located, in some cases within a factory plant itself. In addition to other naval officers, the BAR was staffed with enlisted men and civilian staff as required. BAR personnel included pilots and engineers as well as accountants, analysts, and other administrative personnel. Each BAR worked closely with its assigned contractors to ensure that the requirements of the contract were followed and provide immediate on-site access to the Bureau when questions came up regarding the Navy's understanding of contract requirements, etc.

The BAR was also responsible for relaying BuAer inputs to its contractors concerning integration of BuAer-contracted components with the aircraft, as well as co-ordinating the delivery – and maintaining administrative control – of all Government-Furnished Products (GFPs) such as engines, weaponry, and avionics.

The Bureau assigned a unique number (BuNo) to each aircraft that it procured. Subsequent to delivery, a continuous record of its custodian and nominal location with dates of transfer was maintained by a yeoman on its aircraft history card. The format of and detail required on the card evolved over time and eventually included status codes, number of flight hours, service tour number, etc.

The primary contractor BAR was the initial custodian of all aircraft delivered, as well as aircraft returned to the factory for modification or repair. Their work comprised both the acceptance testing of each aircraft, as well as any experimental flight testing that BuAer deemed appropriate to be conducted by a Navy pilot at point of manufacture. For example, when F7Us were completed at Vought, they were initially flown by company test pilots to determine whether the Cutlass and all its systems functioned as required. Any discrepancies had to be corrected and the aircraft re-flown to ensure they had been. When judged by a company test pilot to be acceptable, the aircraft was

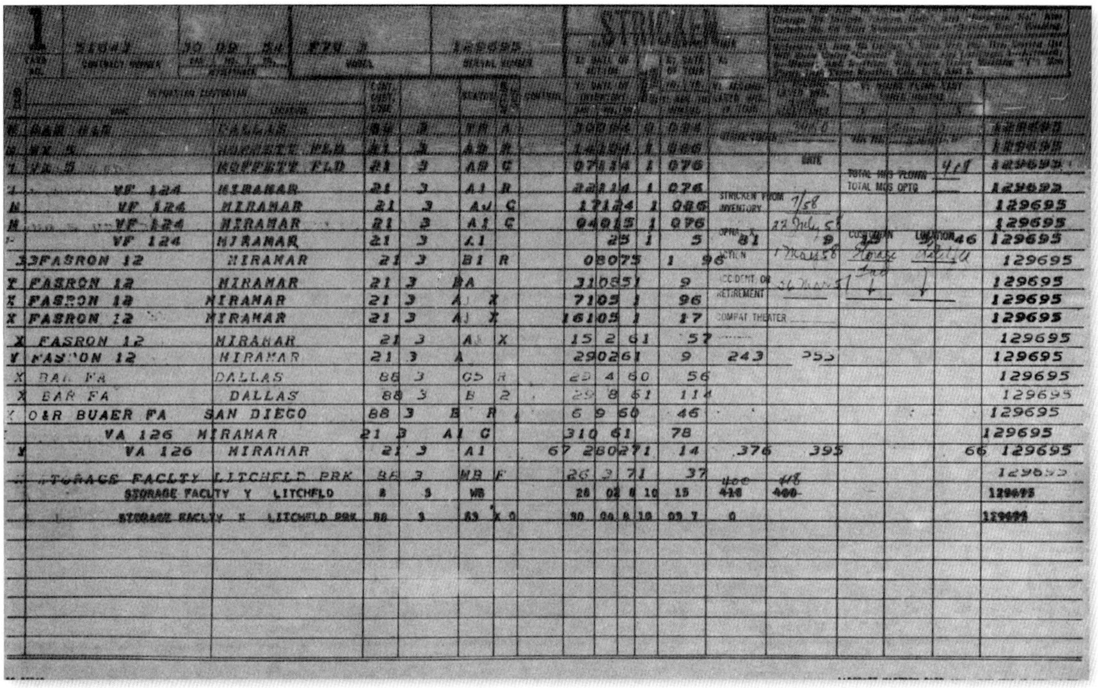

Activity	Location			Status	
BAR R&D	DALLAS	88	3		
VX 3	MOFFETT FLD	21	3	AB	R
VX 3	MOFFETT FLD	21	3	AB	C
VF 124	MIRAMAR	21	3	A1	R
VF 124	MIRAMAR	21	3	AJ	C
VF 124	MIRAMAR	21	3	A1	C
VF 124	MIRAMAR	21	3	A1	
FASRON 12	MIRAMAR	21	3	B1	R
FASRON 12	MIRAMAR	21	3	BA	
FASRON 12	MIRAMAR	21	3	AJ	X
FASRON 12	MIRAMAR	21	3	AJ	X
FASRON 12	MIRAMAR	21	3	AJ	X
FASRON 12	MIRAMAR	21	3	A	
BAR FA	DALLAS	88	3	GD	R
BAR FA	DALLAS	88	3	B	2
O&R BUAER FA	SAN DIEGO	88	3	B	R
VA 126	MIRAMAR	21	3	A1	C
VA 126	MIRAMAR	21	3	A1	
STORAGE FACLTY	LITCHFLD PRK	88	3	WB	F
STORAGE FACLTY Y	LITCHFLD	8	3	WB	
STORAGE FACLTY X	LITCHFLD PRK	88	3	83	X

Aircraft history card for F7U-3 BuNo 129695, accepted by BAR Dallas on 30 September 1954 and stricken at Litchfield Park on 22 July 1958 with a total of 418 hours' flight time. ***Casby Collection***

test flown for official Navy acceptance by a naval aviator assigned to BAR Flight Acceptance Office (BAR FA) at Dallas for that purpose. Acceptance resulted in the creation of an aircraft history card for that Bureau Number, which documented the aircraft's custodians throughout its service. The F7Us to be retained at Vought for test and evaluation were then assigned to the BAR Research and Development Office (BAR R&D) at Dallas. Aircraft that were in need of further acceptance flights, or aircraft that were later returned to the factory for modifications that required subsequent acceptance flights, were administratively reassigned to the BAR FA Office.

In addition to factory-associated BAR R&D assignments, the Bureau also maintained a 'pool' system at selected locations around the country to facilitate the administrative custody of aircraft not currently assigned to fleet units (to include fighter, attack, evaluation, composite, and service squadrons), as well as Overhaul and Repair units (O&Rs), Storage and Reclamation units, and Naval Air Reserve Training Units (NARTUs). These BAR or BuAer Pools were usually administered by a single assigned officer and his staff and were primarily used to effect a continuity of custody. Known as 'Pool BAR M&S', 'Pool BuAer M&S' or simply 'BAR M&S' units (the 'M&S' standing for Maintenance and Storage), these offices were primarily responsible for the custody of aircraft being stored, or in the case of aircraft returning to the factory for modification, awaiting maintenance action performed at a factory level.

Dallas BARs

BAR Dallas, Texas (Chance Vought Aircraft). The BAR located at Vought's Stratford, Connecticut, factory location made the move to NAS Dallas following Vought's legendary cross-country relocation for production of the F6U and continuing development of the F7U. Officially renamed BAR Dallas in December 1948, the office was initially under the command of LCDR Harold S. Nelson, formerly the assistant BAR at Stratford and a project officer in the Service Test Division at NATC Patuxent. Nelson relinquished command of BAR Dallas in September to CAPT Alfred C. Olney Jr., who held the distinction of having flown every Chance Vought aircraft type produced up to that date – he subsequently flew the F7U-1 in January 1951. Olney initially commanded a staff of six officers and ninety civilians.

When the F7U-3 prototype made its first flight on 20 December 1951, the BAR Dallas office was authorised to increase its staffing levels of test and acceptance pilots. The first of many new pilots to join the BAR ranks was LT Donald D. Engen, followed by a change of command with CAPT Charles M. Jett taking over BAR Dallas. It was under Jett's command that the formation of a BuAer-sponsored Cutlass demonstration team was first envisioned. Soon to join the BAR flight ranks was Second World War veteran LT John S. 'Jack' Christiansen, and in May 1953 LCDR George W. 'Red' Brooks, a former 'flying Chief' and recent commanding officer of FASRon-10. Brooks was promptly promoted to full Commander within minutes of his arrival in Dallas and became the BAR Executive Officer. Following him by days was LCDR Ronald G. 'Ron' Puckett, a former Second

World War and Korea veteran, Navy test pilot school graduate, and famed Thompson-Trophy air race pilot flying his own F4U Corsair.

As the BAR in Dallas was getting acquainted with the new F7U-3, BAR pilot LCDR John W. Ryan stole the show at the Detroit International Aviation Exposition on 9 to 12 July 1953 in BuNo 128459 while performing fly-bys at a reported 730mph, slow-flight carrier approaches, and finishing up with taxiing up to cheering crowds in the stands while standing in the cockpit. The reception and goodwill generated by the 160,000 spectators' response to Ryan's performance convinced BuAer to authorise the continuation of the Cutlass demonstrations at airshows all over the country.

On 1 November 1953, LCDR Puckett eclipsed the Blue Angels in the 'people's choice' category when he put the needle-nosed (test probe-equipped) BuNo 128457 through its paces at NAS Dallas for Naval Air Reserve Day. Following Puckett's demonstration, BAR Dallas pilot LCDR Archie P. Stockbrand performed an impromptu 'gunnery run' on a visiting USAF B-36 that was flying over the field, angering the Air Force attendees, but much to the delight of Assistant Secretary of the Navy for Air, James H. Smith Jr. and BuAer Chief RADM Apollo Soucek. Puckett continued with his exciting demonstrations the following weekend with airshows in Milwaukee, Wisconsin and NAS Glenview in Chicago. So impressing with his performance, Puckett received a commendation from RADM Daniel V. Gallery Jr., lauding his flying and extolling the performance of the F7U-3. Puckett would soon deliver F7U-3 BuNo 128477 to Fleet Aircraft Service Squadron Twelve's *Project Cutlass* unit at Miramar, California, to kick off the Navy's integration of the Cutlass to the fleet and form the nucleus of the first west coast Cutlass-equipped fighter squadron, VF-124.

New additions to BAR Dallas' F7U-3 flight department were seasoned Second World War aviators LT Robert C. 'Bob' Woolverton and LT Harold L. 'Hal' Shipley. LT Billy Phillips joined the BAR Dallas cadre in January 1954. Phillips was a former enlisted ordnanceman who applied for flight training and received his wings in 1946. A dashingly handsome aviator, Phillips was chosen to be the face of the Navy in the 1949 motion picture production of *The Naval Aviator*, which was shown in colleges and universities throughout the country as well as on major television networks. Described as one of the finest 'natural pilots' by many, Phillips looked at the BAR assignment as an opportunity to fly the hottest jets in the Navy, and he was not disappointed.

As the 1954 airshow season got started, LCDR's Puckett and Brooks, with LT Christiansen, wowed the crowds at the Navy Relief Festival in Corpus Christi, Texas. Brooks opened the festivities by taking off in Dallas and racing a 1927 Buick that started the race 15 miles away from NAS Corpus Christi. Brooks taxied up to the reviewer's stand one minute and fifteen seconds ahead of the Buick's arrival.

One of the perks of being a naval aviator and airshow performer was the opportunity to meet pretty girls! Here, Billy Phillips straddles the canopy while briefing this one on the controls and instruments in the cockpit of his F7U-3. *Casby Collection via Billy Phillips*

Tragedy struck on 11 June 1954 when LCDRs Stockbrand, Puckett, and LT Woolverton attended the Mid-South Air Festival at NAS Memphis in Millington, Tennessee. Taking off for a practice flight in BuNo 129647, Woolverton inexplicably retracted the leading-edge slats immediately after raising the landing gear – well below the established minimum slat retraction speed of 210 knots. His aircraft stalled and entered a pre-post stall gyration 'slice' (see page107), plummeting his F7U into a Navy schoolhouse that had been vacated by 150 Navy aircraft maintenance students just minutes before. The resulting fireball claimed the lives of LT Woolverton, along with Aviation Maintenance Chiefs Roland F. Brousseau, George F. Hurlburt, and George W. Woodruff, as well as Naval Civilian Employee Mrs Elaine House Branch. Actor George Reeves, star of television's *The Adventures of Superman*, was attending the pre-festivity show and witnessed the crash. He was brought to tears by the children in attendance, who innocently could not understand why Superman could not have saved the pilot.

In late August 1954, Jerome K. Crossman, the president of the Dallas Chamber of Commerce presented Stetson cowboy hats and western boots to BAR pilots Brooks (right), Christiansen (left), and Phillips (on the ladder) as they prepared to attend the National Aircraft Show in Dayton, OH. As ambassadors for the Navy, as well as Chance Vought, they were now tasked with the role of aerial ambassadors for the State of Texas and the City of Dallas. *Casby Collection via Billy Phillips*

It was the final team, nicknamed the 'Silver Streaks' – Red Brooks, Jack Christiansen, and Billy Phillips – that became the faces of Chance Vought and the United States Navy at nine airshows across the country. With full factory maintenance support and full BuAer administrative backing, the team went on to perform flawless airshow performances highlighting the F7U-3's amazing capabilities in the hands of seasoned pilots. Phillips and Christiansen would normally fly the airshow performances, while Brooks would narrate the show and provide his aircraft as a static display. High-speed passes, 'collision-course' passes, and simulated carrier landings were highlights of the team's demonstrations.

LT Phillips developed a personal routine where he would fly inverted across the airfield, pushing up into an outside loop while deploying his landing gear and slats, and once gaining altitude, transitioning into the backside of an inside loop and landing in front of the crowd. Phillips' demonstrated ability to continue a vertical climb while adding the drag of the deploying landing gear and slats speaks positively of the F7U-3's acceptable thrust-to-weight ratio, and should be given consideration when discussions of the type and its engines deteriorate to derisive 'gutless' monikers.

On 22 May 1955, LT Christiansen flew the last show with the BAR prior to his promotion to LCDR and reassignment to Line Officer's School at Monterey, CA. He had logged more than 250 hours in the F7U-3 and was looking forward to assignment to a Cutlass fleet squadron. In August 1955, CAPT Jett (the primary Cutlass airshow proponent) was reassigned and replaced by CAPT Chester A. Briggs as BAR Dallas' Commanding Officer, and newly promoted CDR Red Brooks soon retired from the Navy on 1 February 1956.

There's cool, and then there's Red Brooks (left) and Billy Phillips flying F7Us in cowboy boots cool. *National Archives Photo via Casby*

The 'Silver Streaks', also known as the 'Tennessee Hillbillies', perform a fly-past of the crowd at NAS Buckley, Colorado. The team often drew more attention with their exotic swept-wing, afterburning, tail-less Cutlasses than the Navy's Blue Angels flying pedestrian straight-wing F9F Panthers. *Casby Collection via Billy Phillips*

Resplendent in their polished aluminium and freshly painted magnesium panels, the 'Silver Streaks' utilised BAR Dallas-assigned aircraft like BuNo 129663 and 129648 pictured here. Vought's factory support personnel travelled to the airshows by automobile to attend to any minor maintenance work necessary. The team never missed a performance. *Casby Collection*

The BAR's focus began to shift to the new F8U-1 Crusaders soon to be rolling off the production lines at Vought, and LT Phillips and LCDR Gale C. Burkey both checked out in the new supersonic machines.

The BAR Dallas pilots continued to fly acceptance test flights as the last F7Us came out of the factory, and provided BuAer support for aircraft returning to the factory for modifications. However, the BAR's crowd-thrilling F7U airshow performances that enlivened the summers of 1953–55 were over.

BAR M&S (Pool) Dallas, Texas. Following Navy flight acceptance of newly built aircraft, they were usually administratively transferred to the BAR Dallas Maintenance and Storage (M&S) Office to retain custody prior to their initial assignments. These F7Us were commonly referred to as 'Pool' aircraft.

Plagued by delivery delays of the early J46-WE-8A and -8B engines in 1953–54, the BuAer Pool at NAS Dallas had scores of engine-less F7U-3s, sarcastically known as 'gliders', awaiting power plants. The entire F7U-3 programme was in jeopardy as a result of these delayed engine deliveries, and the BAR M&S was tasked with finding suitable storage space for brand new, yet unflyable aircraft. With the looming spectre of possible contract cancellation, both Vought and the Navy could only store the aircraft in the hope that Westinghouse factories at Essington, Pennsylvania, and Kansas City, Missouri, would achieve success in the ongoing development of the plagued J46s, finding solutions to compressor stall and specific fuel-consumption issues. The initial group of gliders were accepted between July and September 1953 but not ready for delivery until February to November 1954. A second batch of gliders were accepted between March 1954 and November 1954, but not delivered until February 1955.

Sporting black self-adhesive protective plastic over their bare aluminium surfaces, and often equipped with wooden 'fences' designed to disrupt unwanted lift from often very strong winds, these gliders sat nestled together for months. As the delayed engine deliveries eventually took place, the gliders were stripped of their protective coatings and released from the BAR M&S for completion, including Vought acceptance flights, prior to acceptance flights by the BAR Dallas pilots. Barring any anomalies, they would be released for subsequent assignment. Eventually all the aircraft affected received engines and left the BAR's custody.

In addition to pre-delivery custody, the BAR M&S office would also be responsible for temporary custody of all F7U aircraft returned to Chance Vought for engine intake and other modifications.

Other BAR F7U-3 custodians

F7U-3 series aircraft were assigned to eight other BAR custodians between January 1952 and August 1959:

BAR R&D Baltimore, Maryland (Westinghouse Air Arm Division). The BAR in Baltimore was assigned to the Westinghouse Air Arm Division (WAA) that was Westinghouse's test and evaluation branch primarily concerned with the evaluation and refinement of Westinghouse-produced avionics and electrical control systems. F7U-3 BuNo 129547 was flown to the Air Arm Division at Baltimore's Friendship International Airport on 7 June 1954 from BAR Dallas, and remained

Thirteen so-called 'gliders' in temporary storage at Vought, complete except for J46 engines. ***VAHF***

Ex-VX-3 F7U-3P BuNo 129751 used as a backdrop for a personnel inspection at NAS Floyd Bennett Field between the cancellation of its bailment to Grumman and one to Meteor Air Transport Corporation for tests of infrared imaging systems. Note the presence of VX-3's day-go orange band on the nose, and the remnants of the VX-3 '01' side number and 'XC' tail code. *USNAS New York NA15(14)(L)1857/11-56 via Casby*

under the operational control of factory-based BAR Baltimore. Its primary use with the BAR was to test the installation of Automatic Temperature Control (ATC) wiring for the F7U-3M's intended J46-WE-8 engine, using an F7U-3 that was equipped with a revised ATC installation. The majority of these tests were ground-based, however three short shakedown test flights were conducted. Following cessation of the testing, the Cutlass was transferred to the custody of the Naval Ordnance Test Station (NOTS) at Inyokern, California, on 18 August 1954 for participation in weapons testing.

BAR R&D Bethpage, New York (Grumman Aircraft Corporation). The BAR office at Bethpage, NY, was BuAer's liaison to their primary contractor, Grumman. Although not specifically involved in their competitor's F7U programme, Grumman found themselves in need of assistance that a photo-Cutlass could provide. On 4 October 1956, one of VX-3's F7U-3Ps, BuNo 129751, was transferred to BAR R&D Bethpage following its overhaul at NAS Norfolk. It was bailed (a non-ownership transfer of property for a specific purpose) to Grumman in conjunction with a Navy contract for a photoreconnaissance version of the F11F-1 Tiger.

The F11F-1P was subsequently cancelled. No longer needed by Grumman, on 28 February 1957 BuNo 129751 was bailed to the Meteor Air Transport Corporation, for testing to be accomplished by Meteor's Equipment Flight Test Division. Based at NAS New York's Floyd Bennett Field, the Cutlass filled Meteor's need for low-altitude (500ft), high-speed (Mach 0.9) flight test of a classified USAF infrared system being developed by the Servo Corporation of America. On the night of 7 May 1957, according to the *New York Times*, one of the flights caused scores of New York City residents to report seeing or hearing several jet planes 'buzzing' Manhattan while ex-VA-83 F7U-3/-3M pilot Jacob E. 'Jake' Boelhouwer was making three round trips between the Battery and the George Washington Bridge. This resulted in the scramble of a USAF F-94 Starfire from nearby Maguire AFB to investigate; however, the Starfire departed Maguire twenty-eight minutes after the F7U-3P had already landed back at Floyd Bennett Field! The futile interception attempt generated more calls to the authorities, which resulted in its pilot having to return over the city, in effect looking for himself. Although some reports claimed that as many as eight jets were as low as 1,000ft, rattling windows, Boelhouwer was adamant that he was above 3,000ft when over the city.

This F7U-3P was returned to the Navy on 10 March 1958 and subsequently stricken at O&R Norfolk.

BAR R&D Buffalo, New York (Cornell Aeronautical Laboratory). The assignment of a single aircraft, F7U-3 BuNo 129566, to the Cornell Aeronautical Laboratory (CAL) was accomplished on 1 April 1957 when it was flown to Buffalo, NY, from long-term storage at the Naval Air Storage Facility (NASF) Litchfield Park, Arizona. This aircraft was utilised prior to its 10 September 1956 flight to storage for extensive spin and PSG testing at Chance Vought. Already fitted with spin chute apparatus and

BuNo 129556 taking off from the Buffalo airport, NY, for a Cornell Aeronautical Laboratory test flight of its yaw stabilisation system. *Thomason Collection*

structural modifications for the previous testing at Vought, the aircraft was transferred to the BAR office at Buffalo and subsequently bailed to CAL for additional investigation into the PSG phenomenon. Flown by CAL test pilot John C. Seal, the aircraft was equipped with large automated dorsal and ventral vanes mounted just aft of the radome that assisted in preventing uncommanded yaw during post-stall gyration onset. Tests were conducted both with and without the vanes installed (see page 112-114 for a detailed summary of these tests). The tests concluded with one last flight on 24 August 1959, which had the distinction of being the last flight to date of any F7U Cutlass variant. The aircraft was subsequently struck off charge and scrapped in situ.

BAR R&D Inglewood, California (North American Aviation). F7U-3 BuNo 129591 was transferred on 21 September 1955 to BAR Inglewood as a result of its bailment to North American Aviation (NAA). North American utilised the aircraft in support of its further development of the Mighty Mouse Mk 4 folding-fin aerial rocket (FFAR), and the rocket's delivery system. Equipped with the Vought-produced belly-mounted rocket pack and avionics developed by North American, the aircraft remained with NAA conducting developmental duties until 3 October 1956 when its custody was transferred to Naval Air Ordnance Test Station (NAOTS) Chincoteague, where further testing of the unguided rockets ensued.

BAR R&D Kansas City, Missouri (Westinghouse Aviation Gas Turbine Division). Although much early in-airframe engine testing and research was conducted by Westinghouse Aviation Gas Turbine Division (WAGT) during the development of the J46 engine, most of this took place at Vought under the control of BAR Dallas. However, between 1955 and 1957, Kansas City-based WAGT conducted flight testing of the J46-WE-8B and -8 engines at a flight test centre based at NAS Olathe, Kansas. BuAer maintained hangar space for the developmental testing of the J46 engines in bailed

F7Us using facilities originally allocated for their J40 testing that utilised a North American B-45 Tornado.

BuAer approved the bailment to Westinghouse of two Cutlass aircraft, F7U-3 BuNo 128472 on 3 June 1955, and F7U-3M BuNo 129705 on 8 May 1956. Arriving in September 1955, BuNo 128472 was assigned to take part in the testing of the J46-WE-18 engine that was being developed for the A2U-1 ground-attack version of the Cutlass. It utilised a J46-WE-8B engine on the starboard side, and various iterations of the -18 engine to port. On 13 June 1957 it was flown to NASF Litchfield Park and eventually stricken on 1 May 1958.

F7U-3M BuNo 129705 was bailed to WAGT and administrative custody transferred to the BAR at Kansas City on 8 May 1956, being flown in from NATC Patuxent. This aircraft was used in *Project Hot Shot*, a methodical test programme to determine if the J46 engines, both -8B and -8, could withstand operation at turbine outlet temperatures approaching 1,600°F during bolters and go-arounds when the extra thrust was desired. This was especially critical in the -3M during recovery aboard ship due to the increased weight and drag of retained Sparrow I missiles. It was found through extensive testing that the ability to withstand higher temperatures for short periods of time at military power was to be preferred to the use of afterburners during the approach and potential go-around, due to their prodigious use of fuel and the possibility that they would fail to light when called upon. The aircraft was flown to NASF Litchfield following culmination of these tests on 13 March 1957.

Pool BuAer FA Chincoteague, Virginia. Following its service as a rocket test bed with the NAOTS, F7U-3 BuNo 129681 was transferred on 25 March 1958 to the custody of the BuAer 'Pool' at NAAS Chincoteague. The aircraft was struck off charge on the same date and subsequently scrapped on site.

Pool BuAer M&S Memphis, Tennessee. The BuAer 'Pool' at NAS Memphis in Millington, Tennessee, was a repository for many aircraft of all types that were stored either before or after assignment to the Naval Air Technical Training Command schools on base. Joining F7U-1s BuNo 124415, 124424, 124426, and 124427 already struck off charge at Memphis, F7U-3 BuNo 128465 was flown to Millington on 22 September 1955 following repairs made at O&R San Diego. It was intended to be added to the maintenance training department's airframe repair school, and therefore stricken a day later on 23 September. The aircraft languished in the 'Pool' field for more than two years before being reduced to scrap for reclamation.

Pool BuAer M&S Oceana, Virginia. The BAR Pool at NAS Oceana was the repository for many east coast aircraft either waiting for assignment, or found to be no longer serviceable. Following the return of VA-86 from their shakedown cruise aboard *Forrestal* (CVA-59), the surviving eleven of the squadron's thirteen deployed F7U-3Ms were flown to NASF Litchfield. However, two additional aircraft, F7U-3Ms BuNo 139897 and 139900, had been left at NAS Oceana prior to the start of the cruise due to space limitations aboard the ship. Their custody was transferred to the BAR on 15 July 1957 and they were administratively struck off charge on the same date. Remaining on the 'Pool' tarmac for several months, they were eventually scrapped on site.

Pool BuAer M&S Philadelphia, Pennsylvania. The Philadelphia BAR located at Mustin Field maintained a 'Pool' that provided aircraft used in barrier and barricade testing as well as catapult and ejection seat development in conjunction with the Naval Air Material Center (NAMC) and Naval Air Development Center (NADC). Three early F7U-3s were transferred to the custody of the BuAer Pool. F7U-3 BuNo 128452, the second -3, was transferred on 22 April 1955 from Air Development Squadron Three (VX-3) at NAS Atlantic City, New Jersey. It was struck off charge three days later on 25 April. BuNo 128456 was sent to the Pool yard on 18 May 1955 along with F7U-3 BuNo 128458, both coming from the O&R at NAS Quonset Point. Both were stricken on 16 June 1955. All three aircraft remained in the Pool's 'boneyard' for several years with no evidence that they were utilised for any testing prior to their scrapping.

Fleet Aircraft Service Squadrons

The Fleet Aircraft Service Squadron (FASRon) concept became operational in 1946. FASRons were created to provide a source of maintenance and administrative support for co-located squadrons and visiting aircraft that utilised similar aircraft types as well as storage of spare aircraft – new, overhauled, or excess to a deployed squadron's immediate needs. Each FASRon had a distinctive specialisation, depending on its supported squadrons' mission role and aircraft type. The distinctions in roles were accomplished by the separation of FASRons into three categories: Carrier (supporting base and fleet-deployed fighter, attack, and composite; Multi-engine (supporting patrol and transport category squadrons); and Heavy Attack (supporting large multi-engined bombing squadrons). Although these FASRons were each primarily responsible for their specific aircraft type's missions, the greatest benefit to the fleet revolved around the concept that any FASRon could act as an intermediate maintenance source for aircraft types outside the squadron's defined support mission. As a result, many aircraft that were damaged in operational use by fleet squadrons found their custody transferred to the nearest FASRon, either as a point of repair, or as an interim custodian before being shipped off to an Overhaul and Repair (O&R) facility for major repairs or overhaul.

Notwithstanding the efforts of FASRon-12's *Project Cutlass* in providing the initial introduction of the F7U-3 to the fleet and the development of maintenance practices and flight training (see pages 158-161), the presence of Cutlasses in FASRon squadrons can be broken down into two distinctly different roles: the maintenance and administrative custody of aircraft damaged during carrier and shore-based operations and the storage (aka 'pool') of airworthy replacement aircraft. Unlike many large Multi-engine and Heavy Attack aircraft that were in the custody of their respective FASRon squadrons (in many cases these FASRons operated as de-facto operational units, supporting the fleet when necessary), these interim-custody aircraft did not wear any FASRon livery or markings outside of those from the unit or squadron from which they came. Aircraft kept in ready reserve to supplement deployed fleet squadrons were devoid of markings until their transfer to the requesting fleet squadron. Normally the application of the recipient squadron's markings were applied by the FASRon prior to delivery.

Twelve FASRon squadrons had custody of F7U-3 and -3M aircraft during the types' operational history:

Fleet Aircraft Service Squadron Three (FASRon-3). Norfolk, Virginia-based FASRon-3 had custody of six F7Us from April to August 1956, transferring four aircraft to the nearby O&R Norfolk, while striking two aircraft while with the squadron.

They acquired custody of their first F7U-3, BuNo 129613 on 8 April 1956 from VA-66 following its 7 January nose gear collapse aboard *Ticonderoga* (CVA-14). The aircraft was badly damaged in this incident and custody was subsequently transferred to O&R Norfolk on 23 April 1956 where it was ultimately struck off charge on 11 May 1956 without ever being returned to the US. They took custody of their second aircraft, BuNo 129610, a day later on 9 April 1956, from FASRon-104 – a VA-66 victim of a runway excursion accident occurring on 16 February 1956 at NAF Port Lyautey, French Morocco. Transferred to O&R Norfolk custody on 30 April, the aircraft, still at Port Lyautey, was administratively stricken on 31 May to be stripped for spare parts.

After serving without incident with VA-66, F7U-3 BuNo 129696's custody was transferred to FASRon-3 from nearby Oceana-based FASRon-5 on 14 June 1956. On 12 July it was transferred to O&R Norfolk to serve as a BuAer ready replacement aircraft along with BuNo 129643, which FASRon-3 also acquired from FASRon-5. Both aircraft remained at Norfolk without being requisitioned until 30 April 1958, when they were stricken on site and scrapped.

FASRon-3's last two aircraft came directly from VA-83. F7U-3M BuNo 129729 was involved in a barrier engagement aboard *Intrepid* (CVA-11) on 8 March 1956 during the carrier qualifications prior to deployment. Transfer to the FASRon occurred the next day and the aircraft was struck on 23 March 1956 and reclaimed for parts. Its squadron sister-ship, BuNo 129732 made the deployment with VA-83, but was damaged in a gear-up landing and resultant fire during the squadron's time ashore at Port Lyautey. Six days after the incident, FASRon-3 acquired administrative custody of the aircraft and struck it off charge on 13 August 1956, subsequently directing it to be scrapped in situ due to damage in excess of repairable levels.

Fleet Aircraft Service Squadron Four (FASRon-4). FASRon-4 was based at San Diego's NAS North Island and took administrative custody of one early J35-powered F7U-3, BuNo 128462, on 7 September 1955. Acquired from the Naval Air Special Weapons Facility (NASWF) at Kirtland Air Force Base in Albuquerque, New Mexico, the aircraft was deemed obsolete and stricken a day later. Transported by truck to the New Mexico Institute of Mining and Technology in Socorro, New Mexico, the aircraft was cut into sections and used for rip-charge testing under contract to BuOrd and the USAF to ascertain the destructive effects of shaped charges and string charges on aircraft structures.

Fleet Aircraft Service Squadron Five (FASRon-5). Taking custody of its first F7U, BuNo 129641 from VF-81 on 31 January 1955, NAS Oceana-based FASRon-5 came to acquire temporary custody of nineteen F7Us before relinquishing their last F7U-3M on 6 February 1957 to VA-86. The squadron acted as a temporary administrative custodian for aircraft being readied for fleet assignments to VA-12, VA-34, VA-83 and VA-86 following modifications at Vought, or overhaul at nearby O&Rs. On 9 August 1956, FASRon-5 acquired custody of one damaged aircraft, F7U-3M BuNo 129713, following its nose gear collapse while with VA-83 aboard *Intrepid* months before on 17 April 1956. The aircraft was transferred to the custody of O&R Norfolk on 13 August while still aboard *Intrepid*, and struck seventeen days later due to extensive damage.

Fleet Aircraft Service Squadron Six (FASRon-6). Following an accident aboard *Ticonderoga* on 14 December 1955, Jacksonville, Florida's FASRon-6 took custody of VA-66's F7U-3 BuNo 129604 on 6 April 1956. Transferred to O&R Jacksonville on 2 May 1956, the aircraft was deemed uneconomical to repair and was stricken seven days later while still aboard ship.

Fleet Aircraft Service Squadron Eight (FASRon-8). NAS Alameda was home to FASRon-8, and due to its proximity to the adjacent docking of the Pacific Fleet's aircraft carriers it was a primary transfer point of aircraft being shipped overseas. FASRon-8 served as the administrative custodian for thirteen aircraft, ten

of which were being held for transfer to FASRon-11 at Naval Air Facility (NAF) Atsugi, Japan, and one (BuNo 129633) that went to deploying squadron VA-151. In addition, F7U-3 BuNo 129688 was returned to the squadron from NAF (Advance Base) Oppama, Japan, on 21 March 1957 after serving as an unused fleet replacement aircraft in the Fleet Air Japan pool. It was struck off charge on 19 June 1957 and scrapped on site.

ABOVE After LT Corbett's hard landing on 3 August at Atsugi that resulted in the collapse of the main landing gear (but not the nose gear), the Navy decided to strike BuNo 129618. It was scrapped locally by FASRon-11. ***Casby Collection***

BELOW VA-212's F7U-3 BuNo 128473 seen in NAS Moffett Field's Hangar #1 in September 1956 while in the custody of FASRon-10. This aircraft was used for carrier qualification aboard *Bon Homme Richard* (CVA-31) but was transferred to FASRon-10 on 12 July 1956 prior to VA-212's August deployment. It is a rarely photographed combination of the squadron's orange/yellow upper fin treatment combined with a natural metal finish. ***Casby Collection***

The remaining aircraft in custody was accepted by FASRon-117 following an accident while deployed. VA-212's F7U-3 BuNo 129635 was substantially damaged during a 23 August 1956 landing accident aboard *Bon Homme Richard* (CVA-31) and was offloaded to -117 at NAS Barbers Point, Oahu, Hawaii. Custody was assumed by FASRon-8 on 20 September 1956 and subsequently transferred to O&R Alameda four days later. The aircraft was eventually stricken under the custody of O&R San Diego in 1957 after being deemed uneconomical to repair.

Fleet Aircraft Service Squadron Nine (FASRon-9). Supporting F7U Squadrons VA-12 and VA-34, FASRon-9 was home based at NAS Cecil Field, Florida, and took custody of five F7U-3s between March 1956 and April 1957. Two early -3 aircraft, BuNos 128469 and 128471, were acquired by the squadron in March 1956 and subsequently stricken a year later after being used as training airframes for FASRon-9 mechanics as well as visiting mechanic students from the nearby Naval Air Technical Training Center (NATTC) at NAS Jacksonville. Three aircraft, BuNos 129680, 129685, and 129621, were transferred to VA-12 starting in September 1956, with 129621 transferred on 4 April 1957 following repairs from damage incurred while with VA-34.

Fleet Aircraft Service Squadron Ten (FASRon-10). NAS Moffett Field's FASRon-10 was first established in 1951 in support of Korea-bound air groups, and was the Navy's first all-jet FASRon squadron. With the capability for both minor and major repairs, -10 also ferried aircraft between California's Naval Air Stations. Twenty-two F7U-3 and -3M aircraft were assigned to the squadron between July 1955 and November 1956, with all but three arriving from BAR Dallas following modifications. FASRon-10's aircraft were primarily being readied for transfer to VA-151 and VA-212, but three aircraft were actually *acquired* from these two squadrons before transfer to Naval Air Storage Facility (NASF) Litchfield Park, Arizona. One aircraft, F7U-3 BuNo 129671, was acquired from BAR Dallas on 13 January 1956 and involved in an accident while in squadron custody: LT T.A. Wagner suffered a hydraulic failure during his approach and landing at Moffett on 24 January 1956, necessitating the use of the emergency air system to effect suitable braking. The starboard main gear collapsed due to not being fully down and locked and the aircraft received substantial damage. FASRon-10's mechanics made the aircraft ferriable, and following additional repair work at O&R San Diego it was flown to NASF Litchfield for storage.

Fleet Aircraft Service Squadron Eleven (FASRon-11). FASRon-11 was not only the primary aircraft repair unit in Japan, but also maintained Fleet Air Japan's storage pool at NAF Atsugi. Between October 1955 and September 1957, FASRon-11 held custody of fifteen F7U-3 and -3M aircraft. The majority of these aircraft were shipped to the squadron from stateside FASRon-8 at Alameda. Some aircraft were immediately assigned to assume duty with embarked squadrons who lost or damaged aircraft during their voyage, and FASRon-11 was tasked with repainting these aircraft in the recipient squadron's markings. Two aircraft joined the storage pool and never saw further use, being stricken in 1957 while in FASRon-11's custody.

Serving three deployed F7U squadrons, VF-124, VA-212, and VA-116, the FASRon provided heavy maintenance and emergency repairs for them while they were shore-based at NAF Atsugi. Four aircraft were transferred to FASRon-11 following accidents while operating in or near Japan. VF-124's BuNo 129585 suffered a main gear collapse aboard *Hancock* (CVA-19), followed by BuNo 129577's nose gear collapse after the pilot inadvertently taxied off the Atsugi runway into soft dirt. On 3 August 1956, a VA-151 pilot collapsed the left main gear on F7U-3 BuNo 129618 following a long landing that required the use of emergency air brakes, resulting in a blown tyre and an uncontrollable swerve that overstressed the gear. Finally, on 2 February 1957, VX-4's LT Charles E. Hathaway lost control of F7U-3M BuNo 129704 aboard *Shangri-La* (CVA-38) and taxied into the pack, causing extensive damage to his aircraft as well as others. These aircraft were all evaluated by FASRon-11's mechanics, with 129585 being repaired and returned to VF-124 while 129618 was stricken and reduced to spare parts. BuNos 129577 and 129704 were transferred to NAF Oppama for storage and potential transfer state-side.

Fleet Aircraft Service Squadron Twelve (FASRon-12). After its very successful implementation of *Project Cutlass* and transfer of its initial group of F7U-3s to VC-3 and VF-124, FASRon-12 continued to acquire and distribute F7U-3s in accordance with its customary responsibilities. Its second batch of seventeen F7U-3s began arriving on 3 September and continued until 3 December 1954. Between October 1954 and February 1955, ten of these second-batch aircraft were transferred briefly to VF-122 and VF-124 but returned to FASRon-12's custody in July 1955. Four aircraft were transferred to VX-5 between November and December 1954, as well as three aircraft being transferred to VF-212 during that squadron's transition from F7U-3Ms to F7U-3s when they were redesignated VA-212. Similarly, two FASRon aircraft's custody were transferred to VF-151 during their transition to an F7U-3 attack squadron. The third batch of eighteen F7U-3s to join FASRon-12 first arrived on 4 June 1955 and continued until 12 August 1955, with twelve aircraft being transferred to VF-124 custody within weeks.

FASRon-12 transferred their last F7U-3 to VA-126 on 26 July 1956, ending an impressive twenty-nine-month relationship with the type, which saw only one major incident (during *Project Cutlass*) and no injuries or fatalities.

A FASRon-117 hangar at NAS Barbers Pt, Hawaii, on 16 November 1951, filled with an eclectic group of aircraft undergoing maintenance, from a Douglas R4D undergoing engine changes to a Vought F4U on jacks for a landing gear check. *Tailhook via Mark Aldrich*

Fleet Aircraft Service Squadron One Hundred Four (FASRon-104). FASRon-104, home based at Naval Air Facility Port Lyautey, French Morocco, primarily supported the heavy multi-engine community, providing patrol aircraft to the Commander of Fleet Air Mediterranean (COMFAIRMED). Consistent with the FASRon concept, -104 also provided maintenance and logistical support for visiting squadrons. Both VA-66 and VA-83 utilised the services of FASRon-104 concurrently during the extended shore basing of their detachments from *Ticonderoga* (CVA-14) and *Intrepid* (CVA-11) respectively. Although VA-66's CDR Uncas L. Fretwell took his entire twelve-plane F7U-3 squadron ashore and operated out of Port Lyautey during February to August 1956, VA-83 continued to fly from *Intrepid* while still reducing congestion on board by rotating two four-plane detachments to Port Lyautey during its deployment.

The FASRon was kept extremely busy tending to two gear-up landings, one runway excursion, and the 12 March 1956 search and rescue operation to find VA-66's LTJG Stephen O. Hesla after he ejected from BuNo 129603 over the Moroccan desert due to an engine explosion. Racing against time, Hesla was spotted by a FASRon-104 P2V Neptune as well as an USAF SAR aircraft and rescued by helicopter soon after he had encountered a potentially hostile Bedouin tribe. He had been intimidated by the desert dwellers into parting with most of his personal belongings, and only had his wristwatch remaining to offer in return for his life when Pt Lyautey's station helicopter landed and the Bedouins retreated.

FASRon-104 took custody of one F7U-3, VA-66's BuNo 129610, after LTJG Donald E. Schuh's 16 February 1956 departure off the runway, resulting in the collapse of the left main landing gear. His utility hydraulic system, which powered the wheel brakes, had failed on short final, causing him to overtake the Cutlass that had landed before him and was still on the runway.

Although the aircraft was administratively transferred to Norfolk's FASRon-3 on 9 April, it remained in Morocco and was scrapped.

Fleet Aircraft Service Squadron One Hundred Sixteen (FASRon-116). Following the delivery of F7U-3Ms to VA-116, two sustained damage and their custody was transferred to FASRon-116 based at NAS Alameda.

On 23 March 1956 F7U-3M BuNo 139893 sustained damage from a taxi accident at NAS Miramar, California. Its custody was transferred to the FASRon on 27 March and the aircraft was repaired and returned to VA-116 on 9 April 1956. Later that year, F7U-3M BuNo 129716 landed 728ft short of the runway at NAS Miramar following an excessive sink rate that developed while simulating a flameout approach. Fortunately the pilot suffered no injury in this 10 July 1956 accident, but all three landing gear were sheared off and the aircraft caught fire. FASRon-116 took custody of the burned out hulk and it was struck off charge on 12 July 1956 following stripping for spare parts.

Fleet Aircraft Service Squadron One Hundred Seventeen (FASRon-117). NAS Barbers Point on Oahu, Hawaii, was home base for Fleet Air Hawaii's FASRon-117. Their primary purpose was providing small detachments of aircraft to augment Pacific-operating patrol squadrons, but it was also tasked with maintaining a varied selection of aircraft used for instrument and night training. Pilots from deployed carriers stopping in Hawaii often required currency checks that could not be conducted in their squadron's aircraft while their ship was berthed: FASRon-117 offered the use of their aircraft for this purpose. The squadron also provided maintenance in excess of that capable by deployed squadrons due to space and parts availability aboard ship.

FASRon-117 held custody of two F7U aircraft, with F7U-3 BuNo 129592 of VF-124 being the first. Damaged in a 30 August 1955 ramp strike and subsequent barrier engagement aboard *Hancock* (CVA-19), the aircraft was offloaded in Hawaii and the FASRon took custody two days later. Custody was relinquished to O&R Alameda on 29 September 1955 – the aircraft was returned stateside and was stricken. In a similar transitory custody acquisition exactly one year later, VA-212's F7U-3 BuNo 129635 was involved in a 23 August 1956 ramp strike accident aboard *Bon Homme Richard* (CVA-31) while en route to Hawaii on the first leg of its deployment. After it was offloaded in Oahu, custody was acquired by FASRon-117 on 31 August; it was administratively transferred to FASRon-8 in late September.

Other Development Units

Naval Ordnance Test Station, Inyokern/China Lake, California (NOTS). Under the managerial control of the Navy's Bureau of Ordnance – not its Bureau of Aeronautics – the Naval Ordnance Test Station (NOTS) was based at Naval Air Facility (NAF) Inyokern in the high desert north-east of Los Angeles, California. The NOTS was tasked with the research, development, testing and evaluation of naval weaponry, specifically air-to-air and air-to-ground rockets. Although its mission was akin to its east coast counterpart – the Naval Aviation Ordnance Test Station (NAOTS) at Chincoteague, Virginia – the NOTS not only concentrated on aerial rocketry, but missile development: Its engineers and scientists conceived (without formal BuOrd tasking), developed, and perfected the innovative heat-seeking Sidewinder air-to-air missile there. Located on a dry salt bed in the western Mojave Desert known as China Lake, the vast expanse of uninhabited land allowed virtually unrestricted testing of rockets and missiles from air and ground-based launchers. Armitage Field, the station's air operations facility, was home to aircraft assigned to the NOTS, as well as providing support services for visiting fleet squadrons that utilised the test ranges for gunnery and rocket-firing qualification purposes.

As described in Chapter 11, Chance Vought test pilot Angelone ferried F7U-3 BuNo 128463 from NAS Dallas to Inyokern in October 1953 for the initial test and demonstration of the F7U-3's unique belly-mounted rocket pack and returned with BuNo 128467 in August 1954 to complete it with a J46-powered Cutlass. NOTS took custody of two F7U-3s in the summer of 1954. F7U-3 BuNo 129568 was transferred to NOTS custody on 28 July, and was soon followed by BuNo 129547 on 18 August. These two aircraft were assigned to the 'Classified Ordnance Test Programme' (COTP) under LCDR Raliegh E. 'Dusty' Rhodes, commanding officer of the Experimental Operations Division. Although 568 came to the station directly from factory acceptance at BAR Dallas, BuNo 129547 was transferred from BAR Baltimore, where it had special instrumentation added at Westinghouse's Air Arm Division. This aircraft had been utilised for the evaluation of the Automatic Temperature Control (ATC) system designed for the J46-WE-8 engine developed for the F7U-3M, and retained this system when it was transferred to the NOTS. This aircraft could therefore be used to identify any adverse -8 engine issues that firing the rocket pack would cause.

Both aircraft were used to determine the solution to rocket pack problems experienced initially by VF-81 earlier in the year. Although VF-81 pilots reported 80 per cent successful air-to-ground hits with their cannon during demonstrations held off the coast of Cuba, they experienced multiple incidents of rockets getting hung up on the pack's exit door, blast deflector doors failing to open, and intervalometer failures causing both front and

ABOVE **Vought test pilot Joe Angelone flew BuNo 128467 to NOTS Inyokern for rocket-firing tests with the No. 17 F7U-3, the first with J46 engines. Note the unusual inlet markings.** *US Navy via Gary Verver*

BELOW **A naval aviator examines the rocket exit door of the Vought bespoke rocket pack.** *VAHF*

rear rockets to fire simultaneously. On the west coast, VF-124 had a nearly disastrous incident when a rear bank rocket slipped forward in its launch tube and jammed the exit door of the pack, causing an adjacent rocket to burn out within the pack, causing extensive damage. CDR Thomas J. Walker, the NOTS Assistant Experimental Officer, along with LT Ralph W. Stell Jr., the Air-to-Air Weapons Officer, conducted multiple investigatory rocket-firing exercises from September 1954 to January 1956. CVA test pilot Angelone returned to Inyokern to assist in further test flights in the NOTS aircraft in order to gather first-hand knowledge of the issues and act as a liaison to the Vought engineers back in Dallas.

'First hand' was not figurative: On 21 June 1955, Angelone was the pilot for a test of salvo firing – the front row of sixteen rockets first, followed by the second row of sixteen. The pack's normal operation required the exit door at the front of the pack to open, allowing the front bank of rockets to fire. The pack's deflector doors would prevent their exhaust from reaching the warheads on the aft bank's rocket in each tube. When Angelone pressed the trigger, the front exit door opened, but inexplicably began to close and jammed the first sixteen rockets between the door and pack structure. Because the exit door was not fully open, the circuit that normally kept the deflector doors open allowed them to close, causing the front rockets to unleash their fiery wrath upon the aft bank of rockets. Fortunately, the aft rockets (without live warheads) did not explode in spite of being subjected to intense temperatures. However, the belly of the aircraft sustained heat-induced buckling and required extensive repairs. Over the course of this investigation, 800 rockets were fired, with unsuccessful outcomes affecting five

This NOTS F7U-3 is loaded with both a TX-11 shape and a rocket pack. ***US Navy via Gary Verver***

launches and sixty-four individual rockets. The testing identified changes to be made to rocket-loading practices that were deemed to have caused the issues.

In addition to visiting west coast F7U-equipped squadrons conducting gunnery and rocket-firing qualifications, NOTS hosted NAS Moffett-based Air Development Squadron Five's (VX-5's) evaluation of classified 'special weapons' (nuclear) on a regular basis out of Armitage Field – so much so, that they moved into semi-permanent quarters at Inyokern. Although NOTS was not originally tasked to work with nuclear weapons (that was the primary assignment of VX-5 and the Naval Air Special Weapons Facility (NASWF) at Kirtland AFB), they provided support to Atomic Energy Commission research activities tasked with developing these munitions, and aided them in the design and testing of release methods. NOTS was therefore instrumental in the development of the atomic TX 8 and TX 11 armour-piercing nuclear bombs described in Chapter 11 intended for sub-surface detonation for destruction of bunkers, submarine pens, and fortified installations. The nickname of this project was 'Elsie', from the initialism of 'LC' that reportedly stood for Little Child since it was a development of the Mk 1 'Little Boy'. Inyokern initially hosted the drop tests for Elsie using a McDonnell F2H Banshee. Following the TX-11's acceptance and renaming as the Mk 91 MOD 0, an F7U-3 was utilised for additional separation evaluations. The F7U-3 was especially suitable for these tests compared to the smaller F2H: its high stance providing ease of loading the weapon as well as alleviating the need to fold the bomb's fins during ground and take-off operations. The only F7U known to have carried 'nose art', this F7U-3 had the script 'Elsie' painted on its forward fuselage under the windscreen. It took part in Mk 91 weapons drops in April 1955.

On 26 July 1955, CAPT Leonard E. Ewoldt, Commanding Officer of NOTS Inyokern, announced the station's official change of name to Naval Ordnance Test Station China Lake, concurrent with the name change of the Naval Air Facility itself. Both of the station's F7U-3s remained in the custody of NOTS China Lake until BuNo 129568 was transferred to the NASWF on 7 October 1955, followed by BuNo 129547 being returned to BAR Dallas on 30 January 1956. The station's efforts had proved paramount in the development of the necessary fixes to mitigate the fleet's issues with the rocket pack, as well as supporting the tactical nuclear delivery role that the F7U-3 would soon find itself thrust into. Although the NOTS had no further direct involvement with the Cutlass, NAF China Lake continued to host gunnery and rocket-firing qualification visits from Cutlass-equipped squadrons at Armitage Field for the duration of the F7U's use in the fleet.

Naval Parachute Unit, El Centro, California (NPU). Two of the former VX-4 F7U-3Ps, BuNos 129754 and 129755, that had been put into storage at NASF Litchfield Park, Arizona, were subsequently assigned to the Naval Parachute Unit (NPU) at NAAS El Centro, California. BuNo 129755 was used primarily to conduct high-speed drop testing of a dummy to evaluate the feasibility of insertion of clandestine operatives from small high-performance aircraft until being retired. BuNo 129754's oblique cameras were used to record the dummy release testing for review and analysis. These were the last two F7U series aircraft to fly in the Navy's inventory. On 2 March 1959, LT Howard C. Mitchell ferried BuNo 129754 from El Centro back to NASF Litchfield Park to be stricken. It was the last flight of an F7U Cutlass aircraft under active Navy custodianship.

While assigned to the Naval Parachute Unit, BuNo 129755 was flown with a fuselage fuel pod modified to incorporate a large chute for high-speed dummy drop tests. *Casby Collection*

Naval Parachute Unit El Centro publicity photo of F7U-3P BuNo 129754 taxiing out for the last Navy F7U flight to NASF Litchfield Park, Arizona, where it would be stricken and scrapped. *Casby Collection*

Naval Liaison Office, Edwards AFB, California (NLO). The Navy Liaison Office at Edwards Air Force Base (NLO Edwards AFB) was originally established as a tenant unit at Muroc Army Air Field in 1945 to oversee the flight testing of the Chance Vought XF5U-1 Flying Pancake. Although the XF5U-1 never achieved flight due to programme cancellation, BuAer retained the NLO and its lone Naval Liaison Officer to continue inter-service co-operation and scheduling of Navy related projects at the desert base's facilities. Much like the Bureau of Aeronautics Representative (BAR) officers that were assigned to the Navy's prime contractors to co-ordinate contract compliance, testing and acceptance of contracted materials, the Naval Liaison Officer acted as the BuAer representative at Edwards to maintain the Bureau's oversight of station activities as it related to the Navy's interests. The testing of the Chance Vought F6U Pirate was accomplished at Muroc Dry Lake under the watchful eye of the NLO, as was the later XF8U-1 Crusader flight test programme. The F7U, however, was not tested at Edwards AFB; the XF7U-1 conducting flight testing at NAS Patuxent River when Vought was at Stratford, Connecticut, and later Ardmore, Oklahoma, following Vought's move to Dallas. All F7U-3 flight testing was accomplished at the lengthened runway at NAS Dallas.

In 1955, the NLO was comprised of one officer and three Naval Civilian Employee (NCE) administrative support personnel. The office was not only charged with BuAer's administrative oversight of the many simultaneous experimental flight test programmes for the Navy, but also the testing of ancillary equipment. One such test programme involved a novel design for a High-Speed Externally Carried Tow Target (HSECTT).

Armament Components, Inc. (ACI), a subsidiary of the Townsend Company of Santa Ana, CA, were experts in the design and manufacture of flexible chuting used in machine gun and machine cannon belt-fed weaponry. In 1954, the company began to research a solution to the vexing problem of excessive drag and induced turbulence on high-speed jet aircraft caused by the standard fabric cone and sleeve designs of towed targets then in use with propeller-driven aircraft. Severe 'burbling' effects encountered in high-speed flight caused the fabric target cones to disintegrate, or not track properly behind the tow aircraft when physically compromised.

Additionally, a standard catapult launch with a streamed tow target presented operational problems for carrier-based aircraft operations. The result of Armament Components research was an externally carried, stowed tow target with an integral reel and release device that could withstand the rigours of 500-knot flight, and potentially into the realm of Mach 1.0 operations. The concept's design centred around a high-speed dart-type target with foldable pyramid-shaped wings forward, and a conical section aft for streamlining while stowed. It was envisioned to include flotation devices to facilitate recovery following release from a Navy tow aircraft.

The Fletcher Corporation of Rosemead, California, was Chance Vought's contractor for the 150-gallon external fuel tanks used on the F7U-3 series, as well as other aircraft. These tanks were unique in that they were modular in design, consisting of three major components: nose, mid-section, and tail cone. ACI chose the Fletcher tank as the basis for its towable target container, as the modular design allowed them to utilise the nose and mid-section of the existing tanks, adapting the target's release assembly to the nose section and stowing the finned prow of the target as well as the cable drum and associated brake components within the cylindrical mid-section. The container's aft section was horizontally slotted to accommodate two of the stowed target's foldable fins on each side of the tank. The aft section of the target itself was conically shaped to maintain a low-drag design, yet still provide enough slipstream resistance to remove the target from its container once released. The container utilised BuAer's standard 14in lug spacing, making the target easily adaptable to the Navy's Aero-14 and Mk 51 pylon racks. It also included 30in lug spacing to accommodate USAF aircraft, as well as a single hook for British aircraft utilisation.

Initial testing was planned to be carried out at nearby NAS Pt Mugu, but both the Naval Air Missile Test Center (NAMTC) and co-located Air Development Squadron Four (VX-4) were busy with the testing of the Sparrow I missiles and were not operationally free to concern themselves with such matters. With the ACI design being proposed to both BuAer and the Air Force, it was desired to have the testing of the targets conducted and observed at a joint facility. Initially, the F7U-equipped Naval Air Special Weapons Facility (NASWF) was chosen due to their familiarity with the carriage and deployment of special externally carried shapes, and their joint tenancy at Kirtland Air Force Base in Albuquerque, New Mexico. The fact that NASWF's F7U-3s utilised the Fletcher tanks as their standard external fuel tanks was an operational bonus.

However, at the request of ACI and Fletcher Corporation, the proposed flight testing was reassigned to nearby Edwards AFB to facilitate support and timely modifications at the contractor's respective factories.

As was the protocol, administrative and operational control of the tests fell to the NLO at Edwards. Custody of F7U-3 BuNo 129546 was transferred from NASWF to NLO Edwards on 31 July 1955. On 2 August 1955, NASWF pilot LT Frank Asburn Downs flew 129546 to Edwards AFB to commence a three-week test cycle with the ACI team. The F7U-3's high stance and ample ground clearance facilitated the mounting and adjustments of the targets. Initial target payout experiments indicated the need for stronger springs in the target's fin-deployment apparatus.

Following modifications, the targets performed as designed and ACI's newly conceived ballistic guillotine used to sever the used target's cable for jettisoning was found to function impressively well. Following a total of eight flight hours, testing was completed on 21 August with LT Downs returning 129546 to Kirtland AFB that evening. BuNo129546 was transferred back to the custody of the NASWF on 30 August 1955. Sadly, LT Downs would lose his life aboard 129546 three months later while conducting a low-level practise bombing run over the pueblo of Isleta, New Mexico, while on a NASWF test flight.

Although the ACI High-Speed Externally Carried Tow Target did not reach production while the F7U-3 was operational, variations of the design, such as Del Mar Engineering Laboratories' Radar/Optical Target system, would become ubiquitous aboard naval air stations and fleet carriers in the following decade, providing the Navy with improved high-speed gunnery practice capabilities.

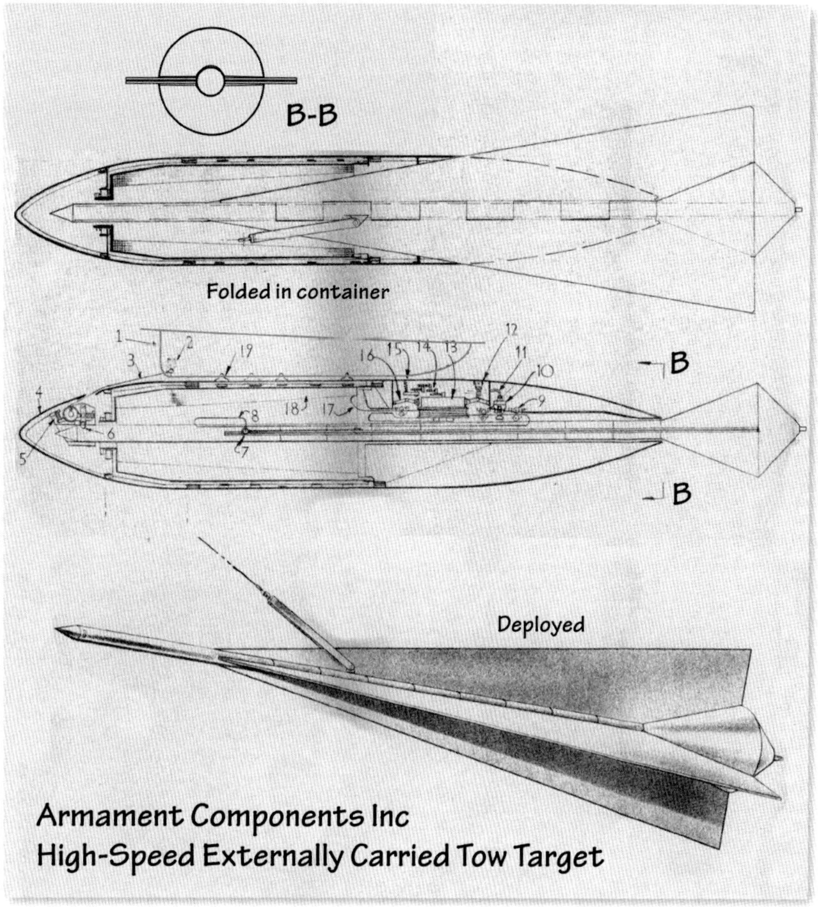

Armament Components Inc
High-Speed Externally Carried Tow Target

Headquarters and Headquarters Squadron Station, Miami, Florida (H&HS-S MIAMI). In spite of the reservations expressed by Marine Corps Maj Marion Carl during the testing of the F7U-1 series, and the subsequent Marine Corps reluctance to utilise the A2U-1, three F7U-3 aircraft were eventually assigned to the Marines in support of a Navy high-speed mine-laying test programme that was being performed in south Florida.

One of the lessons learned early in the Korean War was that establishing a blockade of shipping to and from a harbour by mines was best accomplished by dropping them from low-flying aircraft rather than deploying them from surface ships or submarines, particularly in hostile waters that might have already been mined by the enemy. Moreover, the introduction of transonic enemy jet fighters made the use of lumbering propeller-driven patrol bombers for this purpose inadvisable.

On 25 April 1951, the Chief of Naval Operations had therefore issued an operational requirement for a big, jet-powered seaplane (similar in size to the Air Force's B-47; some think that its primary mission was atomic bombing, not mine laying). One requirement was that it deploy mines at 500ft and at least 500 knots, which was about twice the speed that existing air-dropped mines were qualified for. BuOrd therefore needed to ensure that its new Mk 50 series anti-ship mines were still functional after being dropped by a jet bomber.

Qualification of more capable mines was assigned to Naval Ordnance Laboratory Test Facility (NOLTF) at Fort Lauderdale, Florida. Work began in advance of the seaplane's source selection so that the mines would be available when the new type entered its armament test phase. NOLTF Flight operations were to be conducted from Master Field, part of NAS Miami, in nearby Opa-locka, FL. Test drops were to be accomplished off the coast of Fort Lauderdale. Once deployed, the mine would be recovered by USS *Stallion* (ATA 139), an auxiliary fleet tug based at Port Everglades, located just south of Fort Lauderdale, and returned to NOLTF for evaluation.

However, in February 1952, the air station was transferred from the Navy to the Marine Corps and became Marine Corps Air Station (MCAS) Miami. The Marines inherited the mine-laying tasks. Station-based, propeller-driven Grumman F7F Tigercats were initially used for the mine drop testing but the need for higher-speed performance resulted in the acquisition of three USMC Douglas F3D Skyknight jets. Pilots assigned to the testing programmes came from Station Operations and Engineering Squadron Miami (SO&ES-Miami).

However, the straight-wing F3D was only capable of about 450 knots at sea level even when clean and at combat weight (partial fuel). When carrying a mine with a blunt nose and parachute pack on the tail, it was probably only good for 400 knots. The F7U-3 Cutlass, on the other hand, was big enough and sat high enough off the ground to carry a bulky 2,000lb store and exceed 500 knots at sea level. NOLTF therefore asked BuAer for the bailment of one to the Marines. This resulted in the first of three actual custodial assignments of the F7U-3 series to the Marine Corps.

On 16 August 1954, F7U-3 BuNo 128466 (one of the first sixteen F7U-3s that were powered by non-afterburning J35 engines to expedite Cutlass test and evaluation and now excess to Vought and the Navy's test requirements) was administratively transferred to the custody of the SO&ES-Miami under the control of Headquarters and Headquarters Squadron Station Miami (H&HS-S Miami). With none of the base's four SO&ES pilots qualified in the F7U-3, the station's H&HS-S Intelligence Officer and Provost Marshal, Maj Royce M. Williams USMC, was dispatched to Chance Vought for check-out in the F7U-3. BuNo 128466 had been in the custody of Experimental Squadron Five (VX-5) at NAS Moffett Field, CA; it was subsequently ferried to O&R San Diego at NAS North Island for maintenance work in preparation for transfer to the Marines.

Flown into MCAS El Toro by a Navy pilot from FASRon-4, the aircraft was accepted by Maj Williams and while still wearing its NAVY service designator was flown to MCAS Miami, declaring five emergencies along the way. These were predominantly due to a short in the power control hydraulic pressure warning circuit, which gave Maj Williams spurious 'loss of hydraulic' warning light indications. Arriving at Master Field on Monday, 30 August 1954 with much local fanfare, the aircraft quickly gained the moniker 'hangar queen' due to a lack of spare parts and no preparatory maintenance training or experience with the type. Although it took part in several mine-laying exercises, its 'up status' was dismal: the aircraft accumulated fewer than sixteen hours in the eight months that it was assigned to the Corps. Struck off charge on 12 April 1955, the aircraft was transferred to O&R Jacksonville and became a backdrop for graduation photos from Naval Air Technical Training Center Jacksonville's Marine Corps maintenance training programme.

However, the F7U-3 was still ideal for the mine test requirement because of its size, stance, and speed. As a result, NOLTF therefore requisitioned a replacement. SO&ES Miami received BuNo 129582 on 21 July 1955 (two days, as it happened, after the first flight of the Martin P6M Seamaster for which more capable air-dropped mines were required). This Cutlass proved far more capable and reliable than its predecessor, remaining in service with the Marine Corps for twenty-four months. Maj Royce Williams had assumed command of H&HS-S Miami in December 1954, in preparation for advancement to colonel, and the Marines were once again without a qualified F7U-3 pilot. Maj Edmund 'Edro' Buchser Jr. was the Commanding Officer of Marine Air Base Squadron Thirty-Seven (MABS-37), as well as being the chief test pilot for the 3rd Marine Air Wing, and was chosen to fly 129582 in support of the NOLTF activities.

The size of the Mk 56 mine can be better appreciated by a recent exercise involving the Boeing B-52. ***USAF photo by Staff Sgt Eric Petosky***

The mine was carried on the F7U-3's inboard pylon. Contrary to Buchser's expectation, instead of that wing rising when the mine was released, it tended to drop; he opined that it was being sucked down by the mine due to a venturi effect. At 500ft above the sea, this characteristic was somewhat unnerving but not known to have been experienced by any other Cutlass pilot making bomb or stores drops. It seems more likely that the wing drop occurred because of the significant reduction in drag when the mine was released: the aircraft would yaw away from the wing it had been on, to which both the pilot and yaw damper system would have immediately responded with their respective rudder controls. The duplicative correction could have resulted in a yaw back toward the wing it had been on, which might well have translated into a roll in that direction.

BuNo 129582 continued with SO&ES Miami until 25 April 1956, when its custody was administratively transferred to the H&HS-S. The aircraft continued to be flown by Maj Buchser, as well as Maj Gene W. Morrison, Buchser's Assistant Operations Officer. The aircraft had accumulated 116 flight hours with the Marine Corps when it was stricken with 137 hours total time on 1 July 1957, probably in lieu of a mandatory overhaul. It was eventually towed to Ft Lauderdale's Holiday Park and served as a playground apparatus before being removed due to injury liability concerns.

NOLTF was still in need of a test vehicle in support of its mine qualification programme so on 2 December 1957 H&HS-S Miami received the Marines' third F7U-3, BuNo 129602. It was an ex-VA-66 Cutlass that had undergone overhaul at O&R Norfolk following its return from deployment aboard *Ticonderoga* (CVA-14). H&HS-S pilots flew the aircraft for twenty-eight hours in the eight months prior to its retirement to NAF Litchfield Park on 15 July 1958. At that point, Martin had begun the P6M's armament test phase with qualified high-speed mines and MCAS Miami had been marked for closure by the Department of the Navy. Ironically, a Marine Corps F7U-3 would be the last Cutlass fighter (as opposed to two F7U-3Ps and a spin-test configured one) on flight status.

In all, the Marine Corps' F7U-3s served the needs of the NOLTF well, despite the serviceability pitfalls that accompany a lone type. At no time during their utilisation did the Marines have access to a spare aircraft, and the closest O&R facility was in Jacksonville. Despite these

Major Royce M. Williams, USMC peers down from the cockpit of the Marine Corps' new F7U-3 following his arrival on 30 August 1954 at Master Field, MCAS Miami. Note that the aircraft still carries its NAVY service designator. ***US Marine Corps***

MIAMI
MARINES
466
128466

support challenges, the high-speed mine-laying test and evaluation programme was successful and provided the Navy with the requisite armament capability for the P6M's mission. Although the Seamaster programme was cancelled on 21 August 1959, the Mk 50 series mines continued to be utilised up through the Vietnam War, being dropped by Grumman A-6 and Vought A-7 carrier-based attack planes.

ABOVE **BuNo 129582, one of the few F7U-3s not marked with Navy as the branch of service.** ***Casby Collection***

OPPOSITE TOP **Painted in Marine Corps Air Station Miami markings, BuNo 128466 sits on the Master Field ramp at MCAS Miami in December 1954.** ***US Marine Corps***

OPPOSITE BOTTOM **H&HS-S Miami's F7U-3 BuNo 129582 over Miami Beach, Florida, on 8 June 1956, with Maj Edmund 'Edro' Buchser, USMC at the controls.** ***USMC photo A360065 by SSGT Long***

National Advisory Committee on Aeronautics – Ames Research Center, Moffett Field, California (NACA AMES). The NACA was assigned F7U-3 BuNo 129656 from 10 June to 4 October 1955 and it was used for low-speed handling quality evaluations – with emphasis on determining pilot criteria for a 'minimum comfortable approach speed' – along with nine other USN and USAF jet-propelled fighters. The objective was to be able predict approach speeds quantitatively relative to stall speed, lift-drag characteristics, control power/ response, thrust-to-weight ratio, longitudinal stability, etc. Under Ames Flight Test Engineer's Maurice D. White and Robert C. Innes, and working in close co-operation with test engineer Donald Heile (who previously oversaw LT John Moore's F7U-3 high-sink evaluations while with the Navy), NACA test pilot George E. Cooper was tasked with exploring these flight regimes and developed his final report after forty-four flight hours of testing with the Cutlass. NACA Report RM-A57L11, which did not become available until 1958, eventually compared the approach characteristics of forty-one aircraft to determine the optimal approach speeds for both carrier and land-based operations. However, the

Sporting a complex test probe, F7U-3 BuNo 129656 was assigned to NACA Ames for carrier approach speed evaluations. These tests were conducted with and without the additional instrumentation and probe. ***NACA 255-RF-116-A-20637 Casby Collection***

F7U results were made available to Vought immediately following cessation of the tests, and were later used to corroborate approach speed evaluations that took place during VA-212's carrier qualifications aboard *Bon Homme Richard* (CVA-31) the following summer.

Following the culmination of NACA's testing programme, BuNo 129656 was returned to its pre-test configuration, with the nose test probe removed and its rocket pack re-installed. Its custody was transferred to Moffett Field-based VF-151 on 4 October 1955. Along with his maintenance crew, VF-151's LTJG Eugene A. Corbett drove across the field to perform maintenance checks and perform the squadron's acceptance check flight. Following routine pre-flight maintenance and fuelling, Corbett initiated an afterburner take-off. After rolling approximately 100ft, he felt a shudder in the aircraft and noticed both engine fire warning lights illuminated. The tower advised him that his aircraft was indeed on fire, and he aborted the take-off and abandoned the Cutlass on the runway. Because the aircraft was fitted with a rocket pack, Moffett's fire crew did not attempt to cut into the engine bays in spite of a profuse leakage of fuel from forward of the Station 407 aft fuselage fire seal that fed the flames. The aircraft was completely consumed. It is speculated that fuel contamination was to blame for the loss of the aircraft.

Composite Squadron Twelve (VC-12) – Quonset Point, Rhode Island:.NAS Quonset Point, Rhode Island was initially chosen to become the primary overhaul and aviation supply point in support of east-coast based F7U-3-equipped squadrons. This responsibility included providing an aeronautical outfitting and assembly point for aircraft destined for eastern squadrons, as well as supporting the overseas needs of deployed carriers in the Atlantic. In preparation for Quonset's assumption of this major support role, a single F7U-3, BuNo 129579 was flown from Cecil Field's VA-12 on 26 January 1956 (one day after VA-12 itself took custody of the aircraft) for a facility orientation with the new aircraft type. It is unclear why O&R Quonset Point (previously chosen as the dedicated F7U-3 crash-damage repair depot) did not take custody of the aircraft, but instead 129579's custody was transferred to Quonset-based Composite Squadron Twelve (VC-12), an airborne early warning (AEW) squadron providing detachments to Sixth Fleet carrier deployments. VC-12 temporarily held the aircraft eight days until 02 February when it was returned to VA-12. Subsequently, COMFAIRQuonset and COMNAB-1 chose NAS Norfolk as the east-coast F7U-3 major overhaul and repair facility, as well as ComAirLant's primary aviation supply depot for F7U-3 parts distribution. With the majority of east-coast F7U-3 squadrons home-based within one hour of Norfolk, the decision was sensible.

Fleet Air Transport Squadrons

Air Transport Squadrons (VR) were developed to facilitate the delivery of new aircraft, as well as the repositioning of existing aircraft between custodians. Commonly referred to as 'Ferry' or 'Delivery' squadrons, these units were responsible for the repositioning of all aircraft types within the continental United States, with the exception of large four-engined transport types. Although VR squadrons did not assume administrative custody of aircraft, they retained the aircraft's records for delivery to the recipient squadron or unit.

Pilot transfers to VR squadrons were often initially regarded as unfavourable assignments – lacking the excitement and opportunity afforded by fleet squadrons – but soon came to be appreciated for the variety of aircraft types the naval aviator would gain experience on. It was not uncommon for an aviator to be checked out on fifteen to twenty aircraft types, including helicopters.

When the F7U-3 reached the fleet, a need for prompt delivery of aircraft to squadrons based on both coasts was imperative. Two squadrons were chosen for this task, VR-31 based at NAS Norfolk, Virginia, and VR-32 at NAS North Island in San Diego, California. Despite being on opposite coasts, both squadrons were under the command of Fleet Logistics Air Wing Atlantic Continental (FLAWA) to facilitate common administrative co-ordination of all aircraft transiting the continent. It was not uncommon to have VR-31 pilots receive orders from VR-32 to ferry aircraft back to the east coast after arriving with a west coast-bound delivery, and vice versa. During the 1954–55 fiscal year, VR-31 averaged 218 deliveries per month, with their VR-32 counterpart averaging 205.

Commanding sixty-four pilots in Norfolk's VR-31, CDR James H.R. Fehler worked closely with VR-32 to effect dependable delivery of new F7U-3 series aircraft from Vought's factory at NAS Dallas to fleet squadrons and shore-based units. Considering that 290 aircraft were delivered successfully not only initially, but many were ferried back to Vought for modifications and between custodial assignments, the safety record of the VR squadron's pilots, both officer and enlisted Aviation Pilots (AP), was a testament to the experience that these aviators accumulated. In all VR squadron F7U delivery and ferry operations, only two accidents occurred.

On 7 November 1955, VR-31's LT Oliver F. Brown was ferrying F7U-3 BuNo 129562 from O&R Norfolk to NAS Cecil Field, Florida, when he got behind the power curve during a long straight-in approach. Losing control of the aircraft 500ft short of the runway, his left wing tip struck the ground, followed by the left main gear, causing the aircraft to slam violently down, shearing the nose gear and right main gear off the aircraft. The F7U-3 proceeded down the runway and caught fire, with Brown abandoning the aircraft with minor injury. Following the accident, an investigation initially indicated that the left outer panel slat appeared to be unlocked and retracted, however further analysis found no indication that the slat system had failed. A Control System Malfunction Investigation had been initiated by Vought earlier that year and concluded on 30 December 1955 without identifying any slat system anomalies. Pilot error due to low-altitude manoeuvring was concluded to be the cause of the accident.

Unfortunately, the second ferry accident that occurred on 1 August 1956 had more catastrophic results, with LCDR Robert L. Anderson of VR-32 losing his life in BuNo 128475 during a take-off accident following refuelling at El Paso, Texas. Anderson was delivering the aircraft to Naval Air Storage Facility (NASF) Litchfield Park, Arizona, on a flight that began at BAR Dallas with an intermediate stop at Webb AFB in Big Spring, Texas. During his take-off run in full afterburner, he was notified by the El Paso tower that he was streaming flames, and once gaining 1,000ft in altitude he commenced a left turn to return to the airport. Witnesses reported that he could have ejected, but that the aircraft was headed toward the city of El Paso. To avoid crashing into El Paso's Burges High School, which was filled with students and faculty, he executed a sharp right turn at 200ft – His last words were 'I can't make it', uttered seconds before his right wing struck the ground and the aircraft cartwheeled and exploded in a vacant lot adjacent to the school. Post-crash investigation could not positively determine the cause of the fire, but noted that it was located in the starboard afterburner compartment – a location consistent with afterburner fuel line and fuel vent failures in similar incidents. Given that there was no maintenance performed on the aircraft at any of the intermediate stations, it is surmised that an afterburner fuel line cracked or became detached during his take-off thrust application.

In Memoriam

The Hoofbeats Staff of 1957, dedicates this publication of the Burges yearbook, Hoofbeats, in memoriam of Lieutenant Commander Robert L. Anderson, who sacrificed his own life to spare the lives of the inhabitants of the heavily populated community of Ceilo Vista. The courageous Navy pilot maneuvered his flaming Jet Cutlass out of the area, making his fatal crash only yards from our school.

"Greater love hath no man than this, that a man lay down his life for his friends."
John 15:13

LCDR Anderson was honoured in the Burges High School 1957 yearbook for his heroic decision to save the school. A plaque honouring his selfless sacrifice still graces BuNo's 128475's crash site.

CHAPTER SIXTEEN

F7U-3 series airframe dispositions

In addition to the primary fleet squadrons and units that held custody of the F7U-3 series, there were Navy units that played an important role maintaining, storing, and in the reclamation of the airframes. These units, in most cases, held custody of aircraft that went on to survive their naval service and remain intact for varying lengths of time following being struck off charge (officially removed from the Navy's inventory). Although only five complete F7U-3 airframes remain along with bits and pieces of three others, one of them, BuNo 129554, is destined to fly again.

In the following summary of the disposition of the F7U-3 series survivors, the Bureau Numbers of the airframes still in existence as of 2023, in whole or in part, are identified in ***Bold Italics*** and underlined on the first mention.

Naval Air Storage Facility, Litchfield Park, Arizona

By the beginning of the US government's 1957 fiscal year (1 July 1956–30 June 1957), OpNav and BuAer had concluded that new designs and improved technology were overtaking the F7U series

BuNo 129563 performs gate guard duty under a blanket of snow at NAS Columbus, Ohio, during the winter of 1959. Note the recruiting message 'Fly Navy' painted on the lower forward fuselage. Photo by Robert E. Rogers. ***Casby Collection via James Rogers***

Miss Arizona of 1958 (Donna Riggs) and the 1959 Miss Arizona contestants posing in front of VA-116's F7U-3Ms at Naval Air Storage Facility Litchfield Park, Arizona, in 1959. *Al Casby Collection via Aric Aldrich*

and the time had come to begin to withdraw it from service. Following their squadron and unit assignments, many Cutlass aircraft were flown to the Naval Air Storage Facility (NASF) at Litchfield Park, Arizona, beginning in August 1956 (four F7U-3Ps were the first to arrive a year earlier on 2 August 1955 as they were no longer required for any purpose). These aircraft were stored in the open desert adjoining the base's single 8,500ft runway, some with spray-lat protective coating applied to prevent degradation of the skin and internal equipment, but most without any protection from the harsh desert climate. Although the sun and heat of southern Arizona generally did not present a threat to the aluminium and magnesium airframe components of aircraft (in fact, it was an excellent anti-corrosive environment), the F7U's glue-bonded Metalite skin panels were susceptible to the softening of the early generation resorcinol-type glue used in its construction. De-bonding of the mating edges of surface panels that were not buttressed by riveted supports often led to the penetration of water from the rare rainstorms, which then caused full de-lamination of the panels when the unrestrained balsa wood cores expanded.

Although the function in the NASF's name was 'storage', the scrapping and recycling mission of the unit came in a close second, with many period official documents referring to the facility as the Naval Air Storage and Reclamation Facility. As a result of the type's vulnerability to the elements, F7Us that were sent to Litchfield Park for storage generally had little to no chance of salvation. With the exception of four aircraft, all of NASF's F7Us were stricken from the Navy's register in May 1958, and scrapping commenced shortly thereafter. Only three F7Us managed to leave the NASF: F7U-3Ps BuNos 129754 and 129755, which

F7U-3 survivors – 2023
Whole Airframes
BuNo 129554 – Active restoration to flying condition Cutlass Aeronautics LLC, Falcon Field Mesa, Arizona
BuNo 129565 – Static display USS Midway Museum San Diego California
BuNo 129655 – Static Display National Naval Aviation Museum Pensacola, Florida
BuNo 129642 – Restoration for static display Wings of Freedom Aviation Museum Horsham, Pennsylvania
BuNo 129685 – Restoration for static display MAPS Air Museum North Canton, Ohio
Partial Airframes
BuNo 128451 – Inner wings, ailavator, slat BuNo 128462 – Center section fuselage, inner wing BuNo 129622 – Center section fuselage, cockpit section Cutlass Aeronautics LLC, Falcon Field Mesa, Arizona

were repurposed by the Naval Parachute Unit at El Centro, California (see pages 262-263), and F7U-3 BuNo 129566, which was bailed to Cornell Aeronautical Laboratory for post-stall gyration mitigation tests (see pages 113-114). The -3Ps eventually returned to the NASF's custody in January and March of 1959 for subsequent scrapping, and 129566 was destroyed in situ at Cornell's Buffalo flight facility in late 1959.

In all, 111 F7U-3 series aircraft were stored and eventually scrapped at Litchfield Park, representing 38% of the total airframes delivered. This total consisted of sixty-two of the 180 F7U-3s built, forty-five of the ninety-eight F7U-3Ms constructed, and four of the twelve F7U-3Ps procured. It must be remembered that all 111 of these aircraft were *flown* to Arizona undamaged and fully functional at the time that they were struck from the inventory, some with very few flight hours logged.

Naval Air Reserve Training Units (NAS NARTs and NARTUs)

The Naval Air Reserve Training Units (known as either NAS NART Detachments or NARTUs) were formed at the many Naval Air Stations where Naval Air Reserve squadrons were based to provide on-site training for Naval Reserve aviators, mechanics, and support personnel. In the late 1940s, BuAer came to acknowledge that many of the reserve units soon to be called to action were not proficient in their specialties, and as such operational readiness suffered. Following the armistice in Korea, the formation of NART/NARTUs was intended to breach the gap between regular Navy squadrons and the Naval Reserve. In light of the technological advancements occurring within the fleet, it was difficult to keep line units up to speed with the ever-changing environment, let alone the reserves. As a result, the decision to place recently retired naval aircraft in the custody of the NART/NARTUs was thought to be a fiscally responsible way to bolster the exposure of mechanics and support personnel to the ever-challenging changes reaching the fleet.

With the rapid advancement of aircraft systems, aerodynamics and performance in the 1950s, the F7U-3 was quickly becoming outdated as its service life progressed into late 1956. Systems-wise, the F7U was the most complex Navy aircraft to date, featuring miles of hydraulic lines and electrical harnesses, and very complicated systems found in no other fleet aircraft but a precursor of what was to come. It was thought to be an excellent aircraft for weekend warrior maintainers to learn and practise on, readying them for the future. The presence of a relatively current aircraft type displayed at the local Naval Air Station (which often housed the recruitment office) was considered a secondary benefit of the custody transfers.

Although VA-116 was yet to embark on the last (and very successful) Cutlass deployment with their F7U-3M, the striking of F7U aircraft from the inventory had begun in earnest by August of 1956. Although fast becoming passé performance-wise, the F7U-3's avant-garde design and futuristic appearance was still a harbinger of the coming space age and everything that would come with it. With its tail-less planform, rakish stance, and remarkable aerodynamic agility, the Cutlass represented the future as much in 1956 as it did in 1948. In the daydreams of boys and young men envisioning their future as jet pilots, the Cutlass stood side by side with the North American F-100 and the Lockheed F-104 as the epitome of 1950s aviation 'cool'. It was no surprise that the Navy decided to utilise their soon-to-be obsolete F7Us as recruitment tools, as well as training aids.

Two squadrons would supply the NART detachments and NARTUs with most of the Cutlasses. Both Cecil Field's VA-12 on the east coast and Moffett-based VA-212 were finishing their tour with the F7U-3, and both were planning to transition to their replacement aircraft with little delay. VA-12 transferred ten F7U-3s to NART/NARTUs east of the Mississippi river, while VA-212 transferred seven aircraft to west and Midwest cities following their return from the Far East aboard *Bon Homme Richard*. Along with VA-12 and -212, VA-83 also transferred two aircraft to NART/NARTUs, and two more aircraft came to the reserve units from O&R Norfolk, although their custody never reflected NART/NARTU ownership. All aircraft transfers occurred in April and May 1957, with the last of the deliveries taking place by June.

NAS NART Columbus, Ohio – F7U-3 BuNo 129563. F7U-3 BuNo 129563's custody was transferred to the Naval Air Reserve Training Unit at Columbus, Ohio, from VA-12 on 15 May 1957 with 369 hours on the airframe. Stricken from the inventory in June 1957, the aircraft was not used for maintenance training, but later painted as a roadside billboard advertisement for recruiting naval aviators. Its usefulness waning, the Cutlass was listed for purchase through a government scrap auction. The centre section containing the J46-WE-8B engines was purchased by renowned drag racing and jet-car exhibition driver Fred Sibley of Elkhart, Indiana, in the early 1960s and following his subsequent removal of the engines, the remainder of the aircraft was scrapped.

NAS NART Dallas, Texas – F7U-3M BuNo 139906. Upon their return from *Intrepid*'s Sixth-Fleet Mediterranean deployment, VA-83 readied themselves for the transition to the A4D-1 Skyhawk. Although the majority of their aircraft were flown to NASF Litchfield, two aircraft were transferred to the reserves, with NAS NART Dallas receiving F7U-3M 139906 after amassing only 151 hours of flying time during its service life. Resplendent in VA-83's newly applied, yet short-lived, grey over white scheme, the aircraft was used as a gate guard and recruitment tool at NAS Dallas until it was unceremoniously pushed to the corner of the airfield with a Navy bulldozer. Flipped on its back and heavily damaged, it was eventually scrapped in June 1967.

NAS NART Denver, Colorado – F7U-3 BuNo 129663. Returning from VA-212's Far East deployment aboard *Bon Homme Richard*, F7U-3 BuNo 129663 was retired to NAS Denver's Buckley Field in Colorado. Painted navy blue overall, the Cutlass received large white letters spelling 'DENVER' across its mid-fuselage and bright red warning chevrons in front of the air intakes. The aircraft resided on base as a gate guardian before being towed to Denver's Centennial Park. It quickly became the victim of vandalism, as well as neglect by the city's Parks and Recreation Department. Multiple complaints by concerned parents of children injured on the aircraft resulted in the City of Denver attempting to return the aircraft to the Navy in 1961. This offer was rejected, as NAS Denver had been closed and turned over to the US Air Force on 18 April 1960, becoming Buckley Air National Guard Base. Although the Navy had retained a Naval Air Reserve Facility at the base,

ABOVE A sad end for F7U-3M BuNo 139906, all the more ignominious because it was destroyed virtually within sight of the Vought plant where it was one of the last Cutlasses built. *Photo by Ron Picciani*

BELOW In preparation for its move to Denver's Centennial Park, F7U-3 was adorned with a giant 'DENVER' applied to its mid-fuselage. Prior to the move, the aircraft was entirely painted navy blue except for its IFR probe. *Casby Collection*

After service with NATC, F7U-3P BuNo 129747 was transferred to NAS NART Glenview, Illinois, on 14 May 1957. Tasked with providing the spare parts to keep F7U-3 BuNo 129622 airworthy, F7U-3P 129747 sits forlornly in the parking lot at NAS Glenview on 23 July 1958 along with a Lockheed TV-1 and TV-2 awaiting similar fates. *Casby Collection via Art Kreiger*

they no longer had the ability to display the Cutlass. The aircraft continued to languish in Centennial Park until its removal for scrapping. Rumours persisted that the aircraft was purchased for scrap and moved to a barn in the Buckley area, but to date no substantiating evidence exists in spite of multiple attempts by Casby to locate this Cutlass.

NAS NART Glenview, Illinois – F7U-3 BuNo *129622*/ F7U-3P BuNo 129747. NAS Glenview north of Chicago, Illinois, maintained a robust Naval Air Reserve facility that provided many reserve aviators that lived in the Midwest the ability to keep their skills honed in a variety of propeller and jet aircraft in the mid-1950s. F7U-3 BuNo 129622 was transferred to NAS NART custody on 14 May 1957 following its service in VA-34 and later VA-

BuNo 129622 on the flight line at NAS NART Glenview with LtCol Carl Remmer, one of the F7U-3's few Reserve pilots to fly the aircraft in NART custody. Vought provided the unit with its own field service representative to assist in keeping the aircraft flying. *Casby Collection*

BuNo 129622 being towed into Oaklane Elementary School's playground with an entire class riding on it during simpler times. ***Casby Collection***

12. That same day, F7U-3P BuNo 129747 was transferred to the Reserves from NATC providing Glenview with the distinction of being the only NART facility to have two F7Us in their custody. The photo-Cutlass was soon towed to a grassy area adjacent to the NART ramp, and languished in this spot while acting as a spare parts source for 129622 (the only Naval Air Reserve F7U to continue to be kept in flight status).

BuNo 129622 was delivered to the NART from NAS Cecil Field, Florida, by LCDR Marshal P. Deputy, Jr., the new Commanding Officer of VA-12. He had just recently got checked out in the F7U-3 only to never fly it again due to retraining in the A4D-1 Skyhawk that VA-12 was transitioning to. Shortly thereafter, several Reserve aviators began to sporadically fly 622, including Marine Reserve LTCol Carl Remmer. He had amassed several hours in the aircraft after studying the manuals and speaking with former F7U pilots he knew, and had the most time in the aircraft while in NART custody. Soon, 129622 was no longer able to be maintained due to the unavailability of spare parts and the aircraft became an unflyable fixture on the Glenview tarmac. Used as a backdrop for Boy Scout field trip photos, and infrequently started and taxied during airshows, the Cutlass soon began to show its age after experiencing the Chicago winter exposed to the elements.

On 13 September 1958, a request to the Navy Department at the Pentagon was received from Charles Semel, the president of the Northbrook East Civic Association in Northbrook, Illinois, for an aircraft to be donated for playground recreational use at the city's public Oaklane Elementary School. With F7U-3P 129747 already scrapped at cost to the reserve unit, the 12 November fulfilment of this request was determined to be cost effective over destroying 622's airframe on-base. Still sporting its numeral 3 side number from its VA-12 days, a badly worn radome, and with its internal and external fuel tanks still full, the aircraft was towed by members of the Naval Reserve through the streets of Northbrook in early November 1958 to be placed within the school's playground. Following efforts by members of the Association to mitigate any potential injury sources that proved to be inadequate, the aircraft was towed to the school. Prior to towing it the last 300ft into the playground, the entire third grade class were invited atop the Cutlass with their teacher perched upon the boarding steps adjacent to the canopy, while a member of the Civic Association rode on the left wing. Unfortunately, because of rain and melted snow, the aircraft got stuck in the mud during its initial entrance to the schoolyard despite the prodigious use of boards to prevent the aircraft from sinking. A decision was made to tow the aircraft out of the mud rearward using a borrowed Jeep pick-up from Al Beneventi's nearby Sinclair Service station, which met with mixed results. On 12 November, the ground hardened enough to locate the aircraft in its intended spot, albeit without the initial fanfare or press coverage of the event. The donation did, however, make national news after being picked up by the Associated Press in Chicago's wire office.

Soon after its arrival at Oaklane the injuries to children began to mount, and the school administrators acknowledged that mixing curious elementary school students with an aircraft whose cockpit was 14ft above the ground was a recipe for disaster. The Civic Association requested that the Navy take the aircraft back to Glenview, however the donation was made outright with no legal requirement for the donor to repatriate the Cutlass. As a result, the aircraft was torched apart (still with fuel in its tanks!) and hauled to a field behind the Beneventi service station, where it languished for several years. Its wings and fins were carted off by local scrappers, while the upside-down centre section was obtained by Fred Sibley, the same jet-car campaigner who acquired the remains of the F7U-3 from NARTU Columbus, again for its J46 engines. This left the cockpit section, complete with ejection seat and stripped instrument panel lying on its side in the mud. Famed aircraft collector Earl Reinert acquired the cockpit and moved it to his Victory Air Museum located at Paul Polidori's airstrip in rural Mundelein, Illinois, propping it up with boards to remain erect as a makeshift display. In early 1976, co-author Al Casby (at age 16) learned of the cockpit and purchased it from Reinert, hauling it to his Grosse Pointe Woods, Michigan, home in June, 1977. Two years later, he located the engine-less centre section at Fred Sibley's Elkhart, Indiana, dragster shop and trucked that section home on an imbalanced trailer, which caused the front wheels of his tow vehicle to sporadically leave the ground. The aircraft's remains exist to this day at Casby's Mesa, Arizona, F7U restoration and research facility, and were recently reunited with former Navy LT John 'Jack' Anderson, and retired Navy RADM James 'Mac' Gleim, who both flew BuNo *129622* while it served with VA-34 out of NAS Cecil Field, Florida.

Former VA-34 pilot Jack Anderson visiting the remains of BuNo 129622 at Mesa, Arizona's Cutlass Aeronautics in July 2023. Anderson accumulated eleven flight hours in this F7U-3. *Al Casby Photo*

NARTU Jacksonville, Florida – F7U-3 BuNo 129694. In addition to primary 'A-School' training at the Naval Air Technical Training Center, NAS Jacksonville was also home to the primary F7U-3 Overhaul and Repair (O&R) Facility. As a result, mechanics and pilots in the Naval Air Reserve had the ability to absorb a wealth of knowledge from the co-located units that shared the airfield with them. Jacksonville, Florida's Naval Air Reserve Training Unit, was the busiest of all the reserve facilities on the east coast, and its instructor cadre one of the most experienced.

With 370 hours total on the airframe, F7U-3 BuNo 129694 was transferred to the NARTU on 29 May 1957 from neighbouring NAS Cecil Field's VA-12. Still bearing the squadron's '12' side number, it would be the last of the VA-12 Cutlasses to be transferred and delivered. The aircraft was utilised in the NARTU's advanced hydraulics training shop for a period of two years, ultimately being destroyed in a fire-fighting exercise in June 1959.

NAS NART Lincoln, Nebraska – F7U-3 BuNo 129629. On 19 May 1957, following the culmination of VA-212's Far East deployment aboard *Bon Homme Richard*, F7U-3 BuNo 129629 was flown by LTJG Albert L. Evans to the Naval Air Reserve Training Facility at NAS Lincoln, Nebraska, and retired with 318 hours on the airframe. Although relieved of its VA-212 squadron markings, the aircraft retained LT Carl 'Tex' Birdwell's name below the canopy rail. Shortly after arrival, the aircraft was donated to the Nebraska State Trade School and trucked to its campus in Milford, Nebraska. Displayed proudly in a grassy field at the intersection of Highway 6 and State Street, the Cutlass soon became the target of vandals and souvenir collectors and was deemed a hazard to the public. It was reported to have been dissected and hauled back to Lincoln, where it languished in a railway yard until eventually being scrapped in the late 1970s.

NAS NART Los Alamitos, California – F7U-3 BuNo *129655*. VA-212's F7U-3 BuNo 129655 was the second squadron F7U-3 to wear the '210' side number after BuNo 129597 (the original '210') was retired to FASRon-10. When BuNo 129676 (the first '201' side number nominally assigned to the squadron's commanding officer, LCDR Douglas Hagood), was ditched off Oahu early during its deployment aboard CVA-31, 129655 was repainted as the replacement with the '201' side number. The aircraft was retired on 29 April 1957 and flown to the Reserve Training detachment at NAS Los Alamitos on 30 May 1957 with a total of 414 hours on the airframe. It was subsequently stricken from the inventory one month later on 30 June 1957. After sitting forlornly at Los Alamitos for years, the aircraft was offered to the city of Los Angeles in February 1961

Still retaining VA-212's LT Carl 'Tex' Birdwell's name under the canopy, F7U-3 BuNo 129629 resides on the ramp in the custody of NAS-NART Lincoln, Nebraska. Note the lighter variation in the grey paint on the upper sections of the fins and under the canopy where VA-212's markings were painted out. This aircraft was eventually moved for display to Milford, Nebraska. *Casby Collection*

for display in Los Angeles' Travel Town Museum at Griffith Park.

While displayed in a fenced in circular gravel setting, the aircraft received multiple repaints and eventually was painted white overall. Interestingly, someone at the Parks Department took the time to research the aircraft's history, and reapplied the 'G' tail code of CVG-21, as well as the '201' side number in VA-212's unique location for their side numbers.

On 15 March 1985, Aero Associates, a private aircraft restoration firm, received authorisation to acquire the Cutlass in return for an AT-6 Texan trainer. The Board of Recreation and Park Commissioners felt that the training plane would attract visitors enamoured with the recently released motion picture *Swing Shift*, which featured the aircraft. In 1987 the Cutlass was removed from the park and transported to Paladin Aircraft located at Brown Field, south of San Diego, California. Restoration began in 1988 with stripping of its paint at Paladin and the preliminary re-skinning of the wings taking place in Tehachapi, California. This unfortunately was first completed using bugle-headed drywall screws (!) and sheet steel, and had to be redone. The refurbishment was completed and the aircraft reportedly traded to the Naval Aviation Museum (now the National Naval Aviation Museum) in Pensacola,

BuNo 129655 shared space with several aircraft and trains as part of the Travel Town Transportation display in Griffith Park, California. *Casby Collection via Aric Aldrich*

BuNo 129655 on display at the National Naval Aviation Museum at NAS Pensacola, Florida, the exceptional view downward over the nose very apparent from this angle. ***Don Hinton Photo***

Florida, in return for three flyable T-28 Trojans. With over-the-road transport to Florida deemed to be too expensive, the Cutlass was loaded on a sea-going barge for transport through the Panama Canal to the Gulf of Mexico. During the voyage, the barge fell victim to a Pacific squall and heavy seas, resulting in the aircraft breaking loose from several of its tie downs. Arriving in Pensacola damaged from the voyage, 129655 sat awaiting re-restoration to enable display in the museum. Following restorative work completed by NAS Pensacola's Naval Air Rework Facility, the Cutlass took its spot in the museum, unfortunately mis-marked as a F7U-3M and sporting auxiliary fuel tanks that are incorrect for the type. Although representational, the cockpit was populated with a single throttle, filler instruments, and a gunsight not correct for the Cutlass – it is unwittingly utilised as a reference by enthusiasts and modellers to this day. It is hoped that NNAM will eventually correct the mis-identification and apply an appropriate squadron livery to the airframe.

NARTU Memphis, Tennessee – F7U-3 BuNo 129669. BuNo 129699 was transferred to NARTU Memphis based at NAS Memphis, Millington, Tennessee, on 22 May 1957 from VA-12. The aircraft was stricken from the inventory a day later with 435 flight hours. Retaining VA-12's side number '1', the NARTU applied an international-orange reserve stripe around the rear fuselage with 'MEMPHIS' displayed proudly within, as well as the stations '6M' tail code applied to the fins. The engines were often started for ground run operational training, and the aircraft was reportedly used by NARTU instructors for mechanic taxi phase training. BuNo 129669 was often towed to the flight line for static display at airshows until deemed surplus to the NARTU's needs and scrapped in the station's burn pit.

NARTU Miami, Florida – F7U-3 BuNo 129616. Marine Corps Air Station Miami at Opa-locka, Florida, was host to the NARTU as an on-base tenant located on the station's Master Field. Although the Marines transferred their operations to MCAS El Toro and NAS Jacksonville in 1958–59, the NARTU continued to serve reservists until the Navy transferred the airfield facilities to the

BuNo 129669, another former VA-12 F7U-3, was routinely exercised (but not flown) for a few years by NARTU Memphis for hands-on mechanic ground operation training before finally being scrapped. ***Casby Collection***

After being stricken, F7U-3 BuNo 129549 initially served as a billboard for naval aviation recruiting at NAS Twin Cities, Minneapolis, before its closure. The Cutlass was then abandoned and subsequently scrapped. ***Casby Collection***

City of Opa-locka, Florida. On 22 May 1957, F7U-3 BuNo 129616 was transferred to the NARTU from VA-12 and was subsequently struck off charge seven days later after accumulating 414 hours on the airframe. The aircraft was placed on a grassy triangular-shaped yard adjacent to the NARTU facility until orders to transfer the administrative component of the Miami reserve facility to nearby Ft Lauderdale were received in early 1959. The Cutlass was scrapped on site, however its fuselage was retained by the civilian metal recycler as an advertising prop until being smelted in 1962.

NAS NART Minneapolis, Minnesota – F7U-3 129549. As one of the most photographed F7U-3s during early flight testing of the type, F7U-3 BuNo 129549 later went on to serve with VX-5, VF-212, and VA-212 before being transferred to the NART detachment at NAS Twin Cities in Minneapolis, Minnesota. Flown to Minnesota by LTJG Conrad B. 'Connie' Olson from NAS Moffett Field, California, on 27 May 1957 following VA-212's return from its Far East deployment, BuNo 129549 reached 399 flight hours upon its arrival at the reserve unit, after making four intermediate stops for fuel. Still in its grey over white scheme from VA-212 service, with 'LT Bruce Cobb' stencilled under the canopy, the aircraft was initially painted with an oversized '0' side number on its nose, as well as a reddish-orange reserve stripe aft of the intakes encircling the entire fuselage with 'MINNEAPOLIS' displayed in the band. Additionally, it now carried a recruiting advertisement – 'Fly with the Navy' emblazoned on the underside of its folded outer wings. Utilised as a backdrop for recruiters' enlistee photos as well as airshow static display, the aircraft's original paint was beginning to wear by the mid-1960s. The aircraft was repainted in grey over white with red teardrop intakes and bright red lightning bolts on its fins and was repositioned off the NART tarmac to occupy a grassy area at the entrance to the base. Upon closure of NAS Twin Cities, the Cutlass's engines were purchased by a local farmer for use as corn-driers and were cut out of the aircraft for removal. The eviscerated F7U was towed to a ravine located on what was now the Minneapolis Metropolitan Airport Authority's property and left to rot for years, becoming a plaything for local youths who made their way over, under, or through the airport's perimeter fence. Fearing an eventual liability claim as well as a security threat, the Authority cut the aircraft up and sold its remains as scrap metal to a local recycler in the early 1970s.

NAS NART New York, New York – F7U-3 BuNo 129650. NAS New York's Floyd Bennett Field in New York City's south-east Brooklyn borough was home to the largest Naval Air Reserve Facility in the United States. They received F7U-3 BuNo 129650 from VA-12 following its retirement with 305 total hours flown on 18 May 1957. Still wearing its entire VA-12 livery (minus the 'T' tail code), it was initially chocked at the edge of the base's parking lot, jutting out over the Oldsmobiles, Nashes, and Buicks belonging to the sailors and civilians who occupied the hangar complex. The aircraft deteriorated over the years and was eventually moved off the asphalt into a grassy area, where its tyres soon began to sink into the ground. Its intended purpose as a

One of several VA-12 Cutlasses distributed to NARTs, in this case at Floyd Bennett Field, New York. NART New York relegated BuNo 129650 to its parking lot, where it languished before being unceremoniously scrapped. *Casby Collection via Roger Besecker*

training aid never materialising, the aircraft soon began to lose access panels through being vandalised despite being 'displayed' aboard base. It was subsequently deemed to be an eyesore and reduced to scrap.

NAS NART Niagara Falls, New York – F7U-3 BuNo 129579. BuNo 129579 was delivered to NAS Niagara Falls on 9 May 1957 by a pilot from VA-12. The pilot declared three emergencies en route due to a faulty hydraulic system warning light. However, each time he prepared to divert to a nearby suitable landing field, the problem disappeared and he pressed on. Arriving in Niagara Falls with 193 total flight hours on the airframe, the aircraft was soon adorned with 'NAS Niagara Falls' on its fin tips in place of the VA-12 squadron insignia. It retained VA-12's blue rudder and wing tip trim, as well as the squadron's lightning bolt motif on the canopy and the side number '13'. When it was not displayed in a small park setting aboard the base, the Cutlass was a common static display sight at annual airshows until November 1958, when it was gifted to the Penfield, New York Recreational Commission. The Cutlass was towed on its own tyres behind a semi-tractor from Niagara Falls to the 'New Panorama Plaza of Penfield' located just outside of Rochester, New York, on 23 December 1958. During its trip on the New York Thruway, a frantic call was received by the Batavia, New York Police Department from a woman travelling across an overpass as the

This VA-12 F7U-3 BuNo 129579 was ferried to NAS Niagara Falls as its final resting place. It was quickly personalised with 'NAS Niagara Falls' on the fin tips in place of the VA-12 squadron insignia as well as the standard Navy Reserve markings on the aft fuselage and eventually displayed in a park-like setting adjacent to the air field. *Casby Collection*

NAS NART Niagara Falls' BuNo 129579 being towed on the New York Thruway between Batavia and LeRoy, New York, on 23 December 1958. Note the partially folded wings to allow overpass clearance, as well as the fully deployed speed brakes! *Casby Collection*

partially snow-covered Cutlass made its way towards LeRoy, New York. She stated that 'a jet plane just crashed on the thruway, right under me!' and set off a multi-department search for the crash scene. The aircraft was displayed at the shopping mall – becoming a canvas for artistic vandals – and was eventually cut apart and removed.

NARTU Norfolk, Virginia – F7U-3M BuNo 139907. F7U-3M 139907 came to NARTU Norfolk directly from neighbouring NAS Oceana-based VA-83 upon their retirement of the type and transition to the A4D-1 Skyhawk. Still wearing its '304' side number, the grey over white airframe only accumulated eighty-seven hours of flight time prior to being struck off charge. Essentially a new aircraft, the Cutlass was displayed for a short time in its old VA-83 livery before receiving what is probably the wildest paint scheme to ever grace an F7U. The aircraft was painted overall dark blue, with a white radome that transitioned into white-outlined red flames! The air intakes were similarly adorned with red flames licking back to the wing leading edges, as well as a white scalloped wave motif on the leading edges of the fins. Bright red rudders and wing tips completed this 'hot rod' Cutlass, and it was displayed with bare aluminium wing pylons and belly-mounted rocket pack. Often seen equipped with two red and white Tiny Tim air-to-ground rockets on its inner pylons, this F7U-3M sat on the Norfolk ramp at least until mid-1959, when it is assumed that it was eventually scrapped on site.

Photographed in September 1958, F7U-3M BuNo 139907 sits on the ramp at NAS Norfolk, Virginia, sporting what is probably the wildest 'Hot Rod' paint scheme ever applied to a Cutlass. Seen here with Tiny Tim rockets under its wings, the aircraft was a fixture on the Norfolk flight line for a couple of years. *Photo by George H Stewart via Casby Collection*

NAS NART Oakland's BuNo 129555 sits forlornly on the pierced steel planking ramp mat after delivery from VA-212. Named to LTJG 'Moose' Auer, the aircraft has had its squadron markings painted out, but still displays the black parel-keytone anti-corrosion coating applied to its landing gear. With the canopy left open to the Bay area's weather, the aircraft deteriorated rapidly. *Doug Olson Photo via the CasbyCollection*

NAS NART Oakland, California – F7U-3 BuNo 129555. With 368 hours logged on the airframe, VA-212 flew BuNo 129555 on its short hop across the bay to NAS Oakland, California, from Moffett Field on 1 May 1957 following their return from the Far East. The aircraft had its squadron markings painted over by 212's mechanics prior to delivery to Oakland's 'Weekend Warriors'. Initially placed in a parking lot adjacent to the NART detachment's hangar, the aircraft was often moved to the ramp area during open house activities. It was scrapped in the early 1960s.

NAS NART Olathe, Kansas – F7U-3 BuNo *129565*. If any F7U Cutlass can lay claim to being the most abused, it is BuNo 129565**.** After returning from the deployment aboard *Bon Homme Richard,* VA-212's F7U-3 BuNo *129565* was flown on 19 May 1957 to NAS Olathe, Kansas, just outside the Kansas City metropolitan area. The aircraft sat until October of 1960, when the city of Olathe desired to place the jet in their newly built Navy Air Park at the corner of Harrison Street and US Route 56. Craned onto three low-height steel-reinforced concrete pylons, the Cutlass was marked as 'The City of Olathe' and dedicated as 'a stepping stone into space'. In 1965 it was joined by a retired F-6A Skyray BuNo 134963 (an aircraft that was flown extensively from Olathe) in the city's now-decaying recreation spot.

As years passed, both aircraft suffered the wrath of vandals and weather. On 17 August 1977 Olathe's City Manager Lee Brodbeck received a letter from the Naval Air Systems Command advising that President of the United States Jimmy Carter had received a complaint call on his recently instituted 'hot line' from a local Olathe woman regarding the 'unsightly and dangerous condition' of the two aircraft. The city was admonished to either repair the aircraft or dispose of them. Unable to afford the funds for repairs, the city requested that the Navy dispose of the aircraft, to which the Navy responded by instructing the city to 'demilitarise' the Cutlass and deliver it to Richards Gebaur AFB. Considered to not be of 'historical value' and with pressure mounting from the White House, the Skyray was transported by an Army National Guard Chinook helicopter to the Smokey Hill Air Force Bombing range near Salina, Kansas, and was slated for destruction, with the Cutlass seemingly next in line for the trip to oblivion. With no funding for the destruction, much less the transport, Brodbeck offered the F7U to the Naval Aviation Museum; however, after inspection the Museum rejected the Cutlass in early December 1978.

BuNo 129565 being moved from south Olathe, Kansas, several miles east to the Johnson County Airport in early 1979. *Casby Collection*

Co-author Al Casby, pictured here with BuNo 129565, attempted to acquire it in February 1986, but was advised that the Navy was once again interested in obtaining it, thwarting his efforts. ***Casby Collection***

Fortunately, Joseph Dennis, the Executive Director of the Johnson County Industrial Airport (formerly NAS Olathe, which was decommissioned in 1969), then requested that it acquire the Cutlass for display in its Navy Park, a 3-acre on-airport parcel commemorating Olathe's naval history, which was approved. The F7U-3 was removed from its pylon supports the following spring and transported by truck to the park, where a team of volunteers encapsulated the aircraft in fibreglass cloth and resin. It was then painted overall grey with the Olathe '7K' tail code.

Placed on display within Navy Park, the Cutlass looked strange in its cocoon of polyester; its appearance made worse by the awkward positioning of its nose landing gear leg pointing forward instead of aft. As time progressed, the wisdom of covering the entire aircraft in a plastic shell proved to be ill advised, as the hot and humid Midwest environment caused the aircraft's skin (especially the magnesium panels) to badly corrode from the inside out. Once again, the aircraft needed work with funding unavailable.

Once again, a solution presented itself. Roy Stafford, partner in Black Shadow Aviation in Jacksonville, Florida, offered to trade a presentable A-7 Corsair II for the Cutlass with the intention of restoring it for the Naval Aviation Museum. Stafford was intimately involved with restoring aircraft for the museum, rescuing many basket case airframes (e.g. an F2H-2P Banshee filled with concrete as a children's park attraction) and turning them into museum-worthy jewels. His offer was accepted and 129565 moved by SECO Aviation to Jacksonville. At that point, however, it turned out that the museum had already been in talks with Aero Associates to acquire BuNo 129655 from Griffith Park, California. With no museum contract imminent, it was advertised for sale in Trade-A-Plane (an aircraft-themed classified paper) for $50,000. Due to a lack of interest, the Cutlass remained a fixture for years in the mid-1990s classified ads.

Eventually the Cutlass found a new owner and was taken west to the Santa Rosa Airport in California to be restored for display on the carrier *Hornet*, now a museum ship berthed at the former NAS Alameda docks. William 'Bill' Montegue, an ex-VA-151 F7U-3 pilot, had been instrumental in providing the sponsorship funding for the restoration, as well as the drive to get it completed. Unfortunately, those plans evaporated with the passing of Mr Montegue, and the aircraft was once again without a home.

The Vought Aircraft Heritage Foundation (VAHF), a tax-exempt entity that was involved in the restoration of Vought products through the efforts of members of the Vought Retirees Club, acquired the Cutlass with the intention to restore it for the USS Midway Museum in San Diego, California. Trucked to Hensley Field in Grand Prairie, Texas (the site of the very factory where it was built), 129565 had returned home – for a while. Work commenced on its restoration with the removal of all the fibreglass covering its skin, and was moving along well when the VAHF received word that they were soon to lose their workshop space. With the spectre of having to move all their projects with nowhere to put them, the Cutlass was once again trucked to San Diego's Coronado Island and the NAS North Island home of *Midway*'s aircraft restoration facility. The aircraft's fuselage and wings were placed on wooden cradles along with the remains of prototype F7U-3 BuNo 128451. It sat there for years enduring the salt-ridden coastal air against its now-bare skin, exacerbating the degradation of the magnesium and Metalite panels.

TOP BuNo 129565 at Vought undergoing restoration at the Vought Aircraft Heritage Foundation's hangar in Grand Prairie, Texas, in November 2017. The condition of the airframe suffered beneath the fibreglass coating it received, requiring copious amount of plastic filler to retain its shape. ***Bill Spidle***

ABOVE LEFT Following its last trip to NAS North Island, 129565 is finally completed for display on board the USS Midway Museum's deck. ***Al Casby photo***

ABOVE RIGHT BuNo 129565, now aboard the USS Midway Museum, displayed in the markings of BuNo 128454 except for the aircraft's correct BuNo and Walter Schirra's name on the canopy sill (misspelled as of September 2023 when the photo was taken). In addition, from a configuration standpoint – e.g. sliding canopy shape, engine intakes, cannon installation – it is also not an exact representation of BuNo 128454. ***Clifford Bossie photo***

Now deteriorated even more, it was returned to the VAHF following their securement of a new facility and its restoration work started in earnest. Following completion of the stripping and removal of all unnecessary components, the aircraft had its major flaws refinished with Bondo filler and was partially primed for paint. It was once again transported back to San Diego with the anticipation that the finish work by the Midway Museum's volunteers would take place quickly. Unfortunately, this did not occur and the aircraft once again sat exposed to the elements causing filler to expand and pop, as well as bare aluminium and magnesium panels to begin to corrode once more.

In 2022, sixty-two years after being placed in Olathe's Navy Air Park, BuNo 129565's restoration was finally completed. Dedicated volunteers had worked tirelessly to finish the aircraft, surmounting setback after setback. Hoisted aboard the USS Midway Museum at Navy Pier in San Diego on 14 December 2022, the aircraft took its place on the flight deck with much fanfare to represent F7U-3 BuNo 128454, which was used to accomplish the type's first at-sea carrier suitability testing aboard *Midway* in 1952. It is painted dull silver overall for corrosion protection rather than being primarily unpainted.

NAS NART St Louis, Missouri – F7U-3 BuNo 129680. VA-12's F7U-3 BuNo 129680 was flown to Lambert Field and transferred to the Naval Reserve on 12 May 1957. With complete VA-12 markings minus the tail code, the Cutlass inexplicably had its type designator and Bureau Number covered with black paint. It was towed to a field adjacent to a base operations building and left with the canopy open through two consecutive winters, also sustaining damage to its rudders. When the Naval Air Reserve base at St Louis closed, the aircraft (along with an F2H-1) was repositioned outside the base gate and abandoned. Reportedly towed across town for display at the Jefferson Barracks National Cemetery Park, the aircraft was removed and scrapped in the mid-1960s due to the inability to adequately maintain it.

NAS NART South Weymouth, Massachusetts – F7U-3 BuNo *129685*. F7U-3 BuNo 129685 was retired by VA-12 on 10 May 1957 and flown to NAS NART South Weymouth, Massachusetts, by LT William Doody. Still wearing most of its squadron livery, the aircraft was stricken with 299 hours flown. A fixture on base for years, eventually it was deemed to be in the way and fast becoming no longer display worthy. The aircraft was towed to a grassy basin and let to deteriorate. Following removal of any equipment that the Reserve detachment deemed usable, the Cutlass was placed on the auction block in a Defense Supply Agency (DSA) sale of obsolete equipment and scrap metal. Walter Soplata, a Newbury, Ohio, collector (and saviour of obsolete surplus military aircraft in imminent danger of being scrapped) became aware of the Cutlass from the 1962 DSA catalogue listing the F7U-3 as part of the scrap metal the base wished to rid itself of. With a mail-in bid of $200, Soplata became the owner of an 18,000lb aircraft that he was now responsible for moving to his home in Ohio. Driving a dilapidated, yet functional 1945 White Motors surplus school bus he had acquired and used in the past as a camper, as well as a makeshift parts bin, Soplata set off alone for New England with plans to retrieve the aircraft. With hardly enough money for fuel and food, Soplata was initially rebuffed by the yard managers overseeing the loading of the auction lots. Requesting both a performance bond, as well as liability insurance, they refused to allow him to start the process of dismantling the Cutlass. In addition, the Navy required that he demilitarise the aircraft (mutilate to prevent the possibility of future flight). After much hand-wringing, the Naval Officers at South Weymouth agreed to Soplata's plan to torch various parts of the aircraft to preclude it ever flying again, and offered the use of a dozen Navy mechanics and their equipment to assist Soplata with the disassembly.

With the Cutlasses' size far in excess of what he initially thought, Soplata was forced to completely torch off the back section of his bus, and cut a large slot in the roof – the plan being to ram the aircraft nose first into the bus for transport, with the wings and fins set upon a home-built trailer that he had towed with him. Once the aircraft had been crammed into the school bus, bulging out its sides, it hung out the back over 10ft, precluding the use of the trailer – a second trip (and eventually third) would be required. A drive of a lifetime ensued, with Soplata being stopped by the police for bald tyres, no lights, oversize load, etc, each time being threatened with seizure of the vehicle and arrest. Eventually he made it to Newbury and returned to New England two more times to retrieve the wings and fins. Soplata and his family were then tasked with reassembling the F7U. Using a makeshift set of jacks, bomb hoists, and pole winches, the tenacious Soplata was able to get it back together and on its gear.

Following Walter's death in November of 2010, the fate of his massive collection of recovered aircraft was in limbo. Eventually, sales of the collection's aircraft began and the Cutlass was one of the last to go.

TOP BuNo 129680 before it was virtually abandoned by NART and then evicted from NAS St Louis. Note the damaged rudder and the nose wheel turned 180 degrees after the nose gear scissors link was disconnected for towing. ***Casby Collection***

ABOVE BuNo 129685 proudly displayed at an NAS South Weymouth air show in the golden years of its retirement. ***Tom Cuddy***

PROJECT AND PROJECT ENGINEERS (left to right) Emile H. Jacobs Jr., ADRC; Cmdr. Howard M. Mellblom, Aircraft Maintenance Officer; Walter Soplata, "Cutlass" purchaser; Cmdr. John S. Kuhn; and LT. Cmdr. Wallace E. Miller, pose before the F7U "Cutlass" prior to its disassembly and last ride.

HEADED IN—after removal of the final obstacle, the balky right wing which resisted practically all attempts for removal, the fuselage is started into the cutaway rear of the bus.

bus . . . ?! "Why not?" asked Walter Soplata, part-time aircraft collector who runs an aircraft museum on his 17-acre Newbury, Ohio farm, and who purchased the station's obsolete jet fighter to add to his collection.

And, Walter proceeded to prove to station skeptics it could be done. Of course, it is doubtful his 20-year-old ex-school bus will ever see the highways again, but he did it. The final thrust, which jammed the jet's 30-odd foot fuselage into the bus, peeled the vehicle open like a ripe banana.

During his stay aboard the station, de-militarizing and preparing the aircraft for transportation, Walter slept on a mattress in the schoolbus and cooked his meals on a kerosene stove at the front of the bus.

Navy help was rendered to Walter in readying the Cutlass for its final trip and the man, his hobby and his methods never ceased to amaze all who worked with him.

He expects to have the complete Cutlass (he has several parts-trips yet to make) at his museum before the end of the summer.

Walter's free-of-charge open-air museum presently boasts nine military aircraft and more than 40 aircraft engines on display. Included are an F-82 fighter and a C-82 (R4Q) "Flying Boxcar" transport. He also has hopes for a B-52 bomber.

Walter departed the station with his weird (to say the least) vehicle and cargo on Sunday, April 1.

In a recent letter, received by Cmdr. John S. Kuhn, of the Aircraft Maintenance Dept., Walter stated he was stopped and fined *eight times* between South Weymouth and his Ohio destination . . . *not a bit surprising!*

NOT A SPECTACULAR CRASH . . . just a completely disassembled F7U "Cutlass".

AND IT IS DONE! With the scraping, screeching, grinding sounds of metal giving way under extreme stress, the "Cutlass" is jammed into Walter's old school bus, which peeled open like a ripe banana. ("How Now?" we wonder, in contemplating Walter's removal of the plane at his Newbury, Ohio museum.)

Walter Soplata was never deterred by the degree of difficulty involved in moving one of his acquisitions back to his farm in Ohio. ***Weymouth Warrior, April 1962***

Acquired on 20 November 2021 by the MAPS Museum located at Ohio's Akron-Canton Airport, Walter Soplata's F7U-3 has found a good home. The aircraft is slated for restoration to static display condition.

NAS NART Spokane, Washington – F7U-3 BuNo *129554*. VA-212's F7U-3 BuNo 129554 was one of two replacement aircraft in the squadron (the other was 129565), and upon the unit's return from its Far East deployment this aircraft was transferred to the custody of the Reserve training detachment at NAS Spokane, Washington, on 11 May 1957. Delivered to Spokane's Geiger Field by LT John Rademacher on a two-hour flight with a stop at Mountain Home AFB, Idaho, for fuel, the aircraft landed with 245 total flight hours logged. Leaking hydraulic fluid had presented Rademacher with a hydraulic low-pressure light as he landed. The aircraft was slated to be a maintenance training aid for the Naval Reserves, however, NAS Spokane was preparing to be closed and the facilities turned over to the USAF shortly thereafter.

Meanwhile, Leonard Berryman, an enterprising civil engineer working on the new Chief Joseph Dam project near tiny Bridgeport, Washington, was concerned over the risks taken by town children as they played near the turbulent Columbia river. He decided to spearhead an effort to build a park that the youngsters could play safely in. As was the norm in the 1950s, an aircraft was the playground fixture that every town's parks department desired. Outside of the initial transportation costs, often borne by the government, the acquisition of a surplus aircraft not only pleased the city's manager, but inspired the youth that would soon fly it in their daydreams. Berryman started writing letters in 1954 to the Department of Defense seeking a surplus jet for his park project, envisioning a T-33. In 1956 he was notified that the Navy had a couple of small ships (!) that were available, but obviously the town had no way to transport them.

A year later a jet had become available and was located within a reasonable distance. Berryman drove to NAS Spokane to inspect the aircraft, and as he

Even more amazing than his ability to disassemble his acquisitions for transport with minimal tools and equipment was that Soplata could reassemble them given the crude methods he used to prepare them for the trip. Perched high atop BuNo 129685 in 1983 on a visit to Soplata's collection, author Casby envisioned the day he would own his own Cutlass. *Edward Casby photo*

approached the main gate noticed a huge grey and white Navy fighter. He could only imagine what it would take to move something like that! It wasn't until an officer at Spokane drove him up to that very aircraft and advised him that it was now his that he began to get nervous. A mechanic climbed into the F7U-3 and started both engines, as the officer asked him where he wanted the aircraft delivered, and asked, 'Where is your pilot?' Explaining that Bridgeport didn't even have an airport, Berryman soon realised the enormity of the task that lay ahead. After directing the engines to be shut down, the officer advised Berryman of the Navy's impending relocation, and pointed to an FG-1D Corsair parked off to the side of the airfield; 'You can have that one too!' Overwhelmed by the spectre of having to move not only one huge jet, but now another aircraft, Berryman

Transported to the Akron-Canton airport, BuNo 129685 will finally get refurbished back to presentable static display condition by the restoration team at the MAPS Museum. *Casby Collection*

BuNo 129554 seen at the Berryman Park and War Memorial in the late 1980s. The high desert environment allowed this F7U-3 to survive with little corrosion. *Casby Collection*

Thomas Cathcart made some progress in restoring BuNo 129554 to a flightworthy status. *Casby Collection*

F7U-3 BuNo 129554 in its new home at Cutlass Aeronautics in Mesa, Arizona. *Al Casby*

returned to Bridgeport with the 'good' news. The town had no money allocated for the transport of the aircraft, so Berryman began a six-month long fund-raising campaign to raise the $900 necessary to cover the transport costs. He arranged donations of time and equipment, tirelessly writing letters and making phone calls seeking support. When it came time to finally effect the move, another problem arose. The Washington State Highway Department rejected Berryman's request to haul the aircraft down the wide, flat state highway, causing him to seek permission from four individual counties for permits to utilise narrow, tree-lined county roadways. With permits in hand, the Beardmore Transfer company trucked the planes through the back roads of eastern Washington, arriving at Bridgeport at 7am on Friday, 23 May 1958.

In 1970, co-author Al Casby, (at age 11) learned of the existence of the aircraft from letters received from Arthur Schoeni, Chance Vought's retired Public Relations Director and photographer of most period photographs of the F7Us at Vought. Casby began a letter writing campaign to Bridgeport's city fathers in the attempt to acquire the aircraft – promising the city everything that an 11-year old boy could not possibly produce. Although his offers and pleadings went unfulfilled with multiple mayors and city council members, the effort to acquire this Cutlass for restoration to airworthy condition became his life's goal.

The two aircraft sat virtually unknown to most aviation enthusiasts until restorer David Tallichet learned of the Corsair in 1976 and needed it for use in the *Baa Baa Black Sheep* weekly television series. The Corsair was traded to Tallichet for a piece of playground equipment. Years later, Thomas Cathcart, Director of Restoration at Seattle's Museum of Flight, was flying over central Washington and spotted the Cutlass along with an F-86D that had joined it on display. Intrigued by the find, he began the process of negotiation to acquire the aircraft, eventually trading a Piasecki H-21B helicopter for the F7U. Working on the aircraft on weekends, Cathcart provided electrical power to the Cutlass, and using the auxiliary hydraulic pump easily folded both wings, opened and closed the speed brakes and canopy, and marvelled as everything in the cockpit came to life. On 14 June 1992, Cathcart moved the Cutlass to an old B-17 hangar located at Ephrata, Washington, to begin the process of stripping the paint and performing landing gear swing tests. Eventually it was moved again to the Museum of Flight's restoration facility at Paine Field near Everett, Washington, where Cathcart began the process of restoring the Cutlass to airworthy condition. A run-up of both engines was performed, with the J46s reaching all normal operating parameters without a hitch.

Although much work was completed, the restoration soon slowed and the aircraft became a hangar conversation fixture for the next twenty-two years. In 2014, Al Casby approached Cathcart with an offer to purchase the aircraft after seeing it placed for sale on multiple platforms. A deal was struck, and Casby obtained the very aircraft that he had sought since age 11. Five years progressed as he determined the best way to transport the aircraft to his Mesa, Arizona, home base. Ruling out travel by barge and helicopter, as well as

ABOVE As of the end of 2023, 129554 is undergoing full restoration to flight status at Cutlass Aeronautics at Falcon Field in Mesa, Arizona. The aircraft is being fully stripped, inspected, and repainted internally. *Al Casby photo*

BELOW BuNo 129642, one the most photographed of any F7U-3 survivor, was on display for years at NAS Willow Grove. *Mike Wilson Collection*

airborne transport by Antonov, Beluga, and Guppy large-load transport aircraft, he contracted with Chuck Mosely's All Coast Aircraft Recovery to bring the aircraft to the desert south-west. On 29 September 2019, seventy-one years after the first official flight of the prototype XF7U-1, Casby and his crew set out on a thirteen-day, $143,000 move of his aircraft to Arizona. F7U-3 BuNo 129554 is currently being restored for flight at Casby's Cutlass Aeronautics restoration facility and museum in Mesa, Arizona.

NAS NART Willow Grove, Pennsylvania – F7U-3 BuNo *129642*. Flown to NAS Willow Grove, Pennsylvania, on Thursday, 9 May 1957, F7U-3 BuNo 129642 took part in an annual airshow as a static exhibit the following weekend. Its service life over with a total of 326 hours on its airframe, the Cutlass became a part of an impressive display of aircraft kept on the base by the Naval Reserve, including some ultra-rarities such as a German Me 262, Arado Ar 196, and Convair XF2Y-1 Sea Dart. One of the most photographed of all surviving Cutlasses, the aircraft was easily visible from the adjacent thoroughfare and always attracted a bevy of admirers. Although one of only two complete F7U-3s (both externally and internally with the exception of a couple instruments pilfered over the years), the aircraft has suffered the wrath of time and inclement weather. A botched re-skinning of the upper wing surfaces was effected by Naval Reserve personnel that included pop-riveting sheet metal over the upper wing surfaces, trapping moisture that exacerbated the Metalite's decay. Originally displaying its complete VA-12 markings (minus 'T' tail code), it has seen multiple repaints over the years that have actually trapped moisture – coupled with the weather extremes this has caused delamination of its wing skins and corrosion of its magnesium surfaces.

Upon closure of the Naval Air Station, after a long, arduous hiatus, the displayed aircraft were loaned by the National Naval Aviation Museum to the Delaware Valley Historical Aircraft Association. As of 2023, this Cutlass is in storage awaiting refurbishment. When ready for display again, it will be returned across the field to the Harold F. Pitcairn Wings of Freedom Aviation Museum.

Before the decision was made that the F7U-3 was to be a one-tour aircraft, some were overhauled to like-new condition and configuration. This is BuNo 129684 at NAS Miramar on 13 February 1956, three days after its delivery to VA-126 from O&R San Diego. Freshly painted in light gull grey over insignia white, it awaits its squadron markings to be applied. Note the unique use of Corogard on the tip of the underwing auxiliary fuel tank. *Casby Collection via Doug Olson*

Overhaul and Repair (O&R) facilities

The primary mission of the Overhaul and Repair Facilities (O&Rs) was to return damaged aircraft and those in need of overhaul back to operational readiness, either by repairing damage incurred during use or accomplishing a periodic update/overhaul. The designation of primary repair facilities for the F7U series was an exception to the 'Base Loading' concept instituted in 1954 that assigned bases (and their tenants) specific fleet aircraft mission types. On the west coast, for example, Miramar was the centre for fighter aircraft, Alameda was to handle attack aircraft, while NAS North Island in San Diego was to concentrate on patrol and anti-submarine types. However, North Island's O&R San Diego, not Miramar or Alameda, would handle the entire Pacific fleet's major repairs and overhauls on the Cutlass. Likewise, it was NAS Quonset Point that was originally planned as the F7U's east coast repair facility, but BuAer decided that the Atlantic fleet repair responsibilities for the type be split between Norfolk and Jacksonville (both heavy multi-engine bases), ostensibly to facilitate parts acquisition and transfers between the two, as well as being close to Naval Air Stations Oceana and Cecil Field respectively – both home to multiple F7U squadrons.

Unlike the dedicated mission of the NASF, many O&Rs found themselves taking on an unaccustomed storage role due to the fiscal decision to strike Cutlasses off charge instead of overhauling or repairing them following the decision to classify the F7U as a 'one-tour' aircraft type. Some aircraft transferred to O&R custody were also unrepairable due to accident damage or excessive wear beyond overhaul capabilities. These aircraft were unable to be ferried to NASF Litchfield, causing the O&R to assume the duty of wielding the scrapper's hatchet.

Five F7U-3s and one F7U-3M were struck off charge while in Jacksonville's custody, while Norfolk struck and scrapped thirty-three F7U-3s and -3Ms. It is noteworthy that of these thirty-three aircraft, six were brand-new F7U-3Ms having ten hours or less flight time, with three aircraft having amassed only three hours each! NAS San Diego's O&R took custody of seventy F7U-3/-3Ms, initially repairing and returning thirty-eight aircraft to the fleet, while thirty-two were stricken and salvaged on site. The O&R facility at NAS Alameda, California, assumed custody of seven F7U-3 and -3M aircraft, but transferred all of them to O&R San Diego for eventual disposition. O&R Corpus Christi in Texas likewise transferred the custody of its sole F7U-3 to San Diego. O&R Quonset Point transferred the custody of their four F7Us to Jacksonville's O&R and to the BuAer Pool at Mustin Field in Philadelphia. O&R Lakehurst, New Jersey, received the often-modified and much-photographed BuNo 128454, the first F7U-3 used for carrier suitability evaluation. After it was transferred to their custody it was subsequently scrapped on site. In all, seventy-one F7U-3/-3M series aircraft were salvaged and scrapped while in the custody of the Navy's Overhaul and Repair Facilities, representing 49% of the aircraft assigned to them. However, three aircraft escaped the O&R's torch and were destined for display.

Such was the case with F7U-3 BuNo 129679, which was last assigned to O&R Norfolk and retired on 30 April 1958. Flown to NAS New Orleans in Belle Chasse,

BuNo 129679 on display at NAS New Orleans in May 1967. ***Clay Jansson***

Louisiana, on 1 June, the aircraft was officially stricken from the inventory on 23 June and prepared to be placed on display at a base gate. Previously in the custody of VF-81 (and VA-66 briefly) and bearing the side number '108' from its squadron days, the aircraft was quickly repainted grey over white with all-white rudders. 129679 received a phoney '8' nose number and spurious New Orleans Naval Air Reserve '7X' designators, while its aircraft type designation and Bureau Number were obliterated. Initially retaining 'NAVY', the Cutlass later received both 'NAVY' and 'MARINES' markings on its vertical fins to acknowledge the dual reserve units stationed on base. An eye-catching view for customers of the 7-11 convenience store located adjacent to the base entrance, the Cutlass rested upon concrete pads and was chained down as it would be if aboard ship. After twelve years enduring the harsh coastal environment, the Cutlass began to no longer adequately represent the Reserve units that had expended many man hours attempting to keep it presentable. It was pushed to a deserted portion of the base at the sharp end of a bulldozer blade.

In early 1974, Vermillion, Ohio, aircraft collector Leon Cleaver attempted to salvage the aircraft. He had previously been advised that he would have to demilitarise the aircraft by cutting its wings off (as if it hadn't suffered enough!). Due to adverse weather and

BuNo 129679 in January 1974 after being relocated at NAS New Orleans with the raised blade of a bulldozer. ***Casby Collection via Leon Cleaver***

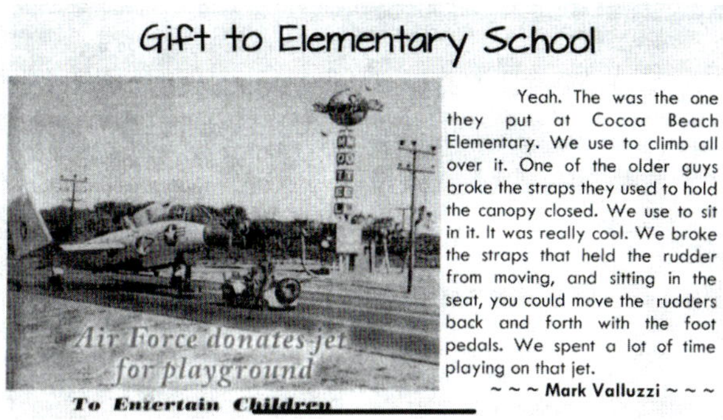
Gift to Elementary School

Air Force donates jet for playground

To Entertain Children

Yeah. The was the one they put at Cocoa Beach Elementary. We use to climb all over it. One of the older guys broke the straps they used to hold the canopy closed. We use to sit in it. It was really cool. We broke the straps that held the rudder from moving, and sitting in the seat, you could move the rudders back and forth with the foot pedals. We spent a lot of time playing on that jet.
~ ~ ~ Mark Valluzzi ~ ~ ~

ABOVE F7U-3M BuNo 129717 became the fantasy conveyance of many elementary school children. It is seen here in January 1960 with a future jet jockey replete with his own P-4A flight helmet atop the wing and a child leaning out of the inlet duct. *Casby Collection*

BELOW Seen on 8 September 1962, NATC Electronic Test's F7U-3M BuNo 129722 (marked as a YF7U-3M) provided playground-bound future aviators with the opportunity to experience their dreams at Maryland's Wheaton Regional Park. *Casby Collection*

unfamiliarity with the dis-assembly process for the Cutlass, the attempt was abandoned after eight days of effort. On 7 May 1975, the bidding opened on Defense Property Disposal Service auction Lot 214, which contained what was described as 'residue of crashed and burned F7U-3 and C-130. F7U-3 twin tail – less engines and afterburner'. The aircraft had been cut to pieces prior to the auction, and was purchased by Edward Levy Metals Inc., a local New Orleans scrap dealer. Its airframe components were subsequently shredded and recycled.

Likewise, with only four hours of flight time on its airframe, F7U-3M BuNo 129717 was received by O&R Norfolk on 21 June 1956 directly from BAR Dallas. It sat idle for more than a year on the NAS Norfolk flight line until being struck on 23 August 1957, and flown off to Patrick AFB for donation to the Cocoa Beach Elementary School in Cocoa Beach, Florida. With local newspapers mis-attributing the benevolent donation to the Air Force (because it was towed to the school by an Air Force tug), it was relocated to the sandy playground of the school. The aircraft continued to deteriorate from the salt air and harsh sun, resulting in it being scrapped in the early 1960s.

Officially in the custody of O&R Norfolk when stricken on 7 November 1956 at Patuxent River, F7U-3M BuNo 129722 had been utilised at the Naval Air Test Center for evaluating the serviceability of the missile carrier's complex electronic and radar systems. No longer needed, the aircraft was flown to NAAS Mustin in Philadelphia, Pennsylvania, and put on base display. Marked as a YF7U-3M and still retaining its NATC and 'ET' (Electronics Test) Division markings, the aircraft was subsequently donated by the Philadelphia Navy Yard Parks Department to the Montgomery County Parks and Recreation Commission and placed in the Wheaton Regional Park in Wheaton, Maryland. Backed up against forested land, the aircraft was installed with its main wheels half buried in the sand, while its nose gear was buried up to the top of the oleo. With a ladder built to enter its cockpit from the right side, and a slide to exit from the left, the aircraft became a favourite of children and parents alike. However, like most playground aircraft, time, vandalism, and the weather took its toll and around 1967 the aircraft became a liability to the county. Its ultimate fate is still unknown – rumours exist that it was buried in the late 1970s after a large hole was dug adjacent to its playground spot, some referring to it being buried whole, while others insist it was chopped to pieces and buried (more likely). Still others insist it was scrapped on site and carted off to the recyclers.

Other survivors ... for a time

BAR Dallas, Texas – F7U-3s BuNo **128451** and **128462.** Following the severe damage incurred during a runway excursion at Hensley Field on 23 June 1953, prototype F7U-3 BuNo 128451 was retained for use as a structural experiment airframe at the Vought factory. When this use was no longer deemed necessary, the aircraft was transported by truck to the New Mexico School of Mines (NMSM) – later renamed the New Mexico Institute of Mining and Technology (NMIMT) – in Socorro, New Mexico. The School of Mines had an ongoing contract with the Navy for the developmental testing of various explosives and 'energetic materials' used in munitions. The Navy's Bureau of Ordnance oversaw the contract, and worked with NMSM laboratory engineers and field representatives to prove (or disprove) the viability of naval weaponry. One of the contracts involved the testing and evaluation of 'rip-charge' explosives used to cut aircraft structure in an emergency. The NMSM had at their disposal many surplus aircraft – including a Vought F6U-1 Pirate. The prototype F7U-3 was to take part in the continuation of the explosives testing to which the Pirate was subjected. In addition to 451, early production F7U-3 BuNo 128462 was added to the test subject inventory after being stricken at NASWF Kirtland in Albuquerque, New Mexico. Although officially transferred to FASRon-4 at North Island in San Diego, California, the aircraft was trucked directly to Socorro. It was cut into pieces that were used in various experiments. Those utilised components were eventually discarded. However, its centre section fuselage and inner wings were spared.

BuNo 128451 was never used for the rip-charge experiments. Instead, it laid on its belly in the New Mexican desert until 21 April 1989, when it, along with the remains of 128462, were acquired by the Frederick Weisbrod Museum in Pueblo, Colorado. Author Casby, after previously being rebuffed years before by the director of the NMIMT in his attempt to acquire these remains, was approached by the Weisbrod museum to provide consultant assistance in the disassembly of the two F7Us. However, upon arrival at the worksite, he found that the team sent to effect the disassembly and removal of the aircraft had not waited for advice or assistance; instead taking buzz saws to both 128451 and 128462 and cutting their wings and fins off. The now ruined remains were transported to Pueblo and placed next to the museum's hangar facility at Pueblo Memorial Airport. Technically, they were still part of the NMIMT contract, meaning that the Navy still retained ownership. The undisplayable artefacts were offered back to BuAer's successor, the Naval Air Systems Command (NAVAIR), in October 1997, who instructed the museum to turn them over to nearby Fort Carson for disposal. Eventually, NAVAIR reconsidered and directed that they be held for the USS Midway Museum in San Diego, California, for use in the restoration of another Cutlass, BuNo 129565.

The remaining parts of both aircraft were initially moved to the VAHF's restoration facility in Grand Prairie, Texas, where their retiree volunteers were tasked with restoring 129565 for the Midway Museum. Following partial completion of restoration work to both airframes, all three airframes were transported to the Midway's NAS North Island restoration centre, with 128451's fuselage being placed in a cradle while its inner wings, fins and remains of 462 lay on the tarmac, seemingly of no use. However, because 128451 was a prototype, none of its mostly hand-made components were able to be utilised as intended in 129565's restoration.

In the early 2000s the Environmental Protection Agency went on a rampage through the museum world and demanded that all aviation museums rid their displays of depleted uranium (DU). Cutlasses and other aircraft contained small amounts of DU in some flight control bob weights, as well as armour plate. The extremely dense and heavy material was only a threat if disturbed, i.e. sanded, sawed, or otherwise disrupted. Its presence encapsulated in displayed aircraft posed no health issue whatsoever, but the EPA was on a mission to see every museum in the country crack open finished aircraft displays to satisfy the Agency's desire to remain relevant. Unfortunately, although this effort was eventually thwarted with regard to aircraft on display or being readied for display, the incomplete

Prototype F7U-3 BuNo 128451 met an inglorious end in the desert pit at the New Mexico Institute of Mining and Technology at Socorro, New Mexico. Although spared of being used for rip-charge testing, the aircraft was butchered apart by the recovery team from the Weisbrod Museum as co-author Casby looked on. *Al Casby photo*

F7U-3 BuNo 128462's mid-fuselage and inner wings after it was unceremoniously hacked apart for transport to the Weisbrod Museum in Pueblo, Colorado. *Al Casby photo*

BuNo 128451 was probably never going to be put to museum use, given the damage done to it in Socorro – thus, the one-of-a-kind prototype F7U-3's fuselage was targeted by the EPA and reduced to scrap (probably resulting in DU exposure!). Its inner wings, along with 128462's inner wings and centre fuselage, were spared and later given to Al Casby by the USS Midway Museum's director in return for his technical assistance in the reconstruction of BuNo 129565. Casby moved the remains of these two early 'bulb noses' to his Mesa, AZ, F7U restoration facility on 2 August 2021 for preservation and eventual display.

MCAS Miami – F7U-3 BuNo 129582. Following the completion of its mine release testing for the Marine Corps, F7U-3 BuNo 129582 sat at MCAS Miami until it was stricken on 1 July 1957. When the Third Marine Air Wing departed Miami for El Toro, California, the aircraft was left on the field, which would become Opa-locka Executive Airport. With the need to populate its playgrounds with suitable play equipment, the City of Fort Lauderdale, Florida, requested the aircraft for use as a children's attraction in its Holiday Park. Placed in a sandy spot within the park, the Cutlass had its main and nose gears buried deep in the ground so that the aircraft would be in a lower and level attitude. A ladder was built leading to the cockpit, where after exploring the jet's controls, a child could then exit the aircraft via a slide protruding from the other side. To allow entry to the cockpit from the top of the fuselage, a ramp was constructed leading from the dorsal spine of the aircraft up over the rear portion of the canopy so a child did not have to balance precariously on the foot pegs. Painted overall navy blue with red trim, the Cutlass also received a side number of '419' based on a photo of F7U-1 BuNo 124419. Its engines were removed during its park installation; the empty engine compartments soon became a hiding spot for teenage drinking, smoking and various other juvenile vices. Remembered in Rita Mae Brown's 1973 book *Rubyfruit Jungle*, the aircraft's use as a privacy location for young lesbian lovers resulted in calls by concerned parents for its removal. Following yet another in a long line of injuries to Park youths, the Recreation Board finally decided that the aircraft had to be removed.

Towed down the streets of Fort Lauderdale in the middle of the night, the aircraft was delivered to Fort Lauderdale Executive Airport where it forlornly sat for years among broken-down equipment and airport refuse. In 1983, co-author Al Casby was contacted by Airport Manager Robert Rawls, who advised him that 582 would soon be heading to the USS Intrepid Museum in New York City for eventual restoration and display aboard the docked carrier. Well aware of Casby's interest in the aircraft and his desire to restore a Cutlass (from years of Casby's constant pestering!), Rawls offered Casby the opportunity to remove anything from the jet that would not detract from its outward appearance. Spending a week camped out under the aircraft's wing, Casby worked day and night removing everything that he could before the window of opportunity expired. During his attempt to extricate the hydraulic reservoirs (which are normally accessed through panels on the upper spine of the aircraft), he entered the right engine compartment armed with a flashlight in his teeth and a set of wrenches and saws. Gingerly navigating the interior encircled with sharp aluminium and jagged hydraulic tubing, he made his way toward the blocked-off air intakes located some 20ft into

Former MCAS Miami F7U-3 BuNo 129582 *circa* 1975. *Mike Wilson Collection*

the bowels of the aircraft. Seeing a strange shape ahead, he made the mistake of poking at it with a box-end wrench. With twenty-three hornet stings to the face, coupled with multiple lacerations to his hands and knees, and a hydraulic line puncture to the shoulder, he frantically attempted to extricate himself blindly from the compartment. Adding to the injuries suffered, he fell out the tailpipe opening onto his head. Fortunately an airport police officer was driving by and noticed that Casby was holding his throat as the venom from the multiple strings had begun to cause anaphylaxis. Following emergency room care to mitigate the impending suffocation, he returned to the airport with every bug bomb pesticide he could acquire and resumed the task at hand.

After successfully removing most of the aircraft's internal components from accessible areas (many access

In 1983, young Al Casby flew down to Fort Lauderdale to salvage many useful internal parts from a derelict 129582 using his Ford Mustang rental car as a work stand when required. *Al Casby* photo

panels were 'welded' shut with corrosion and sand), he departed Florida anticipating that the aircraft would soon be moved to New York. However, within a few months, *Intrepid*'s museum team determined that the airframe was too deteriorated for them to restore; the ex-Marines Cutlass was dissected and loaded onto a truck bound for central Florida's Avon Park Bombing Range. The aircraft was subsequently destroyed in live-fire exercises.

NAAS Kingsville, Texas – F7U-3M BuNo 129735. The Naval Auxiliary Station (NAAS) was recommissioned on 1 April 1951 to address the need for additional naval aviators due to the ongoing war in Korea. In 1954, it was the home for four squadrons providing training in piston-powered fighters, transports, anti-submarine aircraft, and up to eighty-five F9F Panther jets. However, the need for jet-transition training increased as more turbine-powered aircraft reached the fleet. By 1955, fighter training operations were being conducted strictly with F9F-5 and TV-2 jets, significantly increasing the need for maintainers familiar with jet aircraft. In support of the on-field maintenance activities for these aircraft, derelict and soon-to-be struck jet aircraft of multiple types were often trucked or flown (rarely) to the NAAS to provide jet-specific training opportunities for mechanics.

On 8 June 1955, the NAAS took custody of F7U-3M BuNo 129725 following its over-the-road transfer from the Overhaul and Repair (O&R) facility at NAS North Island in San Diego, California. This Cutlass had suffered strike damage due to a runway undershoot accident on 25 March 1955 while in the custody of Air Development Squadron Four (VX-4) at Pt Mugu, California. However, instead of becoming a maintenance trainer, it was used for fire-fighting training. The aircraft was officially struck of charge at NAAS Kingsville one month later on 8 July and scrapped on site.

NAS North Island, California – F7U-3 BuNo 129952. Although custody of a fleet aircraft was rarely assigned to a Naval Air Station or Naval Air Facility outside of an on-station tenant unit, one F7U-3 was assigned to NAS North Island's custody on 30 March 1956. F7U-3 BuNo 129592 was involved in a ramp strike and main gear collapse accident on 30 August 1955 while participating in VF-124's Far East deployment aboard *Hancock* (CVA-19). Initially transferred to FASRon-117 at Barbers Point, Hawaii, it was subsequently shipped stateside to O&R Alameda, before being transported to O&R San Diego, the west coast's F7U-3 primary repair centre. The aircraft was administratively transferred to NAS North Island for a three-month period, most likely in a 'pool' storage capacity. It was returned to O&R San Diego's custody on 28 June 1956 and stricken that day with twenty-nine flight hours.

The NAS Miramar Cockpit Procedures Trainer swims with the fishes. *Casby Collection via Richard Cavicke*

NAF (Advance Base) Oppama, Japan – F7U-3 BuNo 129688. NAF Oppama Japan was used as a storage and maintenance base for aircraft held in reserve for the Seventh Fleet's deployed squadrons. Located near Yokosuka, the Navy's main port in Japan, it often served as the first land base that offloaded aircraft were stored at. Because tarmac space at NAF Atsugi was often filled with visiting squadrons that were temporarily operating there following offload while their ships were in port, Oppama became a 'catch-all' storage facility for aircraft that were shipped to Japan to serve as spares, primarily aircraft intended for Atsugi's FASRon-11. Oppama received nine F7U-3s and -3Ms in the two-year period between 15 September 1955 and 5 September 1957. All but one were transferred to O&Rs or FASRon units. However, one aircraft, ex-VF-124 F7U-3 BuNo 129688, was shipped to Japan after modification work at Vought to fulfil a need for a fleet spare. Never needed, it was scrapped on site at Oppama following its administrative custody transfer to Alameda's FASRon-8.

NAS Miramar – Cockpit Procedures Trainer. One final bit of Cutlass history survived for a while in the form of one of the three original cockpit procedures training aids (CPT) that were used to familiarise aviators with the F7U-3's instrumentation and cockpit controls. After serving as the original trainer used at *Project Cutlass* with FASRon-12, this training aid remained at NAS Miramar for use in assisting the transition of fledgling Cutlass pilots in squadrons VA-116, VF/VA-151, and VF/VA-212. By late 1956, the usefulness of the trainer was waning and it was surplus to the needs of the Navy. It is not known how the trainer's availability to the public was obtained, either through Department of Defense surplus auction or direct donation, but the cockpit ended up sunk in the large fish tank at the Long Beach Aquarium in Long Beach, California. Home to schools of curious aquatic inhabitants, the blue-painted trainer was last seen in 1957 providing an F7U indoctrination to scores of the aquarium's visitors.

CHAPTER SEVENTEEN

Cutlass myths and half-truths

'Gutless': The F7U-3 was definitely not regarded as 'gutless' when it was first introduced, even with the derated J46 engines. That two-word pejorative rhyme probably stems from the Navy's decision to deploy a guided missile-armed fleet air defence fighter as soon as possible combined with the high drag of the Cutlass in landing configuration at approach speed. Both the take-off and landing weight of the resulting F7U-3M were increased significantly by adding back all-weather mission equipment and internal fuel capacity to the F7U-3 day fighter configuration and arming it with four big Sparrow missiles – which required the addition of a missile fire control system and their launch rails.

In addition to not making the Cutlass 'gutless', the J46 was not unreliable, slow to respond to throttle movements, or prone to flame out in rain. It was in fact, at least as reliable as its contemporaries, although it was saddled with a low TBO by virtue of its lack of cumulative operating time discussed elsewhere. With respect to responsiveness, by virtue of being at maximum RPM by the time thrust reached 75% of its continuous rating, it was almost certainly the most responsive jet engine at the time. And the tendency to flame out in rain? The J35 in the first sixteen F7U-3s were responsible for that misunderstanding: its lack of tolerance for water ingestion was exacerbated in the F7U-3 because of the inlet modification required due to the J35's higher mass-flow requirement. The boundary layer removal feature was deleted in order to provide a bigger inlet without changing the outer mould lines, which would affect the Cutlasses' aerodynamics. That increased the amount of water that would be ingested by the engine when being flown through rain.

From the respective May 1955 Standard Aircraft Characteristics charts, the -3 and -3M – both with the 220-gallon fuel pod – and the F7U-3M armed (and landing back) with four Sparrow I missiles weighing 300lb+ each:

One reason that a few F7U-3 accidents were the result of touching down just short of the runway was the much higher seating position of the pilot relative to earlier jets like this Grumman F9F Panther. Another was the need to approach on the backside of the power curve to minimise landing speed. ***US Navy***

	F7U-3	F7U-3M	Increase
Take-off weight (lb)	29,903	34,704	16%
Landing weight (lb)	22,003	25,632	16%

Unfortunately for the Cutlass' reputation, the urgent need to deploy a fighter armed with Sparrows meant that BuAer had to rely on Westinghouse meeting, and preferably bettering, the J46's thrust and SFC specification rather than wait for Vought to redesign and produce the F7U with another engine. As a result, the Cutlass became identified, unfairly and retroactively, as 'gutless' in part due to CDR John Moore's witty description of the shortcomings of the F7U-3M in his book *The Wrong Stuff* about his Navy test pilot career. It should also be noted that the thrust deficiency that CDR Moore described was only significant on a low and flat approach to a carrier landing, ***not* in the other flight regimes or, as Moore himself would demonstrate successfully, on a descending approach to landing**. Otherwise the F7U-3M was not notably 'gutless' compared to its swept-wing day fighter contemporaries: in afterburner at combat weight, including four Sparrows, the F7U-3M still had a thrust-to-weight ratio equal to that of the North American F-86F Sabre and Grumman F9F-8, which were not considered to have inadequate thrust at the time.

'The Ensign Killer': The implication of this frequent Cutlass epithet was that it was hard to fly and therefore dangerous. On the contrary, the Cutlass was not an inherently dangerous aircraft and safer than some. (As Northrop test pilot Max Stanley once said, 'The Piper Cub is the safest aircraft in the world; it can just barely kill you.') In fact, strictly speaking, only one Ensign was killed in a Cutlass accident (the second identified as such had been selected for promotion to LTJG). Moreover, the proportion of F7U-3 accidents of all kinds involving Ensigns was roughly the same as the proportion of Ensign pilots in a squadron. Like any aircraft, the Cutlass was not a respecter of rank as much as experience in flying jets as well as a thorough check out and subsequent time in type – a Vought analysis of F7U-3 accidents up to February 1957 stated that pilots with fifty or fewer hours in the Cutlass were responsible for 40% of them. A LCDR and former patrol bomber pilot made the first and only fatal F7U-3 ramp strike (two others occurred, but were limited to main landing gear tyres and arresting hook strikes), a dramatic example of the shortcomings of the Navy's type transition and duty assignment policies in the early 1950s that did not recognise the degree of difference between flying long-range piston engine-powered patrol planes and transonic carrier-based jets.

The initial development and evaluation of the F7U-3 was relatively free of accidents, certainly by the standard of the time. No Vought or experienced Navy test pilot found it

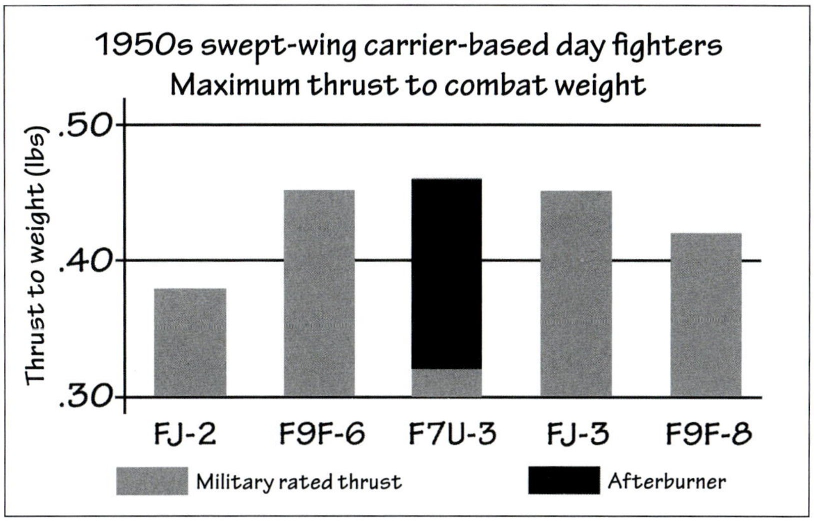

to be hard to fly, much less dangerous. The two fatal accidents in 1952 were the result of a pilot error (not extending the slats for take-off) and a flight control linkage disconnect (an assembly error) at the worst possible moment on an approach to landing. The three incidents in 1953, none of them resulting in injury to the pilot, were the result of landing short, a wheel brake failure that caused a ground loop, and an engine explosion. Even the unexpected appearance of the post-stall gyration that resulted in crashes in 1954 and early 1955 proved to be easily countered by simply letting go of the controls as long as it hadn't been provoked at too low altitude by failure to extend or retract the slats at a high enough airspeed. In summary, the preponderance of F7U accidents, particularly the fatal ones, were errors made by pilots, maintainers, or shore or ship-based equipment failures/mis-settings.

As a day fighter, in afterburner, the F7U-3 had a thrust-to-weight ratio slightly better than the best of its contemporaries. *Thomason*

The primary cause of the horrendous Navy-wide jet aircraft accident rate in the 1950s was that its leadership was slow to fully recognise that the transition to jets required that pilots receive training in the critical differences between their handling qualities, mission planning, and different/more complex systems relative to ones with piston engines and propellers. In the pre-NATOPS days, a cockiness existed that because you had gold wings, you could fly anything with minimal training. The check out could be as limited as reading the flight manual, passing a blindfold cockpit check, and having someone on the ladder beside the cockpit monitor your first engine start. Unlike the US Air Force, the Navy also initially elected to have few dual-control jets and none with swept wings. (The Navy finally procured a two-seat version of the swept-wing Grumman F9F Cougar. It was introduced into the training command in 1957, the same year that the Cutlass deployments were ending.) As a result, naval aviators generally received barely adequate instruction when checking out in the first straight-wing jets: for most their first flight in one was solo. Then, if a pilot had flown any jet, the assumption was that transition to other jet types, including those with swept wings,

The F7U-3 Cutlass was not the Navy's only early swept-wing fighter to sometimes conclude a carrier landing with a trip into the barricade. *US Navy*

required minimal indoctrination, as had been the case with prop planes. As a result, the F7U was introduced to fleet pilots in a disadvantageous culture that permeated Naval Aviation (to be fair, there was a compelling need to transition many pilots rapidly to flying jets since there was a 300% increase in the number of jet fighters in carrier air groups in the early 1950s).

The F7U-3 was not the only poster child for the need for thorough dissemination of best practices by aircraft type to pilots and LSOs. The initial swept-wing jet accident rate proved that they all had handling qualities significantly different from straight-wing ones. As a result, the west coast aviation command initiated the *Cougar College* and *Fury Finishing School* at VC-3; the F7U-3 was subsequently added as *Project Check-Out*, the follow-on to *Project Cutlass* that had been accomplished at NAS Miramar. However, the syllabus was too brief initially and all pilots transitioning to swept-wing jets did not receive orders to take it. Most of VC-3's Cutlass students were a newly F7U-equipped west coast squadron's commanding officer and at most a few of his senior officers who would then, with minimal training themselves, go back and train the rest of the pilots in the squadron.

Inadequate pilot training was particularly ill-advised in the case of the Cutlass. It was probably his first flight in a swept-wing aircraft (almost certainly the first with afterburning engines). An all too traditional brief and informal check out, sometimes given by an ill-informed fellow pilot, occasionally resulted in initial Cutlass flights ending in tears: the 1954 transitions to the Cutlass in the first two fighter squadrons, VF-81 on the east coast and VF-124 on the west, were marred by junior officers having to eject on their first flights after losing control, one fatally when his seat fouled his parachute.

At least five unforced F7U accidents resulted from a pilot touching down short of the runway even though visibility over the nose was excellent and, unlike many jet engines of the time, the response of the J46 to throttle changes was very good. However, it was different from other Navy jets in two critical ways during the landing approach: the pilot was sitting higher above the main landing gear and he was on the backside of a very steep power curve. Also, as good as the J46's throttle response was, at low speed it was still notably less of an immediate increase in thrust than that of any fighter powered by a reciprocating engine turning a propeller that low-time jet pilots would be more familiar with.

The first of the US Navy's late 1950s accident reduction major initiatives was not in place until 1958 – sadly too late for the Cutlass' reputation and the lives of many Navy pilots irrespective of aircraft type. Replacement Air Groups (RAGs, now known as Fleet Replacement Squadrons) were formed that consisted of units dedicated to the comprehensive transition of pilots to a new aircraft type prior to their assignment to an operational squadron equipped with them. The next change that would have particularly benefitted the F7U pilots was the introduction of the Naval Air Training and Operating Procedures Standardization (NATOPS) beginning in 1961.

Most – if not all – of the F7U accidents attributable to pilot error were avoidable because the knowledge base for a safe transition to the F7U was available in 1954. Unfortunately, this knowledge was not promulgated effectively to every F7U-3 pilot as it would have been if RAGs and NATOPs had existed then. NATC had also published detailed guidance for pilots and LSOs on launching and recovering the F7U-3 following its successful, accident-free carrier suitability testing that included deliberately 'bad' landings, e.g. off-centre engagements and ones with sink rates at or even above the design limit. This is exemplified by the training of pilots for the 1954 *Project Cutlass* introduction on the west coast resulting in it being unremarkable, including carrier operations, from an accident standpoint: the only one was caused by a maintenance error during the replacement of a landing gear strut damaged by a catapult bridle.

Accident rate: Unfortunately, the belief that the Cutlass was not only a dangerous but 'the most dangerous' aircraft is primarily due to unquestioning and out-of-context reliance on Navy accident rate data comparing it to other carrier-based fighters in the early to mid-1950s. Two numbers are cited frequently: major accidents per 10,000 hours and percentage of the fleet that was destroyed in accidents. Both are misleading. With very few exceptions, a Cutlass did not kill its pilot; some pilots, maintainers, and/or carrier deck personnel – usually because of inadequate training or procedures – killed Cutlasses.

According to a Vought analysis, Cutlasses were involved in eighty-one major operational service (as opposed to test and evaluation) accidents between May 1953 and February 1957; the cumulative accident rate was 17.5 per 10,000 hours. The average for all Navy jet fighter and attack aircraft during that time was on the order of 10 (better than the F7U's but still worse than the USAF's). Many articles about the Cutlass also usually include the statement that 25% or more of all the F7U-3s were reportedly 'lost' or 'destroyed'.

However, on closer examination, a significantly less damning picture emerges. First, the accident rate of the first Navy carrier-based jets decreased significantly as their flight hours accumulated. The F7U-3 fleet service ended in 1957 after only three years. Its total flight hours were therefore lower than its contemporaries. The high-time Cutlass had only been flown for 477 hours; the average for the fleet was less than 200 hours: the first sixteen F7U-3s that were powered by J35 engines only averaged 129 hours each before all had been stricken as not being production representative; the last production lot of fifty F7U-3Ms averaged 160 hours but six were retired having flown ten hours or fewer (basically production flight test and ferry flights to a storage facility) and a further nine only reached double digits. It is therefore unfair to compare the Cutlass to jets that accumulated many more flight hours, not to mention that they include those of simpler aircraft types (i.e. day fighters) that represented a majority of the overall flight hours.

Some of the accident rates to which the Cutlass is compared also include the introduction of angled decks with mirror-guided descending approaches. From July 1955, the quarter in which operational evaluation and use of the mirror system was begun, up to September 1956, there were 19,202 landings made using the mirror and angled deck. There were nine major accidents, for a rate of 0.47 per 1,000 landings. During the same period, the major accident rate for axial-deck landings was 2.1, 4.5 times as often.

Cutlass pilots benefitted by flying from angled decks: of their fifteen major carrier-landing accidents, ten were on axial-deck carriers versus five on angled-deck carriers. The difference is more dramatic when comparing carrier-landing qualification accidents (with such attempts arguably more likely to result in one as pilots familiarise themselves with an aircraft's landing characteristics) versus deployments: five on axial-decks and only one on an angled deck. During deployments, there were five axial-deck landing accidents during three (1.7 per deployment) and four angled-deck accidents during three (1.3 per deployment and none for the allegedly underpowered F7U-3M on one of those). Moreover, that does not count the accident-free deployments of two four-plane VX-4 detachments flying the F7U-3M on angled decks and the limited experience of VA-86, also flying the F7U-3M, during the *Forrestal* shakedown cruise.

If fleet pilots had initially qualified and deployed in Cutlasses only on angled decks, its carrier suitability

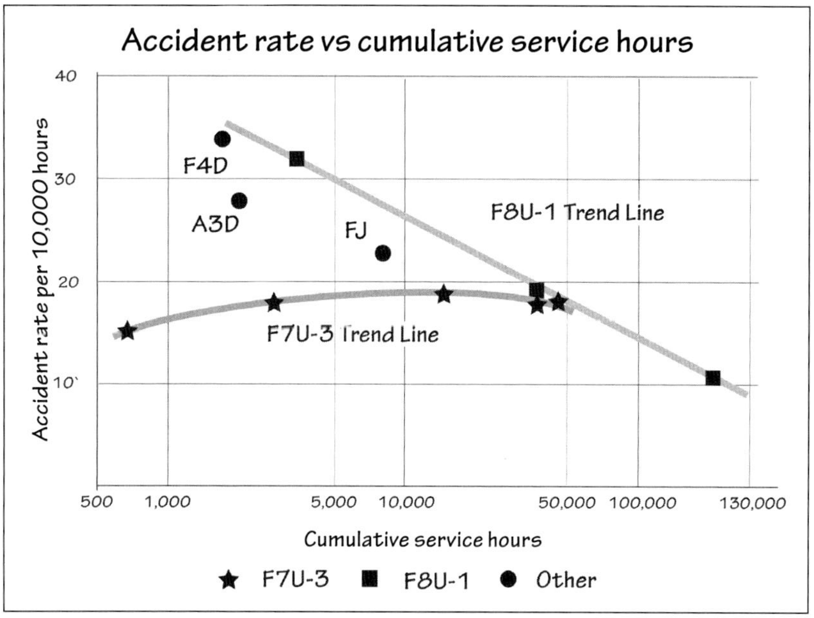

reputation would almost certainly have been very different. Unfortunately that was not the case even though the NATC carrier suitability trials and *Project Steam* landings had all been accomplished accident-free on axial-deck carriers. As it happened, at least five of the subsequent major axial-deck landing accidents would not have occurred or been as severe on an angled-deck carrier. Three squadrons plus two VX-4 detachments deployed on angle-deck carriers (one also participated in *Forrestal*'s shakedown cruise). They suffered only one pre-deployment carrier-landing accident and four during deployment: two hard landings, one the result of a hook point bolt failure, and one the sole F7U-3 ramp strike on an angle-deck carrier. It resulted in substantial but repairable damage to the aft fuselage and tail hook.

When compared to other mid-fifties swept-wing jets at the same point in their introduction with respect to accumulated flight hours, the F7U-3 accident rate was not only *not* significantly worse than most but better than some. Its accident rate in Fiscal Year 1953 (1 July 1952–30 June 1953) was only 14.7 and would have been 0.0 if a VX-3 pilot had not undershot his landing approach at an air show. It increased somewhat during the next Fiscal Year but was still well below other contemporaries with the same cumulative number of flight hours. It stayed about the same the next fiscal year even though three fleet squadrons (VF-81, 83 and 124) began transition to the Cutlass, probably because it included *Projects Cutlass* and *Check-Out*. Many of the aviators involved in *Project Cutlass* were selected Navy test pilots and experienced fleet pilots who received training at Vought in Grand Prairie, and subsequent factory-representative support at Miramar. Several of these experienced Cutlass pilots were then transferred to *Project Check-Out* at VC-3 to form the initial F7U-3

Contrary to its reputation, the F7U-3's initial major accident rate was lower than its carrier-based contemporaries; it subsequently increased as a result of its introduction to service, maintained and flown by inadequately trained personnel. Moreover, while not a significant percentage of the total number of accidents, the rate of Cutlass-specific ones – landing short, post-stall gyrations, and carrier landings – decreased during its operational service. *Thomason*

instructor cadre on the west coast. Similarly, the formal F7U-3 Fleet Introduction Programme at Patuxent River resulted in a cadre of pilots who were then assigned to VF-81 and VF-83.

The F8U's initial accident rate was much worse than the F7U's (although it decreased to be the same at roughly the same number of accumulated hours as the F7U-3 final total) even with at least two advantages: it was only flown from angled-deck carriers and the pilot and LSO were provided with angle-of-attack indication. Its troubled introduction to the fleet in December 1956 would have alone justified the creation of RAGs and NATOPS: the first squadron, VX-3, to receive F8Us had its first fatal accident only two weeks later. The first fleet squadron, VF-32, had seven major accidents in little more than seven months. In less than two years, the second Crusader fleet squadron, VF-154, lost five pilots in fourteen major accidents including two pilots killed during carrier qualifications.

British Royal Navy and Vickers-Armstrongs test pilot Michael Lithgow made two flights in the F8U-1 in October 1958 as part of a Navy exchange pilot programme. He found it challenging to land due to weak low-speed lateral control and difficulty maintaining the desired approach speed. Later that month he discussed his experience with CAPT Bob Elder, then Director of Flight Test at Patuxent River. As he later reported that conversation: 'Another topic touched upon was the very great difficulties squadrons were having in deck landing their F8U-1s. They are breaking them up at a pretty staggering rate.' The subsequent introduction of RAGs was probably a major reason for more than halving the F8U's major accident rate in only a year. There is every likelihood that the Cutlass' overall average would have dropped over time as it did with the rest of the Navy's fleet like the Crusader's.

Another metric for which data is available for both the F7U-3 and the F8U-1 is ejections. For the former – not counting two inadvertent ejections, Milliard's and Montgomery's – it was twenty-four attempts with six fatal: four out of the seat envelope capability (low), one due to an improperly installed firing mechanism, and one attempted in a thunderstorm with the seat fouling the parachute. Of those, twenty-three occurred before 1 March 1957, when the F7U had accumulated 46,192 flight hours, an attempted ejection rate of one per 2,008 hours (note that two of them, both successful, were associated with the early evaluation of the post-stall-gyration phenomenon, one when the spin chute failed to function as intended and the other in an unapproved, misbegotten attempt to demonstrate a conventional spin recovery). With respect to the F8U, twenty-five pilots attempted ejection in its first 37,001 flight hours and six were fatal; while the fatality rate is almost identical, the rate of attempts was more frequent than the F7U's, one per 1,480 hours.

The Fiscal Year (FY) accident rates by type to which the Cutlass has been compared are also misleading because they did not differentiate between similar but significantly different aircraft. For example, the 'F9F' data for the swept-wing F9F-6's first year of introduction (FY 1954) included that of the existing, more conventional straight-wing F9F-2/5 Panther that had been in service for four years. Squadrons flying the -6 experienced a fatal accident rate in that first year that was 50% higher than the more numerous ones flying the -2/5. Similarly, squadrons flying the new heavier, all-weather, more mission-capable F2H-3/4 Banshee initially had a 50% higher accident rate than those flying the F2H-2 day fighter. It should not have been surprising that the F7U-3, with its unusual handling qualities, swept wings, complex flight control and other systems, and afterburners would have a higher accident rate during its initial squadron service than other, simpler jets, particularly those with straight wings.

With respect to the number of Cutlasses destroyed relative to the size of the fleet, usually cited as at least 25%, the actual number is somewhat inflated by two factors. First, relatively few F7U-3s were built and therefore the usual high initial accident rate in the first few years of service had a greater effect on the percentage of total production that was destroyed. For example, sixteen (34%) of the first forty-seven F4H Phantom IIs crashed even though none were ever deployed and they were rarely landed on carriers. Second, as anyone who has had a car accident knows, whether to repair or 'total' a vehicle is sometimes a judgment call. By the end of the 1950s, Navy practice was normally to err on the side of repairable. The F8U is an example. A total of 1,266 were delivered; Crusaders were reportedly involved in 1,106 major accidents, almost 90% of total production. However, when the last Crusader was retired in 1983, there were more than 160 F8Us – the difference between production and major accidents – stored at Davis Monthan AFB, many flown there having been repaired at some point and returned to service, some more than once.

In the case of the F7U, the Navy decided in early 1956 that it was to be a placeholder until the next generation of carrier-based jet aircraft – the F3H Demon armed with the Sparrow III missile, the F8U Crusader and F11F Tiger day fighters, and A4D Skyhawk and FJ-4B tactical nuclear bombers – could be deployed. Further investment in the Cutlass had already been curtailed: there had been no funding for innovations that became standard on the Navy's other jet fighters like angle-of-attack (AoA) indication, the Sidewinder missile, or in-flight refuelling in the case of the F7U-3M. The absence in the cockpit of an AoA gauge was particularly inexplicable: it was the first Vought F7U-3 Engineering Change Proposal, had been present on early Cutlasses, and was even more critical from a safety-of-flight standpoint for F7U pilots

Albeit with damage to the bottom of the F8U's aft fuselage, the pilot managed to bolter after this ramp strike and land ashore; it would have probably been assessed as a major accident even though the Crusader was repaired and returned to service. *US Navy*

than those flying other swept-wing, carrier-capable jets. The heat-seeking Sidewinder was not only a significant improvement in air-to-air armament compared to the 20mm cannon or unguided rocket but adding it was a trivial project, basically the incorporation of wiring and switches. Somewhat more expensive was -3M in-flight refuelling capability that was proposed by Vought. BuAer clearly did not consider it to be essential for the F4D that was to be replaced by F3Hs in carrier air groups since it hadn't funded one for it either (the opinion was not shared by at least two deploying Skyray squadrons; they went to sea with an O&R depot-created kludge involving the addition of a refuelling probe to an external fuel tank).

Also significant from the standpoint of striking (i.e. retiring) versus repairing a crash-damaged F7U, there would not be additional procurement of the usual quantity of airframe or system spares: the Cutlass was officially designated to be a 'one-tour' aircraft in early 1956: Even before then, F7Us with significant but repairable crash damage or that had reached the calendar month tour limit were stored or stricken. There were enough to do so: the number of operational F7U-3 squadrons was at most nine at any given time; each needed to deploy with about twelve aircraft. Assuming 50% attrition for accidents and incidents, the total fleet requirement was only 162. Vought delivered 290 including the -3P and -3M. With respect to the number actually destroyed, as opposed to damaged but repairable, an in-depth review by Bureau Number results in a reasonable (for the mid-1950s) rate for the F7U-3s assigned to squadrons of 17%. Although only 111 F7U-3s, -3Ms, and -3Ps were flown to the Navy's desert storage and reclamation facility following their service, many more were simply stricken, flightworthy or repairable, at the nearest O&R facility; used for barrier/barricade testing; assigned to Naval Air Reserve Training Units (NARTU) for maintainer training; or became static displays at Naval Air Stations.

Ironically, the F3H Demon that the Navy eventually preferred as a missile-armed fleet air defence fighter had a more chequered beginning than the F7U's. Including the two XF3H-1 prototypes, there were eleven Demon crashes between August 1952 and October 1955, with four test pilots killed (one Navy and three McDonnell). Although the Westinghouse J40 engine was considered to be a major cause of the lack of satisfactory Demon development progress, three of the F3Hs that crashed were powered by the Allison J71 replacement. Including the XF7U-1 prototypes and handful of production F7U-1s, which were arguably more susceptible to mishaps, the Cutlass development programme was also marred by ten accidents and five fatalities. However, not counting pre-production prototype crashes in both programmes, the Demon had a far worse record: ten crashes and four fatalities versus five crashes and two fatalities for the Cutlass.

The weak nose landing gear: One of the frequently mentioned Cutlass shortcomings was that it had a weak nose landing gear that was prone to collapse; worse, on occasion in a hard landing the strut would supposedly punch up into the cockpit, killing the pilot. This is an example of speculation eventually and erroneously becoming a 'fact'. Although the nose gear did collapse like any aircraft's when its extension/retraction mechanism was loaded well beyond its design requirement or the strut attachment point was subjected to excessive side loads, the F7U's strut itself never failed, much less ever penetrated the floor of the cockpit and 'speared' or ejected the pilot. In one landing incident, however, the failure that caused the nose gear to collapse tragically resulted in the firing of the ejection seat through a series of freak occurrences.

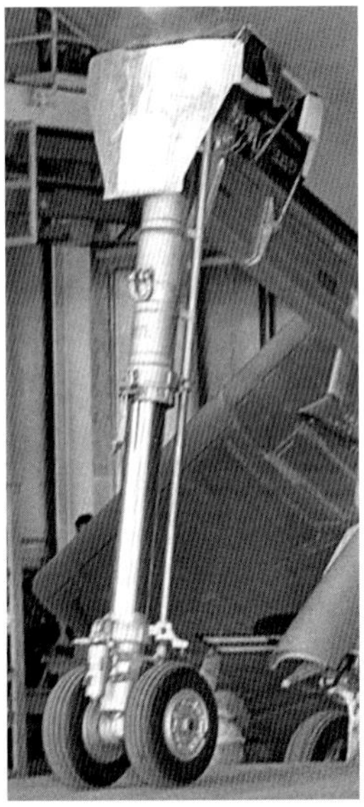

ABOVE The fully extended F7U-3 nose landing gear strut looked long, which it was for the size of the aircraft, and therefore possibly fragile, which it was not. ***VAHF***

BELOW A formal Failure Mode, Effects, and Criticality Analysis (FMECA), a design process instituted by the US Army in 1949 and subsequently adopted by the other military services, NASA, etc. might have highlighted what would happen after a nose landing gear overload resulted in its actuator punching through the turtle deck and knocking off the canopy, arming the ejection seat. ***Thomason***

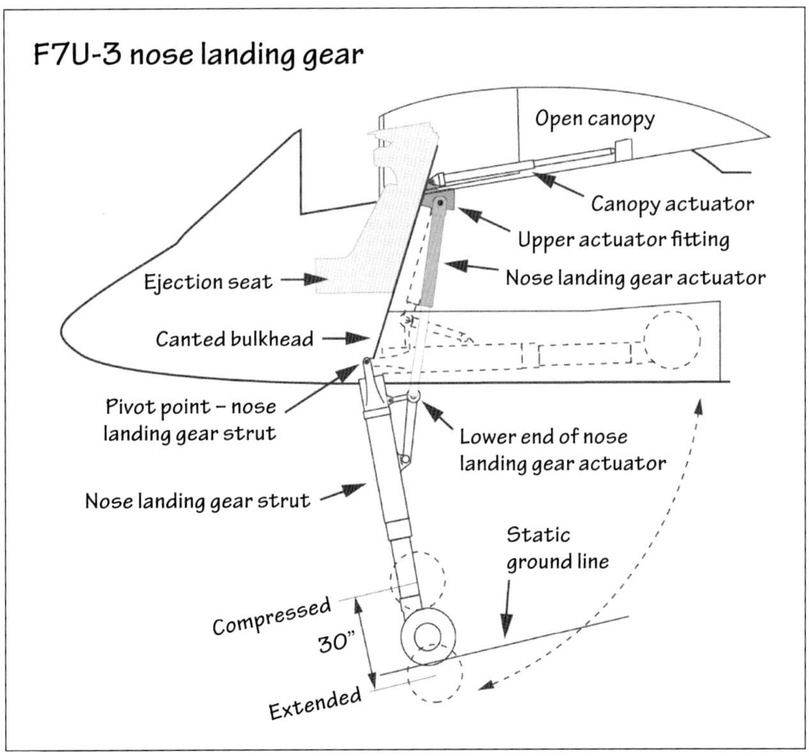

At the time BuAer required a carrier-based aircraft's landing gear to shrug off a 17ft per second (a vertical speed of 10 knots) impact on touchdown at its maximum landing weight. Navy test pilots exceeded that limit on more than one occasion in both the F7U-1 and -3 without damage to the landing gear. What the nose gear could not withstand, *and was not required to*, were loads introduced by 1) pilots running off the runway onto soft ground that restrained the wheels while the aircraft was still moving; landing short and tearing the gear off when it got to the runway; and crash landing in ploughed fields with the landing gear down (it was recommended that gear not be extended in that eventuality) and 2) mis-set or malfunctioning arresting gear engines or crash barriers.

The top of the F7U's nose landing gear strut pivoted on trunnions attached to a strong tubular fitting located at the bottom of the canted, full-depth fuselage bulkhead that was the forward end of the nose gear wheel well and the aft end of the cockpit. The ejection seat was mounted on rails on the front side of this bulkhead. The nose landing gear was retracted and extended by a long hydraulic actuator oriented almost vertically. Its lower end was attached to a triangular frame on the backside of the landing gear strut near its top; the upper end of the actuator pivoted on a forged fitting mounted on the backside of the cockpit bulkhead (the fitting was also the attachment point for the forward end of the canopy actuator).

This actuator, itself larger than nose or main gear struts of many aircraft, contained internal down locks, which had to 'click' into position at the cylinder rod's full extension or retraction. Although the Cutlass's landing gear was incredibly stout, as was the actuator, these small circumferential down locks were prone to failure if multiple or extremely excessive compressive loads were exerted on the actuator.

After static structural tests at Vought, Navy test pilots at Patuxent River verified that the F7U-3's structure and landing gear met the maximum sink-rate requirement without damage as the lighter F7U-'s had. BuNo 128454 was subsequently subjected to sink rates on the order of 20ft per second at gross weights of about 24,000lb in early November 1952 aboard *Coral Sea*. An axle failure on the left main landing gear strut concluded testing. There was, however, no damage to the nose landing gear reported as a result of this test series.

In early 1954, LT John M. Moore, a recent Navy Test Pilot School graduate, was assigned high-sink rate testing in F7U-3 BuNo 128475 by the Carrier Suitability Branch at NATC. His first landing was at 7ft per second, one foot per second shy of his target, which represented a fairly benign carrier landing. On the tenth landing, he touched down at an instrument-

Even a normal landing might use up all the 30in of nose landing gear shock-strut travel (also note the deflection of the left main landing gear wheel). *US Navy*

recorded, bone-jarring 17.5ft per second, slightly in excess of the 17ft per second requirement and without any evident structural damage.

Nevertheless, there was a significant problem associated with F7U nose gear collapses for whatever reason. In a 26 January 1956 message to the CNO – with two F7U-3 squadrons deployed, two F7U-3M squadrons nearing deployment, and six more operating F7Us – the Naval Aviation Safety Center (NASC) documented sixteen nose gear collapses that had occurred by the end of 1955:

- Four as a result of arrested landings, with one fatality, one fractured vertebrae, one sprained back, and one no injury.
- Twelve during field landings, with three fractured vertebrae, two sprained backs, two minor injury not involving the back, and five no injury.

One direct result of the message might have been the minimisation of VA-86's participation in the shakedown cruise of *Forrestal* (CVA-59) in early 1956. The Cutlass squadron spent the majority of the time based at Leeward Point Field, Guantanamo, Cuba. The ship's captain reportedly did not want to risk one of its pilots 'scratching' *Forrestal*'s brand-new deck during a cruise that included members of the worldwide press. Ironically, Navy accident data for FY 1955 (30 June 1955 to 1 July 1956) for swept-wing operations aboard carriers documented that the F7U-3 had an accident rate (all causes) of about forty per 10,000 hours, which is high, but the other swept-wing jets (primarily F9F Cougars and FJ Furies, simpler jets that had been introduced earlier) were crashing during deployments at a rate of almost fifty-seven accidents per 10,000 hours!

The NASC message failed to note that every one of the nose landing gear collapses to that point had been caused by an *overload beyond the design requirement.* Also not mentioned in the message was that there were at least four incidents during that time period similar to the ones cited in which the nose landing gear did not fail. In total there were fourteen take-off or landing incidents between June 1953 and December 1956 similar to the ones that had resulted in a nose landing gear collapse, most of which caused significant damage to one or both main landing gears. Nevertheless, none caused a nose landing gear collapse, a demonstration of its ability to withstand an overload well beyond the design requirement. Moreover, there were only four more nose gear collapses between the January 1956 report and the last one in January 1957. In the final tally, two thirds of all nose gear collapses involved pilot error, about half caused by landing short of the runway and most of the remainder following hard landings or an excursion off the hard surface for various reasons. Other nose gear collapses that contributed to an impression of a lack of adequate strength resulted from an extreme overload caused by an arresting gear malfunction or mis-setting.

Tragically, the chain of events that resulted in the fatal one reported in the NASC message had almost occurred on 17 June 1955 except for the last link. While waiting for a mirror-landing system to become available for further F7U-3M carrier trials, NATC test pilot LT John M. Moore and F7U-3M BuNo 129736 were assigned to a shore-based evaluation of the new Mk 7 Mod 0 'constant runout' arresting gear system in reducing the load on the attachment of the Vought/Fletcher external fuel tank (during an arrested landing one occasionally came off and careened up the deck). In his first high-speed (98 knots) taxi-in arrestment, the system's metering valve that was supposed to modulate the deceleration failed to function as intended. Instead, it 'two-blocked', i.e. jammed. Unfortunately for the

Although the attachment of the nose landing gear strut never failed in compression, a high enough side load on the wheels could cause a failure of the airframe structure in tension, causing the strut to fail to the side. ***US Navy***

F7U-3M and almost fatally for Moore, neither the arresting hook nor its attachment point failed at 190% of their design load (there wasn't even any visible damage to either the arresting hook or the carry-through structure to the fuselage). The nearly instantaneous stop caused the forward fuselage to rotate hard downward due to the restraining hook load acting below the aircraft's centre of gravity. That subjected the nose landing gear to forces far in excess of its design strength.

The weakest point proved to be the attachment of the nose landing gear actuator's upper attach fitting to the backside of the cockpit's aft bulkhead. The fitting was torn loose with the actuator penetrating the deck under the canopy aft of the cockpit, allowing the nose landing gear to fold aft. The sliding canopy was also knocked off because the forward end of its actuating cylinder was attached to the same fitting as the nose landing gear actuator. The sudden stop caused Moore to inadvertently push both throttles forward into afterburner, bending the levers to the point that they could not be pulled back and resulting in the Cutlass careening across the field, on fire, after its initial recoil released the arresting hook from the cable. Moore jumped over the side before it had travelled

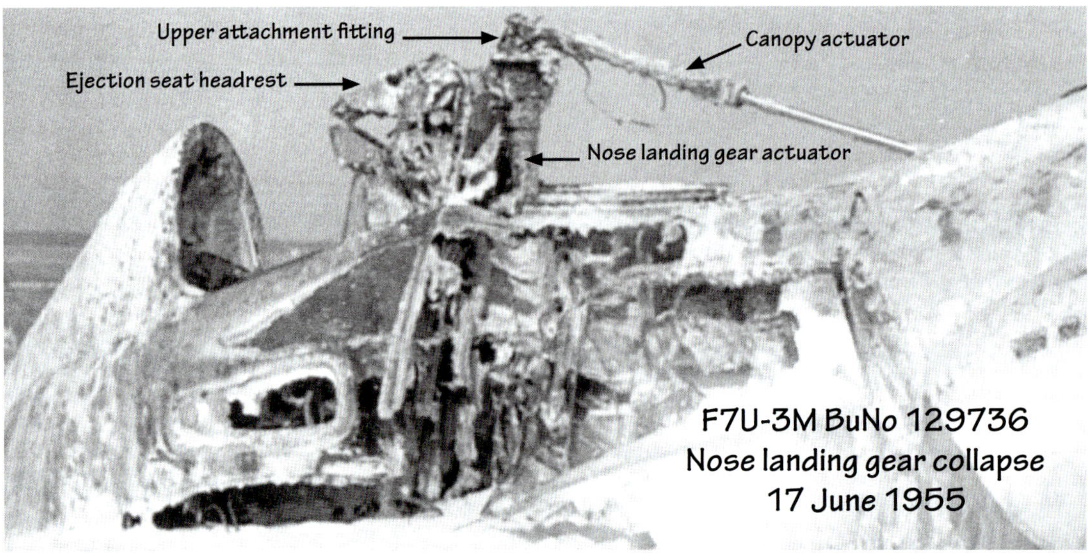

John Moore just missed being seriously injured or killed when his F7U-3M's nose gear collapsed due to a failure of the mounting of its extend/retract actuator, which also knocked off the canopy, arming his ejection seat. ***Thomason***

LTJG 'Barry' Milliard was fatally injured when the collapse of BuNo 129586's nose landing gear, caused by unexpected interactions with the crash barriers and barricade, resulted in his ejection seat being triggered. ***US Navy***

very far and was not seriously hurt. The Cutlass sustained strike damage.

The post-crash investigation report noted that the detachment of the canopy had, as intended, resulted in the safety pin being removed from the seat-firing mechanism 'and for some unknown reason the (seat) catapult firing mechanism arm assembly had rotated to a position which was dangerously close to firing the ejection seat'. Unfortunately this was not alarming enough at the time to initiate corrective action to modify the seat. Subsequent incipient failures of the nose landing gear actuator attachment fitting in September 1955 also occurred: carrier trials of the F7U-3M aboard *Ticonderoga* at the higher landing weights resulting from the addition of Sparrow I fire control system and missiles were halted due to buckled plates and popped rivets in the area following an arrestment during which the nose gear bottomed out. It occurred again during a field arrestment, also when the nose gear bottomed out. The nose gear strut was replaced and examined but no evidence of a malfunction was found.

Although these dots were pretty far apart, the failure to connect them; recognise that a malfunctioning arrestment system and higher landing weights were causing structural damage in a critical area; and take immediate action to place a guard on the ejection seat's firing mechanism so it could only be actuated by pulling the face curtain would soon have a horrific consequence: a 1 November 1955 landing accident in F7U-3 BuNo 129586 aboard *Hancock* (CVA-19) cost LTJG George B. 'Barry' Milliard his life. Instead of touching down in the landing area after the LSO signalled the cut, he had held off and floated over all the arresting wires. Unfortunately the barrier/barricade system provided to stop an aircraft thereafter did not function as intended.

Instead, his tail hook picked up the steel pendant for the number 2 Davis-rigged barrier that was lying flat on the deck since it was set for the much heavier AJ Savage also being operated by the air group. The setting meant that the runout for the F7U was far too abrupt, essentially a repeat of Moore's accident. In addition, the aircraft had engaged the number 5 Davis-rigged barrier and then the barricade, with the nose gear wheels straddling a wide vertical strap of the barricade. The nose gear's strap cutters did not sever the barricade strap, presumably due to fouling by the barrier riser straps, adding to the overload of the nose gear actuator beyond its design specifications. As in Moore's accident, the upper attachment fitting broke loose and penetrated the canopy deck, dislodging the canopy, which armed the ejection seat. Only this time the errant canopy actuator strut also struck the ejection seat firing-cap lever arm, igniting the powder charge that ejected the seat; Milliard was propelled 200ft forward onto the tail of an AD Skyraider parked in the pack and subsequently died of his injuries. Aircraft Service Changes mandated by tragedy resulted: reinforcement of the canopy deck, actuator strut, and bulkhead shelf, as well as redesign of the ejection seat firing mechanism itself and the addition of a guard on

1956 VA-83 nose gear collapse – *Intrepid* (CVA-11)

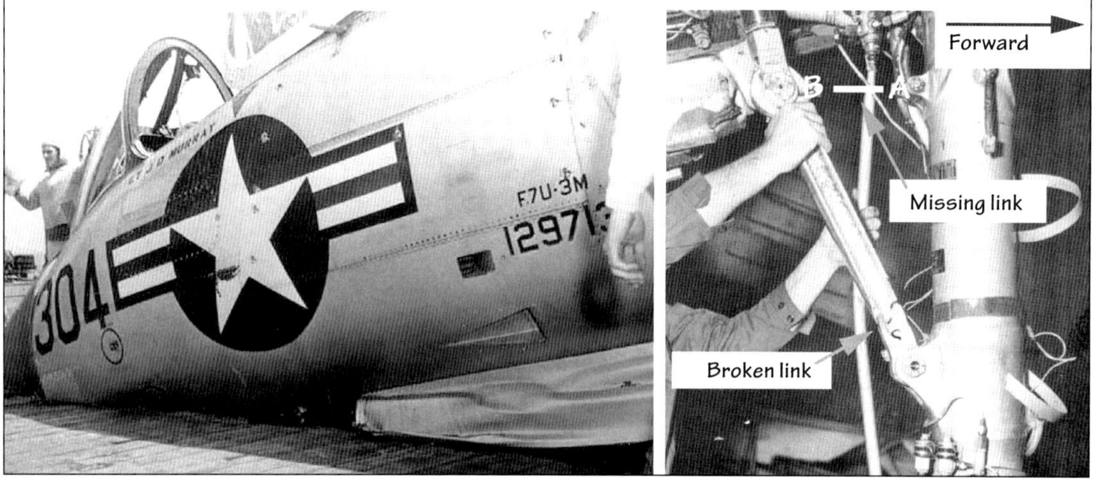

The F7U-3M in which LT Lebert experienced a nose landing gear collapse during VA-83's deployment on *Intrepid* in 1956 had the most carrier landings of the Cutlasses in the squadron and had not yet been modified with a strengthened drag link. *Thomason*

the back of the seat frame to prevent the ejection from activation by means other than the face curtain.

A VA-66 F7U-3 also had a nose gear collapse during an arrested landing aboard *Ticonderoga* on 7 January 1956, with the canopy coming off. Fortunately, the ejection seat firing lever was not struck since the headrest had not yet been modified.

In addition to the design changes initiated by the Milliard accident, Vought was taking action to add a side brace to the nose gear drag link to strengthen it from the standpoint of side loads and beef up the nose gear steering linkage since failures had been experienced. (Vought also recommended in the Flight Handbook that carrier landings not be made with the nose wheel pre-rotation inoperative.) Unfortunately, the changes had not yet been made to at least some of VA-83's F7U-3Ms aboard *Intrepid*. That resulted in the last Cutlass nose gear collapse on a carrier landing to occur on 17 April 1956, only three months after the NASC message. It was also the *only* nose gear collapse due to a material failure that did not result from a load in excess of the original design requirements, although such loads may have been imposed on that nose gear previously without incident that eventually resulted in failure at a nominal load due to metal fatigue. Nevertheless, a misconstrued reputation had been established that the F7U-3 nose gear was prone to collapse even though modifications were accomplished to reduce the incidence of them significantly as a result.

However, there was still the likelihood that pilot error or arresting gear/barrier engine malfunction would occur, causing a nose landing gear collapse and too frequently the pilot suffering a severe back injury due to free-falling 8ft and landing on his tailbone. This was exacerbated by the need for a firm seat cushion in an ejection, with the seat being literally fired out of the cockpit by a repurposed cannon cartridge like a bullet from a gun. If the pilot were seated on a soft cushion, when the seat's catapult was triggered, the inertia of his body would cause him to not move vertically until the cushion was almost fully compressed; in the meantime, the hard seat structure beneath the cushion would have accelerated enough to give him a hard whack in his buttocks at that point. Even with a firm seat cushion, ejections often resulted in a back injury so a soft cushion was more likely to result in a debilitating one. As it happened, the seat cushioning was already minimal. F7U-3 pilots sat on a PK-2 Pararaft Kit, which contained a life raft, canned water, and other hard survival-enhancing items. Only a thin SP-1 seat-pan cushion separated the pilot from the survival kit.

To minimise the incidence of back injuries caused by nose gear collapses, C. T. Koochembere of the Navy's Air Crew Equipment Laboratory at the Naval Air Material Center in Philadelphia suggested the use of an energy-absorbing strap so the downward deceleration of the ejection seat took longer than the airframe's (it's not the fall that hurts you, it's the sudden stop). The result was probably the Navy's first crashworthiness improvement since the introduction of the shoulder harness more than ten years earlier. Chance Vought designed a 3ft-long stainless steel strap attached between the cockpit bulkhead and the bottom of the ejection seat catapult tube, in conjunction with a frangible energy-absorbing foam plastic seat cushion to address the seat pan concerns. In the event of a hard gear-up landing or nose gear collapse, the strap stretched several inches, bringing the seat to a stop much slower than the cockpit. The laboratory did a comparison test of a standard seat and the energy-absorbing seat in 1956 and determined that the latter significantly reduced the risk of injury to the pilot. These modifications were instituted fleet-wide for operating Cutlass units through the Aircraft Service Change programme but due to logistic issues not all F7Us received them before their retirement.

CHAPTER EIGHTEEN

A fact-based assessment of the F7U-3 programme

Some reputations are based on ill-informed gossip; others, unexamined statements, and misconstrued statistics

Ironically, the widely held reputations of the Navy's first three jet fighters equipped with afterburners are not justified. Many aviation enthusiasts hold the Douglas F4D Skyray in high regard, in large part because of its world records for climb and speed performance, while the McDonnell F3H Demon is considered a disappointment and thought to have been retired quickly. The Vought F7U-3 Cutlass? It was described in one error-filled online video as 'The Strangest and Most Dangerous Navy Jet Ever Flown'.

In fact, from a carrier-based fighter standpoint, the F4D was the least effective of the three. To be fair, it was point-designed to fulfil a late 1940s Navy requirement for a deck-launched interceptor. The resulting sacrifice of range and endurance for climb performance was subsequently determined to be ill-advised with respect to defence of

A rare launch of a Douglas F4D without external tanks: 'I'll be right back.' *Bulban*

The F3H-2 armed with Sparrow III missiles was the US Navy's first fully effective all-weather fleet air defence jet fighter. ***US Navy***

the carrier from air attack. The F3H had a long career considering the rapid advancement in aerodynamics and engine performance at the time. The F7U? It was superior to the F4D in every respect except for rate of climb and primarily an also-ran to the F3H because of its shortfall relative to the Demon in range and endurance, which was still better than the Skyray's!

The Douglas F4D Skyray did briefly hold the world record for absolute speed – but contrary to numerous statements in print, it was not supersonic in level flight – and had a spectacular rate of climb, again setting world records, particularly when unencumbered with external tanks or other stores. That, however, was pretty much its only positive attribute. Without drop tanks, the F4D was a one-trick pony with less than one hour of flight time even with limited use of its afterburner. To match the range and endurance of an F7U-3 using only its internal fuel, it needed to be launched with two 150-gallon drop tanks (standard was two 300-gallon tanks).

NATC's final BIS report dated 6 January 1958 was frank about some of its shortcomings: "The F4D-1 (AW) is marginally effective as an all-weather fighter. Major deficiencies are a modest maximum speed capability, poor transonic flying qualities, and armament control system limitations." Supersonic speeds could be achieved and maintained in a dive but there was no effective supersonic manoeuvring capability: "The aircraft decelerates rapidly as soon as g forces are applied." However, at that point not only had most of the F4Ds on contract already been delivered, deployments with the Skyray had even begun to fulfil the need for a high-performance, all-weather fighter in the carrier air group.

The F4D had other shortcomings as well. Its handling qualities on approach were barely adequate (it did not help that forward visibility in heavy rain was poor). It had only one hydraulic system for flight control. If it failed, there was a reversion to manual (unpowered) control, which was only acceptable for a 'deferred emergency', i.e. one not requiring an immediate landing but rendering it no longer capable of its mission. A Douglas test pilot was nearly killed by his discovery that when the F4D was decelerated abruptly from maximum speed, it would pitch up violently; the addition of an electronic trim compensator was required. Although it was equipped with a visual-assist radar, the control stick partially blocked the pilot's view of the radarscope used to aim and fire its unguided rockets, further decreasing the likelihood of hitting even a large, non-manoeuvring target with them. It was never armed with an effective long-range, all-weather missile, i.e. one that was radar-guided.

Before an upcoming deployment in 1959, an Air Group Commander tried unsuccessfully to exchange the F4D squadron that had been assigned to him for one equipped with straight-wing F2H-3 or -4 Banshees that he felt would be more operationally suitable for his all-weather fighter requirement. Its three-year career in the Pacific fleet was only a year longer than the F7U's; in those squadrons, the 'Fords' were replaced by F3H-2 Demons as soon as enough became available; F4D squadrons did deploy with the Atlantic fleet through mid-1962, probably because the carriers were not as far from shore bases. (Given the plan to withdraw it from carrier-based squadrons as soon as practicable, BuAer did not bother with a formal change to provide the F4D with in-flight refuelling.) Only nine deployable Navy squadrons were equipped with the F4D, the same as the F7U-3, although they did make more deployments than the F7U squadrons. F4Ds were also assigned to several Marine Corps fighter squadrons, at least one of which deployed on a carrier, the rest being land-based where its limited range and endurance were not an operational handicap. Not exactly a glowing resume and yet a mention of the F4D Skyray nowadays does not result in sneering, uninformed, knee-jerk remarks about its supposed inadequacies like the F7U Cutlass does.

Unlike the F4D, the F3H provided the Navy with an effective all-weather fleet air defence against bombers when armed with the Sparrow III missile. It had none of the F4D's shortcomings: its handling qualities from approach to supersonic speed (albeit again only achieved in a descent) were excellent and its essential systems, including the engine, fully redundant.

Visibility over the nose was outstanding; its radar scope was large and located high on the instrument panel in a relatively spacious cockpit. Even without external tanks, its range and endurance were more than adequate for carrier operations and it also had in-flight refuelling capability. As a result, the F3H was operated by twenty-three deployable Navy squadrons, more than twice as many as the F4D.

Some of the lack of appreciation of the F3H's contribution to the defence of the aircraft carriers on which it was deployed between 1956 and 1964 undoubtedly results from an emphasis on problems – particularly with both its J40 engine as well as the J71 that replaced it – during its development and first introduction into service. There were several F3H crashes, some fatal, when it was powered by the Westinghouse J40 engine as well as a serious early in-service problem with its J71 engine: before a modification was implemented, it was prone to flaming out in heavy rain, a worrisome tendency for a single-engine, all-weather fighter. It was also considered and nicknamed a 'lead sled' compared to its day fighter counterpart in the air group at the time, the truly supersonic F8U Crusader; opinion of its performance suffered even more by comparison – *after the fact* – to its replacement, the F4H Phantom II.

Responsibility for the F7U-3's brief service life

Many accounts of the F7U-3 programme state that it was a failure: not only lacking in performance (Gutless Cutlass) and dangerous to fly (Ensign Killer) but quickly withdrawn from service: the last F7U-3 was accepted by the Navy in December 1955; the last flights by a deployable squadron occurred only twenty-one months later. While there is some basis for those suppositions, the main reason for the Cutlass' short operational career was its lengthy gestation that allowed for aircraft with more efficient engines and/or optimised for specific missions to become deployable. That allowed McDonnell to recover from the Westinghouse J40 engine programme failure and complete development of the F3H Demon with the Allison J71 and Douglas to accomplish development of the A4D Skyhawk with the Wright J65. Their engines were not the same but shared a common superiority to the J46: the ongoing improvement in jet engine thrust-to-weight and specific fuel consumption. The J46 reflected the performance standard of jet engines qualified in the late 1940s like the J34 that it was based on. By the mid-1950s, however, it had somewhat lower thrust-to-weight and higher SFC performance relative to newer engines. As a result, all other factors being equal, the F7U's range suffered by comparison to tactical aircraft powered by those engines.

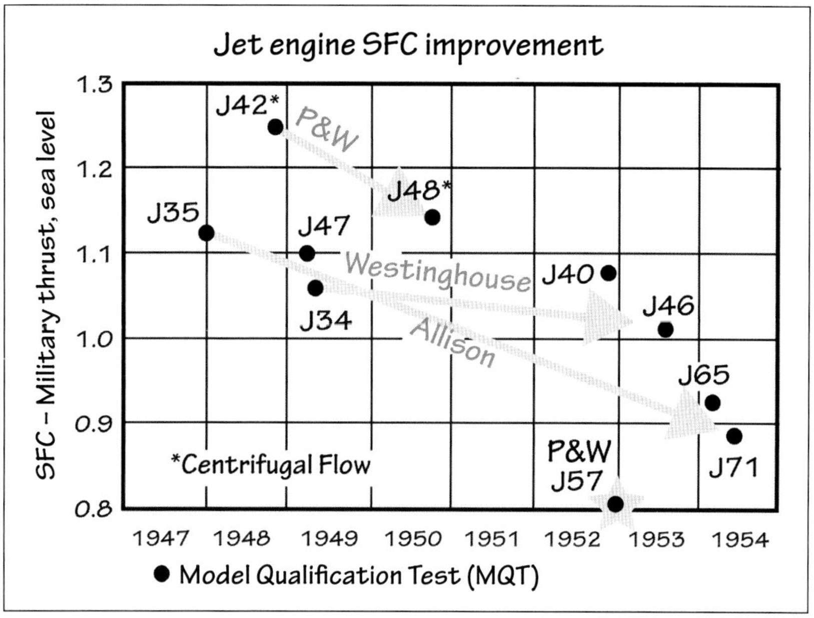

Most jet engine manufacturers were able to significantly improve SFC by the early 1950s. Westinghouse was not one of them. ***Thomason***

A Vought analysis of prospective engines in early 1953 for their day fighter proposal that resulted in the F8U Crusader reflected that. It compared the J57, J65, J71, and J73 along with the J46 (two to meet the thrust requirement). The J46 option was rejected out of hand as having 'quite inferior performance relative to comparable single-engine airplanes'. The J71 and J73 were considered to be inferior to the J57 with its innovative, fuel-efficient two-spool compressor but resulted in 'reasonably satisfactory airplane performance' if a substitute for the J57 was required as it had been for the J40. The J65 provided acceptable performance for a smaller day fighter requirement with a 300nm radius at significantly less total power plant weight (engine + fuel + fuel system) than two J46s.

Responsibility for the time required for F7U-3 development and qualification is shared among the Navy (i.e. BuAer), Westinghouse, and Vought in roughly that order.

The Bureau of Aeronautics decisions and demands: BuAer, after taking a leap of faith in Vought and its radical 1946 proposal for a swept-wing, tail-less, transonic day fighter, proceeded to make successive major changes to the programme – some arguably shortsighted – that in hindsight contributed to the F7U-3 having a short career and also to an extent a poor reputation.

In December 1949, shortly after BuAer deemed it necessary to have Vought beef up the structure of the

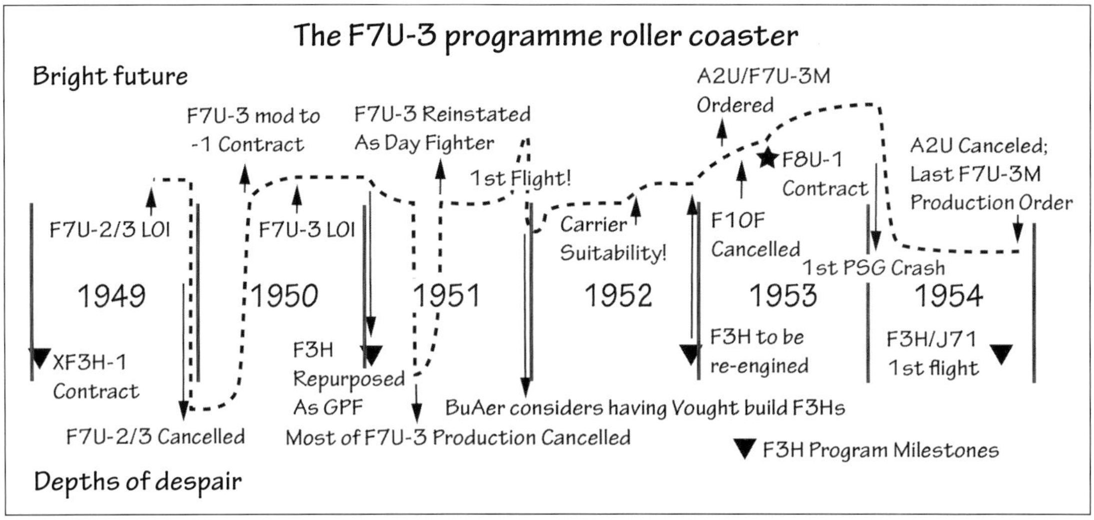

Over the course of the F7U-3 programme, Vought went from a bright future to the depths of despair and back more than once. The status of the McDonnell F3H programme was one of the reasons. *Thomason*

F7U-1 day fighter for production as the F7U-2, it cancelled the programme. President Truman had made draconian cuts in defence budgets. The Navy decided to sacrifice the F7U programme in favour of funding all-weather fighters. Although not likely (as indicated by the F7U-1's brief and unsatisfactory association with the Blue Angels in early 1952 due to maintenance, spare parts availability, and engine development issues), the F7U-2 might have otherwise been available to challenge the swept-wing MiG-15 before the end of the Korean War.

When defence funding was increased in response to the North Korean invasion of South Korea in June 1950, instead of continuing with the F7U-2 as a day fighter, the Navy directed Vought to make major changes to the Cutlass, repurposing it to be a larger, heavier, general-purpose fighter back-up to the relatively high-risk Grumman F10F Jaguar programme. In addition, reacting to shortcomings apparent in its first jet fighters, BuAer now insisted on flight control power redundancy, increased structural strength, and other design requirements that had a significant

From top to bottom, the Navy's front-line fighters in 1955: the Grumman F9F-8 Cougar, Vought F7U-3 Cutlass, McDonnell F2H-3 (or 4) Banshee, and North American FJ-3 Fury. Of these, only the straight-wing Banshee had true all-weather capability. *US Navy*

F7U-3 No. 4 on *Coral Sea*'s deck-edge lift in November 1952, framed by the opening to the hangar bay. *US Navy*

impact on its weight and complexity. The resulting F7U-3 specification negotiation was one-sided. Vought reluctantly acquiesced to BuAer's demands, since it otherwise might soon not have an aircraft in production. Moreover, BuAer had just repurposed the F3H to be a general-purpose fighter.

Less than a year later, BuAer decided that the F7U-3's take-off weight would not allow it to be launched safely from existing carrier catapults (although the more powerful steam catapult was then in development, it was too soon to count on it being adopted). Achieving a satisfactory launch weight primarily involved removing much of its mission capability including a reduction in fuel capacity and elimination of all-weather mission avionics like the visual-assist radar. However, the F7U-3's size, structural requirements, and system specifications remained the same, which meant that the all-weather mission equipment and internal fuel capacity could be restored if more powerful catapults were introduced.

That also meant that the F7U-3 was now a day fighter like the swept-wing FJ-2 Fury and F9F-6 Cougar hastily being developed following the MiG-15's appearance in the skies over Korea but more complex, i.e. more expensive. Worse, improved versions of the Fury and Cougar, the FJ-3 and F9F-8, were subsequently available to deploy a few months before the F7U-3 finally was. What's more, the Cutlass' performance superiority to them in acceleration and rate of climb provided by its afterburners was accompanied by not only less, but marginally acceptable, range and endurance compared to theirs.

The F7U-3 was also bigger and heavier (the first to require nose wheel steering): the initial impression had to be that it was imposing, if not downright huge. On deck, the pilot could look down on the crew of the big multi-engine AJ Savage bomber when he taxied by. Going into the hangar deck for the first time, the pilot or brake rider might very well wonder if there was enough clearance with the overhead. The folded wings were akin to gigantic billboards. More significantly, when configured for parking with the wings folded, the F7U-3 took up roughly 55% more of the limited deck area than the F9F-8 with its wings folded, 40% more than the FJ-3. From the standpoint of procurement cost, it was certainly 'big' relative to a simple, single-engine day fighter like the Cougar and the Fury, not to mention the additional maintenance

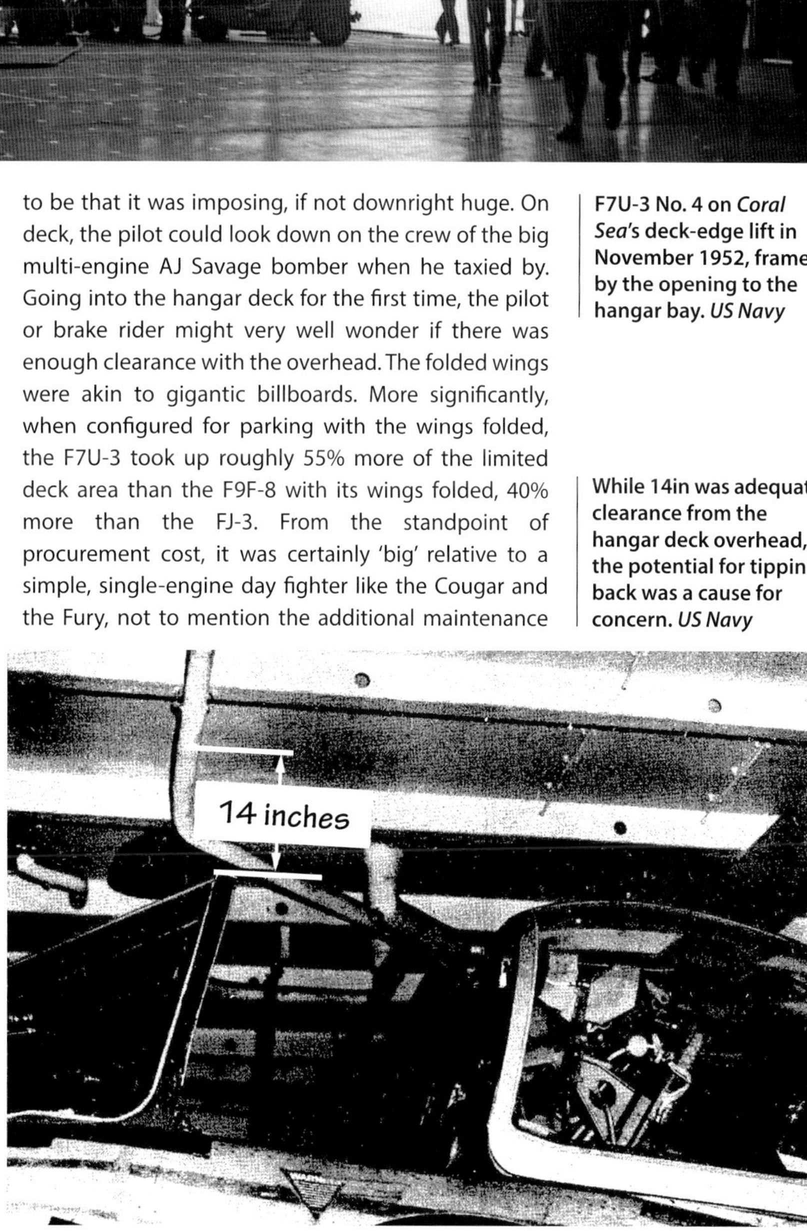

While 14in was adequate clearance from the hangar deck overhead, the potential for tipping back was a cause for concern. *US Navy*

North American General Purpose Attack Weapon (NAGPAW)

In early 1954, North American Aviation had enough confidence in the Westinghouse J46 to incorporate it in an unsolicited proposal, NAGPAW, to BuAer. It was a single-seat, twin-engine carrier-based aircraft about the same size as the A2U, optimised for delivery of a nuclear weapon. Unlike the A4D and A2U, it provided an all-weather capability via an 'inertial autonavigator' that allowed the pilot to fly to a destination at night and in cloud without reference to the ground, stars, or radio signals, utilising a radar for periodic position updates and the final attack. A second innovative feature was the internal carriage of the bomb but rather than dropping it out of the bottom of the fuselage, it was ejected aft out of a tunnel between the engines.

North American's timing was excellent. In December 1954, OpNav directed BuAer to repurpose the big, supersonic McDonnell AH general-purpose fighter then under contract to be the F4H, a Sparrow-armed fleet air defence fighter, now a high priority. OpNav generated a separate requirement for a supersonic attack aircraft as a replacement for the AH. North American quickly responded with a proposal for a significantly bigger and faster two-seat derivative of NAGPAW powered by two J79s like the AH/F4H. It became the Navy's A3J Vigilante.

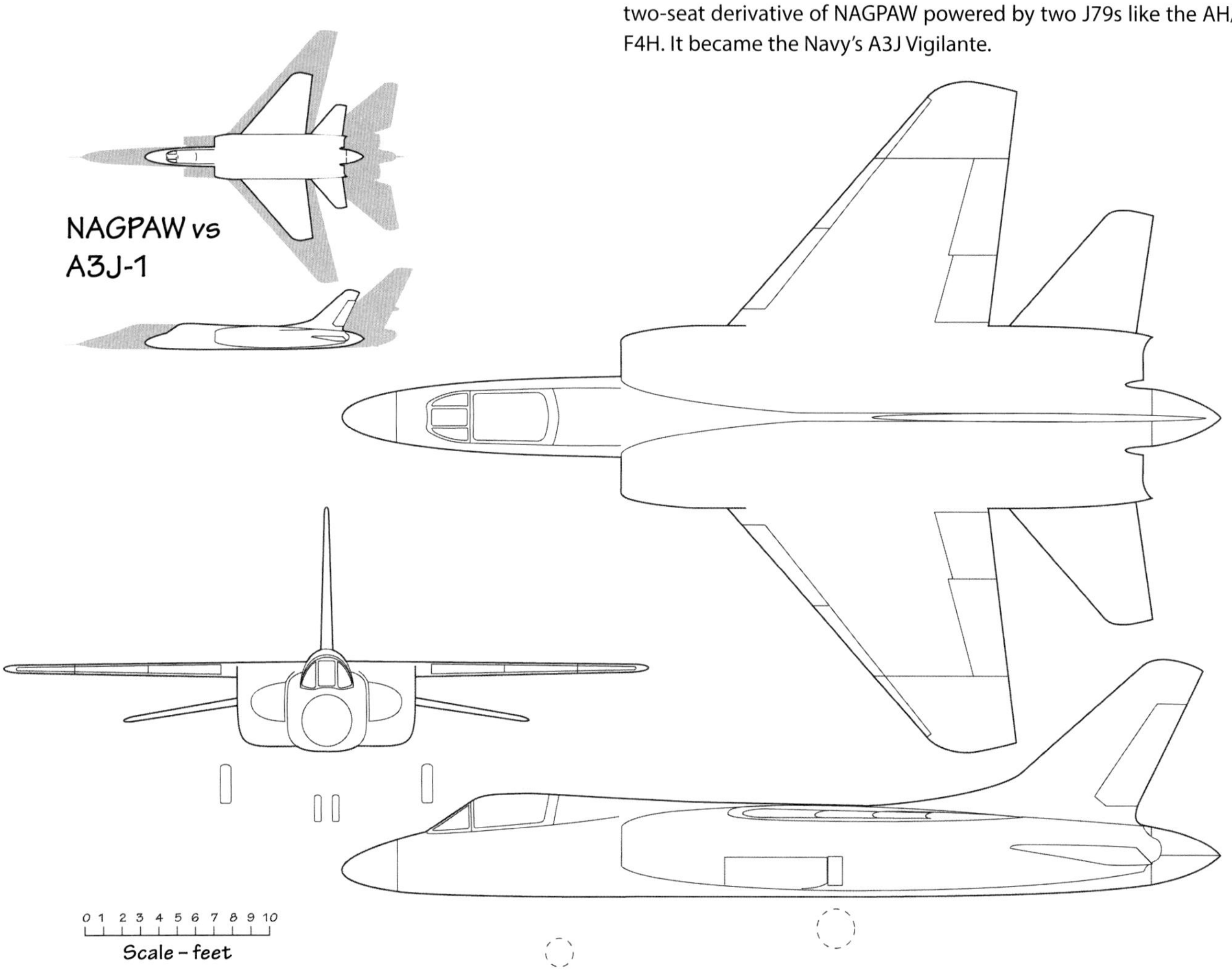

required for the -3's multiple and complex systems dictated by BuAer.

As it turned out, at-sea testing in late 1952 proved that the Cutlass could be launched safely by the most powerful hydraulic catapult at weights that allowed it to be configured as an all-weather fighter with at least adequate endurance, certainly when carrying external tanks as the F4D Skyray, FJ-3 Fury, and A4D Skyhawk almost always did. Although other factors might have delayed its availability in any event, not repurposing the F7U-3 to be a day fighter in 1951 might have resulted in it being the all-weather, transonic replacement for the F2H-3/4 Banshee in the carrier air group well before the F4D and F3H Demon were ready to be. The Skyray, for example, did not fly with its production engine, the P&W J57, until mid-1954. An F4D with a fire control system to aim unguided rockets in all-weather conditions, without which it was a day fighter, was not available for full evaluation by the Navy until July 1957. Similarly, the first F3H flight with the Allison J71 occurred in October 1954.

In early 1953 the Navy, with Vought's help and encouragement, did initiate development of F7U derivatives, the missile-armed F7U-3M and the Mk 7 nuke-carrying A2U-1, that were better suited to its size. This was not entirely altruistic: the F10F, F3H, and F4D programmes that the Navy had continued at the expense of the F7U-2 programme were all floundering at the time. Meanwhile, the Sparrow missile programme was making satisfactory development progress and would soon be in need of a carrier-based transonic fighter to employ it. Similarly, one was needed for the Mk 7 nuclear strike mission.

One might-have-been scenario: in 1953, BuAer cancels the F4D and F3H programmes instead of having Douglas replace the J40 with the J57 and McDonnell, the J40 with the J71. It adds a visual-assist radar to the F7U-3M armed with Sparrow I missiles and subsequently arms it with the more capable Sparrow III. The Cutlass would have had a long career like the F3H and a very different reputation among aviation enthusiasts and historians.

Westinghouse disappoints: Lengthy F7U development and qualification were factors in the F7U having a short operational career. They allowed McDonnell to catch up with its F3H and Douglas to complete development of the A4D. Some would argue that Westinghouse was primarily responsible for that. It should be noted, however, that BuAer, which contracted with the company to develop J46 engines to a thrust/weight/SFC specification and deliver them on schedule on Vought's behalf, had arguably overburdened it with multiple engine programmes: an afterburning J34, the J46, and two different J40 variants. Each of these also required Westinghouse to work with multiple airframe contractors, a drain on management and engineering resources. Moreover Westinghouse – although a jet-engine pioneer with its J30 and J34 (a scaled-up J30) – actually had very limited experience with not only aircraft engine development but also production and support. As it turned out, Westinghouse was not equal to the challenge.

It is also debatable as to how much J46 development and production engine deliveries delayed the F7U-3's deployment. For example, acceptable performance of the cannon installation was not achieved until early 1955, due in part to the problems with the new, government-furnished Mk 12 developed by the Navy's Bureau of Ordnance. At the time, four 20mm cannon were the only air-to-air armament available for day fighters (production of the Sidewinder missile was only then beginning and it was not declared operational until 1956). It is unlikely, given the problems with firing the cannon above 35,000ft, that the Cutlass would have been deployed earlier. Commencing gunfire testing early with the J46 instead of the somewhat different inlet design required for the J35 might have expedited development of the final solution but probably not significantly.

Removing and replacing a jet engine – particularly those lengthened by the addition of an afterburner – in an aircraft carrier's hangar deck required the use of a significant amount of the scarce area available. *US Navy*

The J46 development delay resulted in the F7U-3 being the only aircraft to be powered by it. That, along with much of the F7U-3 flight test and development being accomplished with the J35, resulted in a lack of accumulation of flight time that would have resulted in the J46 TBO being increased above the initial 150 hours. The need for more frequent engine removals had an impact on the maintenance man hours per flight hour and engine overhaul expense for the F7U fleet. However, the TBO was high enough so it did not create an undue maintenance or excessive spare engine storage burden during the standard six-month deployment. The average total hours accumulated per aircraft generally did not exceed 100. An engine removal and replacement at sea was therefore usually not required by the low TBO if the aircraft deployed with low time since overhaul engines and the flight time thereafter was spread evenly among them.

Although there were no unacceptable F7U-3 deficiencies initially identified by BIS testing other than the suitability of its armament, for which resolution of its problems were ongoing, the sheer number of resulting mandatory modifications also delayed its readiness for deployment by fleet squadrons. At the very least, however, for more than a year Vought had to make do with only a close approximation of the F7U-3 while it was powered by J35s until YJ46s were delivered to Vought for flight test. It took almost another year for Westinghouse to deliver production-standard engines. That probably had some impact on Vought's lead over other manufacturers in developing the US Navy's first transonic fighter that it had enjoyed based on its F7U-1 flight test.

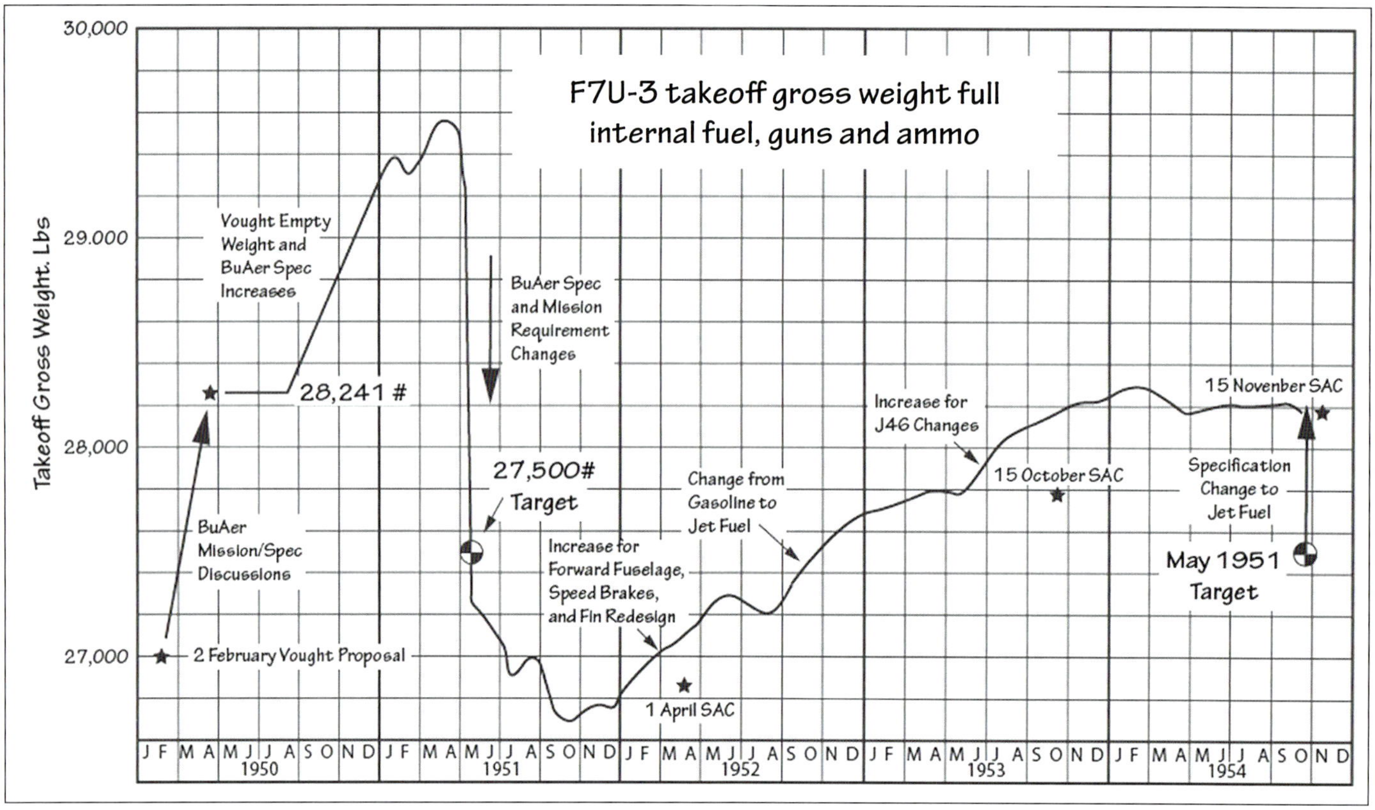

Growth of an aircraft's empty weight is rarely avoided during design and development and inevitable during its service life due to problem/shortcoming resolution and product improvements. Taking into account the 660lb weight increase caused by BuAer's decision to use jet fuel instead of gasoline, however, Vought met its May 1951 gross weight target of 27,500lb for the production F7U-3s. *Thomason*

Westinghouse management could claim that the shortfall in the originally guaranteed J46 thrust was not significant in and of itself:

		Military thrust (SFC)	Combat thrust (SFC)
J46-WE-2	Proposed	4,080 (1.0)	6,100 (2.5)
J46-WE-8	Flight test/production	3,980 (1.1)	5,800 (2.4)
J46-WE-18*	For A2U-1	4,100 (1.0)	6,100 (2.5)

* Demonstrated in a 150-hour qualification test in December 1954 after A2U programme cancellation.

Moreover, although Westinghouse was projecting as early as May 1951 that the engines for flight test would have slightly lower ratings than those proposed for the -2s in September 1948, it was also optimistically projecting that J46 thrust in afterburner might be 7,000lb for F7U-3 initial production and as much as 7,800lb shortly thereafter.

Unfortunately from a thrust standpoint, as the Red Queen said, 'It takes all the running you can do, to keep in the same place. If you want to get somewhere else, you must run at least twice as fast.' The most significant Westinghouse failure was that they were unable to increase the J46's thrust beyond what was originally proposed. Like almost all aircraft, the F7U-3 was heavier than proposed; like all aircraft, its empty weight and the desired useful load increased thereafter. Although Westinghouse did finally demonstrate its initial J46 performance commitments, it was not able to quickly improve on them like P&W and GE did with the J57 and J79 respectively.

Vought did consider other engine alternatives at least six times before the delivery of the first flight-worthy J46 but always concluded that the Cutlass' performance with it would be as good as or superior to them *if* Westinghouse qualified it to the original -2 specification. The Navy did not disagree. Also at that point, the substantial redesign required to replace the J46 was certain to result in production delivery delays that would compromise Vought's competitive position vis-à-vis the other fighters and attack aircraft that the Navy was developing.

While Westinghouse did eventually qualify the J46 at the proposed -2 military and combat thrust performance, and -8 military/combat thrust ratings and SFC shortfalls were not significant, the -8 SFC shortfall was worse at lower thrust ratings; since most of the mission flight time was at throttle settings lower than military or combat, that resulted in a significant reduction in mission radius, exacerbated by higher than predicted F7U-3 drag. The combination of the failure of both Westinghouse and Vought to achieve predicted SFC and L/D respectively resulted in a notable shortfall in range and endurance relative to other carrier-based aircraft in being or development.

Questionable Vought decisions: Besides the usual shortfall in both weight and drag on performance, Vought bore at least some responsibility for the limited career of the F7U-3. That said, it would be unfair to fault it for the unusual 'tail-less' configuration of the Cutlass. It was in fact one of three alternatives that the company proposed in response to the 1946 OS-105 day fighter requirement, the other two being conventional as were all the other contractors' proposals. BuAer selected it rather than any of the other proposals or Vought's alternatives, at least in part because it promised to be an aerodynamic solution for known transonic flight control problems that only *subsequently* proved to be better addressed by the appropriate location of an all-moving horizontal tail relative to the wing.

The company's lack of pushback against BuAer's insistence on arguably onerous specification and schedule requirements was management's judgment call based on the need to keep a badly needed near-term production programme sold (it was only one company of five that the Navy could contract with for its fighter requirements). As Fred Detweiler wrote in a 19 March 1953 letter to the Chance Vought Leadership Team:

> Beginning in 1950, when the F7U-3 airplane was being put together on paper after the F7U-2 project was cancelled, we have had a hard time keeping the F7U-3 configuration firm. At that time we had virtually no prospective business and we were in a mood to try anything the Navy suggested with the Cutlass in order to sell it. We accepted pretty severe requirements for the airplane along with a very difficult production schedule. We tried to swallow our own design troubles without letting them affect the schedule.

For example, Vought made two F7U-3 configuration decisions that in hindsight contributed to its performance and handling qualities shortcomings:

- The F7U-3 wing was essentially the same as the -1's. BuAer had questioned the impact of its thickness on transonic drag and buffet but Vought's chief engineer, in the interest of minimising development /qualification risk, argued against changing it. Making it thinner would also have reduced the internal fuel capacity, possibly more than the decrease in drag improved range.

- Similarly, no change was made to the size of the vertical fins even though the side-facing surface of the forward fuselage was increased not once but twice. To be fair, Vought may have relied on satisfactory results from NACA spin test model trials to justify not adding the weight and drag of bigger vertical fins, but the result of inadequate directional stability at very high angles of attack with the wing leading-edge slats retracted produced a proclivity for a loss of control resulting in what became known as the post-stall gyration, one of the F7U-3's most cited idiosyncrasies.

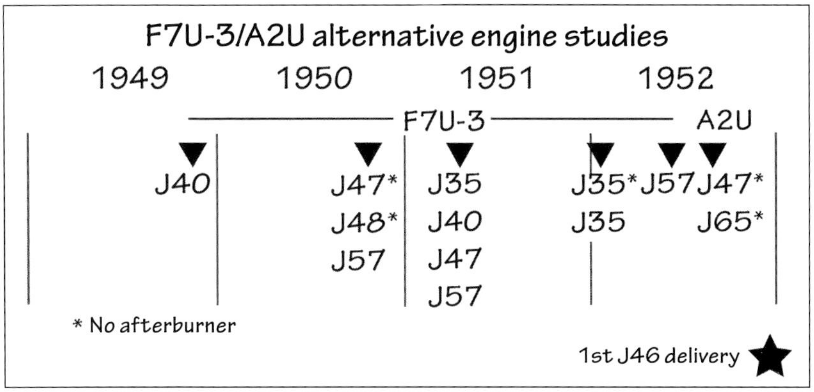

Because of the ongoing J46 development problems and schedule slips at Westinghouse, Vought periodically evaluated substituting other engines in the F7U. BuAer always decided to continue with the J46. ***Thomason***

Another Vought decision, at BuAer's behest, with an impact on performance was to take little, if any, risk in the initial design of the airframe structure from a strength standpoint in order to minimise its weight. In contrast, Douglas deliberately used minimal or even negative margins, betting that what did not break in proof testing was adequate to the task and what did break could be readily beefed up for production. If service use identified additional shortcomings, then redesign, retrofit, and new production would still result in the lightest design. The amount of overweight that resulted from overly strong F7U-3 structure is unknowable but since structure comprised about half of the empty weight, it was probably not trivial. Avoiding the risk of programme schedule delays required for redesign and retest of inadequate structure was of some benefit. Moreover, it resulted in an airframe demonstrated to be unbreakable for all practical purposes and provided the strength that allowed the F7U-3M's gross weight increase required for the fleet air defence mission.

Range and endurance

Somewhat indicative of a lack of knowledge and credibility of pronouncements by most Cutlass critics is that its most significant shortcoming, range and endurance, relative to the other carrier-based fighters is seldom mentioned. An aircraft's range and endurance are primarily determined by a combination of only three factors: fuel fraction, maximum lift divided by drag (L/D), and engine efficiency, i.e. SFC. A deficiency in one can be offset by superiority in another. For example, the A4D Skyhawk had a low L/D as a result of limiting its wing span to 27ft 6in. However, a ruthless approach to minimising empty weight (e.g. elimination of the wing's folding joint and hardware), meant its fuel fraction, the ratio of fuel on board relative to its empty weight, was about 50% more than average for other carrier-based jets. As a result, its range and endurance were comparable to them. The F7U-3 was about average

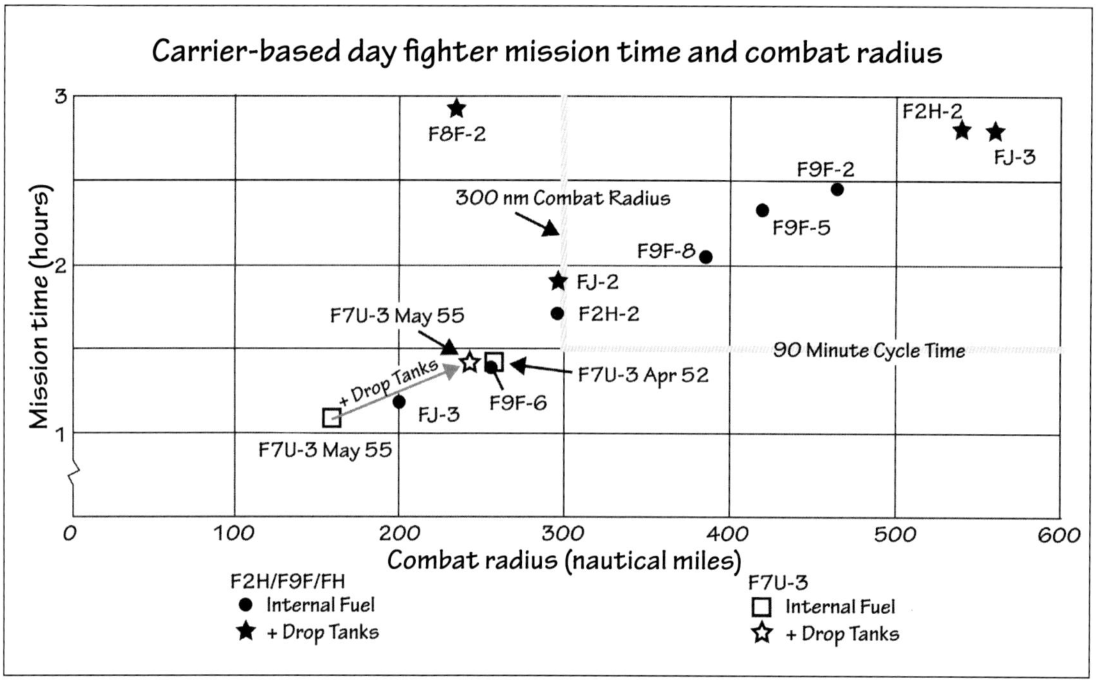

The data on this chart is from the respective SACs with the mission time and combat radius being calculated using the same combat radius problem requirements for altitudes, speeds, thrust, time, etc. The F7U-1 data points are probably optimistic and the SAC mission profile used required less combat time and fuel reserve. *Thomason*

in fuel fraction and L/D compared to the other transonic fighters with axial-flow engines but handicapped by the J46's fuel efficiency.

A first approximation of the relative range and endurance of Navy aircraft is provided by the Standard Aircraft Characteristic charts for each type. In addition to a dimensioned three-view drawing; summary description of the aircraft's mission, powerplant, weights, etc; and speed/altitude performance, it provides data on its combat radius and average cruising speed for one or more mission/armament combinations. The baseline mission armament useful load was usually limited to ammunition. An example (the detailed requirements changes over time), the Mil-C-5011A radius problem for the General Purpose and Escort Fighter With an Afterburner dated 5 November 1951, was defined as follows:

- Warm-up, Take-off, and Rendezvous: Five minutes at normal-rated thrust and one minute at combat-rated thrust
- Climb to cruise altitude: At military-rated thrust
- Cruise out: Maximum-range speed and altitude
- Combat: 15 minutes at military-rated thrust and five minutes at combat-rated thrust
- Cruise back: Maximum-range speed and altitude
- Reserve: 20 minutes at sea level, maximum-endurance speed, all engines operating, plus 5% of initial fuel.

To be conservative, engine specification fuel consumption data was increased by 5% and neither combat nor the descent from cruise altitude to return for landing were to be included in the range calculation. Total mission time included the twenty minutes for combat but not the twenty-minute landing reserve.

The first two day fighter jets that the Navy deployed, the McDonnell F2H-2 and Grumman F9F-2, provided a margin of an hour or more relative to a ninety-minute cycle time after provisions for tip tanks were added to the prototypes; their combat radius was more than 400nm. The F7U-1 capability, as projected optimistically by its 1 June 1949 SAC and based on the less onerous Mil-C-5011 F-5 mission definition, was almost identical to the F2H-2's, which had acceptable endurance without tip tanks and almost three hours with them. By comparison, the Grumman F8F Bearcat, the last piston-engine fighter developed by the Navy, had a mission endurance of almost three hours with full internal fuel and one 150-gallon external tank, although twenty minutes stipulated for rendezvous after take-off and a full hour of reserve before landing reduced its combat mission radius to only 235nm.

In March 1950, BuAer and Vought had agreed on a specification that resulted in the F7U-3 general-purpose fighter powered by the J46-WE-2 engine having a combat radius of 500nm on internal fuel using the Mil-C-5011 F-5 mission definition. The reduced weight specification agreed to a year later removed 390lb of fuel from the outer wing panel, reducing the radius by 50nm. The change to the -8 engine resulted in an initial decrease of 25nm. The next major change was a redefinition of the general-purpose fighter problem in accordance with Mil-C-5011A. It added one minute of afterburning to take-off (465lb of JP-4), five minutes at military for combat (314lb) and the substitution of twenty minutes of loiter on both engines (1,468lb) at sea level for 5% of the reserve

(527lb). That reduced the combat radius by 135nm to slightly under 300nm with two 150-gallon external tanks that would be dropped when empty.

According to the F7U-3 SAC dated 1 April 1952, on internal fuel only it then had endurance and range still the same as the F9F-6's, the first of the Navy's swept-wing fighters to deploy: it was capable of meeting the minimum cycle time requirement in practice. The FJ-2 fell well short, so much so that its SAC did not even provide internal fuel-only data! The addition of two 200-gallon drop tanks almost doubled its fuel capacity, resulting in a combat radius and mission time essentially equal to that of the Grumman F9F-6 on internal fuel. As a result, it was seldom photographed in flight without them and rarely seen on a carrier deck in any event.

The combat radius and mission time of the Cutlass and the Navy's other two swept-wing day fighters diverged dramatically thereafter. The combination of more drag than predicted and a higher J46 engine SFC than expected resulted in the F7U-3's steadily deteriorating; the 15 May 1955 F7U-3 SAC internal fuel-only profile projected a mission time of a little over an hour. The addition of two 150-gallon drop tanks to the -3 improved the Cutlass' combat radius and mission time almost to the original internal fuel-only capability. In the meantime, however, Grumman had stretched the Cougar to create the F9F-8 with more internal fuel capacity, significantly increasing its combat radius and mission time and; North American had replaced the obsolescent J47 with the more fuel efficient J65 in the FJ-3, so now the Fury, with drop tanks, matched the F2H-2's excellent mission time and combat radius with full tip tanks.

Of course, the F7U-3 pilot had options that enabled him to conform to a ninety-minute cycle time with a satisfactory reserve, starting with minimising the use of afterburner and/or combat time. An idle power descent from altitude provided an additional fuel cushion (one F7U-1 pilot in IFR conditions, his destination below minimums, shut down both engines to minimise fuel burn in the descent from cruise altitude to reach his alternate that was almost at minimums). If required to loiter at low altitude, the Cutlass pilot could shut down one engine: the remaining engine would be burning less fuel than two engines for the same amount of thrust because a jet engine's specific fuel consumption improves with increasing thrust until afterburning is employed.

Another alternative, adding two 150-gallon drop tanks, provided a mission time of ninety minutes. Again, judicious use of afterburner increased the cycle time margin. Substituting four and a half minutes of combat thrust for fifteen minutes at military thrust slightly reduced the mission time but increased combat effectiveness with a dramatic increase in acceleration and sustained *g* capability in turning flight.

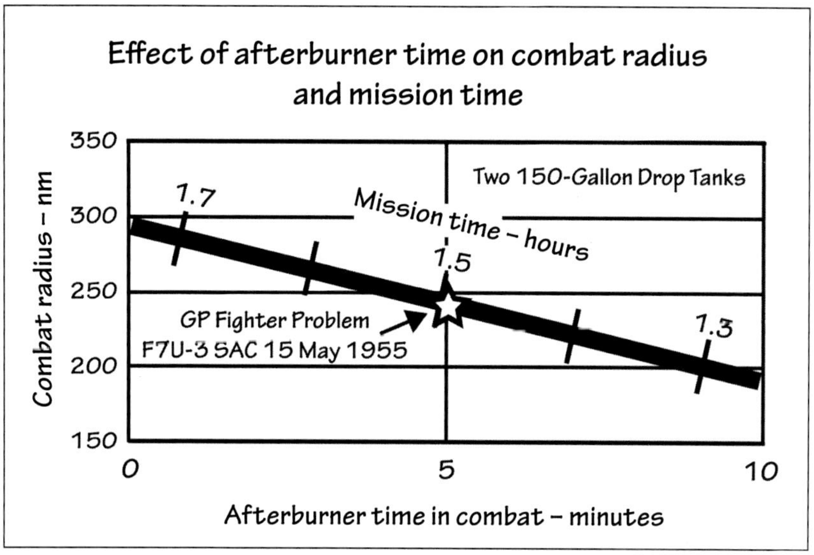

Nevertheless, for the same mission specification, the other swept-wing day fighters available for deployment with the carrier air groups had significantly better range and endurance than the F7U-3. The same would be true for the F3H Demon powered by the J71 engine. In 1952, the Navy also established a combat radius minimum for its next day fighter: 300nm on internal fuel and 400nm with external tanks.

Your mileage may vary: when carrying external fuel tanks, as the F4D and FJ-3 almost invariably did, the F7U-3 had acceptable cycle times with moderate use of afterburner, which significantly increased time to climb, acceleration from cruise speed, and sustained *g* capability. *Thomason*

First-hand naval aviator opinions

Contrary to the reputation promulgated by magazine articles and on the internet (the F7U is seemingly every basement dweller's favourite whipping post), the Cutlass has been praised by virtually all of the more than 200 pilots who flew the F7U-3 that Al Casby has had the pleasure and honour to have interviewed over the last fifty-plus years.

For one thing, the basic airframe is remembered as being incredibly strong – every one that crashed was intact. Vought test pilots claimed that they had pulled 16 *gs* and pushed to -9 *gs* without bending the airframe. They would not have known that absent an instrumented airframe, of course – a standard *g* meter only measures from +10 to -5 *gs*, both well in excess of the Navy's limit-load factor requirement for fighters. Reaching specification limits was expected to result in obvious damage if not structural failure. Withstanding *gs* of +16 and -9 is incredible, both as a claim and a capability, and if accurate this structural strength in excess of specification contributed to the F7U-3s being overweight. Further, the F7U's roll rate was exceptional. In mock air-to-air combat it excelled, with adversary pilots describing it as like 'trying to follow a bat'.

Its performance in a climb when using afterburners was sparkling but a mixed blessing. The Navy's first jet aircraft had required pilots to understand how differently a jet had to be flown compared to a prop plane, most importantly to cruise at high altitudes for best range and endurance; that a jet engine could not be throttled back to significantly increase loiter time like a piston engine could be; and critically from the standpoint of a standard carrier approach, that jet propulsion, even with afterburning, did not provide the immediate acceleration/climb performance that a propeller did at low speed. The F7U provided Navy pilots with initial operational experience with the pros and cons of afterburning engines, which would power the next and all-succeeding generations of fighters. The drawback was that this lighter-weight approach – a smaller engine with its thrust augmented significantly when required by an afterburner – to greatly increased combat thrust from an engine standpoint was very inefficient when afterburning was utilised. It was a critical consideration: an extra five minutes in afterburner rather than military thrust was roughly equal to the twenty-minute landing reserve at maximum endurance speed. In addition, the F7U-3's two J46s, when in afterburner burning almost 500lb of fuel a minute, could drain the engines' feed tank faster than it could be refilled from the other fuel tanks under certain circumstances.

'I liked flying the Cutlass,' wrote Doniphan (Don) B. Shelton, who retired as a Rear Admiral. He was a Navy Test Pilot School graduate who was the F7U-3 project officer in 1954: 'I checked out a lot of guys in it, and for the most part, once you got the guy above the threshold of fear and trepidation and got him in the air and flying, then he liked it.' He acknowledged that the post-stall gyration characteristic was violent and disconcerting but noted 'the recovery technique once the gyration began was to put the stick just aft of neutral – no lateral or rudder input – hang on and the airplane would recover nicely'.

According to Dick Cavicke, he never experienced much fear and trepidation, even on his first day at VF-124 when a classmate from flight school crashed a few minutes into his first Cutlass flight. Cavicke bridled at a local newspaper's attitude in 1956 when announcing the end of the Cutlass: 'The Miramar newspaper said, "VF-124 junks Cutlasses and gets new F3H Demons." That really torqued those of us who were flying the F7U-3,' he says. 'So when the day came, being the maintenance officer of the squadron, I deemed it necessary that one of our Cutlasses needed a test flight, and a few minutes before the Demons were set to arrive, I come smoking by. My squadron buddies said it was a thing of beauty – the plane was totally shrouded in vapour. Soon after, the Demons, which were limited because of some early engine problems, came putt-putting by at a much slower speed.'

Nevertheless, it's not hard to find Cutlass detractors with first-hand knowledge of it although some are clearly mistaken, either misremembering or not aware of subsequent developments. For example, in a February 1983 interview, naval aviator and NASA astronaut Wally Schirra stated that the F7U-3 post-stall gyration 'was not recoverable', which was incorrect. Although he had been part of the original *Project Cutlass* group and was transferred to Moffett Field when VC-3 became a Transitional Training Unit (he was number two to Shelton), he was transferred to the F3H-2N TTU when the F7U-3 transition programme was ended at VC-3. As a result, he may not have been aware of the successful development of a PSG recovery. He also said that it 'was quite an exciting airplane', although that may not have been meant as a compliment. However, in subsequent interviews, he would extol the aircraft's capabilities and spoke quite highly of it.

One naval aviator who lusted to fly the F7U but didn't expect to get the chance due to the aircraft's impending retirement, noticed a Cutlass on the ramp at NAS Floyd Bennett Field, New York. Upon inquiring, he was told that the aircraft needed to be ferried to Norfolk to be stricken. He immediately volunteered, quickly read the manual, and took off. 'I had no problems. The handling was beautiful; it actually was a very pleasant aircraft to fly. But yes, it was underpowered; you could feel the potential it had.' 'Overall, it was like that prom queen you always fantasised about getting into bed … and then you do, and she fails to meet your expectations.'

Conversely, the late RADM Alan B. Shepard Jr., later a Project Mercury and Apollo astronaut and one of the first batch of naval aviators to fly the F7U-3 and perform with it at airshows, bristled at the 'Gutless' moniker. 'All the aircraft could have used more thrust back then! But the Cutlass was the best performing of them all – it was a real hotrod!'

CHAPTER NINETEEN

Summary and epilogue

Horses for courses

Since the F7U-3 was arguably not underpowered, crash-prone relative to its jet fighter contemporaries, unacceptably deficient in range/endurance, or disliked by all who flew it, what was the primary reason for its relatively limited production and short service life? It was definitely not brand bias like your great grandfather's preference for a Ford or Chevrolet: Vought F4U Corsairs filled the decks of escort carriers off Korea in the early 1950s while Grumman F6F Hellcats were being used stateside for lead-in fighter training; Vought was selected in preference to all comers in the 1956 day fighter competition that resulted in the F8U Crusader.

One explanation is the Navy's well-intended but ill-starred attempt in the early 1950s to develop a carrier-based general-purpose fighter, the requirement that the F7U-2 day fighter and XF3H-1 interceptor were repurposed to fill. It proved to be an overly ambitious one. As might be expected of a jack of all trades, both were deficient in some respects to the mission-specific aircraft that the Navy was also developing. As a result, the air groups/wings continued to be comprised of a mix of squadrons employing specialised tactical aircraft: light attack, heavy/all-weather attack, day fighter, and all-weather fighter, while the fast-climbing, short-range interceptor requirement was to be replaced by surface-to-air missiles fired from escorts.

The F7U-3 was not the only carrier-based jet to come in second to an alternative in the Navy's belt and braces approach to ensuring that the fleet got state-of-the-art aircraft. The Grumman F11F Tiger day fighter was deficient in range, endurance, and performance compared to the Vought F8U Crusader: only about 200 were built – versus about 1,200 F8Us – and few deployed (it was subsequently usefully employed in lead-in fighter training and with the Blue Angels flight demonstration team). The North American FJ-4B was superior to the Douglas A4D in some ways but was also more expensive to procure; as a result only 220 were built and its service career was short, only about five years, compared to the A4D's: almost 3,000 Skyhawks were produced and it served with the air forces of several nations, some of which did not have an aircraft carrier.

The general-purpose fighter requirement was subsequently fulfilled by McDonnell's F4H Phantom II, which resulted from an unsolicited proposal of F3H improvement options. However, it was arguably not fully

An F3H-2N returning to McDonnell at St Louis following a test flight with an early Mk 7 nuclear weapon 'shape' under the fuselage, one of the general-purpose fighter missions. ***US Navy***

All the latest Navy jets undergoing NATC service trials in around 1956, with the exception of the Vought F8U Crusader, in one formation. Each was powered by an engine with more thrust per pound and a lower SFC than the Westinghouse J46. *Thomason*

realised even with the introduction of the McDonnell-Douglas F/A-18 in the mid-1980s, three decades later: it was only assigned to light attack and day fighter squadrons. Now, of course, the bigger F-18E/F is not only a true general-purpose fighter, assigned to all four of the tactical squadrons in the air wing, but also a derivative specialised for electronic warfare is flown by a fifth. However, it is the product of significant advancements in propulsion, structure, aerodynamics, and avionics compared to that available to Vought and the other Navy aircraft contractors in the 1950s.

It did not help that some responsible for procurement planning in DCNO (Air)/BuAer and at high levels in the Atlantic Fleet became more disenchanted with the Cutlass during its prolonged development and evaluation than they did with the equally troubled F4D and F3H programmes (for some reason, the Marine Corps had developed an antipathy toward the Cutlass even earlier, most likely due to the less than glowing opinions of Marion Carl regarding the F7U-1). Its procurement cost was not only high relative to the existing single-seat day fighters but its reliability was relatively low and

The F3H-2 had provision for eight external stores stations that could be utilised for close-air support if desired. It seldom, if ever, was. *Bulban*

maintenance demands high (more maintainers, ground support equipment, and spares stock) due to the number of hydraulic systems, the complex flight control system, the afterburner, centre of gravity management system, etc. Most significantly, the F7U/A2U was notably deficient in some way to another aircraft for a mission required of a carrier air group:

- Except for range and endurance, it was equal to or better than the first swept-wing day fighters but also too big and more complex in a role that favoured small size and simplicity for low procurement/maintenance cost.
- For close air support, the A2U was faster than the AD Skyraider and could carry almost as much from a payload standpoint but was very deficient in endurance (it wasn't until the fuel-efficient turbofan jet engine was created that a jet, the Vought A-7 Corsair II, became a suitable replacement for the Skyraider).
- For the new nuclear strike mission involving a relatively small but devastating payload, the A2U was again too big and expensive compared to the A4D Skyhawk for what was most likely a one-way, one-time mission.
- For the missile-armed fleet air defence mission – which the F7U-3 was best suited for since a fighter needed to be big to carry the requisite radar, fire control system, and radar-guided air-to-air Sparrows – it was once again notably inferior in range and endurance to the Navy's other big fighter, the McDonnell F3H Demon, in part because the F3H had a better engine, the Allison J71, which had a lower SFC and higher TBO than the J46. In addition, the J71 was US Air Force funded and powered the B-66 Destroyer as well as the F3H so it was more likely to be product improved than the J46, which had to rely solely on the Navy for funding and only powered one of its aircraft. When the time came to select one or the other to be armed with the Sparrow III missile (upgrading both would have been expensive), the F7U-3M lost the final round of musical chairs, even without the need for the tie-breaker: which Navy contractor needed the work more? That would still have been McDonnell, in need of a Navy production programme as opposed to Vought, which had the F8U contract in hand.

In summary, the jack-of-all-trades Cutlass had been weighed, measured, and found wanting by comparison to forthcoming alternatives for carrier-based missions, specifically the A4D-1 for nuclear strike by a jet and the F3H-2 for Sparrow missile employment. Since both had been aboard *Ticonderoga* in September 1955 for carrier suitability trials along with the F7U-3M and making steady progress in early 1956 toward being declared suitable for service use, there was a diminishing need for a back-up for either. On 30 March 1956, only two weeks after the F7U-3's first deployment ended, BuAer requested CNO concurrence with its decision to not incorporate any future engineering changes (except safety of flight) that had kit delivery dates scheduled

F7U production quantity			
Type	Qty	Bureau Numbers	Remarks
XF7U-1	3	122742-122474	
F7U-1	14	124415-124433	124229-124433 canceled
F7U-2	0	125322-125409	88 cancelled
F7U-3	0	125410-125411	2 cancelled
F7U-3	28	128451-128478	Configuration break #16/1 7
F7U-3	152	129545-129697	129677 counted as F7U-3M*
F7U-3M	48	129698-129744	Count includes 129677
F7U-3P	12	129745-129756	
F7U-3	0	136912-136963	52 cancelled
F7U-3P	0	136964-136965	2 cancelled
A2U-1	0	138368-138417	50 cancelled
A2U-1	0	139822-139867	46 cancelled
F7U-3M	50	139868-139917	
A2U-1	0	140161-140310	150 cancelled
Total	307		17 F7U-1s and 290** F7U-3s

* 129589 and 129590 were utilized as F7U-3M prototypes but counted as F7U-3s
** 180 F7U-3s, 12 F7U-3Ps, 98 F7U-3Ms

after April 1957. A month later, on 24 April 1956, the CNO directed that F7U-3 and -3M Cutlasses would be placed in contingency reserve status upon completion of their present service tour instead of being overhauled for another. In part as a result, no more squadrons were to be assigned Cutlasses.

Continued production justification

Nevertheless, there had been compelling reasons in 1955 for the F7U's continued production and deployment:

- Vought was kept financially viable until the F8U was in full production
- It filled an immediate need for a fleet air defence fighter to deploy the new Sparrow I air-to-air missile until the F3H-2M was available (which was still not a sure thing even in 1956)
- F7U-3Ms modified with the APQ-51 radar and armed with the Sparrow III provided a back-up for the F3H-2
- It was a placeholder available to equip some of the jet attack squadrons tasked with the delivery of tactical nuclear weapons until the A4D or FJ-4B was available

Another reason for continuing production was an imperative to have an adequate quantity of fighter and attack aircraft available for ongoing operations and prospective surges in demand similar to the Korean War requirement. US Navy carriers deployed to the western

Most of the F3H-1Ns in this photo of the ramp at McDonnell Aircraft in St Louis do not have engines installed and never would. ***US Navy***

Pacific and the Mediterranean, among other areas, for approximately six to eight months at a time. They then needed to be replaced on station by another carrier so they could return home for necessary repair, maintenance, and upgrade. The schedule for their replacement was all but sacrosanct and meant an air group with a full complement of fighter and attack squadrons along with the supporting specialist detachments needed to be ready to deploy on a date certain as well. It was therefore essential that BuAer provide the operational squadrons with enough aircraft of the right type for this purpose: having an excess number of a type in inventory was preferable to not having enough. Moreover, having a surplus of operational squadrons with a variety of fighters and attack aircraft types minimised the risk that the readiness failure of a squadron or the grounding of a particular aircraft type for some reason would result in a deploying air group short of a squadron essential to its mission.

Ironically, the F3H Demon programme troubles may have motivated the Navy to keep the F7U-3 (and probably the F4D as well) in service to a somewhat greater extent than it might have wanted to: deploying it avoided the embarrassment of another major and expensive fighter programme fiasco. In September 1955, a Missouri congressman notified the Chairman of the House Committee on Government Operations that 'Demon fighters were sitting idle on the McDonnell ramps at St Louis because the Navy regarded them as unsuitable for flying'. Hearings by the Congressional Military Operations Subcommittee began on 24 October 1955. It established that of the sixty F3H-1Ns built, at least half never had an engine installed; some that did only flew for a few hours if any; and four were completed with Allison J71s instead of Westinghouse J40s for flight. The airframes became ground-bound maintenance trainers instead. As a result of the harsh criticism of their management of the F3H programme that the admirals received in these hearings, building almost 300 F7Us but only equipping a few squadrons with them for a year or so (and only making two deployments) was not an option.

Epilogue

The end for the F7U-3 came fairly quickly after its last deployment in late 1957, by coincidence on the same carrier, *Hancock*, as its first. Nevertheless, a handful of Cutlasses continued to be flown by various test and evaluation units through 1958 and early 1959, valued for its size and performance capability. Most of those not yet stricken or stored in the desert at Arizona's NAF Litchfield Park wound up as gate guards or playground equipment at the last place they had landed. The Reserves got several but the only one known to have remained in flight status was BuNo 129622 that had been acquired by the Naval Air

The only obvious common external feature of the F7U and F8U was the general shape of the vertical fin. ***VAHF***

The Convair F2Y Sea Dart was an early 1950s programme to provide the US Navy with a transonic jet fighter seaplane alternative to one operating from an aircraft carrier due to the perceived difficulty of doing so; it was redesignated F-7 in 1962 even though none had flown since 1957. *US Navy*

Reserve Training Unit at Glenview, Illinois; it was flown several times but finally grounded in November 1957 by the lack of spare parts. The last Cutlass in naval service was F7U-3P BuNo 129754 assigned to the Navy Parachute Facility at NAAS El Centro, California. It was stricken on 2 March 1959. BuNo 129566, which had been bailed to Cornell Aeronautical Laboratory in Buffalo, made its last flight on 19 June 1959 and was stricken there on 24 August 1959.

The main benefit for Vought (and by extension the Navy) was the design and development experience. In 1946, the likelihood of a carrier-based, swept-wing, transonic jet fighter approximated surviving going over Niagara Falls in a barrel – nobody had the requisite knowledge needed to design one. It turned out that a high-performance jet fighter needed a stabilator, irreversible flight controls with artificial control feel, redundant hydraulic systems, pitch and yaw stabilisation, afterburners, pressurisation, ejection seats, air conditioning, engine inlets with boundary layer air removal, and nose gear steering, among other things. Vought learned all about those systems and features with the F6U and F7U. They then embodied them, a low thickness-to-chord ratio wing, a great engine, and as importantly, all the lessons they had learned about what not to do, in the F8U Crusader.

Despite being withdrawn from service and replaced by newer-generation fighters, the F7U received a measure of notoriety even after leaving active service, both negative as well as positive, albeit a case of mistaken identity in the latter instance.

In March 1960, the US House of Representative's Military Operations Sub-Committee Chairman Chet Holifield (D-Calif) launched an investigation into a report from Comptroller General Joseph Campbell, which stated that his auditors had uncovered wasteful spending on the procurement of 'F7U jet fighters' as well as Lockheed T2V Seastar trainers and P5M Marlin radar sets. The audit alleged that the F7U was 'incapable of performing the designated mission', and that 'even after testing uncovered known deficiencies in the planes and equipment, the Navy continued to place volume orders for them'. The Navy rightly responded, 'the knowledge gained is utilised to advantage in latter (sic) procurements'.

On 18 April 1961, during the height of the Cuban 'Bay of Pigs' invasion, Cuban Foreign Minister Raul Roa, while attending an assembly of the United Nation's Political Committee, charged that US Navy 'Cutlass fighters' from a 'US Aircraft Carrier' had escorted a rebel B-26 to safety when it was attacked by Cuban fighters. Obviously alleged in error, it would be the Cutlass's closest brush with combat.

One final slight was to come. In 1962, when the Secretary of Defense decreed that the services use a common designation system for aircraft, all of the F7U's contemporaries were redesignated, e.g. the F9F became the F-9; the F3H, the F-3; and the F4D, the F-6 (F-4 was allocated to the F4H Phantom). By then all of the F7U-3s had been stricken. At that time, however, one of the handful of Convair F2Y Sea Darts built (and fewer flown) had not yet been formally stricken for some reason, even though the jet seaplane fighter had not flown since April 1957, two years before the final flight (so far) of the F7U-3. Apparently wanting to avoid skipping a number in the list of fighters, the DoD committee assigned it the F-7 designation when it would have been more appropriate to recognise the F7U instead.

Paint and markings

Unpainted exterior surfaces evaluation

In early 1950, the Chief of Naval Operations asked BuAer to determine the tactical benefit of unpainted aircraft from a visual acquisition standpoint. An evaluation conducted at Patuxent River had concluded that the maximum detection distance of a natural metal TO-1 (the USAF F-80C) Shooting Star was approximately 14nm compared to 20nm for an all-blue F8F Bearcat.

Engineers in the Maintenance Division at BuAer were concerned about the maintainability impact of not painting carrier-based aircraft, in part because of critical comments in response to a December 1948 questionnaire from VF-52, which was operating bare-metal Lockheed TO-1s from coastal shore bases. In order to evaluate the benefits and shortcomings of bare-metal schemes, BuAer considered but did not implement an elaborate evaluation programme involving thirty-six aircraft: eight all blue; seven with blue upper surfaces and aluminium bottom surfaces; seven with the reverse scheme; seven painted all over with aluminised lacquer; and seven bare, unpainted aircraft.

NATC conducted additional informal tests of the visibility of different paint schemes in 1950. The initial results were reviewed in January 1951 by BuAer, which decided to continue the test programme for six months with formal BuAer direction. The Maintenance Division was initially successful in having unpainted aircraft ruled out as an option:

Although F7U-3s like these appeared to be 'bare metal', much of the external surface was painted like the lower third of the forward fuselage, where an aluminised lacquer finish was applied to magnesium skin to protect it from corrosion. Nevertheless, these Cutlasses were often referred to as being unpainted. ***VAHF***

Unpainted external finish and markings

NOTES

1. Refer to table VIII for exterior prime and finish requirements.
2. Glossy black lacquer is used for serial numbers, service markings and model designations.

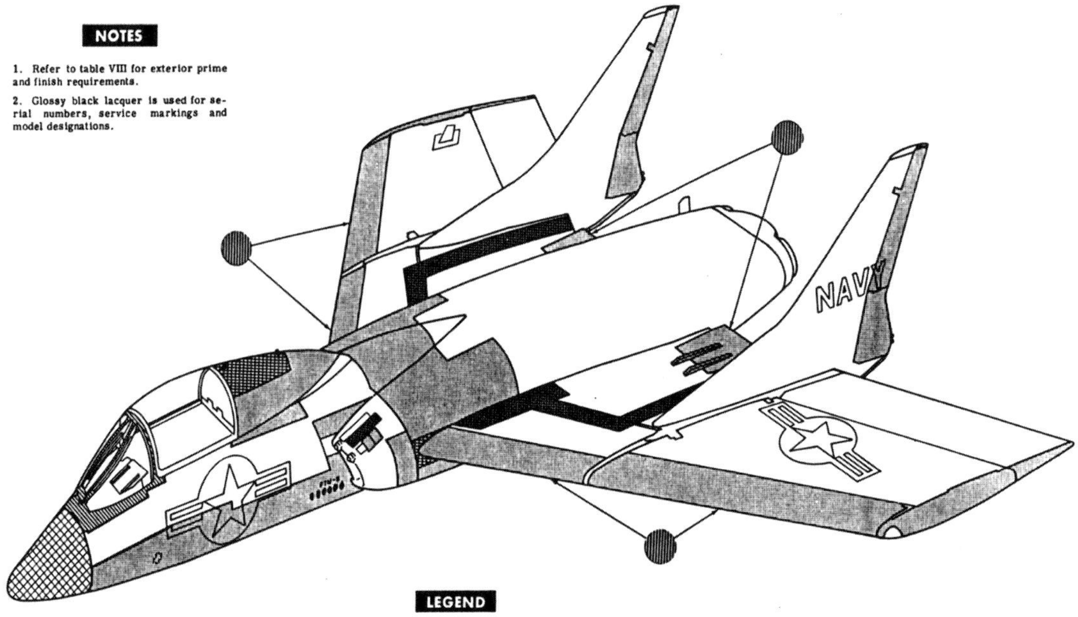

LEGEND

- ALUMINIZED LACQUER (MIL-L-7178)
- RAIN-EROSION RESISTANT COATING (BLACK)
- AIRCRAFT GRAY LACQUER, NO. 512 (MIL-L-7178)
- RED LACQUER (INTERIOR SURFACES OF SLATS AND SPEED BRAKES) NO. 509 (MIL-L-7178)
- SMOOTH TYPE WALKWAY COATING, TYPE I, CLASS II (MIL-C-5044)
- MEDIUM GREEN LACQUER, NO. 612 (MIL-L-6805)
- UNPAINTED AREAS

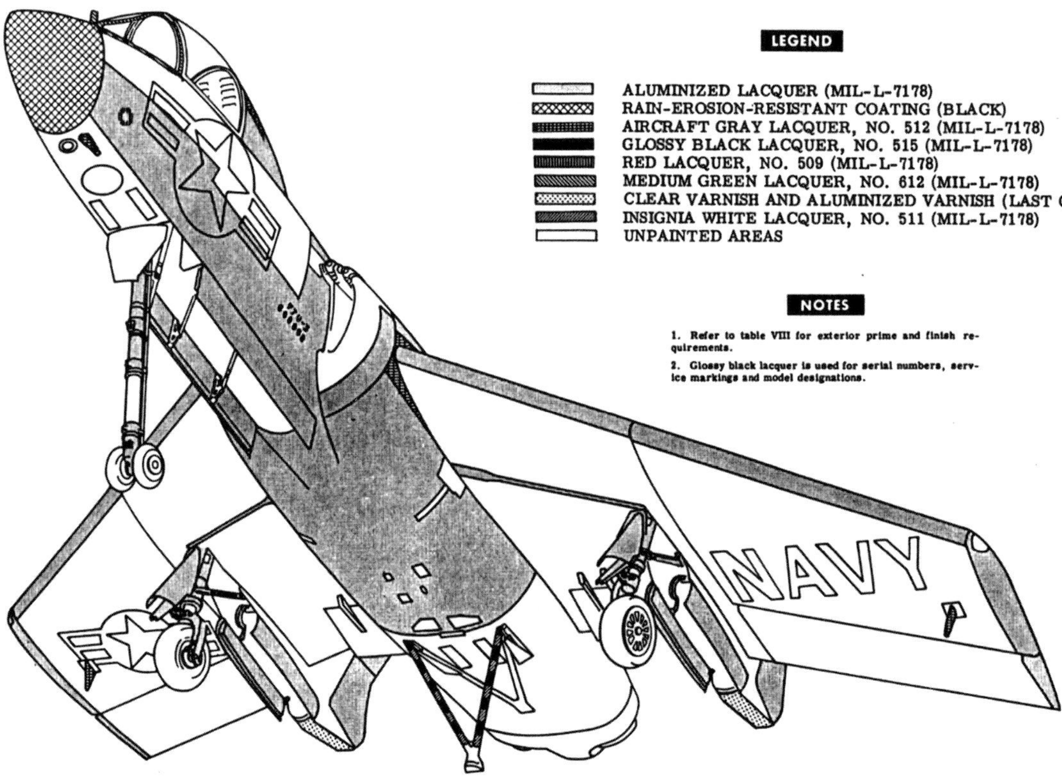

LEGEND

- ALUMINIZED LACQUER (MIL-L-7178)
- RAIN-EROSION-RESISTANT COATING (BLACK)
- AIRCRAFT GRAY LACQUER, NO. 512 (MIL-L-7178)
- GLOSSY BLACK LACQUER, NO. 515 (MIL-L-7178)
- RED LACQUER, NO. 509 (MIL-L-7178)
- MEDIUM GREEN LACQUER, NO. 612 (MIL-L-7178)
- CLEAR VARNISH AND ALUMINIZED VARNISH (LAST COAT)
- INSIGNIA WHITE LACQUER, NO. 511 (MIL-L-7178)
- UNPAINTED AREAS

NOTES

1. Refer to table VIII for exterior prime and finish requirements.
2. Glossy black lacquer is used for serial numbers, service markings and model designations.

ABOVE BuNo 129654 as painted and delivered from Vought. The aircraft in the experimental finish programme were required to be marked with a stencil denoting their special status: 'This is an experimental finish. Do not apply paint without specific authorization. See log book entry.' ***Thomason***

'the desired camouflage effect would be obtained by changes in the colour, reflectance, and gloss of the organic protective coatings on the aircraft exterior'. A separate Maintenance Division memo noted: 'Chance Vought is introducing so much magnesium in the F7U that it would definitely not want to remove all paint.'

One of the Maintenance Division attendees at that meeting, Alfred M. Malloy, who would eventually become the Head of the Materials Protection Section, wrote in an article in the May 1975 issue of *Naval Aviation News* that: 'In the early 1950s, fleet units and commands mounted a campaign to obtain carrier aircraft without exterior paint, somewhat after the fashion of Air Force planes. BuAer was hard pressed to resist the pressure of the arguments of weight saving and exemption from continuous paint touch-ups.' At the time, firmly believing that unpainted aircraft exteriors would impose an undue maintenance burden on fleet units but needing proof to counter the natural-metal advocates, he proposed an evaluation programme involving about 250 unpainted fighters that would be deployed aboard carriers for a one-year service test.

The initial list of guinea pigs included 100 F9F-5s, 100 F2H-3s, and the first 17 F7U-3s along with several F9F-2s, all the FJ-2s, and other combat aircraft to be delivered between April 1952, when BuAer announced the programme, and the end of the year. Magnesium, non-clad aluminium, and fibreglass exterior panels were to be painted with aluminised lacquer. Anti-glare paint was also allowed ahead of and beside the windscreen. These aircraft – with a stencil on the port side of the fuselage below the horizontal stabiliser prohibiting paint application without specific authorisation – were issued to deploying fighter squadrons. The plan was for them to accomplish at least two service tours (about thirty-six months at the time) to provide the data to evaluate the concept. The programme included the requirement for quarterly reports on their maintenance status. Overhaul/repair facilities were also to report on the condition of these aircraft when they inducted one. The experimental fleet would grow to include almost all 400 F2H-3/4s, all the F7U-3s and F7U-3Ps, and about half of the F7U-3Ms.

The first sixteen F7U-3s (BuNo 128451-128466) were delivered with the clad aluminium skin unpainted, aluminised lacquer on the other exterior surfaces, and nonspecular sea-blue anti-glare panels. Starting with BuNo 128467, natural-finish F7Us were delivered with their magnesium anti-glare panels painted with nonspecular medium-green lacquer.

All natural-metal F7Us had their gear struts, interior of landing gear doors, and wing-fold areas painted with aluminised lacquer; the interior of the wheel wells were left in green or greenish-yellow zinc chromate primer.

Vought utilised hundreds of silver-coloured adhesive-backed foil stickers to identify inspection and access panels and other necessary instructional verbiage located on the exterior of the natural-finish aircraft.

The national insignias on the wings and a large service marking ('NAVY') on the underside of the left wing were applied perpendicular to the longitudinal axis of the aircraft, i.e. straight across. (MIL I 6140(ASG) dated 15 September 1954, which was issued subsequent to the F7U-3 go-ahead, stated that on swept-wing aircraft, the national insignia was to be swept, i.e. perpendicular to, and centred, on a line formed by the constant 50% chord of the wing). It appears that changing the orientation of the side number and air group letter on the upper right wing was not addressed at that time, but in any event, probably due to the size, location, and orientation of the national insignia being on Vought's Navy-approved contract documentation, 'swept' national insignia were only present late in the Cutlass' service life.

OPPOSITE In addition to the need to paint the magnesium panels of 'unpainted' Cutlasses forcorrosion control, non-aluminium exterior surfaces were painted for a uniform appearance. Other paint requirements included warning, anti-glare, erosion resistance, etc. ***Thomason***

F7U-3s that had been completed but for which no engines were available were stored outside at Vought with a temporary corrosion protection coating. Since the magnesium skins were already painted, the black areas represent the unpainted aluminium surfaces. *VAHF*

Since there was no aft fuselage for the required sideward-facing service marking, it was located on the outboard side of each vertical fin. Since there was no horizontal stabiliser, the model designation (2in high) and Bureau Number (4in high) were placed on the lower side of the fuselage just ahead of the engine inlet.

Operational squadrons would then add the squadron designation and appropriate tail code to the outboard sides of the vertical fins and upper right wing and the 'unit aircraft numeral' to the forward fuselage, upper right wing, and in other locations like the forward-facing nose landing gear door and auxiliary rudder so its identity could be quickly determined from any angle. The unit aircraft number took three forms at that time: USMC squadrons and Navy squadrons not yet identified to a deployable air group and detachments that deployed with an air group were sequentially numbered from one to however many were assigned; aircraft assigned to units that were not deployable tended to be marked with the last three digits of the aircraft's Bureau Number on the nose; and squadrons (as opposed to detachments) assigned to air groups would have a three-digit side number, the first digit, 1 through 5, identifying a different squadron within the air group.

Some reporting units initially had a favourable view of the concept, reporting less maintenance and minimal corrosion. NAS Alameda submitted a report dated 14 September 1953 for F9F-5P BuNo 126267. It had completed eleven months of its first service tour including at-sea operations. 'The exterior surface appears normal by comparison with painted aircraft of similar service life.' No photographs were enclosed 'since the degree of corrosion is insufficient to show significant deterioration'. Others claimed that careful attention to keeping the unpainted surfaces clean with solvents (basically lacquer thinner), water, and paste wax was effective in minimising surface corrosion even after six months at sea.

More typical of squadron-level experience was a crash-damaged F2H-3, BuNo 126350, inducted at the NAS Jacksonville O&R Facility in October. The report to BuAer dated 1 December 1953 stated, 'This aircraft possessed excessive corrosion throughout and will require a large amount of skin replacement.' In some cases, damage resulted from attempts to buff the unpainted surfaces with an abrasive compound, either for appearance or to remove visible corrosion.

The number of complaints about the unpainted aircraft that had been at sea for more than three months began to increase, especially the effort required to deal with corrosion pitting, stack gas deposit removal, stains, etc. The approved cleaner compound was in short supply and the workload involved in avoiding and treating corrosion was higher than most units could muster or cared to invest. For example, if preventative maintenance failed to prevent corroded or badly discoloured panels, they were to be treated with a cleaner-brightener, basically phosphoric acid, but not more often than once in a twelve-month period. It was supposed to be diluted 50/50 with thinner or water, applied, and the surface scrubbed to loosen the corrosion residue. The cleaning mixture and the corrosion residue was then to be removed after fifteen minutes with a thorough fresh water rinse, which might be practical at a shore base but not on a carrier at sea.

Squadrons would add unit and air group markings to their Cutlasses. Note that VF-124 placed the upward-facing unit aircraft number on the centre of the aft fuselage rather than the standard location, the upper right wing along with the air group letter. The top of each fin was painted black, the assigned trim colour of the fourth squadron in the air group. ***Thomason***

By early 1954 it was increasingly apparent that while there were isolated successes, most experimental finish reports contained similar statements of dissatisfaction:

- Painted aircraft have shown no tendency to corrode compared to unpainted ones
- Maintenance and preservation of unpainted aircraft requires cleaning and polishing three times as often as the painted aircraft to maintain a comparable state of cleanliness.
- The recommended cleaner wax is ineffective in retarding corrosion
- Clad aluminium, anodised or chemically treated, and waxed in accordance with current procedures does not withstand corrosion in normal carrier service.
- Squadrons appear to be unable to maintain unpainted aircraft to current standards, in a practical manner, with present personnel.
- There is no reason to believe that any available wax finish, even though modified to improve the situation, will correct the problems.

In March 1954, the O&R facility at NAS North Island issued a local engineering specification covering fighter aircraft with unpainted exterior surfaces. It allowed for painting corroded or badly discoloured skin panels with semi-aluminised lacquer in accordance with BuAer direction. However: 'If excess corrosion is present, or if the general material condition warrants a full finish scheme, BuAer authority shall be requested to remove the aircraft from the evaluation programme.'

In spite of the mounting evidence that the disadvantages of not painting aircraft far outweighed the benefits, BuAer was slow to act: in July 1954, Vought, Grumman, and Douglas still had or were about to receive production contracts for unpainted A2Us, F9F-9s (to be redesignated F11Fs), F4D-2s (to be redesignated F5Ds), and A4D-1s. In early August, although BuAer discontinued the experimental 'unpainted' finish reporting requirement as of 1 September in letters to ComAirPac, ComAirLant, CNATRA, and the Naval Air Stations with O&R Departments, and implied that the results to that point were conclusive, it also noted: 'A meeting of all interested parties is being considered, to convene in the Bureau of Aeronautics approximately in October to review service data and reports and reach a joint decision based on this review.'

Operating units, particularly on the west coast, continued to press for guidance:

- A Fleet Aircraft Service Squadron Twelve (FASRon-12) letter dated 30 August 1954 cited 'excessive corrosion of the bare exterior surfaces of F7U-3 aircraft (BuNo 129637) after 42 days operation at sea' and 'recommended an investigation to determine if the aircraft should be painted'. BuAer responded: 'Serious consideration is being given by the Chief of the Bureau of Aeronautics to painting F7U-3 aircraft and the Navy aeronautical organisation will be kept

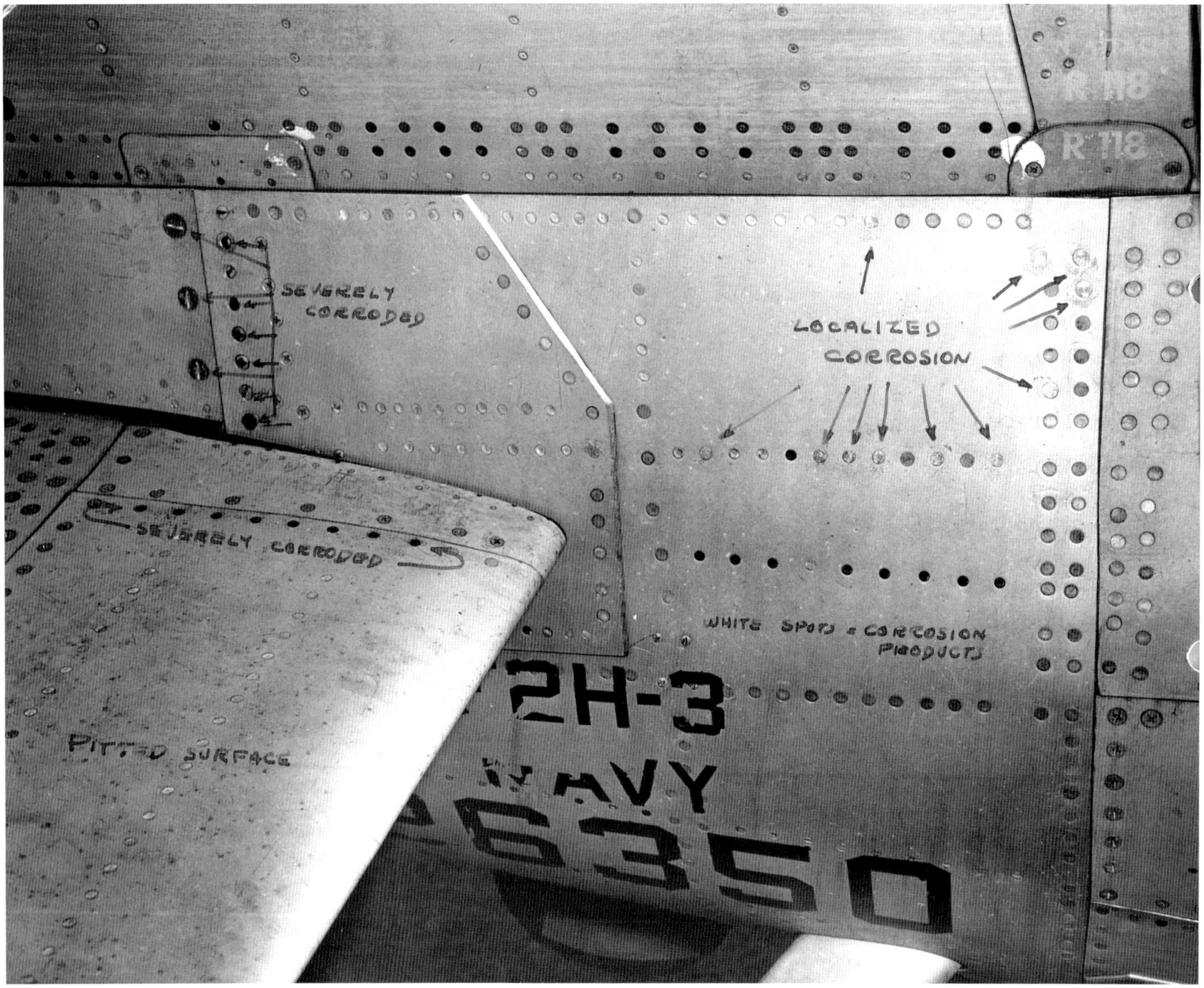

Absent (and sometimes in spite of) significant effort to forestall and combat corrosion, skin damage would result that required significant and expensive repairs. *US Navy*

informed of the changes.' In the meantime, 'compliance with T. N. 5-53 should continue' (Technical Note 5-53 covered maintenance of unpainted aluminium exterior surfaces).

- In October 1954, NAS Alameda also requested direction concerning unpainted aircraft. BuAer responded in early December that a policy to paint all carrier-based aircraft had been established by the Chief of Naval Operations but that specific directives for a new paint scheme were not ready to be released. It did authorise application of an aluminised lacquer finish to all or parts of the exterior of an unpainted aircraft if deemed appropriate by the O&R department because of 'significant deterioration of the surface'. In other words, even though the unpainted surfaces had been proven to be prone to damage, no action other than the maintenance instructions previously issued were to be taken to prevent it.

Change from overall blue to gull grey/white

On 16 February 1955, BuAer finally issued the instruction for a new paint scheme for tactical aircraft, nonspecular light gull grey over gloss insignia white (including white on the upper side of control surfaces). In addition, an erosion-resistant coating, Corogard, was to be applied to the leading edge of the wing and tail surfaces. Tactical aircraft in the unpainted evaluation programme completed by O&R facilities after 1 July 1955 were to be finished in the new scheme. Until then, aircraft that only required partial refinishing or touch-up because of corrosion or damage could be painted with an aluminised lacquer in those areas. If refinishing of the entire aircraft was required, they could be painted aluminised lacquer overall or glossy sea blue. However, aircraft that were assigned to operational squadrons or replacement pools were to remain unpainted until they reached the end of their present service tour or were damaged enough to require induction into O&R. Since unpainted Cutlasses undergoing modification or upgrade at the Vought factory were neither at the end of a service tour or damaged, they were still delivered unpainted after the 1 July deadline, whereas new F7U-3Ms departing the production line were delivered painted.

Citing serious corrosion experienced on the deployed F7Us of VF-124 aboard *Hancock*, in mid-1955 the Commander Air Force Pacific Fleet unilaterally chose to have them painted in the new scheme in mid-deployment while the squadron was operating out of NAS Atsugi, Japan. West coast-based VA-151 and VA-212 were also directed to repaint their F7U-3s in the new colour scheme before they deployed. This took some time so during work-ups and carrier qualifications prior to deployments, these squadrons often had a mix of grey/white and unpainted aircraft.

The anti-glare panels on grey/white F7Us were finished in nonspecular black lacquer. On new production and Cutlasses updated at Vought, the gear struts, interior of landing gear doors, and wing-fold areas were supposed to remain with the aluminised lacquer finish; the interior of wheel wells were left in green or greenish yellow zinc chromate primer. However, F7Us that were refinished at O&Rs or at the individual squadron level often had their gear struts and interior gear doors overpainted in gloss white, which was not an official practice until July 1956. In an ill-conceived Pacific Fleet Command attempt to further reduce corrosion at sea, all exposed areas of the landing gear struts, wheels, interior of the landing gear doors, and the entirety of the wheel wells on the repainted Cutlasses in some squadrons were subsequently over sprayed with par-al-ketone, a black tar-like coating. The addition of this anti-corrosion coating actually hid the development of existing corrosion, and as applied concealed the identification of the wire and tube markings in the wheel wells, resulting in a maintainer's nightmare as everything became indistinguishable. Maintenance down times on deployed aircraft increased exponentially as a result, seriously affecting availability and squadron readiness.

Following adoption of the grey/white scheme, the labelling of inspection and access panels and other permanent notifications reverted to the traditional stencilled lettering as a result of the foil stickers bearing that information being overpainted during the exterior refinishing.

The last revision of SR-2, Military Specification for Insignia and Markings for Naval Aircraft, was replaced by MIL-C-18263(Aer) dated 9 March 1955 (the actual issue date is not known; the BuAer letter announcing it was dated 9 May 1955, two months later). It required a 'radio

For some reason, at least two unpainted, J35-powered F7U-3s had the lower part of their inlets painted red albeit without a warning legend. Inlet warning markings were not then a requirement on either blue or unpainted jets and very rare. *Casby Collection*

ABOVE **VF-124 began their deployment with unpainted F7U-3s and ended it with them painted in the grey/white scheme. They were painted at NAS Atsugi, Japan, with no inlet warnings and a simple straight-line soft delineation between the light gull grey and gloss white on the side of the fuselage. Note the black-coated landing gear on the Cutlass in the foreground.** ***US Navy***

OPPOSITE **While this is the crude 'official' illustration for external finishings and markings, there were detail variations on Cutlasses depending on where and when they were painted, including the size and shape of the inlet warning.** ***Thomason***

call number' (in practice the last four or five digits of the Bureau Number) at least 12in high be marked on the vertical fin. It also dictated the deletion of the branch of service marking, e.g. 'Navy', on the underside of the wings along with all other markings except for the national insignia and small maintenance-related information. Station/air group/side number markings on the upper surface of the wing were to be applied symmetrically along the 50% chord line like the national insignia.

It is believed that F7U-3M BuNo 129714 was the first F7U delivery to be factory painted in the grey/white scheme following the July 1955 BuAer mandated changeover. Although accepted by the Navy in December 1954 with the original unpainted exterior, it was retained at Vought until its delivery to VA-86 in October 1955 in a grey/white paint scheme that featured a wave-patterned hard demarcation line between the grey and white colour on the side of the fuselage and engine inlets. Later, Engineering Change Proposal 460 formally mandated that the grey/white demarcation was to be feathered using a 2in–4in blend. This was present on the next sequential F7U-3M, BuNo 129715, which featured a relatively straight, feathered blend that followed the front fuselage panel lines. This aircraft was also delivered to VA-86, albeit two months later in December 1955. Both aircraft retained their individual demarcations throughout their squadron service. However, there continued to be variations in grey/white demarcation and intake chevron styles seen on subsequent factory-new F7U-3M's as well as previously delivered aircraft exiting factory rework.

As a result of the ongoing changes in marking directives from late 1954 until mid-1955; Vought delivering new F7U-3Ms in different variations of the grey/white scheme; and at least two different overhaul and repair facilities and three squadrons repainting unpainted Cutlasses with no common detailed illustrations, there were variations even within squadrons with respect to jet inlet warnings, the grey/white demarcation on the forward fuselage, exact location of the aircraft designation and Bureau Number with respect to the engine inlet, location and size of side numbers, location of 'NAVY' on the vertical fin, orientation of the national insignia on the wings, landing gear paint/coating, anti-glare area around the windscreen, etc.

Grey/white external finish and markings

NOTES

1. Refer to table VIII A for exterior prime and finish requirements.
2. Glossy black lacquer is used for serial numbers, service markings and model designations per MIL-I-18464 (Aer).
3. Use non-specular lacquer on top surface of national insignia.
4. Use gloss black lacquer, color No. 515 (MIL-L-7178) in 3-inch circles around ground receptacles, plus CVC-3306-6 stencil, gloss white letters on gloss black background.
5. Paint outer surface of skin adjacent to static ports with primer only to edge of static ports. Finish as per specification MIL-I-6115.

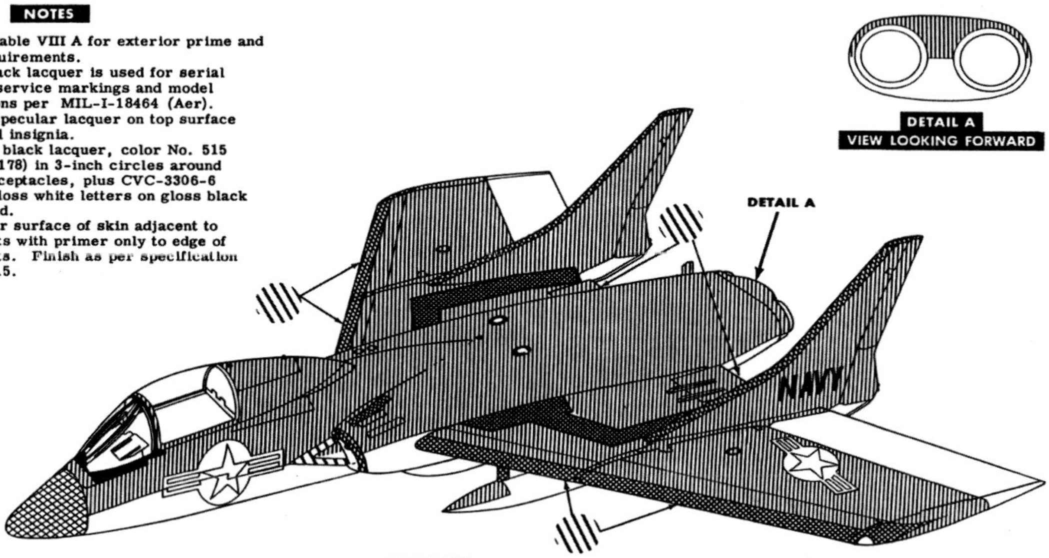

LEGEND

- LIGHT GULL GRAY CAMOUFLAGE LACQUER, NO. 620 (MIL-L-006805)
- RAIN-EROSION-RESISTANT COATING (BLACK COLOR)
- GLOSS INSIGNIA WHITE LACQUER, NO. 511 (MIL-L-7178)
- INSIGNIA RED LACQUER, NO. 509 (INTERIOR SURFACES OF SLATS AND SPEED BRAKES AND JET INTAKE WARNING) (MIL-L-7178)
- SMOOTH-TYPE WALKWAY, MIL-C-5044, TYPE 1, CLASS II, GULL GRAY COLOR, NO. 620 (MIL-L-006805)
- RAIN-EROSION-RESISTANT COATING (ALUMINIZED)
- NON-SPECULAR BLACK CAMOUFLAGE LACQUER, NO. 604 (MIL-L-006805)

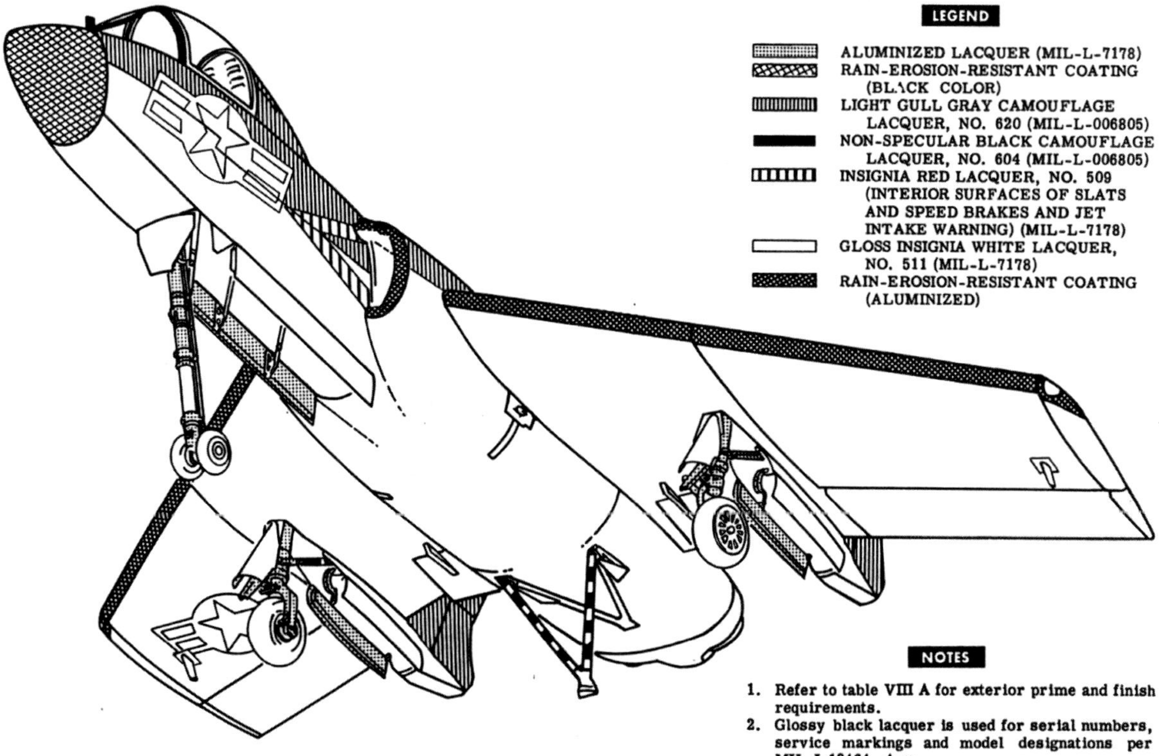

LEGEND

- ALUMINIZED LACQUER (MIL-L-7178)
- RAIN-EROSION-RESISTANT COATING (BLACK COLOR)
- LIGHT GULL GRAY CAMOUFLAGE LACQUER, NO. 620 (MIL-L-006805)
- NON-SPECULAR BLACK CAMOUFLAGE LACQUER, NO. 604 (MIL-L-006805)
- INSIGNIA RED LACQUER, NO. 509 (INTERIOR SURFACES OF SLATS AND SPEED BRAKES AND JET INTAKE WARNING) (MIL-L-7178)
- GLOSS INSIGNIA WHITE LACQUER, NO. 511 (MIL-L-7178)
- RAIN-EROSION-RESISTANT COATING (ALUMINIZED)

NOTES

1. Refer to table VIII A for exterior prime and finish requirements.
2. Glossy black lacquer is used for serial numbers, service markings and model designations per MIL-I-18464, Aer.
3. Use gloss lacquer paint or a decalcomania on lower national insignia. If painting insignia, refer to specification MIL-I-6140.
4. Finish arresting gear with alternate 4-inch bands of glossy insignia white and glossy black lacquer.

While at Vought, F7U-3M BuNo 129714 was used to chase the XF8U-1 that had flown for the first time on 25 March 1955. Note that wave demarcation between the grey and the white was also present on the aft fuselage and the vertical fins. 'NAVY' on the vertical fin is also located lower and farther forward than on the unpainted F7U-3. *Casby Collection*

F7U-3M BuNo 129714 received a wave-pattern variant of the demarcation between grey and white on the side of the fuselage with a single inlet-warning triangle and landing gear struts painted with aluminised lacquer. Corogard, a rain-resistant coating, has been applied to the leading edge of the wings, fin, inlet, and stores pylons. Note that 'NAVY' is no longer present on the underside of the left wing. *VAHF*

These two VA-151 F7U-3s have the last five (more usually four) digits of the Bureau Number on the fin consistent with marking guidance issued in 1955. U.S. Navy

F7U-3 BuNo 129697 fresh out of rework at Vought with a straight line, feathered demarcation between grey and white, Corogard-coated leading edges, double-ended inlet warning triangles, landing gear struts painted white, and the last four digits of the BuNo painted on the vertical fin. Note that it has the lower engine inlet modification to minimise thrust loss at high angles of attack. *VAHF*

A VA-212 F7U-3 on *Bon Homme Richard* in July 1956 with yet another variation of the grey/white demarcation on the forward fuselage, the intake chevrons, and this squadron's unusual side number location, probably so that it could be standard in size. *US Navy*

Even as late as 1956 it wasn't unusual for a squadron to have mixture of natural metal and grey/white aircraft, as here with VA-86 during CVA-59's two-month South Atlantic shakedown cruise. Note the size and font of the side number on the nose necessary to have it fit between the national insignia and the radome, the different relative position of 'NAVY' and the stripe on the vertical fin on the two aircraft, and that the inlet warning was not present on the unpainted F7U-3s. *US Navy*

The VX-4 detachment that deployed on *Lexington* (CVA-16) had a swept national insignia on the wing and did not have the usual, for an air group, side number and *tail code* on the upper right wing. The VA-151 Cutlasses, both painted and unpainted, parked on the port side have the perpendicular orientation of national insignia. *National Archives G-1027741*

Flight and maintenance manual illustrations

Note that some features, e.g. armament, are covered or discussed in more detail elsewhere.

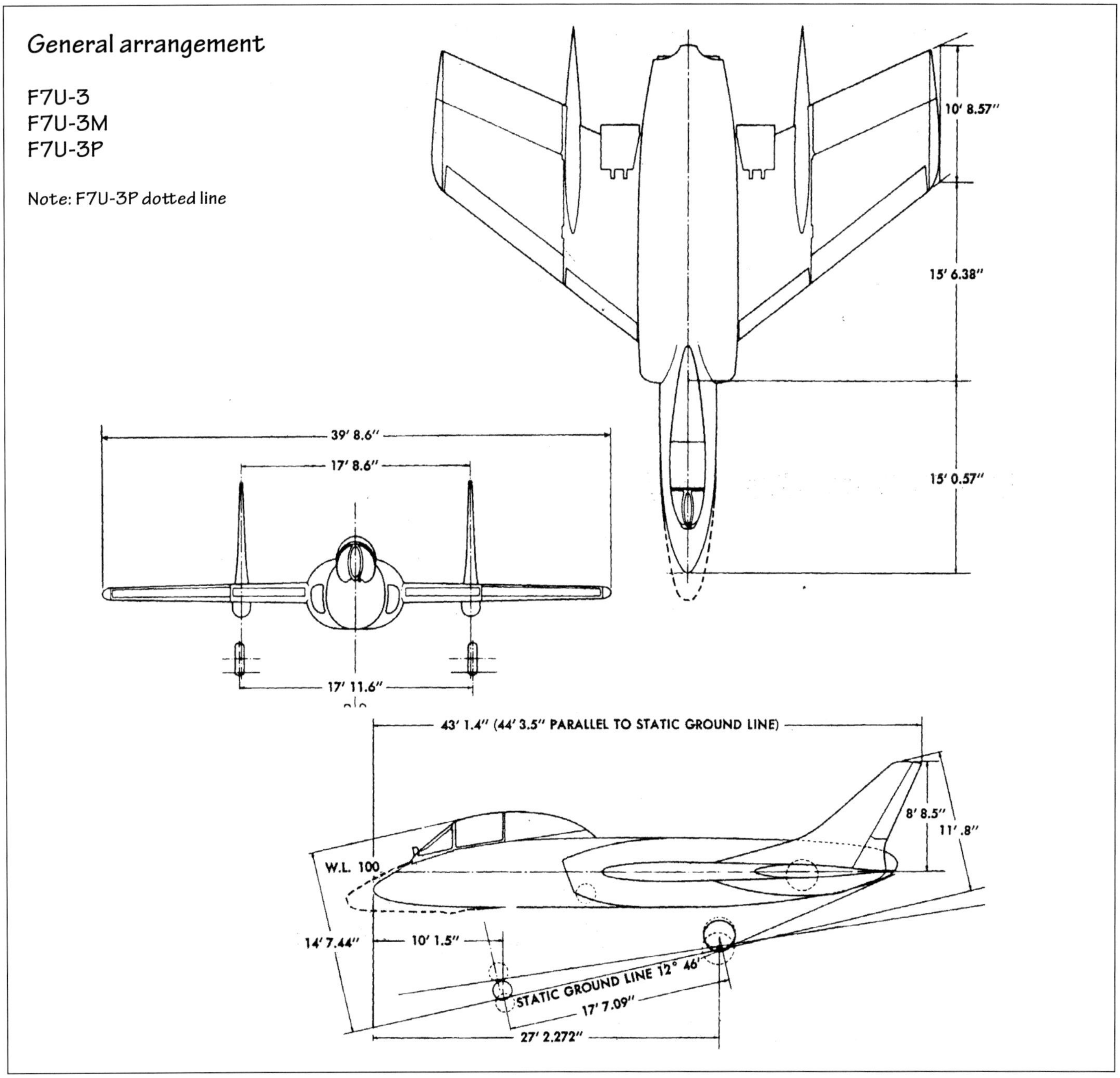

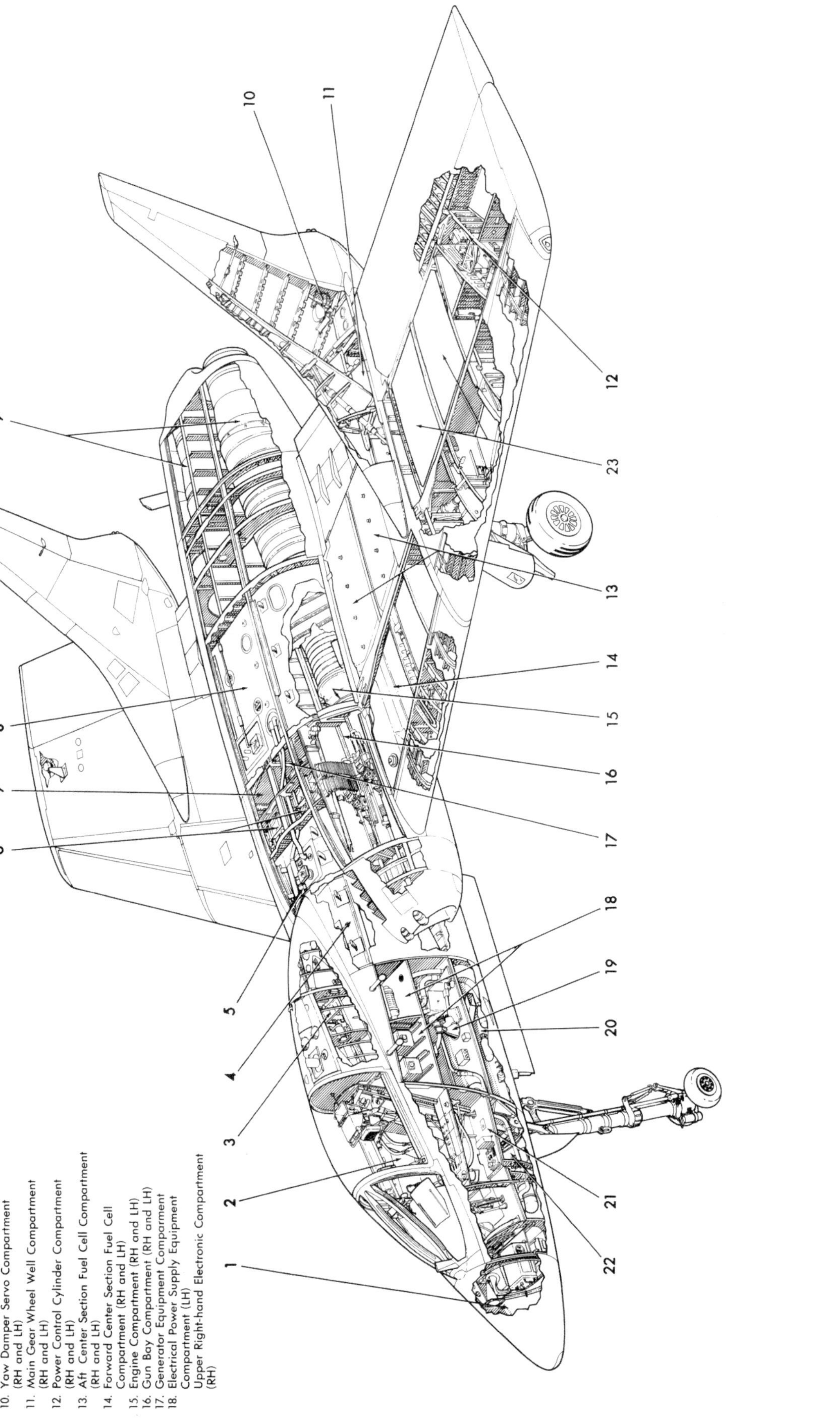

1. Radome Compartment
2. Cockpit Compartment
3. Aft Canopy Compartment
4. Forward Fuselage Fuel Cell Compartment
5. Mid Fuselage Fuel Cell Compartment
6. Ammunition Compartment (RH and LH)
7. Utility Hydraulic Reservoir Compartment
8. Fuselage Aft Fuel Cell Compartment
9. Afterburner Compartment
10. Yaw Damper Servo Compartment (RH and LH)
11. Main Gear Wheel Well Compartment (RH and LH)
12. Power Control Cylinder Compartment (RH and LH)
13. Aft Center Section Fuel Cell Compartment (RH and LH)
14. Forward Center Section Fuel Cell Compartment (RH and LH)
15. Engine Compartment (RH and LH)
16. Gun Bay Compartment (RH and LH)
17. Generator Equipment Comparment
18. Electrical Power Supply Equipment Compartment (LH)
    Upper Right-hand Electronic Compartment (RH)
19. Air-conditioning Compartment (LH)
    Lower Right-hand Electronic Compartment (RH)
20. Nose Gear Wheel Well Compartment
21. Console Compartment (RH and LH)
22. Subcockpit Electronic Compartment
23. Outer Panel Fuel Cells (F7U-3M and 3P only)

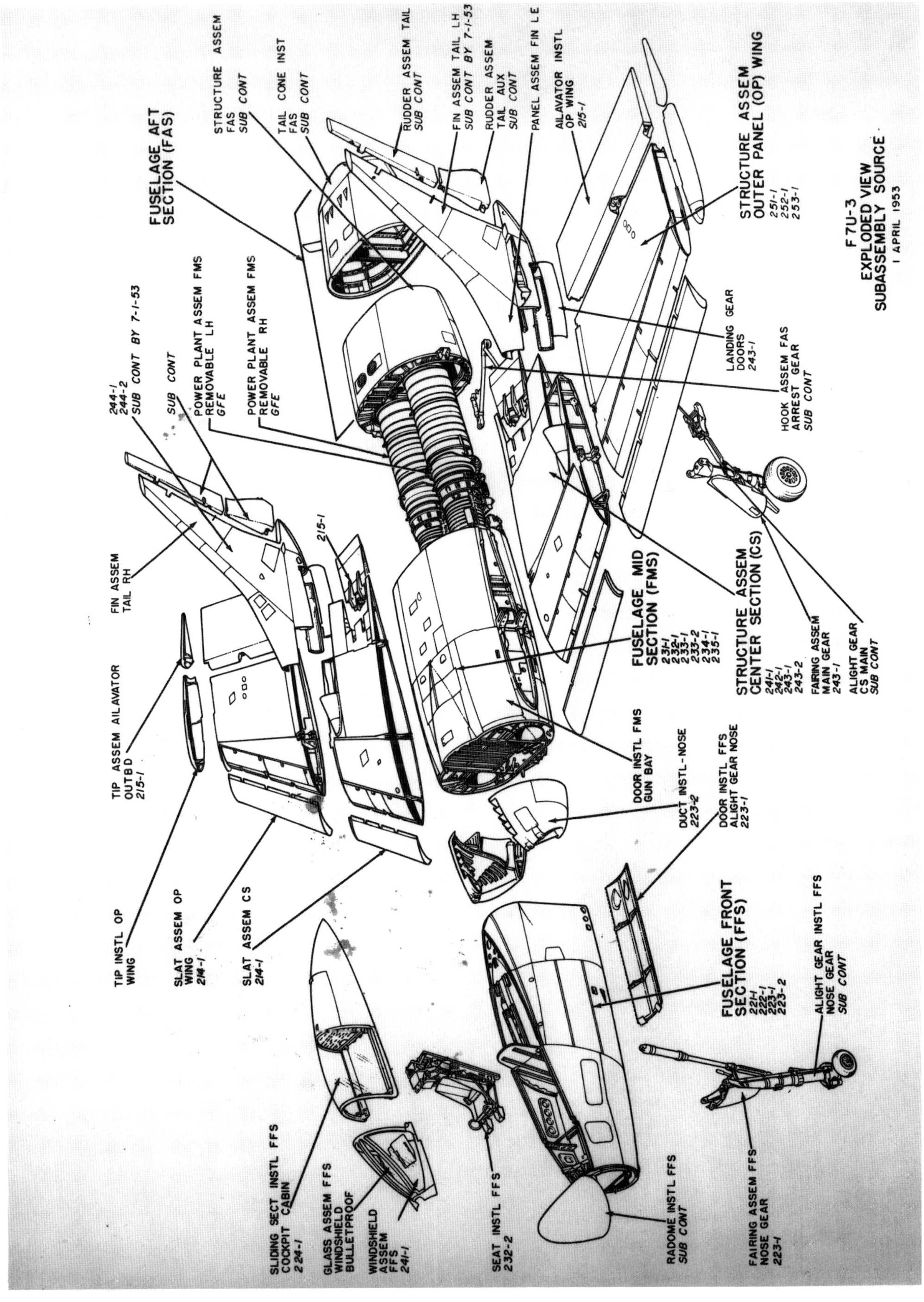
F7U-3
EXPLODED VIEW
SUBASSEMBLY SOURCE
1 APRIL 1953
FUSELAGE AFT SECTION (FAS)
STRUCTURE ASSEM FAS SUB CONT
TAIL CONE INST FAS SUB CONT
RUDDER ASSEM TAIL SUB CONT
FIN ASSEM TAIL LH SUB CONT BY 7-1-53
RUDDER ASSEM TAIL AUX SUB CONT
PANEL ASSEM FIN LE
AILAVATOR INSTL OP WING 215-1
STRUCTURE ASSEM OUTER PANEL (OP) WING
251-1
252-1
253-1
LANDING GEAR DOORS 243-1
HOOK ASSEM FAS ARREST GEAR SUB CONT
244-1
244-2
SUB CONT BY 7-1-53
SUB CONT
POWER PLANT ASSEM FMS REMOVABLE LH GFE
POWER PLANT ASSEM FMS REMOVABLE RH GFE
215-1
FIN ASSEM TAIL RH
TIP ASSEM AILAVATOR OUTBD 215-1
FUSELAGE MID SECTION (FMS)
231-1
232-1
233-1
233-2
234-1
235-1
STRUCTURE ASSEM CENTER SECTION (CS)
241-1
242-1
243-1
243-2
FAIRING ASSEM MAIN GEAR 243-1
ALIGHT GEAR CS MAIN SUB CONT
DOOR INSTL FMS GUN BAY
DUCT INSTL-NOSE 223-2
DOOR INSTL FFS ALIGHT GEAR NOSE 223-1
TIP INSTL OP WING
SLAT ASSEM OP WING 214-1
SLAT ASSEM CS 214-1
FUSELAGE FRONT SECTION (FFS)
221-1
222-1
223-1
223-2
ALIGHT GEAR INSTL FFS NOSE GEAR SUB CONT
SLIDING SECT INSTL FFS COCKPIT CABIN 224-1
GLASS ASSEM FFS WINDSHIELD BULLETPROOF
WINDSHIELD ASSEM FFS 241-1
SEAT INSTL FFS 232-2
RADOME INSTL FFS SUB CONT
FAIRING ASSEM FFS NOSE GEAR 223-1

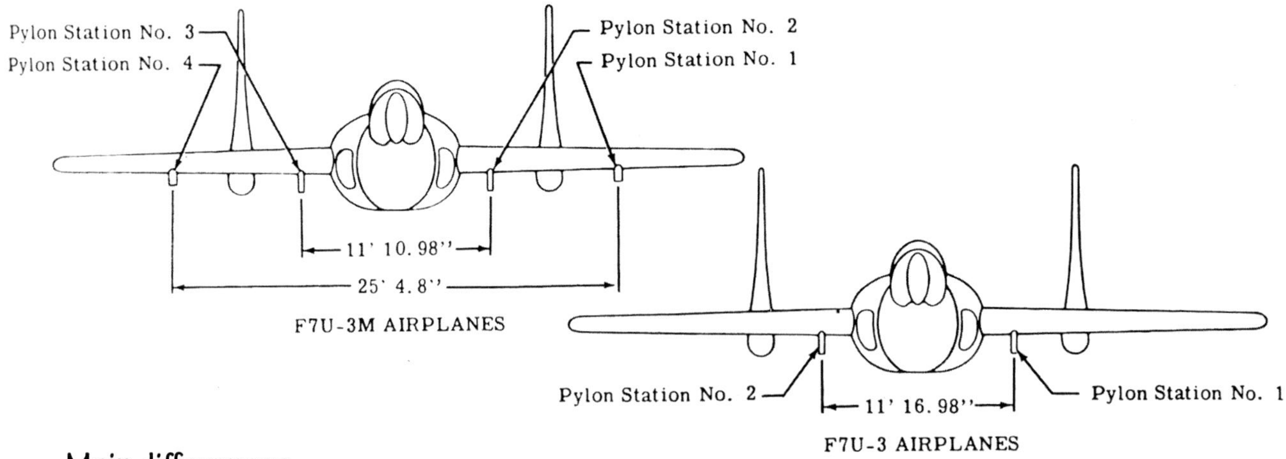

Main differences

	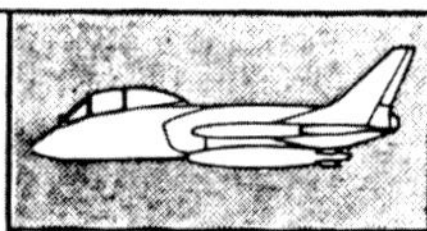	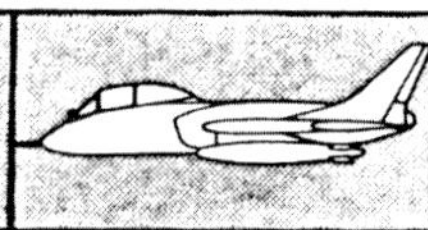	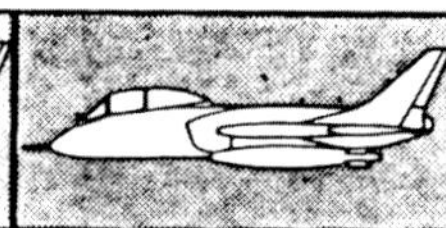		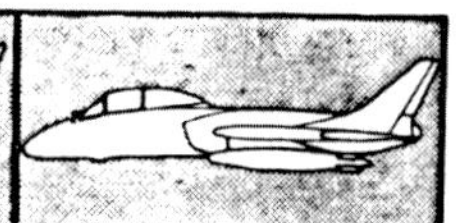
	F7U-3 Airplanes BuNo. 128467 through 128478	F7U-3 Airplanes BuNo. 129545 through 129675	F7U-3 Airplanes BuNo. 129676 and Subsequent	F7U-3M Airplanes	F7U-3P Airplanes
EXTERNAL RECOGNITION FEATURES					Nose section redesigned to accommodate photographic equipment.
	Rocket Pack or Fuselage Fuel Pod when installed.				Fuselage Fuel Pod when installed.
	External Fuel Tanks when installed.	External Fuel Tanks and Inflight Refueling Probe when installed.		External Fuel Tanks when installed.	
				Outer panel pylons to accommodate missiles.	
TACTICAL OPERATION	Carrier-based fighter.				Carrier-based photo-reconnaissance.
POWERPLANT	J46-WE-8B with integral afterburner.			J46-WE-8 with integral afterburner.	J46-WE-8B with integral afterburner.
FUEL SYSTEM	External fuel.	External fuel and inflight refueling.		External and outer panel fuel.	
COCKPIT	AN/ARA-25 Direction Finder Group.				AN/ARR-2A Aircraft Radio Receiver.
	AN/ARR-2A Aircraft Radio Receiver.				
		AN/APA-89 Equipment after ASC 55 (ECP 51).			
	Electrical erection of gyro horizon. Gyro horizon warning light on instrument board.	Manual erection of gyro horizon. Gyro horizon OFF flag on indicator.			
	A-C power control - Main and standby inverters.	A-C power control - main and standby inverters	A-C power control - Main and standby inverters.	A-C power control - Air turbine generator with under-frequency control and two inverters.	A-C power control - Air turbine generator and instrument inverter.
	Aero 10D Armament Control System		Aero 10D Armament Control System.	Aero 10E Armament Control System.	A 20 VF Viewfinder System.
		Aero 18A armament control system after ASC 7 (ECP 223) and temporary kit R82-2-F7U-C7. Aero 14 series stores after ASC 21 (ECP 105), ASC 259 (ECP 433), and conversion kit R82-2-F7U-C21.			
	Emergency engine exhaust nozzle control.				Emergency engine exhaust nozzle control.
	Engine automatic trim controls.			EMERG MILITARY THRUST switch after ASC 301 (ECP 516)	
	Engine AEC power test panel on RH console (one switch and one test light).	Engine AEC power test panel on RH console (two switches and one test light). ◊			Engine AEC power test panel on LH console (two switches and one test light)
	External fuel controls.	External and inflight refueling controls.		External and outer panel fuel controls.	
		Console-controlled preselection of UHF radio frequencies.			

Self-boarding

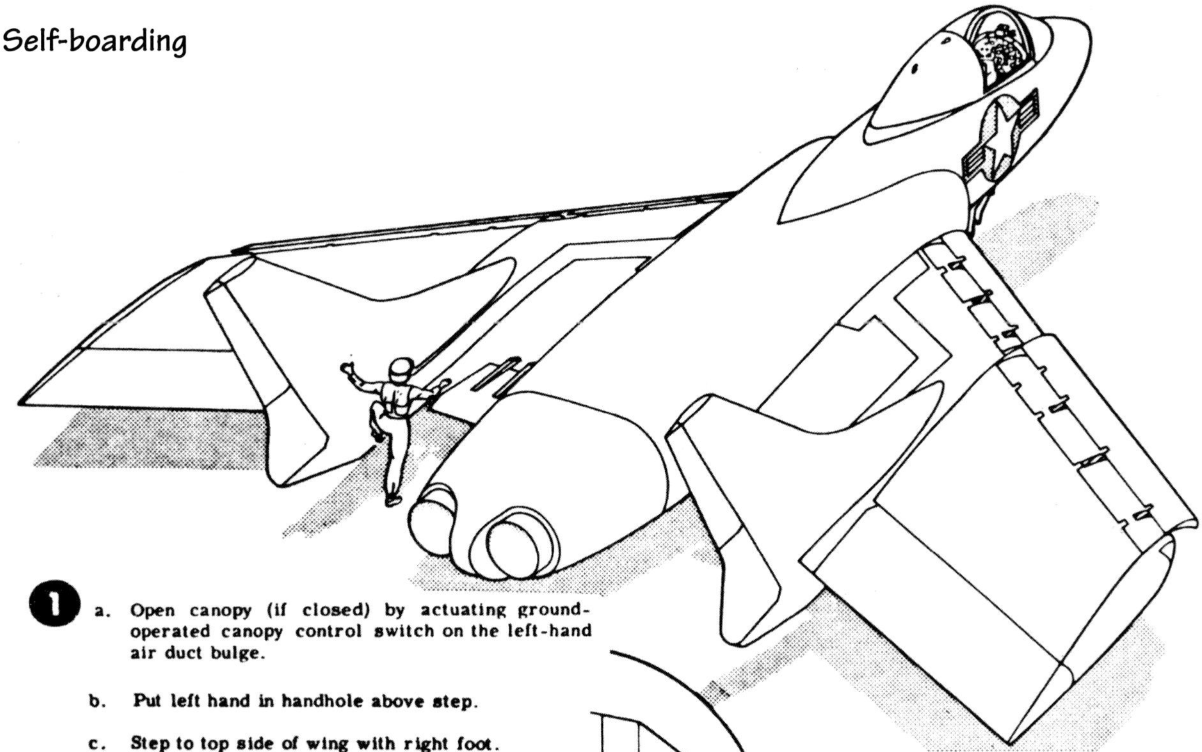

1 a. Open canopy (if closed) by actuating ground-operated canopy control switch on the left-hand air duct bulge.

b. Put left hand in handhole above step.

c. Step to top side of wing with right foot.

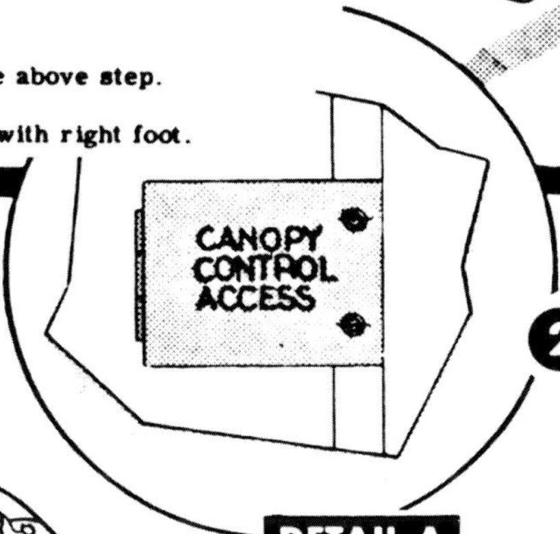

DETAIL A

COCKPIT ACCESS

The two steps on the forward fuselage are extended and retracted along with the nose landing gear doors.

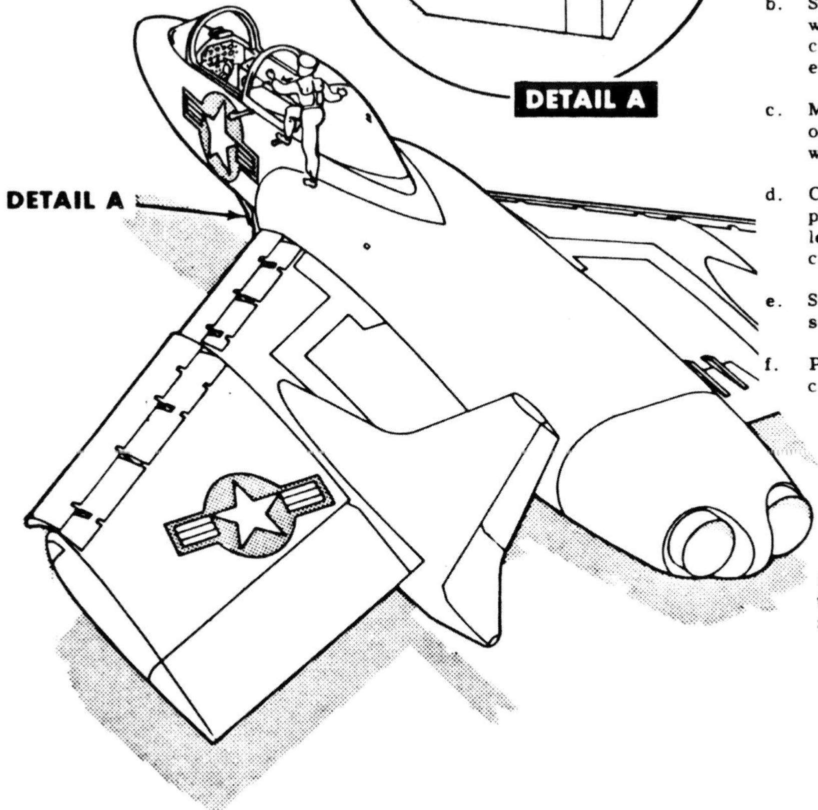

2 a. Walk forward on wing walkway.

b. Step to top of fuselage, grasp handhole in canopy with right hand, and place right foot on first cockpit access step (step should only be out far enough to accommodate foot).

c. Maintain grip on canopy handhole, place left foot on second step, and move step out as far as it will go.

d. Continue to maintain grip on canopy handhole and place right foot in "duckfoot" fashion between left foot and fuselage skin. Grasp front end of canopy simultaneously with left hand.

e. Swing left leg over canopy rail and step on pilot's seat.

f. Put all weight on left foot and bring right leg into cockpit.

CAUTION

Do not use this method to enter cockpit if there is any other means of access available.

F7U-3/3M/3P skin plating

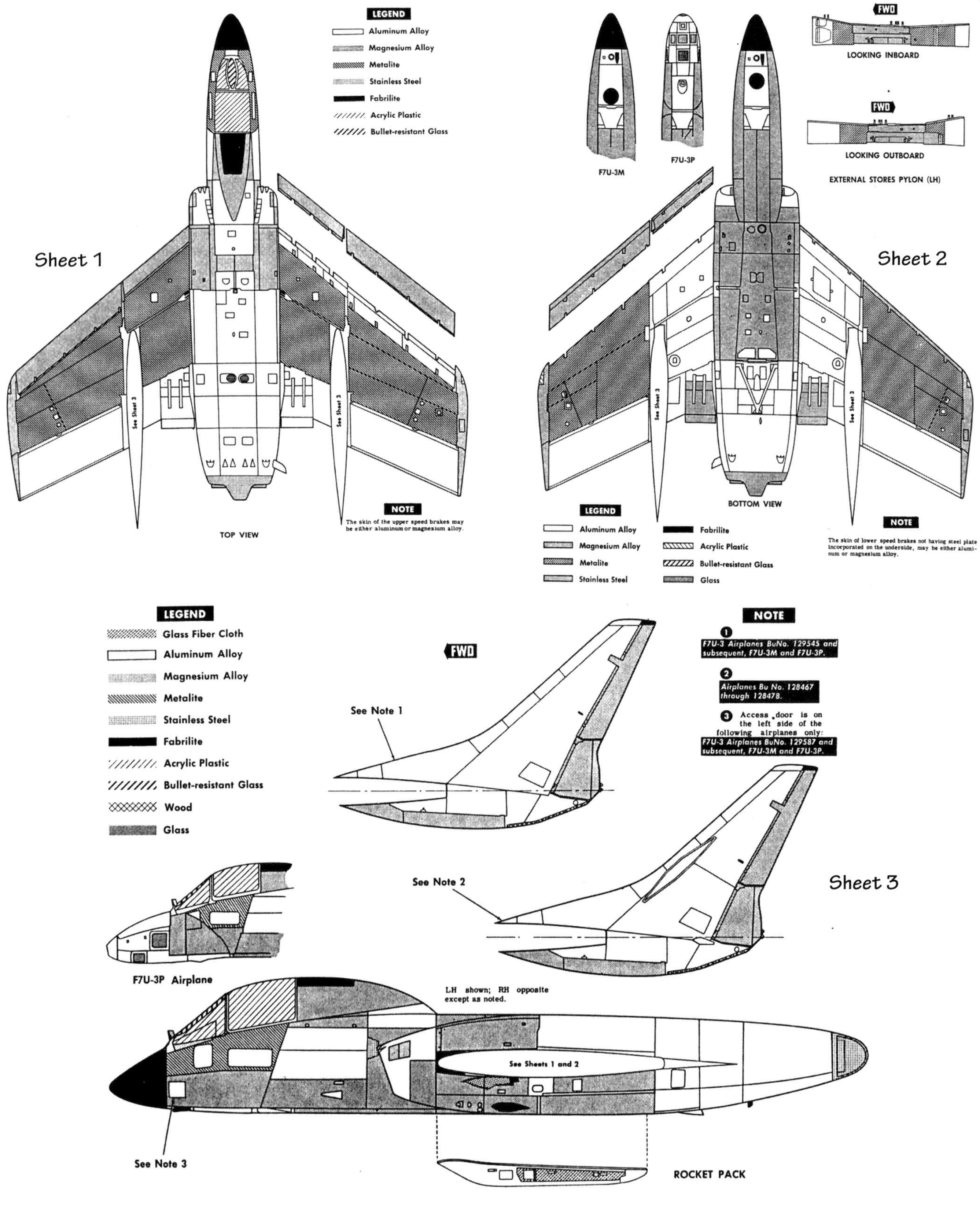

Cockpit

The F7U-3 cockpit in particular varied over time. The following illustrations of the F7U-3, F7U-3M, and F7U-3P should be considered representational since detail changes were made over time, particularly in the case of the F7U-3.

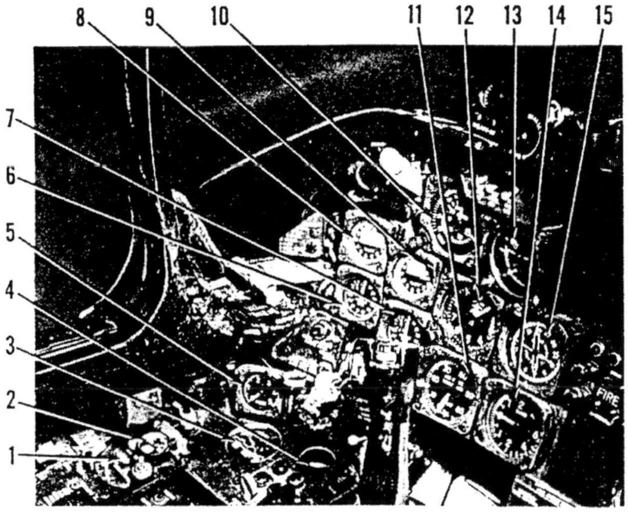

1. Oxygen Flow Indicator
2. Oxygen Pressure Gage
3. Landing Gear and Slats Position Indicator
4. Oxygen Flow Indicator
5. Hydraulic Pressure Gage
6. LH Tachometer Indicator
7. RH Tachometer Indicator
8. LH Exhaust Temperature Indicator
9. RH Exhaust Temperature Indicator
10. Airspeed and Mach Number Indicator
11. Gross Thrust Indicator
12. Altimeter
13. Gyro Horizon Indicator
14. Rate-of-Climb Indicator
15. Radio-Magnetic Indicator
16. Main Fuel Quantity Indicator
17. Fire Warning Panel
18. Transfer Fuel Quantity Indicator
19. Exhaust Nozzle Position Indicators (2)
20. Turn-and-Bank Indicators
21. Elapsed-Time Clock
22. Accelerometer
23. Master Direction Indicator
24. Fuel Flow Indicator
25. Roll Trim Dial
26. Pitch Trim Dial
27. D-C Voltammeter
28. A-C Voltmeter
29. Radio Compass Tuning Dial
30. Radio Compass Band Selector Dial

NOTE

See figures 2-9, 2-10A, or 2-10C for location of cockpit altimeter indicator.

4648-6-1(6)M

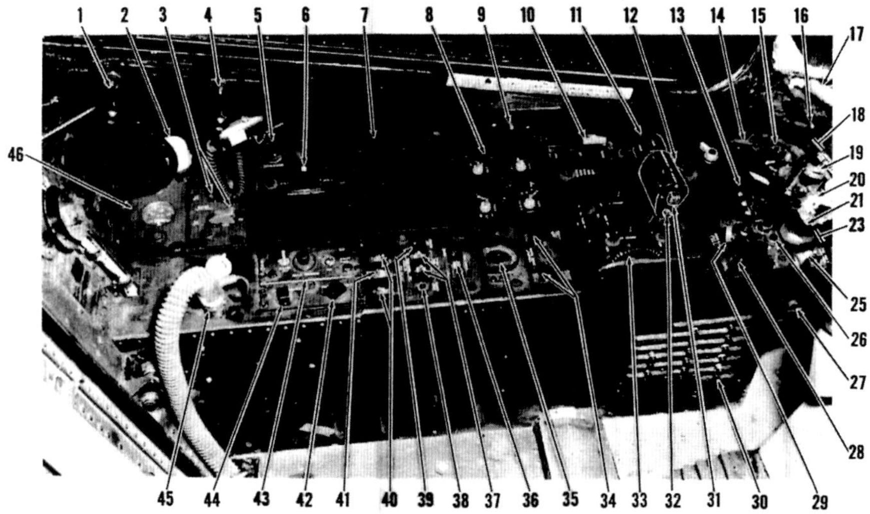

1. Canopy Stop Release Handle (figures 2-5 and 2-6)
2. Antiblackout Pressure Regulating Valve (figure 4-5)
3. Engine Automatic Trim Switches (figure 5-6)
4. Canopy Lock Release Handle (figures 2-5 and 2-6)
5. Pilot's Range Volume Control (figure 9-1C)
6. Emergency Power Control Switch (figure 3-1B)
7. Ejector Rack Test Switches (not shown - see figure 9-2) after incorporation of ASC 259 (ECP 433)
8. Aircraft Fire Control Panel (figure 9-1C)
9. Ejection Seat Control Switch (figure 2-8)
10. Emergency Engine Exhaust Nozzle Control Unit (figure 5-6)
11. Throttle Control Levers (figure 5-11) and Gyro Caging Throttle Switch (figure 9-1C)
12. Oxygen Regulator (figure 4-5)
13. Landing Gear and Slats Position Indicator (figure 2-18 and 2-27)
14. Catapult Handgrip (refer to AN 01-45HFD-1) after incorporation of ASC 227 (ECP 425)
15. Utility Hydraulic Pressure Gage (figure 3-2)
16. Canopy Control Switch (figure 2-5)
17. Emergency Canopy Control Handle (figure 2-5)
18. Speed Brake Warning Light (not shown - see figure 2-16)
19. Landing Gear Handle Lock Solenoid Override Pull Ring (figure 2-27)
20. Landing Gear Control Handle and Warning Light (figure 2-27)
21. Oxygen Flow Indicator (figure 4-5)
22. Deleted
23. External Fuel Control Panel (not shown - see figure 5-8A)
24. Deleted
25. Fuel Tank and Cockpit Pressurization Switch (figures 4-1 and 5-8A)
26. Power Control Hydraulic Pressure Warning Lights (figure 3-1B)
27. Spare Lamps
28. Slat Control Switch (figure 2-18)
29. Emergency Slats Pull Ring (figure 2-18)
30. Circuit Breaker Panel (figure 7-6)
31. Speed Brake Control Switch (figure 2-16)
32. Microphone Switch (figure 8-2)
33. Throttle Lever Friction Control (figure 5-11)
34. Master Engine Switches (figure 5-13)
35. Rudder Trim Control Potentiometer (figure 2-21)
36. Ailavator Trim Control Switch (figure 2-20M)
37. Ailavator Emergency Trim Switches (figure 2-20M)
38. Flight Stabilization Damper Reset Switch (figure 2-21)
39. Flight Stabilization Emergency Disconnect Switch (figure 2-21)
40. Pylon Station Selector Switches (figure 9-2)
40A. Aero 5A Pylon Station Selector Switches (not shown - see figure 9-2) after incorporation of ASC 259 (ECP 433)
41. Fuel Pod Switch
42. Rocket Quantity Selector Switch (figure 9-2)
43. Radar Control Unit (figure 9-1B)
44. Bomb-Rocket Selector Switch (figure 9-2)
45. Oxygen, Antiblackout, and Radio Headset Disconnect Fitting (figure 4-5)
46. Cockpit Altimeter Indicator

4648-2-9AM

Figure No. 2–10A. Left-hand Console—F7U-3 Airplanes BuNo. 129545 through 129675

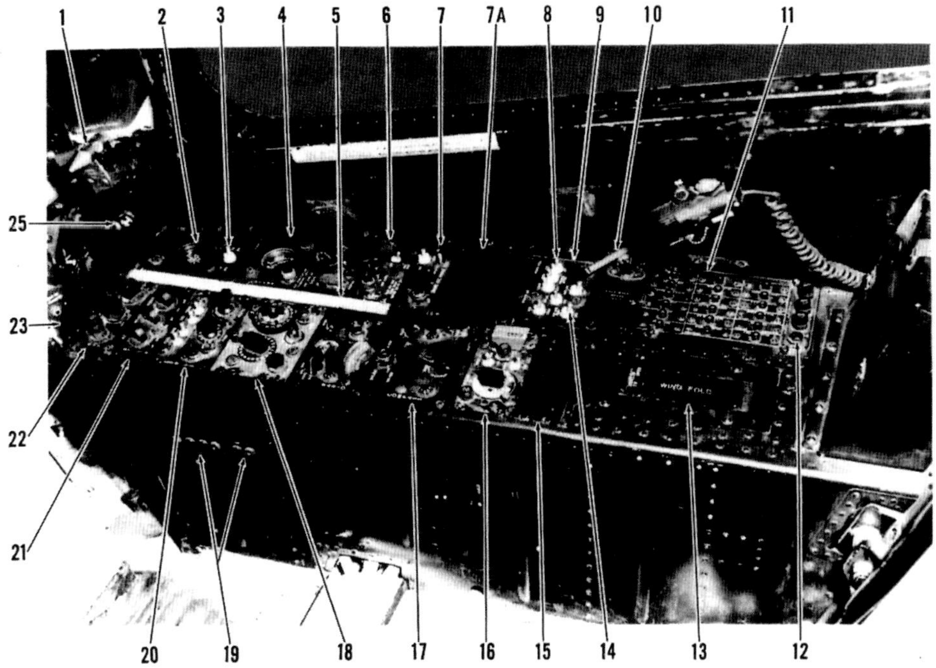

1. Manual Bomb Release Handle (figure 9-2)
2. Voltammeter (figure 7-8)
3. Ammeter Selector Switch (figure 7-8)
4. A-C Power Control Panel (figure 7-5)
5. AN/ARC-27A Frequency Card (figure 8-2)
6. D-C Power Control Panel (figure 7-3)
7. Engine AEC Power Test Panel (reference section V)

7A. D-C Overvoltage Switch Panel (not shown - see figure 7-10) after incorporation of ASC 292 (ECP 514)

8. Rudder Pedal Adjust Switch (figure 2-26) Located here on Airplanes BuNo. 128467 through 129615
9. Cockpit Air Control Panel (figure 4-1) Airplanes BuNo. 128467 through 129615
10. Emergency Wheel Brake Control Handle (figure 2-33)
11. Circuit Breaker Panel (figure 7-6)
12. Interior Lights Fuses (figure 7-13)
13. Wing-Fold Control Unit (figures 1-8 and 2-13)
14. Auxiliary Hydraulic Pump Switch (figure 3-2) Located here on Airplanes BuNo. 128467 through 129615
15. AN/APA-89 Radar Control Panel (not shown, reference section VIII) after incorporation of ASC 55 (ECP 51)
16. IFF Radar Pilot's Control Unit (figure 8-6)
17. AN/ARN-6 Radio Compass Control Unit (figure 8-4)
18. AN/ARC-27A Radio Pilot's Control Unit (figure 8-2)
19. Voltmeter and Ammeter Test Jacks (figures 7-8 and 7-11)
20. Exterior Lights Control Unit (figure 7-12)
21. Interior Lights Control Unit (figure 7-13)
22. AN/ARR-2A Navigation Radio Pilot's Control Unit (figure 8-5)
23. RH External Fuel Control Panel (figure 5-8A)
24. Deleted
25. Arresting Gear Control Handle and Warning Light (figure 2-34)

4648-2-10AM

Figure No. 2–10B. Right-hand Console—F7U-3 Airplanes BuNo. 129545 through 129675

9. Gyro Horizon Indicator
10. Altimeter
11. Radio-Magnetic Indicator
12. Gross Thrust Indicator
13. Rate-of-Climb Indicator
14. Main Fuel Quantity Indicator
15. Fire Warning Panel
16. Turn-and-Bank Indicator
17. Radar Antenna Position Indicator
18. Exhaust Nozzle Position Indicators (2)
19. Radar Range Indicator
20. Accelerometer
21. Elapsed-Time Clock
22. Master Direction Indicator
23. Transfer Fuel Quantity Indicator
24. Fuel Flow Indicator
25. D-C Voltammeter
26. Radio Compass Tuning Dial
27. Radio Compass Band Selector Dial

1. Oxygen Flow Indicator
2. Landing Gear and Slats Position Indicator
3. Oxygen Flow Indicator
4. Hydraulic Pressure Gage
5. RH Tachometer Indicator
6. LH Exhaust Temperature Indicator
7. RH Exhaust Temperature Indicator
8. Airspeed and Mach Number Indicator

NOTE

See figure No. 2-10E for location of cockpit altimeter indicator.

4648-6-1(7)M

Figure No. 6–1. Instruments—F7U-3M Airplanes (Sheet 2)

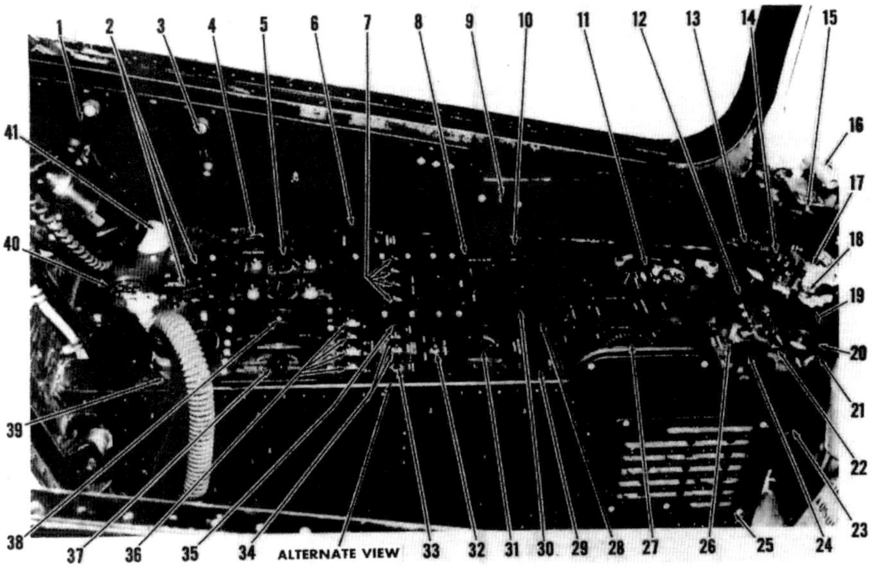

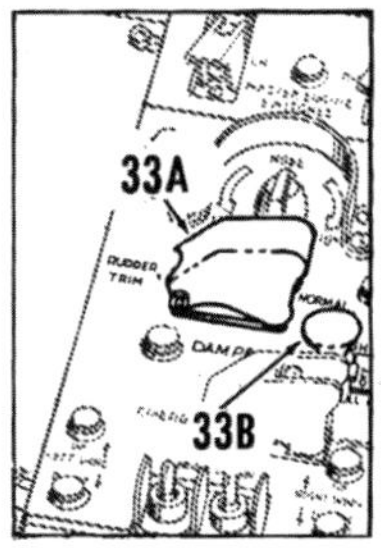

ALTERNATE VIEW

F7U-3M Airplanes
BuNo. 139868
and Subsequent

1. Canopy Stop Release Handle (figures 2-5 and 2-6)
2. Engine Automatic Trim Switches (figure 5-6)
3. Canopy Lock Release Handle (figures 2-5 and 2-6)
4. Pilot's Range Volume Control (figure 9-1C)
5. MK 35 Mod 2 Armament Control Unit (figure 9-1C)
6. Ejector Rack Test Switch (figure 9-2) prior to Incorporation of ASC 23 (ECP 195)
7. Missile Jettison Switches (reference NavAer 01-45HFD-504)
8. APQ-51 Radar Control Panel (reference NavAer 01-45HFD-504)
9. Ejection Seat Control Switch (figure 2-8)
10. Throttle Control Levers (figure 5-11) and Gyro Caging Throttle Switch (figure 9-1D)
11. Oxygen Regulator (figure 4-5)
12. Landing Gear and Slats Position Indicator (figures 2-18 and 2-27)
13. Catapult Handgrip (refer to AN-45HFD-1) after incorporation of ASC 227 (ECP 425)
14. Utility Hydraulic Pressure Gage (figure 3-2)
15. Canopy Control Switch (figure 2-5)
16. Emergency Canopy Control Handle (figure 2-5)
17. Landing Gear Handle Lock Solenoid Override Pull Ring (figure 2-27)
18. Landing Gear Control Handle and Warning Light (figure 2-27)
19. LH External Fuel Control Panel (not shown - see figure 5-8A)
20. Oxygen Flow Indicator (figure 4-5)
21. Fuel Tank and Cockpit Pressurization Switch (figures 4-1 and 5-8B)
22. Power Control Hydraulic Pressure Warning Light (figure 3-1B)
23. Spare Lamps
24. Slats Control Switch (figure 2-18)
25. Circuit Breaker Panel (figure 7-6)
26. Emergency Slat Pull Ring (figure 2-18)
27. Throttle Lever Friction Control (figure 5-11)
28. Microphone Switch (figure 8-2)
29. Master Engine Switch (figure 5-13)
30. Speedbrake Control Switch (figure 2-16)
31. Rudder Trim Control Potentiometer (figure 2-21)
32. Ailavator Trim Control Switch (figure 2-20M)
*33. Flight Stabilization Damper Reset Switches (figure 2-21)
33A. Rudder Trim Selector Switch (figure 2-25A)
33B. Damper Engage Switch (figure 2-25A)
34. Ailavator Emergency Trim Switches (figure 2-20M)
*35. Flight Stabilization Emergency Disconnect Switch (figure 2-21)
36. Pylon Station Selector Switches (figure 9-2) Airplanes BuNo. 129677, 129698 through 129744
37. Armament Selector Switch (reference NavAer 01-45HFD-504)
38. Emergency Power Control Switch (figure 3-1)
39. Oxygen, Antiblackout and Radio Headset Disconnect Fitting (figure 4-5)
40. Cockpit Altimeter Indicator
41. Antiblackout Pressure Regulating Valve (figure 4-5)

*F7U-3M Airplanes BuNo. 129589 through 129744

4648-2-10EM

Figure No. 2–10E. Left-hand Console—F7U-3M Airplanes

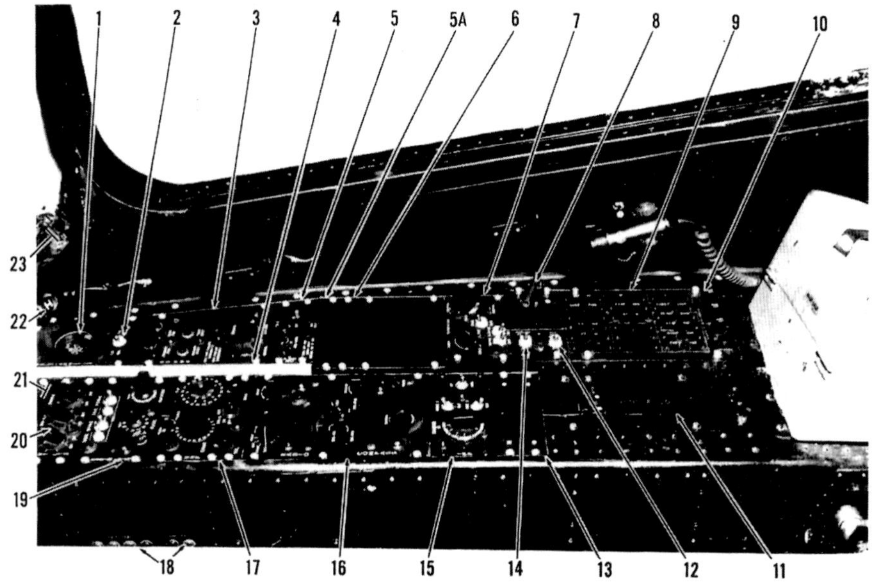

1. Voltammeter (figure 7-8)
2. Ammeter Selector Switch (figure 7-8)
3. A-C Power Control Panel (figure 7-5A)
4. AN/ARC-27A Frequency Card (figure 8-2)
5. D-C Power Control Panel (figure 7-3A)
5A. D-C Overvoltage Switch Panel (not shown - see figure 7-10) after incorporation of ASC 292 (ECP 514)
6. Engine AEC Power Test Panel (not shown - reference section V)
7. Cockpit Air Control Panel (figure 4-1) Except Airplanes BuNo. 129589 and 129590
8. Emergency Wheel Brake Control Handle (figure 2-33)
9. Circuit Breaker Panel (figure 7-6A)
10. Interior Lights Fuses (figure 7-13)
11. Wing-Fold Control Unit (figures 1-8 and 2-13)
12. Auxiliary Hydraulic Pump Switch (figure 3-2)
13. AN/APA-89 Radar Control Panel (not shown, reference section VIII) after incorporation of ASC 55 (ECP 51)
14. Rudder Pedal Adjust Switch (figure 2-26)
15. IFF Radio Pilot's Control Unit (figure 8-6A)
16. AN/ARN-6 Radio Compass Control Unit (figure 8-4)
17. AN/ARC-27A Radio Pilot's Control Unit (figure 8-2)
18. Voltmeter and Ammeter Test Jacks (figures 7-8 and 7-11)
19. Exterior Lights Control Unit (figure 7-12)
20. Interior Lights Control Unit (figure 7-13)
21. RH External Fuel Control Panel (not shown - see figure 5-8A)
22. Arresting Gear Control Handle and Warning Light (figure 2-34)
23. Manual Bomb Release Handle (not shown - see figure 9-2)

4648-2-10FM

Figure No. 2–10F. Right-hand Console—F7U-3M Airplanes

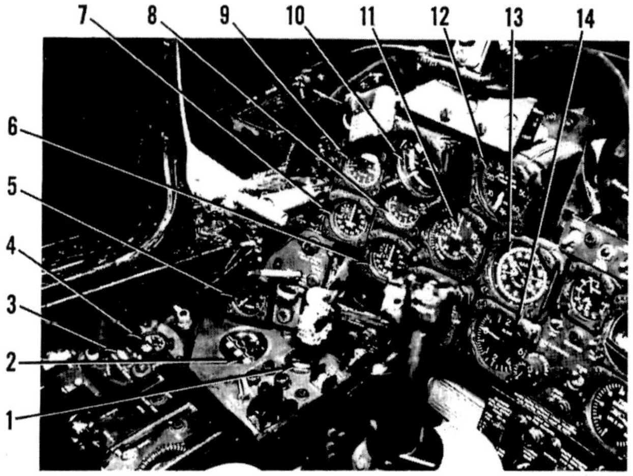

1. Oxygen Flow Indicator
2. Landing Gear and Slats Position Indicator
3. Oxygen Flow Regulator
4. Oxygen Pressure Gage
5. Hydraulic Pressure Gage
6. RH Tachometer
7. LH Tachometer
8. RH Exhaust Temperature Indicator
9. LH Exhaust Temperature Indicator
10. Gyro Horizon Indicator
11. Airspeed and Mach Number Indicator
12. Gross Thrust Indicator
13. Radio-Magnetic Indicator
14. Rate-of-Climb Indicator
15. Transfer Fuel Quantity Indicator
15A. Altimeter
16. Main Fuel Quantity Indicator
17. Elapsed-Time Clock
18. Turn-and-Bank Indicator
19. Radio Altitude Indicator (Inoperative)
20. Exhaust Nozzle Position Indicator
21. Free Air Temperature Indicator
22. Fire Warning Panel
23. Accelerometer
24. Eight-Day Clock
25. Master Direction Indicator
26. Fuel Flow Indicator
27. D-C Voltammeter
28. A-C Voltammeter
29. Radio Compass Tuning Dial
30. Radio Compass Band Selector Dial

NOTE

See figure No. 2-10G for location of cockpit altimeter indicator.

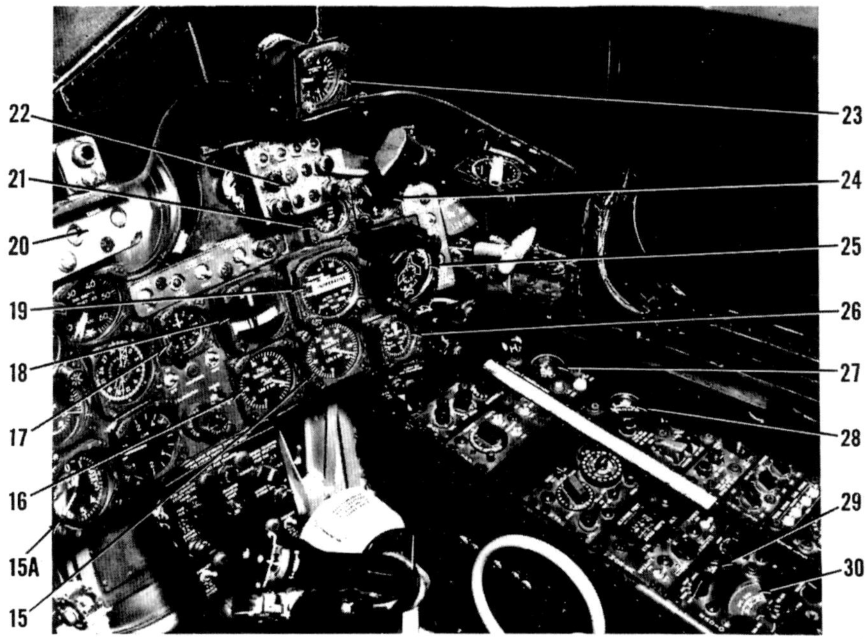

4648-6-1(4)M

Figure No. 6–1. Instruments—F7U-3P Airplanes (Sheet 3)

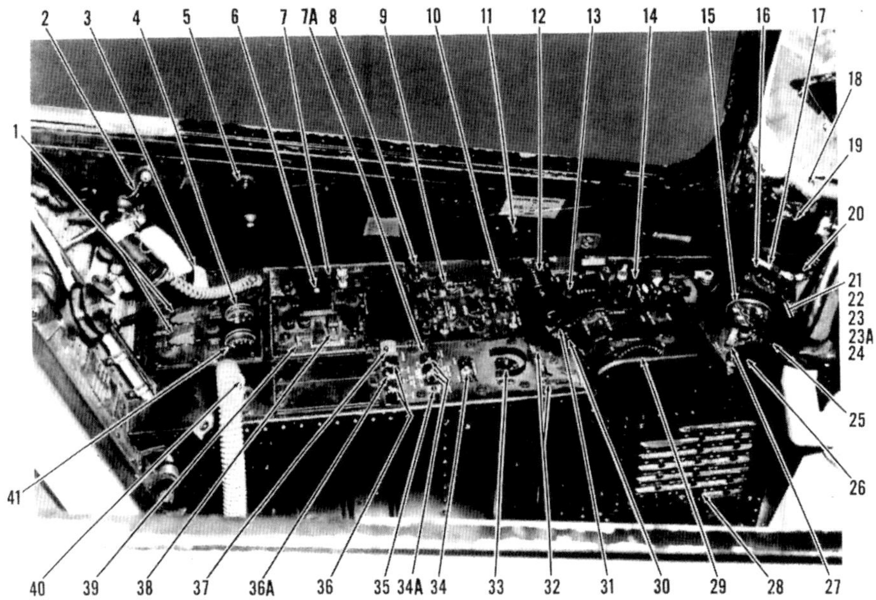

1. Engine Automatic Trim Switches (figure 5-6)
2. Canopy Stop Release Handle (figures 2-5 and 2-6)
3. Antiblackout Pressure-Regulating Valve (figure 4-5)
4. Cockpit Altimeter Indicator
5. Canopy Lock Release Handle (figures 2-5 and 2-6)
6. Emergency Power Control Switch (figure 3-1B)
7. Engine AEC Power Test Panel (refer to section V)

7A. Flight Stabilization Emergency Disconnect Switch (figure 2-21)

8. K-37 Camera Indicator Light (refer to NAVAER 01-45HFD-505)
9. Station 2 Camera Control Panel (refer to NAVAER 01-45HFD-505)
10. Station 1 Camera Control Panel (refer to NAVAER 01-45HFD-505)
11. Ejection Seat Control Switch (figure 2-8)
12. Throttle Control Lever (figure 5-11)
13. Emergency Engine Exhaust Nozzle Control Unit (figure 5-6)
14. Oxygen Regulator (figure 4-5)
15. Landing Gear and Slats Position Indicator (figures 2-18 and 2-27)
16. Utility Hydraulic Pressure Gage (figure 3-2)
17. Catapult Handgrip (refer to AN 01-45HFD-1) after Incorporation of ASC 227 (ECP 425)
18. Emergency Canopy Control Handle (figure 2-5)
19. Canopy Control Switch (figure 2-5)
20. Landing Gear Handle Lock Solenoid Override Pull Ring (figure 2-5)
21. Speedbrake Warning Light (not shown) (figure 2-16)
22. Landing Gear Control Handle and Warning Light (not shown) (figure 2-27)
23. LH External Fuel Control Switch (not shown) (figure 5-8A)

23A. Oxygen Flow Indicator (not shown) (figure 4-5)

24. Fuel Tank and Cockpit Pressurization Switch (not shown) (figures 4-1 and 5-8C)
25. Power Control Hydraulic Pressure Warning Light (figure 3-1B)
26. Slats Control Switch (figure 2-18)
27. Emergency Slat Pull Ring (figure 2-18)
28. Circuit Breaker Panel (figure 7-6A)
29. Throttle Lever Friction Control (figure 5-11)
30. Microphone Switch (figure 8-2)
31. Speedbrake Control Switch (figure 2-16)
32. Master Engine Switches (figure 5-13)
33. Rudder Trim Control Potentiometer (figure 2-21)
34. Ailavator Trim Control Switch (figure 2-20M)

34A. Ailavator Emergency Trim Switches (figure 2-20M)

35. Flight Stabilization Damper Reset Switch (figure 2-21)
36. Pylon Station Selector Switches (figure 9-2)

36A. Fuel Pod Switch

37. Drop Tank Switch
38. Flare Salvo Switch (figures 3-3 and 4-40)
39. Flare Ejector Selector Switch (refer to NAVAER 01-45HFD-505)
40. Oxygen Antiblackout and Radio Headset Disconnect (figure 4-5)
41. Camera Compartment Temperature Indicator (refer to NAVAER 01-45HFD-505)

4648-2-10GM

Figure No. 2–10G. Left-hand Console—F7U-3P Airplanes

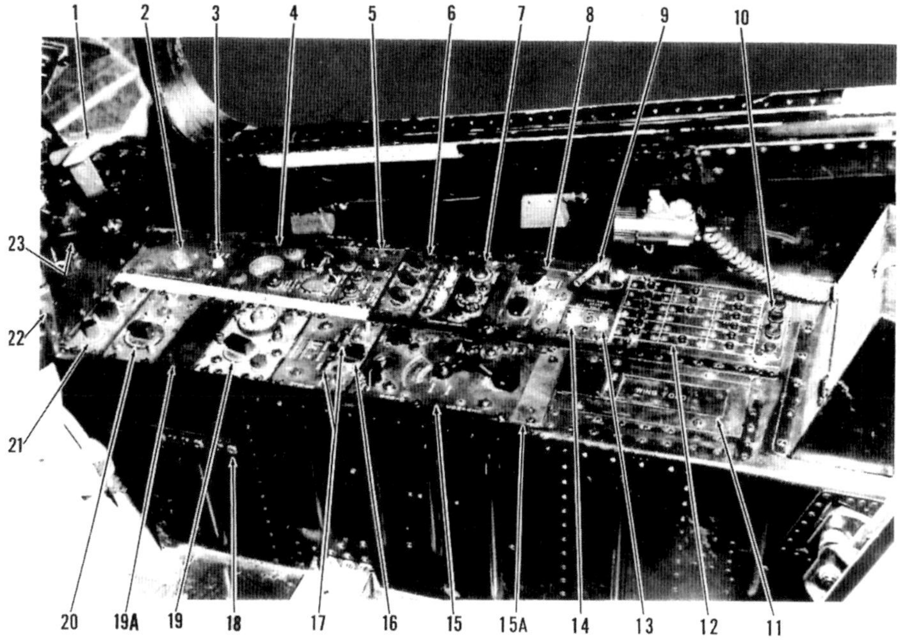

1. Manual Bomb Release Handle (figure 9-2)
2. Voltammeter (figure 7-8)
3. Ammeter Selector Switch (figure 7-8)
4. A-C Power Control Panel (figure 7-5B)
5. D-C Power Control Panel (figure 7-3B)
6. Interior Lights Control Unit (figure 7-13)
7. Exterior Lights Control Unit (figure 7-13)
8. Cockpit Air Control Panel (figure 4-1)
9. Emergency Wheel Brake Control Handle (figure 2-33)
10. Interior Lights Fuses (figure 7-13)
11. Wing-Fold Control Unit (figures 1-8 and 2-13)
12. Circuit Breaker Panel (figure 7-6B)
13. Auxiliary Hydraulic Pump Switch (figure 3-2)
14. Rudder Pedal Adjust Switch (figure 2-26)
15. AN/ARN-6 Radio Compass Control Unit (figure 8-4)

15A. D-C Overvoltage Switch Panel (not shown - see figure 7-10) after incorporation of ASC 292 (ECP 514)

16. Scanner-Computer Selector Switch (refer to NAVAER 01-45HFD-505)
17. Altitude and Speed Computer Knobs (refer to NAVAER 01-45HFD-505)
18. Voltmeter and Ammeter Test Jacks (figures 7-8 and 7-11)
19. AN/ARC-27A Radio Pilot's Control Unit (figure 8-2)

19A. AN/APA-89 Radar Control Panel (not shown - reference section VIII) after incorporation of ASC 55 (ECP 51)

20. IFF Radar Pilot's Control Unit (figure 8-6A)
21. AN/ARR-2A Navigation Radio Pilots Control Unit (figure 8-2)
22. RH External Fuel Control Panel (figure 5-8C)
23. Arresting Gear Control Handle and Warning Light (figure 2-34)

4648-2-10HM

Figure No. 2–10H. Right-hand Console—F7U-3P Airplanes

Ejection seat

Up until the late 1950s, each aircraft company building carrier-based jets for the US Navy was responsible for providing the ejection seat in accordance with a Navy-furnished specification and a government-furnished 'catapult gun' that propelled the seat out of the cockpit.

953e. A safety device shall be provided to assure that all necessary clearances and releases have been accomplished before catapult can be fired. A red warning light shall be installed on the instrument board indicating completed operational sequence which also will provide an alert for firing the catapult. The ejection of each seat is to be accomplished in the following steps:

1. After positioning body and limbs, activate a lever or grip to automatically initiate the following events:
   (a) Decompress the cabin (must be first event)
   (b) Place seat in lowest position
   (c) Retract canopy rear position stops
   (d) Open and release the canopy
   (e) Open catapult safety device
2. After red light on instrument panel flashes on indicating sequence of operation has been completed, the pilot will fire the catapult cartridgewhich releases and ejects the seat from the fuselage, by pulling the wind screen down in front of his face.

ABOVE An early BuAer specification listing the requirements for operation of a manufacturer-furnished ejection seat. *US Navy*

BELOW The Vought seat in the first sixteen F7U-3s featured leg braces that had to be raised to initiate the ejection process; they also minimised leg flailing during ejection. *US Navy*

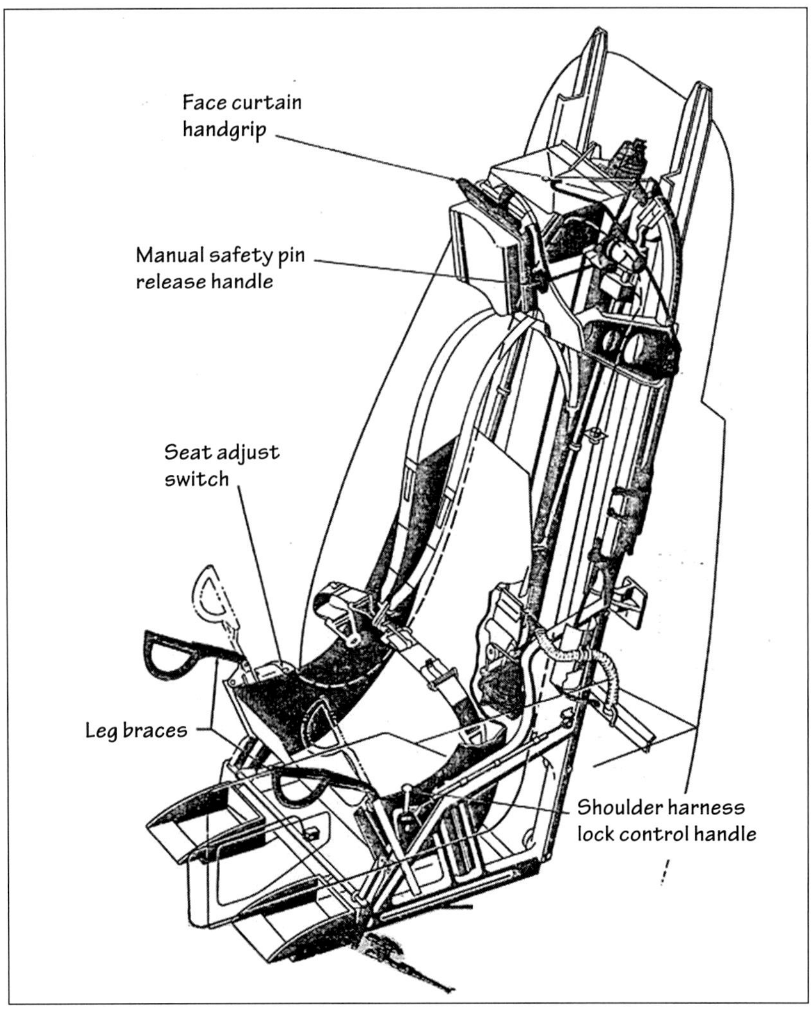

In essence, the seat and its occupant were a projectile, fired out of the cockpit by a 37mm smooth-bore cannon. These seats were basically bailout assists in order for the pilot to get clear of the aircraft at high speeds; ejecting below 1,000ft was almost certain to be fatal. The Navy specification reflected some of the features developed by Martin-Baker for ejection seats, the most notable being the use of a face curtain for the final step for ejection. There was originally a prefatory step that in part served as a safety to assure the pilot seating on the seat that it could not fire accidentally.

The Vought seat installed in the fifteen of the first sixteen F7U-3s, BuNo 128451–3 and 128455–128466, was based on the F7U-1 seat, differing in a few details. The seat bucket sat within a tubular frame that had a set of single rollers outboard of tracks on the ejection seat bulkhead. The headrest, along with redundant armour plate for the pilot's head, was mounted on the frame; the seat bucket was adjustable within a range of 7in up and down; when the seat was full up it was an inch forward from its full-down position. In accordance with the existing specification, these seats provided for a pilot-activated mechanism to accomplish pre-ejection requirements: jettisoning the canopy (which armed the ejection gun) and locking the shoulder harness. This first step required the pilot – in addition to putting his feet in the ejection seat foot rests and activating the emergency oxygen supply if at a high enough altitude – to pull the leg braces up into position; the left-hand brace, which was safety wired to preclude inadvertent actuation, jettisoned the canopy and locked the shoulder harness. The pilot then ejected by pulling down the face curtain.

With the exception of BuNo 128454, which had a redesigned seat and canopy, the Flight Handbook for the first sixteen stated that the seat could be fired through the fully closed canopy if it remained in place after the left-hand leg brace was pulled up. However, in that event the pilot had to manually release the interlock by pulling a handle on the left side of the headrest and then pull the face curtain down (the handle would also have to be pulled in the unlikely event that the departure of the canopy had not armed the seat).

The F7U-3 ejection seat was continuously improved during the Cutlass's development and service life. The seats delivered in F7U-3 BuNos 128467 through 129675 were basically the same as 128454's. There were subsequent small but significant modifications and changes to the seat to improve its functionality. In general, these were retrofitted to the seats previously delivered.

The seat in No. 4, BuNo 128454, which had a modified forward fuselage to improve the pilot's visibility over and to the side of the nose for carrier landings, was extensively redesigned. It had an inner chassis and an outer chassis that allowed the pilot to not only adjust his height but move his head forward for better over-

F7U-3 ejection seat BuNo 128454 and 128467-129675

1. Pilot's Head Armor
2. Outer Chassis
3. Inner Chassis
4. Pilot's Oxygen and Radio Tube (ref)
5. Antiblackout Tube (ref)
6. Left-hand Console (ref)
7. Bucket Seat
8. Pilot's Footrests
9. Pilot's Leg Braces
10. Lap Safety Belt
11. Shoulder Harness Straps
12. Pilot's Headrest

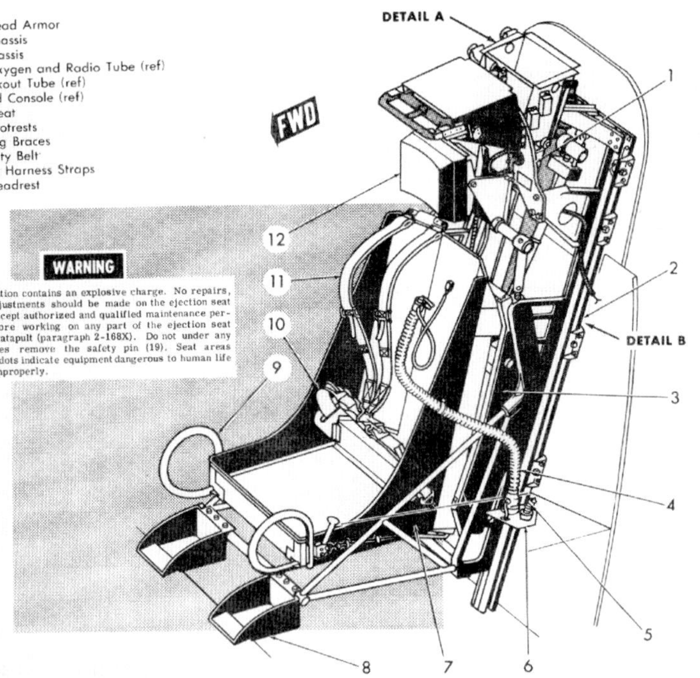

13. Ejection Seat Control Switch
14. Pre-ejection Limit Switch
15. Seat Up Relay
16. Seat Down Relay
17. Catapult Arming and Firing Mechanism
18. Safety Pin Release Cam
19. Safety Pin
20. Firing Piston
21. Firing Yoke
22. Firing Cam
23. Catapult Firing Mechanism and Lock Ring
24. Catapult Holdback Hook Release Handle
25. Inner Chassis Actuator
26. Holdback Hook Lever
27. Catapult
28. Bucket Seat Actuator
29. Catapult Holdback Fitting
30. Terminal Strip No. 80
31. Electrical Plug
32. Harness Reel Control Handle
33. Seat Power Circuit Breaker
34. Seat Control Circuit Breaker
35. Face Curtain Handgrip
36. Deleted
37. Firing Ribbon
38. Firing Ribbon Yoke
39. Catapult Firing Cable
40. Pre-ejection Safety Latch Safety Wire
41. Pre-ejection Safety Latch
42. Warning Tag
43. Catapult Arming Safety Pin Release Cable
44. Pre-ejection Safety Latch Release Cable
45. Manual Safety Pin Release Cable
46. Pre-ejection Air Valve Control Cable
47. Rod (See figure 2-7A)
48. Pre-ejection Air Valve (See figure 2-6A)
49. Pre-ejection Air Valve Control Box (See figure 2-7A)
50. Pre-ejection Control Latch (See figure 2-7A)
51. Pre-Ejection Control Linkage
51A. Pre-Ejection Control Linkage Guard
52. Harness Reel Locking Cable
53. Harness Reel
54. Shoulder Harness Cable
55. Manual Safety Pin Release Handle
56. Landing Eye Relay
57. Terminal Strip No. 57
58. Pre-eject Cruise Eye Relay
59. Pre-eject Relay
60. Cruise Eye Relay

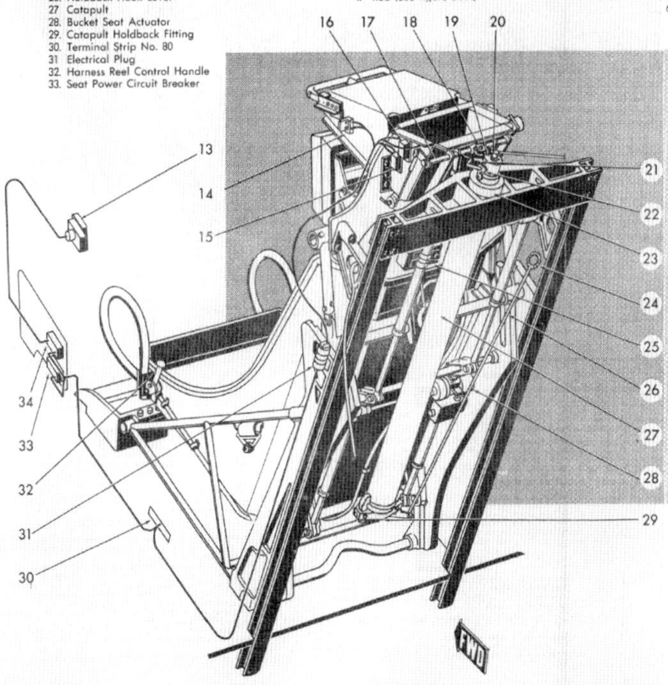

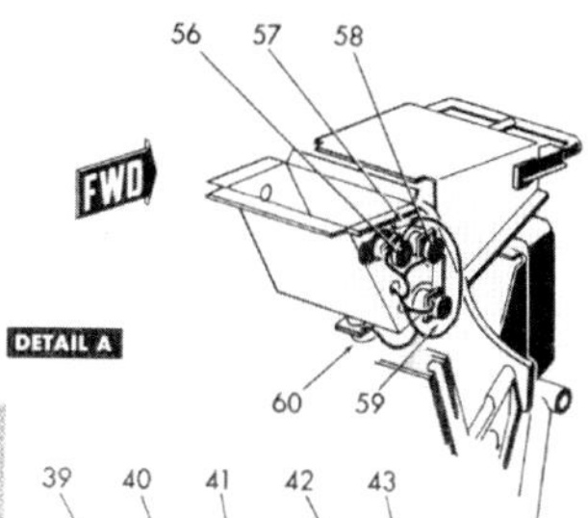

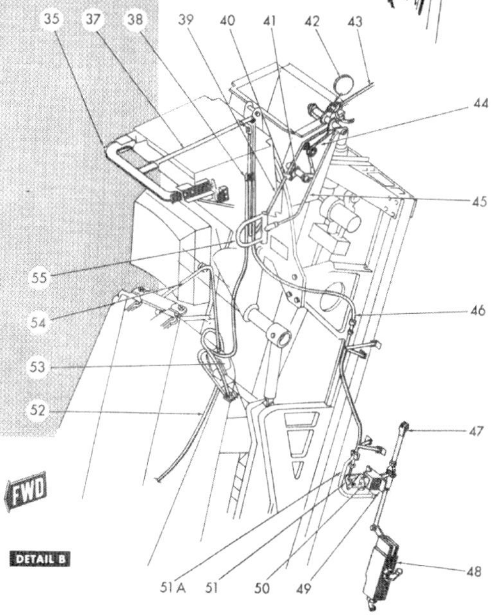

The ejection seats initially installed in F7U-3s BuNos 128454, 128467–128478, and 129545–129675. *VAHF*

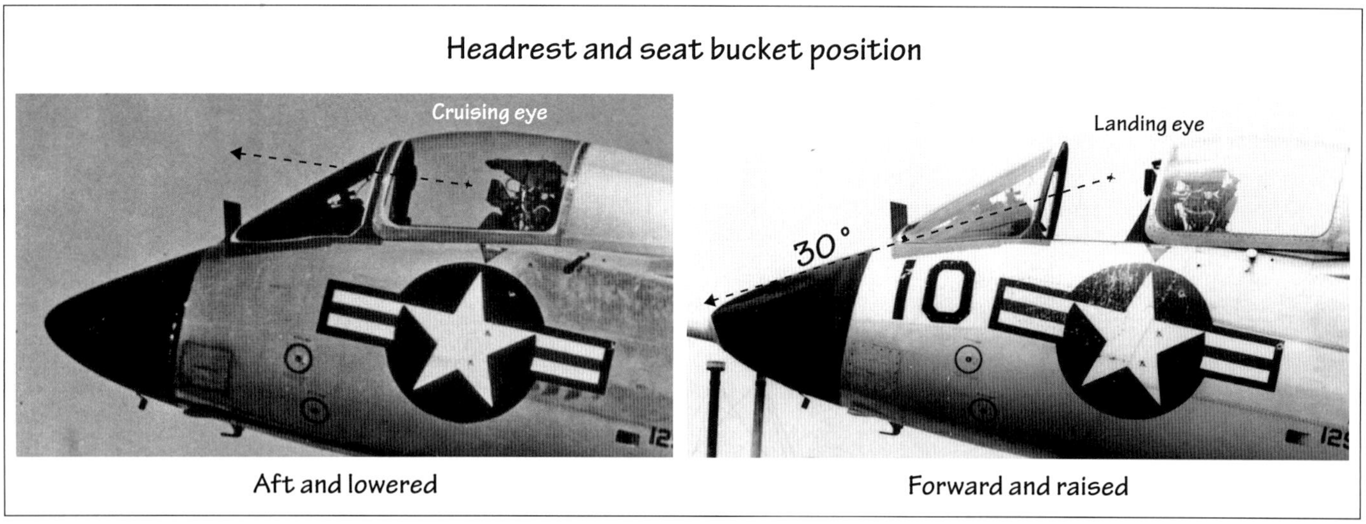

ABOVE To increase the over-the-nose visibility for carrier landings, the F7U-3 forward fuselage was redesigned, including provision for raising and tilting the seat bucket and also repositioning the pilot's headrest forward to the landing eye position. *Thomason*

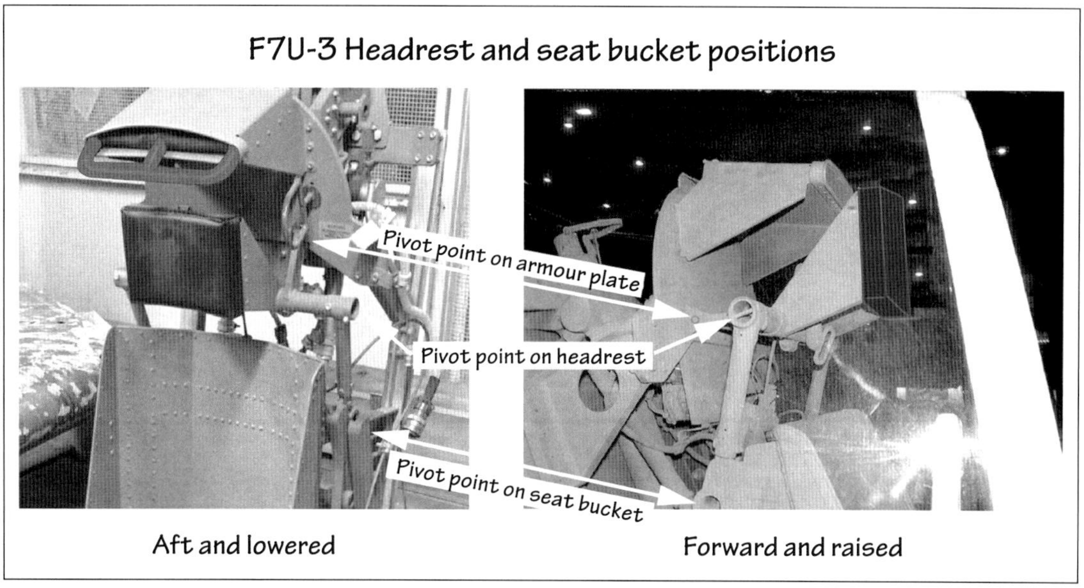

RIGHT The repositioning of the seat bucket resulted in the repositioning of the headrest through a series of links and pivot points. The seat was painted zinc chromate green. The headrest was black leather. The face curtain handle (not present in the righthand picture) was red. *Thomason*

the-nose visibility. The headrest, but not the seat's armour plate or the face curtain mechanism, was now repositioned in concert with a change in the position of the seat bucket. The pilot could now reposition the tilt of the seat and headrest forward and aft in addition to adjusting up and down. There were two standard positions, cruise eye and landing eye. The landing eye position provided for a forward tilt of the seat to increase over the nose visibility, while the cruise eye position returned the seat to the position set prior to flight. The top of the ejection catapult was bolted to the upper end of the outer chassis; the bucket seat was mounted in canted slots on the inner chassis. The pilot could move the bucket seat through a 5in range. Before starting the engines, the pilot selected the cruise eye position and moved the seat up or down as required to centre his head on the headrest. He was then cautioned not to change the seat's position during the remainder of the flight except for landing. However, the landing eye position was not to be used unless the canopy was open because of potential interference between the pilot's helmet and the canopy if it was closed prior to being jettisoned.

The location of the rollers on the seat and the track on the bulkhead was reversed with the substitution of double cam follower rollers located in trunnions on the aft bulkhead, and the track now comprising the vertical portion of the seat assembly's frame. The leg braces were now fixed in place: the pre-ejection steps were accomplished with the pull of the face curtain to its first stop: that returned the seat to the cruise eye position; locked the shoulder harness; and jettisoned the canopy, which armed the seat. After the canopy was jettisoned, the safety latch that stopped further movement of the face curtain was released so the pilot could pull it all the way down to below his chin, which fired the catapult. This interlock was necessary because if the canopy was still present, either closed or open, ejecting would now result in serious or most likely, fatal injury from its structure. However, if the interlock had malfunctioned, preventing the seat from firing with the face curtain pull, the pilot could bypass it manually after verifying that the canopy was gone. In the event the canopy could not be jettisoned, the pilot was to release his seat belt and other attachments, trim nose down, roll the aircraft inverted, and drop out.

1. The seats delivered in F7U-3s BuNos 129676 and up, as well as the F7U-3M and -3P, had a redesigned face curtain mechanism. It incorporated a face curtain roller instead of ribbon activation. The roller utilised two arms that activated the canopy jettison air mechanism and pulled the arming safety pin. This improvement was retrofitted to seats delivered in early F7U-3s.

2. Prior to incorporation of ASC 179 (ECP 472), the pilot had to release his seat belt before rolling forward out of the seat; after incorporation, the belt automatically released three quarters of a second after ejection but the pilot was still responsible for clearing the seat: it was recommended that he not open his parachute for five seconds to allow him to slow to a speed that would reduce the opening shock, as well as avoid the seat becoming entangled with the deploying parachute (after a high-altitude ejection he was also advised to delay opening the parachute until he descended in free fall to a less hostile altitude from a temperature and oxygen standpoint). However, the main benefit was to eliminate the need for the pilot to come to his senses and release his seat belt, hopefully increasing the chances of a survivable ejection at low altitude. (Bud Sickle was almost killed after ejecting from a post-stall gyration because he neglected to get out of his seat before opening his parachute.) Prior to this change, below 2,000ft above the ground the flight manual recommended that unless acceleration forces or violent manoeuvres prevented being well back in the seat for ejection that the lap safety belt be opened, the oxygen-radio tube be disconnected at the attachment point on the left shoulder harness strap, and the shoulder harness straps be off the shoulders prior to ejection.

3. ASC 262 (ECP 490) added a catapult protection shield to eliminate the possibility of an inadvertent firing of the seat like the one that killed VF-124's LTJG Milliard. It was to be locally fabricated from 3/16in aluminium sheet and installed on ejection seats in the fleet.

4. ASC 294 was a redesign of the catapult trigger cap. This modification was also the result of a fatal accident: VF-151's ENS Patrick Edward Harwood had attempted a low-altitude ejection, which failed because the cap was not tightened down far enough during routine maintenance to allow the deployed firing pin to reach the cartridge's initiator.

Ejection seat – F7U-3 BuNo 129676 and subsequent and F7U-3M/P

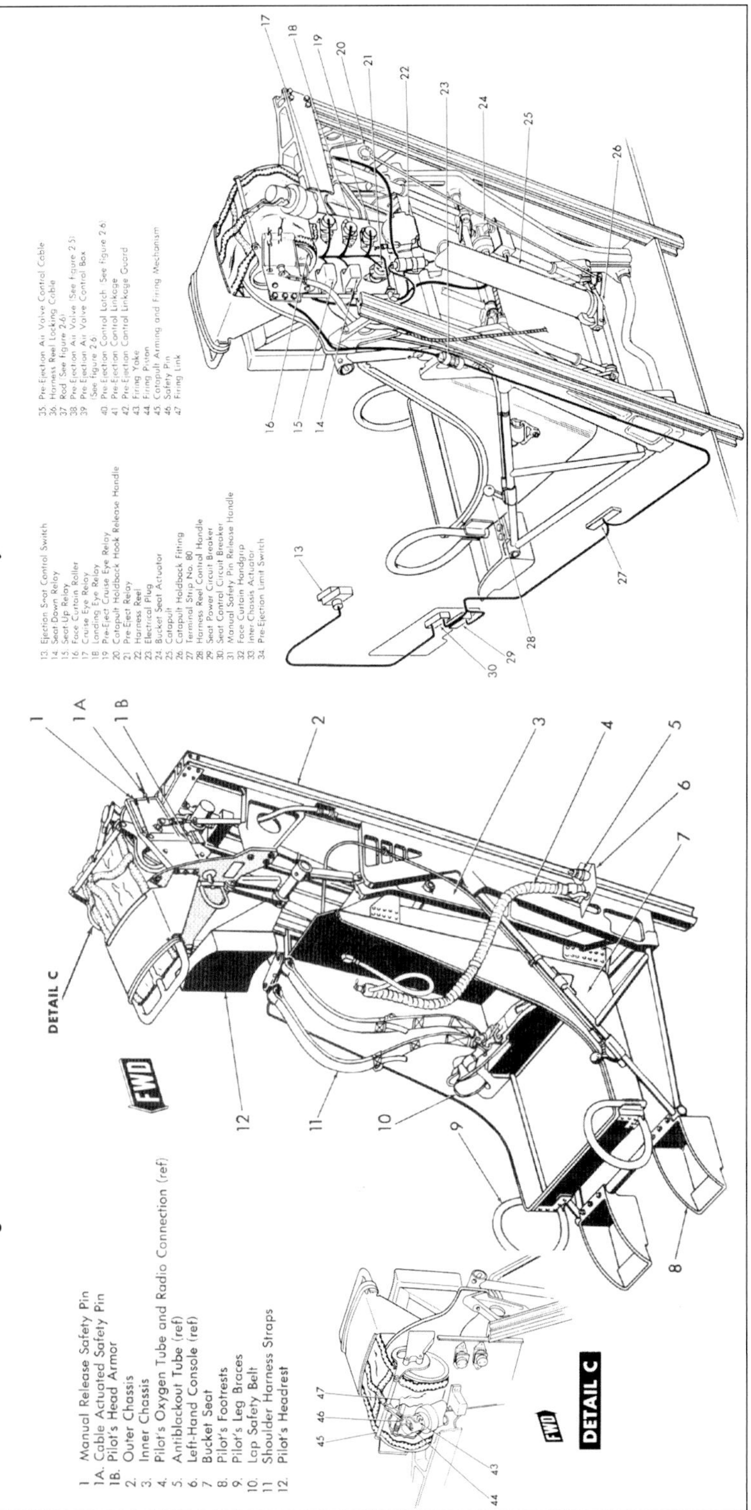

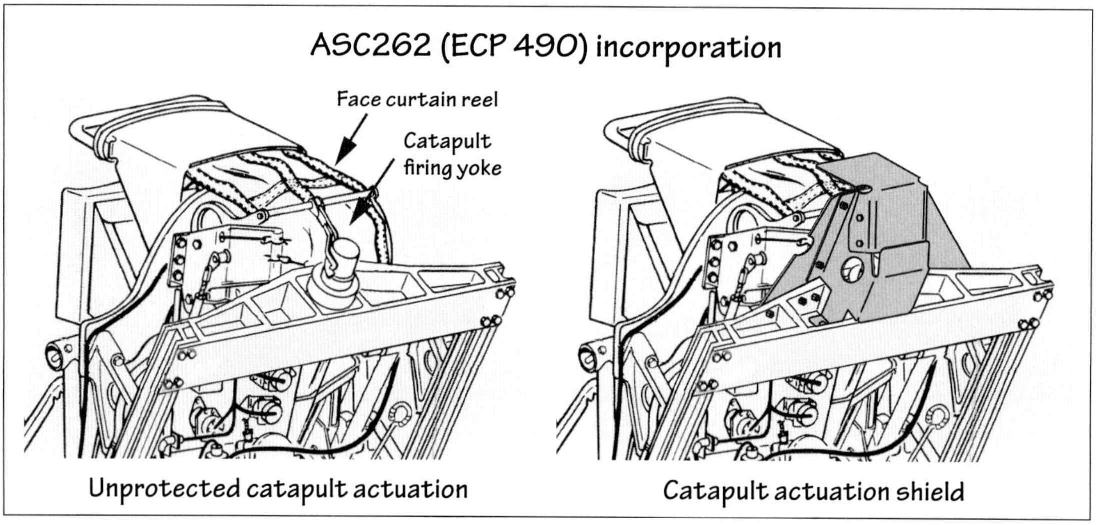

5. ASC 304 added a stretchable strap between the seat's catapult and its bulkhead mounting trunnion as well as a frangible seat cushion to provide shock absorption in the event of either a nose gear collapse or an ejection, reducing the severity of back injuries. It was a very early, if not the first, implementation of ergonomic seat design to minimise the vertical load on a body during non-normal events. The frangible seat cushion also absorbed loads that were previously intended to be absorbed only by the pilot's PK-2 Pararaft and SP-1 seat pan, both of which offered very little protection.

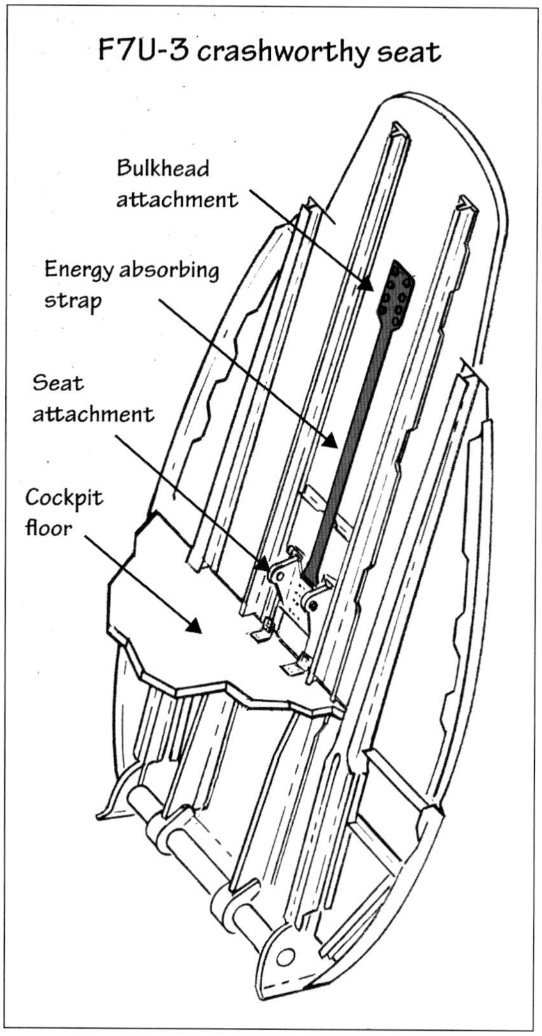

6. The final configuration of the seat included the removal of the foot stirrups and lower seat framework (found to be unnecessary) along with modifications to the catapult attachment point, harness lock attachment location, and protective shield.

A total of twenty-six pilots ejected from F7U-3s and 3Ms. Eight had unsuccessful outcomes: four of those were initiated at too low an altitude; of the other four, one was caused by a mechanic's failure to properly install the catapult cap; one was the result of pilot incapacitation (after inadvertent ejection due to a mid-air collision, he struck the bottom of the lead aircraft that he had just collided with); one was an inadvertent ejection caused by the catapult cap being struck by the canopy actuator following a nose gear collapse; and one was because prior to opening his parachute, the pilot did not clear the seat, which then caused the parachute to fail. Of the remaining eighteen, fourteen pilots were either not injured or suffered only minor injuries. In summary, ejection was 100% survivable when attempted within the capability of a properly maintained seat and following the post-ejection step of clearing the seat prior to opening the parachute.

Landing and arresting gear

Operations from aircraft carriers required significantly stouter landing gears and airframe features not only for catapulting and arresting but for effective retardation of the aircraft by the barriers or barricade in the event that the aircraft landing on a axial-deck carrier was not stopped as intended by hooking an arresting cable (for barrier and barricade engagement features, see pages 76-79).

Nose landing gear

1. Actuator cylinder piston
2. Steering control valve
3. Fairing
4. Stud
5. Glandnut
6. Torque link
7. Ball joint
8. Prerotate tube (telescoping)
9. Fitting assembly
10. Check nut
11. Torque tube fitting

F7U-3 airplanes BuNo. 128475 and Subsequent, F7U-3M and F7U-3P airplanes. F7U-3 airplanes BuNo. 128467 through 128474 similiar.

Left main landing gear

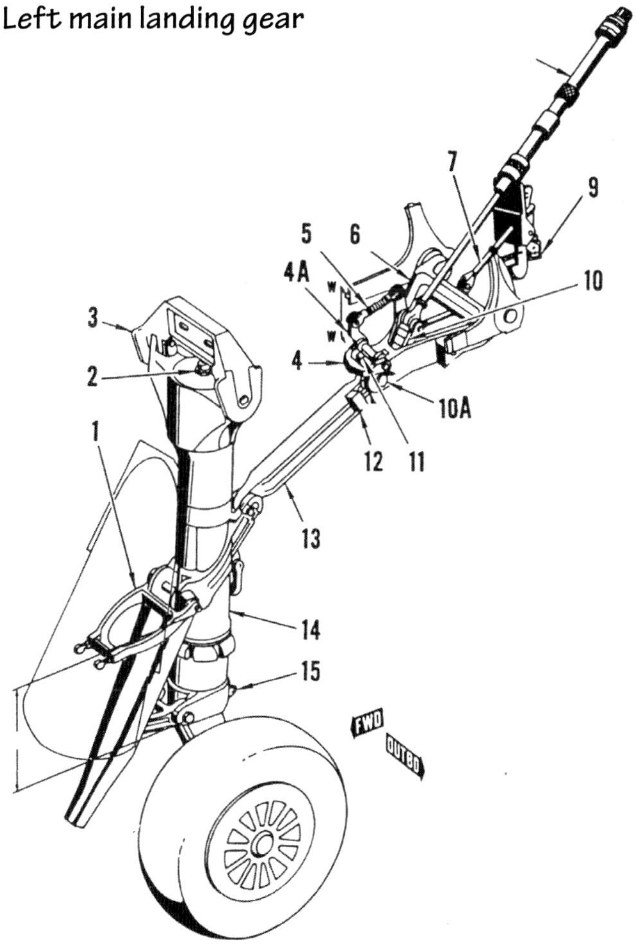

1. Fairing link assembly
2. Air valve
3. Trunnion fitting
4. Down-lock assembly
4a. Down lock torque arm
5. Spring strut
6. Upper drag link
7. Up- lock push rod
8. Main gear actuating cylinder
9. Up-lock switch
10. Stop
10a. Lower drag link bolt
11. Stop lug
12. Down-lock switch
13. Lower drag link
14. Shock strut assembly
15. Up-lock bolt
16. Center of rotation of upper drag link
17. Drag link be 11 crank
18. Up-lock support
19. Up-lock bell crank assembly
20. Up-lock roller
21. Up-lock hook
22. Up-lock spring
23. Retainer
24. Rod
25. Drag link torque arm
26. Down-lock stop bolt
27. Eye bolt
28. Roll pins
29. Insert

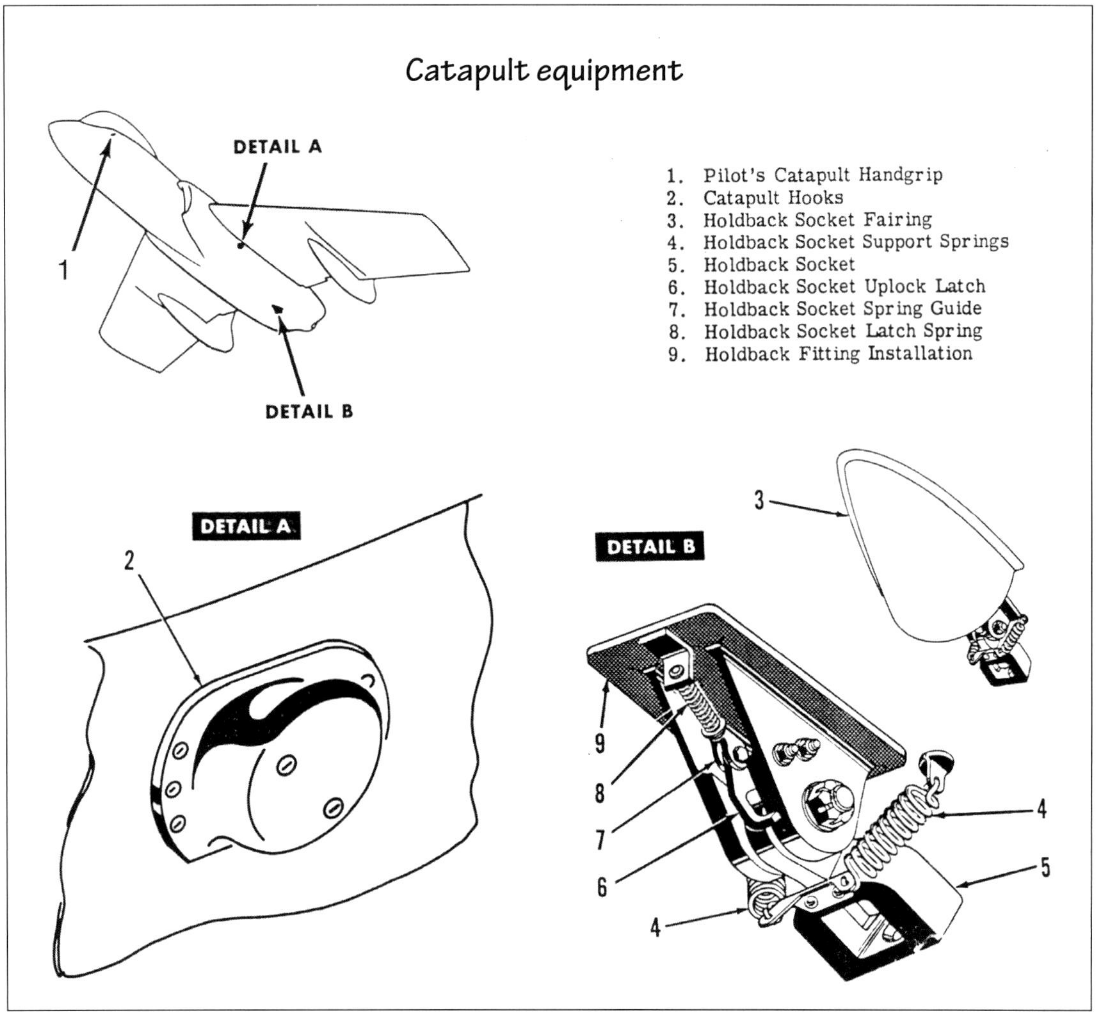
Catapult equipment
DETAIL A
DETAIL B
1
1. Pilot's Catapult Handgrip
2. Catapult Hooks
3. Holdback Socket Fairing
4. Holdback Socket Support Springs
5. Holdback Socket
6. Holdback Socket Uplock Latch
7. Holdback Socket Spring Guide
8. Holdback Socket Latch Spring
9. Holdback Fitting Installation
DETAIL A
2
DETAIL B
3
9
8
7
6
4
4
5

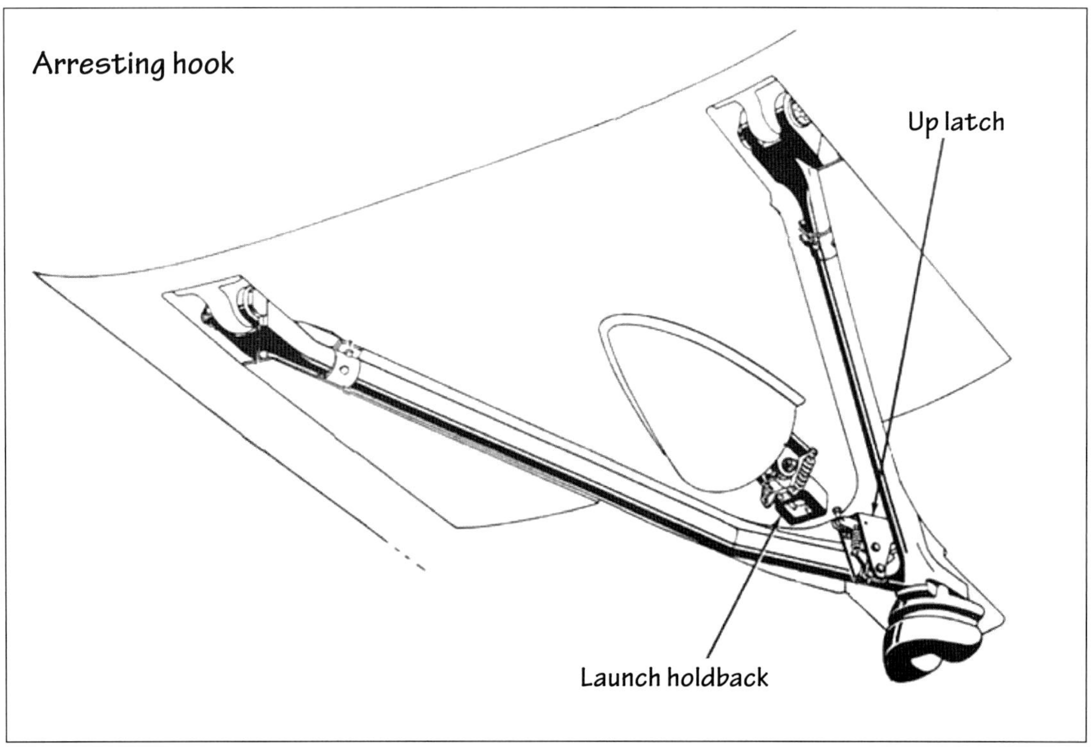
Arresting hook
Up latch
Launch holdback

Control system

The F7U-3 flight control system was necessarily complex because of the need for the control surfaces on the wing to provide both pitch and roll control; satisfactory handling qualities over a very wide speed range; and a high degree of redundancy to meet BuAer's new-found requirement for a fail-operate system. The system consisted of mechanical controls that directed hydraulic actuators to move the ailavators, a control feel system to provide the pilot with feedback of control surface loads, a bob weight and viscous damper to shape the control loads, a ram air-driven device to reduce aileron travel with increasing speed, a pitch and yaw stabilisation system, and a trim system to zero out control moments for a given flight condition.

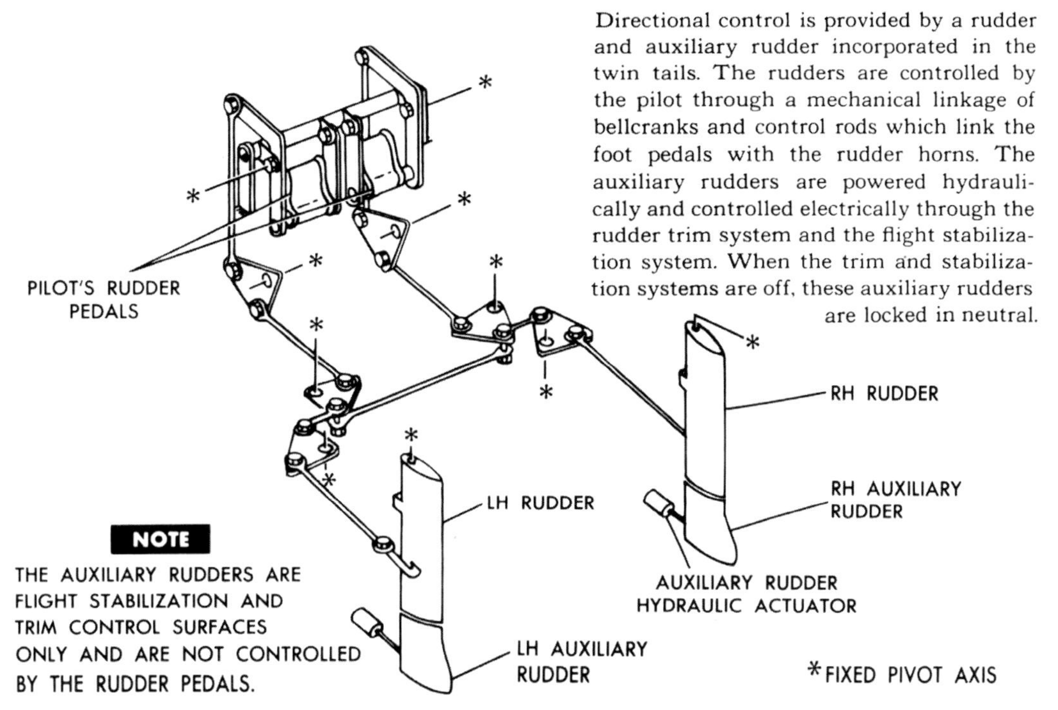

RUDDER CONTROLS SCHEMATIC

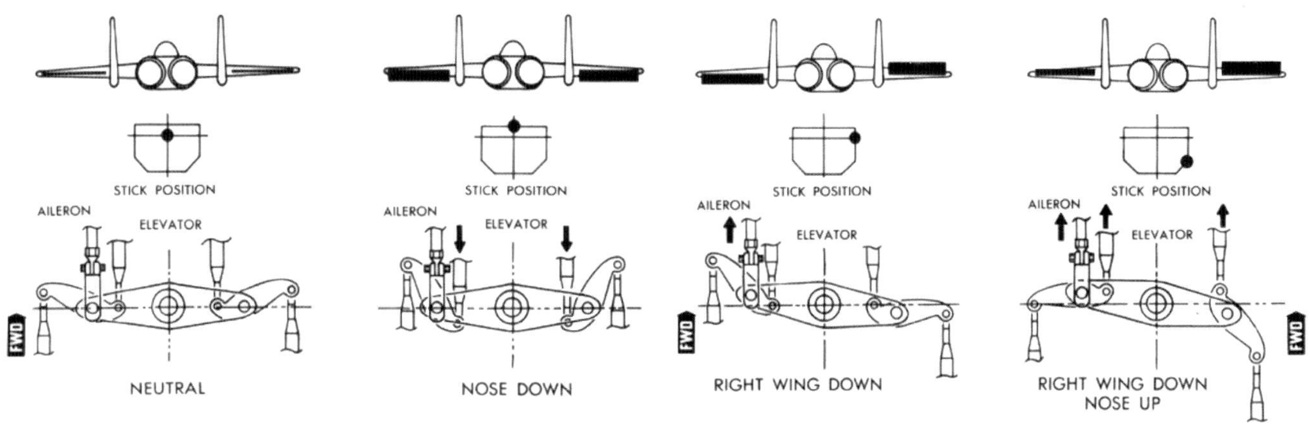

Roll and pitch control mixing linkage

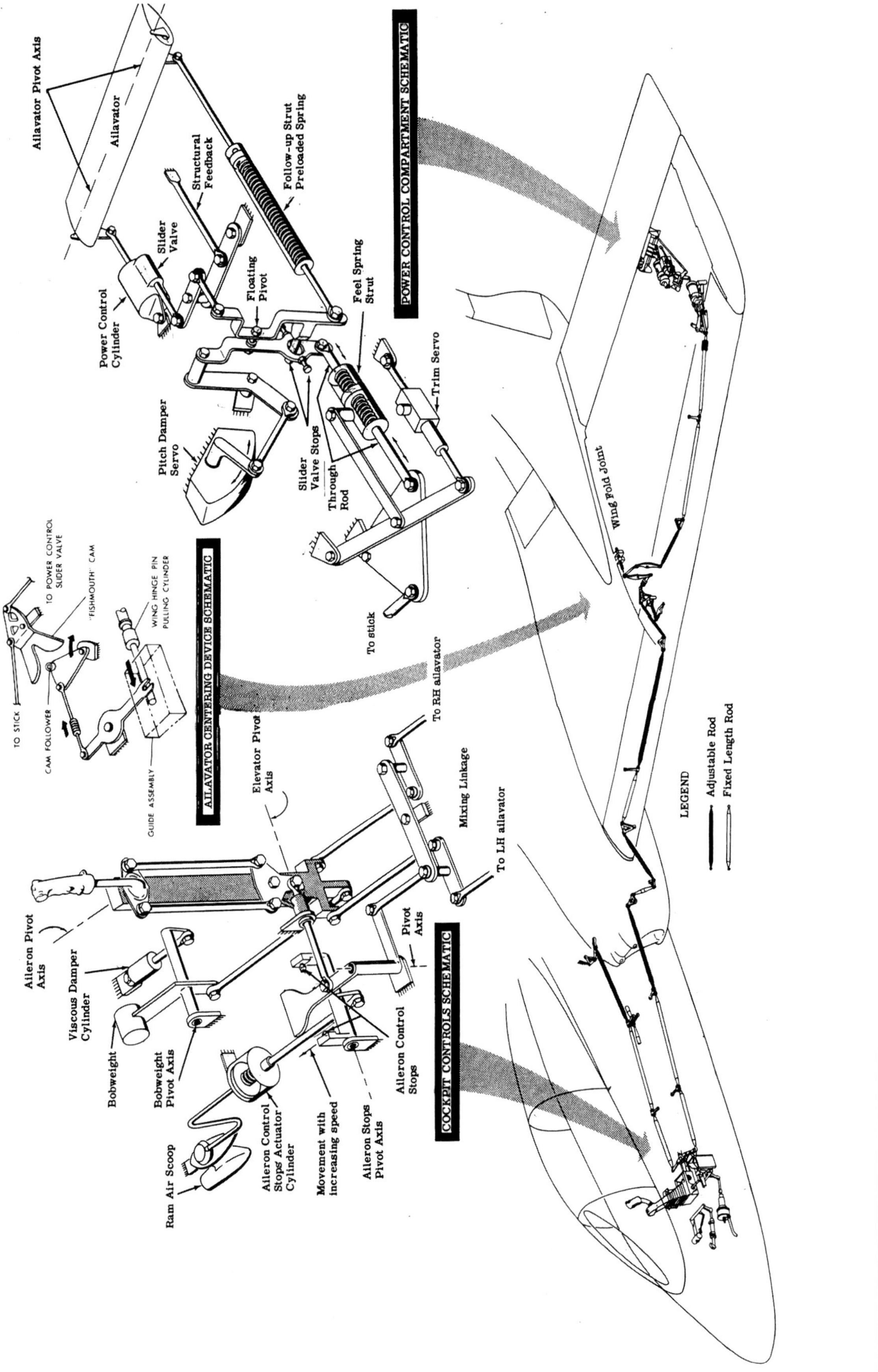

Ailavator control system

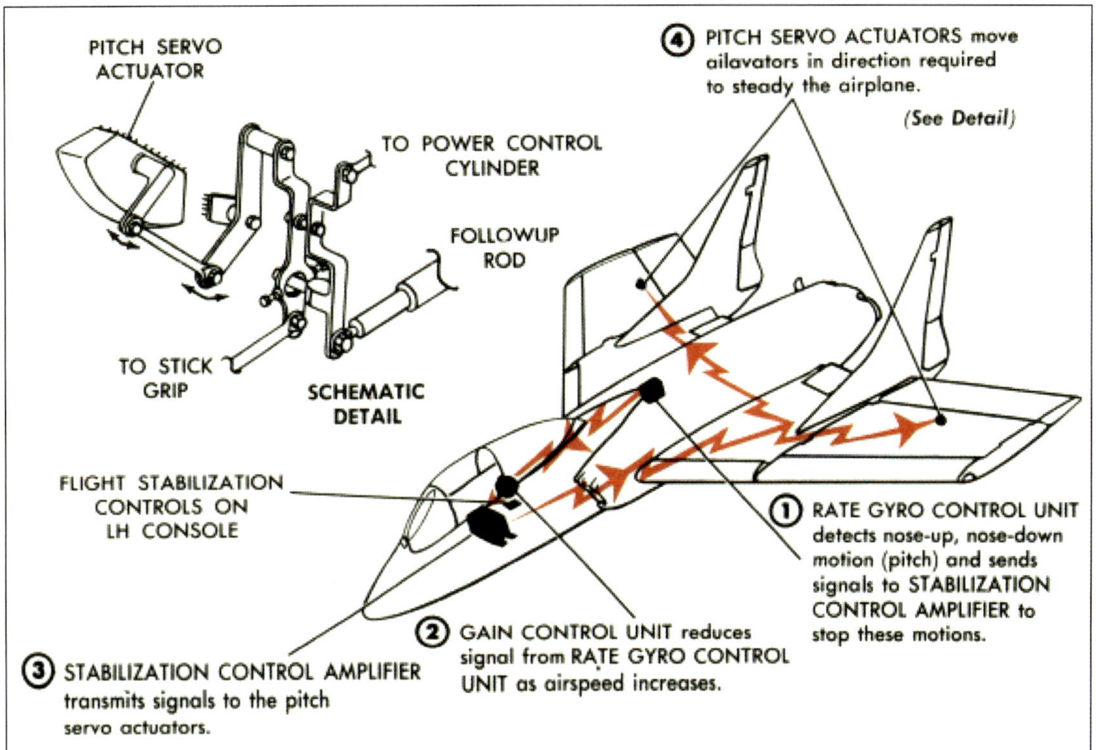

PITCH STABILIZATION

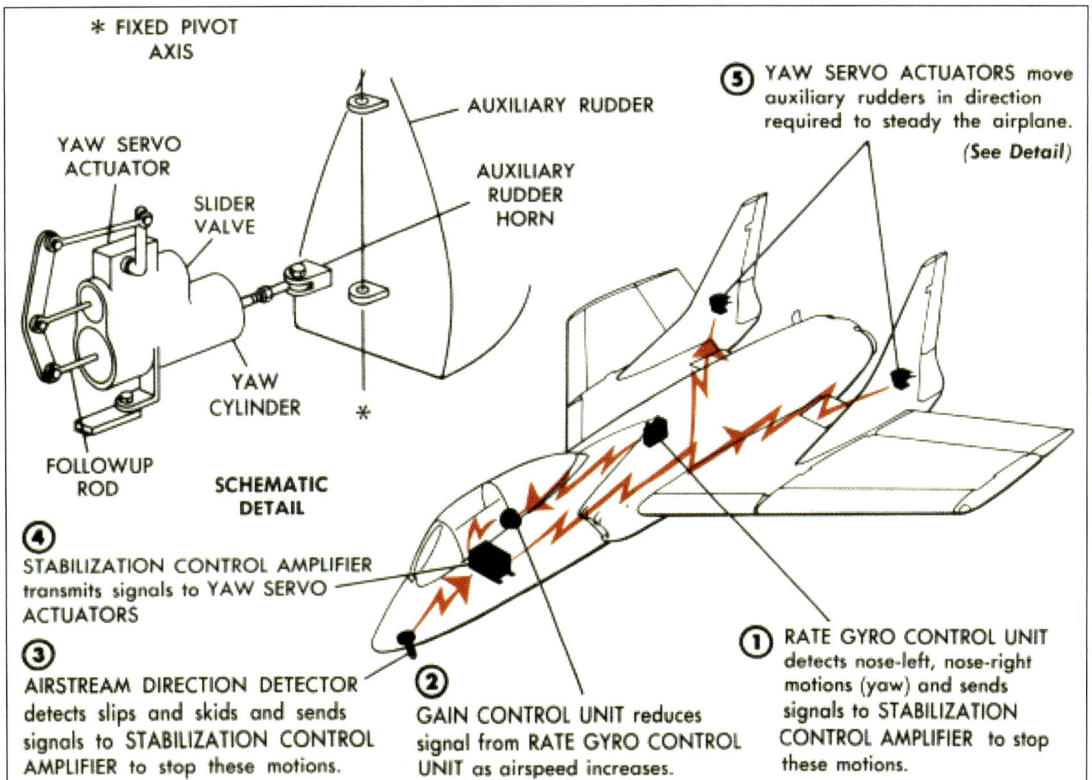

YAW STABILIZATION

Fuel system

The basic F7U-3 internal fuel system consisted of nine separate cells clustered around the aircraft's centre of gravity. Three of the cells comprised the main fuel system and six the transfer system.

Capacity (gallons)		
Main fuel system cells	**Pressure**	**Filler neck**
Mid fuselage	182	184
Aft fuselage	341	343
Right forward wing centre section	92	92
Total	615	619
Transfer fuel system cells		
Forward fuselage	234	244
Left forward wing centre section	104	107
Aft wing centre section (4)	347	350
Total	685	701
Total fuel capacity	**1,300**	**1,320**

The engines received fuel from the mid-fuselage fuel cell.

The transfer cells were emptied first, the fuel being pumped into the mid-fuselage fuel cell. The transfer of fuel from the transfer system to the main system was automatic, sequenced to minimise centre of gravity movement unless the pilot chose to control it manually because of fuel system component failures (in that event, the pilot was cautioned that it was critical to maintain the centre of gravity within limits). The transfer began with the emptying of the left forward wing centre section and the four aft wing centre section cells. Fuel began transferring from the forward fuselage cell when the left aft wing centre section outboard cell was empty.

When the transfer cells were empty, fuel began draining from the aft fuselage and right forward wing centre section cell into the mid-fuselage cell, primarily by gravity (the aft fuselage fuel cell was pressurised to ensure it was emptied when the aircraft was nose up), into the mid-fuselage fuel cell.

The pilot was provided with two fuel system gauges, one selectable for either total main fuel or mid-fuselage cell and one for total transfer fuel. There was also a mid-fuselage cell low-warning light when the amount of fuel in it reached 63 gallons; in addition to serving as a low remaining fuel warning (this was the last cell to empty), if the indicated fuel total was greater than 63 gallons, its illumination during engine afterburning indicated that the fuel transfer rate to it was insufficient to provide adequate fuel for continued afterburner operation; the engines could be expected to flame out in about thirty seconds after the light illuminated if afterburning was not discontinued.

The F7U-3M and -3P were provided with four additional transfer fuel cells, two in each outboard wing panel, with a total capacity of 248 gallons. In this case, the fuel from the forward fuselage cell did not begin to transfer until all three centre section transfer

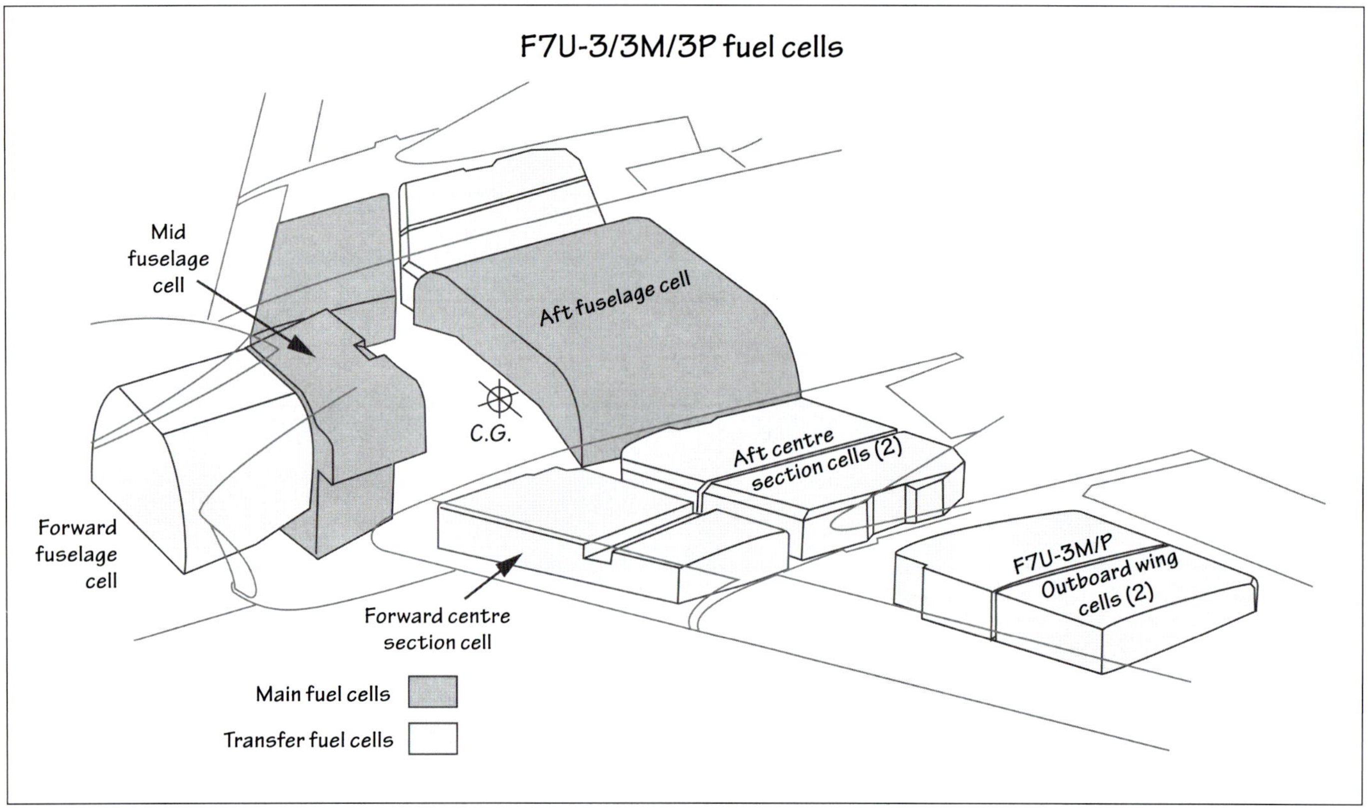

fuel cells were empty. Then, when the forward fuselage fuel cell was down to 72 gallons, its transfer was stopped and the outer wing panel fuel transfer cells, which were the farthest aft, began to empty. When they were empty, the transfer from the forward fuselage fuel cell resumed until it was empty.

External fuel options consisted of two 150-gallon external tanks, one under each wing centre section, and one 210-gallon external fuel pod that could be attached directly to the belly. Transfer of fuel in the external tanks and pod to the main fuel cells was accomplished manually. The external tanks and fuel pod could be jettisoned. It was envisaged that two 300-gallon external tanks could be carried, however this resulted in a 2,197lb pylon load – somewhat more than the pylon's weight limit – and there is no evidence that they were used operationally.

All the internal fuel cells could be filled during in-flight refuelling along with the belly-mounted fuel pod (BuNo 129545 and subsequent). The external fuel tanks under the wing centre section could not be refilled by the in-flight refuelling system.

TOP RIGHT The external, jettisonable fuel tanks provided for the F7U-3 were procured from the Sargent Fletcher Company. They weighed 127lb and had a capacity of 150 US gallons. *VAHF*

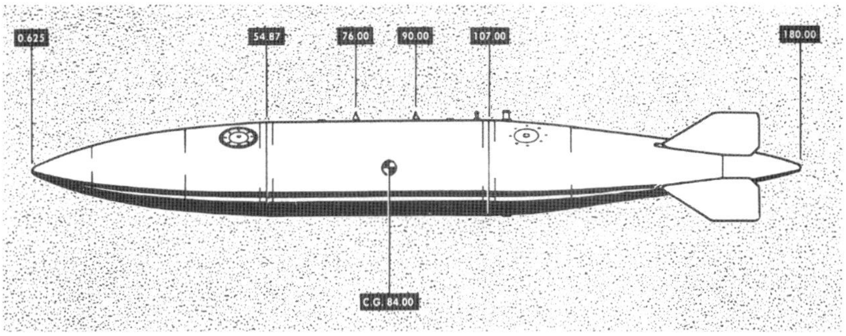

ABOVE RIGHT The dimensions provided in this illustration of the 150-gallon auxiliary fuel tank are in inches. It had a constant section diameter of 21.00in. *US Navy*

RIGHT The 210-gallon jettisonable fuel tank that could be attached to the bottom of the fuselage was identical in shape to a 2.75in rocket pack. *VAHF*

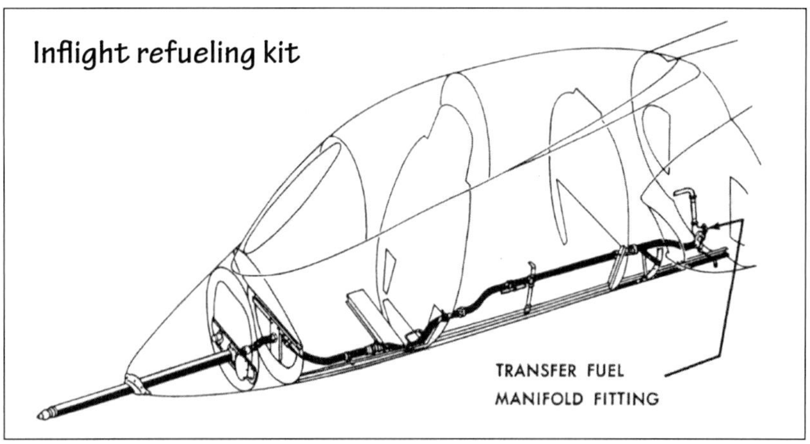

BOTTOM RIGHT In-flight refuelling capability was provided by an F7U-3 kit that could not be installed on the F7U-3M or -3P. *VAHF*

BELOW Westinghouse flight qualified the J46 well behind the schedule to which it had initially committed, forcing Vought to initiate F7U-3 flight test with Allison J35 engines. More development was then required to qualify a production configuration. *Thomason*

J46 configuration summary

The Westinghouse J46 was a turbojet engine with a single-entry, twelve-stage, axial-flow compressor; a single annular through-flow combustion chamber; and a two-stage turbine. The afterburner was equipped with a variable-area nozzle and was an integral part of the complete engine.

The J46, like the J40, was originally intended to have an electronic engine control system. Westinghouse's engineers had attempted to create an automated system of engine power control management whose underlying concept would be refined years later to become the ubiquitous Full Authority Digital Engine Control (FADEC) that is an integral part of all modern turbine engines. They attempted to create a 'set and forget' throttle control, which included among other features, full thrust modulation in afterburner, rather than it being an all-or-nothing, on-off selection. Although they had incredible foresight, the technology of the day did not provide the necessary tools (digital computers and electronics) to allow this concept to come to fruition until decades later. It was the tenacious desire to perfect this system that added to the J46's delivery delays, which in turn delayed the F7U-3's delivery to fleet units.

After insurmountable development problems with the electronic control system, a more reliable, primarily hydro-mechanical one was substituted for the engine's flight qualification and production. It still incorporated many features that reduced pilot workload in managing and monitoring engine operation. For example, it regulated the rate of fuel increase during acceleration to prevent excessive turbine-out temperatures and the rate of decrease during deceleration to prevent flameout. It regulated the rate of fuel flow to the afterburner to compensate for air density, altitude, airspeed, and temperature changes. It automatically switched from the primary pump element to the emergency (standby) pump element of the dual fuel pump if the primary pump element failed.

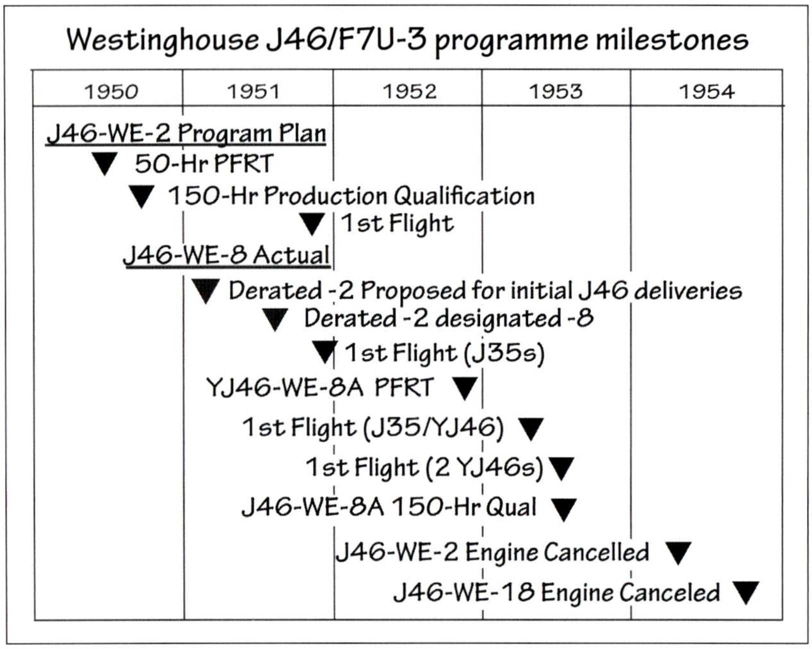

RIGHT Shortly before the F7U-3's first flight (with J35s) in December 1951, Vought requested that the J46 exhaust nozzle be canted slightly (3° 7′ 36″ upward. As a result of initial flight tests, Vought subsequently determined that a straight nozzle would reduce the stall speed in the landing configuration. However, Westinghouse delivered the first few Y engines with the cant due to the lateness of the change. They were also delivered with the so-called short-coupled afterburner. Short vs Long refers to the (coupling) distance between the fuel spray rings and the front face of the flame holder. An increase resulted in increased thrust and high-altitude performance.

Derated J46 configurations

		YJ46-WE-8A	J46-WE-8A	J46-WE-8B	J46-WE-8
		Flight test	Flight test	F7U-3I3P	F7U-3M
Quantity	Aircraft[1]	2	9	153/12	98
	Engine	6	21[2]	437	436
Combat thrust (lbs)		5,300[3]	5,500	5,800	5,800
Exhaust nozzle (sq in)		360	375	375	375
Compressor		C75	C75	C75/C89	C89
Turbine		T3	T3	T3/T39	T39
Thrust control (nozzle)		Mechanical?	Electrical	Electrical	Hydro-mechanical
Afterburner					
TOT trim		Manual	Automatic	Automatic	Automatic
Coupling		Short	Long	Long	Long
3° Cant		Yes	No	No	No
50-Hr Qual		Nov 52	NIA	NIA	NIA
150-Hr Qual		None	July 53	Oct 53	Mar 54
1st Delivery		Dec 52	Aug 53	Oct 53	Sept 54

[1] Does not include 16 F7U-3s powered by J35s

[2] Some converted to -8B

[3] Subsequently 5,500

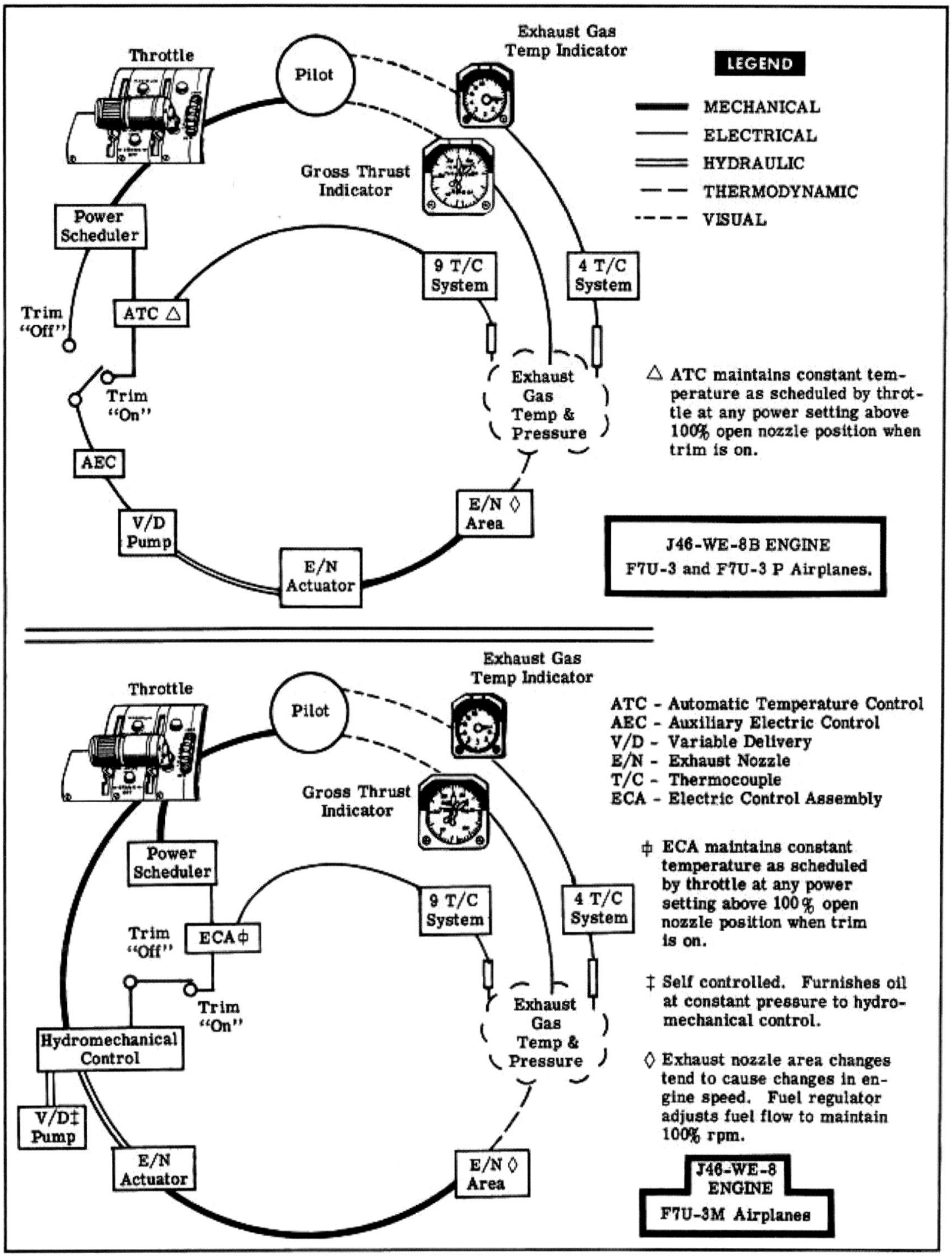

The major difference between the J46-WE-8B and -8 engine-control systems was the mechanism and electronics that scheduled the afterburner nozzle. *US Navy publication*

Unlike axial and centrifugal flow engines that lacked variable nozzles required by afterburning, the J46 could operate at a constant rpm at throttle settings that were a fraction of the normal rated thrust, reducing the lag in throttle response significantly. *Thomason*

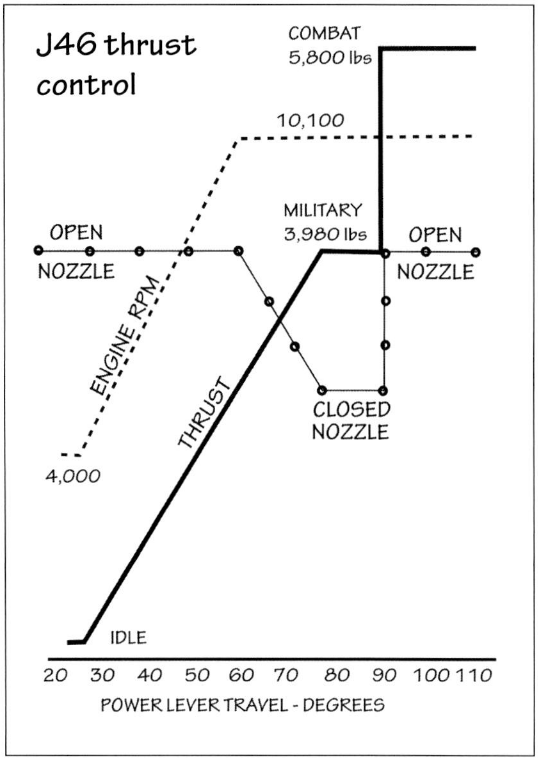

Most importantly, and not well known now, was that the J46 was running at 100% rpm when the thrust was more than about 67% of the military rating, which was nominally 4,000lb. Thereafter the fuel control maintained it at 100% regardless of air density, altitude, or airspeed. Simply put, J46 thrust management was controlled based on exhaust gas temperature. As a result, there was little lag in J46 thrust response at approach throttle settings up to the military throttle stop compared to most of the other jet engines at the time that were controlled based on rpm. The variable-area nozzle was the key: it was fully open until the engine reached 100% rpm; additional throttle resulted in both more fuel and the nozzle beginning to close down to provide the additional thrust desired.

Decreasing the nozzle area resulted in an increase in exhaust gas temperature in addition to increasing the thrust; for military thrust, it was intended to be fully closed. Since the maximum allowable temperature was regulated (trimmed) by control of the nozzle area, which was virtually instantaneous, the thrust response to the throttle was much quicker than by speeding up and slowing down the compressor/turbine. The F7U-3 and -3P were powered by the J46-WE-8B engine; the -3M by the J46-WE-8 engine. The control of the nozzle was slightly different. On the -8B, an 'Automatic Temperature Control' regulated the exhaust nozzle area to keep the turbine-out temperature at its limit via an 'Auxiliary Electric Control'; on the -8, an Electric Control Assembly regulated it.

While there was minimal lag in response to throttle changes at military thrust and below, going into afterburner was not as straightforward. When the pilot selected afterburner by moving a throttle outboard and forward after reaching the military stop, the nozzle needed to go immediately from fully closed (military thrust) to fully open while fuel was being provided to the afterburner spray nozzles and then ignited. It was necessary that both nozzle movement and fuel ignition occurred for the expected increase in thrust. If the nozzle opened but the afterburner did not ignite, there would actually be a loss in thrust; if the nozzle stayed closed but the afterburner did ignite, the compressor was very likely to stall from the resulting back pressure, causing a significant lack of thrust. As a result, features incorporated to detect either failure complicated the afterburner control system (the pilot could also override it and either open or close the nozzle). It was also biased toward ensuring the nozzle opened because engine thrust recovery from a compressor stall took longer than simply closing the nozzle.

The fact that afterburner was either on or off, a significant difference in thrust, was generally only a consideration in the event that it was required for a single-engine approach and landing. It was normally only used if desired for take-off, climb, and acceleration, taking into the dramatic increase in the rate of fuel consumption that resulted. Another consideration was its use in a wave off; the Flight Handbook contained this warning:

> Selection of maximum power is accompanied by a slight thrust delay lasting up to 2 seconds. Therefore for the first three seconds following power increase, more aircraft acceleration can be attained by increase to military power than by igniting afterburners. For time increases greater than 3 seconds a very marked acceleration advantage is obtained by igniting both afterburners.

Although its development was troubled, the J46, by the standards of the time, was reliable. Engine failures – absent running out of fuel, over-temping in a botched recovery from a post-stall gyration, sloppy maintenance, etc – were relatively rare. And although a single-engine carrier landing was not recommended, when attempted they were successful.

J46-WE-8 Quick Change Assembly.

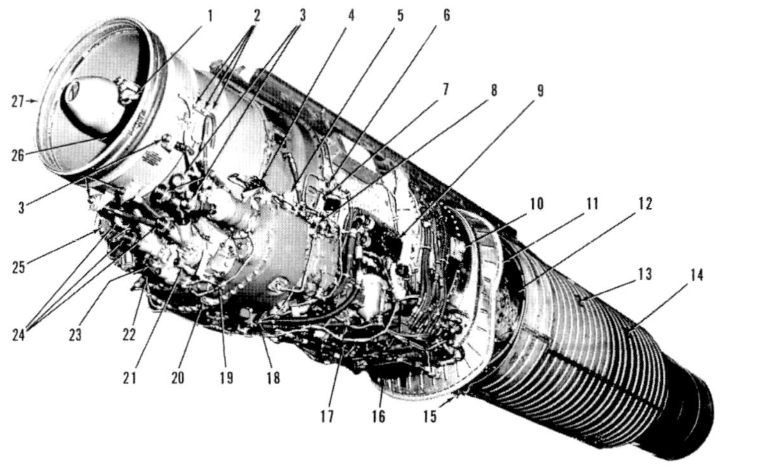

LH ENGINE SHOWN

1. Starter Fairing Island
2. Starter Generator Bus Bars
3. Hydraulic Quick-Disconnect Units
4. Oil Pressure Switch
5. Oil Reservoir Filler Line Connection
6. Oil Pressure Tap
7. Fuel Pressure Tap
8. Oil System Dipstick
9. Fuel Flow Transmitter
10. Engine Mount Adapters
11. Fire Seal
12. Engine Insulation Blanket
13. Forward Afterburner Shroud
14. Aft Afterburner Shroud
15. Exhaust Nozzle Position Switch Actuator
16. Exhaust Nozzle Actuator Cam Box
17. Throttle Control Connection (Bracketed to Afterburner Fuel Control)
18. Overspeed Relay, Booster Pump, Dual Fuel Pump Seal Drainline
19. Hydraulic Pump Seal Drain Line
20. Engine Installation Bracket
21. Utility System Hydraulic Pump (Refer to section III)
22. Tachometer Generator
23. Power Control System Hydraulic Pump (Refer to section III)
24. Hydraulic Quick-Disconnect Units
25. Engine Afterburner Pump Inlet Connection
26. Starter-Generator Assembly
27. Removable Engine Air Duct

4648-5-421J

Figure No. 5–3A. Quick-Engine Change Assembly (J46-WE-8)

J46-WE-8B Quick Change Assembly.

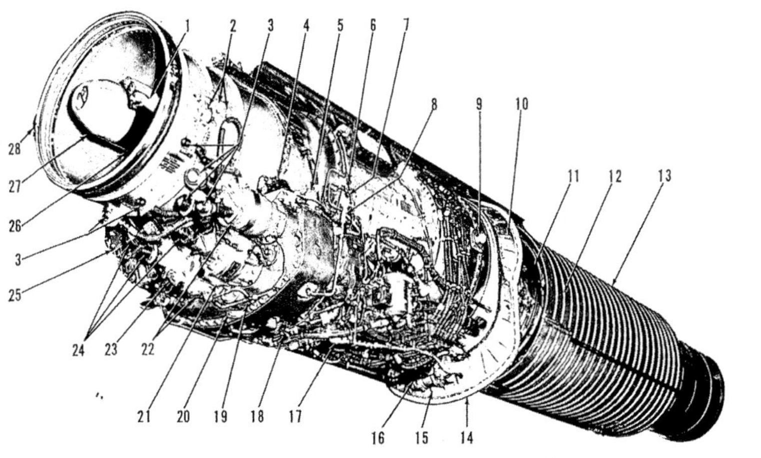

LH ENGINE SHOWN

1. Starter Fairing Island
2. Starter-Generator Bus Bars
3. Hydraulic Quick-Disconnect Units
4. Oil Pressure Switch
5. Oil Reservoir Filler Line Connection
6. Oil Pressure Tap
7. Fuel Pressure Tap
8. Oil System Dipstick
9. Engine Mount Adapters
10. Fire Seal
11. Engine Insulation Blanket
12. Forward Afterburner Shroud
13. Aft Afterburner Shroud
14. Exhaust Nozzle Position Switch Actuator (Aft of Fire Seal)
15. Manifold Fuel Dump Tank (Engine-mounted on F7U-3 airplanes BuNo. 128467 through 129586 only)
16. Fuel Flow Transmitter
17. Emergency Exhaust Nozzle Control Connection (On Variable Delivery Pump RH Underside)
18. Overspeed Relay, Booster Pump, Dual Fuel Pump Seal Drainline
19. Hydraulic Pump Seal Drainline
20. Engine Installation Bracket
21. Utility System Hydraulic Pump (Refer to section III)
22. Power Control System Hydraulic Pumps (Refer to section III)
23. Tachometer Generator
24. Hydraulic Quick-Disconnect Units
25. Engine Afterburner Pump Inlet Connection
26. Starter-Generator ✳
27. Forward Starter Generator Fairing (Prior to ASC 211 [ECP 387]). ✳
28. Removable Engine Air Duct

✳ After ASC 211 (ECP 387) starter-generator with permanently attached fairing is supplied as Starter-Generator Assembly.

4648-5-420J

Figure No. 5–3. Quick-Engine Change Assembly (J46-WE-8B)

Another downside of afterburning was that the length of an engine was almost doubled, requiring more deck area to remove it and special attention to the support of the afterburner during engine removal and installation. *US Navy*

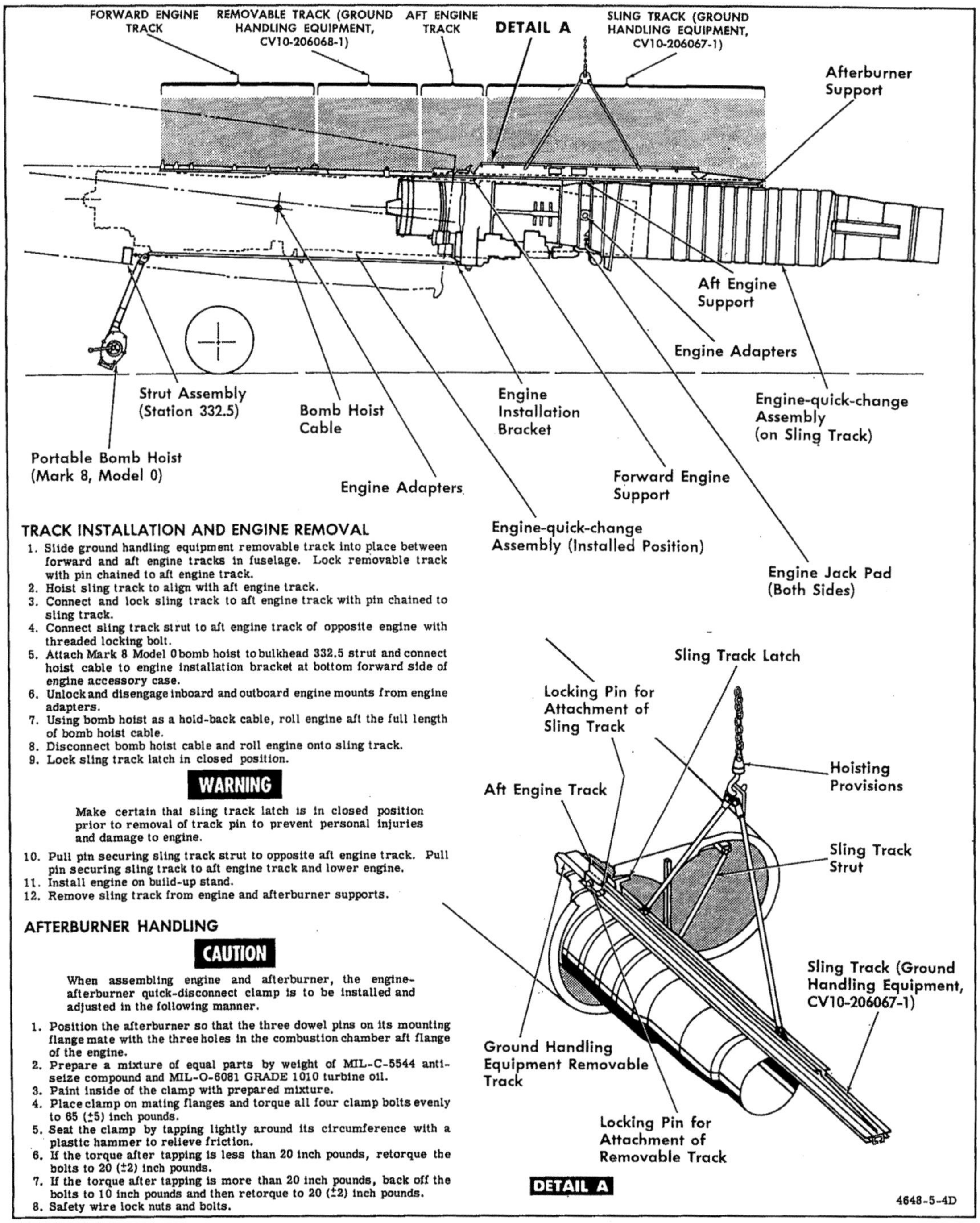

TRACK INSTALLATION AND ENGINE REMOVAL

1. Slide ground handling equipment removable track into place between forward and aft engine tracks in fuselage. Lock removable track with pin chained to aft engine track.
2. Hoist sling track to align with aft engine track.
3. Connect and lock sling track to aft engine track with pin chained to sling track.
4. Connect sling track strut to aft engine track of opposite engine with threaded locking bolt.
5. Attach Mark 8 Model 0 bomb hoist to bulkhead 332.5 strut and connect hoist cable to engine installation bracket at bottom forward side of engine accessory case.
6. Unlock and disengage inboard and outboard engine mounts from engine adapters.
7. Using bomb hoist as a hold-back cable, roll engine aft the full length of bomb hoist cable.
8. Disconnect bomb hoist cable and roll engine onto sling track.
9. Lock sling track latch in closed position.

WARNING

Make certain that sling track latch is in closed position prior to removal of track pin to prevent personal injuries and damage to engine.

10. Pull pin securing sling track strut to opposite aft engine track. Pull pin securing sling track to aft engine track and lower engine.
11. Install engine on build-up stand.
12. Remove sling track from engine and afterburner supports.

AFTERBURNER HANDLING

CAUTION

When assembling engine and afterburner, the engine-afterburner quick-disconnect clamp is to be installed and adjusted in the following manner.

1. Position the afterburner so that the three dowel pins on its mounting flange mate with the three holes in the combustion chamber aft flange of the engine.
2. Prepare a mixture of equal parts by weight of MIL-C-5544 anti-seize compound and MIL-O-6081 GRADE 1010 turbine oil.
3. Paint inside of the clamp with prepared mixture.
4. Place clamp on mating flanges and torque all four clamp bolts evenly to 65 (±5) inch pounds.
5. Seat the clamp by tapping lightly around its circumference with a plastic hammer to relieve friction.
6. If the torque after tapping is less than 20 inch pounds, retorque the bolts to 20 (±2) inch pounds.
7. If the torque after tapping is more than 20 inch pounds, back off the bolts to 10 inch pounds and then retorque to 20 (±2) inch pounds.
8. Safety wire lock nuts and bolts.

Figure 5–4. Engine Handling Without Ground Handling Carriage

The J46 iris-type afterburner and its actuation mechanism were housed in a cooling shroud. Note that the afterburner is fully open when shutdown for ease of engine starting. *Don Hinton photos*

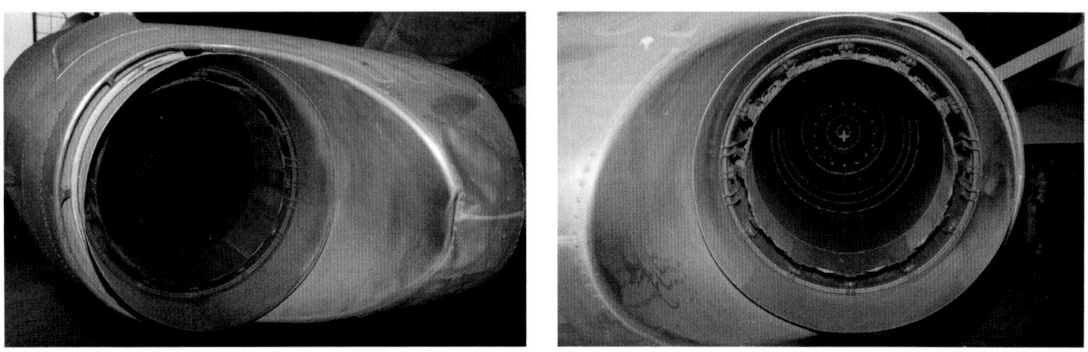

Roll attitude light

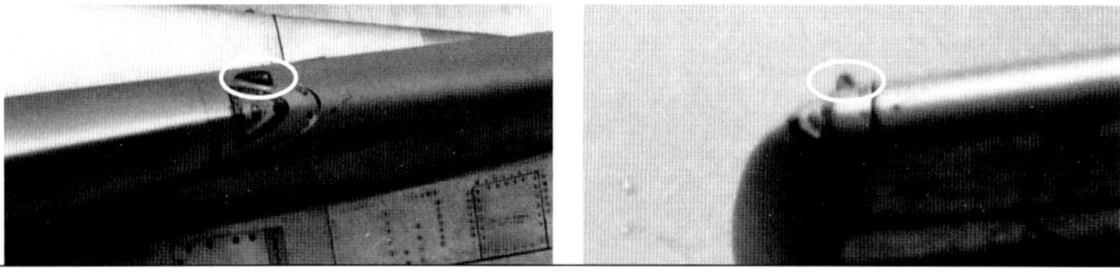

External lights and antennas

Standard external lights

Position/Navigation/Running Lights. These are the standard lights: red (left wing tip), green (right wing tip), white and orange (aft end of both auxiliary rudders), and white (top and bottom of the fuselage). The two different colour tail lights was a holdover from a pre-Second World War CAA (the forerunner of the FAA) requirement for separate orange and white tail lights that would flash alternately (white-orange-white-orange) to improve visibility at night. A white light was provided on the bottom of the rocket and fuel pods to substitute for the white light on the belly.

Formation Lights. These were instituted for night formation flight safety and sometimes referred to, along with the fuselage lights, as 'section' lights. They originally consisted of a flush blue light in the upper surface of the outer wing panels and a protruding blue light on the top of the fuselage. On the F7U, they consisted of a flush 'lunar white' light on the bottom of the outboard wing panels just aft of the UHF antenna.

The Cutlass was withdrawn from service before the requirement for anti-collision lights was instituted in the late 1950s.

LSO-Specific lights

In addition to the existing position/navigation/running lights, the LSO was provided with two additional lights for determination of the Cutlass' pitch and roll attitude during night operations as well as the position of the landing gear and arresting hook.

The standard angle of attack light was located on the forward-facing left main landing gear door. At the time, this was a single bulb shining through different-coloured lenses. Depending on the pitch attitude of the aircraft, the LSO would see a green (too fast), amber (about right), or red (too slow) light (the meaning of green and red appears to have been reversed when the existing three-light system was adopted). If it was on, both the landing gear and the tail hook were down; if it was flashing, the landing gear was extended but the arresting hook was not down; if the light was off, the gear was not down.

An auxiliary approach light was subsequently added by Service Change No. 154 to the upper surface of the right-hand wing tip to permit the landing signal officer to establish the angle of bank at night of an F7U-3 by the time it had reached a position 10 degrees beyond the base leg during a carrier approach (the existing position light on the right wing tip would not be readily visible during the initial part of the turn from base to final). It was covered by green lenses like the right position light.

Antennas

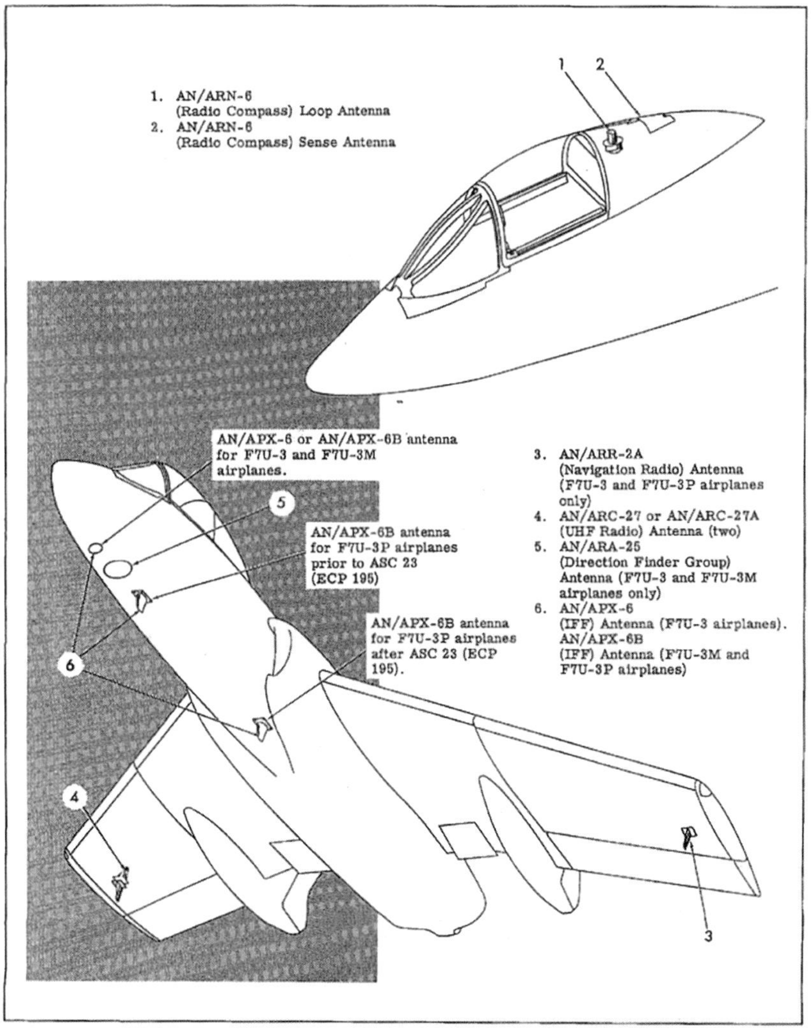

F7U squadron allocation

F7U-3 / -3M / -3P Operational Squadron / Unit Allocation								
Squadron / Unit	**Air Group - Command / "Tail Code" / (Unit Side #) Additional Unit Identification**	**First F7U-3 Acquired**	**First F7U-3M Acquired**	**First F7U-3P Acquired**	**Last F7U-3 Relinquished / Stricken**	**Last F7U-3M Relinquished/ Stricken**	**Last F7U-3P Relinquished /Stricken**	**Squadron/Unit Custody Totals, Fate and Pertinent Notes**
VC-3	**ComFAirAlameda (CVG-21) / "NP" / (7x)**	23 Sep 54	7 Nov 55	- - -	28 Feb 56	9 Dec 55	- - -	11 aircraft in custody
VC-12	**ComNAB-1 / None / None**	26 Jan 56	- - -	- - -	2 Feb 56	- - -	- - -	1 aircraft used for F7U-3 support-point orientation
VX-3	**ComOpTevFor / "XC" / (0x)**	17 Apr 53	- - -	3 May 55	23 Mar 56	- - -	22 May 56	14 aircraft in custody. Jet aircraft tactics and procedures development
VX-4	**ComFAirAlameda (ComOpTevFor) / "XF" / (1x) (2x)** **CVG-2 / "XF" / (2x) (3x)** - *DET A* **ATG-1 / "XF" / (3x)** - *DET H*	- - -	26 Jan 55	14 May 55	- - -	2 May 57	2 Aug 55	29 aircraft in custody. Air-launched guided missile development VX-4 Detachment A aircraft offloaded mid-cruise to NAF Oppama / Fasron-11
VX-5	**ComFAirAlameda (ComOpTevFor) / "XE" / (x)**	6 May 53	- - -	- - -	19 Apr 56	- - -	- - -	10 aircraft in custody. Special weapons and tactics development
VA-12	**CVG-1 / "T" / (x) (1x)**	21 Dec 55	- - -	- - -	29 May 57	- - -	- - -	21 aircraft in custody
VA-34	**CVG-3 / "K" / (3xx)**	6 Oct 55	- - -	- - -	4 Mar 57	- - -	- - -	15 aircraft in custody
VA-66	**CVG-3 / "K" / (0x) (1xx) (3xx)**	1 Jul 55	- - -	- - -	15 Aug 56	- - -	- - -	29 aircraft in custody
VF-81	**CVG-6 / "C" / (1xx)**	22 Apr 54	- - -	- - -	1 Jul 55	- - -	- - -	27 aircraft in custody. VF-81 re-designated VA-66 on 01 July 1955
VF-83	**CVG-8 / None / (4xx)** - *F7U-3* **CVG-8 / "E' / (3xx)** - *F7U-3M*	24 Aug 54	6 Apr 55	- - -	27 Jun 55	1 Jul 55	- - -	29 aircraft in custody. VF-83 re-designated VA-83 on 01 July 1955
VA-83	**CVG-8 / "E" / (4xx)** - *F7U-3* **CVG-8 / "E" / (3xx)** - *F7U-3M*	10 Dec 55	1 Jul 55	- - -	21 Dec 55	25 Apr 57	- - -	25 aircraft in custody
VF-84	**CVG-8 / None / (None)**	- - -	29 Jun 55	- - -	- - -	1 Jul 55	- - -	1 aircraft in custody. VF-84 re-designated VA-86 on 01 July 1955
VA-86	**ATG-181 / "I" / (3xx)**	- - -	1 Jul 55	- - -	- - -	15 Jul 57	- - -	15 aircraft in custody
VA-116	**CVG-11 / "V" / (6xx)** **ATG-2 / "W" / (2xx)** **ATG-2 / "NB" / (2xx)** *on CVA-19*	- - -	7 Dec 55	- - -	- - -	29 Oct 57	- - -	23 aircraft in custody
VF-122	**CVG-12 / None / (x)**	15 Dec 54	- - -	- - -	24 Mar 55	- - -	- - -	5 aircraft in custody
VF-124	**CVG-12 / "D" / (x) (xx) (4xx)**	13 Oct 54	- - -	- - -	10 Apr 56	- - -	- - -	35 aircraft in custody
VA-126	**CVG-12 / "D" / (3xx)**	11 Apr 56	- - -	- - -	9 Apr 57	- - -	- - -	27 aircraft in custody
VF-151	**CVG-15 / "H" / (3xx)**	25 Jun 55	26 May 55	- - -	7 Feb 56	7 Feb 56	- - -	21 aircraft in custody. VF-151 re-designated VA-151 on 07 February 1956
VA-151	**ATG-1 / "U" / (3xx)**	7 Feb 56	7 Feb 56	- - -	2 Jan 57	25 May 56	- - -	14 aircraft in custody
VF-212	**CVG-21 / "G" / (2xx)**	19 Aug 55	19 Jul 55	- - -	1 Apr 56	1 Apr 56	- - -	22 aircraft in custody. VF-212 re-designated VA-212 on 01 April 1956
VA-212	**CVG-21 / "G" / (2xx)**	1 Apr 56	1 Apr 56	- - -	22 May 57	30 Apr 56	- - -	17 aircraft in custody
FASRON-3	**ComFAirNorfolk / None / (None)**	8 Apr 56	9 Mar 56	- - -	12 Jul 56	13 Aug 56	- - -	6 aircraft in custody
FASRON-4	**ComFAirAlameda / None / (None)**	7 Sep 55	- - -	- - -	8 Sep 55	- - -	- - -	1 aircraft in custody
FASRON-5	**ComFAirNorfolk / None / (None)**	31 Jan 55	23 Mar 56	- - -	21 Sep 56	6 Feb 57	- - -	19 aircraft in custody
FASRON-6	**ComFAirJacksonville / None / (None)**	6 Apr 56	- - -	- - -	2 May 56	- - -	- - -	1 aircraft in custody
FASRON-8	**ComFAirAlameda / None / (None)**	9 Jul 56	16 May 56	- - -	17 Oct 56	19 Jun 57	- - -	13 aircraft in custody
FASRON-9	**ComFAirJacksonville / None / (None)**	9 Mar 56	- - -	- - -	4 Apr 57	- - -	- - -	5 aircraft in custody
FASRON-10	**ComFAirAlameda / None / (None)**	1 Aug 55	18 Jul 55	- - -	14 Nov 56	12 Sep 55	- - -	22 aircraft in custody
FASRON-11	**ComFAirJapan / None / (None)**	13 Oct 55	7 Sep 56	- - -	14 Feb 57	5 Sep 57	- - -	15 aircraft in custody
FASRON-12 (PROJECT CUTLASS)	**ComFAirAlameda / None / (x)**	2 Feb 54	- - -	- - -	13 Oct 54	- - -	- - -	13 aircraft used in Project Cutlass
FASRON-12 (Regular)	**ComFAirAlameda / None / (None)**	31 Oct 54	- - -	- - -	26 Jul 56	- - -	- - -	46 aircraft in custody including Project Cutlass aircraft
FASRON-104	**FAW-5 / None / (None)**	4 Mar 56	- - -	- - -	9 Apr 56	- - -	- - -	1 aircraft in custody
FASRON-116	**ComFAirSeattle / None / (None)**	- - -	27 Mar 56	- - -	- - -	12 Jul 56	- - -	2 aircraft in custody
FASRON-117	**ComFAHawaii / None / (None)**	31 Aug 55	- - -	- - -	20 Sep 56	- - -	- - -	2 aircraft in custody
BUAER BALTIMORE (WESTINGHOUSE BAILMENT)	**BAGR Eastern District**	7 Jun 54	- - -	- - -	18 Aug 54	- - -	- - -	1 aircraft used for J46-WE-8 Automatic Temperature Control Testing
BUAER BETHPAGE (GRUMMAN BAILMENT) (METEOR AIRCRAFT LOAN)	**BAGR Eastern District**	- - -	- - -	4 Oct 56	- - -	- - -	10 Mar 58	1 aircraft intended for chase plane photography of Grumman F11F. Subsequent bailment to Meteor Aircraft Corporation
BUAER BUFFALO (CORNELL AERO LAB BAILMENT)	**BAGR Eastern District**	1 Apr 57	- - -	- - -	24 Aug 59	- - -	- - -	1 aircraft used for spin/PSG research
BUAER POOL DALLAS (VOUGHT BAILMENT)	**BAGR Central District**	- - -	- - -	28 Jan 57	- - -	- - -	15 Sep 59	1 aircraft used for chase-plane and photographic research testing
BUAER INGLEWOOD (NORTH AMERICAN BAILMENT)	**BAGR Western District**	21 Sep 55	- - -	- - -	3 Oct 56	- - -	- - -	1 aircraft fitted with North American avionics for NAOTS Chincoteague ordinance tests
BUAER KANSAS CITY (WESTINGHOUSE AGT BAILMENT)	**BAGR Central District**	3 Jun 55	8 May 56	- - -	13 Jun 57	13 Mar 57	- - -	2 aircraft used for Westinghouse's NAS Olathe Flight Test Facility for engine research
BUAER POOL CHINCOTEAGUE	**ComNAB-5 / "NAOTS CHINCOTEAGUE" / (last 3# of BuNo)**	25 Mar 58	- - -	- - -	25 Mar 58	- - -	- - -	1 aircraft retired from rocket testing at NAOTS
BUAER POOL MEMPHIS	**BuAer**	22 Sep 55	- - -	- - -	23 Sept 55	- - -	- - -	1 aircraft intended to be used for maintenance training
BUAER POOL OCEANA	**BuAer**	- - -	15 Jul 57	- - -	- - -	15 Jul 57	- - -	2 aircraft from VA-86 stricken at NAS Oceana
BUAER POOL PHILADELPHIA	**BuAer**	11 Oct 53	- - -	- - -	16 Jun 55	- - -	- - -	3 aircraft used for barricade and catapult testing
SO & ES / H & HS MCAS MIAMI	**ComNAB-6 (3rd MAW) / "MIAMI" / (last 3# of BuNo)**	16 Aug 54	- - -	- - -	15 Jul 58	- - -	- - -	3 aircraft used for mine release testing

F7U-3 / -3M / -3P Operational Squadron / Unit Allocation

Squadron / Unit	Air Group - Command / "Tail Code" / (Unit Side #) Additional Unit Identification	First F7U-3 Acquired	First F7U-3M Acquired	First F7U-3P Acquired	Last F7U-3 Relinquished / Stricken	Last F7U-3M Relinquished/ Stricken	Last F7U-3P Relinquished /Stricken	Squadron/Unit Custody Totals, Fate and Pertinent Notes
NAAS (NAATC) KINGSVILLE	**CNAVanTra / None / (None)**	- - -	8 Jun 55	- - -	- - -	13 Jun 55	- - -	1 aircraft salvaged following accident
NACA MOFFETT (NACA AMES BAILMENT)	**NACA / None / (None)**	10 Jun 55	- - -	- - -	4 Oct 55	- - -	- - -	1 aircraft used for low-speed controllability testing
NADC JOHNSVILLE	**Com-4 / None / (None)**	- - -	- - -	25 Aug 55	- - -	- - -	13 Feb 56	1 aircraft used for reconnaissance tactics development
NAF OPPAMA	**ComNAB Japan / None / (None)**	15 Sep 55	1 May 57	- - -	21 Mar 57	13 Nov 57	- - -	9 aircraft offloaded from carrier deployments
NAMC PHILADELPHIA	**ComNAMC Phila / None / (None)**	2 Sep 54	- - -	- - -	10 Jun 55	- - -	- - -	4 aircraft used for barricade and catapult testing
NAMTC POINT MUGU	**Com-11 / "POINT MUGU" / (None)**	- - -	27 Sep 54	5 Aug 55	- - -	19 Jan 56	3 Aug 56	5 F7U-3M aircraft used for missile development and 1 F7U-3P used for chase plane photographic duty
NAOTS CHINCOTEAGUE	**ComNAB-5 / "NAOTS CHINCOTEAGUE" / (last 3# of BuNo)**	22 Nov 54	- - -	- - -	25 Mar 58	- - -	- - -	4 aircraft used for ordinance testing and development
NAS NORTH ISLAND	**ComNAB-11 / None / (None)**	30 Mar 56	- - -	- - -	28 Jun 56	- - -	- - -	1 aircraft salvaged following VF-124 ferry flight accident
NATC PATUXENT	**BuAer Mat Div / "NATC" / (None)** (normally) (some carried last 3# of BuNo)	1 Aug 52	11 Jan 55	4 Mar 55	10 Aug 56	11 Mar 57	14 May 57	34 aircraft used for research and development
NASF LITCHFIELD	**ComNAB-11 / None / (None)**	4 Aug 56	18 Aug 56	3 Aug 55	21 Jul 58	1 May 58	3 Mar 59	111 aircraft in custody
NASWF KIRTLAND	**BuAer - BuOrd / "NASWF" / (last 3# of BuNo)**	31 Mar 53	- - -	- - -	4 Oct 57	- - -	- - -	7 aircraft used for special weapons testing and development
NLO EDWARDS AFB	**ComNAB-11 / "NASWF" / (last 3# of BuNo)** *(carried NASWF due to temporary assignment)*	31 Jul 55	- - -	- - -	30 Aug 55	- - -	- - -	1 aircraft utilized for testing of target-tow underwing store.
NOTS INYOKERN	**ComNOTS Inyokern / None / (None)**	28 Jul 54	- - -	- - -	26 Jul 55	- - -	- - -	2 aircraft used for ordinance testing. Unit re-designated NOTS China Lake 26 July 55
NOTS CHINA LAKE	**ComNOTS Inyokern / None / (None)**	26 Jul 55	- - -	- - -	30 Jan 56	- - -	- - -	2 aircraft used for ordinance testing. Unit re-designated from NOTS Inyokern 26 July 55
NPU EL CENTRO	**ComNAB-11 / "NPU" / (last 3# of BuNo)**	- - -	- - -	8 Nov 55	- - -	- - -	2 Mar 59	2 aircraft used for human (dummy) drop testing
O&R ALAMEDA	**ComNAB-12 / na / na**	29 Sep 55	13 Nov 57	- - -	20 Dec 56	10 Feb 58	- - -	7 aircraft in custody
O&R CORPUS CHRISTI	**CNAVanTra / na / na**	23 Oct 56	- - -	- - -	19 Dec 56	- - -	- - -	1 aircraft in custody
O&R JACKSONVILLE	**ComNAB-6 / na / na**	12 Apr 55	23 Nov 55	- - -	2 Aug 56	31 May 56	- - -	16 aircraft in custody
O&R LAKEHURST	**CNATE / na / na**	22 Jun 56	- - -	- - -	22 Jun 56	- - -	- - -	1 aircraft stricken in custody and moved to Mustin for storage and scrapping
O&R NORFOLK	**ComNAB-5 / na / na**	15 Nov 54	6 Jun 56	10 Apr 56	20 Jun 58	20 Jun 58	20 Jun 58	47 aircraft in custody
O&R QUONSET PT	**ComNAB-1 / na / na**	30 Jun 54	- - -	- - -	22 Jun 56	- - -	- - -	4 aircraft in custody
O&R SAN DIEGO	**ComNAB-11 / na / na**	7 Jul 54	28 Jan 55	24 May 55	30 Jul 58	30 Jul 58	25 Aug 55	70 aircraft in custody
NAS NART COLUMBUS	**CNAResTra / None / (2)** - *when acquired - later removed)*	15 May 57	- - -	- - -		- - -	- - -	Ex VA-12 / Displayed NAS Columbus, OH DESTROYED - engine at Cutlass Aeronautics
NAS NART DALLAS	**CNAResTra / None / (302)**	- - -	25 Apr 57	- - -	- - -	Jun 67	- - -	Ex VA-83 / Displayed NAS Dallas, TX DESTROYED
NAS NART DENVER	**CNAResTra / None / (None)**	17 May 57	- - -	- - -		- - -	- - -	Ex VA-212 / Displayed Centennial Park, CO DESTROYED
NAS NART GLENVIEW	**CNAResTra / None / (3)** - *F7U-3* **CNAResTra / None / (None)** - *F7U-3P*	14 May 57	- - -	14 May 57	Gifted to Northbrrok East Civic Association 12 Nov 58	- - -	Scrapped Oct58	F7U-3 / Displayed Oaklane Elementary School **SURVIVED (partial) - Cutlass Aeronautics, Mesa AZ** F7U-3P / used as parts source for F7U-3 DESTROYED
NARTU JACKSONVILLE	**ComNAB-6 / None / (12)**	29 May 57	- - -	- - -		- - -	- - -	Ex VA-12 / Displayed NAS Jacksonville, FL DESTROYED
NAS NART LINCOLN	**CNAResTra / None / (None)**	19 May 57	- - -	- - -		- - -	- - -	Ex VA-212 / Displayed Milford, NE DESTROYED
NAS NART LOS ALAMITOS	**CNAResTra / None / (None** - *Initially*) **LACPD / "G" / (201)**	29 Apr 57	- - -	- - -		- - -	- - -	Ex VA-212 / Displayed Griffith Park, CA **SURVIVED - NNAM, Pensacola FL**
NARTU MEMPHIS	**CNATechTra / "6M" / (1)** **"MEMPHIS"** *in aft fuselage band*	22 May 57	- - -	- - -		- - -	- - -	Ex VA-12 / Displayed NAS Memphis, TN DESTROYED
NARTU MIAMI	**ComNAB-6 / None / (7)**	22 May 57	- - -	- - -		- - -	- - -	Ex VA-12 / Displayed MCAS Opa Locka, FL DESTROYED
NAS NART MINNEAPOLIS	**CNAResTra / None / (0)** **"MINNEAPOLIS"** *in intake band*	22 May 57	- - -	- - -		- - -	- - -	Ex VA-212 / Displayed NAS Minneapolis, MN DESTROYED
NAS NART NEW YORK	**CNAResTra / None / (14)**	18 May 57	- - -	- - -		- - -	- - -	Ex VA-12 / Displayed Floyd Bennet Field, NY DESTROYED
NAS NART NIAGRA FALLS	**CNAResTra / None / (13)**	9 May 57	- - -	- - -		- - -	- - -	Ex VA-12 / Displayed Niagra Falls Park, NY DESTROYED
NARTU NORFOLK	**ComNAB-5 / None / (304)**	- - -	10 May 57	- - -	- - -		- - -	Ex VA-83 / Displayed with Navy/Red Flame Livery at NAS Norfolk DESTROYED
NAS NART OAKLAND	**CNAResTra / None / (None)**	1 May 57	- - -	- - -		- - -	- - -	Ex VA-212 / Displayed NAS Oakland, CA DESTROYED
NAS NART OLATHE	**CNAResTra / "7K" / (None)**	19 May 57	- - -	- - -		- - -	- - -	Ex VA-212 / Displayed Olathe, KS **SURVIVED - Midway Museum, San Diego**
NAS NART ST. LOUIS	**CNAResTra / None / (5)**	12 May 57	- - -	- - -		- - -	- - -	Ex VA-12 / Displayed NAS St Louis, MO DESTROYED
NAS NART SOUTH WEYMOUTH	**CNAResTra / None / (10)**	10 May 57	- - -	- - -		- - -	- - -	Ex VA-12 / Displayed Soplata Farm **SURVIVED - MAPS Museum, Akron/Canton OH**
NAS NART SPOKANE	**CNAResTra / None / (None)**	11 May 57	- - -	- - -		- - -	- - -	Ex VA-212 / Displayed Bridgeport, WA **SURVIVED - Cutlass Aeronautics, Mesa AZ**
NAS NART WILLOW GROVE	**CNAResTra / None / (11)**	9 May 57	- - -	- - -		- - -	- - -	Ex VA-12 / Displayed NAS Willow Grove **SURVIVED - DVHA Pitcairn Museum, Willow Grove PA**

na = not applicable

Glossary

ADM: Admiral
AEC: Atomic Energy Commission
AERO: Aeronautical Equipment Reference Ordinal
ALF: Auxiliary Landing Field
AoA: Angle of Attack
ASC: Aircraft Service Change
ASW: Anti-submarine Warfare
ATG: Air Task Group

BAR: Bureau of Aeronautics Representative
BIS: Board of Inspection and Survey
Bolter: Taking off again after not picking up an arresting cable when landing on an aircraft carrier with an angled deck.
BuAer: Bureau of Aeronautics
BuNo: Bureau Number (a unique number assigned to each aircraft purchased by the US Navy)
BuOrd: Bureau of Ordnance
BuShip: Bureau of Ships

CAG: Commander, Air Group
CAL: Cornell Aeronautical Laboratory (subsequently Calspan), Buffalo, New York
CAP: Combat Air Patrol
CAPT: Captain, US Navy
Capt: Captain, USMC and USAF
CDR: Commander, US Navy
CG: Centre of Gravity
CINCLANTFLT: Commander in Chief, Atlantic Fleet
CNO: Chief of Naval Operations
ComAirLant: Commander Air Forces, Atlantic Fleet
ComAirPac: Commander Air Forces, Pacific Fleet
COMFAIRJAX: Commander of Fleet Air, Jacksonville
ComOpTEvFor: Commander Operations Test and Evaluation Force
CPT: Cockpit Procedures Trainer
CRP: Combat-Rated Thrust (Afterburner)
CVA: Aircraft Carrier – Attack
CVG: Carrier Air Group

DCNO (Air): Deputy Chief of Naval Operations for Air Warfare
DoD: Department of Defense

ECP: Engineering Change Proposal
ENS: Ensign, US Navy

FASRon: Fleet Aircraft Service Squadron
FAWTUPac: Fleet All-Weather Training Unit – Pacific
FCLP: Field Carrier Landing Practice
FIP: Fleet Introduction Programme
FRI: Flight Refueling Incorporated
FSR: Field Service Representative (aircraft company)
FY: Fiscal Year (the US Federal Government accounting period; for example FY1951 began on 1 July 1950 and ended 30 June 1951; beginning with FY1977, the fiscal year began on 1 October 1976 and ended on 30 September 1977.

***g*:** The acceleration of gravity on the surface of the earth. Aircraft and pilots making steep turns or sudden pull-ups are subjected to multiples of *g*.
GCA: Ground-Controlled Approach
GFP/GFE: Government-Furnished Property/Equipment
GP: General purpose

HMS: His/Her Majesty's Ship

JATO: Jet-Assisted Take-Off (actually provided by a solid-fuel rocket)

KIAS: Knots, Indicated Air Speed in knots

LABS: Low-Altitude Bombing System (for delivery of nuclear weapons)
LCDR: Lieutenant Commander, US Navy
LSO: Landing Signals Officer
LT: Lieutenant, US Navy
Lt: Lieutenant, USMC
LTJG: Lieutenant Junior Grade, US Navy

Mach: The speed of sound (varies with air temperature)
Maj: Major, USMC
MCR: Master Change Record (Vought)
MRT: Military-rated thrust

NAAS: Naval Auxiliary Air Station
NACA: National Advisory Committee for Aeronautics
NADC: Naval Air Development Center, Johnsville, Pennsylvania
NAF: Naval Air Facility
NAMC: Naval Air Material Center, Philadelphia, Pennsylvania
NAMTC: Naval Air Missile Test Center, Point Mugu, California
NAOTS: Naval Air Ordnance Test Station, Chincoteague, Virginia

NAVAIR: Naval Air Systems Command
NART: Naval Air Reserve Training detachment
NARTU: Naval Air Reserve Training Units
NAS: Naval Air Station
NASF: Naval Air Storage Facility, Litchfield Park, Arizona
NASWF: Naval Air Special Weapons Facility, Kirtland AFB, New Mexico
NATC: Naval Air Test Center, Patuxent River, Maryland
NATOPS: Naval Air Training and Operating Procedures Standardization
NATTC: Naval Air Technical Training Command
NATF: Naval Air Testing Facility
NLO: Naval Liaison Office
NOLF: Naval Outlying Field
NOLTF: Navy Ordnance Laboratory Test Facility, Fort Lauderdale, Florida
NOTS: Naval Ordnance Test Station, China Lake, California
NPU: Naval Parachute Unit, El Centro, California
NTPS: Naval Test Pilot School

OinC: Officer-in-Charge (detachment)
O&R: Overhaul and Repair
OpNav: Office of the Chief of Naval Operation
ORI: Operational Readiness Inspection

P&W: Pratt & Whitney engine company
PFRT: Preliminary Flight Rating Test to establish safety of flight
PSG: Post-Stall Gyration

RADM: Rear Admiral
RAG: Replacement Air Group

SAC: Standard Aircraft Characteristics (a set of charts)
SFC: Specific Fuel Consumption (pounds of fuel per hour per pound of thrust)
SWUPAC: Special Weapons Unit – Pacific

TBO: Time Between Overhaul
TRANSTUPAC: Transitional Training Unit Pacific
Trap: An arrested landing

USAF: United States Air Force

VA: Attack Squadron
VADM: Vice Admiral
VAH: Heavy Attack Squadron
VAHF: Vought Aircraft Heritage Foundation
VC: Composite Squadron
VF: Fighter Squadron
VF(AW): All-Weather Fighter Squadron
VMF: USMC Fighter Squadron
VR: Transport Squadron
VX: Air Development Squadron

WAA: Westinghouse Air Arm Division
WAGT: Westinghouse Aviation Gas Turbine Division
WOD: Wind over Deck

Index

Air Groups

Air Fields/Stations

Companies

Engines

Organisations

People

Projects

Radar

Ships

OVERLEAF ***Hancock*, CVA-19, making a ceremonial arrival at a port—possibly Yokosuka, Japan—with VF-124 aboard, the first squadron to deploy with F7U-3 Cutlasses. *US Navy***

406
404
5
407